MULTILEVEL GOVERNANCE OF GLOBAL ENVIRONMENTAL CHANGE

This collection is the outcome of an interdisciplinary research project involving scholars in the fields of international and comparative environmental law, the sociology and politics of global governance, and the scientific study of global climate change. Earth system analysis as developed by the natural sciences is transferred to the analysis of institutions of global environmental change. Rather than one overarching, supranational organisation, a system of 'multilevel' institutions is advocated. The book examines the proper role of industrial self-regulation, of horizontal transfer of national policies, of regional integration, and of improved coordination between international environmental organisations, as well as basic principles for sustainable use of resources. Addressing both academics and politicians, this book will stimulate the debate about the means of improving global governance.

GERD WINTER is Professor of Public Law and Sociology of Law at the University of Bremen.

MULTILEVEL GOVERNANCE OF GLOBAL ENVIRONMENTAL CHANGE

Perspectives from Science, Sociology and the Law

Edited by
GERD WINTER

CAMBRIDGE
UNIVERSITY PRESS

CAMBRIDGE UNIVERSITY PRESS
Cambridge, New York, Melbourne, Madrid, Cape Town,
Singapore, São Paulo, Delhi, Tokyo, Mexico City

Cambridge University Press
The Edinburgh Building, Cambridge CB2 8RU, UK

Published in the United States of America by Cambridge University Press, New York

www.cambridge.org
Information on this title: www.cambridge.org/9780521173438

© Cambridge University Press 2006

This publication is in copyright. Subject to statutory exception
and to the provisions of relevant collective licensing agreements,
no reproduction of any part may take place without the written
permission of Cambridge University Press.

First published 2006
First paperback edition 2011

A catalogue record for this publication is available from the British Library

Library of Congress Cataloguing in Publication data
Multilevel governance of global environmental change : perspectives from science, sociology and the law / edited by Gerd Winter. – 1st ed.
p. cm.
Includes bibliographical references and index.
ISBN-13: 978-0-521-85261-6 (hardback)
ISBN-10: 0-521-85261-7 (hardback)
1. Environmental law, International. I. Winter, Gerd. II. Title.
K3585.M85 2006
344.04′6 – dc22   2005020131

ISBN 978-0-521-85261-6 Hardback
ISBN 978-0-521-17343-8 Paperback

Cambridge University Press has no responsibility for the persistence or accuracy of URLs for external or third-party internet websites referred to in this publication, and does not guarantee that any content on such websites is, or will remain, accurate or appropriate.

In Memoriam
Konrad von Moltke

The group of authors which first met at Bremen in March 2001 to initiate and assemble this volume has sadly lost one of its most respected members: On 19 May 2005, Professor Konrad von Moltke passed away in Vermont after a brief but valiant battle with cancer.

Dr. von Moltke will be remembered for outstanding contributions to global environmental policy and governance. Trained as a mathematician and historian (PhD Goettingen 1970), he became founding director of the interdisciplinary *Institute for European Environmental Policy* (Bonn, Paris, London), then moved to the United States as Senior Fellow of the *World Wildlife Fund* in Washington/DC and Adjunct Professor of Environmental Studies at Dartmouth College. From 1989 to 1998, he was editor-in-chief of the quarterly, *International Environmental Affairs*; he also was a Senior Fellow at the *International Institute for Sustainable Development* in Winnipeg/Canada (where he focused on issues of world trade and environment); and Visiting Professor, *Institute for Environmental Studies*, at the Free University of Amsterdam in the Netherlands (where part of his family lives).

Konrad came from an old Prussian family. When he was only three years old, his father – international lawyer Helmut James Graf von Moltke – was executed by the Nazis for his participation in the resistance movement and in the abortive 1944 plot to assassinate Hitler (today, the family's ancestral home in former Silesia, where several of the secret resistance meetings took place during World War II, is a seminar centre for Polish-German and European reconciliation). What Konrad certainly inherited was a standard of absolute human integrity. He also had, in the most difficult times, a great sense of humour – and above all, a big heart. To his memory, this book is dedicated.

PREFACE

This book is the outcome of an interdisciplinary research group called Transnational Institutions on Evironment (TIE) involving scholars in the fields of international and comparative environmental law, the sociology and politics of global govenance, and the scientific study of global climate change. It is meant as a contribution to Institutional Dimensions of Global Environmental Change (IDGEC), one of the core projects of the International Human Dimensions Program (IHDP). The idea to launch the project was born in the National Committee Global Environmental Change Research of the Deutsche Forschungsgemeinschaft (DFG) which also sponsored some of the meetings of the group. The DFG Collaborative Research Center 'Transformations of the State' at the University of Bremen provided an intellectual background for the project.

We are grateful for this support. We would also like to thank Antje Spalink for assisting in keeping the herd together, Kate Levy for transposing many Germanisms into decent English, and the production team at CUP for delightful cooperation and incredible scrutiny

Gerd Winter
Bremen
November 2005

CONTENTS

List of figures   *page* xii
List of tables   xiv
Notes on contributors   xv
List of abbreviations   xix

1   Introduction   1
GERD WINTER

PART I   **Earth system analysis**   35

2   Dimensions and mechanisms of global climate change   37
PETER LEMKE

3   Global climate change: what can we learn from the past?   67
STEFAN RAHMSTORF

PART II   **Society and institutions of global environmental change**   77

4   The social embeddedness of global environmental governance   79
KARL-WERNER BRAND AND FRITZ REUSSWIG

5   Globalising a green civil society: in search of conceptual clarity   106
ASHER ALKOBY

PART III   **Self-regulation of industry and the law**   147

6   Private authority, global governance, and the law   149
MARTIN HERBERG

7   Responsibility of transnational corporations in international environmental law: three perspectives   179
ANDRÉ NOLLKAEMPER

8 Transboundary corporate responsibility in environmental matters: fragments and foundations for a future framework 200
JONAS EBBESSON

PART IV   The potential of the state   225

9 The diffusion of environmental policy innovations   227
KERSTIN TEWS

10 Process-related measures and global environmental governance   254
CHRISTIAN TIETJE

11 The impact of the USA on regime formation and implementation   275
THOMAS GIEGERICH

12 Transnational bureaucracy networks: a resource of global environmental governance?   305
MICHAEL WARNING

PART V   The potential of world regions   331

13 The EU: a regional model?   333
LUDWIG KRÄMER

14 Transition and governance: the case of post-communist states   358
STEPHEN STEC, ALEXIOS ANTYPAS, AND TAMARA STEGER

PART VI   Formation and implementation of international regimes   385

15 Multilateral environmental agreements and the compliance continuum   387
JUTTA BRUNNÉE

16 On clustering international environmental agreements   409
KONRAD VON MOLTKE

17 Institutions, knowledge, and change: findings from the quantitative study of environmental regimes   430
HELMUT BREITMEIER

PART VII **Improving the instruments of global governance** 453

18 Regulatory competition and developing countries and the challenge for compliance push and pull measures 455
JOYEETA GUPTA

19 Policy instrument innovation in the European Union: a realistic model for international environmental governance? 470
ANDREW JORDAN, RÜDIGER K. W. WURZEL, AND ANTHONY R. ZITO

20 Financial instruments and cooperation in implementing international agreements for the global environment 493
CHARLOTTE STRECK

PART VIII **Fundamental concepts of institutionalising common concern** 517

21 Global environmental change and the nation state: sovereignty bounded? 519
PETER H. SAND

22 Whose environment? Concepts of commonality in international environmental law 539
MICHAEL BOTHE

23 Globalising environmental liability: the interplay of national and international law 559
A. E. BOYLE

24 The legal nature of environmental principles in international, EU, and exemplary national law 587
GERD WINTER

Index 605

FIGURES

1.1	Interrelations between institutions, society, and the natural earth system	page 3
1.2	Network of interrelations characterising the overexploitation syndrome	6
2.1	Variations of global surface temperature of the Earth since 1860	38
2.2	Reconstructions of the mean surface temperature of the northern hemisphere	39
2.3	Climate variations from instrumental records, historical sources, and proxy data	41
2.4	Increase of CO_2 concentration in the atmosphere since 1958 and natural variations during the last 450,000 years	43
2.5	Sea ice cover and sea surface temperature in the North Atlantic in fall	48
2.6	Schematic depiction of the climate system	49
2.7	Cell structure of Earth's atmosphere	51
2.8	Time series of ocean temperature	53
2.9	Components of the global hydrological cycle	54
2.10	Oceanic thermohaline circulation	56
2.11	Components of the cryosphere	57
2.12	Arctic and Antarctic sea ice extent	60
3.1	The Mueller Glacier in the Southern Alps of New Zealand	68
3.2	Climate history of the past 400,000 years from the Vostok ice core in Antarctica	70
3.3	Temperature in the northern hemisphere during the past millenium	73
3.4	Simulation of glacial climate in the CLIMBER-2 model	75
6.1	Schematic representation of transnational self-regulatory systems	161
9.1	Sum of annual environmental policy innovations	232
9.2	Environmental policy adoptions in the USA and Canada	234
9.3	Comparison of the patterns of spread of media-related and 'new' environmental policy innovations	240
9.4	Diffusion in the shadow of international institutions	247

18.1 Regulatory competition	466
20.1 Multilateral Fund for the Implementation of the Montreal Protocol, project example	501
20.2 Global Environmental Facility, project example	508
20.3 Prototype Carbon Fund, project example	514
21.1 Trusteeship	532
21.2 International environmental trusteeship	533

TABLES

1.1	Causation of global environmental problems by syndromes	page 8
2.1	Pre-industrial and present concentrations of some anthropogenically influenced greenhouse gases	46
2.2	Area and volume of cryospheric components	56
17.1	International regimes database: regime elements	434
17.2	Level of understanding of the nature of the problem	440
17.3	Completeness of information on policy options	446
17.4	Institutional mechanisms in regime elements	449
18.1	Elements of compliance push and compliance pull	463
19.1	The distribution of NEPIs by country	475

NOTES ON CONTRIBUTORS

Asher Alkoby is a doctoral candidate at the University of Toronto Faculty of Law. He received his LLB from the University of Haifa and his LLM from the University of Toronto. His doctoral project is an interdisciplinary examination of the impact that cultural diversity has on compliance of states with international law.

Alexios Antypas is Associate Professor of Environmental Policy at Central European University (CEU), and Director of the CEU Center for Environmental Policy and Law.

Michael Bothe is Professor Emeritus of Public International Law and Co-Director, Environmental Law Research Centre, at the J. W. Goethe University, Frankfurt, and head of the research group on International Organisation, Democratic Peace, and the Rule of Law, Peace Research Institute, Frankfurt.

Alan Boyle is Professor of Public International Law at the University of Edinburgh School of Law and General Editor of the *International and Comparative Law Quarterly*. He represents governments in international legal disputes.

Karl-Werner Brand is Professor of Sociology at the Technical University of Munich and Director of the Munich Institute of Social and Sustainability Research (MPS). He specialises in environmental sociology, sustainable consumption, and politics of sustainability.

Helmut Breitmeier is Senior Research Scholar at the Institute for Political Science (Darmstadt University of Technology) where he specialises in research on global governance issues.

Jutta Brunnée is Professor of Law and Metcalf Chair in Environmental Law at the Faculty of Law of the University of Toronto. Her teaching and research focus on public international law and international environmental law.

Jonas Ebbesson is Professor of Environmental Law and Director of Stockholm Environmental Law and Policy Centre at Stockholm University. He specialises in international, European, and Swedish environmental law.

Thomas Giegerich is Professor of Public Law, European Community Law, and Public International Law at the University of Bremen, and Director of Bremen Institute of Transnational Constitutional Law. His reseach focuses on the constitutional developments of the EU, the constitutionalisation of public international law, and comparative constitutional law.

Joyeeta Gupta is Professor of Policy and Law on Water Resources and the Environment at the UNESCO-IHE Institute for Water Education in Delft and Professor on Climate Change Law and Policy and head of the Programme on International Environmental Governance at the Institute for Environmental Studies at the Vrije Universiteit in Amsterdam.

Martin Herberg is Junior Research Fellow at the Collaborative Research Center 597 'Transformations of the State' at Bremen University. His doctoral dissertation is a sociological analysis of environmental self-governance of multinational corporations.

Andrew Jordan is Philip Leverhulme Prize Fellow and Reader in Environmental Policy at the School of Environmental Sciences at the University of East Anglia.

Ludwig Krämer is Honorary Professor for European Environmental Law at the University of Bremen, and Lecturer at the College of Europe, in Bruges. He is also a former official in the Environmental Department of the European Commission, where he worked for more than thirty years.

Peter Lemke is Professor of Physics of the Atmosphere and Ocean at the Alfred Wegener Institute for Polar and Marine Research and the University of Bremen. He is also Chairman of the Joint Scientific Committee for the World Climate Research Programme (WCRP), and Chairman of the IIASA Program Committee (Laxenburg, Austria).

Konrad von Moltke (deceased) was Senior Fellow at the International Institute for Sustainable Development (Winnipeg, Canada). His work focused on international environmental relations. He contributed to developing the agenda on trade, investment, and sustainable development at global and regional levels. He was also a Senior Fellow at the World Wildlife Fund in Washington, DC, and Senior Fellow at the Institut pour le Developpement Durable et les Relations Internationales (Paris).

André Nollkaemper is Professor of Public International Law and Director of the Amsterdam Center of International Law at the University of Amsterdam.

Stefan Rahmstorf is Professor of Physics of the Oceans at Potsdam University and the Potsdam Institute for Climate Impact Research, where he specialises in studying the role of the oceans in climate change, past, present, and future. He is also a member of the German Advisory Council on Global Change.

Fritz Reusswig is Senior Research Fellow in the Social Science Department of the Potsdam Institute for Climate Impact Research (PIK). He is leading a research platform on Lifestyle Changes and Sustainable Development (LSD). His current research activities focus on the emergence of a global consumer society, the modelling of the global lifestyle dynamics, and the public perception of climate change.

Peter H. Sand is Lecturer in International Environmental Law at the Faculty of Law, University of Munich, and was formerly Chief of the Environmental Law Unit, United Nations Environment Programme (UNEP), and Legal Adviser (Environmental Affairs), World Bank.

Stephen Stec is Visiting Professor at the Central European University, Budapest, and also Associate Scholar at Leiden University and Senior Legal Specialist at the Regional Environmental Center.

Tamara Steger is Visiting Professor at the Central European University (CEU), Budapest, and Programs Director, CEU Center for Environmental Policy and Law.

Charlotte Streck is Director at Climate Focus B. V. Rotterdam. Until February 2005, she was Senior Counsel with the World Bank, and Adjunct Lecturer at the University of Potsdam.

Kerstin Tews is Research Fellow and coordinator of the working group on Pioneer Policy and Diffusion of Environmental Policy Innovations at the Environmental Policy Research Centre, Freie Universität Berlin.

Christian Tietje is Professor of Public Law, European Law, and International Economic Law, and Director of the Institute for Economic Law and the Transnational Economic Law Research Center (TELC) at the Faculty of Law at University Halle-Wittenberg, Germany.

Michael Warning is Junior Research Fellow at the Collaborative Research Centre 597 'Transformations of the State' at the University of Bremen where he participates in a project concerned with transnational governance and international law.

Gerd Winter is Professor of Public Law and Sociology of Law at the University of Bremen, and Director, Research Center for European Environmental Law. His research focusses on comparative, European, and international environmental law.

Rüdiger K. W. Wurzel is Jean Monnet Chair in European Studies and Senior Lecturer at the University of Hull where he is the Director of the Centre for European Union Studies (CEUS).

Anthony R. Zito is Reader in Politics at the University of Newcastle where he specialises in EU politics, policy, and decision-making. He is the Assistant Director of the Jean Monnet Centre of Excellence at the University of Newcastle.

ABBREVIATIONS

AOSIS	Alliance of Small Island States
ASEAN	Association of South-East Asian Nations
CBD	Convention on Biological Diversity
CDM	Clean Development Mechanism
CEE	Central and Eastern European
CER	Certified Emission Reduction
CFC	chlorofluorocarbon
CFI	Court of First Instance
CIS	Commonwealth of Independent States
CIT	country in transition
CITES	Convention on International Trade in Endangered Species of Wild Fauna and Flora
COP	Conference of the Parties
COP/MOP	Conference of the Parties serving as the Meeting of the Parties
CSD	Commission on Sustainable Development
DSB	WTO Dispute Settlement Body
ECJ	European Court of Justice
ECOSOC	UN Economic and Social Council
ECtHR	European Court of Human Rights
EEA	European Environment Agency
EECCA	East Europe, Caucasus and Central Asia
EEZ	exclusive economic zone
EIA	environmental impact assessment
EIT	economies in transition
EMAS	Environmental Management and Auditing System
ERU	Emission Reduction Unit
ETS	Emissions Trading System
EU	European Union
FAI	free access to environmental information
FAO	Food and Agriculture Organization
GATT	General Agreement on Tariffs and Trade
GCC	Global Climate Coalition
GEF	Global Environment Facility

GEG	global environmental governance
GEN	Global Eco-labelling Network
GETF	Global Environment Trust Fund
GHS	Globally Harmonized System for Hazard Classification and Labelling of Chemicals
GLP	good laboratory practice
IAEA	International Atomic Energy Agency
ICCA	International Council of Chemical Associations
ICCS	International Conference on Chemical Safety
ICCt	International Criminal Court
ICJ	International Court of Justice
IFCS	International Forum on Chemical Safety
IGO	intergovernmental organisation
IIA	international investment agreement
IL	international law
ILC	International Law Commission
ILO	International Labor Organization
IMO	International Maritime Organization
IOMC	Inter-Organization Programme for the Sound Management of Chemicals
IPCC	Intergovernmental Panel on Climate Change
IPCS	International Programme on Chemical Safety
IR	international relations
IRD	International Regimes Database
ISO	International Standards Organisation
ITLOS	International Tribunal for the Law of the Sea
IWC	International Whaling Commission
JI	joint implementation
LRTAP	long-range transboundary air pollution
MAD	mutual acceptance of data
MARPOL	International Convention for the Prevention of Pollution from Ships
MBI	market-based instrument
MEA	multilateral environmental agreement
MLF	Multilateral Fund
MNC	multinational corporation
MNE	multinational enterprise
MoU	memorandum of understanding
NAAEC	North American Agreement on Environmental Cooperation
NAFTA	North American Free Trade Agreement
NCP	non-compliance procedure
NEPA	National Environmental Policy Act 1969 (USA)

NEPI	new environmental policy instrument
NGO	non-governmental organization
NIS	newly independent state
ODS	ozone-depleting substance
OECD	Organisation for Economic Cooperation and Development
OSCE	Organisation for Security and Cooperation in Europe
PCF	Prototype Carbon Fund
PIC	prior informed consent
POP	persistent organic pollutant
ppbv	parts per billion by volume
PPM	process and production measures
ppmv	parts per million by volume
PVS	public voluntary scheme
QELRC	Quantified Emission Limitation and Reduction Commitment
SADC	Southern African Development Community
SEA	strategic environmental assessment
SEM	Single European Market
SIDS	screening information data set
TACIS	Technical Assistance to the Commonwealth of Independent States
TBT	Technical Barriers to Trade
TCS	transnational civil society
TNA	transnational actor
TNB	transnational network of bureaucracies
TNC	transnational corporation
TNE	transnational enterprise
TPRM	Trade Policy Review Mechanism
UNCC	United Nations Compensation Commission
UNCED	United Nations Conference on Environment and Development
UNCETDG	United Nations Committee of Experts on the Transport of Dangerous Goods
UNCHE	United Nations Conference on the Human Environment
UNCTAD	UN Conference on Trade and Development
UNDP	United Nations Development Programme
UNECE	United Nations Economic Commission for Europe
UNEP	United Nations Environment Programme
UNFCCC	United Nations Framework Convention on Climate Change
UNIDO	United Nations Industrial Development Organization
UNRTDG	United Nations Recommendations on the Transport of Dangerous Goods
USEPA	US Environmental Protection Agency
VA	voluntary agreement

WBGU	Wissenschaftlicher Beirat Globale Unweltveränderungen (Advisory Council on Global Change)
WHO	World Health Organisation
WMO	World Meteorological Organization
WSSD	World Summit on Sustainable Development
WTO	World Trade Organization

1

Introduction

GERD WINTER

I. Overview

Within the interaction between humans and their natural environment four stages are prominent.

The first stage is characterised by the presence of subsistence economies. These largely exist in a circular relationship with nature by extracting or depositing no more than that which grows anew in or can be absorbed by the local environment.

The second stage is marked by an overburdening of natural resources through their exploitation for extraction or waste disposal purposes. However, the burdensome events and their effects remain local, even though this may have disastrous consequences for the local population. As a result, social and governmental measures to mitigate the damage remain local or national and often rather weak.

The third stage is characterised by an increase in the severity of burdens. One such burden is that the causation chain of environmental issues transgresses local borders and spreads over a wider area; another is that single incidents of local damage accumulate and contribute to the endangering of overarching entities, such as whole species or the ozone layer. Both of these burdening effects have triggered regional and international institutions of environmental protection.

It seems that a fourth stage has been reached. The domestic and the cross-border causation chains have multiplied to the extent that the complex bio-physical-chemical mechanics of the biosphere as a whole are put under strain. Not only do environmental 'problems' of a planetary magnitude appear, but the earth is afflicted as a system. The causation is less visible but, at the same time, more and more severe, a fact which has caused some to say that the present Holocene Age may mutate into an Anthropocene Age. Whilst the human impact on the environment led to an immediate and often mono-causal response from nature during the earlier stages, the new stage is marked by more complex and concealed causation trails. Consequently, the phenomenological description of 'global environmental change' is moving towards a more structural analysis of the earth system, extending both to long-term natural causes as well as to the contribution of mankind.

If the fundamental mechanics of the earth as a whole are affected, a new kind of institution and, with them, institutional analysis is needed. Just as earth system analysis, the analysis of institutions must be holistic. This is not to mean that international law must now develop towards a supranational organisation endowed with managing the fundamental laws of the globe. On the contrary, a holistic view requires us to look at the full scale of institutions because all levels contribute to the systemic whole.

This means, first of all, that given the preoccupation of institutional research with international regimes, the structures beneath the international layer must be rediscovered, i.e. regional integration, the state, and the self-regulatory potential of societies and transnational societal actors and networks. It is one of this book's central assertions that many institutions other than those on an international level must be considered in order to reach a truly global approach. Before considering the integration of state-based and societal governance into international regimes or even a worldwide superstructure, one should try first of all to make them reflective of their proper role on a global scale. The most progressive view on global institutions is the vision of a community (rather than society) of states, based on both the states and civil society. The ideal of this vision is an overall well-ordered unity, the global federal union. By contrast, what is advocated in this book is the concept of a polyarchy of institutions located at several organisational levels, divided into many issue-related sections and dispersed over various geographical zones. This polyarchy would be self-organisational in order to reflect the common concern of preserving an inhabitable earth system.

Secondly, it should systematically be considered that institutions have played a dualistic and often contradictory role in bringing about the kind of man-nature constellation we are facing today. There are institutions which foster human technological and economical inventiveness. By organising economic growth they have contributed to human welfare but also to an ever-increasing exploitation of nature as a resource for extraction and waste disposal. In contrast, there are institutions struggling to protect nature against overexploitation. This tension between promotion and limitation of nature exploitation cross-cuts all levels of institutions. It is innate in societies themselves, represented in state bodies, and reappears on the international level as a split between international economic and ecological organisations. The challenging question is how the opposing structures can be interrelated in order to sustain the earth system.

A third aspect of institutional analysis concerns the overall orientation of research. Is it still the idea of preserving a livable earth, or is the focus shifting towards resilience and adaptation to change? The overburdening of the earth's bearing capacity is, by some observers, seen as unavoidable. They

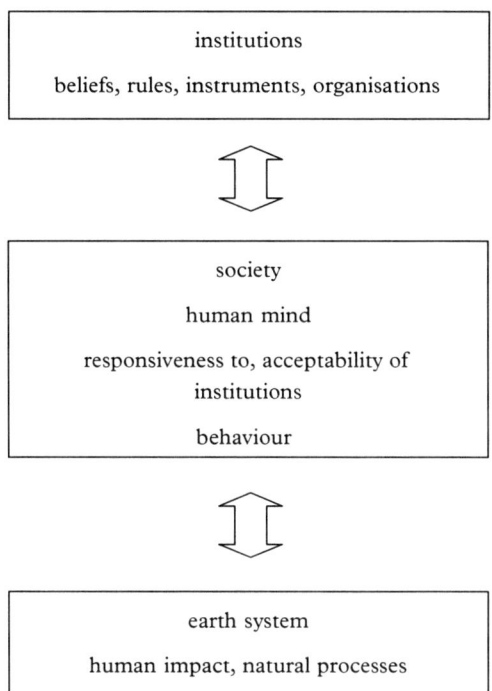

Figure 1.1 Interrelations between institutions, society, and the natural earth system

promote instead the potential of institutions that are capable of adapting societies to the consequences of global change as, for example, the new patterns of societal stratification, migration, incidence of disaster effects, etc. Whilst the importance of this task is not refuted, this book focuses instead on institutions that abate environmental decline. The decline of soil, water, biodiversity, and the atmosphere cannot be repaired by new technologies. Admittedly, there is a fundamental incongruence between the speed of the Promethean exploitation of the biosphere and the slow institutionalisation of mitigation measures. But this does not in itself render global change ungovernable because global change is a product of institutional settings too. The challenge for institutional development is to determine how to bring these settings in line with the long-term preservation of nature. Ideally, measures of long-term mitigation would at the same time be able to contribute to short-term adaptation.

Fourthly, clarity is necessary about the relationship between institutions, society, and nature. Of course, there is no direct link between institutions and the earth system: a law cannot command the climate not to change, neither can climate change make laws. The link is represented by society, i.e. human mind and the patterns of human behaviour. Based on its perception of the state of the earth system and depending on the existing social structures, human mind will respond (or not) to institutions of global change, and it will accept (or not) the institutions as legitimate.

The present book – and this introduction to it – is based on this model. We begin with a summary account of earth system analysis focussing on human impact and an analytical tool of its identification. We proceed by looking at society in its double role of responding to and legitimising institutions of global change. The remaining and most extensive part is concerned with the variety of institutions and their interlinkages.

II. The earth system

The mechanics of the earth system are demonstrated in the example of the climate, as offered in the contributions of Peter Lemke, Chapter 2 and Stefan Rahmstorf, Chapter 3. An adequate climate is a fundamental precondition to human life. The major components of the climate system include the atmosphere (acting through gas, clouds, and aerosols), the ocean (acting through its temperature, salinity, pressure, and velocity), the cryosphere (consisting of ice covers on land and ice shields on water), the lithosphere (acting e.g. through volcanoes), and the biosphere (acting through the production of gases including carbon dioxide and oxygen). The components work on a fundamental external impact, i.e. solar radiation. The laws determining how they interact are complex and far from fully understood. Some of these interactions are represented in Figure 6 in Lemke's Chapter 2. A particularly important mechanism for maintaining living conditions in moderate climates are the oceans. They serve as a huge energy pump, storing heat in the south and transporting it to the north (see Figure 10 in Chapter 2). Another major climate-determining factor is the albedo (i.e. rate of reflection of solar radiation) of different land covers. The cryosphere has a high albedo, thus keeping the temperature low which leads to snowfall, enabling the cryosphere to reproduce itself. By contrast, water and forested land have a low albedo, thus producing evaporation and, consequently, rain. A third factor is the composition of gases in the atmosphere, and in particular the percentage of carbon dioxide which accounts for the storing of heat at higher or lower levels.

In the past, this complex system has undergone fundamental changes triggered by variations in solar radiation, continental drift, ocean salinity, and natural factors within the system.

These changes were not induced by human activities. However, as Rahmstorf demonstrates in Chapter 3, human activities did induce new changes in the twentieth century. Carbon dioxide levels in the atmosphere increased by 30 per cent, resulting in a temperature rise of 0.7 °C. Indicators point to a further increase in the twenty-first century, all the more so in the light of changes in land use as, for example, deforestation and its implications for the function of the land cover as a sink for carbon dioxide. Models of the climate system enable us to predict the consequences of these human-made changes. The study of causation chains can go so far as envisaging the halting or diversion of the great oceanic currents, thus affecting the system responsible for the moderate climate of vast regions of the earth. Other changes may result in an increase of extreme weather conditions (already verified by statistics), an acceleration of desertification, a loss of habitats for plants and animals, etc.

The German Scientific Advisory Board on Global Environmental Change has proposed syndrome analysis as an intellectual tool to understand the complex interaction between deviant states of the climate and other parts of the earth system. Syndromes are defined as 'undesired, characteristic, negative trajectories (or environmental degradation patterns) of natural and civilizational trends and their interplay, which can be identified in many regions of our world'.[1] The particular merit of syndrome analysis is that it takes systematic account of the effect of the human factor of global environmental change. Figure 1.2 shows an example of a syndrome, namely that of the overexploitation of the biosphere. The human factor is presented in the boxes entitled social organisation, economy, and science/technology.

The WBGU has identified sixteen such syndromes, but more could be proposed. Three groups can be distinguished:

- *'utilisation' syndromes*: syndromes which are the consequence of the inappropriate utilisation of natural resources;
- *'development' syndromes*: human/environmental problems resulting from non-sustainable development processes;
- *'sink' syndromes*: environmental degradation due to inappropriate disposal of human effluent.

The full list as identified by the WBGU includes the following:[2]

Utilisation syndromes:

- *Sahel Syndrome*: overcultivation of marginal land;
- *Overexploitation Syndrome*: overexploitation of natural ecosystems;
- *Rural Exodus Syndrome*: environmental degradation caused by abandonment of traditional forms of land use;
- *Dust Bowl Syndrome*: non-sustainable industrial management of soil and water resources;
- *Katanga Syndrome*: environmental degradation caused by extraction of non-renewable resources;

---

[1] Wissenschaftlicher Beirat Globale Umweltveränderungen (WBGU) (Advisory Council on Global Change), *New structures for global environmental policy*, London (Earthscan) 2000, p. 21.
[2] WBGU, op. cit. p. 22.

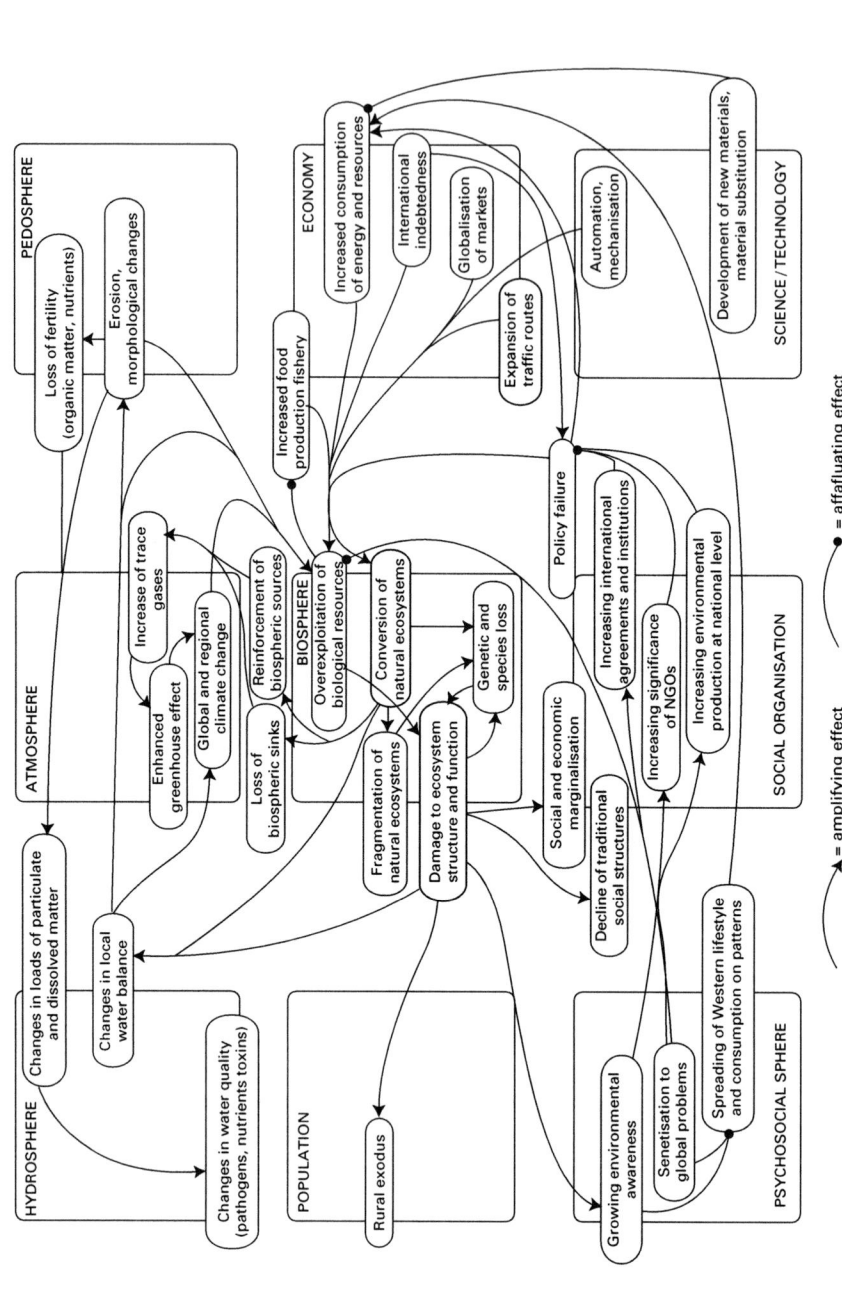

Figure 1.2 Network of interrelations characterising the overexploitation syndrome.
Source: WBGU, Welt im Wandel: Erhaltung und nachhaltige Nutzung der Biosphäre, Berlin (Springer) 2000, p. 279

- *Mass Tourism Syndrome*: development of and damage to near-natural areas for recreational purposes;
- *Scorched Earth Syndrome*: environmental degradation through military activities.

Development syndromes:

- *Aral Sea Syndrome*: environmental damage caused by large-scale projects aimed at restructuring natural landscapes;
- *Green Revolution Syndrome*: environmental degradation caused by the introduction of site-inappropriate farming methods;
- *Asian Tigers Syndrome*: neglect of environmental standards in the course of highly dynamic economic growth;
- *Favela Syndrome*: environmental degradation caused by uncontrolled urbanisation;
- *Urban Sprawl Syndrome*: landscape degradation caused by planned urban and infrastructure expansion;
- *Major Accident Syndrome*: singular anthropogenic environmental disasters with long-term impacts.

Sink syndromes:

- *Smokestack Syndrome*: environmental degradation caused by long-range, diffuse dispersal of mostly persistent substances;
- *Waste Dumping Syndrome*: appropriation of environmental space through the controlled and uncontrolled dumping of wastes;
- *Contaminated Land Syndrome*: local contamination of environmental assets, mainly at industrial production sites.

These and other syndromes – one could, for example, imagine a syndrome focussing on Western lifestyles – can be employed to explain climate change as well as other global environmental problems such as the chemical contamination of air, soil, and water, the overexploitation of the oceans, the degradation of the soil, the loss of biodiversity, and the scarcity of fresh water. Whilst descriptive information on the state and development trends of these problems is more and more available,[3] syndrome analysis can help to trace the much demanded causal chains behind the phenomena. Table 1.1 shows how in the view of the WBGU[4] the syndromes are related to the six large global problems.

Syndrome analysis achieves two objectives in the study of institutions: first, if developed further, by the insertion of a special box on institutions and allowing for genuine syndrome trajectories within institutions (see Figure 1.2), it can help to identify how much of an impact institutions have as a part of the human

---

[3] See in particular the comprehensive global and regional Environment Outlooks published by UNEP (www.geo.org/GEO/index.htm).
[4] WBGU, op. cit. p. 53.

Table 1.1 *Causation of global environmental problems by syndromes*

	Climate change	Stratospheric ozone depletion	Oceans at risk	Biodiversity loss and deforestation	Soil degradation	Fresh water scarcity and pollution
Sahel	●			●	●	●
Overexploitation	●		●	●	●	●
Rural Exodus	○			●	○	
Dust Bowl			●	●	●	●
Kalanga			○	○		●
Mass Tourism	○			○	○	
Scorched Earth				●	○	
Aral Sea	○				○	●
Green Revolution	●		●	●	●	●
Asian Tigers	●	●	●	●	○	●
Favela			●	●	●	●
Urban Sprawl	●	●	●	●	●	●
Major Accident			●	●	○	○
Smokestack	●	●	●	●	●	
Waste Dumping			●	○	●	○
Contaminated Land			○	○	●	○

● means that the syndrome plays a leading role in the causation of the environmental problem ○ indicates a less marked influence.

causation of global change. Secondly, syndrome analysis allows the identification of the strategic points in the causal chains best suited to institutional intervention.

III. The global mind

The scientific community is preoccupied with understanding the individual syndromes, their configuration as a whole, their contribution to the major global environmental problems, and in all of these respects – the role of human impact. However, if the emerging knowledge is to become actively relevant, it must be known by the global population. Therefore, the analysis of human knowledge of and perspective on global environmental change must start with a genuine sociological enquiry into the inner logic of societies, their beliefs, rules, and structures. Devising measures of influencing this perspective can only occur after this has been accomplished. However, the vision of a global subject as proposed by John Schellnhuber[5] must be considered with caution and not be understood as the rule of a new philosopher king. The global subject may well turn out to be a mere metaphor for a common concern based on the prevailing fundamental differences of perception.

There are two dimensions of the human mind of interest in the institutional context: in one sense, the human mind is a factor determining human behaviour towards nature, and as such institutions must take it into consideration in order to find the appropriate means of action. For instance, if the Western lifestyle is tabooed by institutions propagating modesty, these institutions are doomed to fail. In another sense, the human mind is the political basis required for institutions to come into existence and be legitimate. The human mind is therefore a condition of both the effectiveness and legitimacy of institutions.

In their contributions to the present volume, Karl-Werner Brand and Fritz Reusswig in Chapter 4 focus on the first condition and Asher Alcoby in Chapter 5 focuses on the second.

Brand and Reusswig explore the societal preconditions of a successful institutionalisation of global environmental governance. They describe how institutions are embedded in societies. In order to become effective their problem solution must take the interest and power structure of society into account, their core idea must be related to basic cultural values, and the basic hypotheses they assume must correspond to 'storylines' widely shared by society. They also have to meet the criteria of procedural and distributional 'fairness' which prevail in society. These conditions of anchoring institutions in society apply also to those institutions – national as well as international – which contribute to global environmental change. If they are to be reoriented towards more

---

[5] Schellnhuber, H. J., Earth sytem analysis and management, in Ehlers, E. and Krafft, T. (ed.), *Understanding the Earth System*, Berlin (Springer) 2001, p. 17 *et seq.*

sustainable utilisation of natural resources the human mind and its construction of risk must become aware of the globality of environmental problems in order to 'green' interest and power structures, societal values, and perceptions.

The authors argue that such awareness is indeed emerging, but that its perseverance will depend on some broader developments of modern societies. These can be reconstructed in terms of structure and agency. As to the first aspect, Brand and Reusswig show that macrostructural trends such as detraditionalisation, individualisation, globalisation, or the emergence of the 'knowledge society' have ambivalent effects on the social acceptance of environmental regulations. On the one hand, they erode traditional ways of life and pave the way for the spread of Western lifestyles; moreover, they increase the probability of cultural conflicts and the salience of social problems. On the other hand, they favour participation, the spread of information and a worldwide networking of concerned citizens and non-governmental organisations (NGOs).

Structural opportunities for the required change towards sustainability are no guarantee for a real change. This demands powerful agents. The authors therefore go on to analyse the societal key actors who will – or could – be the hosts of the required 'greening' of human society. Leaving business and the media aside, they focus on transnational civil society as represented by NGOs, science as a social phenomenon, and the consumer. Acknowledging certain flaws of NGOs, the authors nevertheless insist that NGOs do pave the way towards a world society. As for science, they show its precarious role between uncertainty and the practical need for definite answers. Concerning consumers, whilst revealing the burdensome impact on global change of consumerism, they nevertheless are positive about the prospects of environmentally concerned consumption, provided the consumer's mind is supported by adequate institutions.

Asher Alkoby embarks upon answering the question whether and if so in what way civil society within the nation state can develop into a global civil society and as such become the source of legitimacy for international institutions. Whilst there is substantial empirical information about the kinds of transnational actor (TNA) appearing on the international stage, such as NGOs, social movements, advocacy networks, and transnational corporations, and about the way in which TNAs act, e.g. by participating in agenda-setting, norm creation and norm implementation, the theoretical explanation of why TNAs emerge and may constitute a global civil society is still underdeveloped.

The author believes some approaches are counter-empirical, such as the 'power theory' which does not accept any influence of NGOs etc. on institutions, and the 'institutionalist theory' which regards NGOs etc. as pure instruments of states. Whilst the author considers 'constructivist theories' to be generally of more substance, nevertheless some variants are flawed, such as the 'old social movements' concept which explains such movements by experiences of deprevation, and 'rational choice' concepts which overlook the moral and cultural elements of the social fabric. Alkoby concentrates on the concept of 'new social movements' which emerge on the basis of principled ideas (human rights, environmental concern, etc.) rather than on depravation or the purpose of gaining benefits. This concept is also widely accepted by scholars of international law who see NGOs as legitimate entities able to fill the democracy deficit of international institutions.

However, the author finds the interpretation of the emergence of TNA on the whole rather too narrowly conceived. A more comprehensive understanding of the relationship between international institutions and societies is possible if TNA are discussed as part of the broader civil society. The question is not only whether there can be global social movements but whether there can be a global civil society. The history of the conception of civil society shows that it has mostly been proposed as a sphere opposed to the state or at least mediating between the private sphere and the state. This preoccupation with the state lurks also behind the major modern theories of civil society, i.e. the liberalist and the communitarian conceptions. They presuppose the existence of concentrated power 'against' which civil society is built. This is hardly a route to the transnational stage where no such power centres exist. In that realm, civil society must be conceivable as an agent working 'with' the newly emerging institutions.

Alkoby finds discourse theory better suited to conceive of such a globalised civil society. Discourses do not assume the existence of a power 'against' which legitimation occurs, rather this power can be a source of institutions. They also do not assume there to be consensus on certain material values, thus avoiding the risk of domination of some values over others. They only need consensus on some formal requirements of an 'ideal speech situation'. As Alkoby asserts: 'The procedural model of communicative action, which prescribes the ideal *formal* requirements for developing a consensus (rather than prescribing what that consensus ought to be) is the only way of developing the cross-cultural solidarity that would open the possibility of arriving at common norms.' In the view of the author, however, these requirements should be reformulated somewhat in order to integrate economic actors into civil society. Economic actors are often seen as practising 'strategic' argumentation which is alien to the 'discursive' style of discourse theory. The author is of the opinion the distinction should not be overemphasised because in practice often both styles are used; industry often participates in discourses whilst NGOs also employ strategic arguments. Concluding his chapter, the author adds the cautionary note that civil society of the discursive kind is not yet there but rather 'becoming'.

IV. The global view on governance

Governance, organisations, and institutions are terms widely used in our context but very differently defined. Therefore, we start with a terminological clarification. For the purposes of this work an 'institution' is defined as common values, perceptions of the real world, and rules of behaviour established (from the Latin 'instituere' – to establish) for (but not necessarily by) a group of persons.[6] For instance, marriage is an institution in most societies, as is the UN prohibition of force in the international arena.[7] Often institutions are supported by specialised personnel, acting bodies, a budget, etc. In this sense they are also organisations. If organised institutions within the international arena fulfil certain additional requirements such as being based on a founding treaty and having an (at least partial) international personality, they are called international organisations. The term 'international regimes' employed by political science is largely identical to the term 'international organisations' defined by international law doctrine, but the term is both wider and narrower: whilst neither a treaty nor international personality are required, the organisation must have some real world effectiveness. For instance, an apparatus set up by soft law and managing some informally agreed tasks can be a regime, but not an international organisation. International regimes are thus (effective) organised institutions.

Institutions can be a framework for self-regulation by the actors concerned. If organised, they are often more active in steering the behaviour of their clientele. In this case one speaks of 'governance'. If formal powers of command are involved, the arrangement is called 'government', be it that of a state or supranational organisation. The term 'institution' is therefore broader than the term 'governance'. Looking for 'multilevel governance' of global change would assume that there is an actor consciously steering the action whilst in fact global change is widely also the unintended result of common arrangements. For example, private property is a powerful institution affecting global change and as such a framework but not a steering device. For this reason, the present book might rather have been titled 'multilevel institutions'. But as the general focus of the contributions is on the steering element of institutions, 'multilevel governance' is also appropriate.

As explained above, the institutional response to global change is not just seen in global institutions. Many levels of institutions contribute to global change, and actors on many levels must be employed in order to redirect it. Therefore, the perspective rather than the object of inquiry must be global.

There are two elements to be considered in relation to institutional impact on global change, one relating to geographical and physical variations and the other to the organisational scale. The geographical and physical dimension can

---

[6] This definition is widely used in the social sciences but also in legal theory. A narrower variant defines institutions as acting entities. For instance, the European Community organs are called institutions in Article 234 of the Treaty founding the European Community.

[7] Examples taken from WBGU, op. cit. p. 69. The WBGU defines institutions somewhat differently, as common arrangements established by actors to regulate their relations. See WBGU, op. cit. p. 69.

be described by further use of and elaboration upon syndrome analysis. For instance, the Asian Tiger Syndrome tells much about Chinese and South Korean institutions – that they prioritise economic growth; the Smokestack Syndrome reveals US, Japanese and EU institutions are aimed at the wide utilisation of chemicals; the Sahel Syndrome points to African communal institutions allowing overutilisation of land, etc. The organisational dimension can be explored by distinguishing between different levels of institutions and analysing the genuine characteristics of each level.

The organisational dimension was taken as the basis for this book. Hence, the analysis progresses from institutions of societal self-organisation to the state and from there onto international institutions. The geographical dimension will be reflected (but of course not fully covered) on each of these levels.

It does not, however, suffice to show that there is a multitude of institutions acting on global change. Whilst post-modernist thought may halt in amazement at the number of institutions, the challenge is to explore whether there are patterns of interaction between institutional levels, allowing us to speak of a structured whole. Ideally the analysis of the 'natural laws' of the earth system would be complemented by an analysis of the 'social laws' of the institutional system. Important points to be raised in this regard are:[8]

- the question of scale: which functions are fulfilled at what level, and how do these levels relate to one another?
- the question of interplay: how do exploitative and protective institutions relate to one another and how can the gap between them be bridged?
- the question of fit: which rules and instruments are most appropriate to solving an environmental problem?
- the question of structural coupling: are there basic ideas and structures that pervade all of the levels of governance and geographical/physical variants, such as, in particular, certain legal principles of common concern like liability for damage or even precaution?

Some of these questions will be explored in the following contributions, but the overall analysis remains a task for future research.

V. Societal self-regulation

There are many societal institutions which direct human behaviour towards the environment, ranging from the Japanese belief in the sexual potential of whale oil to the German preoccupation with separating different kinds of household waste for recycling. We have treated those as part of the societal culture in which more formal institutions must be established in order to meet compliance with

---

[8] Most of these points are taken from Young, O., *The institutional dimensions of environmental change: fit, interplay, and scale*, Cambridge, Mass. (The MIT Press) 2002.

themselves (see Chapter 4 by Brand and Reusswig), however, it goes without saying that such societal institutions also work without support (or opposition) by formal institutions.

In the book we have focussed on self-regulation by economic actors. Informal institutions of this kind can take different forms: self-organisation within multinational corporations (MNC) (or multinational enterprises (MNE)), self-coordination of transnational networks of companies on contractual or portfolio bases (transnational enterprises, TNE),[9] and self-regulation by business associations and normalisation organisations at national, regional, and global levels, such as the International Standardisation Organisation (ISO). In the present work we take MNE and TNE as an example.

We propose to distinguish self-organisation in the private interest from that in the public interest. Whilst a wealth of studies have been produced on the self-interest of MNEs and TNEs regarding their self-organisation and the commercial transactions between each other, less research has been done on the potential self-organisation has to transcend short-term profit orientation and include public concerns such as environmental protection within the goals of MNEs and TNEs.

In Chapter 6, Martin Herberg gives an empirically founded account of the modes and potential of self-regulation of MNEs in relation to health and environmental protection. Based on interviews and their methodologically sophisticated interpretation he finds German chemical concerns' self-established regulation to consist of three components: publicly announced codes of conduct, auditing schemes, and concrete technical and organisational standards. They allow the mother company to control her subsidiaries. Exploring the auditing schemes in more detail, Herberg shows that the corporate environmental managers display neither a laissez-faire nor a hierarchical attitude but concede rather a kind of autonomy, which, however, also allows for a possible resort to command and control. The self-regulatory auditing of MNEs is more effective than the kind of auditing proposed by rule 14001 of ISO, the latter being criticised by managers themselves as paper work containing mere descriptions of self-descriptions.

---

[9] The terminology varies. 'MNC' (or MNE) and 'TNC' (or TNE) are often used interchangeably as a generic term for all kinds of economic entities or clusters of entities operating in two or more states. See for 'TNC' the Subcommission on the Promotion and Protection of Human Rights, *Norms on the Responsibilities of Transnational Corporations and Other Business Enterprises with regard to Human Rights*, UN Doc. E/CN.4/Sub.2/2003/12/Rev.2 (2003), para. 20, and for 'MNE' the OECD *Guidelines for Multinational Enterprises* 2001 (also at www.oecd.org). We suggest to reserve 'MNE' or 'MNC' for a cluster which is in some way directed by a parent company, thus providing ground for guided self-organisation but also for home state control, and 'TNE' for a more loosely connected network which more easily evades home state control and has (intentionally?) more difficulties to self-organise concern for public interests.

According to Herberg, the 'operative autonomy under reservation' (of intervention) is a proof that organisational learning has made ground during the past decades in MNEs. The Bophal catastrophe illustrates the risks of the 'steering at arm's length' approach as compared to control by the mother company. The company now often takes responsibility for the 'user gap', i.e. for ensuring that dangerous technology exported to other countries is safely operated by the personnel of the subsidiary. It is interesting to note that the author explains this change in direction by the challenge for the MNE's professionals rather than by their concern for a positive image (as many would assume).

Relating his study of societal rules to questions of legal rules, Herberg argues that the transnational rulings of MNEs make good that which is lacking in national regulation and enforcement in many countries in which they invest. If practised by many MNEs, self-established internal rules may constitute transnational fields of practice (in German: *transnationale Verkehrskreise*) indicative of a standard of control over the subsidiary which may justify 'piercing the corporate veil' and making late-comers or those concerns violating their own standards liable. However, the author adds a cautionary note. According to his own research, self-regulation focuses on the prevention of accidents whilst the 'normal' environmental impact (air and water pollution, waste disposal, etc.) is under less strict control. Although more self-regulation might be developed in this regard, an improvement of state-based control is a necessity.

Continuing this train of thought on an international level, André Nollkaemper in Chapter 7 addresses the question of how MNEs and TNEs are related to international law. For the sake of terminological clarity he proposes two definitions of responsibility bearable by a company, state etc. The first distinguishes between primary rules of expected behaviour and secondary rules of the consequences of breaching such rules. The second, much broader, definition defines responsibility as any kind of obligation a person or body will respect. *Nollkaemper* then explains the legal value of self-regulation by MNEs and TNEs. Acknowledging the potential persuasive and influential authority of such regulation in the social world, he insists that there is a gap between self-regulation and formal law. Self-regulation is not based on international law obligations and neither are the consequences of the breaches of self-made rules determined by international law. To speak, as some authors propose, of a global overarching constitution (in German: *Gesamtverfassung*) embracing different layers of informal and formal law disregards the different sources of these orders. The usual manner in which international law becomes relevant for MNEs and TNEs is through addressing states which in turn impose obligations upon the corporation. There are, however, a few examples of international treaties which can be interpreted as directly addressing corporations and, in any case, state law may open itself up to accept direct applicability of international provisions. However, the author finds consideration of this point odd because in most cases domestic law will be more clearly defined than the broad language of international treaties anyway.

Nollkaemper's central argument is that there is nevertheless the potential to develop international law to involve directly MNEs and TNEs. As seen in the examples of international human rights and criminal law, there is no conceptual barrier to international law addressing private actors. Illustrative examples include the 'Norms on the Responsibilities of Trans-national Corporations and other Business Enterprises with regard to Human Rights' concluded by a Subcommission of the UN Commission on Human Rights in 2003,[10] which despite being soft law nevertheless demonstrate that the international community is willing to impose obligations upon private actors. This also extends to the sphere of environmental protection. He also discusses the pros and cons of developing 'international' law towards an order accepting multinational private actors as its subjects.

Jonas Ebbesson in Chapter 8 pushes this approach further by proposing a methodology of how an international treaty on transnational business relations in view of health and environmental protection could be designed. Rather than embarking on wishful thinking he builds on what has already been achieved by international treaties, national laws with extra-territorial reach, international soft law, and self-binding codes of industry. 'Fragments' of this growing body of law at different levels and of different degrees of validity can be assembled and formed into a more consistent, ambitious, and binding text. Much of what legal doctrine would understand as profoundly divergent worlds becomes a kind of joint construction ground in this study. Ebbesson distinguishes between fragments concerning the substance, procedures, and 'subjectivity' of the addressee of the treaty.

'Substance' means principles, performance standards, and liability criteria. Already now there are treaties which establish rather concrete duties, e.g. in the areas of dumping of waste at sea, transnational shipment of hazardous waste, trade in endangered species, marketing of certain hazardous substances, etc. Some of these may even be understood as self-executing in national laws, thus directly binding companies and giving rights for affected third parties. The same is true for civil liability schemes. These concrete institutions are, however, issue-specific and would need to be generalised. There is also a wealth of international documents, binding or more often soft, universal or more often regional, which reflect general principles such as precaution, polluter pays, environmental impact assessment, transparency, etc. The author also considers if, rather than harmonising substantive law, the envisaged treaty should be confined to harmonise the rules on the conflict of laws. He cites an ambitious model found in the Nordic Environment Protection Convention ruling that a case of compensation for environmental harm must not be

---

[10] See n. 9 above.

decided by rules less favourable to the plaintiff than those in the state of the activity.

As for 'procedure', Ebbesson observes that in liability cases jurisdiction outside the state of activity and harm is more and more accepted, thus giving the plaintiff the choice of the most effective forum. Less developed is access to courts outside the state of activity or harm concerning injunctions and mandamus actions aiming at preventing harm by MNEs/TNEs. The author refers to the system of national contact points and 'soft' means of dispute resolution established by the OECD Guidelines on Multinational Enterprises. As far as criminal acts are concerned, the OECD Bribery Convention is noteworthy for its principle to refer to the home state forum. International fora, the author explains, are, however, not yet accessible for disputes over MNE/TNE activities, except for the singular case of war crimes heard by the International Court of Criminal Justice.

The author goes on to questions of 'subjectivity', i.e. the legal construction of the MNE/TNE and its implication for who should be the addressee of the envisaged obligations and who should bear responsibility for failure. Following the principle also advocated by Martin Herberg in Chapter 6 that responsibility should follow de facto control, the way is opened for liability of the parent company in MNEs. More creative drafting would be required to find appropriate solutions for TNEs, drawing on advice from the 'Draft Norms on Responsibility of TNC' of the UN Subcommission on Human Rights.

Ebbesson concludes his contribution by delineating the structure and basic content of the envisaged treaty.

VI. Transnational bureaucratic networks

In addition to the societal layer of transnational self-regulation, a layer of bureaucratic transnational networks, capable of producing institutions of global environmental change, has emerged. Located 'beyond' the nation state but 'below' international organisations they have the potential to fill the gap left by the lack of international harmonisation between state institutions. There are such networks which promote economic growth and such which protect against the related exploitation of natural resources. One example of the 'protective' network is presented by Michael Warning in Chapter 12.

Taking hazardous chemicals as a case in point, the author begins with the observation that whilst few chemicals are regulated, a tremendous number of others are marketed and used without the availability of adequate risk information and assessment. This problem of 'toxic ignorance' is of a global nature because the chemicals are used everywhere. National systems have proved to be incapable of solving the problem, acting too slowly, applying different test methods and parameters, and often repeating substance risk assessments already completed by other countries. An international joint venture is therefore long overdue. As an international treaty to tackle the problem was beyond sight, the professional staff from many states have formed informal structures, thus bypassing the formal roads of treaty-making and implementation.

The author reveals that within these structures exist agenda-setting networks formulating basic orientations, rule-making networks developing technical rules, e.g. on tests, good laboratory practice, and the classification and labelling of chemicals, and administrative networks collecting, assessing, and publishing risk information on single substances. It is possible for industry and public interest NGOs to participate in the networks, but voting is reserved to government representatives. Most of the networks establish their own rules, which further proves their potential for self-organisation.

The networks described by Warning are not entirely freely floating but attached to and organisationally supported by intergovernmental organisations such as OECD, WHO, FAO, and ILO. These supporting organisations sometimes also lend their decision-making capacity to give added weight in the international sphere to unusual results. Examples of this include the OECD adoption of recommendations on test guidelines and the ECOSOC subcommittee adoption of a decision on the harmonisation of the classification of chemicals.

Warning concludes by posing some evaluative questions. The first relates to efficacy: the networks are still slow, but they have led to some acceleration of the assessment of chemicals and have the potential to be improved further. Secondly, in spite of the seemingly technical character of the matter, 'political' decisions are involved in the process, and therefore legitimation is required. The author argues that such legitimation cannot be provided by domestic structures, but needs to exist on the transnational level itself. Thirdly, despite being soft law, the products of the networks can bind the private interests of industry or third parties, which means that legal protection must be provided. Again, national court review would not reflect the genuine rationality of the transnational networks. Therefore, new conflict resolution institutions must be founded.

VII. Self-regulation by states

State analysts agree that the globalised economy and its global environmental effects have largely escaped the jurisdiction of the state, and that for these reasons an internationalisation of the legal order imposes itself. More precisely, the political-economic 'laws' of the role of the state are often seen to be that:

- in order to compete on production costs a state will only introduce high production standards if these are internationally harmonised;
- in order to compete on product prices a state will only prescribe high product standards if these are internationally harmonised;

- in order to compete on best infrastructure for investment a state will only protect nature if nature protection standards are internationally harmonised;
- in order to maintain a high level of demand for domestic products (and in order to secure its basis for tax income) a state will generally be hesitant to impose consumption charges and, if at all, agree to such impositions only upon international harmonisation.

In this highly internationalised view, the state is increasingly more bound to act as a member of international fora and as an implementer of what has been agreed on the international level. Nevertheless, if things go wrong this is inevitably attributed to either the slow process of international harmonisation or to flaws in implementation.

This view cannot be entirely accepted. Even if one accepts its rationalistic assumption, it is quite possible that states act on a different rationale. Efficiency considerations may motivate them to pioneer environmental protection. For instance, progressive production standards may trigger more efficient technology, ambitious product standards may create new promising markets, a high level of nature preservation may attract tourism, and consumption charges may not reduce but reorient consumption. A clear prohibition combined with a grace period for adaptation can be an effective device inducing innovation in production or products. All this has been experienced in the development of the EU. Most significantly, fears that the state of origin principle (which forces importing states largely to accept the products standards of the exporting state) would induce a 'rush to the bottom' have not materialised.[11]

More fundamentally, the rationalistic approach itself raises objections. Explaining the behaviour of states in terms of rational actors disregards the variety of geographical conditions, economic development, organisational capacity, tradition, culture, corruption, and political processes which may lead states to take other routes than those the rational models predict.

Of course, states do not only act in response to internal causes, but also to those from the international sphere. But the pivotal factor is very often not international 'vertical' institutions but rather 'horizontal' pioneering, imitation, and pressure.

For these reasons the impact of state institutions on global environmental change must take account of the complexity of external and internal conditions. The global perspective on the state needs to integrate comparative with international studies of both social sciences and the law. It is likely that a typology referring to some of the syndromes previously mentioned will emerge from such analysis. For instance, in consideration of the types of institutions, the environmental impact of a state like China, which is rushing towards industrial

---

[11] See the classical analysis by Rehbinder, E. and Stewart, R., *Environmental protection policy*, Berlin (de Gruyter) 1985.

growth, is certainly different in substance and cause than that of a state like Germany, which is struggling against the loss of investment, or a state with a dominant ethos of resource exploitation like the Russian Federation, or a state both idiosyncratic and missionary, like the USA. In view of geographical conditions, state institutions will differ profoundly according to whether the state's natural resources are minerals, forests, arid land, arable soil, mountains, coasts, or none of the above. Cultural and religious traditions will only further diversify the picture. In view of these differences there can be very different models of how to make state policies respond to environmental concern.

The present work cannot, of course, cover all of these models. The development of the former communist countries during their transition is used to example the type of approach necessary in analysing the role of states in global change.

Stephen Stec, Alexios Antipas, and Tamara Steger in Chapter 14 delve into the environmental development of the former Soviet block. The revolutionary and post-revolutionary period demonstrated strong public and political concern about environmental issues. Environmental matters were at the same time a learning ground for participation in general. First drafts and codifications of environmental law were very ambitious. But concerns of economic recovery quickly gained influence and resulted in more realistic environmental legislation. Conflicts over shared resources which had been previously solved by the central government in the former USSR became conflicts between new states and made regional agreements essential but difficult to acquire. Simultaneously, the unity of the Soviet period made way for increasingly more divergence along the geographical lines of the old East and West Roman empires.

The central European states wishing to accede to the EU were obligated to adapt their legislation to comply with the EU's *acquis communitaire*. In some sectors such as industrial pollution this led to significant improvements. However, as the authors state, 'governments sacrificed their creativity and initiative to the overriding, and overwhelming, task of readying their countries for entry into the EU'. The EU, on the other hand, was hesitantly, if at all, prepared to learn from achievements of the communist or post-communist periods. For instance, the legal standing of collectives such as the citizens' initiative, environmental duties complementing environmental rights, citizen enforcement, EIA requirements and NGO consultancy concerning the drafting of legislation and treaties, achievements in the areas of waste recycling, public transportation, agriculture, and nature preservation, were not considered worthy of adoption by EU legislation. Eastern approaches had only one major success in establishing the basis of the Aarhus Convention of 1998 and its far-reaching participation and standing rights.

Whilst the accession states have or will soon have a modern environmental law, the situation has become even more diverse within the other post-communist states. The Russian Federation, after years of *perestroika* and environmental concern, took a step backwards, reinstalling the 'octopus of state power' and the politics of maximal exploitation of resources with little concern for effective environmental protection. Environmental legislation is well developed but the style of the laws is often loose and the participation rights are more concerned with an 'appreciation of governmental issues' rather than genuine critique. The authors add some remarks on the development of environmental law in the remaining CIS states. Some of them follow the Russian path closely, whilst in others generic governmental issues supersede environmental governance issues.

In their conclusion, the authors claim that the development of a civil society is crucial to effective environmental protection. However, the role of NGOs must be redefined with more autonomy, as watchdogs rather than consultants.

VIII. Mutual influence between states

The potential of states to influence each other 'horizontally' rather than 'vertically' through building and implementing international regimes is a further source of global governance. The potential to influence is usually based on either the cultural leadership of the influencing state or its purchasing power on the world market. The vehicles of influence range from the media and the instigation of discourses to technical assistance and market restrictions.

In Chapter 10, Christian Tietje addresses the question of how and to what extent the purchasing power of states can be used, via trade restrictions, to press other states to observe environmental protection requirements in their own territory. This question approaches the issue of free world trade from an unusual perspective. Whilst it is normally discussed whether free trade *erodes* national environmental standards due to competition from imported products, or whether it enables the improvement of environmental performance due to increased income from exportation, the present question is whether free trade can be used to *impose* environmental standards. The most effective way of doing this is to impose certain production or extraction standards on the exporting state (so-called processes and production measures (PPM)). In this way the importing state can discourage process-based pollution, degradation of nature, energy consumption, etc.

Given the international legal framework of world trade, the use of PPMs is not only a question of politics but also of law. Tietje therefore explores the room for manoeuvre left by GATT and related agreements. This margin depends on a number of checks. The first is whether the imported product subject to PPM is similar to a product free of PPM. The author propounds a negative answer to this question, which would widely free PPMs from the applicability of GATT restrictions and thereby create a broad discretion to apply PPMs. However, if it is decided in the first step that PPMs do fall within the GATT regime, a further step must be taken, i.e. the measure must not treat domestic and external products differently. Should the importing state deem it expedient to impose special measures on external products (e.g. because the environmental problem is peculiar to the exporting state, such as the occurrence of certain endangered species), the third step applies, the proof of necessity of protection. Tietje spells out that if a link to the regulating state exists, the fact that one state interferes in matters within the territory of another state through PPMs contradicts neither GATT nor general international law. Finally, the fourth step requires the regulating state to have first of all attempted to enact a bilateral or multilateral agreement on the matter.

At this point the author widens the question to a broader legal discussion on the proper place of unilateral trade measures in relation to international cooperation and international standard-setting. Although it is clear that international cooperation is preferable, the author remains more sceptical about its effectiveness, pointing to the regulatory potential of the country of origin principle. In conclusion, he submits that unilateral PPMs can be a powerful instrument of global environmental governance.

Kerstin Tews in Chapter 9 addresses the mechanisms of environmental policy transfer among states from the broader perspective of political science. Based on a quantitative empirical study on the adoption of twenty-one environmental policy innovations in forty-eight countries over a time period of fifty years, she identifies the dissemination patterns of certain types of instruments among states. 'Weak' instruments such as environmental planning spread faster than 'hard' instruments, 'new' instruments such as economic incentives were introduced later than hard instruments, but at about the same time as weak instruments.

Tews offers various explanations of these patterns. The data do not support the popular view among scholars of international law and international relations that states usually adopt environmental laws following international treaties. Nor does it support the hypothesis that the diffusion of policies results from the geographical and/or cultural proximity of states. Rather, she identifies international discourse based on, but not commanded by, international organisations as the primary factor determining adoption, such as the global debates around the 1972 Stockholm Conference and the 1992 Rio Conference. This kind of debate can also be instigated by international bureaucracies such as the OECD, which acts via persuasion rather than formal means of law-making. Sometimes, policies unfold during the run-up to or parallel to negotiations about new treaties.

However, international institutions are not the only cause of policy diffusion. Sometimes an international institution can even hamper the 'horizontal' learning processes when states anticipate policy formation at the international level and 'wait and see', giving up their own pioneering action. More importantly, the fact that some types of policies spread more easily than others indicates that policy transfer is heavily dependent on the content of the instrument. Tews calls this the diffusibility factor. A policy must fit the problem it is designed to solve, it must be compatible with the style of instruments already adopted by a state, it must be acceptable in the light of internal political priorities and debates, etc. However, the author believes that in spite of these obvious 'objective' factors, the power of 'constructivist' discourses is significant.

Policy learning by one state from another, directly or via regional or international facilitation or harmonisation, is addressed in Chapter 19 by Andrew Jordan, Rüdiger Wurzel, and Anthony Zito. The authors focus on the European experience, as related to new environmental policy instruments (NEPIs), i.e. market-based instruments (MBIs) such as eco-taxes and tradable permits, voluntary agreements (VAs) and informational devices such as eco-labels. They analyse the overall pattern of NEPI use and more traditional (or 'older') tools of environmental policy (i.e. regulation) in seven Member States and the EU. They then explain what role or roles the EU has played in the selection and diffusion of policy instruments, and relate this to the actual use of NEPIs both at the EU and Member State level. Finally, they assess what lessons could be learnt from the EU's experience of adopting and implementing NEPIs to aid the development of environmental governance in other states and regions.

The authors found that most NEPI activity takes place at a national level, even though most target and policy framing activity is now undertaken at an EU level. Although the EU has greatly influenced Member State environmental policies, this influence does not extend to the selection and implementation of 'new' policy tools such as NEPIs. In some cases the opposition to giving the EU a greater role is simply due to technical (i.e. efficiency and effectiveness) concerns. For example, voluntary agreements are difficult to engineer, monitor, and 'enforce' beyond the state level, especially in policy sectors which are characterised by a large number of relatively small firms. Concerns about free-riders are magnified at the supranational and, even more so, at the global level. However, there are also important economic and political impediments which work against certain NEPIs being taken up at the supranational and/or global level, as can best be seen in the EU's continuing failure to adopt a carbon dioxide/energy tax. The EU's influence in shaping the prevailing pattern of NEPI use has been and remains very mixed. A strong entrepreneurial influence on the part of the EU can only really be detected with respect to tradable permits and, to a much lesser degree, eco-labels.

IX. Integration of world regions

Given the slow emergence of effective institutions on a global level, regional integration is a means of global governance worth considering. The major regions of the world – North America, South America, North Africa, Sub-Saharan Africa, the CIS states, and East Asia – are in a process of economic integration. The question is whether the prevailing focus on free trade may create such widespread consequences that social and environmental policies become part of the emerging institutions.

The most developed example is, of course, the European Union. In Chapter 13, Ludwig Krämer explores what can be learned from the EU experience. He first gives a concise summary of what has been achieved, stressing the most significant organisational characteristics of the EU as a quasi-federal state: the Community organs, the major instruments of policy elaboration, the decision-making structures including remaining margins of action by the Member States, the mechanisms of implementation, dispute settlement, the involvement of the public, and the integration of environmental concerns into other (i.e. not primarily environmental) policies.

Observing the state of environmental institutions at the global level in the areas of water, air, biodiversity, and waste, Krämer argues that what has been achieved is far from effective in halting environmental deterioration. One criticism he raises is the broad language used by many international conventions. Even if they were implemented, he submits, they would not really improve the situation. The major flaw is therefore the lack of precise standards.

Looking at the reasons for the unsatisfactory state of global governance (as seen in the principle of sovereignty and the rule of unanimity accompanying it) the author sheds some light on the role of the USA. Given its hegemonic status, this country has had the chance to push towards more effective environmental protection. However, Krämer shows that for approximately twenty years, the USA has not only not acted upon this opportunity but even hampered initiatives started by other regions. (The subject is further developed by Thomas Giegerich in Chapter 11). For these reasons, the author proposes that regional integration independent of the consent of the hegemonic state may be more promising.

Reiterating his summary of EU characteristics, Krämer points to those which might be most effectively imitated. He is sceptical about the potential of the existing economic integration in regions outside Europe to become the basis of effective environmental governance. Rather he suggests that regionalisation should be sector-related (i.e. focussed on the environmental issue) and based on the UN regional conventions and organisational nuclei. The most important lesson to be learnt from Europe is that it is not just conventions that are concluded but also that a body is established to act as a trustee of the general regional interest, such as the Commission in the European case. These regional environmental agencies should begin – as did the EEC – by setting up environmental action programmes; they should be given rule-making powers, initially in tandem with the Member States, but progressing to making decisions by majority voting, and they should be endowed with powers and auxiliary bodies to oversee the correct implementation of the law. In addition to such agencies, dispute resolution bodies should be founded at a regional level which can be invoked by the environmental agency in cases of law violation. The EU treaty violation procedure might serve as a model in this respect. It would provide a forum and also allow negotiation with the Member States in its 'shadow', thus obtaining amicable solutions.

X. International regimes

There is no doubt that international law and global organisations have had a major influence on global environmental change in relation to both the exploitation and the protection of natural resources. A vast body of literature has been produced on the structures and functions of international regimes, those organising economic growth and those ensuring sustainability. International lawyers discuss whether and in what forms the classical international 'society' of states moves towards a 'community' of states legitimated by both states and peoples and endowed with supranational powers. For a long time political science has focussed on the conditions of international regime formation proposing power, constructivist discourse, individual interest maximisation, and institution-building, as major factors. Compliance with and implementation of regimes have attracted more interest of late. The sociology of law has discovered societal self-regulation as a further source of governance.

If anything critical can be said about this highly sophisticated research it is its fascination with forms rather than substance. Intrigued by the creativity of international regime formation, scholars have somewhat neglected the question 'cui bono?'. We are well informed about the mechanisms of the WTO system, but what do we know about its impact on the global environment? There is plenty of research about the formation and structure of the climate protection regime, and tremendous political effort is spent on the implementation of its new instruments, but the actual effect of the grand design on halting climate change is hardly measured.

Although, of course, this book cannot fill the gap entirely, its contributions address questions of effectiveness of regime formation and implementation on an international level. On this point, one article offers suggestions for reorganising the international environmental organisations, another discusses the most embarrassing obstacle to regime formation of recent times, namely the hegemonic role of the USA, and others focus on improving compliance with and implementation of regimes.

In Chapter 16, Konrad von Moltke begins with the observation that the hundreds of environmental conventions and tens of international organisations lack coordination because they have developed in a non-systematic way. The vision of a World Environmental Organisation being unpragmatic and even doubtful, he discusses more realistic options for reorganisation. Finding the merger of conventions and organisations difficult for reasons including differing memberships and constituencies, he proposes to form a limited number of clusters.

The tools of each cluster are to colocate conferences of parties to different conventions and to integrate secretariats, technical bodies, budgets, implementation reviews, and capacity-building, most appropriately under the supervision of a coordinator. The clusters themselves would be formed to fit between institutional design and problem structures. In discussion of the difficulty of conceptualising this interaction, the author bases his proposal on his experience in suggesting five clusters of conservation: nature preservation, global atmosphere, hazardous substances, marine environment, and extractive resources.

The author further submits that UNEP should be entrusted with tasks that span a number of clusters and may help them to perform their duties more effectively. Such tasks would include integrated science assessment, monitoring, and implementation reviews. He also discusses whether a horizontal treaty on public participation should be made. Regarding dispute settlement structures, he warns against making easy analogies with the mechanisms of the WTO. Differences to be noted include: trade disputes concern cross-border transactions, whilst environmental disputes relate mainly to domestic phenomena; trade claims attack national laws, environmental claims very often factual behaviour; further, and most importantly, in environmental disputes, unlike trade disputes, the claimant is often also a 'sinner' thus facing blame if raising a complaint and accused of failure in other areas of the law. Therefore, compliance with environmental regimes will rather be secured by administrative and political means.

The success of an international regime undoubtedly rests on a common understanding of the contracting parties of the problem at stake and the policy options available. The theme of Helmut Breitmeier's Chapter 17 is to what extent such understanding is present in the framework of various international regimes. Incidentally, the quantitative research on which the chapter is based is the second of its kind presented in this book, the other example being Kerstin Tews' Chapter 9 study on policy diffusion. In the comparison of these contributions with one another, and in turn with the qualitative study on multinational enterprises by Martin Herberg in Chapter 6, the reader may form his/her own opinion on the debate of methodologies and yield of quantitative and qualitative research.

Breitmeier first describes the method of his research. Twenty-one international regimes were selected and broken down into regime 'elements' (i.e. components of regimes and periods of development). For the resulting 170 elements questions were asked, relating to the understanding of (a) the problem underlying the regime, (b) the most important policy options, and (c) the activities of the monitoring and research activities undertaken by the different regimes. The changes in understanding during the period of observation were investigated, as well the final results and differences of understanding among individual states. The questions were answered by carefully selected experts.

The data derived from the research shows that, in general, knowledge of the problem structure and policy tools has increased in most regimes. However, differences in achievement can be identified between different regimes. For example, the Antarctic regime with its subregimes are well understood whilst the tropical timber, hazardous waste, and North Sea pollution regimes are less understood. Correlating the degree of understanding with regime activities, Breitmeier shows that strongly established understanding of the nature of a problem only results if the regime has conducted scientific monitoring and research. This means that the provisions in many environmental treaties asking for monitoring and research but being often neglected and sometimes mocked, have more importance than often assumed.

Thomas Giegerich's Chapter 11 is a contribution to the discussion of regime formation and performance. Giegerich addresses the problem of the hegemonic state which, because of its domination of both economic transactions and cultural exchange, possesses the potential to introduce a sustainable utilisation of natural resources. Against widespread discontent with the role of the USA, he presents a more differentiated view. His central argument is that internal politics determine external policies in the USA much more than in many other states where the executive branch enjoys a broad margin of manoeuvre in external matters. This is reflected in the constitutional requirement of a two-thirds majority consent of the Senate for international treaties to be ratified, a hurdle which is reinforced by certain facilitating procedures, the rejection of direct applicability of treaties, and the constitutional prohibition of a transfer of powers to international organisations. As the author says, sovereignty here is a twin of democracy.

According to Giegerich, the North American attitude towards environmental treaties and international law-making in general is a mixture of isolationism, unilateralism, and multilateralism, three elements which the author traces back to their historical roots. Multilateralism in particular began largely with the US intervention in the First World War and has often remained 'à la carte' since, as demonstrable with regard to the issues of human rights on the one side and free trade on the other.

In global environmental law development, the USA has sometimes been the protagonist of environmental law instruments, motivating other states to copy them, such as environmental impact assessment and freedom of information; or sometimes forcing them to do so through its purchasing power, such as in the case of Californian automobile standards. With regard to international treaty-making, Giegerich identifies a 'sense of mission' in some cases such as the foundation of UNEP, the Convention on International Trade in Endangered Species, the Antarctic Treaty, and the Montreal Protocol, although sometimes economic considerations have also played a role. Since the 1980s such considerations have often come to dominate the US attitude and led to isolationism, such as in the cases of the Antarctic Environmental Protection Protocol, the

UN Convention on the Law of the Sea, the Convention on Biological Diversity, the Cartagena Protocol on Biosafety, and the Kyoto Protocol on Climate Protection. The latter is particularly significant because the USA has imposed its instrumental philosophy of emission rights on the contracting states but finally refused to expose its own population to the demands of cutting back on the American way of life.

Unilateralism, on the other hand, has sometimes been used in the environmental interest, such as in the *Gasoline, Dolphin,* and *Turtle* cases brought before the GATT and WTO dispute settlement bodies, trade sanctions concerning products from whales, and the submission to EIA of credits issued by US banks. The potential lying in the US Alien Tort Claims Act has, however, not been realised in the environmental domain. Conversely, the USA has also used bilateral action to fight environmental standards it found unjustified. Giegerich mentions the growth hormone case and the controversy over genetically modified organisms in feed and food, taking them as examples of differences in risk perceptions in Europe and the USA.

Summarising his contribution, the author says that the USA may well not be more egotistical than other states, but because of the dominant position it holds its attitude has much more serious consequences on the environment and the law governing it. Due to the importance of internal politics he claims it is crucial to convince the US population that the preservation of the global environment is also in its own long-term interest.

In Chapter 15, Jutta Brunnée addresses the core means of compliance of states with international regimes. Giving an overview of different theories she distinguishes between a managerial and rationalistic explanation which, grouping them together as institutionalist, she compares with an interactionist explanation. Whilst compliance will result if the causes of non-compliance were identified and treated with tailor-made measures according to the managerial approach, the rationalistic approach predicts compliance if the blend of incentives and disincentives best suited to the individual interest of the actor was found. Brunnée instead advocates an interactionist view. Compliance is based on a shared understanding achieved by the characteristics of law such as its generality, clarity, and consistency rather than by strategic manipulation. Institutions of this sort provide legitimacy and with it compliance, but using the pull rather than push approach. The understanding emerges continuously during the full process of designing, adopting, and implementing the law. According to the author, an advantage of her approach is that it also explains compliance with soft as well as formal law.

Taking the Kyoto Protocol as an example, Brunnée expects that whilst the legal quality of its resulting secondary rules is at best unclear, and will in fact be non-binding 'guidelines', they will nevertheless be followed by the contracting parties, because, as the author submits, they meet the states' understanding. This will also be true regarding important issues such as the details of the so-called Kyoto mechanisms (emission trading, joint implementation, clean development, etc.) and of the compliance procedures and mechanisms. Interactionist thought is also present in the planned compliance measures. A compliance committee will be established which, in addition to an 'enforcement branch' will also have a 'facilitative branch' which will proceed by persuasion rather than sanction. The author, however, admits that the very far-reaching tools given to the enforcement branch (including the suspension of a party from the trading mechanism, and the deduction of a quota from a party's allowable emission rights) rather point in the direction of forcing compliance. But, as she says, both approaches – the institutionalist and the interactionist – can coexist, and it is not yet clear whether facilitation or enforcement will prevail.

Whilst Brunnée's views seem to be particularly suited to explaining compliance by Northern countries, Charlotte Streck in Chapter 20 and Joyeeta Gupta in Chapter 18 look at what induces developing and threshold countries to comply.

Charlotte Streck focuses her study on financial instruments. Given the preponderant responsibility of industrialised states for the major global environmental threats and the economic and institutional weakness of many developing countries to comply with environmental obligations, a mechanism organising financial transfers from the North to the South is necessary to fill the gap. The polluter pays principle, as well as the innovative principle of common but differentiated responsibilities as included in Principle 7 of the Rio Declaration have laid the intellectual and ethical grounds for systems that include financial transfers from the North to the South. Streck describes how the different financial mechanisms and funding schemes have developed. The first was the Multilateral Fund (MLF) under the Montreal Protocol. It was virtually extorted by the developing from the industrialised world, and proved very effective in making the regime successful. The organisational design corresponds to the 'political' type characteristic for UN institutions. For instance, in the bodies of the fund not only the donor countries but also the recipient countries have significant influence.

Next to the MLF, the Global Environmental Facility (GEF) was founded. Being closely attached to the World Bank, its initial organisational structure was of the 'banking' type, with the donor countries deciding according to their shares in the fund. However, when the GEF became the designated financial mechanism for the Framework Convention on Climate Change and the Convention on Biodiversity, a pragmatic compromise between the more World Bank-driven GEF pilot facility and the UN-driven Conventions was found in the governance structure of the restructured GEF. The GEF can be involved for projects providing benefits to the global environment, including the climate, biodiversity, international waters, and the ozone layer. It is therefore crosscutting the related international regimes. Both MLF and GEF do not just open another window of aid. Instead, the fund as well as the facility are to meet the incremental costs encountered by developing countries when undertaking a project with additional global benefits. Or, looked at from a different angle, development should not be penalised by expenses that could not be justified by domestic benefits

The so-called flexible mechanisms under the Kyoto Protocol are the third type of funding Streck describes. In particular, the Clean Development Mechanism (CDM) if viewed from the side of development provides a means to mobilise private funds for environmentally sound investment. The author explains how these mechanisms work in practice. It is worth noting that they have started operations before the Kyoto Protocol has entered into force. Although Streck does not neglect shortcomings, such as that the funding will concentrate on 'low hanging fruits', the author defends the approach of, in times of public poverty, directing private money to fulfil environmental goals, and doing so in an economically and environmentally efficient way. Similar approaches should complement the Kyoto type, such as user charges and insurance requirements. Another facet of the new approach Streck finds promising is the network structure of the organisational setting, including industrialised and developing countries as well as public and private entities. Concluding, she points out that flexibility and private sector involvement in addressing environmental problems is essential; however, a reliable framework of formal law is an indispensable prerequisite for such mechanisms to function.

Joyeeta Gupta in Chapter 18 broadens the view on factors ensuring compliance by developing countries. The success of an international treaty is dependent on its 'compliance push' and 'compliance pull' aspects. The compliance push measures include monitoring, reporting, reviewing, dispute resolution, enforcement, and other mechanisms to ensure implementation. The compliance pull idea is based on goodwill, *pacta sunt servanda*, and the legitimacy of the agreement.

The problem of countries, namely developing countries, defaulting on their legal obligations within various international environmental regimes is often being attributed to the lack of administrative capacity. Because of this, compliance-pull mechanisms are now being redefined to include non-compliance mechanisms and capacity-building activities within the regimes to enable developing countries to implement the agreements. These in themselves are useful instruments.

However, Gupta argues that non-compliance with environmental treaties by developing countries can be explained not just by post-negotiation explanations (lack of technology and finance or 'new capacity' problems) but also by prenegotiation issues ('old capacity' problems). She further argues that the 'new capacity' problems emerge more as a result of regulatory competition between countries. The author points out that non-compliance mechanisms and capacity-building programmes in treaties tend to focus on 'new capacity' problems and are likely to be at best self-serving and at worst self-defeating.

The lack of attention paid to 'old capacity' issues is likely to be an enduring problem.

XI. Overarching principles

In the previous sections, the structures and functions of institutions on various levels of governance have been expounded as agents of global environmental change. The final section is concerned with principles overarching the different levels and – at each level – the different segmental institutions. These principles – structural coupling by systems theory – are widely debated and accepted within and between the different sections of this system. Normally they are not strategically employed by any level or segment in order to influence another but constitute a globalised discourse of world society, experts, and politicians. They represent fundamental concepts of responsibility, more concrete but still general propositions of environmentally sound behaviour and common understandings about best instruments. They may be promoted and reinforced by mechanisms of horizontal diffusion between societal actors or states, or by codification in an international treaty or rule of international customary law.

There are four chapters looking at overarching principles. Peter Sand in Chapter 21 offers public trusteeship as a fundamental concept, Michael Bothe discusses in Chapter 22 various general principles of common concern, Alan Boyle in Chapter 23 elaborates on variants of liability, and Gerd Winter outlines in Chapter 24 different notions and roles of principles. Instrumental concepts are presented by Jordan, Wurzel and Zito and Tews, whose chapters, however, appear at another place in this volume.

In his contribution, Peter Sand analyses and develops the public trust as a concept emerging at all levels of institutions. In spite of early hopes for a 'fading out' of sovereignty in the face of global environmental challenges, recent codifications of international law have confirmed the creeping national enclosure of what were once considered common assets, e.g., exclusive economic zones under the Law of the Sea Convention 1982, and access to genetic resources, under the Biodiversity Convention 1992 and the FAO Treaty 2001. Yet, because of their explicit limitation and qualification by 'common interest' obligations, the author suggests that these expanded sovereign rights of nation states must be considered *fiduciary* rather than proprietary. The emerging legal institution is one of international public trusteeship (sometimes referred to as guardianship or stewardship) over a widening range of environmental resources. The author points to proposals suggesting a new environmental mandate for the UN Trusteeship Council to demonstrate that the concept of public trust may also have organisational implications.

Sand traces the evolution of public trusteeship in modern national environmental laws, where it serves to hold public authorities (as trustees) accountable for their management of environmental resources. Furthermore, it characterises more recent self-regulatory undertakings such as the Marine and the Forest Stewardship Councils. This shows trust to be a principle cross-cutting all levels of governance.

Michael Bothe in Chapter 22 presents a contrasting view of how institutions are injected with environmental concern. From the understanding that the earth system is in a fundamental sense communal to humankind, sovereignty is so to speak a secondary institution relativised by concerns of commonality. Bothe demonstrates that international environmental law has developed a number of leading principles in order to deal with the problem of externalities, both interlocal and intertemporal. These principles are specific to particular conflict situations and types of externalities and reflect the idea of commonality in different ways. In his view, these principles are more meaningful than certain private law analogies, for example, the construction of a trust. The most important principles are: *sic utere tuo*, equitable utilisation, duty to cooperate, common concern, common but differentiated responsibilities, common heritage, common heritage of mankind, sustainable development, and precaution.

Looking at the more concrete concepts of liability as elaborated by the UN International Law Commission (ILC), Alan Boyle introduces the reader to a method of law creation which gives credit to all institutional levels and allows for a coevolution of national and international law. The earlier proposals of the ILC concentrated on interstate liability whilst more recent considerations have been found unsatisfactory on the ground of the polluter pays principle and in view of effectiveness of remedy for the plaintiff. Therefore, the scheme will be complemented by rules on transnational liability between the private actors concerned.

Taking national law into account as well as the international instruments already in existence (which, however, either have a narrow field of application or have proven to be too ambitious), Boyle considers the major components of such harmonising rules, such as the appropriate forum, the choice of law, negligence or non-fault, the channelling of compensation to appropriate defendants, including residual duties of states, and the impact of interindividual schemes on interstate claims. Further questions might address environmental damage and liability in purely domestic cases. Speaking in terms of the legal framing of the envisaged harmonisation, Boyle applauds the ILC for not recommending an international treaty but rather a model legislation states should follow when developing their domestic liability legislation.

Gerd Winter in Chapter 24 starts with the observation that much has been said about the semantic content of various environmental and other principles, but that there is less clarity about the legal nature of principles. Many a discussion is hampered because different meanings are used at the same time without explanation. A proposition can be a principle of policy or of law. Principles of law are to be distinguished from rules of law; they are basic ideas informing rules, and whilst rules are conclusive, principles are capable of being balanced with opposing principles. Principles of law can be ordinary or fundamental principles, the latter often having a constitutional or higher level status. Looking at principles in the context of both the systems of separation of powers and equality of states provides insight into why courts sometimes support a very broad interpretation of a principle and sometimes narrow it down to a minimalist core. Winter suggests that this terminology can be applied to all levels of the law, national, regional, and international.

Distinguishing between different kinds of principles can also improve the understanding of the development of law. Principles of policy and of law serve as a point of interaction between common experience and common sense on the one side and legal rules on the other. Principles and rules as defined by the author may also help accelerate the creation of international law so desperately needed in the globalised world. Principles may be more readily accepted as having legal value if their potential to be balanced with countervailing principles is taken into account. For example, the precautionary principle can be formulated as a principle of law and even as a rule of international customary law if allowing for a balancing of environmental against economic concerns. Distinguishing between ordinary and fundamental principles may help to clarify and foster the evolution of constitutional or peremptory law as control for ordinary law, both on the national and international level.

XII. Conclusion

In 1992 the global community in Principle 7 of the Rio Declaration expressed the need that 'States shall cooperate in a spirit of global partnership to conserve, protect and restore the health and integrity of the Earth's ecosystem.' The 'health and integrity of the Earth's ecosystem' is a holistic concept that was to be reflected in the institutional design. Meanwhile, ecosystem analysis has mutated into an earth system perspective which integrates the human factor, and the modest duty to cooperate has been developed towards more ambitious organisational, instrumental, and material devices of global governance. But much more work must be done in order to alert the many levels and territorial units of governance dividing the earth system to the common whole. The editor hopes that this book can make a useful contribution to this question.

PART I

Earth system analysis

2

Dimensions and mechanisms of global climate change

PETER LEMKE

I. Introduction

The present characteristics of the Earth system, and in particular of the climate system, in which human societies are embedded, are a product of a long-term evolution: a current snapshot in a six-billion-year movie that is still running. After colonisation of the continents by plants and animals, the Earth has developed a climate system – composed of atmosphere, ocean, cryosphere, land surfaces, and the marine and terrestrial biosphere – which very effectively, through complex interactions, has produced a rather stable equilibrium state, around which climate variations evolve.

Until 250 years ago, the interference of man was small, and climate variations were a product of natural processes and interactions alone. Since the beginning of industrialisation, the composition of the atmosphere, especially the concentrations of greenhouse gases like carbon dioxide and methane, have significantly increased. In addition, the character of the land surface has been largely modified through human activities. Part of the observed global warming during the past 100 years is attributed to these anthropogenic impacts.

One of the most important characteristics of the climate system is its variability, which extends on timescales ranging from days to millions of years. Short-term variations of atmospheric variables – such as air temperature, pressure, humidity, the three wind components, precipitation, and cloud cover – on the order of days denote the weather. Climate variations are associated with long-term (months and longer) changes of the atmosphere, which mostly originate from interactions with the slow components of the climate system. The distinction between weather and climate is, therefore, not just a matter of timescales, but involves also the conditions of ocean, cryosphere, land surfaces, including the marine and terrestrial biosphere.

Short-term stochastic variations of the atmosphere induce – in analogy to the slow erratic Brownian motion of particles suspended in a fluid – long-term changes of ocean and ice. Variations of sea surface temperature (SST) and sea ice extent in turn modify the atmospheric variables. In order to assess the present

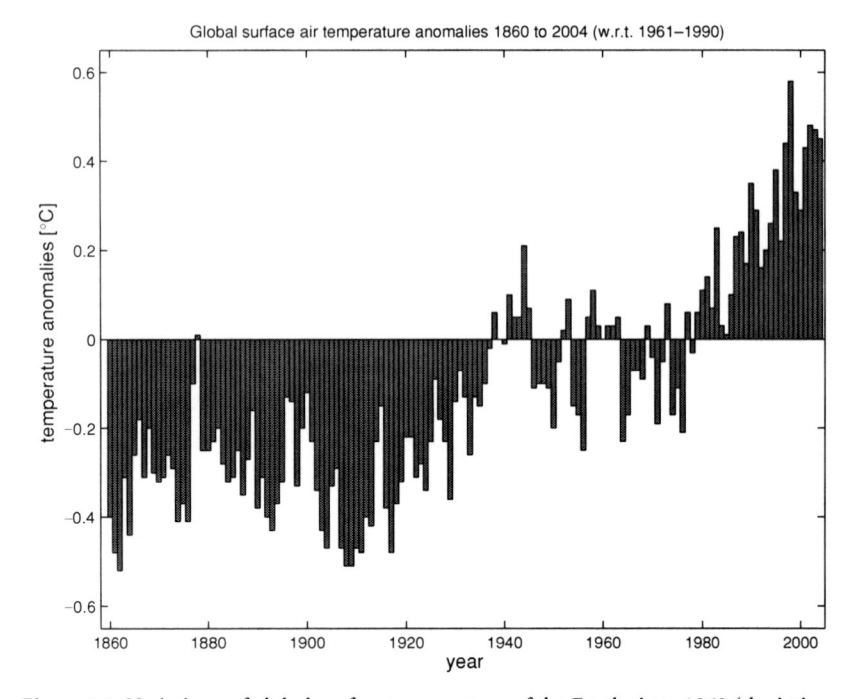

Figure 2.1 Variations of global surface temperature of the Earth since 1860 (deviations from the 1961–1990 mean value)
Source: Jones, P. D. and Moberg, A., Hemispheric and large-scale surface air temperature variations: An extensive revision and an update of 2001, *J. Climate* 16 (2003), pp. 206–223.

climate variations the historical evolution of climate has to be investigated. Information about climate parameters on historical and geological timescales is available from different sources with different accuracies.

Observations of meteorological variables date back to the invention of the thermometer and the barometer by Galileo Galilei (1597) and Torricelli (1643), respectively. The longest continuous time-series cover approximately 300 years. Long time-series require a careful calibration, since instruments and measurement techniques have been modified, and stations have been relocated and may have been affected by urbanisation. Consequently, they have to be interpreted with care. Because of the sparsity of observing stations before the nineteenth century, global temperature averages can only be generated for the period 1860 to 2001 (see Figure 2.1).

Instrumental records are also used to reconstruct longer time-series from comparison with tree ring, coral, and ice core data. Figure 2.2 displays such a reconstruction for the last 600 years using historical records and data from

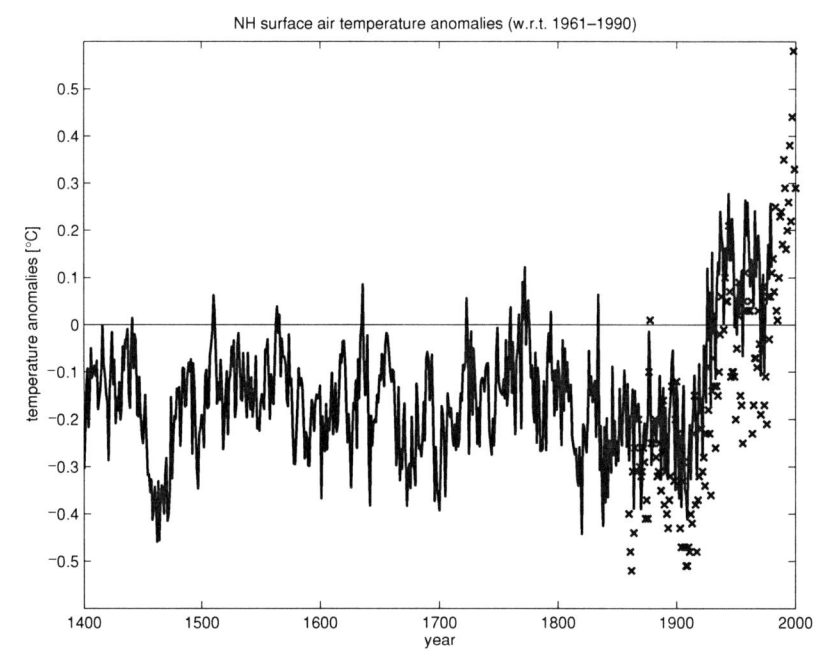

DIMENSIONS AND MECHANISMS OF GLOBAL CLIMATE CHANGE

Figure 2.2 Reconstructions of the mean surface temperature of the northern hemisphere from tree rings, corals, ice cores and historical records
The instrumental record (equivalent to Figure 2.1) is represented by crosses.
Source: Mann, M. E., Bradley, R. S., and Hughes, M. K., Global-scale temperature patterns and climate forcing over the past six centuries, *Nature* 392 (1998), pp. 779–787.

corals, tree rings, and ice cores. The historical analysis of such data sets indicates a strong impact of climate on human society, i.e. the period of mass migration in Central and Northern Europe around AD 400 under cool and wet climate conditions; the colonisation of Iceland and Greenland around AD 900, and the loss of the Viking settlements, and crop failure, famine, and decrease of the population in Europe during the Little Ice Age (1350–1850).

Knowledge of past climate variability is crucial for understanding and modelling current and future climate trends. The growing body of palaeo-climatic tools and data, developed and gathered over the past fifty years, has enormously increased our knowledge of past climates. Although palaeo-climatic tools are far from being perfect, they are tremendously useful because they represent the only source of information on the behaviour of the climate system on long timescales (Stefan Rahmstorf, Chapter 3). The great value of palaeo-climate methods lies in the fact that information about the climate system has been recorded in natural materials, which have been deposited in sediments, in snow and ice, and in trees and corals. The generation of this information requires two steps: first, the determination of the age of the sample (dating problem), and secondly, the retrieval of the climate information, i.e. the development of an algorithm that relates the proxy[1] data, e.g. isotope ratios ($\delta^{18}O$), to geophysical variables such as temperature and ice volume on continents.

II. Climate variations

Summarising the information from instrumental records, historical sources, and proxy data it is evident that climate has changed on all timescales. The amplitudes of the variations increase with increasing periods, i.e. the temperature deviations during the ice ages were larger than those of the Little Ice Age, and these were larger than present decadal variations (see Figure 2.3). From these data we can identify the following past climate regimes.

The last millennium: global temperature was slightly higher than average during the *Medieval Warm Period* or the *Little Climatic Optimum* (around AD 1000 to 1250). The *Little Ice Age* (1350–1850) was cooler than the average, where the mean seventeenth-century temperature was about 0.5°C lower than between 1961 and 1990. The last three decades (1970–2000) were likely the warmest of the last millennium, with the strongest warming (about 0.6°C per century).

Holocene (the last 10,000 years): global temperature during the Holocene was relatively stable compared to glacial-interglacial variations. Yet, the middle Holocene was appreciably warmer than today. In Europe this phase has been called the Climatic Optimum. It began about 9,000 years ago, peaked about 6,000 years ago, and ended about 2,500 years ago.

Last Glacial Maximum (LGM, 18,000 years BP (before present)): atmospheric circulation was different, global temperature was about 5 to 8°C colder. The ocean probably showed a weaker and shallower overturning in the North Atlantic. Sea ice extent was greater and large ice caps built up on Scandinavia, Russia, and North America. As a result, sea level was about 120m lower than today. Concentrations of atmospheric greenhouse gases were different, indicating reorganisations of biogeochemical cycles.

Pleistocene (1.6 million years (Ma) to 10,000 years BP): during this period a succession of glacial and interglacial climatic cycles occurred, which has been informally referred to as the Great Ice Age. The periodic waxing and waning of

---

[1] The word 'proxy' is commonly used to describe a stand-in or substitute. In palaeo-climatic reconstructions proxy variables, or short *proxies*, are measurable descriptors, which stand in for desired, but unobservable, variables such as temperature, salinity, ice volume, etc. These are the target parameters. The concept of proxies relies on a physical relationship between a proxy and the target variable. Therefore, each proxy is associated with a rule (a transformation algorithm), which relates it to the target variable. These algorithms have to be established through calibration, e.g. using the instrumental records.

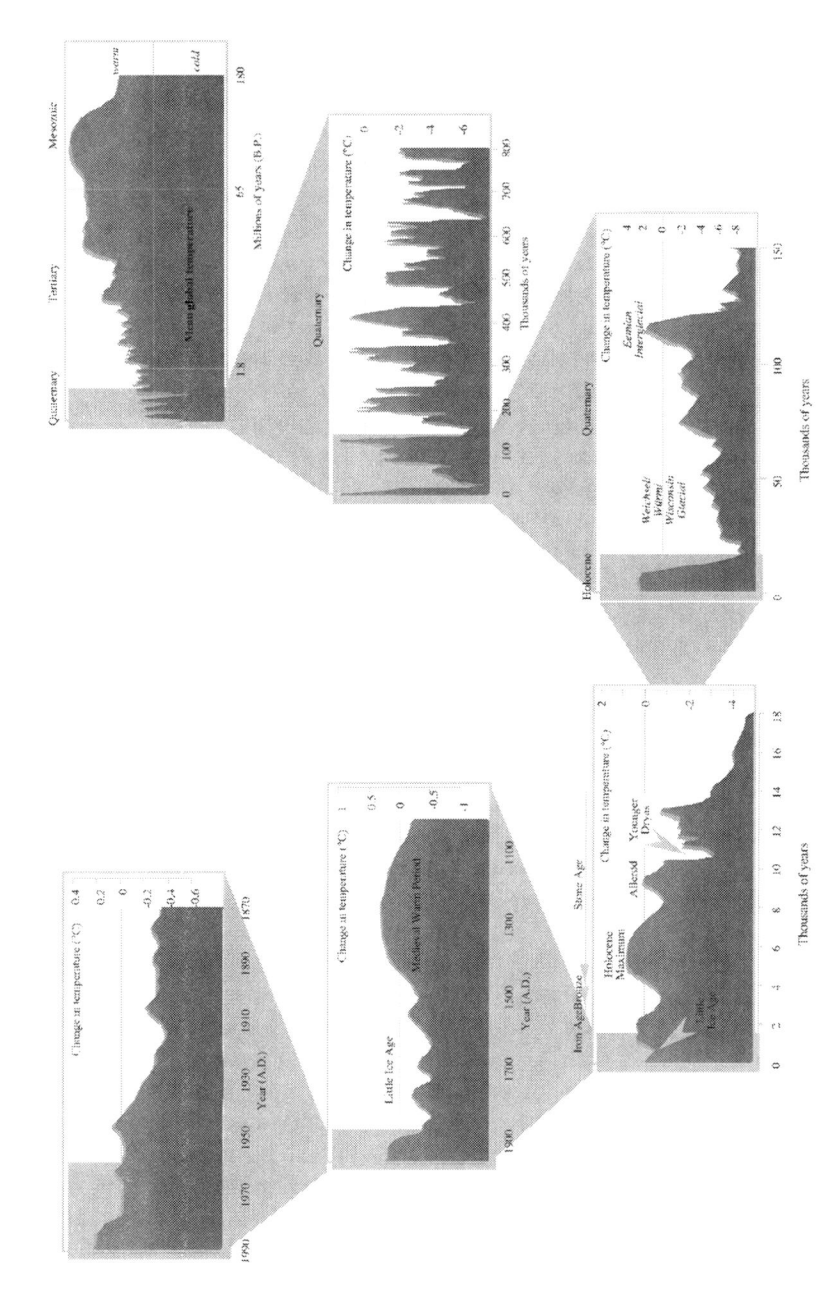

Figure 2.3 Climate variations from instrumental records, historical sources, and proxy data

ice sheets appear to be unique to the Pleistocene. Modern research, however, has shown that large glaciers had formed prior to the Pleistocene.

Cenozoic (65 Ma BP to present): over the Cenozoic period, Earth has experienced a general cooling trend. Global temperature has probably fallen by about 10°C. However, the cooling was not continuous but interrupted by gradual trends of warming and cooling. Periodic cycles are driven by orbital forcing (so-called Milankovitch frequencies).

Typical examples of climate variations on different timescales are the El Niño phenomenon, the Little Ice Age, and the ice ages. The El Niño phenomenon occurs on time intervals of three to eight years in the tropical Pacific with global impacts. The characteristic feature of El Niño is the occurrence of anomalously warm water in the generally cold upwelling regions in the tropics off the South American west coast. Along with the oceanic surface temperature the wind systems (the trade winds) and the precipitation patterns are changing dramatically. El Niño is accordingly a coupled atmosphere-ocean phenomenon.

During the Little Ice Age (1350 to 1850) the temperatures in Europe were approximately 1.5°C lower than today and the glaciers were significantly larger. Since 1850 temperatures are rising and glaciers are shrinking significantly.

From the distribution of oxygen isotopes in marine sediment cores, time-series of the global ice volume on the continents can be generated. These data show that ice ages occurred at intervals of 100,000 years (see Figure 2.3). There is an apparent asymmetry: slow build-up and fast decay, indicating different physical mechanisms involved.

Instrumental observations during the past 150 years show the following changes in the climate system. If not indicated otherwise these changes apply to the period 1901 until 2000. The global average surface temperature has increased by 0.6°C. The 1990s was the warmest decade and 1998 the warmest year in the instrumental record, since 1861 (see Figure 2.1). Reconstructions from proxy data (tree rings, corals, etc.) indicate that the 1990s was the warmest decade and 1998 the warmest year of the last millennium (Figure 2.2).

Because of the rising temperatures the snow covered area has decreased by 10% since 1960. Similarly, nearly all glaciers (with a few exceptions in maritime climates like Norway) have retreated significantly, and the sea ice covered area in the Arctic has reduced by 10 to 15%. In response to warming of the oceans and melting of glaciers sea level has risen by 0.1 to 0.2m.

Precipitation in the northern hemisphere has increased in middle and high latitudes (30N to 90N) by 0.5–1% per decade, and in the tropics (10S to 10N) by 0.2–0.3% per decade. In the subtropics (10N to 30N) it has decreased by 0.3% per decade. The precipitation extremes have increased by 2–4% since 1901.

In the atmosphere, carbon dioxide has increased since 1750 by 31% (Figure 2.4). The present concentration is the highest during the last 420,000 years. About 75% of this increase is due to fossil fuel burning and 25% to land use changes. The methane concentration has risen by 151%. The N_2O

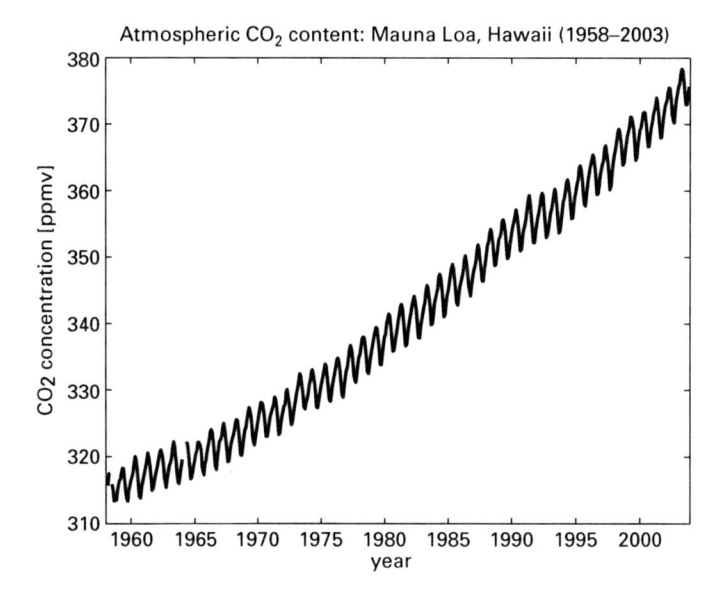

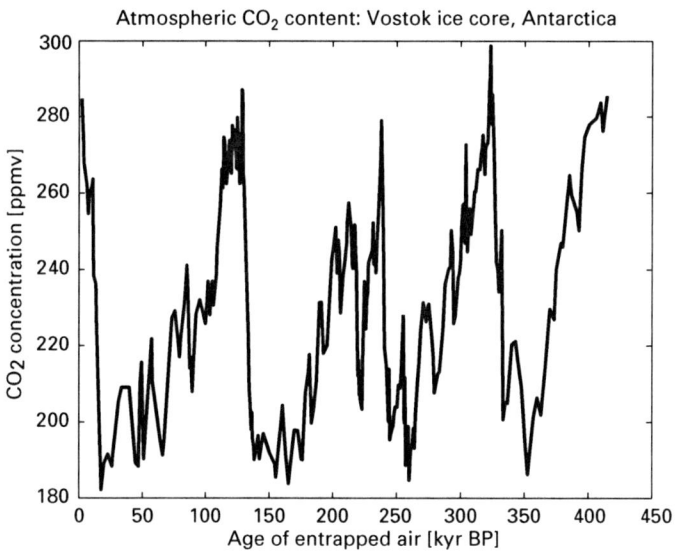

DIMENSIONS AND MECHANISMS OF GLOBAL CLIMATE CHANGE   43

Figure 2.4 Increase of CO_2 concentration in the atmosphere since 1958 and natural variations during the last 450,000 years from investigations of the Vostok ice core
Source: top: Keeling, D. and Whorf, T., *Atmospheric carbon dioxide concentrations at 10 locations*, La Jolla, Cal. (Scripps Institution of Oceanography) 2004. bottom: Barnola, J.-M., Raynand, D., Lorius, C., and Barkov, N. I., Historical CO_2 record from the Vostok ice core, in Carbon Dioxide Information Analysis Center, Oak Ridge National Laboratory, *Trends: a compendium of data on global change*, Oak Ridge (US Department of Energy) 1999.

(laughing-gas) concentration has increased by 17% since 1750. In the lower atmosphere, the ozone concentration has increased by 36% since 1750. In the stratosphere it has diminished substantially (ozone hole).

Earth's climate has changed significantly in the past and will change in the future. In contrast to the past there will not only be natural causes for climate change, but also man-induced impacts on the climate system, like modifications of the composition of the atmosphere through input of greenhouse gases, and land use changes. The expected warming through the coming 100 years is 2 to 5°C.[2] Detailed investigations of the response of the climate system to anthropogenic impact represent presently a main topic of international climate research.

III. The energy balance of the Earth

The prime source for climate variations is the regional and temporal change of the solar radiation. The radiation balance of a planet determines to a large degree the state of the climate system. In thermodynamic equilibrium the amount of solar energy absorbed by a planet is emitted as thermal radiation, which is described by the Stefan-Boltzmann law. The total radiation hitting the planet is given by its cross-section (a circle of radius r) multiplied with the solar radiation flux density S. A certain fraction α of this incoming radiation is reflected by the planet, especially by clouds and other bright surfaces like ice and snow. The reflectivity α of a planet is also called *albedo*. The total emitted radiation is given by the surface of the planet multiplied by the Stefan-Boltzmann constant σ and the fourth power of the absolute temperature T. The radiation balance of a planet is, therefore, given by:

$$\pi r^2 (1 - \alpha) S = 4\pi r^2 \sigma T^4 \tag{1}$$

Solving this equation for the global radiative equilibrium temperature T we find:

$$T = \sqrt[4]{S(1 - \alpha)/(4\sigma)} \tag{2}$$

It is obvious that the radiative equilibrium temperature T is independent of the size of the planet. It is only determined by the albedo of the planet and the energy flux supplied by the sun.

The solar radiation flux density at the distance Sun–Earth (solar constant) is $S = 1368$ W/m^2 and the global albedo of Earth is $\alpha = 0.3$. With these values the radiative equilibrium temperature is calculated as: T = 255 K = −18°C. This is the temperature which a space traveller would measure

---

[2] Houghton, J. T., Ding, Y., Griggs, D. J., Noguer, M., Van der Linden, P. J., and Xiaosu, D., *Climate change 2001: the scientific basis*, Cambridge (Cambridge University Press) 2001 (see also www.ipcc.ch).

aiming his radiation thermometer at the Earth. The thermal radiation lost to space originates mostly from the upper layers of the atmosphere and from the cloud top surface. Without the atmosphere this cold temperature (hostile to life) would also prevail at the Earth's surface.

IV. The greenhouse effect

The observed surface temperature, T_S, is, however, about 288K (+15°C). The reason for the difference between the cold radiation temperature and the warm surface temperature is that the Earth naturally has an atmosphere including greenhouse gases such as water vapour, CO_2, CH_4, etc. While the atmosphere is largely transparent to the visible wavelengths, it is largely opaque to long-wave radiation mainly due to absorption by water vapour and CO_2. In this way, the atmosphere acts like a blanket that tends to trap the heat inside, keeping the surface warm. Mathematically this effect can be described by assuming that the thermal energy emitted by a planet to space is given by a fraction β of the surface radiation. Then the radiation balance at the top of the atmosphere is given by:

$$\pi r^2 (1-\alpha) S = 4\pi r^2 \beta \sigma T_S^4 \qquad (3)$$

For the surface temperature T_S we find accordingly:

$$T_S = \sqrt[4]{S(1-\alpha)/(4\beta\sigma)} \qquad (4)$$

Applying the surface temperature T_S = 288 K = 15°C, the constant β is given by β = 0.6, i.e. only 60% of the surface thermal radiation are lost to space. The remaining 40% are absorbed by the natural greenhouse gases in the atmosphere, especially by water vapour and CO_2.

Greenhouse gases in the Earth's atmosphere are trace gases, i.e. they are not major constituents such as nitrogen or oxygen. The most important greenhouse gas is water vapour. The concentration of water vapour is highly variable, surface annual-mean values are about 0.1–2%. The other important greenhouse gas is carbon dioxide (0.03%). These two gases are mainly responsible for maintaining an average surface temperature of +15°C on Earth. Other natural and anthropogenic greenhouse gases are methane (CH_4), nitrous oxide (N_2O), chlorofluorocarbons (CFCs), and ozone (O_3). The pre-industrial (prior to 1750) and today's concentrations of some greenhouse gases that are anthropogenically influenced are given in Table 2.1.

In 1958, Charles Keeling began to measure the atmospheric carbon dioxide concentration continuously. This has generated the famous Mauna Loa curve. The measurements are carried out at the Mauna Loa Observatory on the island of Hawaii (see Figure 2.4 and http://cdiac.esd.ornl.gov/trends/trends.htm). The data show that since 1958 CO_2 has increased from 315 ppmv to about 376 ppmv in the year 2003 as a result of fossil fuel burning and changing land use by

Table 2.1 *Pre-industrial and present concentrations of some anthropogenically influenced greenhouse gases (ppmv/ppbv = parts per million/billion by volume)*

Greenhouse gas	Pre-industrial	Present
CO_2	280 ppmv	376 ppmv
CH_4	700 ppbv	1700 ppbv
N_2O	285 ppbv	310 ppbv

humans. The Mauna Loa curve also shows large annual variations. This is due to the *breathing* of the biosphere, which mainly takes up CO_2 in the northern hemisphere summer and respires it during the winter.

By measuring the concentration of CO_2 in gas bubbles enclosed in polar ice cores, the CO_2 record can be extended back into the past. The pre-industrial CO_2 (prior to 1750) was fairly constant since the year 1000. Ice core measurements have also revealed that the current CO_2 concentration of 370 ppmv is higher than any CO_2 concentration in the pre-anthropogenic atmosphere over the past 400,000 years or more (see Figure 2.4, bottom). In addition, the current rate of increase (about 1.5 ppmv per year) is unprecedented over this period of time. The CO_2 rise at the termination of the last ice age from 200 ppmv to 280 ppmv took in the order of 5,000 years, which gives a rate of 0.016 ppmv per year. The anthropogenically caused increase is hence about a hundred times greater.

From the analysis of gas bubbles in ice cores from Vostok, Antarctica, it has been demonstrated that atmospheric CO_2 has varied between 180 ppmv and 280 ppmv over the past 400,000 years. Typical values are 280 ppmv during interglacials (warm periods such as today) and 180 ppmv during maximum glaciation (such as the maximum of the last ice age, 18,000 BP). These variations have now been known for twenty years. Yet, nobody has come up with a completely satisfying explanation of what caused these variations to occur within the observed limits. The greenhouse potential of carbon dioxide has been estimated to produce a 2°C temperature increase for a doubling of its concentration.

Over the coming 10,000 years, the deep ocean will have absorbed most of the fossil fuel produced by humans. There are two important *carbon pumps* by which carbon dioxide can be transported into the deep ocean. The first one is the *physical carbon pump*. CO_2 is a gas that dissolves in seawater and if the concentration in the atmosphere increases, so does CO_2 in the surface ocean, simply as a result of its solubility. The extra dissolved CO_2 is then transported into deeper layers by mixing (vertical diffusion) and the mean circulation (deep water formation).

The second carbon pump is the *biological pump*. Through absorption of light (photosynthesis) and uptake of (inorganic) CO_2 and nutrients, algae in the surface ocean produce organic matter. This organic carbon is carried through the food chain, and part of it is finally sinking into the deep ocean as dead organic matter accumulating in the sediments. This process reduces the total dissolved inorganic carbon (DIC) in the surface ocean and thus the atmospheric CO_2 concentration. If the biological pump were to shut down completely, the atmospheric CO_2 would probably rise to more than 500 ppmv. It is a matter of debate whether or not the biological pump and its effect on atmospheric CO_2 concentrations will change in the future.

Generally, there is a large potential of the oceans to absorb CO_2. However, there are limitations on the timescale over which this can be accomplished. The first has to do with the time required to mix the CO_2 into the deep ocean (about 1,000 years), the other has to do with the chemistry of CO_2 in seawater.

V. The climate system

Observations demonstrate that climate variations occur on all timescales. This has been the case in the past and will continue in the future. Climate variations are a result of both external impacts, such as changes of the solar radiation or volcanic eruptions, and internal interactions within the climate system.

There are various mechanisms of climate change. The incoming solar radiation varies with latitude. As a consequence, the tropics receive more solar energy than they emit by long-wave radiation, whereas the opposite is true for high latitudes. This leads to regional temperature differences, which cause motions in atmosphere and ocean (winds and currents) that transport energy poleward. As an example: the Gulf Stream is a gigantic heating system which, for instance, produces a very mild climate in Northern Europe compared to climates of similar latitudes at the east coasts of the continents. For example, in February, the average temperature in Goose Bay (Labrador, 53N) is −15.5°C, and in Bremerhaven (53.5N) it is +1.7°C (see Figure 2.5). The motion and, therefore, the heat transport in both the atmosphere and the ocean is not uniform but turbulent due to high and low pressure systems and oceanic eddies, respectively.

There are pronounced temporal variations in the incoming solar radiation, e.g. seasons caused by the tilt of Earth's axis. Variations of the orbital parameters (obliquity (tilt), precession, eccentricity) due to the gravitational forces of the other planets occur on longer timescales (Milankovitch Theory).[3] The periods of the obliquity (41,000 years), the precession (19,000 and 23,000 years), and

---

[3] McGuffie, K. and Henderson Sellers, A., *A climate modelling primer*, Chichester (Wiley) 1997.

48   PETER LEMKE

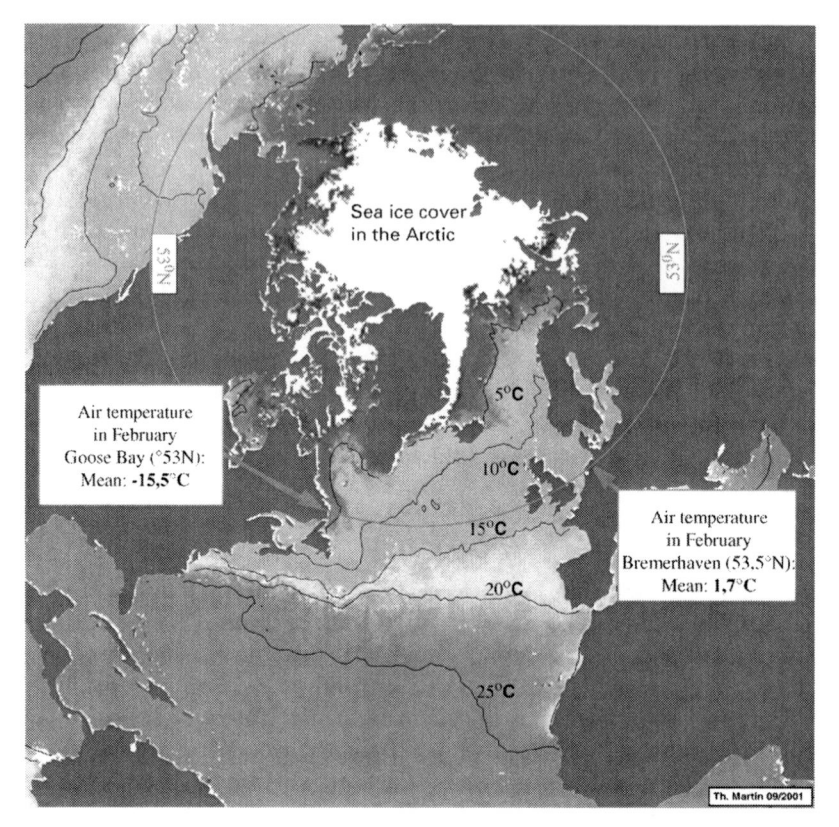

Figure 2.5 Sea ice cover and sea surface temperature in the North Atlantic in fall

the eccentricity (100,000 years) are also found in the variance spectra of climate variations.

Atmosphere, ocean, ice, land surfaces, and the marine and terrestrial biosphere are not independent, but interact with each other forming the components of the climate system (Figure 2.6). They exchange heat, momentum, and matter and subsequently modify each other's state of motion, heat content, and composition. In addition, the components of the climate system vary on different timescales ('fast' atmosphere, 'slow' ocean), which has a profound effect on their interaction.

Interactions and feedbacks in the climate system can be amplifying (positive, i.e. destabilising) or damping (negative, i.e. stabilising). Examples are:

- temperature-ice-albedo feedback (positive): an initial temperature reduction leads to an increase of the ice and snow covered areas; this in turn causes lower temperatures due to increased reflection of solar radiation (higher albedo);

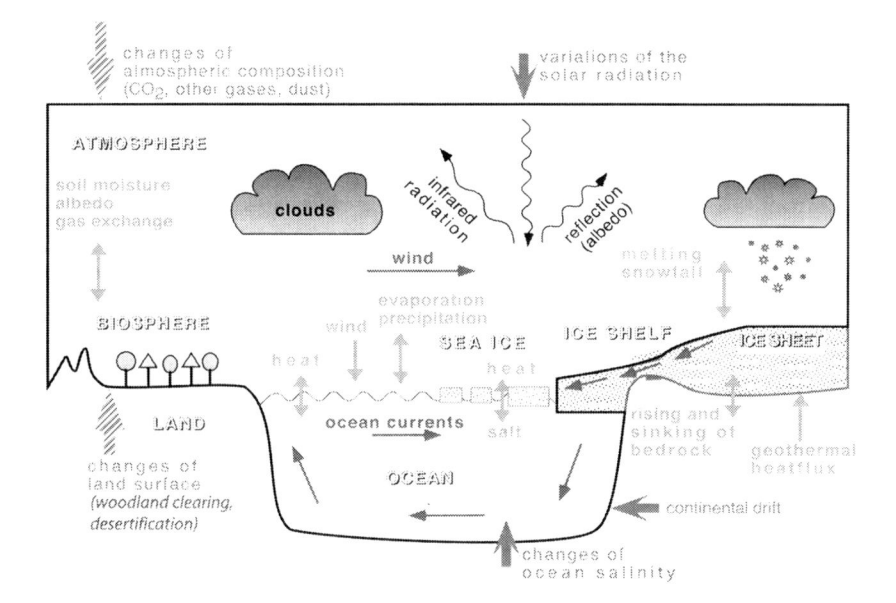

DIMENSIONS AND MECHANISMS OF GLOBAL CLIMATE CHANGE 49

Figure 2.6 Schematic depiction of the climate system
Thin black arrows denote radiative processes; black arrows show advection processes, grey arrows indicate interactions within the climate system, bold black arrows represent changes of the boundary conditions, and the hatched arrows show impacts of human activities on the climate system.

- temperature-water vapour (greenhouse) feedback (positive): a temperature increase causes higher evaporation, increased humidity in the atmosphere, and, therefore, an increased infra-red absorption, which in turn leads to higher temperatures;
- infra-red emission (negative): a warmer Earth emits more infra-red radiation, thereby cooling off;
- cloud feedback (negative): an increased cloud cover leads to reduced solar radiation at the Earth's surface, which causes less evaporation, and, therefore, less cumulus convection.

In the climate system, feedbacks do not work separately, but are linked through interactions in a web of feedback loops. Perturbations of the system can, therefore, be amplified or damped in many ways.

VI. The components of the climate system

Ocean and atmosphere are geophysical fluids that both display organised circulation patterns, chaotic motion, and statistical turbulence. The origin of this motion is the differential heating from the sun. Only half of the solar radiation entering the top of the atmosphere reaches the Earth's surface. The remaining part is either reflected to space (30%) or absorbed in the atmosphere (19%).

As a consequence of the temperature differences caused by the differential heating of the sun, pressure gradients are generated that induce motions in atmosphere and ocean (winds, currents), which transport energy (as in a giant heat engine) from the warm tropics to the cold poles. Both fluids act as collectors in the tropics and radiators in high latitudes. They represent a very effective medium for the transport of energy to high latitudes.

This transport is controlled by many interactions within the climate system (Figure 2.6), i.e. the components of the climate system do not react independently to the forcing of the sun. Winds and currents are in addition modified by the rotation of the Earth about the sun and about its own axis, which is tilted by 23 degrees with respect to the orbital plane (ecliptic). This introduces a time-dependent solar radiation (day and night cycles, seasons), and the Coriolis and centrifugal forces enter the momentum balance as apparent forces in the rotating coordinate system fixed to the Earth.

1. Atmosphere

The atmosphere influences climate through radiative, chemical, and dynamical processes, which are all interconnected. The atmosphere consists of three components:

(1) a gas mixture (78% nitrogen, 21% oxygen, and 1% water vapour, CO_2, ozone, and other trace gases), called *air*;
(2) water and ice particles (*hydrometeors*), which appear as clouds and precipitation (rain, snow);
(3) suspended particles (soot, dust, etc.), called *aerosols*.

The gaseous composition of the air has a pronounced influence on the behaviour of the atmosphere in the climate system. This is especially true for water vapour, cloud liquid water, aerosols, CO_2, ozone and other trace gases. These components determine – although they comprise less than 1% of the atmosphere – the absorption, transmission, and reflection of solar radiation and terrestrial emission, and, therefore, control the energy budget of our planet. In weather prediction and climate models, this gas mixture is usually described as a binary fluid consisting of two components, dry air and water vapour. The reason for this division is the major role that the water vapour plays in weather and climate processes.

A size comparison: if one reduces the Earth to the size of a normal globe (ca. 40 cm in diameter), then the troposphere (the lower 10km of the atmosphere), which is the home of the weather, would have a thickness of only 0.3mm. The atmosphere, therefore, represents a very thin shell around the solid and liquid parts of our planet. The large-scale motion is consequently

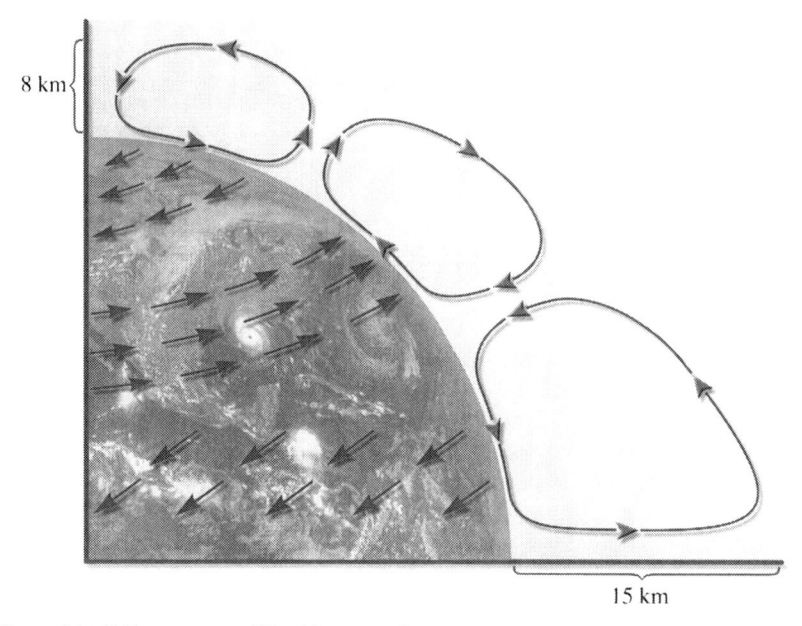

DIMENSIONS AND MECHANISMS OF GLOBAL CLIMATE CHANGE 51

Figure 2.7 Cell structure of Earth's atmosphere

horizontal, i.e. parallel to Earth's surface. Vertical motion is only locally significant, but there it is very important, e.g. for cloud evolution, precipitation, and thunderstorms.

The origin of atmospheric motion is the regional and temporal variability of the incoming solar radiation. These differences create temperature, i.e. density gradients, and, therefore, pressure gradients, which together with gravitation and friction represent the dominant forces acting on an air parcel. The rotation of the Earth induces three cells per hemisphere: the *Hadley cell* in the tropics, the *Ferrel cell* in the mid-latitudes, and the *polar cell* (see Figure 2.7). The Hadley and the polar cells are direct cells, which are driven by warming and cooling, respectively, whereas the Ferrel cell is an indirect cell driven by the two other cells. All cells are not pure meridional (south-north) cells, but have a strong zonal (west-east) component, indicated by the surface winds also shown in Figure 2.7.

Oceans and continents represent the lower boundary of the atmosphere. At this interface a turbulent boundary layer (the planetary boundary layer) develops, where intense interactions occur (see Figure 2.6). Therefore, the atmosphere is not a closed system but represents a part of the coupled climate system, in which many processes are occurring on different temporal and spatial scales (atmosphere – days, biosphere – months to decades, ocean – months to centuries, cryosphere – months to thousands of years).

2. Ocean

In analogy to the atmosphere the ocean is also described as a binary fluid consisting of water and salt. The most important state variables are temperature, salinity, pressure, and the three velocity components. As for the atmosphere, the prognostic equations for the ocean are derived from the conservation equations for momentum, energy, and mass (water and salt separately). These equations represent a system of coupled partial differential equations, which is solved numerically on a geographical grid. The most important problem in ocean modelling is the representation of small-scale processes that are not resolved explicitly on the numerical grid. These processes have to be parameterised in terms of the prognostic variables. These parameterisations are presently the main topic of internationally coordinated ocean and climate modelling activities.

The relevant spatial scales in the ocean are an order of magnitude smaller than in the atmosphere (low pressure system in the atmosphere $\sim$ 1,000km; ocean eddies $\sim$ 100km). Therefore, the grid spacing in ocean models has to be a factor of 10 smaller than in atmospheric models to achieve a similar resolution. This puts a high demand on computer storage and speed.

The oceanic motion is driven at the surface. Changes of the oceanic state are a response to local forcing (heating, cooling, precipitation, evaporation) and to advection of horizontal gradients of velocity, temperature, and salinity. Signals penetrate only slowly into the deeper parts of the ocean, and they are reduced in amplitude by diffusion.

Time-series of temperature taken at *Weather Ship M* in the Norwegian Sea clearly indicate the effect of the seasonal cycle at the sea surface; with temperature variations of 3 to 4°C (see Figure 2.8). At a depth of 600m, the impact of the seasonal cycle is not apparent and the temperature fluctuations are of the order of 1°C, mainly caused by variations of the ocean currents. At a depth of 2,000m, temperature variations are rather small and amount to 0.1°C only. Large changes of the heat content are, therefore, limited to the surface mixed layer.

The ocean influences the climate through the following.

(a) Heat storage

The ocean represents the largest heat reservoir on Earth. Because of the large specific heat and density of water, the upper 3m of the ocean store as much heat as the whole atmosphere. In summer in mid-latitudes the oceanic mixed layer warms up by 5°C down to a depth of approximately 100m. The heat content of the mixed layer at the end of summer is 556kWh/m^2, determined by the product of specific heat, density, mixed layer depth, and temperature difference.

The heat stored in summer is released in winter, which results in a reduction of the seasonal cycle of temperature in maritime regions. If the heat stored in

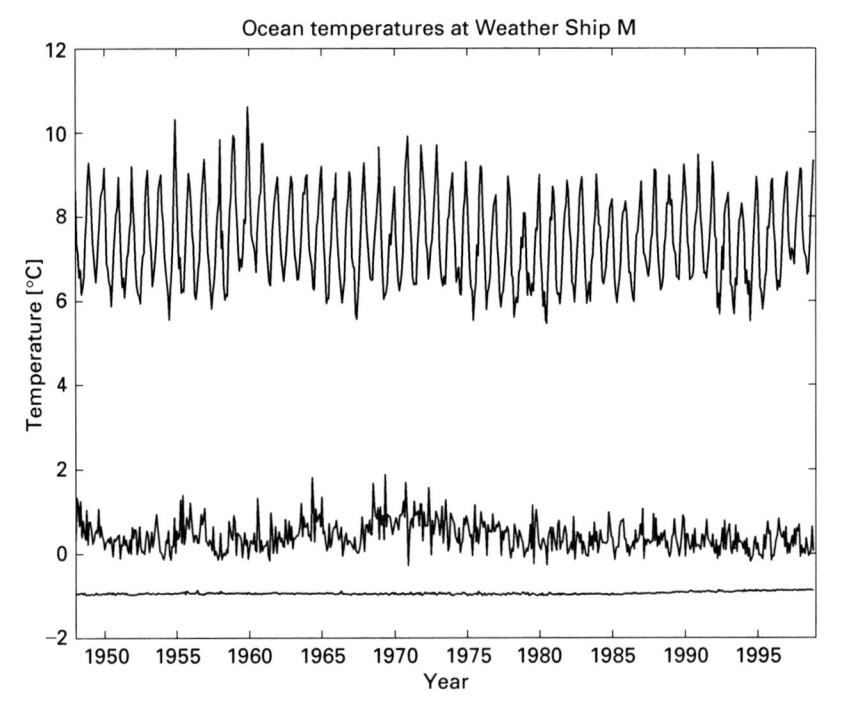

DIMENSIONS AND MECHANISMS OF GLOBAL CLIMATE CHANGE 53

Figure 2.8 Time series of ocean temperature at 50m (top), 600m (middle) and 2000m depth (bottom) observed at *Weather Ship M* in the Norwegian Sea
Source: S. Østerhus, Bjerknes Center, Bergen.

the oceanic mixed layer could be converted completely into electricity, the monetary value (using the present price of 0.11 euro per kWh) would be 63 euro per m^2. A typical European family could satisfy the annual demand for electricity (6,000kWh) from 11m^2 of ocean surface area. For home heating and warm water supply (40,000kWh) 72m^2 are additionally required. In addition to the seasonal cycle, the ocean heat storage affects also long-term climate variations through its thermal inertia in deeper layers.

(b) Heat transport

As a consequence of the oceanic heat transport, the west coasts of the continents exhibit relatively warm winters. This is especially true for Western Europe, which is affected by the Gulf Stream and its extension, the North Atlantic Current. Here, the winter temperatures are more than 15°C warmer than in the corresponding regions on the east coast of North America (see Figure 2.5). The Gulf Stream transports approximately 1 peta-Watt (10^{15} Watt, i.e. the output

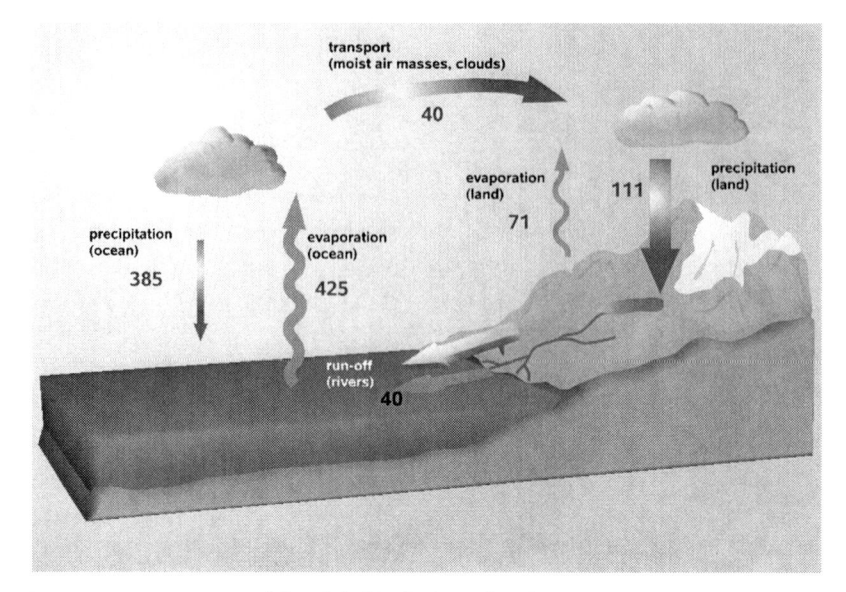

Figure 2.9 Components of the global hydrological cycle
The numbers indicate water transports in $10^{12} m^3$/year

of one million nuclear power plants). Converting it with the present price for electricity (0.11 euro/kWh) this amounts to 31 million euro per second.

(c) Water source (regulation of the hydrological cycle)

Water is one the most important and most active substances in the climate system. Water constitutes the ocean, glaciers, and ice sheets, and it is present in the atmosphere as vapour, and in the clouds as droplets and ice crystals.

The ocean represents the largest water storage on Earth. It contains 97% of the water on our planet, and dominates the hydrological cycle (Figure 2.9). This cycle begins with the evaporation at the surface of the oceans and continents. Carried away by the wind systems, the water vapour condenses in the clouds forming water droplets and returns to the surface with the precipitation starting the new cycle directly or after a long detour through glaciers, rivers, or ground water.

The essential water on the continents originates mostly from the evaporation at the ocean surface, where $42.5 \times 10^{13} m^3$ enters the atmosphere annually. The evaporation at the continental surface amounts to only $7.1 \times 10^{13} m^3$/year. Estimates of the sizes of the reservoirs yield for the ocean $1350 \times 10^{15} m^3$, for the continents $33.6 \times 10^{15} m^3$, and for the atmosphere $0.013 \times 10^{15} m^3$. Dividing the sizes of the reservoirs by the exchange rates, the residence times are determined as 3,000 years for the ocean, 300 years for the continents, and 10 days for the atmosphere.

Associated with the water cycle is the energy cycle. The radiative energy received from the sun is mostly used to evaporate water at the ocean or land surface. This latent heat is gained by the atmosphere during the condensation of water vapour in the clouds. The latent heat flux from the Earth's surface to the atmosphere is more than three times larger than the sensible heat flux, and represents one of the most important energy sources for the atmospheric motion.

(d) Gas storage (regulation of the chemical composition of the atmosphere)

In addition to water, other substances are exchanged at the sea surface: trace gases, which are exchanged in both directions, and dust particles carried by the wind enter the ocean and are finally deposited in the marine sediments. The dust is of importance for the interpretation of sediment cores with respect to palaeo-climate information. From the size of the dust particles and the distance of the core site from the dust source, the wind velocity can be inferred.

Because of the exchange of CO_2 and other trace gases, the ocean is of major importance for the evolution of climate. As a storage medium for gases, the ocean regulates the chemical composition of the atmosphere and, therefore, determines the radiation and energy budgets of our planet.

Approximately 71% of the Earth's surface are covered with oceans, which are on average 4,000m deep. Ocean and atmosphere are intensely connected via the exchange of heat, momentum, and mass (water and gases). Particularly the salinity of seawater is coupled to precipitation and evaporation at the sea surface.

The oceanic currents at the sea surface are predominantly driven by the wind stress, and, therefore, mostly reflect the patterns of the global wind systems. The trade winds in the tropics push the water towards the east coasts of the continents (*equatorial currents*) where it piles up, and an east-west surface slope is maintained (approximately 4cm per 1,000km increase towards the west). The water piled up at the western edge of the oceans either flows back to the east (partly below the surface) as *equatorial counter-currents*, or enter the so-called *western boundary currents* (Gulf Stream, Kuroshio). In the eastern parts of the tropical oceans the water pushed towards the west is replaced by cold water from deeper layers of the ocean (*upwelling*).

Similar to the atmosphere, the large-scale motion in the ocean is superimposed by small-scale eddies. These eddies are visible in the surface temperature pattern and also in the drift pattern of oceanic surface buoys. The size of the oceanic eddies is an order of magnitude smaller (100km) than the atmospheric analogue, the low pressure systems (1,000km).

In addition to the wind, oceanic currents are driven by density variations of the different water masses. Whereas surface currents are mainly generated by the wind, the deep ocean circulation is influenced by gradients of the density,

Table 2.2 *Area and volume of cryospheric components*

	Area [10^6 km^2]	Volume [10^6 km^3]	Volume [relative]
Ice sheets	14.8	28.8	600
Ice shelves	1.4	0.5	10
Sea ice	23.0	0.05	1
Snow	45.0	0.0025	0.05

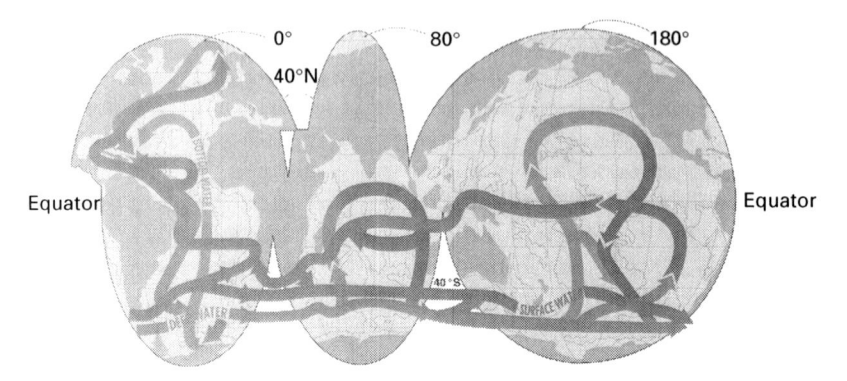

Figure 2.10 Oceanic thermohaline circulation

or more precisely by the gradients of the pressure field. The density of seawater is determined by temperature and salinity (and pressure). Therefore, the deep ocean circulation is also called *thermohaline* circulation.

Dense water is predominantly produced in polar regions through cooling and brine rejection during the freezing of seawater. The dense water produced at the surface of the high latitude oceans sinks to greater depth replacing the less dense water. The most important areas of deep and bottom water production are the northern North Atlantic and the Weddell Sea in the Southern Ocean. From these regions the dense water flows into all ocean basins (Figure 2.10).

3. Cryosphere

Concerning its mass and heat capacity, the cryosphere represents the second largest component of the climate system (after the ocean). The main components of the cryosphere are snow, sea ice, ice shelves, and ice sheets (Figure 2.11).

Presently, ice covers 11% of the land surface (15.7 × 10^6km^2), and on an annual average approximately 6.5% of the oceans (23.0 × 10^6km^2) (see Table 2.2). In spite of its larger area, the volume of sea ice relative to that of

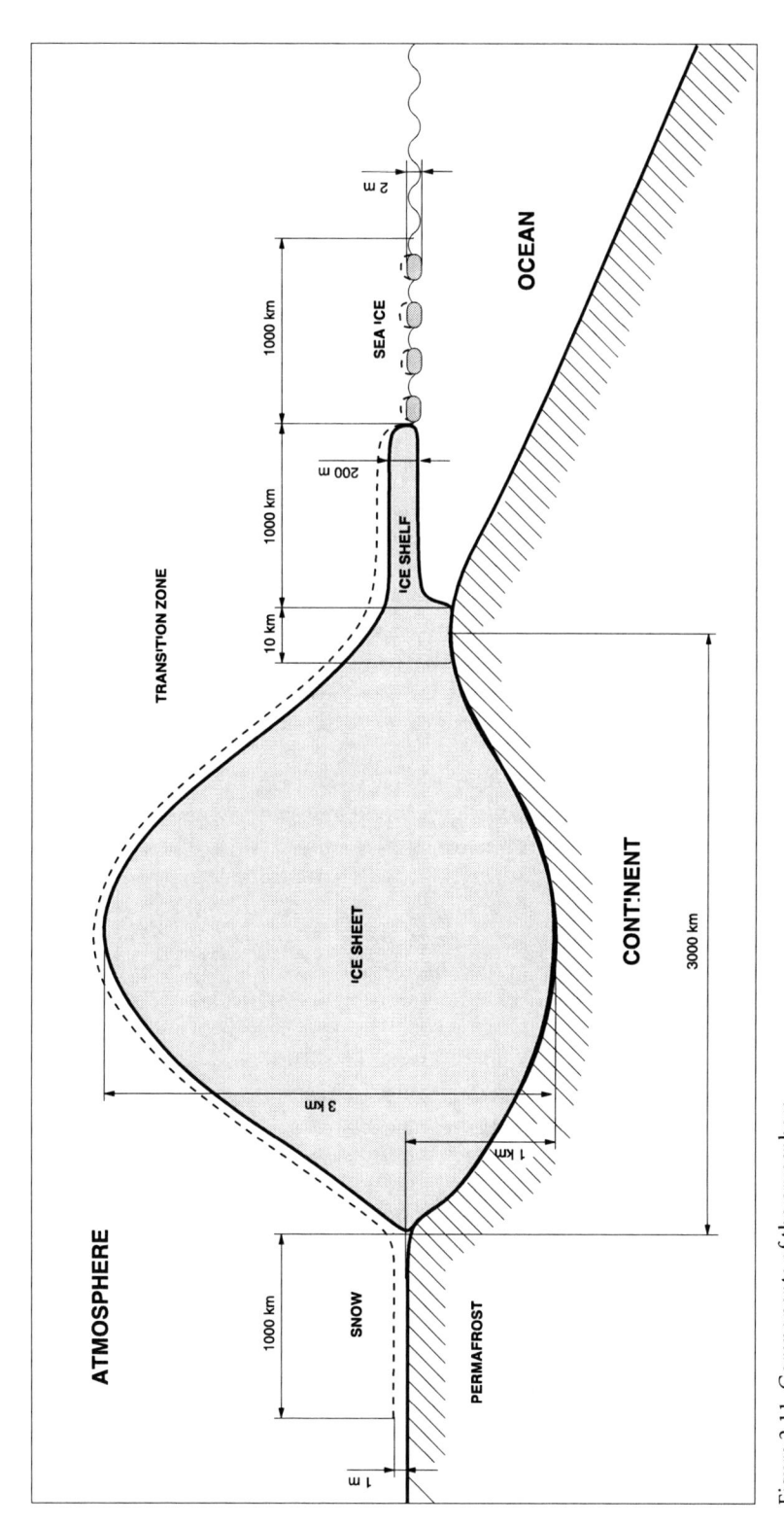

Figure 2.11 Components of the cryosphere

ice sheets is only 1:600. Ice shelves, mostly present in Antarctica, cover $1.4 \times 10^6 \text{km}^2$, which is far less than the area of sea ice. The ice shelf volume is approximately $0.5 \times 10^6 \text{km}^3$, ten times the volume of sea ice. All mountain glaciers amount to $0.24 \times 10^6 \text{km}^3$, a little less than 10% of the Greenland ice sheet. Because of their small area, the climatic impact is rather minor and will not be discussed here. Snow covers in winter – in addition to sea and land ice – approximately 50% of the land surface in the northern hemisphere. The snow volume is, on the other hand, rather small: $2.5 \times 10^3 \text{km}^3$.[4]

The components of the cryosphere are characterised by rather different timescales. Snow and sea ice anomalies exist for days to weeks and several months, respectively. The lifetime of ice shelf variations is several centuries, and that of ice sheets several tens of thousands of years. Short-term climate variations are, therefore, influenced by snow and sea ice, and long-term changes by ice shelves and ice sheets, which determine the ice age variations.

An important property of snow and ice with climatic relevance is its high reflectivity (albedo). Up to 90% of the incident solar radiation is reflected by snow and ice surfaces. Only a small part of this reflected energy is absorbed in the atmosphere, most of it is lost to space. Over the open ocean, on the other hand, 90% of the solar radiation is absorbed and is used to heat the climate system.

Because of the spherical shape of the Earth and the high albedo of snow and ice, the polar regions absorb significantly less solar radiation than the tropics. The resulting temperature differences induce winds and currents, which are influenced by many interactions within the climate system (Figure 2.6). The cryosphere plays a major role in these interactions, because the tracks of low pressure systems are influenced by the large temperature gradients at snow and ice margins, and the formation of sea ice affects the oceanic deep water formation, and, therefore, the thermohaline circulation in the ocean.

The cryosphere is also involved in one of the most important feedback processes, the positive (i.e. destabilising) temperature-ice-albedo feedback. An initial cooling in the polar regions leads to a larger snow and ice extent, which induces further cooling through the increased global albedo and decreased absorption of solar energy. On the other hand, an initial warming leads to a smaller snow and ice extent, which induces further warming through the decreased global albedo. The climate system is regulated by a large variety of positive and negative (i.e. stabilising) feedbacks. The cryosphere plays an important role in this climatic feedback system.

---

[4] Untersteiner, N., The cryosphere, in Houghton, J. (ed.), *The global climate*, Cambridge (Cambridge University Press) 1984, pp. 121–140.

(a) Snow

Among all components of the cryosphere the snow is characterised by the largest areal extent and the smallest total mass. In winter snow covers the sea ice, all ice masses on land, and a substantial part of the land surface (i.e. 50% of the continents in the northern hemisphere). Snow has the highest albedo (up to 0.9 for dry snow). This high reflectivity for solar radiation is the most important climate property of snow. In addition, snow has a low heat conductivity, thereby reducing the upward heat flux from the underlying soil or ice surfaces to the atmosphere. Because of the large reflection of solar energy and the low heat conductivity, less heat is available in the atmosphere. The air above snow surfaces is, therefore, significantly cooled. Snow-covered areas act as strong energy sinks on our planet.

(b) Sea ice

Sea ice plays a special role within the cryosphere, since – in contrast to all other forms of ice – it does not originate from fresh water, but consists of frozen seawater. Sea ice covers in March 5% and in September 8% of the ocean surface (Figure 2.12). On average, it is in the Arctic Ocean 3m and in the Southern Ocean 1m thick.

Because the sea ice – even without snow cover – has a relatively high albedo, it acts in the climate system (like snow) as an energy sink. This role is amplified through the isolating effect of the sea ice cover, which results in a reduction of the exchange of momentum and heat between atmosphere and ocean. Above sea ice, the air is significantly colder than above open water surfaces. As a result of increased cooling of air in high latitudes through advancing sea ice, the meridional temperature gradient is enhanced and the westerlies in mid-latitudes are amplified. Less sea ice would reduce the meridional temperature gradient and consequently weaken the westerlies. This effect has been confirmed by experiments with atmospheric circulation models using very large sea ice anomalies. Observed variations of sea ice mostly initiate a local response. Because of the large natural variability in the atmosphere, global effects of sea ice variations are difficult to detect.

Sea ice influences not only the atmosphere but also the ocean. It affects the ocean through isolation against the atmosphere, reducing the heat and mass exchange because of the lid effect. It also modifies the momentum exchange because of deformation processes occurring in the sea ice, which can be described as a two-dimensional viscous-plastic material.[5] The most important impact of sea ice on the ocean is the formation of deep and bottom

---

[5] Lemke, P., Hibler, W. D., Flato, G., Harder, M., and Kreyscher, M., On the improvement of sea ice models for climate simulations: the sea ice model intercomparison project, *Ann. Glaciol.* 25 (1997), pp. 183–187.

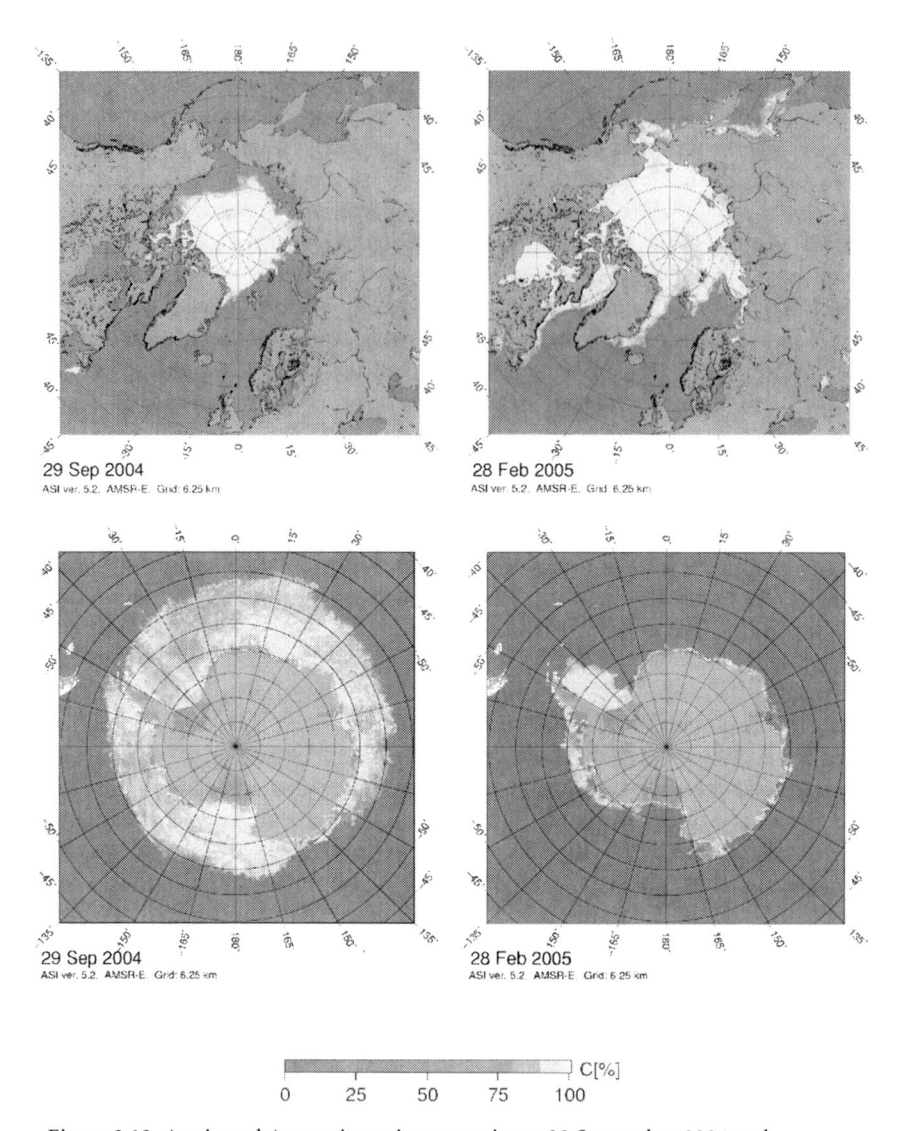

Figure 2.12 Arctic and Antarctic sea ice extent in on 29 September 2004 and 28 February 2005

water. The salinity of seawater is on average 34.7 per mille; the salt content of sea ice, on the other hand, is only 5 per mille. During the freezing process a substantial amount of salt is released into the ocean. Because of the saltier surface water, convection is initiated and may reach into the deeper parts of the ocean. Cooling and brine rejection in polar regions are the main processes driving the global thermohaline circulation.

In polar regions, the oceanic temperature at the surface is near freezing point, whereas the water is warmer at depth. Therefore, warm water reaches the surface during convection. In regions with a weak stability like in the Weddell Sea near the Antarctic continent, convection reaches deep oceanic layers, such that enough heat is entrained into the mixed layer to prevent the formation of sea ice.[6] Then a *polynya*, i.e. a large area of open water within the pack ice, is created. Such a polynya – 1,000km long and 350km wide – was observed in the Weddell Sea during winter in 1974 and 1975.

The stability of the sea ice cover is, therefore, strongly dependent on the stability of the oceanic stratification. In the Arctic Ocean, the high oceanic stability is a consequence of the fresh water supply by the river run-off from Asia and North America. Old plans exist in Russia to divert some of the north-flowing rivers to the south, where there is a large demand of fresh water for household supply and irrigation. These plans have led to a wide discussion about the impact of the river diversion on the stability of the Arctic sea ice cover. A weakening of the oceanic stratification would lead to deeper mixed layers in winter, favouring enhanced entrainment of warm Atlantic water into the surface mixed layer with subsequent reduction of the sea ice cover. Experiments with a coupled sea ice-mixed layer model have shown that a 30% reduction of the river run-off may cause a reduction of the sea ice thickness of 3cm. A 50% reduction would lead to a substantially stronger response. In this case the sea ice thickness reduces by 30cm. This is approximately 20% of the average sea ice thickness on the Eurasian shelf.[7] The old Soviet plans, which included up to 10% of the Russian river run-off, are in the meantime postponed.

(c) Ice shelves

Ice shelves are a characteristic feature in Antarctica. Ice shelves are floating, with thicknesses of 200m at their northern edge and 1,000m at the grounding line near the continent (Figure 2.11). Here, the ice thickness is given by the water depth multiplied with the density ratio water/ice. The ice shelves gain mass through the inflow from the ice sheet, and they lose mass through calving of icebergs and melting at their underside, which is in contact with the ocean.

The largest ice shelves are the Ronne-Filchner and the Ross Ice Shelves, each covering an area of about 500,000km². Ice shelves are located in huge bays and are stabilised by friction at their lateral boundaries. The ice velocities are a few kilometres per year at the edge and a few hundred meters per year near the grounding line.

In contrast to snow and sea ice, the ice shelf is a very slow system. Approximately every fifty years, a large tabular iceberg calves at a given location and

---

[6] Lemke, P., A coupled one-dimensional sea ice – ocean model., *J. Geophys. Res.* 92 (1987), pp. 13164–13172.
[7] See Lemke, op. cit.

changes the extent and shape of the ice shelf. Another timescale is the residence time of an ice particle in the ice shelf. Travelling from the grounding line to the edge lasts about 1,000 years, which is comparable to the overturning time of the deep ocean.

Because of their small area, the influence of ice shelves on the atmosphere is rather limited and is dominated by the high albedo. For the ocean, the ice shelves play a more pronounced role, because in their vicinity – particularly in the Weddell Sea – deep and bottom water is produced which is found in all major ocean basins. On the other hand, ice shelves are sensitive to changes of ocean properties. During warming of the atmosphere-ocean system, e.g. due to increased greenhouse gas concentrations, the ice shelves are losing mass. An additional sea level rise would lift the ice shelves, move the grounding line south towards the continent, and increase the contact surface to the ocean, which would result in an enhanced melting. Depending on the bottom topography, i.e. the slope of the bedrock, parts of the ice shield may become unstable and glide into the ocean. This scenario has been suggested for the West Antarctic Ice Sheet. The stability of ice sheets partly depends on the stability of the ice shelves.

(d) Ice sheets

Ice sheets grow through accumulation and compression of snow. There are two large ice sheets on Earth: the Greenland Ice Sheet with a height of about 3,000m and the Antarctic Ice Sheet with an elevation of more than 4,000m. The bedrock under the Greenland Ice Sheet is formed like a bowl, with an elevated rim of mountains and a deep centre that is approximately 130m below sea level. The volume of the Greenland Ice Sheet amounts to 8m sea level rise. The Antarctic continent below the ice sheet shows a variety of features. West Antarctica would consist of a collection of islands after removing the ice sheet. Presently, the West Antarctic Ice Sheet still rests on the bedrock, mostly below sea level, in parts down to 2,500m. This has caused speculation that the increased hydrostatic pressure of a rising sea level may lift most of the West Antarctic Ice Sheet, which would then in parts swim and disintegrate. The volume of the total West Antarctic Ice Sheet is equivalent to a 5m rise of sea level. The East Antarctic Ice Sheet, separated from the West Antarctic Ice Sheet by the Trans Antarctic Mountains, contains approximately 80% of the Antarctic ice mass. The bedrock under the ice sheet is in most regions mountainous, only a small part is below sea level (up to 1,000m). The volume of the East Antarctic Ice Sheet is equivalent to a 55m sea level rise.

Concerning their mass balance the Greenland and Antarctic Ice Sheets are totally different. There is no surface melting observed in Antarctica. There, the mass balance is achieved through outflow of ice into the ice shelves. For the Greenland Ice Sheet the accumulation of snow in the central part is balanced through large melting areas at the edges, particularly in the south. As on mountain glaciers, there is an equilibrium line with a positive mass balance above and a negative one below. In addition, the Greenland Ice Sheet is losing mass through the calving of icebergs at many glacier tongues. There are no larger ice shelves in Greenland.

Variations of ice sheets have a significant impact on the global energy balance. Two processes are important in this regard. The main effect is the influence on the radiation budget through the high albedo of the high elevation, cold, and snow-covered ice masses. In addition, the atmosphere gains latent heat during the condensation of water vapour and subsequent snow fall. This latent heat has to be supplied to melt snow and ice. In order to melt the present ice sheets completely, 9.3×10^{24} Joule are required. In comparison: the total solar energy absorbed by the Earth amounts to 3.8×10^{24} Joule per year. The transition from glacial to interglacial periods requires 1.6×10^{25} Joule. This is a large amount, but considering the transition time of about 5,000 years, only 0.085% of the absorbed solar energy has to be taken for the melt-back of the Laurentide and Scandinavian Ice Sheets. Considering further that the ocean has warmed during this transition period by about 4°C, then the total energy for melting the ice sheets and warming the ocean amounts to only 0.2% of the absorbed solar energy.[8] It seems that the short retreat phase of the ice age cycle does not heavily stress the overall energy budget of the Earth. In addition to the impact on the energy budget, the ice sheets modify the atmospheric circulation through their significant height. Like huge mountain ranges they act as barriers and influence the planetary waves.

There is also a strong influence of the ice sheets on the ocean. During the advance phase of the ice age, more water evaporates from the oceans than runs off from the continents. The difference is stored in the ice sheets. Due to the excess evaporation, the surface layers of the ocean get saltier, and enhanced deep convection significantly modifies the global ocean circulation. Because of the lower sea level (by about 150m), the ocean circulation is also modified, e.g. no flow through Bering Strait. During the retreat phase of the ice sheets, huge amounts of meltwater are flowing into the ocean, increasing the stability and reducing deep and bottom water formation significantly. Impacts of fresh water anomalies on the oceanic overturning have been investigated in great detail.[9]

Radiation anomalies originating from the variation of Earth's orbital parameters are supposed to be the initiators of the ice age cycles (Milankovitch Theory). A simple calculation shows that the annual snow equilibrium line may be shifted by 10 degrees latitude taking the extremes of the radiation anomalies.

---

[8] Oerlemans, J. and van der Veen, C. J., *Ice sheets and climate*, Dordrecht (D. Reidel) 1984.
[9] Marotzke, J., Welander, P., and Willebrand, J., Instability and multiple steady states in a meridional-plane model of the thermohaline circulation, *Tellus* 40A (1988), pp. 162–172. Rahmstorf, S., The thermohaline ocean circulation: a system with dangerous thresholds?, *Climatic Change* 46 (2000), pp. 247–256.

A new ice age sets in when the snow balance is positive over a longer time. The period of successive ice ages is dependent on radiation anomalies, on the dynamics of ice and lithosphere, and the interaction with the other components of the climate system (atmosphere, ocean, and biosphere). Recent investigations indicate also that the carbon cycle, in particular the CO_2 concentration in the atmosphere, has changed with the ice ages. However, a conclusive theory of the ice ages is still missing. Ice ages represent a climate anomaly which affects all components of the climate system.

(e) Land

The upper 100km of the Earth's mantle are referred to as the lithosphere, which includes the continents and the ocean floor. The maximum age of the ocean floor is about 160Ma because of seafloor spreading and subduction of oceanic plates. On the continents, rocks have been found that are as old as 3.8 billion years. Continents are 'lighter' (the density is smaller) than the underlying asthenosphere on which they float (like sheets of ice on water).

On short timescales, the lithosphere may be considered as a constant boundary condition for atmosphere and ocean. On longer timescales, however, the continental drift leads to dramatic changes of the distribution of continents and oceans. The typical timescale is of the order of 10 to 100 million years (the seafloor spreading rate is 3cm per year). Earth's surface is subject to continuous change through plate tectonics, weathering, erosion, uplift, mountain-building, volcanism, and seafloor spreading. Atmospheric and oceanic circulations are significantly affected by the distribution of continents, mountains, ocean passages, and continental features such as the Isthmus of Panama. Changes in the rate and pattern of the mantle's flow lead to changes in the rate of CO_2 degassing and its release into the atmosphere. Hence, on long timescales, the Earth's climate is also linked to its tectonics.

Volcanoes eject particulate matter and sulphate-bearing gases, forming aerosols which affect the radiation balance of the atmosphere and thus climate. As an example, Mount Pinatubo, Philippines, erupted in 1991 (for the first time in 600 years) and caused widespread devastation and resulted in measurable cooling worldwide (about 0.5–0.6°C surface cooling in the northern hemisphere).

In contrast to the long-term effects of the land-ocean distribution, the character of the land surface impacts on the climate system on shorter timescales (seasons to decades). The land surface can be divided into three parts: the bare soil, the regions covered with vegetation, and the ice-covered areas. Land surfaces represent the lower boundary condition for approximately one-third of the atmosphere, and there they determine the exchange of momentum, heat, water, and gases. The most important effect on the climate system is caused by the vegetation. There are two types of interactions: a biogeochemical interaction between the vegetation and the chemical composition of Earth's atmosphere, and a biophysical interaction that affects the exchange of momentum, heat, and water.

The biosphere on land (and in the oceans) plays a major role in the carbon cycle on Earth. It has a pronounced effect on atmospheric composition. Nitrogen, oxygen, and carbon dioxide concentrations in Earth's atmosphere are very different from those on Venus and Mars. Also, fluxes of other greenhouse gases such as CH_4 and N_2O (nitrous oxide) are very different from abiotic conditions. Organisms are also involved in the so-called carbonate-silicate cycle which acts as a thermostat keeping the surface temperature of Earth relatively constant and preventing the Earth becoming completely frozen.[10]

On the biophysical side, Earth's vegetation affects the albedo through its darker colour as compared to bare soil in a desert. This reduced reflectivity leads to enhanced absorption of solar energy, which affects the surface energy balance and increases the temperature. In addition, the water cycle is affected by the vegetation through transport of water from the ground water level to the surface of the leaves, where it is transpired. The storage of water on vegetated land is strongly enhanced. In particular in forested areas this leads to an increased humidity of the air.

Compared with the ocean, the heat storage on land is small and the horizontal heat transport is negligible. In contrast to the ocean, the land surfaces are very heterogeneous and rough. Its pronounced topography affects local wind systems through differences in the vegetation and the large-scale atmospheric circulation through mountain ranges.

VII. Outlook

The climate on Earth has changed in the past and will change in the future. In contrast to past changes, future variations will be caused naturally and additionally also by mankind. These anthropogenic impacts result mainly from changes in the composition of the atmospheric and from modifications of the land surface. The projections for the next 100 years indicate a temperature increase of approximately 3°C. Detailed investigations of such scenarios are currently a matter of national and international climate projects.

In the framework of these activities, numerical climate models consisting of atmosphere, ice, ocean, and land surfaces modules are developed, which are forced with energy scenarios that determine the expected rise in atmospheric CO_2. These climate models follow the basic physical laws such as the conservation of momentum, energy, and mass. They include radiation components, which distribute the solar radiation to the different climate components. The

---

[10] Lovelock, J., *The ages of gaia: a biography of our living Earth*, Oxford (Oxford University Press) 2004, p. 277.

resulting temperature distribution is the origin of atmospheric winds, ocean currents, and changes in the ice masses on Earth.

Given the different scenarios of fossil fuel consumption, climate models predict an increase of the global surface temperature of $+1.5°C$ to $+5.8°C$ by the year 2100, with the strongest warming in winter on the continents and in polar regions. According to these studies precipitation will increase in high latitudes (especially in winter), sea and land ice will retreat significantly, and sea level will rise by 0.1m to 0.9m. These changes will significantly affect human societies and mitigation will only be successful with international cooperation.

3

Global climate change: what can we learn from the past?

STEFAN RAHMSTORF

Evaluating the human effect on climate requires a good understanding of past climatic changes. We have to turn to history in order to understand the present. However, myths and misunderstandings about past climate changes abound and ill-informed or simplistic conclusions are often drawn.

Has climate not changed at all times, and much more than we are presently witnessing, so that humans cannot be blamed? Is climate change mostly controlled by the sun, with all human influence insignificant in comparison? Does CO_2 really affect climate, or was it just the other way round in the past? Aren't humans responsible only for 2% of the greenhouse effect, and 98% is perfectly natural? And is the next ice age inevitably approaching?

A thorough analysis of what we know about climate history gives answers – sometimes surprising ones – to these and similar questions.

Many signs of past climate changes are clearly visible in the landscape, for example, the moraines of glaciers long gone (Figure 3.1). Most of our knowledge on past climate changes, however, is the result of painstaking detective work with increasingly sophisticated methods. Wherever lasting deposits form – be it sediments on the seafloor, snow layers on glaciers, stalagtites in caves, or growth rings in trees and corals – scientists will find a way to derive climatic information from these. They drill for years through the ice caps of Greenland and Antarctica until they hit bedrock, they bring up sediment cores from thousands of metres below the ocean surface, they analyse the isotopic composition of snow with precision instruments, or they identify and count pollen or tiny shells under a microscope for months on end.

Climate is the result of a simple energy balance: the long-wave radiation from the Earth into space balances the incoming solar radiation; ocean and atmosphere redistribute heat within the climate system. Climate changes result from changes in this energy balance. Incoming solar radiation may change through changes in the Earth's orbit or within the sun itself. The portion reflected into space (the albedo) depends on cloud cover and brightness of the surface, i.e., on ice cover, land use, and the distribution of continents. And the emitted long-wave radiation depends not only on surface temperature

Figure 3.1 The Mueller Glacier in the Southern Alps of New Zealand
The Mueller Glacier is seen in the foreground. Clearly visible are the moraines marking its extent in the late nineteenth century. Like most glaciers in the world, the Mueller is collapsing rapidly.
Source: photograph by the author

but is also influenced by the concentration of absorbing gases and aerosols in the atmosphere. All these factors play a role in the roller-coaster history of climate.

Fortunately, the calculation of climatic variables (i.e., long-term averages) is much easier than weather forecasting, since weather is ruled by the vagaries of stochastic fluctuations, while climate is not. Imagine a pot of boiling water. A weather forecast is like the attempt to predict where the next bubble is going to rise (physically this is an initial value problem). A climate statement would be that the average temperature of the boiling water is 100°C at normal pressure, while it is only 90°C at 2,500m altitude in the mountains, due to the lower pressure (that is a boundary value problem).

So what are the causes of past climate changes? Let us start with the planetary motions. The Earth is like a spinning top that tumbles a little. Her position in relation to the sun changes in the so-called Milankovich cycles; these change the distribution of solar radiation in a calculable manner. Their characteristic frequencies (23,000, 41,000, and 100,000 years) are clearly visible in most long climatic time-series. They are found in 50-million-year-old deep sea sediments just as in the Vostok ice core from Antarctica, which spans the past 400,000 years. For the past two million years the Earth has been so cold that ice has covered the polar areas. The amount of ice waxes and wanes in the rhythm of the Milankovich cycles: this is the coming and going of ice ages.

In the 1970s, when climate research was still in its infancy, a few scientists even saw the risk of a new ice age coming. The reasoning was simple: previous warm periods had lasted around 10,000 years; our current warm period, the Holocene, has already lasted that long, thus it should end very soon. Today, the Milankovich cycles are better (though not completely) understood, and we can assume that the Holocene will last much longer. Such exceptionally long warm periods usually occur when the Earth's orbit is going through an eccentricity minimum (i.e., the orbit is almost a perfect circle). It will probably take at least another 50,000 years until the next ice age starts – that at least is the result of calculations with simple models, which successfully reproduce the start of the past ten glaciations from the Milankovich cycles.[1] The example illustrates that a physical understanding is required in order to draw proper conclusions, simple analogies do not carry us very far.

A theory of the ice ages further needs to explain, in a quantitative sense, how the changes in the radiation budget caused by the Milankovich cycles lead to glaciers forming with the observed size, in the right places, and the right time sequence. This is a difficult problem, but it has recently been solved in important parts. One of the problems is that the Milankovich cycles hardly change the total amount of solar radiation received by the Earth, they just change its distribution over the seasons and latitudes. In order to cool the whole planet by 4–6°C in this way, feedback mechanisms must play a major role.

It turned out that snow is crucial here: ice sheets start to grow when solar radiation during northern summer is too weak to melt the snow of the previous winter. That leads to a strong positive feedback: snow reflects much sunlight and cools the climate further, and the ice slowly grows to a thickness of several thousand meters.

But when summer sun in the north is weak, then it is strong in the southern hemisphere – so why should the latter cool simultaneously? The answer is found in tiny air bubbles enclosed in the Antarctic ice: carbon dioxide (Figure 3.2). Those air bubbles reveal the CO_2 content of the atmosphere of the past 400,000 years.[2] It oscillated between ∼190 ppm at the peak of glaciations and 280 ppm during warm periods (present value: 380 ppm). The radiative effect of this gas has been known since the calculations of Svante Arrhenius, published in 1896, and has been confirmed by laboratory measurements. When this radiative effect is included in climate models, one obtains realistic simulations of ice age climate, including the otherwise inexplicable cooling in Antarctica.

---

[1] Paillard, D., The timing of Pleistocene glaciations from a simple multiple-state climate model, *Nature* 391(1998), pp. 378–381.

[2] Petit, J. R. *et al.*, Climate and atmospheric history of the past 420,000 years from the Vostok ice core, Antarctica, *Nature* 399 (1999), pp. 429–436.

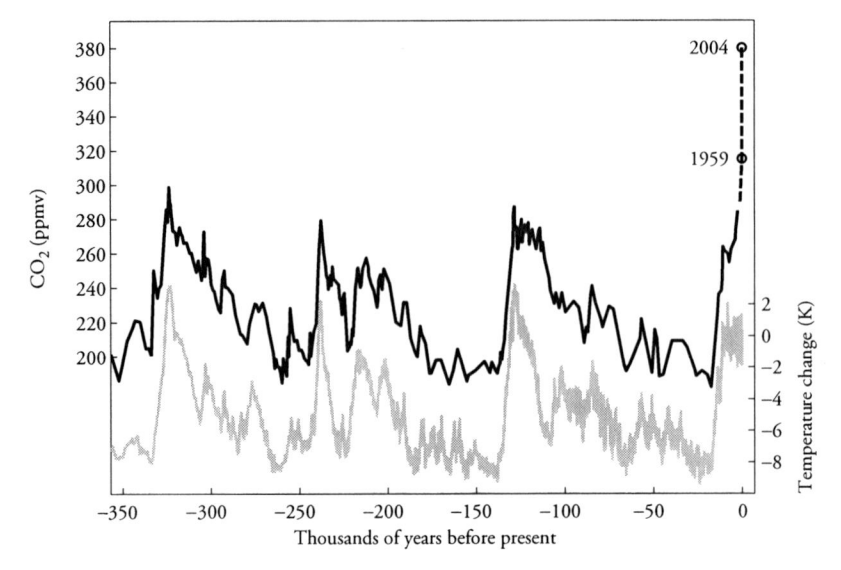

Figure 3.2 Climate history of the past 400,000 years from the Vostok ice core in Antarctica
Local temperature deviation from present is shown in the grey curve (scale on right in °C). CO_2 content of the atmosphere is shown in the black curve (scale on left in ppm). Anthropogenic emissions have now increased the CO_2 concentration to 380 ppm.
Source: Petit, J. R. et al., Climate and atmospheric history of the past 420,000 years from the Vostok ice core, Antarctica, Nature 399 (1999), pp. 429–436.

CO_2 operates here as part of a feedback loop: if temperature drops, so does the atmospheric CO_2 content, and this in turn amplifies and globalises the cooling. In contrast to the second part of this feedback (i.e. the well-known effect of CO_2 on temperature), the first part is still hotly debated. Why does CO_2 concentration drop when it gets cold? Apparently the CO_2 vanishes in the oceans, but which mechanisms play which part in this is still not settled. But one thing is certain: this feedback works. When temperature is changed (e.g., through the Milankovich cycles) then CO_2 follows with some delay; when CO_2 is changed (e.g., by anthropogenic emissions), then temperature follows soon after.

'Climate sceptics', who dispute the need for reducing CO_2 emissions, sometimes claim that a small lag of CO_2 values behind temperature in the Vostok core argues against the climatic effects of this gas. In reality this only confirms the known fact that CO_2 is not the primary cause of the glacial cycles. The delay with which the CO_2 feedback kicks in tells us about the response time of the carbon cycle, but nothing about the effect of CO_2 on climate. Not even the amplitude of the curves shown in Figure 3.2 gives away the sought-after value of global climate sensitivity with respect to CO_2 (misinterpreting it in this way would lead to far too high a sensitivity value). There are two main reasons for this. While the CO_2 values apply globally, the temperature curve applies only to local conditions in Antarctica; and the temperature changes shown are not the result of changes in CO_2 alone; other parts of the radiation budget change as well, e.g. insolation (due to the Milankovich cycles) and the Earth's albedo (due to the presence of large ice sheets).

Sceptics also like to point out periods in climate history during which CO_2 and temperature did not change in such close lockstep as during the past 400,000 years. However, this also does not speak against the climatic effects of CO_2, but simply confirms that CO_2 has not been the dominant factor in all climatic changes. Such examples usually relate to the Holocene, during which CO_2 hardly varied and thus could not be the major factor in climatic variability. Or they refer to timescales of millions of years, for which CO_2 concentration is not well known and where other factors, like continental drift, become important. The general cooling trend during the past 65 million years, however, fits well with the decline in CO_2 over this time due to tectonic processes. Times in climate history where temperature and CO_2 run counter to each other are an interesting exception – we can learn much from those times about other climatic driving forces, but they do not rule out the climatic effect of CO_2.

One of those other driving forces is the luminosity of the sun. The sun is a self-regulating fusion reactor, the radiative output of which undergoes slight variations. Shortly after the invention of the telescope in 1609, dark spots were discovered on the sun and in 1611 Johann Fabricius published his book *De Maculis in Sole*. Since the late 1970s, solar luminosity is measured by satellites: it varies with the eleven-year sunspot cycle by about 0.08% (corresponding to 0.2 W/m^2 at ground level). To reconstruct earlier solar variations, the satellite data are combined with recordings of sunspots and with data of the cosmogenic isotopes ^{10}Be and ^{14}C in tree rings and ice cores. Estimates for the Maunder minimum, a period without sunspots around the year 1700, suggest that solar luminosity was 0.24% weaker than compared to today (which is about 0.6 W/m^2 at ground level – for comparison, the anthropogenic increase in greenhouse gases since 1700 has changed the radiation budget by about 2.4 W/m^2). These solar variations can explain a significant fraction of the observed climate variations of the past millennium, but not the unusual warming during the twentieth century.

In 1991 the Danish scientists Friis-Christensen and Lassen created a stir when they claimed the opposite.[3] In *Science* they published a curve showing variations in the length of the sunspot cycle, which looked surprisingly similar to the global temperature variation during the twentieth century. This seemed to explain why the 1990s were the hottest decade of the century, since the

---

[3] Friis-Christensen, E. and Lassen, K., Length of the solar cycle: an indicator of solar activity closely associated with climate, *Science* 254 (1991), pp. 698–700.

solar curve pointed steeply upwards for the past few decades. But other Danish researchers revealed this to be the result of improper data treatment: the data up to about 1960 were averaged over fifty-five years, the later ones not. Only by joining filtered and unfiltered data together did the curve rise towards the end; according to the unfiltered raw data (or consistently filtered data), the 1940s should have been warmest. Knud Lassen withdrew his curve and together with his colleague Peter Thejll published a corrected and updated curve in 2000.[4] This time he concluded: the warming of the past decades cannot be explained by the solar variation. In spite of this, the old solar curve is still publicised by 'climate sceptics' in the popular media.

Recent research has focused on evaluating the combined effect of different forcing factors during the past millennium.[5] For this purpose palaeo-climatic reconstructions of the major forcing functions are compiled: solar luminosity, CO_2, volcanic eruptions, deforestation, and orbital parameters. Climate models are driven with these forcing functions and the resulting climatic evolution is compared with reconstructions of the actual temperature changes. Models and data reconstructions are in reasonable agreement; key features are a general cooling trend up to the nineteenth century and a rapid warming after that; medieval temperatures are reached in the mid-twentieth century. Such a model simulation by Bauer, Claussen et al.[6] showed that increased solar radiation had contributed 0.13°C to the warming of the twentieth century, while anthropogenic greenhouse gases contributed 0.59°C. Other models arrive at similar numbers.

The history of climate also has some surprises in store. During the last glacial about twenty abrupt and dramatic warmings occurred, during which Greenland temperature increased by up to 10°C within a couple of decades. These so-called Dansgaard-Oeschger events lasted for centuries and had global repercussions – a recent compilation lists 183 sites where palaeo-data show synchronous climate changes.[7] The combination of such data with model simulations has in recent years led to a theory of these events which can explain most of the data, e.g., their characteristic time evolution and the spatial patterns of warming and cooling.[8] According to this theory, Dansgaard-Oeschger events

---

[4] Thejll, P. and Lassen, K., Solar forcing of the northern hemisphere land air temperature: new data, *J. Atmospheric and Solar-Terrestrial Physics* 62 (2000), pp. 1207–1213.

[5] Mann, M. E. et al., On past temperatures and anomalous late-20th century warmth, *Eos* 84(27) (2003), pp. 256–258.

[6] Bauer, E., Claussen, M. et al., Assessing climate forcings of the Earth system for the past millennium, *Geophysical Research Letters* 30 (2002), p. 1276.

[7] Voelker, A. H. L. and workshop participants, Global distribution of centennial-scale records for marine isotope stage (MIS) 3: a database, *Quaternary Science Reviews* 21 (2002), pp. 1185–1214.

[8] Ganopolski, A. and Rahmstorf, S., Rapid changes of glacial climate simulated in a coupled climate model, *Nature* 409 (2001), pp. 153–158.

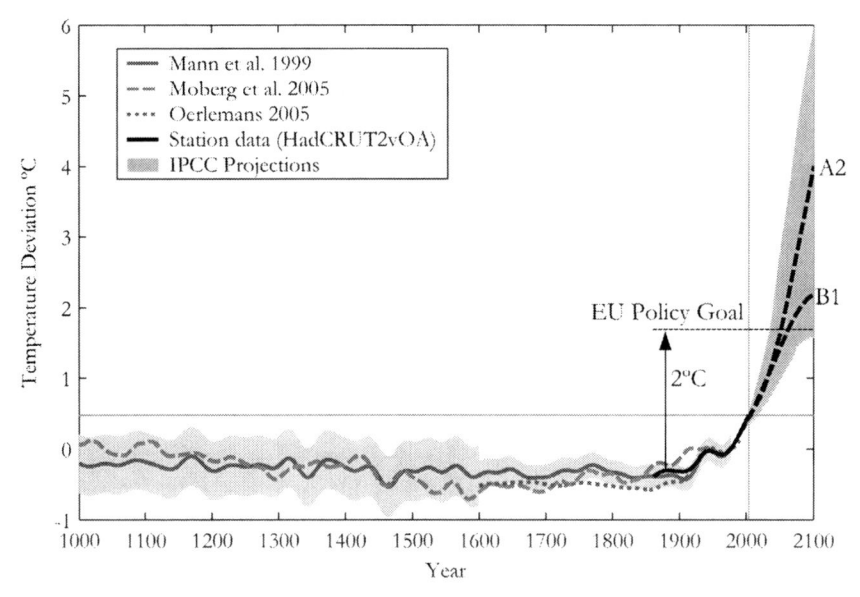

Figure 3.3 Temperature in the northern hemisphere during the past millennium
Shown is the classic reconstruction of Mann *et al.* (1999) (with its uncertainly band in grey, as shown in the 2001 IPCC report) as well as two new reconstructions including sediment data (Moberg *et al.* (2005)) and using glacier extensions (Oerlemans (2005)). Black is the observations from weather stations, with the cross-hair at the 2004 value. The curves are smoothed over 20 years and show deviations relative to 1931–1990. For the future, the range of IPCC scenarios is shown with two examples (A2, B1) and the 2°C policy goal of the European Union.
Source: Mann, M. E., Bradley, R. S., and Hughes, M. K., Northern hemisphere temperatures during the past millennium, *Geophysical Research Letters* 26 (1999), pp. 759–762; Moberg, A., Sonechkin, D. M., Holmgren, K., Datsenko, N. M., and Karlen, W., 2005: Highly variably Northern Hemisphere temperatures reconstructed from low- and high-resolution proxy date, *Nature* 433 (2005), pp. 613–617; Oerlemans, J., 2005: Extracting a climate signal from 169 glacier records, *Science* 308 (2005), pp. 675–677.

are abrupt shifts in the northern Atlantic ocean currents. Probably these current shifts required only a minimal trigger – this is suggested by model simulations, and there is no sign in palaeo-data of any large external forcing causing the events. It seems that the glacial climate was 'on the edge': close to a bifurcation point where the currents flipped easily between two different states. Another type of drastic climate events are Heinrich events, during which large chunks (estimates go up to 10%) of the Laurentide Ice Sheet slipped into the Atlantic (Figure 3.4).

Even during the rather quiet Holocene there was one large climate change: the Sahara turned from a populated savannah with open water into a desert. The cause was apparently a change in monsoon circulation triggered by the 23,000-year orbital cycle. When Claussen, Kubatzki et al.[9] simulated the climate of the past 9,000 years including Milankovich forcing, the Saharan vegetation withered around 5,000 years before the present. This turned out to be a correct 'forecast': soon afterwards new sediment data from the Atlantic coast off northern Africa became available which show a sudden increase in Saharan dust around that time. That is a sure sign of the drying of the Sahara.

These examples show that the investigation of climate history has matured from a descriptive to a quantitative, mechanistic science, based on the fruitful interplay of refined data analysis and the evolution of physical climate models. Only a quantitative understanding of cause and effect of past climate changes allows us to draw robust conclusions from climate history. This is the basis for an evaluation of anthropogenic effects in comparison to natural forcings of climate.

So what can we conclude from climate history? The most important conclusion is perhaps the following: the climate system is a sensitive system that responds strongly to small perturbations of the energy balance. The roller-coaster history of climate shows that climate is like an angry beast, as climatologist Wally Broecker once phrased it. We shouldn't poke at it with sticks.

Climate history confirms strongly the important role of CO_2 as a greenhouse gas, already which was recognised by Arrhenius in the nineteenth century. Climate history further shows that during the past 400,000 years – the interval for which we have accurate data – the CO_2 content of the atmosphere has never remotely been as high as we have pushed it today: it is now already 30% above the normal value for interglacials, with a strongly increasing trend. It is sometimes claimed that the human contribution to the greenhouse effect is only 2% – that is formally correct but misleading. This number holds in relation to the total (natural) greenhouse effect, which warms the Earth by about 33°C compared to a hypothetical Earth without atmosphere at all but with the same albedo (2% of 33°C incidentally makes 0.7°C, showing with a simple linear estimate and without use of a complex model that the anthropogenic change to the radiation budget is of the right magnitude to have caused the observed global warming.)

Climate history further shows that the warming by 0.7°C during the twentieth century probably exceeds any natural variations during the past 1,000 years. This is, of course, not true for every region, e.g. for Europe – climate sceptics are quick to point out anecdotal evidence like medieval wine-growing in England.

---

[9] Claussen, M., Kubatzki, C. et al., Simulation of an abrupt change in Saharan vegetation in the mid-Holocene, *Geophysical Research Letters* 26 (1999), pp. 2037–2040.

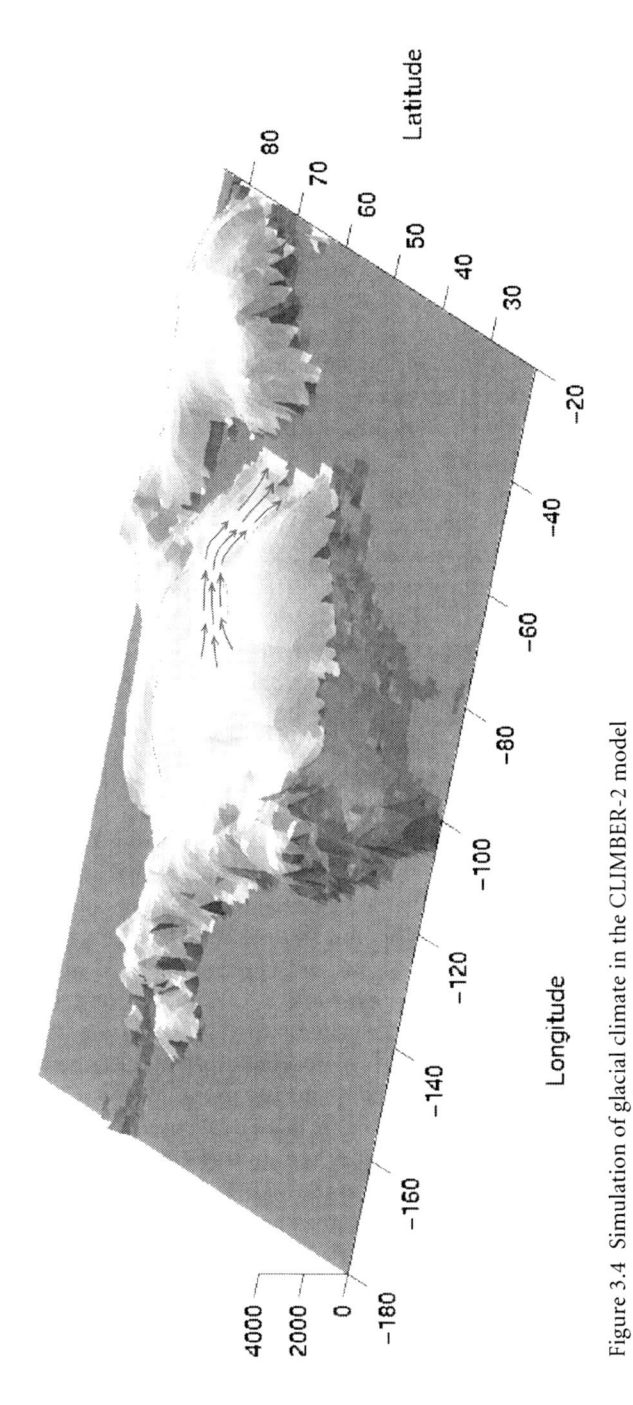

Figure 3.4 Simulation of glacial climate in the CLIMBER-2 model
The image shows the simulated Laurentide and Greenland ice sheets. Part of the ice is sliding into the Labrador Sea at the time of this snapshot (arrows); such Heinrich events occurred several times during the last glacial.

But considering the northern hemisphere as a whole, all the existing quantitative compilations of proxy data (Figure 3.3) show that the 1990s were warmer than the so-called 'Medieval Warm Period'.

Our growing understanding of climate history thus gives us a clear warning. It shows that human influence on climate is no longer negligible; it probably has already become the dominant reason for climate change. The exceptional warming of the twentieth century has been mostly caused by humans; if emissions continue unabated the global temperature will most likely rise by several degrees centigrade this century. The Earth has not experienced such high temperatures for hundreds of thousands of years.

Past climate changes have had serious consequences: the ice ages have wiped out the forest cover in much of Eurasia and North America, and when they came to an end, sea level rose by over 100m, inundating vast areas of continental shelf. Even small fluctuations, like the cold phases of the 'Little Ice Age', have caused failed harvests and famine in Europe. The warming of the twentieth century has already caused glaciers to decline strongly around the world, arctic sea ice to thin and shrink, many animal species to change their geographical range, and plants to extend their growing season. The warming expected for the twenty-first century is several times larger and will have a major effect on ecosystems. Unlike during ice ages, however, many ecosystems are fragmented today due to human land use, and the scope for plants and animals to migrate with shifting climate patterns is very limited. The rate of climate change is also much faster than the warming at the end of the last ice age (a 5°C global warming back then took around 5,000 years) and will very likely exceed the capacity of many ecosystems to adapt. Thus, many species of plants and animals would probably face extinction. Many coral reefs may not survive a warming by more than 2°C, and the Greenland Ice Sheet may melt down completely if local warming exceeds 3°C (which is likely already for a global-mean warming of 2°C).

Human society is more vulnerable to extremes than to a change in mean climate. More frequent or intense storms, droughts, forest fires, and flooding disasters are likely adverse impacts. Some effects of global warming may also be beneficial, but since human society is in many ways highly adapted to past climate conditions, the overall effect of a major change will be negative. A simple illustrative example is a shift in rainfall pattern; this could in one region (or season) reduce water availability below what is currently used, while in another it could exceed established river capacities and cause flooding.

The Earth will not mind – she is used to a varied history. Ice caps, deserts, and forests come and go, species of animals spread and disappear again, continents drift around. But it is we humans who will suffer the consequences of the self-inflicted climate change, unless we are intelligent enough to learn in time from climate history.

PART II

Society and institutions of global
environmental change

4

The social embeddedness of global environmental governance

KARL-WERNER BRAND AND FRITZ REUSSWIG

I. Introduction

Facing the challenges of global environmental change is more than a political and legal problem – it is also a social one. New institutions of global environmental governance have to be rooted in the emerging 'world society'.[1] However, what are the societal preconditions for the institutionalisation of new patterns of governance that allow for an environmentally effective and socially acceptable way of dealing with global environmental problems? One might argue that the new and sometimes threatening nature of these problems[2] will almost automatically lead the 'world society' to develop efficient institutional forms of dealing with them, following a kind of rational logic of problem pressure and interest in survival. Yet it is a well known fact that there is no deduction from problems (i) to problem perceptions and (ii) to solutions. Especially if complex and far-reaching problems are at stake, as in the case of global environmental change, even the very definition of the nature and the scope of the problem is contested, forcing social science research towards reconstructing the process of their social construction. The same holds for the solutions: what might be regarded as a reasonable (effective, feasible, acceptable . . .) solution varies according to the different actors involved and their views of nature and society, interests, and institutional and national backgrounds. One might even doubt whether 'rational' solutions have a chance against those that merely reflect power structures and actual interests of the parties involved. In addition, addressing global environmental problems often requires the involvement of non-state actors in markets, firms, and private households that are supposed to change their consumption patterns and lifestyles significantly in order to mitigate a problem.

The concept of 'global governance' which has gained wide acceptance in the wake of the UNCED Rio Conference reflects this demand for wider, more

---

[1] We use the concept 'world society' in a rather loose and descriptive manner, well aware of the fact that neither a global polity nor a global demos exist.
[2] Cf. the contributions of Peter Lemke (Chapter 2) and Stefan Rahmstorf (Chapter 3).

encompassing institutional solutions. It is not only the basis for central UN documents such as Agenda 21 but has also shaped the institutional design of the follow-up process to Rio and the implementation of the *Leitbild* (guiding vision) 'sustainable development'. The distinct characteristic of 'global governance' lies in its assumption that the effective handling of problems is no longer the exclusive responsibility of governments but of 'joint activities by governments, international and supranational institutions, business and other nongovernmental organizations, bound together in a web of formal and informal connections'.[3]

It is by no means certain, however, that institution-building in the new field of global environmental governance will come to a successful solution − successful in the double sense of (a) contributing to the improvement of the state of the Earth's environment and (b) being implemented in the 'fabric' of national societies or even an eventually emerging 'world society'.

The main focus of this chapter is therefore the societal preconditions for the development and embedding of successful participatory and cooperative forms of global environmental governance. This will be explored in five sections. First, we identify three general preconditions of successful institution-building (section II). The question is if and how far these preconditions can be met in view of the given societal macrotrends (section III), the evolution of environmental awareness and risk perception (section IV), and the strengths and weaknesses of societal actors that push the emergence of a new institutional arrangement of global environmental governance (section V). In order to answer the latter question we will have a closer look at three such actor groups: transnational civil society, science, and consumers. The final section (VI) draws some conclusions regarding the chances of a stable social embedding of global environmental governance.

II. Societal conditions for successful institution-building

The social and political sciences widely agree on the importance of institutions for social development and problem-solving in general. Institutions, understood as formal and informal rules and organisational mechanisms regulating and structuring social interactions and the interactions with natural systems, do matter. Institutions do not only *constrain* but also *enable* social action, and they do not exist apart from human agency.[4] They constitute a strategic corridor in which political and societal actors form their preferences and make and justify their decisions. At the same time, these actors try to shape institutions and the

---

[3] Brand, U., Brunnengräber, A., Schrader, L., Stock, C., and Wahl, P., *Global governance: Alternative zur neoliberalen Globalisierung?* Münster (Westfälisches Dampfboot) 2000, p. 13.

[4] Cf. Giddens, A., *The constitution of society: outline of the theory of structuration*, Cambridge (Polity Press) 1984.

rules of the game according to their particular interests. Still, as the social sciences are rather pluralistic and influenced by different schools and paradigms, different aspects of institutions are emphasised and others neglected by different approaches. The most influential focuses of conceiving institutions are thus 'interests', 'culture', and 'power'. In order to identify conditions for institutional success it is necessary to run briefly through these concepts and the related approaches.

Interests and the mutual, conditioned exchange of appreciated goods, services, or capabilities are, as (neo-)liberals have pointed out, a clear base to institutions and need to be used and met for institution-building. Who benefits from institutions and institutional change, and who will lose (power, money, influence, information, recognition . . .) is an important question that needs to be addressed by social analysts. This question is especially salient in the domain of environmental institutions (regardless of scale) – and might have 'demystifying' qualities, given the fact that many proponents of environmental regulations either tend to focus mainly on their effectiveness (in social or ecosystems terms) or are sometimes inclined to highlight the beneficial effects for 'humankind' in general – leaving aside the adverse effects on specific social groups or systems' performances. According to this approach, successful institutions are those that meet existing interests of the actors involved, or at least help to create compromises among different interests.

Neo-realists also stress the importance of power, particularly the power of nation states in the process of institution-building. Institutions depend on the power to enforce a behaviour conforming to rules and to impose sanctions against behaviour deviating from them. Power is a basic category of social life and different actors dispose of very different forms and degrees of power. Not only political, military, or economic power, but also cultural and social capital, formal competences, informal relations, or relevant information are rather unevenly distributed. Successful institutions are those established or maintained by the most powerful actors.

But power – especially if institutionalised over time – is always in need of legitimacy. The more credible the 'myths of justification' appear to those that have less power, the more probable a specific power arrangement (or regime) will stay in place. Thus, power is in itself constitutively intermingled with other aspects of social reality. Changes in the systems of knowledge and meaning clearly affect the 'legitimacy beliefs' (Max Weber) of existing power structures. For example, it was the massive and eventually rather rapid breakdown of the belief that socialist parties, their programmes, and their leadership, are a good, historically legitimate, and personally advantageous political system that led to the end of the socialist regimes in Central and Eastern Europe at the end of the twentieth century.

This brings *culture* into play. In a wider, sociological understanding, institutions do not only regulate behaviour, but also structure the perception of reality, define the normative standards of action, and create specific social identities.[5] Institutions are based on systems of knowledge, beliefs, narratives, rituals, and symbolic events that enforce the central 'core ideas' (*Leitidee*, *idée directrice*) of institutions. Such 'core ideas' motivate action, create commitments, and provide legitimacy – but only insofar as they are rooted in everyday culture and life. From this viewpoint, conflicts are not only seen as rooted in diverging interests (as neo-liberals would put it), but also in conflicting, sometimes mutually exclusive, values, world views, and convictions that make up the social identity of groups. From this point of view, successful institution-building requires the creation of a common cultural framework, including shared values, symbols, and rituals.

How this can be brought about is discussed in more detail by *discourse-theoretical approaches* to institution-building. Most of these approaches draw upon either the work of Foucault or symbolic interactionism. A prominent example is Maarten Hajer's study on the acid rain controversy in Great Britain and the Netherlands. His 'argumentative approach' conceives politics as a struggle for discursive hegemony in which actors try to gain and secure support for their definition of reality. He introduces two middle-range concepts into discourse analysis: the concept of 'storylines' and 'discourse coalitions'.

> A storyline . . . is a generative sort of narrative that allows actors to draw upon various discursive categories to give meaning to specific physical or social phenomena. Key function of storylines is that they suggest unity in the 'bewildering variety' of separate discursive component parts of a problem like acid rain.[6]

Storylines essentially work as 'discursive cement that create communicative networks between actors with different or at best overlapping perceptions and understandings'.[7] Thus, they provide the basis for 'discourse coalitions' which are seen 'as the ensemble of (1) a set of storylines; (2) the actors that utter these stories; and (3) the practices in which this activity is based'.[8] Such discourse coalitions are formed when actors cooperate to promote a common political project on the basis of a specific narrative on the problem in question.

Altogether, institutions imply culture, interest, and power simultaneously. It makes little sense to look at them from only one of these viewpoints. In particular, discourse-theoretical approaches have made great progress in including

---

[5] See March, J. G. and Olson J. P., *Rediscovering institutions: the organisational basis of politics*, New York (Free Press) 1989; Powell, W. and DiMaggio, P. J. (eds.), *The new institutionalism in organisational analysis*, Chicago (Chicago University Press) 1991; Rehberg, K. S., Institutionen als symbolische Ordnung, in Göhler, G. (ed.), *Die Eigenart der Institutionen: Zum Profil politischer Institutionentheorie*, Baden-Baden (Nomos) 1994, pp. 47–84; Risse, T., 'Let's argue!' Communicative action in international relations, *International Organization* 54(1) (2000), pp. 1–39.

[6] Hajer, M., *The politics of environmental discourse: ecological modernization and the policy process*, Oxford (Clarendon Press) 1995, p. 50.

[7] Ibid., p. 57.   [8] Ibid., p. 58.

most of the aspects discussed so far and will serve as a reference point for further argumentation.

Thus, we can identify at least three preconditions for a successful social 'anchoring' of new institutional arrangements of global environmental governance:

(1) *Normative validity and cultural fit ('culture')*. New institutions must be able to gain normative acceptance and to give orientation in daily and organisational routines. For this reason, they need a legitimising basic narrative or storyline which convincingly suggests that the new institutional arrangements are a 'reasonable', 'appropriate', and 'fair' answer to the socially perceived problems.

(2) *Social resonance ('interests')*. New institutions must find a reasonable degree of resonance with the interests of the actors involved; usually, this is connected with the emergence of a new class or coalition of collective actors as the 'natural' proponents of institutional changes. New institutions also have to provide a mechanism to balance oppositional interests and to ensure a fair distribution of costs and benefits among the members of society (or the international community).

(3) *Compliance resources ('power')*. In order to be successful, new institutions need sufficient authoritative and allocative resources to gain compliance and to sanction non-compliance. This requires political authority and a broad, powerful coalition of societal actors.

Whereas the latter aspect will be dealt with more in detail by many other contributions to this book, our focus will primarily be on the first two aspects of institution-building. The question we are addressing in the next three sections is, how far societal macrotrends, the international state of environmental awareness, and the emergence of new societal key actors in the arena of global environmental governance provide a real possibility of meeting these preconditions and of 'embedding' new institutional arrangements of global environmental governance in society.

III. Social macro-trends and global environmental governance

The scientific debate on the main driving forces of global environmental change includes issues such as population growth, increasing population density, industrialisation of the agricultural sector, or the global proliferation of the Western model of prosperity with its high resource and energy intensity. While these macrotrends increase the sense of urgency, others influence the societal acceptance of responses to these problems. Four such processes deserve mention: (1) detraditionalisation, individualisation, and cultural pluralisation, (2) fundamentalist backlashes, (3) globalisation, (4) emergence of a 'knowledge society'.

1. Detraditionalisation, individualisation, and cultural pluralisation

Progressive processes of detraditionalisation, rationalisation, and cultural pluralisation are main features of modern and partially modernised societies. Traditional ways of life have lost their power to create social cohesion in most (not only in the highly industrialised) countries.[9] New differentiations of lifestyles gain importance, which has many causes: the spread of mass consumerism, development of the welfare state, removal of educational barriers, urbanisation, progressive commercialisation, spread of mass media, mass migration, increasing mobility and tourism, etc.

The erosion of traditional forms of societal cohesion does not remove social disparities, however; they only change their structural basis. New criteria of social inclusion and exclusion such as lifestyles and value systems gain importance. Biographies become more individualised. Education and profession, the form and type of personal relationships, belief, habitation, and consumption patterns are increasingly a matter of choice and have to be chosen.[10]

This also produces new subcultural differentiations across nations. Various studies have shown that, for instance, bankers, teachers, technicians, nursing staff in hospitals, or homeless people from different countries and cultures have more in common – in terms of the perception of technologies and risks – than members of different social groups in the same country.[11] On the one hand, this benefits transnational networks of specific subgroups of the civil society or transnationally coordinated environmental campaigns. On the other hand, it can complicate the embedding of these activities within national societies.

2. Fundamentalist backlashes

However, the Western model of social and cultural modernisation has not remained undisputed. Whereas its correlation with economic growth and prosperity has made it a global blueprint for societal progress between the 1950s and 1970s – to rival that of the socialistic model of modernisation – it has in the meantime lost much of its attractiveness for Third World countries. Apart from the South-East Asian 'tiger states' urbanisation, technical modernisation, and integration into the world market did not generate prosperity but growing mass poverty, social polarisation, mountains of debt, and new forms of dependence. This produced a backlash: the more dominant the Western model became, the stronger fundamentalist counter-movements that tried to reframe

---

[9] Cf. Giddens, A., *The consequences of modernity*, Cambridge (Polity Press) 1990.

[10] Cf. Beck, U., *Risk society: towards a new modernity*, London (Sage) 1992; Giddens, A., Living in a post-traditional society, in Beck, U., Giddens, A. and Lash, S., *Reflexive modernisation*, Cambridge (Polity Press) 1994.

[11] Renn, O. and Rohrmann, B., *Cross-cultural risk perception*, Dordrecht and Boston (Kluwer) 2000.

social identities through the revitalisation of ethnic or religious traditions grew.

Islamic fundamentalism is the most salient case. Its highly visible impact on the globalisation process and discourse might not only be due to the fact that Muslim societies around the globe are, or at least perceive themselves, as 'losers' of Western-oriented globalisation – here resource-poor and/or land-locked Sub-Saharan African countries would have much more reason to complain – but also and even more so due to the fact that in the self-perception of fundamentalist leaders, the tradition of Islam (which sometimes is more a mixture of true tradition and very recent political ideas) is culturally and politically seen as superior to Western ideas, either in reference to Christianity or mundane, secular, and often perceived as morally 'corrupt' ways of life.

The institutionalisation of global environmental governance has to do justice to these culturally polarised conditions. Issues of cultural identity play an important role in the development of environmental regimes, the assignment of responsibilities, the regulation of competences, the distribution of costs and benefits, and the social acceptability of political measures.

3. Globalisation

Many of the afore-mentioned trends have been accelerated by globalisation.[12] During the past ten years its economic aspects have received the greatest public attention, yet one must not neglect other aspects. The radical innovations of information and communication technologies, the liberalisation of the world market, and the growing possibilities to exploit comparative cost advantages regardless of space, have sped up the economic integration and reconstructed multinational corporations and their suppliers on a global scale. This in turn reduced the scope of national governments to regulate economic and social conditions of life. These developments not only contributed to the decline of the post-war model of the welfare state. Additionally, there is also the tendency of a new social and socio-spatial polarisation which results in new hierarchies between the winners and losers of globalisation.[13]

From socio-cultural perspectives, globalisation is discussed from two opposite points of view. For some, globalisation brings the world of mass culture and homogenised capitalism to its perfection ('McDonaldization').[14] For

---

[12] Cf. Albrow, M., *The global age: state and society beyond modernity*, Cambridge (Polity Press) 1996; Beck, U., *Was ist Globalisierung?* Frankfurt (Suhrkamp) 1997; Featherstone, M., Lash, S., and Robertson, R. (eds.), *Global modernities*, London (Sage) 1995; Robertson, R., *Globalisation: social theory and global culture*, London (Sage) 1992.

[13] Cf. Sassen, S., *The global city*, Princeton (Princeton University Press) new edn. 2001; Stieglitz, J., *Globalisation and its discontents*, New York (Norton & Company) 2002.

[14] Cf. Ritzer, G., *The McDonaldization of society*, Thousand Oaks, Calif. (Pine Forge Press) 1993.

others, globalisation may lead to a resurgence of the local and it might bring regional idiosyncrasies to the fore.[15]

In any case, new media and information technologies have speeded up a process of networking and socio-cultural globalisation which reduced not only the relevance of frontiers between national societies, but also, and more fundamentally, the relevance of time and space for production, consumption, and communication. This opens up new opportunities for a worldwide networking of individuals, organisations, and social movements.[16] Thus, the past five years saw a rapid rise of strong, transnational protest movements against neo-liberal globalisation and its negative social effects.[17] As societies are increasingly experiencing economic, political, and cultural conflicts which have their origins in contexts that are no longer governed by national regulations, debates on such questions also contribute to the emergence of a – at least rudimentary – world public.

4. Emergence of a 'knowledge society'

Most scholars and politicians agree that knowledge has become the most crucial production factor in modern societies.[18] This has two paradoxical effects.

First: the existing knowledge gets revised and devalued in ever faster cycles, precisely because the global production of knowledge expands. Societies lose their capabilities to actively shape their future unless they permanently renew and adapt their knowledge base. Knowledge becomes 'reflexive', which assigns a central political significance to investments in research and education.

Secondly: together with knowledge grows non-knowledge. Scientific knowledge increasingly influences societal action, which lends special importance to scientific consultancy. However, due to the fact that knowledge and non-knowledge go hand in hand, far-reaching decisions have to be made more frequently under conditions of uncertainty. This opens the door for a politicisation of scientific debates. At the same time, it restores value to non-scientific local knowledge. Conflicts about the definition of risks become focal points of

---

[15] Cf. Robertson, R., Globalisation: time-space and homogeneity-heterogeneity, in Featherstone *et al.*, op. cit. pp. 25–44.

[16] Cf. Castells, M., *The rise of network society*, Oxford (Blackwell Publishers) 1997.

[17] Andretta, M., della Porta, D., Mosca, L., and Reiter, H., No global – new global: Identität und Strategien der Antiglobalisierungsbewegung, Frankfurt/New York (Campus) 2003; Della Porta, D., Kriesi, H., and Rucht, D. (eds.), *Social movements in a globalizing world*, London (MacMillan Press) 1999; O'Brian, R., Goetz, A., Scholte, J., and Williams, M. (eds.), *Contesting global governance: multilateral economic institutions and global social movements*, New York (Cambridge University Press) 2000; Walk, H. and Böhme, N. (eds.), *Globaler Widerstand: Internationale Netzwerke auf der Suche nach Alternativen im globalen Kapitalismus*, Münster (Westfälisches Dampfboot) 2001.

[18] Cf. Stehr, N., *Knowledge society*, London (Sage) 1994.

the public discourse ('risk society') and push the transformation of industrial to reflexive modernity.[19]

The necessity to make decisions under conditions of uncertainty not only changes the relation between science and politics in the context of global environmental governance. Also, the societal acceptability of global environmental regulations (and their national consequences) is shaped to a considerable degree by the perception of risks and the way problems are 'framed' in different societies.

5. *Summary*

New forms of global environmental governance have to gain societal acceptance under conditions of intensified cultural conflicts and an accelerated erosion of traditional ways of life. The possibility of linking them to traditional sources of legitimacy (belief systems, authorities, common norms) is therefore limited. This increases the importance of public framing of environmental problems and communicative linkages with social problems, questions of power, or cultural conflicts. The likeliness of successfully embedding environmental policies and regulations in the social fabric grows in proportion to their capability to provide answers to concrete practical problems and to incorporate the experiences of those affected. The more abstract and distant problems are, the more their perception depends on the way they are framed by mass media. Regulations that do not seem urgent, in comparison with all the other practical problems of everyday life, or that appear unfair are hardly likely to gain societal acceptance.

However, the global electronic network makes it also possible to mobilise counter-information and challenge hegemonic discourses. In addition, the global emergence of societal subgroups with common cultural orientations facilitates the formation of transnational environmental discourse coalitions and alliances of social actors.

IV. Environmental awareness

Another decisive factor in the social acceptance of global environmental governance is the changing awareness of environmental problems. Since the 1970s, public concern in Western industrial societies on ecological problems and technological risks has grown considerably. Throughout the 1970s and the early 1980s, ecological conflicts were marked by a high degree of polarisation and a clash of two contradictory cultural patterns – 'catastrophists'

---

[19] Beck (1992), op. cit. Beck, U., Giddens, A., and Lash, S., *Reflexive modernization: politics, traditions, and aesthetics in the modern social order*, Cambridge (Polity Press) 1994.

vs. 'cornucopians'.[20] Today, nobody seriously doubts the urgency of ecological problems. We have experienced a process of 'normalisation' of ecological concerns which have been adopted (and transformed) by different kinds of actors, social subsystems, and narratives. Although there still exist very different and even contradictory attitudes towards nature and technological risks, concerns for the environment have become more or less institutionalised in politics, in organisational and everyday life.

A crucial role for the distribution of environmental awareness and institutional practices is played by the public discourse about environmental problems in the mass media.

1. Environmental concerns

In contrast to a widely held opinion, environmental concern is no longer a matter concerning merely wealthy, highly industrialised countries. Comparative surveys show that environmental concern has spread all over the world. This observation contradicts a thesis of Inglehart that has gained followers primarily among political scientists, that the rise of environmental awareness and related movements is a reaction to the emergence of 'post-materialistic' values, which is explained as an effect of growing prosperity.[21] However, the claim that environmental concerns are a 'phenomenon of luxury' cannot be upheld in light of the vitality of ecological grass-root organisations in many poor countries. The results of international comparative studies about environmental awareness show that the Inglehartian assertion describes – at best – the situation in Western countries during the 1970s and 1980s.

Data on the development of environmental consciousness is collected in many countries worldwide. Due to different survey techniques and wordings of questions applied to different social and cultural contexts, these country-specific data are difficult to compare. Comparative data on the perception of environmental problems in the member countries of the European Union is produced by the regular surveys of the European Commission (Eurobarometer). There are only a few systematically surveyed, globally comparable data sets, however.[22] What are the findings?

A more conventional approach argues that environmental concern is positively correlated with income: the higher per capita GDP, the higher

---

[20] Cotgrove, S., *Catastrophe or cornucopia: the environment, politics and the future*, New York (John Wiley & Sons) 1982.

[21] Inglehart, R., *The silent revolution: changing values and political styles among Western publics*, Princeton (Princeton University Press) 1977; Inglehart, R., *Culture shift in advanced industrial society*, Princeton (Princeton University Press) 1990.

[22] e.g. Environment survey 1993 and 2000 of the International Social Survey Programme (ISSP). Dunlap, R. E., Gallup, G. H., and Gallup, A. M., Of global concern: results of the health of the planet survey, *Environment* 35 (1993), pp. 7–15, 33–39.

environmental concern, which might then be regarded as a luxury good.[23] Other studies find that environmental concerns might take very different forms and affect peoples' livelihoods more directly in poorer countries and are mostly framed in a livelihood context, not in an environmentalist one.[24] The latter argument is strongly supported by the 'Health of the Planet' survey[25] which included a selection of twenty-four very different, poor and rich countries.

His central findings can be summarised as follows:

- In general, throughout all twenty-four countries, environmental questions are regarded as a more or less serious problem. People in poorer countries almost consistently rank environmental problems higher in comparison to other urgent problems than people in richer countries. (Only Germans appraise these problems similar to the inhabitants of countries like South Korea, Poland, and Mexico.)
- The 'personal concern' through environmental problems is on average lower in rich, industrialised countries than in poorer countries. The Philippines, Brazil, and Mexico rank highest in this regard.
- A general pattern is that remote environmental problems are perceived as more serious than those close by (with Russia as an exception.) However, there are again significant differences between poor and rich countries. The level of poverty correlates with the perceived severity of local and national environmental problems. This also applies vice versa, in that people in rich countries consider the quality of their local environment relatively intact whereas they consider the state of the global environment as bad.
- Environmental problems are perceived much more as a threat to individual health and quality of life nowadays than ten years ago; this trend is expected to intensify.
- Asked whether economic growth or environmental protection should be given priority in case of conflict, surprisingly a majority in all countries (except Nigeria) gave priority to environmental protection. There are also only slight differences between industrialised and developing nations in the willingness to pay higher prices to protect the environment. The willingness to support environmental measures (even if they increase the costs of living) is even higher in poorer than in rich countries.
- 'Residents of the developing nations are more likely than their counterparts in the industrialized nations to think that citizens can play an effective role in solving environmental problems (with the three East European countries

---

[23] Franzen, A., Environmental attitudes in international comparison: an analysis of the ISSP surveys 1993 and 2000, *Social Science Quarterly* 84(2) (2003), pp. 297–308.
[24] Brechin, S. R., Objective problems, subjective values and global environmentalism: evaluating the postmaterialism argument and challenging a new explanation, *Social Science Quarterly* 80 (1999), pp. 793–806.
[25] Dunlap *et al.*, op. cit.

being strict exceptions).'[26] Interviewees from industrialised countries, however, assign this responsibility rather to government and business.

Many of these findings refer to the very different health impacts of environmental problems in rich and poor nations. Western countries managed to remedy the most urgent pollution problems of water and air through technical measures in the 1970s and 1980s, whereas in many developing countries social, sanitary, and environmental problems still cumulate – particularly in the growing slums of mega-cities – and affect the immediate lifeworld. The economic resources, technical infrastructure, and administrative capacities to alleviate these problems in an efficient manner are lacking. At the same time, the aforementioned results demonstrate that an awareness of environmental problems and the necessity to tackle them exists in all countries. The same holds to a particularly high degree for global environmental problems. Thus, global environmental governance can count on broad support, at least in general terms. Among large sections of the population in rich and poor countries, there also seems to exist the willingness to bear the costs of the necessary measures and to contribute directly to the solution of environmental problems.

2. *The patchwork of environmental behaviour*

This means neither that this willingness exists in all societal groups to the same extent, nor that it can easily be transferred into institutional practices and concrete patterns of behaviour. Social environmental studies emphasise a specific correlation between environmental awareness and social group parameters, such as age, gender, education, social class, ethnicity, etc. on the one hand.[27] On the other hand, they show that the link between environmental awareness and environmentally friendly behaviour is rather weak. Environmental behaviour always exhibits the characteristic of a heterogeneous patchwork, even among people with a high environmental awareness.[28] There is a pronounced environmental sensitivity in one field of behaviour combined with an astonishing indifference in others. Accordingly, environmental considerations mostly play a very diverse role in the decision of what groceries, clothes, or durable goods to buy, how to use water and energy, what means of transport to choose, or where to spend the vacation. This may be explained by cost-benefit theories,

---

[26] Ibid., p. 36.
[27] e.g. Brand, K.-W., Environmental consciousness and behaviour: the greening of lifestyles, in Redclift, M. and Woodgate, G. (eds.), *The international handbook of environmental sociology*, Cheltenham/Northhampton, Mass. (Edward Elgar) 1997, pp. 204–217; Haan, G. de and Kuckartz, U., *Umweltbewusstsein: Denken und Handeln in Umweltkrisen*, Opladen (Westdeutscher Verlag) 1996; Gardner, G. T. and Stern, P. C., *Environmental problems and human behavior*, Boston (Allyn and Bacon) 1996.
[28] Reusswig, F., *Lebensstile und Ökologie: Sozial-ökologische Arbeitspapiere 43*, Frankfurt (Institut für sozial-ökologische Forschung) 1994.

psychological mechanisms of denial, cultural habits, or the necessity to find a personal balance between a lot of competing demands. Yet, the eclectic forms of environmental behaviour display typical social patterns, which can be reconstructed as environmental mentalities[29] or – in terms of behaviour – as specific styles of consumption, mobility, or nutrition. However, these patterns vary greatly among different countries and cultures, which is why the international comparison of such qualitative typologies is as yet relatively undeveloped.

The overall findings (which are primarily derived from studies in Western societies but probably transferable to other cultural settings) are not very surprising if one considers the extreme difficulty in making actual choices in compliance with strict ecological criteria in a society geared to the Western way of life, economic growth, material affluence, and technological progress. Institutional efforts to establish new and more environmentally friendly practices encounter a host of structural barriers, the predominance of economical short-term logics, vested interests, established powers, and sector-specialised ways of dealing with problems. Individual choices, too, are complicated by incomplete and overly complex information, adverse price incentives, bad supply, practical inconveniences, and contradictory behavioural norms which render the ideal of environmental behaviour a very intricate venture.[30]

These observations have led social scientists to conclude that the search for *the one*, ecologically sound lifestyle is futile. Rather, they argue, one should try to harness the ecological potentials of all the different societal lifestyles in the various areas of everyday life (food consumption, mobility, energy use etc.) Another important lesson from many studies on the trajectory of ecological initiatives is that a widespread and lasting change to everyday routines towards sustainability is only realistic if different strategies and policy instruments join forces in a coordinated manner in order to support the new practices from different angles.[31]

A more radical, macrostructural approach to understand the inconsistencies of environmental behaviour is Wolfgang Sachs' critique of the hegemonic Western model of 'development'.[32] Focusing on a Southern 'community perspective' from below he argues that the 'environmental crisis' and the 'crisis of equity' are tightly connected with each other on the international level. The major rift in his view is not between North and South but between the global

---

[29] e.g. Poferl, A., Schilling, K., and Brand, K.-W., *Umweltbewusstsein und Alltagshandeln*, Oplanden (Leske + Budrich) 1997.

[30] Lange, H. (ed.), *Ökologisches Handeln als sozialer Konflikt: Umwelt im Alltag*, Oplanden (Leske + Budrich) 2000; Poferl *et al.*, op. cit.

[31] Cf. Kaufmann-Hajos, R. and Gutscher, H., *Changing things – moving people*, Basel (Birkhäuser Verlag) 2001.

[32] Sachs, W., *Planet dialectics: explorations in environment and development*, London (Zed) 1999; Sachs, W., Development: the rise and decline of an ideal, in Munn, T. (ed.), *Encyclopedia of global environmental change*, vol. IV, London (John Wiley) 2001.

consumer class on the one side and the localised poor on the other. Only a reduction of the ecological footprint of the consumer classes around the world and more democracy and livelihood (community) rights for the poor can provide a sustainable solution for both the environmental and the equity crisis.

3. The social construction of environmental risks

Not only the inconsistent implementation of ecological demands in everyday routines is problematic, however, the interpretations of these demands are in themselves contradictory. Both the urgency of given problems and the 'appropriate' solution strategies are contested. There are numerous and often highly polarised conflicts on these questions which involve various conflict dimensions at the same time: struggles between different economic and political interests, North and South, causers and affected groups, conflicts over a fair burden-sharing, and disputes over national and cultural identities.

The constellation and dynamics of interest conflicts in national and international negotiation systems have been a traditional focus of political sciences. In contrast, sociological studies have examined more the group-specific perception of environmental problems, questions of risk communication, and competing cultural orientations in conflicts on environment and technology. One of the results is that these cultural orientations do not vary arbitrarily but exhibit typical features which are linked systematically to particular patterns of social life and different institutional practices.[33]

A well known example of this kind of approaches is *cultural theory*.[34] It has differentiated four basic views or 'myths' of nature (better: forms and degrees of resilience of anthropogenically-influenced natural systems) and traced them back to four different social archetypes. We subscribe to neither the theoretical background of cultural theory nor to its conception of social institutions. Nevertheless, this approach has rather successfully challenged the hegemony of natural science and engineering-dominated risk discourses and brought to the fore the social and cultural base of risk awareness and risk management.

Ulrich Beck[35] has treated risks in a much more subtle way. He emphasises a core aspect of the debate on global environmental problems: their social construction in a controversial public discourse that includes science, social

---

[33] Cf. Jaeger, C., Dürrenberger, G. Kastenholz, H., and Truffer, B., Determinants of environmental action with regard to climatic change, *Climate Change*, 23 (1993), pp. 193–211; Macnaghten, Ph. and Urry, J., *Contested natures*, London (Sage) 1988. Thompson, M. and Rayner, S., Cultural discourses, in Rayner, S. and Malone E. (eds.), *Human choice and climate change*, vol. I, Columbus, Ohio (Batelle Press) 1998.

[34] Douglas, M. and Wildavsky, A., *Risk and culture: an essay on the selection of technical and environmental dangers*, Berkeley, Calif. (University of California Press) 1982; Thompson, E. and Wildavsky, A., *Cultural theory*, Boulder (Westview Press) 1990.

[35] Beck (1992), op. cit.

movements, politics, and the mass media. These disputes are the venue for different societal actors to enforce their specific definition of problems. Such struggles can become explosive if oppositional groups (e.g. critical scientists, environmentalists, etc.) succeed in reframing problems in a way that challenges the dominant institutional practices. Oppositional movements constitute themselves and develop in this environment of cultural conflicts. Myths, symbols, slogans, and rhetorical questions play a central role in these disputes.[36] Mass media serves as the central filter and sounding board of these public debates on risk.[37] The frames which become hegemonic in these discursive struggles then provide the legitimating basis for the establishment of a particular set of rules which promise to deal with the problems in question in an adequate way.

Drawing on these theoretical insights we can see that the general framing of environmental problems has significantly changed during recent decades. Basically we can distinguish a succession of three 'master frames',[38] the first of which dates back to the late nineteenth century ('nature conservation'), the second to the 1960s ('environmental protection'), and the third to the 1990s ('sustainable development'). Whereas *conservationism* aims at the preservation of attractive parts of nature and 'wilderness', modern *environmentalism* is preoccupied with the harmful effects of industrialisation on natural human environments, with pollution and technical risks, the exhaustion of resources, and the limited 'carrying capacity' of the earth. S*ustainable development*, again, relates the ecological discourse systematically with social and economic aspects of development.

This new master frame has made an astonishing career in the last ten years. It has not only restructured the perception of problems and spawned a host of programmes at the international, national, and local level; it has also triggered an abundance of bottom-up activities in all parts of the world. It facilitates the integration of different issues and actors. It stresses the importance of cooperation, win-win potentials, and broadened participation. Processes under the banner of sustainability are not about radical criticism of the capitalist system or spectacular protest actions. Rather, sustainable development strives to develop institutional solutions in a cooperative setting.

This integrated perspective guides most local initiatives and issue-specific cooperations in sustainability networks. However, the emphasis on cooperation and participation cannot conceal that most politics in the area of global

---

[36] Gamson, W. A., *Talking politics*, Boston, Mass. (MIT Press) 1992.
[37] Cf. Eder, K., The institutionalisation of environmentalism: ecological discourse and the second transformation of the public sphere, in Lash, S., Szerszynski, B., and Wynne, B. (eds.), *Risk, environment and modernity*, London (Sage) 1996, pp. 203–223; Hannigan, J. A., *Environmental sociology*, London and New York (Routledge) 1995.
[38] Snow, D. A. and Bedford, R. D., Master frames and cycles of protest, in Morris, A. D. and Mueller, C. M. (eds.), *Frontiers in social movements theory*, New Haven, Conn. (Yale University Press) 1992, pp. 133–155.

environmental change is characterised by highly controversial positions. The master frame of sustainable development has merely created a new discursive arena where the struggles about 'appropriate' institutional forms of regulation take place. No one would deny that this has increased the opportunities for societal groups to participate in the various settings of global governance. The question is whether these new forms of civil participation (a) provide a real chance of influencing the core of power plays and (b) manage to achieve a sufficiently broad legitimacy of transnational regulations in civil society.

V. Emerging key actors in the arena of international environmental politics

From a sociological point of view, the process of institution-building is closely connected to the type of actors involved and the forms of their social interaction. Are there new actors in the emerging field of global environmental governance (GEC)? We will focus on three of them: transnational civil society, science, and the individual as consumer. None of these actors is new with regard to environmental policy on a national level. The challenging point is that they are entering the scene of *global* governance whilst still in initial forms, sometimes rather weak, hard to conceive and predict with regard to the future evolution of the world system.

In highlighting these cases we do not state that other actors such as national states, transnational organisations, business, or media are not important in order to manage GEC in a sustainable manner. Quite the opposite: state actors and intergovernmental organisations will remain important – and even have to increase their responsibility and role. But in order to come to successful institution-building, it will be necessary to include the interests, views, and contribution of transnational civil society, science, and individuals as consumers in some form.

1. *Transnational civil society*

Non-state actors enter the stage of global environmental issues in various forms and shapes. They are often termed as 'non-governmental organisations' (NGOs), but this collective term is misleading given the differences among them. Profit-oriented actors from the business sector are of undoubted importance (e.g. with regard to environmental standards).[39] Often accused as being

---

[39] Cf. Clap, J., ISO environmental standards: industry's gift to a polluted globe or the developed world's competition-killing strategy?, in Stokke, O. S. and Thommessen, Ø. B. (eds.), *Yearbook of international co-operation on environment and development 2001/2002*, an independent publication from the Fridtjof Nansen Institute, Norway, London and Sterling (Earthscan) 2001, pp. 27–33.

a main part of the problem, many globally acting business corporations have in recent years been trying to become part of the solution. The 'greening of industry' on a global scale may sometimes be a public relations myth; in many others it is a powerful driver of institutional change, especially in cases where the business sector teams up with its ancient adversaries, environmental NGOs in 'green alliances' or public-private partnerships (e.g. in the Marine Stewardship Council, MSC, initially founded by Unilever and WWF). It seems that the influence of scientific arguments and the 'moral entrepreneurs' of the NGO world has had an influence on business actors.[40] Sometimes even governmental bodies are part of such – then trisectoral – networks, e.g. the World Commission on Dams.[41]

Our focus here is on the emerging transnational civil society (TCS) as constituted by self-organised advocacy groups that undertake voluntary collective action across state borders in pursuit of what they deem the wider public interest. This includes transnational NGOs, transnational networks, coalitions, and advocacy campaigns and is often rooted in social movements in at least one country.[42] The *Yearbook of International Organisations*[43] counts 38,000 international NGOs and almost 6,000 intergovernmental organisations and networks by the year 2004. There was a growth from 150,000 to more than 250,000 members in non-governmental organisations worldwide between 1990 and 2000, with the strongest growth in middle and low income countries.[44]

TCS actors are involved in different kinds of activities: (1) agenda-setting and knowledge construction – identifying a problem of international concern and producing information, explanation, and framing; (2) developing solutions – creating norms or recommending policy change; (3) building networks and coalitions of allies; and (4) implementing solutions – employing tactics of persuasion and pressure to change practices and/or encourage compliance with norms. TCS actors usually have the goal of influencing other relevant

---

[40] See Asher Alkoby, Chapter 5.
[41] Dingwerth, K., Globale Politiknetzwerke und ihre demokratische Legitimation: Eine Analyse der Weltstaudammkommission, *Zeitschrift für Internationale Beziehungen* 10(1) (2002), pp. 69–109.
[42] Arts, B., Noortmann, M., and Reinalda, B. (eds.), *Non-state actors in international relations*, Aldershot (Ashgate) 2001; Florini, A. M. (ed.), *The third force: the rise of transnational civil society*, Washington DC (Carnegie Endowment for International Peace Press) 2000; Higgott, R., Underhill, G., and Bieler, A., *Non-state actors and authority in the global system*, New York (Routledge) 2000; Keck, M. and Sikkink, K., *Activists beyond borders: advocacy networks in international politics*, Ithaca, NY (Cornell University Press) 1998; Khagram, S., Riker, J. V. and Sikkink, K. (eds.), *Restructuring world politics: transnational social moments*, Minneapolis (University of Minnesota Press) 2002.
[43] See www.uia.org
[44] Anheier, H., Glasius, M., and Kaldor, M., (eds.), *Global civil society*, Oxford (Oxford University Press) 2001, p. 6.

actors – their interests and their identities – and the environments, in which they operate, that is, the structure of power, meaning, and action itself.

Crucial points with regard to TCS actors relate (1) to their effectiveness and (2) to their legitimacy. Optimistic views of their *effectiveness* see a global public policy on the horizon and emphasise vertical and horizontal subsidiarities.[45] Others remain more sceptical with regard to remaining power deficits, especially with regard to 'hard issues', such as climate and energy policies, where only symbolic participation – if at all – seems possible.[46] The study of impacts or effects of social movements on policy outcomes presupposes an understanding of the social and political mobilisation processes. Here the identification of collective action frames[47] and the construction of legitimate meanings through social actors[48] is crucial. NGOs play a key role in the process of agenda-setting and public awareness. They exert influence neither by 'money' nor by 'power', but by using moral authority, expertise, public credibility, or other forms of discourse and persuasion.

Bas Arts[49] has assessed the political influence of global environmental NGOs in the case of the UN Framework Convention on Climate Change (UNFCCC) and the Convention on Biological Diversity (CBD) in an empirical manner. He found that in both cases NGOs did have substantial (e.g. submission by the Alliance of Small Island States (AOSIS) of the draft Protocol on climate gas reduction, financial mechanism of CBD) or at least some influence (e.g. emissions targets, marine biodiversity). Only in some cases or aspects of the two regimes was no influence detected (e.g. implementation of UNFCCC, genetic resources in CBD). If 'power' is defined in a wider sense, allowing for a broader set of resources than only political or state power, TCS actors may even be regarded as powerful actors. Arts[50] distinguishes decisional power, discursive power, and regulatory power. The former concept refers to the capacity to influence decision-making processes in a given set of institutions, the second to the capacity to (re)frame the discourse that goes along with decision-making processes, and the latter to the capacity to (re)make the rules of institutional

---

[45] Reinicke, W. H., *Global public policy*, Washington, DC (Brookings Institution Press) 1998.
[46] Haufler, V., Crossing the boundary between public and private: international regimes and non-state actors, in Rittberger, V. (ed.), *Regime theory and international relations*, Oxford (Clarendon Press) 1993, pp. 94–111; Rucht, D., Global governance: eine Antwort auf Steuerungsprobleme internationalen Regierens?, in Allmendinger, J. (ed.), *Entstaatlichung und Soziale Sicherheit, Verhandlungen des 31. Kongresses der Deutschen Gesellschaft für Soziologie in Leipzig 2002*, vol. II, Opladen (Leske + Budrich) 2002, pp. 1010–1023.
[47] Snow and Bedford, op. cit. [48] Morris and Mueller, op. cit.
[49] Arts, B., *The political influence of global NGOs: case studies on the climate and biodiversity conventions*, Utrecht (International Books) 1998; Arts, B., The political influence of NGOs on international issues, in Cerny, C., Goverde, H., Haugaard, M., and Lentner, H. (eds.), *Power in contemporary politics*, London (Sage) 2000, pp. 132–148.
[50] Arts, B., *Non-state actors in global governance: three faces of power*, Preprint No. 4, Bonn (Max-Planck-Projektgruppe Recht der Gemeinschaftsgüter) 2003.

settings. Non-state actors in general and TCS actors in particular have achieved power in this broader sense in recent years. They might even speak the 'language' of money, as in the case of consumer boycotts;[51] or, as Alkoby puts it, 'civil society has civilizing effects on rational, economically driven entities as well'.[52]

With regard to *legitimacy* issues, the emergence of TCS actors and their growing involvement in policy-making might arouse serious criticism. Government actors are – at least in democracies – accountable to their *demos*, in most cases represented by national Parliaments and other institutions of checks and balances. NGO representatives may have been elected by some organisational bodies, but mostly there are no clear-cut accountability structures. In addition, the claimed mandate goes far beyond the NGO membership and addresses public interest issues, the planet, and our common future. Neither are NGO leaders held accountable to business boards and/or representatives of well-defined shareholders, as in the case of business. So there seems to be good reason for a sceptical view on NGOs in the global arena; the looming danger of a privatisation of international environmental governance seems real.[53] Even the more or less unintentional support for 'hegemonic', non-democratic, and power-dominated policies by NGO activities has been criticised.[54]

This is a noteworthy criticism. Still, we would like to think in a different direction. Of course many national governments have been elected by their *demos*, whereas NGOs represent their members. However: (1) not all governments have this democratic legitimacy; especially in many developing countries, we still observe a lack of freedom and democracy that, among others, NGOs criticise and try to change. (2) Even democratically legitimised national governments might fail to recognise the urgency of social problems or tend to narrow the understanding of the common good in the eyes of some groups of citizens – that is a classical reason for the emergence of social movements and has fostered the environmental movement in many countries. (3) Based on national governments and not on a global demos, which is still lacking, the UN system – the cornerstone of international policy-making – lacks democratic legitimacy itself. NGOs as key actors of the TCS represent at least a small spectrum of the so far non-existent global demos and might thus well open up their voice in the diplomatic arena. (4) Profit-oriented business actors, even if part of the 'green business' segment that we can observe emerging from the markets, have only very limited democratic legitimacy, if at all. Oriented towards

---

[51] Cf. the Brent Spar affair and Shell in 1995.   [52] See Asher Alkoby, Chapter 5.
[53] Brühl, T., The privatisation of international environmental governance, in Biermann, F., Brohm, R., and Dingwerth, K. (eds.), *Proceedings of the 2001 Berlin Conference on the Human Dimensions of Global Environmental Change: 'Global Environmental Change and the Nation State'*, Potsdam (Potsdam Institute for Climate Impact Research) 2002, pp. 371–380.
[54] Ford, L. H., Challenging global environmental governance: social movement agency and global civil society, *Global Environmental Politics*, 3(2) (2004) pp. 120–134.

shareholder values and shifting opportunities on global (financial) markets it is by no means clear if their engagement in international environmental policy will assist the public good – the opposite baseline assumption is often closer to the true hypothesis, at least for the 'grey' industry cluster. Exerting counter-influence (or even counter-power) seems necessary and appropriate, a view that is shared by far more people than by environmental activists, as surveys on the trustworthiness of different kinds of organisations clearly show. This is by no means a charter for each and every action of an NGO: they definitely should invest more in processes, mechanisms, and standards of accountability, both to external actors/agencies and to their own members.[55] But it provides sufficient arguments against an exclusion of NGOs from legitimate participation in international institutions.

The emergence of a transnational civil society is a global *fait social* and, with regard to the state of the global environment, a rather positive one. One might regard it as a kind of foreshadowing of a new global democracy, based on a true demos and true representation.[56] The important point from our viewpoint is the conceivable role of TCS actors in the current transition of international environmental policy and their contribution to new, more successful, and more socially 'anchored' institutions. The more transnational policy-making affects national domains and the 'lifeworld' of national civil societies, the more the growing demand for democratic support and legitimacy cannot be confined to the political spheres of nation states, but has to encompass transnational and national civil society actors.[57]

2. Science

The diagnosis that we are living in a 'knowledge society' is, in hardly any other domain, as true as in the case of GEC. This holds with respect to two directions: diagnosis and action. Research input constitutes a key component in the development of effective international environmental regimes. Scientific knowledge is called for not only in the design of policies that are effective in terms of solving the problems for which they were designed, but also (increasingly) in the identification of the problem itself. As most GEC problems are perceivable only by means of statistics, long-term observation, satellite images, model runs, and computer experiments, their perception and assessment almost exclusively depends upon scientific expertise – in many cases by interdisciplinary endeavours and newly built-up research fields. We would like to highlight two aspects

---

[55] Ebrahim, A., Accountability in practice: mechanisms for NGOs, *World Development*, 31(5) (2003), pp. 813–829.

[56] Held, D., *Democracy and the global order: from the Modern State to Cosmopolitan Governance*, Stanford (Stanford University Press) 1995.

[57] Zürn, M., *Regieren jerseits des Nationalstaates: Globalisierung und Denationalisierung als Chance*, Frankfurt (Suhrkamp) 1998.

of scientific knowledge that are crucial to GEC and, at the same time, have the potential to transform the relation between science and society: uncertainty and the role of computer models.

Uncertainty is a key feature of GEC research, but, of course, of many other research areas (such as genetic engineering, the epidemiology of new diseases, or the causes of unemployment) as well. At the same time, the stakes are high and the need for decisions appears pressing. Assessment of the world's biodiversity is very difficult; a once extinct species cannot be retrieved, however. In the case of climate change we are facing uncertainties despite substantial progress in recent years, mainly due to sources such as the following:[58]

- weather as a main basis for the object 'climate' has intrinsically stochastic components, displays non-linear behaviour, and is – in the long term – influenced by orbital and solar cycles;
- existing climate models are but approximations to the 'real' object and do not mirror it in its entire complexity;
- parts of our knowledge are vague;
- human action and possible adaptation and mitigation strategies are hard to model;
- scientists and modellers views about future social, economic, and technological change influence the outcomes, at least the interpretation of models.

Far from being preliminary or accidental, uncertainty is a key feature of our knowledge base with regard to the climate system. Waiting for scientific progress eventually eradicating uncertainty could mean postponing necessary mitigating and adaptive action – a procedure ruled out by the UN Framework Convention on Climate Change stating that 'lack of full scientific certainty should not be used as a reason for postponing (. . .) measures'.[59] A main point for successful institution-building is the question of whether societies in general and decision-makers in particular succeed in building a culture of dealing with scientific uncertainties despite the general expectation that science should reduce them.

But how is science, impeded by uncertainties and the shaky outputs of computer models, able to inform and advise modern societies in crucial questions? While science (ideally) is conceived of as a truth-seeking endeavour whose norms and guidelines for behaviour are directed towards the generation of 'objective' and disinterested knowledge, politics is characterised by strategic reasoning and an often instrumental utilisation – as well as manipulation and distortion – of knowledge. This tension is reinforced, moreover, by the

---

[58] Cf. Edwards, P. N., Representing the global atmosphere: computer models, data, and knowledge about climate change, in Miller, C. A. and Edwards, P. N. (eds.), *Changing the atmosphere: expert knowledge and environmental governance*, Cambridge, Mass. and London (MIT Press) 2001, pp. 31–65; Webster, M., Communicating climate change uncertainty to policy-makers and the public, *Climatic Change*, 61 (2003), pp. 1–8.

[59] UNFCCC, Article 3(3).

traditional image of the relationship between science and politics, where science is attributed the (innocent) role of 'speaking truth to power'. We doubt both characterisations: (1) that politics is only about 'power' (or strategic behaviour) and never about 'truth' (or communicative, argumentative behaviour), and (2) that science is only about 'truth' and not about 'power'. Their relation is much more complex in the field of GEC and so is their internal structure.

Some analytical tools have been offered by the sociology of science to keep pace with recent developments, and the blurring of traditional boundaries. Nowotny et al.[60] speak of 'mode 2' research, where science has to develop 'social robustness' facing the new coevolution of science and society, extended expertise throughout society, and validity criteria that go beyond desks and laboratories. Science is an actor on the 'agora' of the (post-) modern knowledge society.[61] The analysis of Funtowicz and Ravetz goes in a similar direction: 'post-normal science' is entering the scene of post-modern risk societies. Such a science is characterised by high decision stakes and high uncertainties alike.[62] This new characterisation of science is embedded in a new relationship between science and society: no longer do scientific experts seem to be able to analyse real world problems and to offer clear-cut options of problem-solving to politics and society. Instead, we are witnessing a coevolution of scientific knowledge and social processes defining problems and framing solution spaces more and more.[63] The transformation of the whole field science–society raises the question of new models of scientific research as well as of 'scientific citizenship'.[64]

This is no simple endeavour. In order to become influential in the political arena – or for stakeholders in general – scientific knowledge has to meet three different, sometimes even conflicting criteria: it has (a) to be *salient* (relevant to current choices of policy- and decision-makers), (b) *credible* (based on research by those with expertise and trustworthiness), and (c) *legitimate* (accounts for concerns, perspectives, and interests of stakeholders).[65]

---

[60] Nowotny, H., Scott, P., and Gibbons, M., *Re-thinking science: knowledge and the public in an age of uncertainty*, Cambridge (Polity) 2001.

[61] Nowotny, H., Democratising expertise and socially robust knowledge, *Science and Public Policy*, 30(3) (2003), pp. 151–156.

[62] Funtowicz, S., and Ravetz, J., Science for the post-normal age, *Futures* 25(7) (1993), pp. 739–755; Funtowicz, S. and Ravetz, J. (eds.), Post-normal science, *Futures* 31(7) (1999) (special issue).

[63] Jasanoff, S. and Wynne, B., Science and decisionmaking, in Rayner and Malone, op. cit. pp. 1–87; Miller, C. A. and Edwards, P. N., Introduction: the globalisation of climate science and climate politics, in Miller and Edwards, op. cit. pp. 1–30.

[64] Elam, M. and Bertilsson, M., Consuming, engaging and confronting science: the emerging dimensions of scientific citizenship, *European J. Social Theory* 6(2) (2003), pp. 233–251; Pellizoni, L., Knowledge, uncertainty and the transformation of the public sphere, *European J. Social Theory* 6(3) (2003), pp. 327–355.

[65] The Social Learning Group, *Learning to manage global environmental risks*, vol. I, *A comparative history of social responses to climate change, ozone depletion, and acid rain*; vol. II, *A functional analysis of social responses to climate change, ozone depletion, and acid rain*, Cambridge, Mass. (MIT Press) 2001.

How is salient, credible, and legitimate knowledge to be construed? Haas[66] has been one of the scholars to underline the importance of science for international environmental decision-making. According to him, 'epistemic communities' are the key for ensuring this: groups of experts who believe in the same cause-and-effect relationships and share common values with regard to the problem they are facing. Still, scientific uncertainties and controversies are typical of GEC problems, most of which have to be dealt with in inter- and transdisciplinary projects and institutes. The scientists engaged in GEC research often do not meet the preconditions of forming an 'epistemic community'.

An interesting and paradigmatic example here is the Intergovernmental Panel on Climate Change (IPCC), a large, international body of climate and climate impact scientists mandated by UNEP and the World Meteorological Organization (WMO) in 1988 to assess the state of the art in climate change and to provide the knowledge basis to deal with climate change politically.[67] IPCC resides exactly at the interface between politics and science, as both ends have to be met: good science and policy advice. Additionally, it has already been described as an example for post-normal science.[68] The institutional design and the performance of this body is thus quite complicated and unique,[69] as one would expect for a body that so much embodies the new coevolution of science and society. Not surprisingly, there has been harsh criticism with regard to the procedures of the IPCC and the type of science it provides. Some argue that 'true science' would be compromised by political interests (e.g. the environmental movement), or by the self-serving interests of climate scientists, or both.[70] Others argue that IPCC is still too close to the old model of experts 'speaking truth to power'.[71] Taken together, both criticisms show that a new form of science–policy interaction could be on the rise: simultaneously being cautious about scientific credibility, exactness, and rigor – indicated by the extensive process of international peer review[72] – and about questions of policy

---

[66] Haas, P. M., *Saving the Mediterranean*, New York (Columbia University Press) 1990; Haas, P. M., Introduction: epistemic communities and international policy coordination, *International Organization* 46(1) (1992), pp. 1–37.
[67] See www.ipcc.ch
[68] Saloranta, T. M., Post-normal science and the global climate change issue, *Climatic Change*, 50 (2001), pp. 395–404.
[69] Skodvin, T., *Science-policy interaction in the global greenhouse: institutional design and institutional performance in the Intergovernmental Panel on Climate Change (IPCC)*, Working Paper 1999: 3, Oslo (Center for International Climate and Environmental Research (CICERO)) 1999.
[70] Boehmer-Christiansen, S., Uncertainty in the service of science: between science policy and the politics of power, in Fermann, G. (ed.), *International politics of climate change: key issues and critical actors*, Oslo (Scandinavian University Press) 1997, pp. 110–152.
[71] Jasanoff and Wynne, op. cit.
[72] Edwards, P. N. and Schneider, S. H., Self-governance and peer review in science-for-policy: the case of the IPCC Second Assessment Report, in Miller, C. A. and Edwards, P. N. (eds.), *Changing the atmosphere: expert knowledge and environmental governance*, Cambridge, Mass./London (MIT Press) 2001, pp. 219–246.

relevance, salience, and public perception of science – indicated by the careful drafting of summaries for policy-makers, the explicit communication of uncertainties (since the Third Assessment Report in 2001), and the use of multiple emission paths due to very different scenarios of possible economic and social development (the so-called SRES scenarios in the Third Assessment Report). The credibility of the IPCC is considerable, and the biodiversity research community is trying hard to copy this paradigm with regard to the Convention on Biological Diversity (CBD). Even hardline industry representatives who initially doubted the scientific credibility of the IPCC find its work increasingly compelling. 'We have stopped paying the climate skeptics since IPCC is hard to fight – and may be they are right' is a personal communication we heard from a representative of the German chemical industry. This is anecdotal evidence for the concept of influence and for the blurring of the boundaries between scientific and strategic forms of argumentation[73] that appear requisite to new institutions facing GEC problems with high stakes and high uncertainties.

3. Consumers

All scientific endeavour possible will not lead to successful institutions if the majority of society is not willing (or able) to follow the policy advice given by scientists. This does not only hold for industry – a powerful, but rather 'simple' actor in terms of manageability, as their number is rather small and their action patterns are rather predictable – it holds for society as a whole or for virtually all of 'us'. This brings the 'consumers' into play.

The emergence of the 'consumer society' started with the USA in the early twentieth century and encompassed most parts of the developed world after the Second World War. A new dynamic impulse has come about due to the restructuring and recovery of the ex-communist world after 1989, and by the economic growth processes of some developing countries in the last two or so decades, a process that still is in the making and in part covered by the processes of globalisation. Myers and Kent[74] have calculated that we experienced the emergence of 1 billion 'new consumers' recently in developing and transition countries, endowed with a purchase power that equals the USA, and mostly with preferences for more goods, more resources, and more emissions.[75] But also in OECD countries a growth of 30–35% in the total motor vehicle stock and in energy use is expected till 2020.[76]

---

[73] Risse, op. cit.
[74] Myers, N. and Kent, J., New consumers: the influence of affluence on the environment, *Proc. Natl. Acad. Sciences USA*, 100 (8) (2003), pp. 4963–4968.
[75] Princen, T., Maniates, M., and Conca, K. (eds.), *Confronting consumption*, Cambridge, Mass./London (MIT Press) 2002.
[76] Dziubinski, O. and Chipman, R., *Trends in consumption and production: household energy consumption*, DESA Discussion Paper No. 6, 1999 (available at www.un.org/esa/sustdev/sdissues/consumption/esa99dp6.pdf).

The environmental effects of consumption process and lifestyle changes are twofold: direct and indirect. Direct effects are externalities of individual or household consumption activities like heating, cooking, driving by car, and the like. Indirect effects are those that are directly caused or initiated by other actors (e.g. businesses, state agencies), but serve consumers' needs and wants (e.g. public transportation, energy supply for homes). Data for the direct effects is rather easy to obtain for the developed world, data for indirect effects is rather difficult to obtain for both the developed and the developing world; often they require extra calculation from different sources, generalisation from single case studies, or simple estimation. Useful tools and approaches help to fill existing data gaps, e.g. the concept of 'material flow analysis' that traces exact resource and energy use required for products and services (or, more widely, for whole economies) at all stages from production to consumption, including 'hidden flows' (like extraction) that do not enter in the 'fabric' of a product.[77] Some statistical offices have started to open their systems of national accounting (SNA) for material and energy flows. The decomposition of these national aggregates to different consumer or lifestyle groups is still a desideratum, calling for a closer cooperation between sociology, market research, material flow analysis, and statistics people.[78]

There is no doubt that a 'greening of lifestyles',[79] a fundamental change in consumption patterns, is a prerequisite for sustainable development. But consumers are hard to influence – their 'sovereignty' is a core element of free market societies and their liberal ideology. And socially and culturally dispersed consumers around the globe seem even harder to influence. It is all the more astonishing that consumers have emerged as new, more or less influential actors in the domain of GEC in the past decade.

There are some signs of change here. (1) Market shares of sustainable products (green labels, certified products, fair trade products) are small, but growing. (2) The revealed preferences of people in terms of what they would like to see happening in market and production exceed revealed preferences in the market. Some criticise this as discrepancies between attitudes and behaviour, blaming the consumers. A more favourable way of interpretation would read this as a call for more social and political action towards enabling consumers to buy sustainable products within the range of given possibilities (e.g. prices and income). Survey and experimental data have made it clear that having

---

[77] Duchin, F., *Structural economics: measuring change in technology, lifestyles, and the environment*, Washington, DC (Island Press) 1998.

[78] See e.g. Lutzenhiser, L., Social and behavioral aspects of energy use, *Annual Review of Energy and the Environment* 18 (1993), pp. 247–289; Reusswig, F., Lotze-Campen, H., and Gerlinger, K., Changing global lifestyle and consumption patterns: the case of energy and food (available at www.populationenvironmentresearch.org/papers/Lotze-Campen˙Reusswig˙Paper.pdf) 2004; Weber, C. and Perrels, A., Modeling lifestyle effects on energy demand and related emissions, *Energy Policy*, 28(8) (2000), pp. 549–566.

[79] Brand, op. cit.

products that are produced under 'fair' working and environmental conditions is for many consumers part of their 'utility function'. Consumers are willing to pay between 5% and 10% more for a 'sustainable product' and expect a large discount (over 30%) if a product has been made under poor working or environmental conditions.[80] (3) There are small groups of consumers that already practise more sustainable lifestyles (e.g. living without a car, low energy housing, vegetarian diet). Sometimes they are regarded as hopeless minorities, but they might also be the spearhead of a new mass phenomenon. (4) Even in the developing world we observe criticism with regard to 'overconsumption' and resource intensive consumption patterns.[81] (5) An important point for a successful institutionalisation of sustainable consumption will be the interplay between innovative and environmentally friendly basic technologies and new forms of buying and using them by consumers. The idea of a 'sufficiency revolution', i.e. the reflection on 'how much is enough'[82] and what would be a more appropriate level of material input for wellbeing is a forceful driver for new institutional patterns, but by itself – without the backing of new technologies and policy support – is not able to diffuse widely in society.

VI. Conclusions

What conclusion does the aforesaid permit? What are the chances of building successful institutions with regard to their necessary social embedding? Are there promising hints that new institutional arrangements of global environmental governance can find broad social acceptance in highly industrialised as well as in less industrialised countries?

Referring to the social preconditions of successful institution-building discussed in section II (normative validity and cultural fit; social resonance; compliance resources) we can at least say that the prospects are not hopeless. Macrostructural trends such as individualisation, globalisation, and the emergence of 'information', 'network', or 'knowledge' society clearly have ambivalent effects. On the one hand, they accelerate the erosion of traditional ways of life and the spread of Western lifestyles, they increase the probability of cultural conflicts and the salience of social problems (social polarisation and exclusion). On the other hand, they favour participation, the spread of information, a worldwide networking, the emergence of new proactive groups of concerned citizens, and of transnational environmental discourse coalitions.

---

[80] Freeman (1998), op. cit.
[81] Consumers International, *A discerning middle class? A preliminary enquiry of sustainable consumption trends in selected countries in the Asia Pacific Region*, Penang (Consumers International Regional Office for Asia and the Pacific (CI-ROAP)) 1998.
[82] Durning, A., *How much is enough? The consumer society and the fate of the earth*, Washington, DC (Worldwatch Institute/W. W. Norton) 1992.

Empirical findings also show a spreading environmental awareness worldwide. The idea of a global vulnerability of ecosystems and social systems depending upon them has gained some kind of cultural hegemony among experts and the public. The new master frame of 'sustainable development' provides a widely accepted ideological basis for the development of new cooperative strategies and institutional arrangements in dealing with global environmental problems.

Of course, different groups have different interpretations of 'sustainable development', some of them conflicting. Still, the main advantage from a sociological point of view is the fact that it creates a common framework of reference, which binds the involved political and societal actors, to a global and integrated perspective for a lasting protection of the those conditions that enable human development. Normative validity might gain even further support from the strong participatory element of the sustainability discourse. The concept of global governance has, as we discussed above, opened up the social and the instrumental solution space for global environmental problems. Business, TNC actors, and consumers were our main examples here.

At the same time, questions regarding the 'fairness' of environmental regulations gain significance. Solutions focusing on the protection of the environment and the preservation of ecosystems lose their legitimacy if environmental problems are not systematically linked to social and economic development. On the one hand, this is a matter of procedural fairness. New participatory forms of global environmental governance can meet this requirement relatively well. On the other hand, this implies questions of distributional fairness which are defined very differently depending on particular interests or institutional and cultural backgrounds. This is certainly the crux for the development of appropriate responses to problems of global change. The perception of fairness is inextricably linked to the historical experience of colonialism, the lack of synchronisation of development and modernisation in various parts of the world, the blatant global and national social disparities, and the lack of credibility of many political elites. Fair solutions are only possible if these various and mutually linked dimensions are acknowledged.

Other problems refer to the 'cultural fit' and 'social resonance' criterion. The process of industrialisation and the emergence of the consumer society has created standards of living, patterns of thinking, of institutional routines and of individual behaviour, which are opposed to a consequent ecological modernisation of societies. Win-win options or strategic alliances are possible here and there and they are supported by many initiatives and the diffusion of best practice cases. However, the greening of industry and lifestyles is a protracted process. Institutionalising sustainable patterns of consumption and production requires coordinated efforts of political, economic, technological, and societal incentives and development strategies. There are promising beginnings at many levels pushed forward by networks and strategic alliances of the transnational civil society – but these are still beginnings.

5

Globalising a green civil society: in search of conceptual clarity

ASHER ALKOBY

I. Introduction

Over the past decade or so, frequent use of the term 'global civil society' can be found in the writings of scholars who study the pluralisation of global politics and international law, especially in the area of environmental protection.[1] While adding prefixes such as 'emerging' or 'nascent' to the term, many seem to agree that there now appears to be a realm of collective life at the global level, inhabited mainly by non-governmental organisations (NGOs).[2] And indeed, the growing scholarly interest in the concept of global civil society began with the explosion of NGO activity in global politics, including law-making fora. In what has been so far a Westphalian state-centric system, these new non-state actors seem to have increasing influence on the processes and outcomes of international

---

[1] See generally Otto, D., Nongovernmental organisations in the United Nations system: the emerging role of international civil society, *Human Rights Q.* 18 (1996), p. 107; Mathews, J. T., Power shift, *Foreign Affairs* 76 (1997), p. 50; Cox, R. W., Civil society at the turn of the millennium: prospects for an alternative world order, *Rev. Int'l Stud.* 25 (1999), p. 3; Scholte, J. A., Civil society and democracy in global governance, *Global Governance* 8 (2002), p. 281; in the environmental context see Lipschutz, R. D., Reconstructing world politics: the emergence of a global civil society, *Millennium J. Int'l Stud.* 21 (1992), p. 389; Lipschutz, R. D. with Mayer, J., *Global civil society and global environmental governance: the politics of nature from place to planet*, Albany (SUNY) 1996; Raustiala, K., The 'participatory revolution' in international environmental law, *Harv. Envt'l L. Rev.* 21 (1997), p. 537; Wapner, P., Horizontal politics: transnational environmental activism and global culture change, *Glob. Envt'l. Pol.* 2 (2002), p. 37. Any attempt to provide a full account of the attention given to global civil society across disciplines would not do it justice. These are only examples of a fast growing body of literature, and others will be cited throughout my discussion.

[2] Some even use the terms 'global civil society' and 'NGOs' interchangeably. See e.g. Falk, R. and Strauss, A., On the creation of a global people's assembly: legitimacy and the power of popular sovereignty, *Stan. J. Int'l L.* 36 (2000), p. 191 at 194 n. 13, and also Charnovitz, S., Two centuries of participation: NGOs and international governance, *Mich. J. Int'l L.* 18 (1997), p. 183 at 188 (observing that the term 'NGOs' is on the decline and that 'the emerging nomenclature seems to be "civil society"').

negotiations. They interact with each other, with states, and with international organisations, successfully using different tactics to promote their agendas.[3]

Much of the global civil society literature addresses three key questions. All three have been explored both empirically and normatively, although as will be argued below, many of the normative aspects remain undertheorised. At the descriptive level, these questions are:

- Who are the members of what has come to be known as 'global civil society'?
- What do the members of 'global civil society' do? How are they involved in world affairs? How do they influence global governance?
- Why do they become involved in global politics? And once they do, under what conditions do they become influential?

Much of this data has been collected by social scientists, who study the emergence of NGOs and other collectivities at the global level, their patterns of participation in global political discourses, and their influence on policy outcomes. Legal scholars have also examined these issues, but have mostly focussed on civil society's involvement in institutional arrangements (i.e. their influence on law-making processes in international organisations). Taken together, the existing studies allow us to make theoretically founded normative statements when considering the following corresponding enquires:

- Who should be included in the definition of 'global civil society'?
- What roles should 'global civil society' play in global governance?
- Why should 'global civil society' be involved in what has been thus far the domain of sovereign states alone?

These questions are, of course, intimately related. Any answer given to one clearly has some bearing on the response to the other. The last of the three seems to be a good place to begin theorising global civil society: once we determine the reasons for opening up global governance to entities other than sovereign states, it would become relatively easy to defend a proposed definition of the concept 'global civil society'. It would also allow us to consider the roles these members of global civil society ought to play in order to be most effective, and to suggest, from an institutional design perspective, what they should be *allowed* to do. This seems to be the common methodology in the current debate.[4] But the concept 'civil society', as we know, was invented in territorially bound societies, and its import from national social ordering to the global level demands clarification.

---

[3] See Keck M. E. and Sikkink, K., *Activists beyond borders: advocacy networks in international politics*, Ithaca/London (Cornell University Press) 1998.

[4] See e.g. Bodansky, D., The legitimacy of international governance: a challenge for international environmental law?, *Am. J. Int'l L.* 93 (1999), p. 600; Ebbesson, J., The notion of public participation in international environmental law, *Y. Int'l Envt'l L.* (1997), p. 51; Raustiala, op. cit.

In this chapter I thus take a slightly different approach by asking: 'Can civil society be globalised?'

I proceed as follows. Section II provides a brief overview of the global civil society debate in international law (IL) and international relations (IR) theory, along the lines of enquiry outlined above. These two fields of study have had the benefit of a fruitful scholarly interplay in recent years, but IL and IR scholars ought to consider stepping further outside the confines of the two disciplines and be more open to available insights from other fields of study, especially when making use of concepts that were first conceived of in those fields. In other words, any search for a civil society that is not bounded by national borders should not be bounded by disciplinary constraints.

In section III, I begin the theoretical discussion by tracing the origins of 'civil society' as it emerged in Western thought and as political thinkers understand it today. This is not a mere terminological investigation, of course: exploring the meaning of the term in its original context involves a discussion of all questions listed above: What is 'civil society'? Who are its members? How is their role conceptualised in political theory and what is the nature of their relationship with political authority? Why is their involvement in social and/or political life considered valuable for social ordering?

After clarifying the elements of the original definition(s), section IV presents a thesis that the concept of civil society can be globalised, and that it has the potential to serve as a real democratising force in international law. That would only be possible, however, when democracy is understood in a meaningful, deliberative sense. Both the liberal and the communitarian interpretations of the concept in political theory, I argue, are ill-suited to the global realities: to import the liberal model employed by contemporary Western thinkers is to overlook the plurality of world societies; to adopt the communitarian variant is to ignore the fact that a sufficient level of global social cohesion is still lacking.

A detailed discussion of this critique, as well as an alternative conception of global civil society, will be framed by three questions. First, can civil society be globalised in the absence of a world state? This chapter suggests that it would be possible only by adopting a conception of democratic legitimacy that centres on discourse and deliberation rather than on elective representation. Secondly, should economic entities be considered a part of an ideal-type global civil society? I suggest that the common negative answer provided by scholars across disciplines to this question is deeply problematic, for it is based on the assumption that economic actors cannot be socialised in the same way that other individuals can. It also implies that social interactions are generally either 'discursive' or 'strategic' and cannot consist of both.

Finally, I ask what kind of social bonds are required at the planetary level for us to imagine a global civil society. In answering this question, I borrow the notion of solidarity from the critical perspective in political theory to propose a procedural approach to cross-cultural dialogues. This approach prescribes the ideal *formal* requirements for developing a consensus rather than prescribing what that consensus ought to be.

While my discussion may have broader implications, my focus is on the international law and politics of the environment. If there is any basis for the claim that there exists an 'international' or 'transnational' or 'global' civil society, nowhere is it more evident than the environmental realm. When reviewing the practice of transnational actors I will draw on empirical work done in the environmental field when available, and when considering the possibility of globalising civil society I will use the environmental lens to consider the 'greening' effect that civil society could have on international cooperation.

II. Global civil society: empiricism and interpretations

1. Who is 'global civil society'?

The term 'global civil society' typically refers to a variety of non-state actors, including many forms of voluntary associations, most prominently NGOs.[5] There is a tendency to define the members of global civil society as 'non-profit entities', and by that excluding all forms of economic actors,[6] although this is not uncontroversial.[7] But for now I will begin by listing the *transnational actors* who are currently involved in global politics and/or law-making, giving special attention to environmental cooperation. After concluding the conceptual discussion offered in this chapter, it will be possible to suggest which of these actors would be the members of an ideal-type 'global civil society'. For the sake of clarity, I will employ the term transnational actors (TNAs) when referring to the non-state entities listed below.

NGOs receive most of the attention in recent studies, given their increasing involvement in international politics and law-making.[8] Their number is

---

[5] See e.g. the sources listed in n. 1 above. Mary Kaldor suggests helpful typology (however, informed by her own normative definition of 'global civil society'): Kaldor, M., *Global civil society: an answer to war*, London (Polity Press) 2003, pp. 78–108.

[6] See for example Otto, op. cit. n. 2 ('networks, movements, and organisations of nonprofit interest groups which form to assert interests, identities, or causes outside state-based and controlled political institutions') and also Wapner, P., The normative promise of nonstate actors: a theoretical account of global civil society, in Wapner, P. and Ruiz L. E. J. (eds.), *Principled world politics: the challenge of normative international relations*, Maryland (Rowman & Littlefield Publishers Inc.) 2000, p. 260, at 269 ('they are non-profit in the sense that they are not businesses seeking economic gain but rather are animated by social, cultural, or normative concerns').

[7] See Keane, J., *Global civil society?* Cambridge (Cambridge University Press) 2003, pp. 75–88, and see my discussion in Alkoby, A., Non-state actors and the legitimacy of international environmental law, *Non-State Actors and Int'l L.* 3 (2003), p. 23, at 47–50, 95–96. And more on this in section IV.

[8] See e.g. in the area of environmental cooperation, Oberthür, S. *et al.*, *Participation of non-governmental organisations in international environmental governance: legal basis and practical experience*, Berlin (Ecologic and FIELD) 2002, as well as the vast empirical literature that they review.

difficult to establish, but it is estimated that the twentieth-century witnessed a two-hundred-fold increase in the number of international NGOs.[9] Broadly speaking, NGOs are associations of individuals or groups of individuals with an organisational structure, who are engaged in legal, political, or social action to promote different goals and objectives at the global level.

Since many of their activities are in institutional settings, one way to find out which NGOs are currently operating at the planetary level is to consider their definition and their eligibility criteria in international institutions. This may not be an easy task, however, since there does not seem to be a single agreed definition of the term NGO in international law. Article 71 of the United Nations Charter does not define the term NGO, stating that '[t]he Economic and Social Council may make suitable arrangements for consultation with NGOs'.[10] A UN report from 1994, which introduced proposed rules to regulate the participation of NGOs in UN conferences, suggested the following definition:

> An NGO is a non-profit entity whose members are citizens or associations of citizens of one or more countries and whose activities are determined by the collective will of its members in response to the needs of the members or of one or more communities with which the NGO cooperates.[11]

This formulation excludes entities with a profit-making aim. However, the resultant resolution by the UN's Economic Social Council makes no mention of the non-profit requirement when establishing the eligibility criteria for NGOs. Article 12 of the resolution merely states that an NGO is an organisation that is not established by a governmental entity or an intergovernmental agreement.[12] The Council of Europe has also made an attempt to formalise the accreditation process for NGOs and defined them as associations, foundations,

---

[9] See Anheier, H. et al. (eds.), *Global civil society 2001*, Oxford (Oxford University Press) 2001, pp. 283–286. The data brought there indicate that the number of NGOs registered as international organisations has reached the number of 13,206.

[10] Charter of the United Nations, 26 June 1945, Can T.S. 1945 No. 7.

[11] *General review of arrangements for consultations with non-governmental organisations: report of the Secretary General*, UN. ESCOR, UN Doc. E/AC.70/1994/5 (Open-Ended Working Group on the Review of Arrangements for Consultations with Non-Governmental Organisations, 1st Sess. Prov. Agenda 3). For a detailed discussion of this report see Otto, op. cit.

[12] *Consultative relationship between the United Nations and non-governmental organisations*, 49th plenary meeting, UN Doc. E/RES/1996/31, 25 July 1996. The main eligibility requirements are that the NGO is concerned with matters falling within the competence of the Economic and Social Council and its subsidiary bodies (Article 1), that its aims and purposes are consistent with the work of the United Nations (Articles 2, 8); that is has a recognised standing within the particular field of its competence or of a representative character (Article 9); and that it has a representative and democratic structure (Articles 10–12).

and private institutions, which 'have a non-profit aim of international utility'.[13] In most multilateral environmental agreements (MEAs), however, such non-profit requirement does not apply. These agreements typically define NGOs as any body, national or international, that is qualified in the regulated subject matter.[14]

As a result, NGOs of various kinds can be found in international environmental institutions, with different aims, types of activities, and organisational structure.[15] Their motivation could be promoting a public interest cause (environmental, human rights, development) or a private interest (business and industry). Their type of activity might also vary (lobbying, providing aid, providing expertise) as we will see below, although most of them are involved in a wide range of activities. At the organisational level, they could be representing individuals from one country or have a broader constituency across countries; they could derive their funding from member contributions and donations, or from financial support provided by governments.[16]

It should be noted that the definition of NGOs provided by international organisations can only tell us which actors are granted access (limited as it is) to the organisations' institutional arrangements. The fact is, however, that much of the NGO activity that can be witnessed in relation to the generation, interpretation, and implementation of international agreements remains informal,[17] and so there could be other forms of associations involved in international negotiations and outcomes of various kinds that are not covered by these formal definitions.

A second, non-institutional form of collective action is a social movement. A social movement may be defined as an informal interaction network between a plurality of individuals, groups, and/or organisations. They have a shared set

---

[13] European Convention on the Recognition of the Legal Personality of International Non-Governmental Organisations, Article 1 (see http://conventions.coe.int/Treaty/en/Treaties/html/124.htm). The meaning of the phrase 'international utility' is implied in the Preamble to the Convention, where the work of NGOs is recognised as being 'of value to the international community, particularly in the scientific, cultural, charitable, philanthropic, health and education fields'. The Convention's Explanatory Report points out that the element of international utility 'also makes it easier to circumscribe the concept of "non-profit making" aim'. See http://conventions.coe.int/Treaty/en/Reports/html/124.htm

[14] See Oberthür et al., op. cit. pp. 26–27 (Table 1).   [15] Ibid., pp. 32–38.

[16] Ibid. For studies of NGO practice in international environmental institutions, see Raustiala, op. cit.; Yamin, F., NGOs and international environmental law: a critical evaluation of their roles and responsibilities, RECIEL 10 (2001), p. 149, and more specifically in the climate change negotiations, in Giorgetti, C., The role of non-governmental organisations in the climate change negotiations, Colo. J. Int'l Envt'l L. and Pol'y 9 (1998), p. 115; Giorgetti, C., From Rio to Kyoto: a study of the involvement of non-governmental organisations in the negotiations on climate change, N.Y. U. Envt'l L. J. 7 (1999), p. 201; and Oberthür, S. and Ott, H., The Kyoto Protocol: information policy for the 21st century, Berlin (Springer) 1999, pp. 29–32.

[17] See e.g. Alkoby, op. cit. pp. 32–41 and the sources cited there.

of beliefs and a sense of belonging and they are engaged in political or cultural conflict meant to bring about social change. Social movements typically use protest or disruptive action to mobilise their constituencies.[18] A *transnational social movement* is a 'set of actors with common purposes and solidarities linked across country boundaries that have the capacity to generate coordinated and sustained social mobilisation in more than one country to publicly influence social change'.[19] One current example for such a transnational actor is the anti-globalisation movement.[20]

An even more fluid form of association at the global level is what Margaret Keck and Kathryn Sikkink have termed 'transnational advocacy networks', which they define as 'forms of organization characterized by voluntary, reciprocal, and horizontal patterns of communication'.[21] Transnational advocacy networks do not involve mobilisation of large numbers of people as social movements do, but they also share certain values and act jointly to promote their agendas, mainly through information exchange, in areas such as human rights, environment, women, infant health, and indigenous peoples.[22] Transnational networks could include

> (1) international and domestic nongovernmental research and advocacy organizations; (2) local social movements; (3) foundations; (4) the media; (5) churches, trade unions, consumer organizations, and intellectuals; (6) parts of regional and international intergovernmental organizations and (7) parts of executive and/or parliamentary branches of governments.[23]

Yet another type of actor that ought to be considered in this inventory-taking stage is the transnational corporation (TNC) – a business entity that operates in more than one country, usually by having companies in different locales that are linked and coordinated. TNCs are said to influence world affairs by playing a major role in the integration of national economies into one single global market economy,[24] and also by forming associations and interest groups that have become involved in international negotiations similar to non-profit

---

[18] Della Porta, D. and Diani, M., *Social movements: an introduction*, Oxford (Blackwell Publishers) 1999, pp. 14–15; and see Khagram, S., Riker J. V., and Sikkink, K., From Santiago to Seattle: transnational advocacy groups restructuring world politics, in Khagram, S., Riker J. V., and Sikkink, K. (eds.), *Restructuring world politics: transnational movements, networks and norms*, Minneapolis (University of Minnesota Press) 2002, p. 3, at 8.
[19] Khagram *et al.*, op. cit. p. 8.
[20] See Kaldor, op. cit. pp. 101–104 (names it the 'anti-capitalist movement'). For another example see Thompson, K. B., Women's rights are human rights, in Khagram *et al.*, op. cit. p. 96 (speaks of an international women's social movement).
[21] Keck and Sikkink, op. cit. p. 8.   [22] Ibid.   [23] Ibid., p. 9.
[24] See Risse, T., Transnational actors and world politics, in Carlsnaes W. *et al.* (eds.), *Handbook of international relations*, London (Sage Publications) 2002, p. 255, at 262–263.

NGOs. In most MEAs, as mentioned above, business associations could qualify as NGOs and be given equal access to negotiating fora.[25]

2. What does 'global civil society' do?

I have thus identified a variety of transnational actors involved in world affairs: NGOs, transnational advocacy networks, social movements, and TNCs, as well as the individuals who comprise them, of course. The following is a brief description of their functions as observed in recent empirical work. Following Thomas Risse, I divide the categories of policy cycles where TNA activity can be observed into three: agenda-setting, international norm creation, and international norm implementation.[26]

(a) Agenda-setting

All of the transnational actors listed above are involved in this category of activities, with the possible exception of business entities (who typically respond to NGO or state initiatives that are perceived as threats rather initiate change by themselves). Two kinds of activities contribute to bringing normative issues onto the international agenda by these actors: provision of information and advocacy.[27] Since NGOs and transnational advocacy networks do not posses the might of states, they must 'use the power of their information, ideas, and strategies to alter the information and value contexts within which states make policies'.[28] Sometimes provision of the facts or the scientific data is all that is required to promote change. This typically happens in the field of environmental protection, where lack of information and scientific uncertainty often become barriers to global efforts to combat environmental degradation. By providing scientific expertise, NGOs often act to shape the global environmental agenda.[29] Such expert NGOs sometimes become a part of what Peter Haas has termed epistemic communities: 'a community of experts, sharing a belief in a common set of cause and effect relationships as well as common values to

---

[25] Alkoby, op. cit. pp. 37–38.
[26] Risse, op. cit. pp. 265. For more on international norms' 'life cycle', see Finnemore, M. and Sikkink, K., International norm dynamics and political change, Int'l Org. 52 (1998), p. 887.
[27] See Risse, op. cit. and Oberthür et al., op. cit. pp. 40–44.
[28] Keck and Sikkink, op. cit. p. 16. They speak of TANs, but this surely holds for NGOs as well.
[29] See e.g. Keck and Sikkink, op. cit. pp. 121–164; Raustiala, K., States, NGOs and international environmental institutions, Int'l Stud. Q. 41 (1997), p. 719; Princen, T., Ivory, conservation, and environmental transnational coalitions, in Risse-Kappen, T. (ed.), *Bringing transnational relations back in: non-state actors, domestic structures, and international institutions*, Cambridge (Cambridge University Press) 1995, p. 227; the contributions in Haas, H. P. M. (ed.), Knowledge, power and international policy coordination, Int'l Org. 46 (1992) (Special Issue).

which policies governing these relationships will be applied'.[30] A few examples of expert NGOs are the World Watch Institute, the International Institute for Sustainable Development (IISD), and the Foundation for International Environmental Law and Development (FIELD).[31]

In other cases, reporting the facts or providing information is not all that is required to draw attention to an existing problem, and TNAs need to use the information they have in a strategic manner in order to 'make the need for action more real for ordinary citizens'. They do this by dramatising the testimonials they may have collected, thereby giving the campaign a human face, or reframing issues in a way that draws more attention and support. Keck and Sikkink show, for example, how the issue of land use rights in the Amazon gained more support when it was framed by TNAs as a deforestation concern rather than a matter of social justice or regional development.[32] Other examples where TNAs served as 'moral entrepreneurs' in the field of environmental protection are the ozone regime, the climate change regime, and wildlife conservation.[33]

(b) International norm creation

Advocacy and lobbying by TNAs continues after a concern is successfully placed on the international agenda. Typically, this is when states decide to convene and discuss possible solutions to the perceived problem, towards the signing of a treaty. Oberthür and his colleagues define advocacy as the phase where TNAs promote their cause formally, within the institution established by the treaty or within an existing institution in charge of implementing the solution. Lobbying, on the other hand, is understood as the informal influence on states and international organisations exerted by TNAs in the institutional setting ('corridor diplomacy') or outside of it (parallel conferences held by NGOs, for example).[34]

On the formal side, activities of TNAs in international conferences and international organisations include making statements during official meetings, submitting written statements and position papers to state delegations, and generally, attending the meetings and deliberations under their 'observer

---

[30] Haas, H. P. M., Do Regimes Matter? Epistemic Communities and Mediterranean Pollution Control, *Int'l Org.* 43 (1989), p. 377, at 384. One recent example for such a community of experts is the Intergovernmental Panel on Climate Change (IPCC), which played a key role in the removal of uncertainty and scepticism from the climate change agenda, and contributed to the perceived legitimacy of the emerging legal regime in the eyes of state actors. See Oberthür and Ott, op. cit. pp. 3–10.

[31] See Yamin, op. cit. pp. 156. [32] Keck and Sikkink, op. cit. pp. 17 and also ch. 4.

[33] See respectively, Liftin, K., *Ozone discourses, science and politics in global environmental cooperation*, New York (Columbia University Press) 1994; Tolbert, D., *Global climate change and the role of international non-governmental organisations*, in Churchill, R. and Freestone, D. (eds.), *International law and global climate change*, London/Boston (Graham and Troman/M. Nijhoff) 1991; and Princen, op. cit.

[34] Oberthür *et al.*, op. cit. pp. 42–43 (following Bas Art).

status', and often making the information they receive public.[35] As a result of a relatively inclusive approach taken by states in recent years, one can witness an increasing participation of NGOs in many of the major international conferences.[36] The ratio of NGO participants and government officials at the June 1992 United Nations Conference on Environment and Development in Rio de Janeiro, for example, was approximately one to one.[37]

During advanced stages of negotiations, states and international organisations assume centre stage and TNAs are usually pushed aside. States tend to adopt a less inclusive approach for TNA participation, in order to ensure the secrecy of the negotiations.[38] TNAs have three main courses of lobbying action in this rule creation phase: domestically, working to change government preferences in powerful states; internationally, by coalescing with international organisations to pressure states 'from above'; or by building coalitions with smaller states, thereby indirectly continuing to be involved in the process of negotiations.[39] In what remains a state-centred international political process, TNAs have to devise creative strategies in order to remain key players in the norm creation phase. One of the powerful instruments that NGOs used during the climate change negotiations, for example, was the publication of daily newsletters such as *ECO* and the *Earth Negotiation Bulletin*.[40] These publications, especially the more critical of the two, *ECO*, served as an important source of information on the deliberations in the conference of the parties leading to the signing of the Kyoto Protocol. They ensured transparency by revealing the state of the negotiation process and helped 'prevent the obscure language of

---

[35] The permitting provisions in the legal instruments have almost identical language. See Montreal Protocol on Substances that Deplete the Ozone Layer, 16 September 1987, I.L.M. 1541, Article 11; United Nations Framework Convention on Climate Change, 9 May 1992, I.L.M. 849, Article 7(2)(l); United Nations Convention on Biological Diversity, Article 23; Convention on the Control of Transboundary Movements of Hazardous Wastes and their Disposal, 22 March 1989, 28 I.L.M. 649, Article 15(6). For earlier conventions see Raustiala, op. cit. p. 545.

[36] See Waak, P., Shaping a sustainable planet: the role of non-governmental organisations, *Colo. J. Envt'l L. and Pol'y* 6 (1995), p. 345.

[37] Tarlock, D., The role of non-governmental organisations in the development of international environmental law, *Chi-Kent L. Rev.* 68 (1992), p. 61, at 63.

[38] Raustiala, op. cit. p. 570.

[39] Risse, op. cit. p. 265. One example for the latter is the advice provided by business NGOs to OPEC countries during the climate change negotiations. See Oberthür and Ott, op. cit. p. 31.

[40] The first is published by the Climate Action Network (available at www.climatenetwork.org/eco/); the second is published by the International Institute on Sustainable Development (IISD) (available at www.iisd.ca/). Whereas *ECO* is more of an openly critical review of negotiations, the *Earth Negotiation Bulletin* has virtually become a de facto official source of information, and links to it have even been incorporated into the UNFCCC's websites. See, e.g. the COP-7 website, at http://unfccc.int/cop7/

international diplomacy from shielding governments from accountability for their actions'.[41]

Yet another 'back door' through which TNAs manage to remain involved in the norm creation process is by participating in national delegations. They sometimes serve as members of the delegations with no specific task, and at times they are even recruited as direct advisors, or function as negotiators.[42] As Oberthür and his colleagues point out, this direct involvement comes at a price: 'Not only are NGO representatives acting as negotiators on national delegations unable to pursue their usual NGO activities, they may even have to act under government instructions that do not necessarily conform to the positions otherwise taken by them'.[43]

'Norm creation' in the context of MEAs is more than treaty-making. Many international environmental regimes today are based on the 'Convention-Protocol' model, which treats law-making as a progressive activity.[44] Under this model, participating states first negotiate a framework convention, consisting of an initial set of principles, procedural provisions, and information-sharing mechanisms, and only later develop a more substantive set of binding commitments, usually in the form of protocols. This model allows for work to proceed in an incremental manner, and to 'produce positive feedback loops'[45] by establishing institutions where actors interact. Thus, there is not always a clear (temporal or substantive) separation between 'creation' and 'implementation' of norms. TNA activity in the forms discussed above continues throughout this jurisgenerative process of norm creation, clarification, implementation and interpretation.

(c) International norm implementation

Nonetheless, some TNA activities can be distinctly classified as part of the 'implementation' phase of the norms. NGOs are frequently involved in monitoring and enforcement of state's obligations, as agreed upon in signed treaties and ratified domestically. They rarely have direct access to international dispute settlement mechanisms, but even when they do not, they either submit the

---

[41] French, H., The role of non-state actors, in Werksman, J. (ed.), *Greening international institutions*, London (FIELD/Earthscan) 1996, p. 1. This would be true especially with regard to the more critical of the two, *ECO*. See also Betsill, M., Environmental NGOs meet the sovereign state: the Kyoto process negotiations on global climate change, *Colo. J. Int'l Envt'l L. and Pol'y* 13 (2002), p. 49, and Oberthür et al., op. cit. pp. 46–48.

[42] Oberthür et al., op. cit. pp. 44–45.   [43] Ibid., p. 45.

[44] Two notable examples are the ozone regime and the climate change regime. See generally E. B. Weiss, International environmental law: contemporary issues and the emergence of a new world order, *Geo. L. J.* 81 (1993), p. 675, at 687–688. See also Lang, W., Is the ozone depletion regime a model of an emerging regime on global warming?, *UCLA J. Envt'l L. and Pol'y* 9 (1991), p. 161 and Bodansky, D., The United Nations Convention on Climate Change: A Commentary, *Yale J. Int'l L.* 18 (1993), p. 451, at 494.

[45] Bodansky, op. cit. p. 495.

relevant information to state actors that can trigger a non-compliance complaint, or make the information public, aiming to 'shame' governments into compliance.[46] NGOs can also resort to national courts in cases where international norms are being breached.[47]

TNA involvement in the enforcement of international agreements can often be crucial, since most compliance mechanisms for international agreements are based on self-reporting by governments, who may distort the information or fail to report at all. State agencies and international organisations often rely on TNA expertise and information-gathering capacity, especially in regimes that lack detailed and intrusive verification mechanisms.[48]

It should be noted, however, that while many of TNA activities are aimed at the international political processes, they are not exclusively so. Many NGOs are involved with attempts to change people's behaviour without the mediation of legal norms. They work on educating individuals and groups or shaping public opinion by launching media campaigns, conducting workshops, and are often 'engaged in conversation projects "on the ground", thereby linking local knowledge and local concerns to the national and international levels of policy making'.[49]

3. Interpretations of empirical findings in IR and IL literature

What can the empirical work on TNAs teach us about the reasons why they are involved in world affairs? In answering this question, IL scholars, as well as IR theorists of the rationalist bent, have tended to focus on the political conditions that explain the explosion of TNA activity in international policy-making, namely on structure. To the extent that they are interested in the agents involved, it is in *state* actors, and the question they would typically ask is 'What can TNAs do for the state, or for the state-system?'. Some IR scholars, in contrast, are shifting their attention from questions of 'structure' to 'agency',

---

[46] See generally Bothe, M., Compliance control beyond diplomacy: the role of non-governmental actors, *Envt'l Pol'y and L.* 27 (1997), p. 293. NGOs have not yet been granted standing in non-compliance procedures under MEAs. Under the Montreal Protocol, however, NGOs may participate as observers in the Multilateral Consultative Procedure (MCP), provided that two-thirds of the parties assent to their participation. See Barratt-Brown, E. P., Building a monitoring and compliance regime under the Montreal Protocol, *Yale J. Int'l L.* 16 (1991), p. 519, at 564. See also, on the monitoring roles of NGOs in the CITES and the Basel Convention, Handl, G., Compliance control mechanisms and international environmental obligations, *Tul. J. Int'l and Comp. L.* 5 (1990), p. 29, at 43. NGOs will not be permitted to submit questions of implementation to the climate change regime's compliance committee, as the agreed upon draft of the procedures suggests. See Alkoby, op. cit. pp. 40–41; Oberthür op. cit. pp. 45–46.

[47] See e.g. in the climate change context, Hodas, D. R., Standing and climate change: can anyone complain about the weather?, *J. Land Use and Envt'l L.* 15 (2000), p. 451.

[48] Risse, op. cit. p. 266.   [49] See Oberthür *et al.*, op. cit. p. 49.

and exploring how the two interact. While they remain interested in the political opportunities that allow for (as well as necessitate) the increasing pluralisation of world politics, they also ask what motivates *non-state* actors to coalesce and become active globally? What are the goals they seek to achieve, and under what conditions do they become influential? I begin by discussing the agent-centred interpretations in IR, and equipped with their understanding of the motivations for global collective action, I turn to the structural changes that stand at the centre of IL discourse on TNAs.

The focus on *non-state* agency is a relatively new development in IR theory. Two of the leading IR theories, neo-realism and institutionalism, have long been 'agent-centred', but as mentioned above, they remain focused on interactions between *states* at the global level. The first downplays the role of non-state actors in a system where material power is the determining factor, and the latter views TNA involvement in global governance in instrumental terms. Under an institutionalist framework, the reason why states are increasingly receptive to TNA input and influence, especially in institutional settings, is the fact that they increase the efficiency of the political process. The interests of governments are served when TNAs deliver technical expertise to interested parties, facilitate negotiations by providing data and competing ideas, help secure ratification and implementation of treaties on the domestic level, and monitor compliance of states' obligations. By playing these roles, TNAs are essentially being *utilised* by governments to their benefit, mainly by minimising research and implementation expenditures.[50]

A growing body of research in IR theory looks beyond the instrumentality of TNAs. These scholars are commonly termed constructivists, and they are concerned with the influence of ideas and norms on world politics.[51] Their research programme challenges both of the above-mentioned theories. First, they show how material power is not a precondition for shaping behaviour at the global level, which implies that TNAs can no longer be deemed irrelevant. Secondly, by demonstrating how norms and values matter, constructivists show how TNAs who take part in the generation and application of these norms seek (as well as offer) much more than instrumental benefits.

Since there are no existing transnational collective action theories to test the empirical work against, social scientists tend to use a methodology often termed

---

[50] See Alkoby, op. cit. pp. 64–67 and also Nowrot, K., The legal consequences of globalisation: the status of non-governmental organisations under international law, *Ind. J. Global Legal Stud.* 6 (1999), p. 579, at 605–606.

[51] See Risse-Kappen, T. (ed.), Bringing transnational relations back in: non-state actors, domestic structures and international institutions, Cambridge (Cambridge University Press) 1995; Klotz, A., *Norms in international relations: the struggle against apartheid*, Ithaca, NY/ London (Cornell University Press) 1995; Finnemore, M., *National interests in international society*, Ithaca (Cornell University Press) 1996; Keck and Sikkink, op. cit.; Risse, T. et al. (eds.), *The power of human rights: international norms and domestic change*, Cambridge (Cambridge University Press) 2001; Khagram et al., op. cit.

'grounded theory' in explaining the observed behaviour of collectivities at the global level (i.e. generating theories through qualitative research). As some of these social scientists acknowledge, however, insights provided by previous sociological research on collective action in the domestic sphere might prove helpful in explaining TNA behaviour, if only because many TNAs are often simultaneously international and domestic actors.[52]

The scholarly ground where one is most likely to find theoretical insights on collective action is social movement theory. Very broadly speaking, there are three theoretical orientations in this field of study. In attempting to explain why social movements emerge, the first provides a psychological explanation; the second adopts a rational approach; and the third provides a non-rational explanation.

The school of 'collective behaviour' defines social movements as responses to experience of deprivation by actors in society: 'When traditional norms no longer succeed in providing a satisfactory structure for behaviour, the individual is forced to challenge the social order through various forms of non-conformity'.[53] 'Forced' would be the operative word here: the act of resistance by individuals (in the form of collective action) is not purposeful and deliberate, but rather an irrational psychological response to frustrated expectations.

Under the 'resource mobilisation' paradigm, social movements are viewed as extensions of (rational) political action. Collective action derives from cost–benefit calculations, influenced by the presence of resources, either material or non-material. Within this rationalist paradigm is placed the 'political process' approach, which seeks to explain why collective movements develop by exploring the political and institutional conditions under which they emerge and operate. They thus focus on the 'opportunity structure' of the political system and its level of openness to the social and political goals and tactics of social movements.[54]

Finally, the 'new social movements' approach, more associated with European sociologists, examines the social transformations that brought about the emergence of new types of collective movements. The rationalist approaches, these theorists observe, are informed by past conflicts among the industrial classes from the nineteenth century onward. But these types of conflicts now have decreasing relevance. The conflicts that characterise the post-industrial society are those of a social rather than economic nature.[55] These movements are concerned with issues such as human rights, environmental protection, gender equality, and peace. Their motivation for collective action according

[52] Keck and Sikkink, op. cit. pp. 5–8, 30–32, and Khagram *et al.*, op. cit. pp. 5–6.
[53] Della Porta and Diani, op. cit. p. 6. [54] Ibid., pp. 9–11, and also ch. 8.
[55] Some of the representative works are Touraine, A., *The voice and the eye: an analysis of social movements*, Cambridge (Cambridge University Press) 1981; Cohen, J., Strategy or identity: new theoretical paradigms and contemporary social movements, *Social Research* 52 (1985), p. 663; Melucci, A., *Challenging codes: collective action in the information age*, Cambridge (Cambridge University Press) 1996.

to this approach lies not necessarily in achieving material gains, but rather in resisting and defending individual autonomy.[56]

IR theorists who study transnational activity consciously draw upon social movement theory insights, and while they are interested in the link between domestic political opportunity and the emergence of global collective action (similar to the 'political process' approach), they understand it not as motivated by rational pursuit of material gains, but by principled ideas and values. Like 'new social movement' theorists, they show how these movements do not target the state or the economy and demand inclusion or material benefits, but seek to reshape social and political institutions. According to Khagram, Riker and Sikkink, 'the third sector, or nongovernmental sector, could be characterized by the search for meaning. The individuals and groups in this sector are primarily motivated to shape the world according to their principled beliefs'.[57]

But the search for meaning, while it could explain why people choose to act collectively in a given community, still does not account for *transnational* activism. In trying to explain the reasons for which domestic collective actors make use of international norms and international institutions by linking with other activists across borders, IR scholars have looked at the domestic opportunity structure and its impact on transnational activism. Keck and Sikkink suggest, based on their empirical findings, that when channels between domestic groups and their governments are blocked or when they prove ineffective, a 'boomerang effect' is triggered. Domestic groups try to bypass their governments and seek allies to bring pressure on their governments from the outside by linking with international NGOs and transnational networks of activists. TNAs work to convince international organisations to put pressure on the norm-violating state 'from above'.[58] This hypothesis has been confirmed by other scholars as well, in a series of case studies on the impact of TNAs' activity on the internalisation of human rights norms in repressive regimes.[59]

In repressive regimes, the lack of domestic political opportunity to influence policy-making is what brings collective actors to seek allies transnationally. Their allies in democratic regimes cooperate with them in an effort to bring about change in the repressive target state. But what motivates TNAs that are based in democracies to initiate collective political action? If the domestic

---

[56] Della Porta and Diani, op. cit. pp. 12–13.
[57] Khagram *et al.*, op. cit. pp. 11. [58] Keck and Sikkink, op. cit. pp. 12–13.
[59] Risse, Ropp, and Sikkink build on this notion of 'boomerang effect' when they develop a 'spiral model', which consists of several 'boomerang throws'. They show how, in the human rights field, international norms go through several phases in the processes of socialisation in repressive regimes: repression, denial, tactical concessions, prescriptive status, and finally, rule-consistent behaviour. See Risse, T. and Sikkink, K., The socialization of international human rights norms into domestic practices: introduction, in Risse *et al.*, op. cit. pp. 1 at 17–34. See also the case studies in Khagram *et al.*, op. cit.

political opportunity exists (as it does in democracies), and domestic collectivities can find channels of influence in their own countries, why would they resort to international norms and institutions as well?

A possible answer is that easy access to the political system might be a precondition to, but does not guarantee policy outcome.[60] And so when local NGOs in democracies find it difficult to reach the desired policy changes domestically, they too seek global channels of influence to achieve their goals. Another possible explanation, which stands at the centre of IL discourse on civil society participation, concerns the consequences of globalisation on the national policy-making capacity of democratic governments.[61] International lawyers identify a growing shift in the decision-making authority from states to international institutions, which creates a 'democratic deficit' in international law.[62] The dramatic developments at the global level, associated with the end of the Cold War and the globalisation of the economy, technology, and the environment, are changing the meaning of sovereignty.[63] In national democracies, it is argued, the justification of authority derives from the participation of publics in the decision-making processes. Citizens may hold governments accountable for their actions through elections, and the political process allows for pathways of public participation and ensures transparency.[64] But these domestic channels of influence have decreasing relevance, since many decisions that have direct impact on the lives of citizens in national democracies are being made at the global level, in international institutions that were formed by governments. And so domestic groups that want to promote the principles and ideas that they share must act transitionally in order to have impact on the policy outcomes.

IL scholars view this growing involvement of TNAs in global governance favourably. The way to address the 'democratic deficit', they argue, is to allow for participation of the individuals and groups in international policy-making. An increased involvement of the interested public in global governance would contribute to the popular legitimacy of international institutions and advance their effectiveness as a result.[65]

---

[60] See Risse, op. cit. p. 266.   [61] See in detail Alkoby, op. cit. pp. 43–44, 52–64.
[62] In the environmental context see e.g. Dunoff, J., From green to global: towards a transformation of international environmental law, *Harv. Env'l L. Rev.* 19 (1995), p. 241. These concerns are not voiced only by international lawyers, of course. A broad range of 'globalisation theories' in political science literature make similar observations. See Held, D. and McGrew, A., The great globalization debate: an introduction, in Held, D. and McGrew, A. (eds.), *The global tranformations reader: an introduction to the globalization debate*, Cambridge/Oxford (Polity/Blackwell Publishing) 2003, p. 1, as well the contributions in Part I of that volume.
[63] See Falk, R., Towards obsolescence: sovereignty in the age of globalization, *Harv. Int'l L. R.* 17 (1995), p. 34.
[64] See e.g. Bodansky, op. cit.   [65] See ibid. and also Raustiala, op. cit.

This approach seems logically flawed, for it suggests that the cure for the democratic deficit is simply to ignore it;[66] namely, while claiming that the international political structure is far from resembling a democracy, it posits that what works for national democracies should work at the international level as well. However, in a horizontal legal system, where there is no government and no demos, the basis for justified authority cannot simply be imported from hierarchical democratic legal systems.

The dismissal of the implied analogy between domestic and global structures, however, is based on a straightforward (not to say equally simplistic) proposition: since there is no 'world state' to be found, imagining the international system as a democratic liberal state is highly problematic. A possible response to this claim is that certain concepts *can* be imported when it is possible to conclude that 'the conditions of order within states are *similar* to those of order between them'.[67] When considering the possibility of globalising 'civil society', this argument goes, such similarities *do* exist. While there is no 'demos' at the global level, there exists an international community; a global consciousness; a 'we' feeling. And while there is no world government, there is a political authority in the form of the institutions of global governance. Global civil society, similar to its domestic version, fulfils a mediating role between political authority and society, and could serve as a powerful democratising force.[68] And so, by exploring the meaning of 'civil society' in the next section, I examine a more nuanced version of a domestic analogy. My aim is to see whether the relevant structural features in the domestic sphere, which, according to some, make 'civil society' a helpful concept in theorising political legitimacy, have equivalents in the global structure.

III. Civil society in political theory

Since the revival of the concept in the early 1990s, several scholars have explored the history of 'civil society' in detail, and many have begun exploring its modern meaning and implications.[69] While the concept has been fraught with ambiguity throughout its transformations, three observations can be made on the different meanings it has received over the years. First, often it reflected (or responded to) the societal conditions that it sought to describe (or prescribe).

---

[66] For this critique in detail, see Alkoby, op. cit.
[67] Suganami, H., *The domestic analogy and world order proposals*, Cambridge (Cambridge University Press) 1989, p. 1 (emphasis added).
[68] Versions of the argument can be found in Kaldor, op. cit. and Keane, op. cit.
[69] See e.g. Cohen, J. L. and Arato, A., *Civil society and political theory*, Cambridge (MIT Press) 1992; Hall, J. A., *Civil society: theory, history, comparison*, Cambridge (Polity Press) 1995; Seligman, A., *The idea of civil society*, Princeton (Princeton University Press) 1992; Keane, J., *Civil society: old images, new visions*, Stanford (Stanford University Press) 1998, and Walzer, M. (ed.), *Toward a global civil society*, Providence (Berghahn Books) 1995.

Secondly, controversies over the definition and boundaries of 'civil society' also reflect the political views of those engaged in the debate. In each of the earlier interpretations, however, theorists have stressed the *emancipatory potential* of 'civil society': in freeing individuals from coercive feudal or religious authority; liberating them from a capitalist hegemony; or safeguarding them from oppressive governmental powers. It seems, however, that this is no longer the common thread in liberal contemporary thinking.

1. The current discourse on civil society

The return of 'civil society' is associated with the struggles against totalitarian regimes in Central-Eastern Europe that eventually resulted in the 1989 revolutions and the end of the Cold War.[70] The term was adapted to refer to social movements and leading intellectuals who sought to create a vocal, organised, and politically informed public in opposition to state policies. Since the main aim of these reformers was democratisation and a transition to free market economies, their success has brought some thinkers in the West to view the concept of civil society as something that liberal democracies have already achieved, and to declare communism's collapse as the end of ideology, or alternatively an emerging ideological consensus. Other scholars have drawn on the East European experience to support their call for further democratisation of Western societies, while stressing the advantages of conceptualising civil society as distinct from both the state and the economy in achieving that goal (as opposed to using state or market reforms).[71]

But even theorists who do not consider the East European experience to have much import for liberal democracies have been invoking the term since its rebirth over a decade ago. Many political theorists of different theoretical orientations use it for their own purposes. Classic liberals (also referred to as libertarians) consider it to be a useful tool to counter-balance the dangers of an overbearing state. Communitarians espouse it as a less loaded term for their ideal type 'good society', with predefined shared values, which serves to counter the dangers of liberal individualism. In a sense, they view civil society as a school of good citizenship.

---

[70] As well as upheavals against dictatorships in Latin America. See Kaldor, op. cit. pp. 50–77.
[71] See Cohen and Arato, op. cit. pp. vii–viii, 15–16, and compare Fukuyama, F., *The end of history and the last man*, New York (Free Press) 1992. For an illuminating juxtaposition of these two works see the review essay by Binder, G., Post-totalitarian politics, *Mich. L. R.* 91 (1993), p. 1491. Referring to the ideological crisis in the West following the end of the Cold War, Binder notes: 'When a society's ends are supplied by a foreign threat, ideology is unnecessary and military mobilization supplants political mobilization . . . Now that we have made the world safe for liberalism, democracy and capitalism, we must decide what these fine phrases mean': ibid., p. 1501. Cohen and Arato's voluminous book has attempted to do exactly that.

Classic liberalism finds its roots in the writings of John Locke and the Scottish Enlightenment scholars. But while the latter had monarchs as their foes, contemporary liberals target the welfare state, or what they would prefer to call 'unlimited government'. Their policy prescription, in the words of Scalet and Schmidtz, is:

> Nurture voluntary associations. Limit the size, and more importantly, the scope of government. So long as the state provides a basic rule of law that steers people away from destructive and parasitic ways of life and in the direction of productive ways of life, society runs itself. If you want people to flourish, let them run their own lives.[72]

Law is thus viewed as largely instrumental, procedural, and does not reflect specific community values but 'universal' ones.[73]

Liberals wish to leave most choices and decisions in the hands of individuals rather than in the hands of society or the state, because 'the preferred setting for the good life is in the marketplace, where individual men and women, consumers rather than producers, choose among a maximum number of options. The autonomous individual confronting his, and now her, own possibilities – this is much the best thing to be'.[74] From this assumption follows the principle of political neutrality as the standard for legitimacy of political authority, and a strong emphasis on individual rights.[75] Under this approach, civil society could typically be defined as 'the community that delegates authority to government . . . [It] refers to anything *but* government: businesses, schools, clubs, unions, media, churches, charities, libraries, and any other nongovernmental

---

[72] Scalet, S. and Schmidtz, D., State, civil society, and classical liberalism, in Rosenblum, N. L. and Post, R. C. (eds.), *Civil society and government*, Princeton, N J (Princeton University Press) 2002, p. 26, at 26, 28–29. See also Palmer, T. G., 'Classical liberalism and civil society: definitions, history, and relations, in Rosenblum and Post, op. cit. p. 48, and Lomasky, L., Classical liberalism and civil society, in Chambers, S. and Kymlicka, W. (eds.), *Alternative conceptions of civil society*, Princeton, NJ (Princeton University Press) 2002.

[73] Cohen and Arato, op. cit. p. 9.   [74] Walzer, op. cit. p. 12.

[75] John Rawls is most associated with 'rights-oriented liberalism', and sometimes confused with classic liberalism. See Rawls, J., *A theory of justice*, London (Oxford University Press) 1971 and Rawls, J., *Political liberalism*, New York (Columbia University Press) 1993. See Cohen and Arato, op. cit. p. 3 n. 4, 8; and also Etzioni, A., Law in civil society, good society, and the prescriptive state, *Chi.-Kent L. Rev.* 75 (2000), p. 355, at 360 (who claims that Rawls 'seems to be' a classical liberal and explains it, oddly, by stating, 'I do not join here the very elaborate debate concerning what Rawls says, or what he meant to say, and how he changed his mind from one volume to the next.' ibid., n. 26). A more nuanced understanding of Rawls's theory is suggested by Kymlicka, who labels Rawls a liberal egalitarian, to the extent that he would support an 'equality of resources' view of liberal equality. See Kymlicka, W., Civil society and government: a liberal egalitarian perspective, in Rosenblum and Post, op. cit. p. 79. See also in the same volume Galston, W. A., Liberal egalitarianism: a family of theories, not a single view, in Rosenblum and Post, op. cit. p. 111 at 111–112).

forms of organization through which a community's members relate to each other'.[76]

A liberal civil society then comprises roughly two main forms of association that ought to be free from government intervention: individuals interacting for the purpose of economic activity, and those who form voluntary organisations for any purpose they wish. The market is there, of course, because 'the state is not competent as a direct producer of ordinary private goods'.[77] The role of the state is to facilitate the efficacy of markets by providing the framework that allows productive competition in civil society. The second component of the definition, voluntary associations, also plays a role in improving people's lives. It is because 'the associational life of civil society is the actual ground where all versions of the good are worked out and tested'.[78] Classic liberals would tend, however, to encourage associations with *private aims* rather than public interest advocacy groups, since the demands that the latter typically make from the state work against the desirable neutrality of the political order.[79]

But the idea of civil society can also receive a communitarian interpretation, which emphasises associational solidarity rather than individualism. Communitarians (sometimes referred to as 'republicans') view individuals as 'situated into communities through which they derive their individual and collective identity, language, world concepts, moral categories, etc'. They claim that liberals fail to see that not all values are universal (if there *are* any); they are community-specific, and many communal duties (of loyalty, civic virtue) are owed by individuals to other members of the community, not to 'abstract humanity'.[80] But this does not imply that the role of law in an ideal-type communitarian society is greater than the vision of a procedural, 'blind' law under the classic liberal model. Communitarians would try to minimise reliance on law because 'it often undermines . . . informal social controls by replacing them'.[81] They put great emphasis on persuasion and conviction rather than coercion, on bringing people to serve their community and uphold its values because it is 'the right thing to do', not because the law says so.[82]

---

[76] Scalet and Schmidtz, op. cit. p. 27 (emphasis in original). And see Palmer, op. cit. pp. 49, 57 (supporting Scalet and Schmidtz's definition).
[77] Scalet and Schmidtz, op. cit. p. 32. Kymlicka suggests, however, that libertarians consider the markets to encourage civility. Kymlicka, op. cit. p. 90.
[78] Walzer, op. cit. p. 16.
[79] See Lomasky, op. cit. But see Scalet and Schmidtz, op. cit. p. 40 (suggesting that classic liberals are divided on the issue, and some might consider civil society to have a role in forming 'good citizens' as well).
[80] Cohen and Arato, op. cit. pp. 8–9.
[81] Etzioni, op. cit. p. 362. He does realise, however, that law has 'an expressive role to state and underscore the values that society cherishes'. Ibid.
[82] Ibid. Naming the figures who subscribe to this approach would not be an easy task, since it really is a family of theories rather than a single coherent one. However, the list of editors of a quarterly journal established by Etzioni, *The Responsive Community: Rights*

The liberal and communitarian variants in the above discussion are on the two extremes of the political axis, of course. Many theorists are located somewhere in the middle. And so for example egalitarian liberals, who are sometimes labelled 'neo-Tocquevilleans' or 'welfare state defenders'[83] hold that 'formal principles of economic and political liberty are necessary but not sufficient to define a morally adequate political outlook'.[84]

Many of the Western democracies, it may be argued, are situated on the right half of this axis. The embodiment of liberal principles can be found in Bills of Rights of many constitutional democracies.[85] This could explain why political thinkers in the West no longer express complete mistrust in governments typical of the liberal tradition, and rather than speaking of 'civil society *against* the state' they now try to suggest how the two can go together. While they continue to stress the importance of keeping clear boundaries between the state and civil society as much as possible (although a certain degree of overlap is inevitable), they also speak of mutual dependency of state and society and ask 'what does the state need from civil society' as well as 'what does civil society need from the state'.[86] The concept has thus lost much of its emancipatory potential in political thought, partly due to the post-Cold War Western triumphalist currents alluded to above.[87] Civil society is perceived as a tool for reinforcing and enriching democracy (in its individualist or communitarian versions) rather than a challenge to it.

I will now sketch out an alternative to the classic liberal and the communitarian conceptions of civil society, offered by critical theory. Jean Cohen and Andrew Arato's book on civil society and political theory provides the most detailed and comprehensive contemporary account of the civil society argument. As shown below, their model has two advantages in considering the possibility of globalising civil society: its emphasis on the process of generating legitimacy in highly complex, *pluralist* societies, and the *transformative* role civil society can play in this process.

2. Civil society in critical theory

Like thinkers before them, Cohen and Arato develop a theory of civil society that is informed by their theoretical commitments, in their case to post-Marxism.[88]

---

and *Responsibilities*, might serve as an indication. They include Charles Taylor, William Galston, Benjamin Barber, Robert Bellah, Martha Minow, and Philip Selznick, among others. See www.gwu.edu/~ccps/rcq/rcq_index.html

[83] See Kymlicka, op. cit. pp. 79–80, who discusses the 'equality of resources' variant of this approach and puts under that category theorists such as Rawls, Dworkin, and others. See also Cohen and Arato, op. cit. pp. 8–15.

[84] Galston, op. cit. p. 111. [85] Palmer, op. cit. p. 62.

[86] See Introduction to Rosenblum and Post, op. cit. p. 2 (framing the basic inquiries around these questions, among others).

[87] Binder, op. cit. [88] Cohen and Arato, op. cit. p. 2.

They understand civil society as a tool for achieving radical political projects, not only in authoritarian regimes but in liberal democracies as well. 'Now that the radical rhetoric of communism has at last (and deservedly) been discredited', they argue, 'the question confronting political theorists is whether utopian thought and corresponding political projects are conceivable at all'.[89] The answer they provide is affirmative, and civil society, they argue, is the arena for the project of democratisation.[90]

Cohen and Arato define civil society as 'a sphere of social interaction between economy and the state, composed above all of the intimate sphere (especially the family), the sphere of associations (especially voluntary associations), social movements, and forms of public communication'.[91] It is thus a three-part model, which differentiates the 'civil' from the 'economic' sphere as well as from the state. They share the liberals' concern about the need to strengthen civil society vis-à-vis the state, but following Gramsci, argue that it needs to be differentiated from the economy as well. The experience in Western democracies, they contend, has taught us that economic power can pose as great a danger to social solidarity and justice as the power of the state.[92]

Their model is introduced as an alternative to both liberal and communitarian conceptions of civil society. They do this by putting forward the thesis that moral autonomy does not presuppose possessive individualism:

> [R]ights do not only secure negative liberty, the autonomy of private, disconnected individuals. They also secure the autonomous (freed from state control) *communicative interaction* of individuals with one another in the public and private spheres of civil society, as well as a new relation of individuals to the public and political spheres of society and state.[93]

As their terminology makes clear, Cohen and Arato draw extensively on Jürgen Habermas's social theory of communicative action.[94] His approach rejects, on the one hand, the liberal vision of the political process as an agglomeration of private preferences, and posits an intersubjective, interactive conception of individuality and autonomy. On the other hand, it perceives the communitarian vision of social ordering as based on a shared conception of the

---

[89] Ibid., p. xi.   [90] Ibid., p. xii.   [91] Ibid., p. x.

[92] Under their model, it should be added, civil society is not identified with all social life outside the state and the economy. They further distinguish civil society from 'political society' and 'economic society'. The first includes parties, political organisations, Parliaments, and others involved in the political discourse. Economic society includes firms, cooperatives, labour unions, and all other entities involved in economic production. The concepts of political and economic society serve as mediating categories between the three main spheres.

[93] Ibid., p. 23 (emphasis in original).

[94] See ibid., pp. 21–22, and in more detail at 345–420. Habermas' more recent work on deliberative democracy further develops these themes. Habermas, J., *Between facts and norms: Contributions to a discourse theory of law and democracy*, Cambridge (MIT Press) 1996.

good life as ill-suited to pluralist societies. Modern societies are heterogeneous and structurally differentiated; they are not communities integrated around a single conception of a common good. Instead of a shared ethos, Habermas introduces the notion of 'institutionalised discourses' as the processes through which political consensus is formed.[95]

This discursive activity takes place not only in political society but in civil society as well: 'A deliberative practice of self-determination can develop only in the interplay of, on the one hand, the parliamentary will-formation institutionalized in legal procedures and programmed to reach decisions, and, on the other, political opinion-building in informal circles of political communication'.[96]

From here comes the distinction between 'strong publics' – formally organised institutions of the political system – and 'weak publics' – the informally organised public sphere located within civil society, which includes voluntary associations and the mass media among others.[97] The realm of 'weak publics' (or the 'lifeworld') is where social problems are identified, interpreted, and resolved. They are then further filtered through the political discourse (the Habermasian 'system'), which assumes the decision-making responsibility and addresses these problems at the level of policy change.

The dominant mode of communication in civil society is moral argumentation. This is when agreements are reached in an 'ideal speech situation', which has several demanding preconditions: all parties must have access to the dialogue; all parties must be able to participate in it on equal terms; and all parties must be open to be persuaded to change their positions or change existing norms.[98] This mode of interaction would produce a consensus that is formed on the basis of adequate information and relevant reasons, to which all those affected can agree.[99] Unlike social contract theories, what Habermas refers to as 'deliberation' is not a virtual dialogue but an *actual* one, and thus it requires, for example, 'designing institutions of political will-formation so that they reflect the more complex preference structure of individuals rather than simply register the actual preferences individuals have at any given time'[100] (i.e. what is required is an active participating citizenry, and not only in the ballot). Civil society is thus viewed as a terrain of democratisation, where legitimacy of norms can be attained. Political and economic actors are not considered part of it because they 'cannot subordinate strategic and instrumental criteria to the patterns of normative integration and open-ended communication characteristic of civil society'.[101]

---

[95] See Habermas, op. cit. p. 298.   [96] Ibid., p. 275.
[97] See Baynes, K., A critical theory perspective on civil society and the state, in Rosenblum and Post, op. cit. p. 123 at 125.
[98] These are the 'meta-norms' that prescribe the validity of norms. Ibid., pp. 347–348.
[99] See Baynes, op. cit. p. 127.   [100] Ibid.
[101] Cohen, J., Interpreting the notion of civil society, in Walzer, op. cit. p. 35, at 38. This short piece provides a useful and concise summary of Cohen and Arato's model.

This distinction between the political-strategic and the civil-normative modes of action fits nicely into Cohen and Arato's understanding of collective action. They suggest a way of reconciling the two competing paradigms in social movement theory by making the following proposition. Social movements, they contend, have a double political task: they struggle simultaneously for the defence and democratisation of the institutions of civil society and for the inclusion within political institutions.[102] Civil society is the realm where social movements defend the 'lifeworld' from economic and political 'colonisation'. This is where they construct new identities, reshape institutions, and create and legitimate norms through a process of social learning as the 'new social movement' theory suggests. The *political* sphere is where social movements act strategically, in order to gain recognition, achieve benefits, and influence the political discourse. This mode of action is more in line with the 'resource mobilisation' paradigm in social movement theory.[103] At the same time, the offensive, political mode of action is not all about material gains; it also involves 'the politics of influence' – targeting political and economic actors and making them more receptive to the needs and self-understandings of actors in civil society.[104] As I will later argue, this dual logic of collective action and the distinction between two 'modes of argumentation' is not without its problems.[105]

Let me sum up. What has become clear from the outset is that 'civil society' has no single definition in political thought. The concept has travelled far over the centuries, and while not much is left from its ancient original definition (of a well-governed, legally ordered way of life), its early modern conceptualisation still resonates in contemporary theorising, although with the adjustments that the conditions of modernisation have entailed. From the eighteenth century onwards, 'civil society' became distinct from the state and was identified with the new capitalist market. This remains the classic liberal understanding of the term: civil society as a sphere that is free from government intervention, and therefore includes all *non*-governmental bodies, interacting in the market of commodities and ideas. Post-Marxist theorists, however, view civil society as a tool for radical political projects. Like Marx, they emphasise the transformative potential of the concept. But they 'turn Marx on his head' when they exclude the economy from the definition of civil society, since the market, under their analysis, is no longer a tool for emancipation but an instrument of domination.

The following section, which forms the core of my argument, both draws on and challenges the critical perspective on civil society. The first part argues that civil society could be globalised in the absence of a world state only if democracy is understood as a process of continuous deliberation (i.e. communicative action) rather than formal representation. The second part questions the exclusion of economic actors from the definition of civil society, shared

---

[102] Cohen and Arato, op. cit. p. 523.   [103] Ibid., pp. 525–526.
[104] Ibid., p. 532.   [105] See nn. 142-143 below and accompanying text.

by critical theorists, and the final part explores the usefulness of the critical perspective in 'universalising' discourses.

IV. Globalising a green civil society

1. Global civil society and (the absence of) the state

The idea of civil society has always been linked to democracy. In each of the interpretations it has received in Western political thought, as well as in the intellectual resistance to dictatorships in the East, civil society has been viewed as a democratising force, even if there has not been much agreement on what 'democracy' means or how it can be achieved. Either way, democracy in theory and practice has always had ties to *the state.*

Theories on democracy, writes Michael Zürn, have assumed a 'spatial congruence' between rulers (the nation *state*) and subjects (the national *society*).[106] But as soon as the nature of the relevant political community begins to transform, this assumption becomes problematic. A common argument made by sceptics is that 'beyond the nation state, the political prerequisite for a democratic political community – the political space – is missing', and thus in the absence of an international political authority, stretching the reach of democracy to the global (or regional) level is not a possibility.[107]

Against these sceptics, others have begun exploring the possible institutional bases for a 'cosmopolitan democracy'.[108] David Dryzek shows how these proposals to extend democracy to the global level are essentially an extension of *liberal* democracies.[109] When David Held speaks of a cosmopolitan democracy, he imagines a democracy that 'results from, and only from, a nucleus, or cluster, of democratic states and societies'.[110] Yet even setting aside the objections such proposals raise at the normative level, this vision is not politically feasible. Even the existing international institutions, which arguably form the basis for a future world government, are not especially democratic today and are not likely to be in the foreseeable future.[111]

---

[106] Zürn, M., From interdependence to globalisation, in Carlsnaes *et al.*, op. cit. p. 235, at 244.

[107] Ibid., p. 245. Two examples for this critique are Offe, C., The democratic welfare state in an integrating Europe', in Greven, M. T. and Pauly, L. W., *Democracy beyond national limits: the European dilemma and the emerging global order*, Lanham (Rowman and Littlefield) 2000, p. 63, and Dahl, R., Can international organisations be democratic? A sceptic's view, in Shapiro, I. and Hacker-Cordon, C. (eds.), *Democracy's edges*, Cambridge (Cambridge University Press) 1999.

[108] See e.g. Held, D., *Democracy and the global order: from the nation state to cosmopolitan governance*, Oxford (Polity Press) 1995. See also Falk and Strauss, op. cit.

[109] Dryzek, D. S., Transnational democracy, *J. Pol. Phil.* 7 (1999), p. 30, at 32.

[110] Ibid. and see Held, op. cit. p. 22.

[111] One obvious example is the World Trade Organization. See Dryzek, op. cit. pp. 32–33.

Nonetheless, as Dryzek argues, there might still be a way to democratise global governance, and this can be done by making two conceptual moves. First, one must abandon the ideas of a world *government* or any other constellation of world federalism in favour of decentralised systems of *governance*. Secondly, the notion of global democratic legitimacy must rest not on voting or representation of persons and interests, but rather on deliberation.

The first proposition is not a novel one. It can be found in the writings of many students of world politics. 'Governance without government' is the common efficiency-based formula for state cooperation in conditions of interdependence. Keohane and Nye define governance as:

> the processes and institutions, both formal and informal, that guide and restrain the collective activities of a group. Government is the subset that acts with authority and creates formal obligations. Governance need not necessarily be conducted exclusively by governments and the international organizations to which they delegate authority. Private firms, associations and firms, non-governmental organizations (NGOs), associations of NGOs all engage in it . . . to create governance.[112]

And thus with the growing number of international institutions and 'regimes', authority is becoming 'parcellised' on the basis of issues rather than on a territorial basis, be it the human rights regime, the climate change regime, or global financial regulation.[113] In these processes, global civil society 'provides an alternative vehicle for deliberation, for introducing normative concerns, for raising the interests of the individual and not just the state'.[114] David Dryzek emphasises the importance of international discursive fora in the following elegant metaphor:

> Discourses are intertwined with institutions; if formal rules constitute institutional hardware, then discourses constitute international software. In the international system, the hardware is not well developed, which means that the software becomes more important still . . . it may turn out that [the] absence [of international hardware] can be turned to good democratic use, especially if institutional software is less resistant to democratization than is the hardware.[115]

The notion of deliberative democracy has the potential of severing the link between democracy and the state, and is thus superior to older versions of democracy. If the measure for legitimacy of norms and principles is the degree to which they were produced in a process of reasoned deliberation between the

---

[112] Keohane, R. O. and Nye, J. S., Governance in a globalising world, reprinted in Keohane, R. O., *Power and governance in a partially globalised world*, London/New York (Routledge) 2002, p. 193, at 202.
[113] Kaldor, op. cit. p. 141.   [114] Ibid.   [115] Dryzek, op. cit. p. 44.

affected actors, then the absence of a representative government at the global level becomes less important.

Global civil society may play an important role in this discursive activity. According to Dryzek, it consists mostly of questioning, criticising, and publicising the practice of states.[116] As we have seen, however, the involvement of TNAs in international political processes extends well beyond that, and they do not always work 'against' international institutions but sometimes 'with' them as well. They provide information and expertise, they participate in negotiations within institutional settings, they bring new issues and values and contribute to reproducing the political consensus, and they are actively involved in the implementation of international norms. How can their more direct involvement in the political process be understood?

Dryzek argues that compared to the realm of states, civil society is a realm of unconstrained communication; free of power, fear, and economic concerns. He therefore believes that governmental institutions are not likely to promote a deliberative process.[117] But empirical studies suggest otherwise. As we have seen above, constructivist IR scholars have shown that this grim view on how states behave is far from accurate, and that external threats or material constraints are not always determinative factors in how states relate to each other. As Martha Finnemore points out, 'state interests are defined in the context of internationally held norms and understandings about what is good and appropriate. That normative context influences the behaviour of decision-makers and of mass publics who may choose and constrain those decision-makers'.[118] The role of international institutions in the socialisation of states has received special attention, and constructivists have demonstrated how social learning and emulation 'may enable institutions to establish, articulate and transmit norms across nations, to define what constitutes legitimate behaviour, and shape the identities of their members'.[119] Thus, deliberation is far from being a foreign concept to international politics, and international institutions, undemocratic as they may be in the liberal-representative sense, can serve as effective deliberation fora.[120]

---

[116] Ibid., p. 45.

[117] Ibid., p. 46. Recall that Cohen and Arato similarly propose a dual organising logic of collective action. One consists of 'defensive' struggles for defending the 'lifeworld'. This is where communicative action takes place and new meanings and identities are being created. Second is an 'offensive' struggle against the political and economic society, aimed at achieving institutional reforms, where bargaining and negotiation take place. But they also argue that collective actors sometimes act discursively to 'persuade' political actors when employing 'the politics of influence'. See n. 104 above and accompanying text.

[118] Finnemore, op. cit. p. 2.

[119] E. Adler, Constructivism and international relations, in Carlsnaes *et al.*, op. cit. p. 95, at 104, and the sources cited there.

[120] See Risse, T., Let's argue! Communicative action in world politics, *Int'l Org.* 54 (2000), p. 1.

To be sure, TNAs that are involved in international discourses, both in and outside of international institutions, may not always act 'discursively'. Their 'collective action logic' may indeed be dual, as Cohen and Arato suggested (i.e. both strategic and discursive), but *both* of these modes of operation are employed *both in and outside* the political process; they are not mutually exclusive.[121]

In international environmental regimes, the potential for discourse in institutional settings is especially evident, and one might say that with the increasing legalisation of international relations, the international 'hardware' and 'software' are becoming truly intertwined. As discussed above, under the framework protocol model, decision-making in environmental regimes is typically incremental. In institutions that are established to solve complex environmental problems, law-making is an ongoing activity and norms and principles are the product of continuous deliberation. The extensive review of NGO participation in MEAs by Oberthür and his colleagues demonstrates how engaged NGOs are in these discourses, and the extent of their influence on the outcomes of the negotiations.[122]

This does not imply that the distinction between global civil society and political authority should be abandoned, of course. As Mary Kaldor stresses, 'NGOs have a voice, not a vote'.[123] Collective actors can and should *supplement* and not aim to replace political actors. This is why one of the common practices in MEAs is alarming. Oberthür *et al.* report how increasingly, environmental NGO representatives become members of national delegations, and while the final decisions rest with government representatives, NGO members are still left with significant room for designing substantive positions.[124] This raises serious concerns of cooption by governments, as Oberthür and his colleagues recognise. Participation in the international discourses allows the members of global civil society to exercise the politics of *influence*, not to 'take over' political institutions.

In sum, it appears that the first hurdle in our way to globalise civil society – the absence of a world state – may be overcome if we imagine a global polity headed by political authority made up of a diffused, decentralised web of governance structures (rather than a world government), and by adopting a conception of democratic legitimacy that centres on discourse and deliberation (rather than on formal representation). Global civil society could play a crucial role in these international discourses by providing an alternative deliberation vehicle to that of states alone and in that sense they are 'non-governmental' or 'non-state' actors, although they do not necessarily act *against* the state.

---

[121] See section II.
[122] See also Ellis, J., The regime as a locus of legitimacy, *Int'l Insights* 13 (1997), p. 111, at 121, 126.
[123] Kaldor, op. cit. p. 141.   [124] Oberthür *et al.*, op. cit. pp. 44–45.

2. Global civil society and its colonisers

Section II of this chapter surveyed the empirical terrain. We have seen how TNAs are engaged in a wide range of activities that can be largely divided into three categories: agenda-setting, norm creation, and norm implementation. Empirical work also demonstrates that these activities take place both in and outside of global governance institutions. When carving a normative definition, theorists across the board seem to agree that NGOs, transnational advocacy networks, social movements, and other forms of associational life are included in the definition of global civil society. The inclusion of for profit entities, however, is controversial.

Similar to liberal political theorists, many IL and IR scholars view global civil society as 'laissez-faire politics'; a market of NGOs that conveniently carry out many of the functions that states can no longer perform.[125] Global governance institutions today also espouse this definition and typically do not distinguish between non-profit NGOs and those who act to promote the business interests of their constituents.[126] But against this practice, the vision shared by many global civil society theorists can be characterised by what John Keane has termed 'purism': 'They give the impression that global civil society is a loosely woven net which can be used to catch various fish – so long as the fishing is restricted to non-governmental, not-for-profit ponds.'[127]

Global civil society 'purist' theories often draw on Gramsci in conceptualising the role of 'the third sector'.[128] Under Gramsci's definition, civil society is the ground that sustains the hegemony but it is also the ground on which an emancipatory counter-hegemony could be built. John Keane dismisses Gramsci's relevance to the present-day meaning of the term, claiming that his approach was bound up with all sorts of revolutionary 'communist presumptions' that have no place in a sophisticated theory of civil society.[129] However, even when Cohen and Arato make use of Gramsci's three-part model, they qualify it by using the notion of 'self limitation' vis-à-vis the political authority: the purpose is not to dismantle the state but to achieve an alternative social order within the existing institutional framework.[130]

But what is it about the world order that is being challenged? If we consider the context of environmental governance, Steven Bernstein has shown how current discourse is dominated by 'liberal environmentalism', which links environmental values to liberal markets and economic growth.[131] If the first

---

[125] See Kaldor, op. cit. p. 9.
[126] As shown with regard to MEAs by Oberthür *et al.*, op. cit.
[127] Keane, op. cit. p. 63.   [128] See e.g. Cox, op. cit.; Wapner, op. cit.
[129] Keane, op. cit. p. 63.
[130] Cohen and Arato, op. cit. ch. 3 (on Gramsci) and on social movements' 'self-limiting radicalism' at 492–493.
[131] Bernstein, S., *The compromise of liberal environmentalism*, New York (Columbia University Press) 2001.

global environmental conference in 1972 centred on notions such as 'loyalty to the Earth', the 1992 Rio Conference, following the Brundtland Report, has turned the concept of 'sustainable development' into common parlance and institutionalised the view that trade liberalisation is consistent with, and even necessary for, environmental protection.[132] Paul Wapner observes that the Johannesburg World Summit on Sustainable Development (WSSD) in 2002 marks yet another shift in the strategy of powerful Northern countries, headed by the USA. Historically, wealthy countries used to put environmental concerns front and centre at international conferences (while Southern countries emphasised developmental goals). Today, it seems, economic globalisation is key.[133] This economic orientation in international environmental policy-making is alarming for obvious reasons. Liberal environmentalism, cautions Bernstein, 'risks justifying inaction if tough regulatory choices, which imply trade offs with market values, are necessary to get the desired ecological effects'.[134]

Similarly, for neo-Gramscians, global governance is seen as embedded in the neo-liberal political economy, which is hegemonic in the sense that power relations are maintained through the orthodox discourse.[135] Global environmental discourse, this argument goes, makes frequent use of the term 'global civil society'. The Commission on Global Governance in its report from 1995, *Our Global Neighbourhood*, defines global governance by using a highly inclusive language, and considers practically everyone as stakeholders in global environmental governance.[136] The UNCED Agenda 21 similarly acknowledges the importance of non-state actors (including the *business community*) to the protection of the global environment.[137] The members of global civil society who typically have access to global institutions, however, are the professional and established NGOs who are being gradually coopted and 'their engagement in this setting could be seen as reproducing the existing hegemony, especially with the tendency to adopt the technical-rational discourse'.[138] Rather than talking

---

[132] Stockholm Declaration on the Human Environment, 16 June 1972, 11 I.L.M. 1416 ('Stockholm Declaration'); World Commission for the Environment and Development Staff, *Our Common Future*, Oxford (Oxford University Press) 1987 ('Brundtland Report'); Rio Declaration on Environment and Development, 16 June 1992, 31 I.L.M. 874 ('Rio Declaration').

[133] Wapner, P., World summit of sustainable development: toward a post-Jo'burg environmentalism, *Glob. Envt'l Politics* 3 (2003), p. 1, at 5–6.

[134] Bernstein, S., Liberal environmentalism and global environmental governance, *Global Envt'l Politics* 2 (2002), p. 1, at 14. And see in more detail in Bernstein, op. cit. pp. 234–242.

[135] See Ford, L. H., Challenging global environmental governance: social movement agency and global civil society, *Global Envt'l Politics* 3 (2003), p.120, at 122–123.

[136] Commission on Global Governance, *Our global neighbourhood*, Oxford (Oxford University Press) 1995.

[137] *Report of the United Nations Conference on Environment and Development*, UN GAOR, 47th Sess. Agenda Item 21, 12 UN Doc. A/CONF/151/26 (1992).

[138] Ford, op. cit. p. 130.

about civil society as a democratising force (in the liberal sense of the term), we ought to think about radicalising the discourse by putting emphasis on social movement agency as a counter-hegemonic challenge.[139]

Radicalising the discourse may be a wise strategic move, but the exclusion of for profit entities from the definition of global civil society is a normative judgment that needs to be justified on a firmer ground. As discussed above, Cohen and Arato justify the exclusion of the market from their definition of civil society by claiming that (a) civil society is the target and the terrain of democratisation; (b) norms are validated and legitimated within the realm of civil society in a process of communicative action, where values, principles, and ideas are debated in an equal and reasoned manner; (c) economic actors cannot take part in such discourse, since they operate by a different logic, of power relations guided by rational instrumentality.[140] Cohen and Arato do acknowledge that the 'politics of influence' would *perhaps* have some influence on economic actors, as a separate category, and would make them more receptive to the needs of civil society, but they do not clarify how and where this dialogue would take place.[141] The danger is, of course, that the exclusion of the economy from the institutions of civil society might lead to a blocking of potential channels of influence and such dialogue is not likely to take place at all.

The civil/economic society dichotomy cannot be easily defended, however well it fits into the current trend of demonising multinational business corporations.[142] For it builds on two problematic assumptions, that (a) economic actors cannot be socialised in the same way that individuals can, and (b) that social interactions are either 'discursive' or 'strategic', and cannot consist of both. At first glance, these assumptions have a certain appeal. Communicative action can only take place when actors are prepared to be persuaded and try to convince each other to change their principled beliefs in order to reach a reasoned consensus about validity claims. While this could be true for entities such as environmental NGOs, how can we say the same for purely rational actors like business entities, whose only desire tends to be to realise their individual preferences? One's first instinct is that attributing 'truth-seeking' behaviour to profit-seeking actors is an absurd idea.

Still, as Thomas Risse has argued, there could be a way to accommodate rational actors in a discursive framework. Rational actors must be interested in correcting false information and cognitions about the costs and the benefits of their behaviour. It is not unlikely that they would be willing to receive new

---

[139] See ibid., drawing on Cox, op. cit., and see also Lipschutz (1992), op. cit.
[140] See n. 101 above, and accompanying text.   [141] Cohen and Arato, op. cit. p. 532.
[142] For two popular examples, see Klein, N., *No logo: taking aim at the brand bullies*, Toronto (Vintage Canada) 2000, and Hertz, N., *The silent takeover: global capitalism and the death of democracy*, London (Heinemann) 2001.

information and be open to persuasion. Furthermore, the two rationalities of social interaction are not mutually exclusive and in many cases actors act strategically and discursively at the same time.[143] So the empirical question should not be whether actors behave strategically or argumentatively, but which mode captures more of the action in a given situation.

An example might help explain this point. Transnational corporations are generally not afforded a legal status in international law.[144] For many years, while the international system has moved towards greater regulation of international business, direct participation of the regulated entities was not allowed.[145] In the climate change negotiations, however, business NGOs, comprised of national and transnational corporations, have been very active in the lawmaking fora, both in and out of the institutional setting. They work to promote a specific industrial activity, and represent different points of view and different business sectors.[146] At times, business NGOs outnumbered the environmental NGOs at the conferences.[147] Several observable facts regarding business entity involvement in the Kyoto process indicate that rational actors involved in lawmaking sometimes use argumentative modes of behaviour.

Many of the business NGOs attempted, first, to thwart the chances of reaching an agreement and then to influence the form and content of the commitments.[148] But ever since the climate change debate gained momentum, one can observe a diversity of views held by different segments of the industry. The business community was divided into 'grey' industry groups, which were concerned with the economic impacts of the forming agreement,[149] and the 'light green'

---

[143] Risse, op. cit. pp. 9–12 (Risse names the two modes of interaction 'the logic of consequentialism' and 'the logic of appropriateness').

[144] See Artz, D. E. and Lukashuk, I. I., Participants in international legal relation, in Ku, C. and Diehl, P. F. (eds.), *International law: classic and contemporary readings*, London (Lynne Rienner Publishers) 1998, p. 157, at 166–169.

[145] This could have negative effects on the outcome of state negotiations, according to Jonathan Charney. In the UNCLOS III negotiations, the international community limited its own access to industry information that would have been available had it allowed for the participation of the industry in the negotiations. In turn, the industry reacted by applying pressure on local governments in order to undermine the negotiations. Charney, J. I., Transnational corporations and developing public international law, *Duke L. J.* (1983), p. 748, at 754.

[146] See Giorgetti, op. cit.; Oberthür and Ott, op. cit. pp. 31–32.

[147] Giorgetti, op. cit. p. 220.

[148] The corporate community in the USA was particularly active in Congressional lobbying and starting advertising campaigns against Kyoto. See Grubb, M., Vrolijk, C., and Brack, D., *The Kyoto Protocol: A guide and assessment*, United Kingdom (The Royal Institute of International Affairs) 1999, p. 261.

[149] One influential conservative group of business entities, representing the coal and oil companies, was the Global Climate Coalition (GCC), which initiated and financed economic studies about the impacts and costs of greenhouse gas emission reductions, and helped the OPEC countries' delegations drafting interventions. See Oberthür and Ott, op. cit.

groups, representing renewable energies, cogeneration, natural gas, and other energy efficient industries.[150] Insurance companies comprise another example of a 'green' sector, aligned with progressive industry forces on the issue of climate change. Their involvement stems from the fact that they are expected to suffer major financial losses in a changing climate.[151] Thus, the business sector has not presented a united front to oppose emissions reduction goals.

Furthermore, the increasing scientific findings have arguably made business entities realise that climate change is an issue of great concern that should be addressed.[152] In recent years, even some of the hardline segments of the corporate community have changed their perspective on global warming. This was partly a result of interaction with environmental groups and a response to the political reality. Eileen Claussen gives some instructive examples for this interesting shift in the US industry sector.[153] Ford Motor Company and Daimler Chrysler announced in 1999 that they were resigning from the GCC, a business NGO that has consistently questioned the science of climate change. A large group of companies became affiliated with the Pew Centre on Global Climate Change, and developed a joint statement that accepts the science of climate change.[154] They have decided to set their own emissions reduction goals. These multinationals also acknowledge the importance of the Kyoto Protocol as a first step of the international community to tackle climate change, and they believe that climate change mitigation and economic growth are not necessarily contradictory terms.[155]

---

p. 31. Other major members of the 'Carbon Club' include the World Business Council for Sustainable Development (WBCSD) and the American Petroleum Institute (API). Giorgetti, op. cit. p. 221, and Oberthür and Ott, op. cit. p. 31.

[150] This sector is represented in the USA primarily by United States Business Council for Sustainable Energy (USBCSE), and in Europe by the European Business Council for a Sustainable Energy Future (e5). See Giorgetti, op. cit. p. 224.

[151] Although they tend to be less active in the negotiating process. See ibid., p. 223.

[152] See Grubb et al., op. cit. pp. 257–258. See also Giorgetti, op. cit. p. 225 (noting the influence that the IPCC Second Assessment Report in 1995 had on the industry's vocal scepticism regarding the scientific uncertainty of climate change).

[153] Claussen, E., Responding to global warming problem: climate change: present and future, *Ecology L.Q.* 27 (2001), p. 1373, at 1375–1377.

[154] These are multinational corporations and household names such as American Electric Power, Boeing, British Petroleum, Amoco, Lockheed Martin, Shell International, Sunoco, Toyota, United Technologies, and Whirlpool. Ibid., p. 1376.

[155] See Statement of the Business Environmental Leadership Council, available at the Pew Center website (www.pewclimate.org/press_room/sub_press_room/1998_press_release/pr_major.cfm). An even more striking example comes from the European continent. A European NGO, Germany's Federation of Chemical Industry (which includes firms like BASF A.G. and Bayer A.G.), has called upon the USA to support the Kyoto Protocol and rejoin the process. See Andrews, E. D., Frustrated Europeans set to battle U.S. on climate, *New York Times*, 16 July 2001.

One might argue, of course, that the measures taken by greenhouse gas-emitting firms are also economically driven: they believe that environmental awareness 'sells', because it contributes to the public image of a firm. Nonetheless, it is important that an argumentative discourse is taking place, even by egoistic actors. Moreover, the civilising effect that a public discourse has on actors makes it almost impossible to raise selfish arguments. This is why 'even actors such as profit-seeking multinational corporations must justify their actions on the basis of some common goods or shared values'.[156]

The point is, in short, that while it may have varying degrees of success, civil society has a civilising effect on rational, economically-driven entities as well. These 'entities', let us not forget, are made up of human beings, who are not only themselves socialised in the realm of civil society but within the market settings as well. John Keane reminds us how:

> those who go about their business and do their work chronically draw upon *endogenous* sources of sociability. Their activities are always embedded within civil society interactions that are lubricated by norms like punctuality, trust, honesty, reliability, group commitment and non-violence ... Markets are always and everywhere *human creations embedded in social and political relations.*[157]

To be sure, as Keane concedes, much of the claims against global capitalism are a case in point, for it both nurtures and disorders the institutions of global civil society within which it operates.[158] But the exclusion of market forces from public discourse is not a viable option, since paradoxically, whether we like it or not, our 'lifeworld' could not exist without its so-called colonisers – the forces of the market. Thus, the idea that placing the market outside the category of global civil society would necessarily transform the neo-liberal agenda stands on shaky normative ground.

3. Towards a global solidarity: the promise of discourses

Civil society, let us recall once more, is a project closely related to democracy. A democracy assumes not only the existence of a political authority, but of there being a 'demos' as well. Within nations, the existence of community, however plural it may be, is taken for granted. At the global level, however, the existence of a community becomes an empirical question. But the difficulty is not only that mapping the actual contours of the 'global community' is arguably an impossible task, given the complexity and richness of social interactions at the planetary level. The difficulty is compounded by the fact that normatively

---

[156] Risse, op. cit. p. 22. [157] Keane, op. cit. p. 77 (emphasis in original).
[158] Ibid., p. 82. Keane also finds examples for 'socially embedded market activity' such as corporate philanthropy, which seem anecdotal but prove his case nonetheless; that it is empirically impossible to divide the market neatly from civil society. Ibid., pp. 78–80.

speaking, 'society' or 'community' are contested concepts in themselves. Any empirical finding would still need to face the challenge of defining 'what counts as a community', or in other words, how socially integrated does a group of persons need to be in order to be considered a community. These questions are not new, of course. They have been the topic of numerous books and articles by scholars across disciplines for many years, and addressing them here thoroughly is, of course, not a possibility. I will instead call attention to two distinctions, recount a sceptic position, and suggest where I see the promise.

The forerunners of the sociological approach in IR theory were the 'English School' scholars, who viewed the international society as a 'true society' sharing a common culture.[159] Hedley Bull has written that:

> a society of states (or international society) exists when a group of states, conscious of certain common interests and common values, form a society in the sense that they conceive themselves to be bound by a common set of rules in their relations with one another, and share in the working of common institutions.[160]

This state-centric view of the international system may be explained by the limited scope of Bull's enquiry. His concern was how to 'mitigate the inevitable conflicts that would arise from the existence of a multiplicity of sovereignties'.[161]

In contrast to this view stands the Grotian conception of international society, which Bull characterised as solidarist.[162] 'The members of the international society in the view of Grotius are not merely states or the rulers of states but include groups other than states and, indeed, individual humans beings'.[163] In other words, this is a vision of a world society, which rests on common interests and identities held by individuals across the globe.

Bull was initially sceptical of this ambitious version of international society and believed that in the twentieth century, the Grotian conception has proved premature'.[164] But as Alderson and Hurrell show, in his later writings he seemed to have accepted that the state-centric conception is no longer adequate in the changing reality of growing economic and environmental interdependence, and in view of the emerging 'cosmopolitan moral consciousness'.[165] Globalising

---

[159] Wight, G. and Porter, B. (eds.), *International theory: three traditions*, London (Leicester University Press) 1991, p. 39.

[160] Bull, H., *The anarchical society: a study of order in world politics*, New York (Columbia University Press) 1977, p. 13.

[161] Ibid, p. 8.

[162] Bull, H., The Grotian conception of international society (1966), reprinted in Bull, H., Kingsbury, B., and Roberts, A. (eds.), *Hugo Grotius and international relations*, Oxford (Clarendon Press) 1990, p. 65.

[163] Ibid., p. 83.   [164] Ibid., p. 117.

[165] Alderson, K. and Hurrell, A. (eds.), *Hedley Bull on international society*, London (McMillan) 2000, pp. 11–14.

civil society in the sense proposed by this chapter, then, would only be possible under a human-centred view of the international society.

At the level of rhetoric, it appears that the state-centred view of the international system is gradually being discarded in much of international parlance,[166] as well as in liberal IL and IR scholarship, in favour of a frequent reference to the 'international community' broadly defined.[167] But to the extent that liberal scholars value normative individuality and consider it to be the basis for the legitimacy of international law, they see its manifestation mostly within the boundaries of states.[168] Few are the scholars who espouse a truly human-centred approach when conceptualising the international system. Richard Falk, for example, believes we are now in a 'Grotian moment'.[169] 'The prime world order imperative', he writes, 'is ecological in the broadest sense of interdependence amid scarcity'.[170] But the state system, which prevailed since the Peace of Westphalia, has proven inadequate to deal with the problems facing humankind in the era of globalisation. 'Under these circumstances, a new normative order will almost certainly not evolve from the primary agency of the state'. Falk claims that two main features mark this paradigm shift: increased central guidance and increased roles for 'non-territorial' actors in the international realm, in the form of grass-root organisations.[171]

But the question remains: What level of social integration is required so that global civil society could fulfil its potential as a democratising force? A helpful distinction used in IL literature is the one between an 'international *society*' and an 'international *community*'.[172] It contrasts a functional vision of

---

[166] See Kwakwa, E., The international community, international law, and the United States: three in one, two against one, or one and the same?, in Byres, M., and Nolte, G. (eds.), *United States hegemony and the foundations of international law*, Cambridge (Cambridge University Press) 2003, p. 25.

[167] See Franck, T. M., *The power of legitimacy among nations*, New York (Oxford University Press) 1990 and Franck, T. M., *Fairness in international law and institutions*, Oxford (Clarendon Press) 1995. For a discussion of Franck's conception of 'international community', see Kritsotis, D., Imagining the international community, *Eur. J. Int'l L.* 13 (2002), p. 961. See also Tesòn, F. R., *A philosophy of international law*, Boulder, Colo. (Westview Press) 1998; Slaughter, A. M., International law in a world of liberal states, *Eur. J. Int'l L.* 6 (1995), p. 503.

[168] For this critique see Alkoby, op. cit. pp. 50–64. For a similar argument see Paulus, A., The influence of the United States on the concept of 'international community', in Byres and Nolte, op. cit. p. 57 (who argues, more generally, that while US IL scholars espouse the notion of an international community made up of individuals, they centre their attention on the spread of liberal values rather then global institutional design).

[169] Falk, R., The Grotian moment: unfulfilled promise, harmless fantasy, missed opportunity?, *Int'l Insights* 13 (1997), p. 3.

[170] Falk, R., *Revitalizing international law*, Ames (Iowa University Press) 1989, p. 26.

[171] Ibid., p. 3, and see Falk and Strauss, op. cit.

[172] See Simma, B. and Paulus, A., The 'international community': facing the challenge of globalisation, *Eur. J. Int'l L.* 9 (1998), p. 266.

the global system (individualist, if you may) against a more communitarian one. In explaining the two ways in which an international society/community may come into existence, Barry Buzan uses the distinction drawn by the German sociologist Ferdinand Tönnies between a 'civilisational model' (*Gemeinschaft*) – a community involving historical bonds of common sentiments, experience, and identity, and a 'functional model' (*Gesellschaft*) – society as a rational long-term construction process, based on contractual relations.[173] A human-centred approach is linked, of course, to the civilisational model, since including individuals and groups in an imagined global *Gemeinschaft* implies that it would involve more than a coordinating function; it would require a subjective feeling of commonality.

But can this vision of common values be attained at the global level? Post-modernists answer this question with a resounding 'no'. As Andreas Paulus notes, for post-modernists, '"community" may be used as an ideological construct for the maintenance of structures of power, excluding the "other", the marginal, the different. Postmodernists criticize both the social-democratic enthusiasm for new international bureaucracies and the neoliberal reliance on liberal values.'[174]

Similarly, the rivals of global civil society consider it to be a Eurocentric concept. According to these critics, '"civil society" is not just a geographically specific concept with pseudo-universal pretensions; it also has a strong elective affinity with "the West", and even potentially plays the role of an agent of Western power and influence in the world'.[175] But as Mary Kaldor rightly points out, the fact that civil society was invented in Europe and that its development was associated with conquest, domination, and exploitation still does not negate its potential.[176] Furthermore, as stressed throughout this chapter, conceptualising the project of global civil society is a great challenge, especially because it

---

[173] Buzan, op. cit. p. 333.
[174] Paulus, op. cit. p. 75. For an example of this critique in IL scholarship, see Kennedy, D., The disciplines of international law and policy, *Leiden J. Int'l L.* 12 (1999), p. 9. For other critiques see Paulus' excellent exposition in Paulus, A., International law after postmodernity, *Leiden J. Int'l L.* 14 (2001), p. 727.
[175] See Keane, op. cit. p. 29. These critics include Chatterjee, P., On civil and political society in post-colonial democracies, in Kaviraj, S. and Khilnani, S., *Civil society: history and possibilities*, Cambridge (Cambridge University Press) 2001, p. 172, and Mamdani, M., *Citizen and subject: contemporary Africa and the legacy of late colonialism*, Princeton (Princeton University Press) 1996. See also Gellner, E., *Conditions of liberty: civil society and its rivals*, London (Hamish Hamilton) 1994 (recounting the Eurocentric critique with a sympathetic view to civil society, albeit a rather pessimistic one), and Brown, C., Cosmopolitanism, world citizenship and global civil society, in Caney, S. and Jones, P. (eds.), *Human rights and global diversity*, London/Portland (Frank Cass) 2001, p. 7 (arguing that while it might make sense to think of an emergent North Atlantic civil society, the extension of the metaphor to global civil society is profoundly misleading).
[176] Kaldor, op. cit. p. 44.

requires a critical examination of existing models and testing them against the global realities rather than automatically importing them. In this sense, the post-modernist critique is right in claiming that to import a neo-liberal model of civil society to the global level is to deny the diversity and plurality of world societies. Since we are discussing an ideal-type, however, such blind importation can and should be avoided.

A discursive approach to international politics could be the way to avoid the dilemma that the controversy between the liberal and the post-modernist approaches raise. As mentioned earlier, Habermas understands discursive action not as a deliberative process in which citizens seek to achieve the community's predefined shared values. The meta-norms, or the preconditions for ideal argumentative speech, are the only regulative principles that guide participants when they debate on which values and principles ought to be institutionalised as common norms. When thinking of a heterogeneous, pluralist, society (or societies, in the global context), this notion of a procedural discursive framework with no culture-specific conceptions of the 'good life' seems especially attractive.

But this supposedly universal applicability of communicative action as a basis for democratic legitimacy is vulnerable to some objections. As Kenneth Baynes points out, Habermas does not claim that a healthy polity can be maintained without any recourse to civic virtues. Habermas has argued that the institutional infrastructure of civil society must be complemented by 'liberal political culture' and the 'supportive spirit of consonant background of legally noncoercible motives and attitudes of a citizenry oriented toward the common good'.[177] As this typical abstract language suggests, Habermas does not say much about the kind of civic virtues he has in mind. He describes his approach as 'constitutional patriotism', and as Baynes shows, one can find scattered references that he has made to terms such as civility, fairness, toleration, and reasonableness.[178] Baynes' discussion of the possible meanings of these terms in the context of liberal polities is illuminating, but I am more interested in the 'thinner' version that Cohen and Arato provide in their response to Habermas' critics, with a view to 'universalising' communicative action. They borrow from Habermas the notions of solidarity and identity, and explore how the two are linked. Communicative action, as Habermas sees it, is the process where individual as well as collective identities are constructed. Human beings:

> acquire an individual identity only as members of a collective, and simultaneously, as it were, they acquire group identity... To be sure, both collective and individual identities established through socialization processes need to be reaffirmed, since they require ongoing mutual recognition and are continuously open to challenge and change.[179]

---
[177] Baynes, op. cit. pp. 134–135 (quoting Habermas, op. cit. p. 499).
[178] Ibid., p. 135.   [179] Cohen and Arato, op. cit. pp. 377–378.

Building and maintaining collective identities, then, require *solidarity* among individuals as members of a community in which they are socialised.[180] Solidarity, argue Cohen and Arato, is no more than 'the acceptance of the other as an other, as one who must be accorded the same chance to articulate identity needs and arguments as one would like oneself'.[181] The preexistence of a certain form of collective identity is what enables one to imagine oneself in the place of the other. But the ability to put oneself in the place of the other as required by this notion of solidarity is possible in a *single society*, with shared lifeworld. Could it be argued that there exists a *global* single society with a shared lifeworld as well?

When two societies share the same institutionalised discourse and principles of democratic legitimacy, a similar solidarity can be found between them. For cultures who do not have an institutionalised discourse or rights, 'we must still show respect if not solidarity', claim Cohen and Arato.[182] Nonetheless, solidarity across political cultures can still be conceivable in the context of universal human rights (even if rights cannot be secured in a given polity, we may feel solidarity with those who invoke them).[183] Furthermore, when a discourse across cultures takes place, 'the principles of rational dialogue among equals represent the only normatively acceptable form of conflict resolution'.[184] In other words, the procedural model of communicative action, which prescribes the ideal *formal* requirements for developing a consensus (rather than prescribing what that consensus ought to be) is the only way of developing cross-cultural solidarity that would open the possibility of arriving at common norms. This is perhaps the most valuable insight that the current discourse on civil society can offer, and any attempt at expanding civil society in a universal direction ought to consider its potential advantages.

Some years after Cohen and Arato commented on the possibility of globalising civil society, Habermas himself further developed this notion of 'cosmopolitan solidarity'.[185] Responding to ideas of cosmopolitan democracy, he first denies the possibility of a world polity. Any political community that wants to understand itself as a democracy, he argues, must be able to distinguish between members and non-members. In other words, there cannot be a 'we' feeling in the absence of 'them'. A world state would necessarily be all-inclusive, and unable to develop a self-referential collective identity. The existing substantive framework for a global community may only build on the existing core of universal human rights, and that would not be enough for a development of true *civic* solidarity.[186]

---

[180] Ibid., p. 378.   [181] Ibid., p. 383.   [182] Ibid., p. 384.
[183] Ibid.   [184] Ibid., pp. 384–385.
[185] Habermas, J., *Postnational constellation*, Cambridge (Polity Press) 2001.
[186] Ibid., p. 107, and see also at 53–57.

But Habermas is also somewhat optimistic about the ability to develop international discourses, and the role that both international norms and TNAs may play in them: 'As normative framing conditions delimit the choice of rhetorical strategies, they effectively structure negotiations just as much as the influence of "epistemic communities".'[187] These 'weak forms of legitimation' would help develop a cosmopolitan solidarity that is still lacking. Such solidarity would be weaker and less binding than civic solidarity that can only develop in nation states, but it is nonetheless capable of generating collective will formation.[188] Loyal to his deep suspicion of the potential for socialising governments, Habermas adds that the first addressees for this project of cosmopolitan solidarity are not governments, but 'the active members of civil society that stretches beyond national borders'.[189]

The development of principles of international environmental law since the 1972 Stockholm Declaration is arguably a reason to be further optimistic about the emergence of a global solidarity.[190] These principles serve as 'normative framing conditions' for international discourses on environmental matters. The 'no harm' principle, for example, holds that states must ensure that activities within their jurisdiction will not cause damage to the environment of other states. The underlying rationale for this principle is not only the need to protect the global environment, but also the vision of mutual dependability of states.[191]

Another such solidarity-based norm is the principle of 'common but differentiated responsibilities', according to which higher standards of conduct are set for developed countries 'on the grounds that they have both contributed most to causing problems such as ozone depletion and climate change and that

---

[187] Ibid., p. 109.   [188] Ibid., p. 111.   [189] Ibid., p. 57.
[190] For an argument that solidarity is now a fundamental principle of international law, see Macdonald, R. St. J., Solidarity in the practice and discourse of public international law, *Pace Int'l L. Rev.* 8 (1996), p. 259 (providing examples from international economic law and international environmental law to show how solidarity 'reflects and reinforces the broader idea of a world community of interdependent states' at 259).
[191] Principle 21 of the Stockholm Declaration, later stated again in Principle 2 of the Rio Declaration, which now reflects customary law as confirmed by the International Court of Justice in the 1996 Advisory Opinion on the Legality of the Threat or Use of Nuclear Weapons 35 I.L.M. (1996) 809. See Sands, P., *Principles of international environmental law*, Cambridge (Cambridge University Press) 2nd edn. 2003, pp. 235–236. Louis Sohn, in his account of the negotiating history of the Stockholm Declaration and Principle 21 in particular, stated: 'The development of the new notion that international law should no longer be purely an interstate system but should bring both individuals and international organisations into the picture, and the impact of the other modern idea – that international law should have much more social content and should become an instrument of distributive justice – have led to a new way of expressing the basic rules of international law . . . conveying the feeling of the international community that the time has come to attend to certain common tasks through common means and in accordance with generally agreed guidelines': Sohn, L. B., The Stockholm Declaration on the Human Environment, *Harv. Int'l L. J.* 14 (1973), p. 423, at 513–514.

they also possess greater capacity to respond than is usually available to developing states'.[192] This principle has taken root to the extent that the entire design of several key international environmental agreements in built upon it.[193] It reflects 'the spirit of global partnership' towards the achievement of sustainable development, as articulated in Principle 7 of the Rio Declaration.[194]

V. Conclusion

The search for conceptual clarity thus leaves us with a paradox: for a global civil society to exist and fulfil its potential as a democratising force (in the meaningful, deliberative sense), there needs to be global solidarity (and most observers would agree it is still lacking). Global solidarity, in turn, can only evolve out of genuinely deliberative interaction between all the affected actors, civil society included. But this paradox is easily resolved when the project of global civil society is viewed as an ongoing process. Civil society is not created in a moment; you may say it is 'becoming'. From an institutional design perspective, policy-makers need to realise that it will continue to 'become' from 'below', for all the reasons recounted in this chapter. A policy-maker's responsibility, however, is to help civil society 'become' from 'above', by opening up the channels for meaningful deliberation in institutional settings.

To conclude, even if the answer to the question 'Is there a global civil society?' may be empirically contested, any observer of world politics, in the environmental field in particular, would have to admit that it is 'becoming'. Should civil society be globalised? Yes, and it could definitely have a 'greening effect' on international law. But while there is much to learn from the theorising and history of the concept in territorially bound societies, an ideal-type global civil society may look quite different than its (Western) domestic counterpart. Finding complete conceptual clarity just might be an impossible task; in a complex world, theoretic complexity cannot be avoided, and perhaps *should* not. Recalling Michael Walzer's sage words: 'I have no desire for simplicity, since a world that theory could fully grasp and neatly explain would not, I suspect, be a pleasant place'.[195]

---

[192] Birnie, P. and Boyle, A., *International law and the environment*, Oxford (Oxford University Press) 2nd edn 2002, p. 101.

[193] A few examples are the Montreal Protocol, the Biological Diversity Convention, and the Climate Change Convention (all cited in n. 35 above). For a detailed discussion on global solidarity as a key element of the 'common but differentiated principle', see Birnie and Boyle, op. cit. pp. 100–104.

[194] See French, D., Developing states and international environmental law: the importance of differentiated responsibilities, *Int'l and Comp. L.Q.* 49 (2000), p. 35, at 55–56.

[195] Walzer, op. cit. p. 8.

PART III

Self-regulation of industry and the law

6

Private authority, global governance, and the law
The case of environmental self-regulation in multinational enterprises

MARTIN HERBERG

I. Environmental protection in multinational enterprises: a dilemma of globalisation

The discussion about corporate governance in multinational enterprises refers to a social problematic of ground-breaking historical significance, which characterises the contemporary stage of globalisation in general. This problematic consists in the tension of parallel processes of ever-increasing economic interweaving and a dynamic of legal, cultural, and technological homogenisation on the one hand, as well as a series of countervailing developments, disintegrative tendencies, and increasingly porous legal and political structures on the other.[1] As far as the multinationals are concerned, they are perceived by the Third World as an indispensable agent of modernisation, as promoters of global economic integration, and as representatives of the modern technological universe, yet at the same time economic expansion can lead to the result that developing countries are played off against each other, that their steering capacity will be ever more limited, and that existing regulatory gaps and low standards will be used by enterprises to externalise costs and negative outcomes

---

This chapter presents some of the results from the research project Environmental Double Standards concerning Foreign Direct Investment in Developing Countries, conducted from 2000 until 2003 at the Bremen Research Center for European Environmental Law (Forschungsstelle für Europäisches Umweltrecht, FEU). Important ideas came from Prof. Gerd Winter, Dr. Katja Böttger, ass. jur. Olaf Dilling, ass. jur. Carola Glinski and many other members of the institute. The text was translated in collaboration with Eric Allen Engle, D.E.A., LL.M.Eur., University of Bremen.

[1] In the present discussion about globalisation, most contributions either focus on the aspects of homogenisation, emphasising the increasing chances for economic growth, widespread modernisation, and international coordination, or on the contrasting aspects of heterogenisation – describing globalisation, roughly speaking, as the most destructive force of our epoch. For an attempt to overcome this one-sidedness in each of these approaches, see Robertson, R., *Globalization: social theory and global culture*, London (Sage) 1992.

to a great extent.[2] The legal construction of the independently managed subsidiary can be strategically employed to hide behind the sovereignty of the host state and to immunise the parent enterprise against possible legal risks and consequences of damages.

In the absence of a 'world state', 'world government', or international institutions empowered to define and realise binding minimum standards directly addressed to non-state actors, the question arises whether the existing need of governance can be satisfied, at least in part, through reflexive governance mechanisms, patterns of 'regulated self-regulation' on the global level, and new ways of connecting the corporate world and the state-centric world: briefly, through manifestations of what is currently discussed under the catchword 'global governance'.[3] It is often stated in the literature that the conception of appropriate problem-solving mechanisms on the global scale requires as a precondition well-founded empirical insights into the structures of private self-regulation, but that goal is only seldom reached: in political science, private actors appear only rarely as (semi-)autonomous rule-makers;[4] instead, they are regarded primarily in the role of participants in the framework of (inter)state initiatives. In the economic sciences, empirical questions such as this are usually neglected in favour of formal models and theoretical reflections, and sociology is also far from that position where it could contribute seriously to the contemporary global governance questions because its research practices are too often obviously bound to the old coordinates of the nation state.

Environmental protection concerning foreign direct investment is a policy field which bears good chances of revealing some of the new private forms of corporate self-regulation, since in many multinational enterprises a fundamental change of perspective has taken place: because of the frequency of user errors, mistakes, accidents, damages, and environmental scandals in the foreign subsidiaries, many enterprises have given up on their old, rather decentralised, model of leadership. Instead, they have instituted special organs at the corporate headquarters, usually under the title 'Corporate Representative (*Konzernbeauftragter*) for Safety, Health and Environment'. These managers

---

[2] 'The logic of existing law, based as it is on the concept of the single unit enterprise, fails to grasp the realities of interdependence between affiliated enterprises in the national or multinational group ... Significant legal and practical obstacles remain for the effective protection of those who make claims against multinational enterprises': Muchlinski, P., *Multinational enterprises and the law*, Oxford (Oxford University Press) 1999, p. 339.

[3] Compare Rosenau, J. N., *Along the domestic-foreign frontier: exploring governance in a turbulent world*, Cambridge (Cambridge University Press) 1997; Zürn, M., Das Projekt 'Komplexes Weltregieren': Wozu Wissenschaft von den Internationalen Beziehungen?, in Leggewie, C. (ed.), *Wozu Politikwissenschaft? Über das Neue in der Politik*, Darmstadt (WBG) 1994, p. 77.

[4] As cornerstones of the recent departure towards this direction, see Hall, R. B. and Biersteker, T. J. (eds.), *The emergence of private authority in global governance*, Cambridge (Cambrige University Press) 2002; Cutler, C. A., *Private power and global authority: transnational merchant law in the global political economy*, Cambridge (Cambridge University Press) 2003.

are assigned the tasks of developing a fixed stock of internal environmental and safety standards and constantly to develop them further, to reveal possible weaknesses in the operational units, to correct these deficiencies, and regularly to inform the corporate leadership about the overall situation in the individual subsidiaries.[5]

Apparently, top managers in the home countries have recognised that it is not sufficient to limit the headquarters' function to the role of a technical consultant or provider of technical expertise. Should further accidents in the foreign establishments be avoided, appropriate mechanisms of surveillance and influence must be installed. These phenomena refer to a process of organisational learning, which appears to have escaped the notice of most authors engaged with questions of transnational environmental management, although this process takes on a central significance in the self-definition and the self-perception of the newly-created internal steering departments:

Interviewer: Can you describe with a little more precision the particular difficulties in running an existing plant? Why is this so much more problematic than the conceptualisation of a new factory?

Interviewee: When creating the conception of a new plant you make active decisions. You have a question, I need that, you decide this, build that – and that is in principle very logical. When you run a plant however, then you don't even notice that you need decisions to be made somewhere. And then the decision is made by non-decision. Some things just won't get done – and eventually that totally screws up the entire plant (Interview, 30 June 2000).

Environmental managers in the countries of origin describe the situation in the foreign establishments as a permanent source of dangers and risks, the minimisation of which demands constant efforts. Enterprises which are not interested in an exploitation of the regulatory gaps between North and South, which are more concerned with sustaining an acceptable and stable level of protection, are faced with particular challenges by the existing national differences and developmental deficits. It is a basic rule of transnational environmental management that the technologies in service, even when not always at the cutting edge of technology, must demonstrate a reasonable degree of development. In the chemical sector the basic technical outfitting of the overseas plants is almost always drafted by professionals at the home base, which is known as

---

[5] The old, decentralised model expresses itself clearly in the argument which Union Carbide brought up after the catastrophe of Bhopal (the biggest accident in the history of the chemical industry) – as a supporter of the 'steering at arm's length' model, one did not have any influence over the foreign subsidiaries. There are many indications that a company today in a similar situation would be unable to raise a justification like this in order to exculpate itself. See Rublack, S., *Der grenzüberschreitende Transfer von Umweltrisiken im Völkerrecht*, Baden-Baden (Nomos) 1993, p. 104.

'global engineering'. However everything which serves a certain protective function can be handled in a way which in fact undermines these functions.[6] Errors slip into the process but are not discovered and only receive attention once the damage has already been done. In the description of the interviewee, the parent company cannot rely on the argument that at the time of plant installation, the technical preventative measures were in an orderly state. The option to insist on the operational and legal independence of the subsidiaries would be equivalent to an utterly irrational disavowal of responsibility ('the decision is made by decision') – an eventuality which apparently does not represent the normal case and which is to be avoided by means of regular surveillance and control over the corporate subdivisions.

The empirical reconstruction of those transboundary forms of governance within an analytic framework, including questions of effectivity, normative anchoring, and the driving forces behind these arrangements, is the aim of the following considerations. As in all analyses of organisational learning, it is desirable here first to sketch the set of problems to which the organisational structures must be properly tailored to fulfil their task. What are the systematic causes of the fact that the application of modern production processes under the conditions found in developing countries lead to greater dangers, additional risks, and unanticipated damages? One important explanation of the causes of these dangers is the incomplete or even failed modernisation of the legal and administrative structures in those countries. Often, there is an absence of concrete standards and limits through which the environmental law texts would be implementable. Where such standards exist, they often do not aim high enough. In many cases there is even a lack of particular laws for the separate fields of regulation like problems of waste water, air pollution, or pollution of the soil. Insofar as legal regulations exist, these are often annulled by a variety of factors such as missing competencies on the part of the authorities, ubiquitous enforcement deficits, political patronage, the absence of independent courts, and many other structural deformations.[7] The fact that many serious

---

[6] In some contributions, this aspect is strikingly captured by the concept 'user gap'. It refers to the particular susceptibility of modern technologies to service errors, which requires certain organisational counter-measures, since such errors cannot simply be eliminated through the development of user-friendly or fail-safe systems. See Jasanoff, S., Introduction, in Jasanoff, S. (ed.), *Learning from disaster: Risk management after Bhopal*, Philadelphia (University of Pennsylvania Press) 1994, p. 9.

[7] For an overview of environmental law and policy in the Third World see Desai, U. (ed.), *Ecological policy and politics in developing countries*, New York (State University Press) 1998; Edmonds, R. L. (ed.), *Managing the Chinese environment*, Oxford (Oxford Universiy Press) 2000; Lyska, B., *Umweltpolitik in Indien*, Aachen (Alano) 1991. Regarding the existing regulatory gaps and their persistence, it is difficult to understand how some authors can speak of a worldwide diffusion of Western environmental standards as the 'bright side' of globalisation. But see Weidner, H. and Jänicke, M., Konvergenz umweltpolitischer Regulierungsmuster durch Globalisierung?, in *WZB-Jahrb.* (2001), p. 294.

environmental damages in the Third World are legally permissible and the high rate of legal impunity – in many regions less than half of the firms hold the legally required permissions and licences[8] – create a climate which heavily reduces the motivation of the individual firm to apply more diligence than the average of the local firms.

Furthermore, the state in the Third World is often unable to present basic infrastructural preconditions such as public dumps and waste treatment centres in sufficient numbers necessary for industrial environmental management. That leads to a dramatic proliferation of irregular dumps and also to an extreme waste load on surface and subsurface waters.[9] Another factor for the industrially conditioned environmental problems of the Third World lies in the limited availability of up-to-date environmental technologies on the local markets, and also a lack of the necessary knowhow and appropriate machinery, materials, and spare parts. A final aspect of the problem, which is both the least concrete factor and presumably the most important of all, is the particular lack of environmental consciousness in the population: as far as ecological demands play a role in the cultural perception of the developing countries, protection of wildlife and nature dominate while the risks posed by pollutants resulting from industrial production are hardly noticed. This perceptual shortcoming is also clearly recognisable in the legislative structure of these countries.

If the internal corporate governance mechanisms are intended to respond to these problems, internal monitoring and control cannot simply rely on the prevailing legal standards of the host country with all their gaps and deficiencies. Instead, an independent stock of organisational and technological standards has to be developed and implemented company-wide. Standards are required that guarantee a single minimum level of environmental protection and safety in all the subsidiaries and which are suited for the particular difficulties predominating in less developed countries. Thus, self-regulation in multinational enterprises does not mean, despite some literature to the contrary, initiating selective ecological improvements or conducting some exemplary activities in individual parts of the corporate group (e.g., 'best practices'),[10] self-regulation implies the implementation of appropriate minimum standards on a broad front, and that task cannot be accomplished without the necessary amount of precision, scrutiny, and a certain degree of intervention.

---

[8] For the example of the situation in Latin America, see Kürzinger, E. *et al.*, *Umweltpolitik in Mexiko*, Berlin (Deutsches Institut für Entwicklungspolitik) 1990, p. 83.

[9] For example, in the ten water purification plants of Mexico City, only 5% of accumulated waste water is treated. See Kürzinger, op.cit. p. 66.

[10] See the contributions in Fichter, K. and Schneidewind, U. (eds.), *Umweltschutz im globalen Wettbewerb*, Heidelberg (Springer) 2000; as well as Conrad, J. (ed.), *Environmental management in European companies: success stories and evaluation*, Amsterdam (Gordon & Breach) 1998.

Another set of problems, which is additionally accentuated by the geographical distance between the parent company and its subsidiaries, is the latency of many environmental and safety problems, the danger of cover-ups of forbidden practices, and the opacity and subtlety in the diffusion of chemical pollution. Many damaging practices such as illegal dumping of toxic waste are almost impossible to trace back to the polluter. The use of cheap, inadequate materials is often not visible to the naked eye, and also procrastination as to necessary renovation or maintenance can go long undiscovered. For this reason, if the internal and company-wide control systems are to be effective, it is not sufficient to rely on any form of standardised and quantitative data-gathering such as emission values, energy consumption, or the volume of waste in the various subunits. Although such surveys are common practice in many multinationals today, the corporate representatives themselves admit the superficiality and limited informational power of these instruments – one could only identify breaches and excess emissions which are going 'far too far and which are ten times higher than normal', as was stated in one of the interviews.

In order to develop a reliable and independent database and to keep control over the subsidiaries, multinationals are compelled to conduct regular checks and audits in the field, since serious problems such as leaks, errors in construction, or the disrespect of basic safety rules might be hidden even from the eyes of the local foremen and managers. In the past, a significant amount of mistakes, accidents and several variations of irrational and dysfunctional behaviour took place at the foreign operation units. Many of those mistakes in running and maintaining the plants are characterised by the circumstance that they could not be the result of economic calculation or an overeager desire to save costs but rather were the result of negligence, gaps in the internal structure of competencies, and serious organisational deformations. Accordingly, they can be discovered and corrected only on the basis of specialised methods of monitoring and influence. The insight into the extent of such irrationalities and erroneous practices created, corresponding to the thesis of the following reflections, a collective field of experiences (in German: *kollektiver Erfahrungsraum*), in which the question of the relationship between parent companies and their subsidiaries had to be entirely reconsidered. The internal, cross-border regulatory systems (in German: *transnationale Regulative*) of many multinational enterprises arose in reaction to the practical failure of the old decentralised model.

II. Methodological notes: some problems of empirical research on multinationals

The following reflections are limited to multinational enterprises of a single economic sector, namely the chemical industry, and within that sector, they are restricted to companies of only one country of origin, namely Germany.

This is because, first, the chemical industry shows a degree of integration in the world economy which is far above the average of the whole industrial sector. In the German chemical branch, the flow of capital to foreign production centres has long exceeded the investment into the stocks at the German home country base.[11] Enterprises such as Bayer, BASF, Beiersdorf, Celanese, Degussa, Henkel, Merck and Wacker today occupy, in addition to their factories in other OECD countries, several foreign subsidiaries in the developing countries of Latin America, Asia, Africa, and Eastern Europe, in which the attempt at bridging the gaps, the tensions and the asynchronicities of economic globalisation in a self-regulatory way can be studied in detail, with all its possibilities and limitations. Secondly, the chemical sector is, concerning the environment, still a rather polluting industry, containing a broad spectrum of possible environmental dangers and risks, from 'creeping' poisoning in small doses to the danger of large explosions and serious accidents.

The high level of internationalisation and the enormous potential for damages in the chemical industry taken together have led to a number of voluntary protective measures. Each of the named enterprises regularly publishes individual environmental reports on aspects of minimisation of emissions, on product safety, safety in factories, safe waste disposal, and recycling. The descriptions in the firms' brochures are clearly directed to the creation of appropriate environmental management systems with the function of improving the activities of all foreign establishments of the company. That fact again shows the fruitfulness of the sector as a field of research. Yet the same aspects which appear so promising for the branch as an object of research, can also turn up in a rather disturbing way: while doing research on multinationals, the observer is confronted with several rationalisations, official accounts, and the 'corporate identity' of the firm under research that can transform themselves into a symbolic veil limiting the ability to look into the operative processes and structures of corporate governance with all its problems and problem-solving capacities. The various symbolic artefacts which every experienced manager holds ready for interaction with outsiders cannot necessarily be taken at face value in sociology. That is so even where (or perhaps: especially when) terminology is borrowed from the social or economic sciences. The methodological arsenal of qualitative social research provides numerous measures to take into account the multiple layers of everyday life's reality[12] – roughly speaking it is necessary, besides focusing

---

[11] See Verband der Chemischen Industrie (VCI), *Chemiewirtschaft in Zahlen*, Frankfurt (VCI) 2000, p. 12. From a historical perspective, the giants of the chemical branch are noteworthy in that much of what today is discussed under the rubric 'globalisation' was already laid out at a much earlier point in time. See the contributions in Abelshauser, W. (ed.), *Die BASF: Eine Unternehmensgeschichte*, München (C. H. Beck) 2002.

[12] On the position of interpretative sociology see, primarily, Bohnsack, R., *Rekonstruktive Sozialforschung: Einführung in Methodologie und Praxis qualitativer Forschung*, Opladen (Leske & Budrich) 1991; Oevermann, U. et al., Die Methodologie einer 'Objektiven

on the self-descriptions of the actors, to develop content-rich insights into the practical context on which the statements are grounded and which supplies them with their specific meaning (a task, which, in any event, cannot be mastered with the instruments of the prevailing 'variable'-oriented approaches or any of the decontextualising techniques of standardised social research).

This warning against an uncritical reproduction of ideas and artefacts must not, however, be confused with the view – which is widespread especially throughout research on multinationals – that the task of empirical research should be, primarily, to 'unmask' the subject of research.[13] What is necessary is not an update of the old pseudo-analytical critique on multinationals by means of 'see-through sociology', which permanently 'celebrates itself for identifying the prevailing strategies and forms of symbolic representation and self-positioning in the public, while ignoring the authentic forms of practice, which are expressing themselves in these artefacts, and letting them fall to oblivion'.[14] Rather, a style of research is desirable that principally touches upon the same problems which the practitioners inside the internal corporate task forces are confronted with, a style of research that does not develop the intended abstract concepts before empirical observation has reached a satisfactory degree of saturation. From the perspective of qualitative social research, multinational enterprises, as every other social unit in the world, principally possess the ability to reflect their behaviour before the background of past experiences in order to control it and eventually overcome deformations. So long as the gathered empirical material does not contain compelling indications of structural deformations, the task of reconstruction is a matter of identifying, as precisely as possible, the characteristics of the case as a possible and plausible form of mastering the underlying problems and challenges. The stimulation of content-rich reports and descriptions based on actual experiences during the questioning creates a useful database for the reconstructive analysis in the evaluation phase, which implies that in choosing the relevant interviewees the focus should be on those who themselves are carriers of the praxis to be investigated. In the present case those persons are the corporate representatives

---

Hermeneutik' und ihre allgemeine forschungslogische Bedeutung in den Sozialwissenschaften, in Soeffner, H. (ed.), *Interpretative Verfahren in den Sozial- und Textwissenschaften*, Stuttgart (Metzler) 1979; Schütze, F., *Die Technik des narrativen Interviews in Interaktionsfeldstudien*, Bielefeld (Fakultät für Soziologie) 1977.

[13] The titles of various contributions from the anti-globalisers' position speak for themselves, for example, Corten, D., *When corporations rule the world*, London (Earthscan) 1995; Mitchell, L., *Corporate irresponsibility*, Yale (Yale University Press) 2001; Werner, K. and Weiss, H., *Schwarzbuch Markenfirmen: Die Machenschaften der Weltkonzerne*, Wien/Frankfurt (Deuticke) 2001.

[14] Oevermann, U., Die Methode der Fallrekonstruktion in der Grundlagenforschung sowie in der klinischen und pädagogischen Praxis, in Kraimer, K. (ed.), *Die Fallrekonstruktion: Sinnverstehen in der sozialwissenschaftlichen Forschung*, Frankfurt (Suhrkamp) 2000, p. 58 at 78.

(*Konzernbeauftragte*) for environmental protection and safety in the named enterprises, and their colleagues.

The valid reconstruction of the self-regulatory structures and their specific *modus operandi* necessitates various analytical points of comparison and empirical demarcations (in German: *empirische Gegenhorizonte*):[15] first, a systematic contrast of the self-regulatory structures under research versus the functional logic of other existing or hypothetical forms of governance; secondly, several cross-comparisons between the different enterprises in the sample in order to discover the interfirm differences as well as the similarities and the familiar structures of the entire branch. The approach outlined opens the possibility to appreciate the growing significance of non-state actors in the process of transnational problem-solving and to supply the global governance debate with the well proven, but scarcely used, methodological arsenal of interpretative sociology. Where this is successful, sociology can take on an important function as a provider of new information and independent expertise. Sociology can thereby initiate an increased substantive rationality of future discussions on new governance forms and can inform the various interested parties which degree of self-regulation can and cannot be expected from the enterprises. Finally, the empirical insights into the internal structure of competencies and the factual duties of care inside the companies can also prove themselves to be useful for legal practitioners in the various national or international contexts.

III. The anatomy of corporate governance: private self-regulatory systems (*private Regulative*) as transnational law?

The self-regulatory activities of transnational non-state actors are not only generating various resonances and responses in the dimension of formal legal structures, they also feature a series of similarities and structural analogies to the formal law of the state-centric world.[16] In the course of the expansion and consolidation of translocal networks and fields of interaction, a number of non-state norm-makers and institutionalised forms of dispute settlement, surveillance, and implementation, have developed. These institutions contain a capacity of structuring social action not less effective than the ordering function of classical formal law, as several authors even in legal science are gradually acknowledging. That the existence of such paralegal structures should not lead to an inflationary or completely relativistic use of the concept of law must no longer be justified. Regardless of the differences and conceptual ambiguities in

---

[15] On this concept see Bohnsack, op. cit. p. 41 *et passim*.
[16] See Sousa Santos, B. de, *Toward a new common sense: law, science and politics in the paradigmatic transition*, London (Routledge) 1995; Teubner, G. (ed.), *Global law without a state*, Aldershot (Dartmouth) 1997; Winter, G., *Transnational governance und internationales Recht: Projektbeschreibung im Rahmen des Sonderforschungsbereichs 597 'Staatlichkeit im Wandel'*, Bremen (Universitätsdruck) 2002.

the literature of legal sociology, a basic set of criteria can be given which must be fulfilled in order to mark a given normative system as a 'paralegal order'[17] or as 'quasi-law':

(1) *Internal differentiation.* The various bundles of societal norms and rules can only be sensibly described as (quasi-) law if they display a coherent inner structure, which puts each individual norm in its proper place. Often this will be accompanied by a division of the paralegal system into a level of higher ranking norms and a meshwork of concretising norms which can at all times be modified, which allows the system, with relatively little effort, to adapt itself to new conditions while maintaining its general orientation and identity.

(2) *Effectiveness.* The norms concerned not only define and describe the discourse and the expectancy horizon of their addressees, they must also display a demonstrable causal effect on the activities exercised in the relevant field of praxis.[18] Where the effectiveness of a normative order is clearly disavowed through serious errors of construction or ubiquitous evasive strategies, it is hardly sociologically appropriate to speak of a legal or paralegal system.

(3) *Problem proximity and capacity to learn.* The inner structure of a normative order results, at least in part, from the character of the social problems at hand. Concrete structuring often contains considerable degrees of freedom. However, where the appropriate relation between the normative structure and the problems to be solved is disturbed, this is most often directly notable as the necessity to restructure the entire apparatus.

(4) *Normative anchoring.* Just as with the state's laws, informal orders must have at their disposal stable foundations of validity in order to be convincing and durable. The binding power of a given normative system partly results from the basic substantive necessities in the field of action, partly it is based on various forms of general exercise and common practice. The result is that the individual actor can no longer ignore them or argue them to be just voluntary.

(5) *Specialised organs.* Additionally, we can only speak of a (para)legal order when clear-cut competencies have emerged which are especially made to supervise the implementation of the norms and, when ambivalences and normative dissonance occur, to make binding decisions and to intervene

---

[17] Merry, S. E., Anthropology, law, and transnational processes, *Annu. Rev. Anthro.* 21 (1992), pp. 357–377.

[18] In the classic definition of Max Weber, the object of legal sociology is 'what is factually happening inside a given community for the reason that the possibility exists that the participating persons subjectively consider certain orders valid and thus practically act, orienteering their individual actions around them': Weber, M., *Wirtschaft und Gesellschaft*, Tübingen (Mohr) 5th edn 1980, p. 181.

in the case of violations. This idea has already been mentioned by Weber ('coercive apparatus', in German: *Erzwingungsstab*)[19] and it is thanks to Luhmann that we have the concise formula 'differentiation of particular roles'.[20]

In the close interplay between the empirical material on corporate governance in the chemical branch and the contemporary debate on economic, legal, and political globalisation, an analytical concept was generated in which the above mentioned aspects are conceptually summarised and which seems to be adequate to serve as a guide for further research on the emergence of private governance structures on the global scale, namely the concept of 'transnational self-regulatory systems' (in German: *transnationale Regulative*). These paralegal regulatory orders are relatively long-lasting and stable. At the same time, however, they are also adaptable, dynamic, multilevel systems of norms and rules which allow non-state norm-makers to present solutions to politically relevant problems in separate fields of action. They represent systems of norms, which meet a sufficient degree of acceptance by their addressees to become factually effective. At the same time they can, if necessary, be enforced even against reluctance. This also implies that implementation will be supervised and accompanied by specialised organs intentionally created for this function.[21] Insofar as economic actors make use of their private autonomy in order voluntarily to undertake tasks which are in the public interest but not explicitly required by the formal legal order, the mechanisms called *transnationale Regulative* (self-regulatory systems) represent an important supplement to the state-created legal norms.

For the empirical reconstruction of these regulatory systems, it is desirable to decode the different elements and levels of norms step by step, carefully moving from the 'outer' layers to the 'inner' content. The outside layer consists of the various statements, announcements, and promises addressing a broader public (in the case here, enterprise guidelines and codes of conduct) through

---

[19] Ibid., p. 17 and passim.
[20] Luhmann, N., *Rechtssoziologie*, Wiesbaden (VS Verlag für Sozialwissenschaften) 1987, p. 79.
[21] Their multilevel structure, problem proximity, and capacity to learn are all characteristics, which transnational self-regulatory structures (*transnationale Regulative*) – as products of the business world – share with international regimes, the latter being products of the state-centric world. Unlike the various international conventions ('regimes') with their various flanking measures, transnational self-regulatory structures show several elements of direct, sometimes even authoritarian intervention, and various procedures for corrective intervention. This is an important reason for the introduction of a separate analytic concept tightly connected with the self-governance of transnational non-state actors and not merely to speak of 'private regimes', such as Haufler, V., Crossing the boundary between public and private: international regimes and non-state actors, in Rittberger, V. and Mayer, P. (eds.), *Regime theory and international relations*, Oxford (Oxford University Press) 1993, p. 94.

which the informal duties, tasks, and rules of diligence receive an additional binding power.[22] The connection between this external and highly symbolic layer and the normative and organisational structures inside the companies might be rather loose, but in their external presentation enterprises constitute themselves – to address only one of the various sociological implications of private codes of conduct – as relatively coherent units of action. They can present themselves to the public as environmentally conscious and integrated actors because, internally, they have company-wide effective environmental management mechanisms at their disposition. The challenge for sociological analysis is to determine precisely whether and how enterprises manage, on the basis of everyday life's language, to establish stable structures of expectations, and which concrete external claims are created and covered by the relevant texts. At the same time, sociological analysis provides an important toolbox for the juridical practitioner who is concerned with the legal evaluation of the prevailing codes of conduct. Even when the documents lack direct legally binding effect, they can, in certain cases, be mobilised to underpin the demands and claims of external interested parties. The clearest example of this is when the recipient of a self-binding statement, as a consequence of his legitimate trust in the announced activities, is affected by losses or damages.[23]

Penetrating further into the inner context of the arrangements called *transnationale Regulative*, the interpreter will discover a layer of internal checks, audits, and correction mechanisms. These are the operative basis of private self-regulation and fulfil the function of equipping the company's headquarters with sufficient options to influence the activities of the foreign subsidiaries. Here, one is in the dimension of the above-mentioned specialised organs, professional roles, and elements of Weber's 'coercive apparatus' for the implementation of existing norms. The outlined model corresponds with the sociological convention, that the term 'implementation' should be reserved for situations where 'deviant behaviour will trigger particular activities which serve the preservation of law and the restoration of a permissible and norm-compatible state of affairs'.[24] Transnational self-regulatory systems establish a border between admissible and inadmissible practices and this border must be protected from violations if the normative order is not to be given up or left to the addressees'

---

[22] See Köpke, R. and Röhr, W., *Codes of conduct: Verhaltensnormen für Unternehmen und ihre Überwachung*, Köln (PapyRossa Hochschulschriften) 2003; Jenkins, R., *Corporate codes of conduct: self-regulation in a global economy*, Geneva (United Nations Research Institute for Social Development) 2001.

[23] The development of the various national legal systems to a greater sensitivity towards such 'soft' and legally difficult to classify phenomena cannot be demonstrated here. As an overview, see Köndgen, J., *Selbstbindung ohne Vertrag*, Tübingen (Mohr) 1981, p. 91; Loges, R., *Die Begründung neuer Erklärungspflichten und der Gedanke des Vertrauensschutzes*, Berlin (Duncker & Humblot) 1990.

[24] Luhmann, op.cit. p. 79.

Outside layer:
Enterprise guidelines

Middle layer:
Internal checks and audits

Self-regulatory 'core':
Internal environmental and safety standards

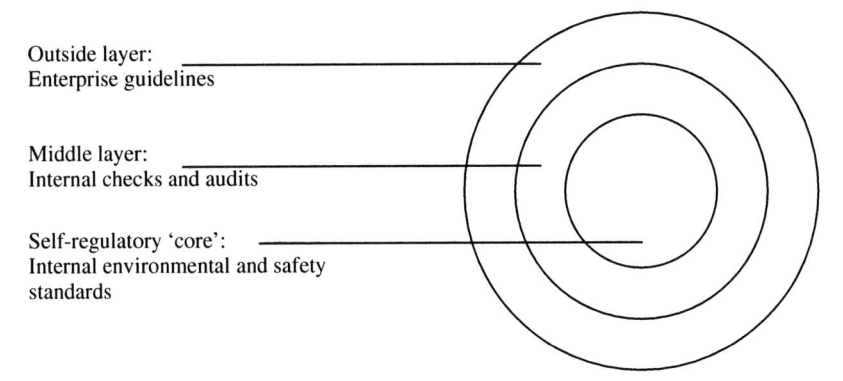

Figure 6.1 Schematic representation of transnational self-regulatory systems

disposition. The empirical task is to reconstruct how internal implementation is organised; how implementers manage to create an independent knowledge base, which depth of investigation they reach conducting the various on-site controls and internal audits, which direct or indirect steering mechanisms they use, and which (new) division of responsibility between the parent company and the subsidiaries can be read or derived from these new regulatory structures. Here, again, a number of questions with legal connection are to be found: empirical reconstruction can help to reconsider the misleading contemporary picture of multinational enterprises, which is still strongly influenced by the old decentralised paradigm. The possibilities for intervention of the parent company can in certain cases be a legitimate trigger to penetrate the 'corporate veil' (i.e. the protective legal construction of separate 'parent' and 'subsidiary' companies), in order to assign a juridical duty to compensate damages caused by the subsidiary directly to the headquarters, where corporate governance was characterised by provable mistakes and acts of negligence.[25]

The most detailed part – roughly speaking the 'core' of the self-regulatory systems – consists of a mesh of relatively narrow and concrete standards defining the particular duties imposed on the various subdivisions, giving detailed information on which points the norms and rules of corporate governance exceed the level of care defined by the formal legal standards in the different host countries. Sociologically, a variety of different types of rules can be identified which must be interlocked in a functional way if the project of corporate

---

[25] On the problem of tort or, in particularly extreme cases, criminal liability concerning multinationals, see Anderes, S., *Fremde im eigenen Land: Die Haftbarkeit multinationaler Unternehmen für Menschenrechtsverletzungen an indigenen Völkern*, Zürich (Schulthess) 2000; Meier, W., *Grenzüberschreitender Durchgriff in der Unternehmensgruppe nach US-amerikanischem Recht*, Frankfurt (Lang) 2000; Teubner, G., Unitas Multiplex: Das Konzernrecht in der neuen Dezentralität der Unternehmensgruppe, *ZGR* (1991), pp. 189–217.

governance is to succeed: technical rules (such as the velocity of waste water flow in a water purification plant) will be combined with organisational requirements (such as the division of competencies and the intervals of measurements, maintenance and repair); partly, the relevant rules are formulated in a result-oriented manner (most often in the form of threshold values, for example, the concentration of pollutants in a medium), but more often they appear to be structured in a rather process-oriented manner (e.g., regulations as how to operate the equipment at hand in an orderly way); partly, it is a matter of dealing with optimisation rules for the augmentation of environmental performance, but it is also partly a question of elementary commonsense demands which no one can violate without accepting the probability of serious damages and disturbances. Where the empirical analysis succeeds in reconstructing the stock of precautionary criteria and diligence rules which characterise the translocal activities of a branch in their crucial dimensions and baselines, that can help the juridical practitioner in the various host lands to concretise the general clauses and rather abstract concepts in their own formal legal system such as due diligence, common practice, proportionality, or reasonableness with regard to the multinationals and their extraordinary problem-solving capacity.[26]

The detailed reconstruction of the prevailing explicit or even implicit rules and norms of the different transnational branches and separate fields of practice must be handed over to further sociological research. The following reflections will focus on only one of the three layers, namely the forms and elements of the internal control and implementation mechanisms; this, first and foremost, because the literature on cross-border environmental management in multinational enterprises is rather superficial and, moreover, because the implementation process represents the dimension where the *modus operandi* of corporate environmental governance can be observed 'in action', manifesting and reproducing itself in various concrete situations and sequences of organisational interaction.

1. *State of research, empirical points of comparison and analytic demarcations*

As outlined above, guaranteeing an accident-free and environmentally friendly operation represents, in comparison with the setting-up of a new factory and the design of adequate protective equipment, a relatively difficult task. Because of the latency and the complexity of potential deficiencies, effective surveillance

---

[26] On integrating informal criteria of diligence into the structure of formal law, see Kötz, H. and Wagner, G., *Deliktsrecht*, Neuwied (Luchterhand) 2001, p. 116; Rehbinder, M., *Rechtssoziologie*, München (C. H. Beck) 4th edn 2000, p. 19; Teubner, G., Generalklauseln als sozio-normative Modelle, in Stachowiak, H. (ed.), Bedürfnisse, *Werte und Normen im Wandel*, München (Fink) 1982, p. 87.

without specialised on-site monitoring is hardly conceivable. In fact, this instrument constitutes in each of the surveyed enterprises an indispensable element of company-wide environmental management, often termed as internal 'audits', 'checks', or 'reviews'. As a starting point for sociological reconstruction, a brief inventory of the objective parameters which represent the external conditions of self-regulatory monitoring is advantageous, particularly because these characteristics are nearly identical in all surveyed enterprises: in a regular three to four year cycle, each part of the enterprise undergoes an inspection which lasts from four to five days. This is done partly through two environmental specialists from the German parent company and partly under the direction of German specialists working with a specialist from a third land of engagement. The auditors review various documents, they conduct inspections of the physical equipment and they report their findings directly to the top management of both the parent company and the foreign establishment. As the regularity and steadiness of internal auditing demonstrate, the headquarters makes constant demands on the subsidiaries to obey the internal rules and standards: the foreign subdivisions must, in a metaphor often used in the interviews, 'do their homework'. At the same time, the considerable intervals between the separate audits and the tight time-budget during the investigation show that any form of a completely centralised control or a concentration of all environmentally and safety-relevant decisions in the hands of the companies' headquarters are clearly not intended.

Thereby, a first important point of comparison is identified: although internal controls mark a decisive step toward overcoming the old fragmented and decentralised enterprise structure (such as *Union Carbide*'s 'steering at arm's length' concept), the efforts towards a stronger integration of the individual parts of the corporate group do not take the form of a pyramidal hierarchy or a tightly centralised organisation. 'We don't try to undertake anything on our own initiative', as was stated in one of the interviews, 'our work is based on the understanding that the organisation needs supportive activities' (Interview, 13 December 2000). The audits operate, one could say, according to a falsifying or fallibilistic logic. Ultimate certainty as to whether in fact all deficiencies and sources of error have been identified is not to be reached with this method. Monitoring is based on sampling and thus it is unavoidably selective: the auditors, as was indicated during the interviews, do not conduct chemical or quantitative measurements, rather, their tests fulfil the task of supervising the testing done by the foreign subsidiary. In many cases, the auditors have to rely on the relevant information, descriptions, and explanations which they get from the local representatives, although it is always possible to probe those data critically and partially scrutinise their validity.

Despite the selectivity of the audits there is a considerable probability that, when appropriate strategies and methods of investigation as well as a selection based on substantive and well-founded criteria are applied, the most serious defects at a foreign establishment will in fact be discovered. The flexibility and openness of investigation also impose some pressure on the local managers to find the major mistakes themselves, looking through their operations on a broad front in anticipation of the next audit. The underlying modus of regulation can thus be quite rightly described as indirect regulation, as 'controlling self-control', or as 'second order review'. In some of the interviews this method is also strikingly characterised as monitoring following the principle, 'two heads are better than one'. The tasks of the corporate representatives for environment and safety serve as the keystone in a complex meshwork of roles, duties, and competencies; they function as a kind of supervisor and as 'initiators of organisational learning'.[27] If a certain degree of distance between them and the local actors was not maintained this could gradually lead to a rather passive 'wait and see' attitude through which dangers and potential risks would be increased.

The mode of indirect control must not in any event – and herein consists a further contrasting point – evoke the idea that the safety and environmental protection managers hold a purely advisory and supportive role without authorisation and competence to intervene. However, this is the view of the current discourse in the business management literature on transnational environmental management. Some of these contributions tend to exaggerate the dangers of the centralist and interventionist elements of corporate governance in an almost excessive manner, as if each form of inspection and influence, be it as careful as possible, would necessarily suffocate any aspect of individual initiative and responsibility on the ground.[28] At times, the multinational enterprises are, ironically enough, described as a decentralised forum of mutual learning, a setting of network-like quality, in which the individual units permanently bring each other to the newest state of the art without the need for any authority or supervising unit above them.[29] Although during the interviews the corporate environmental managers also place great importance on removing all echoes of authority from their self-description – probably not the least of reasons for which is the maintenance of a cooperative framework of interaction between them and the local actors, which eases the task of monitoring – a closer examination reveals a number of elements which are diametrically opposed to the often quoted non-binding and decentralised model.

Just the fact that the cycle of checks and controls is fixed indicates that the local managers' participation in the control system is not voluntary but obligatory: in one of the interviews this is emphasised with the words 'in our company the subunits don't need any "motivation", they simply must do

---

[27] Argyris, C. and Schön, D., *Organisational learning: theory, methods and practice*, Reading, Mass. (Addison-Wesley) 1996, p. 229.

[28] See Brodel, D., *Internationales Umweltmanagement: Gestaltungsfelder – Determinanten – Ausprägungen*, Wiesbaden (Gabler) 1996, p. 449.

[29] Hansen, M. W., *Cross border environmental management in transnational corporations*, Occasional Paper 5, Copenhagen (Copenhagen Business School) 1999, p. 6.

it' – a circumstance that also characterises the anatomy of corporate governance in the other enterprises in the sample, although that point is not always made so bluntly. Auditing is in no way limited to counselling in the sense of offering solutions for problems which the local managers have already recognised as such, the job of monitoring consists in detecting the whole variety of prevailing weaknesses and errors, including those which are unknown to the practitioners on the spot and those that are already discovered but not admitted voluntarily. The internal controllers hold the power of defining with binding authority what has to be regarded as faulty or as a breach of the norms. With the definition that a fact is deficient they do not, however, themselves take on the position of operational management, although it nonetheless must be seen as an exertion of influence to arrange the observations along the demarcation of admissible/inadmissible and to establish the points where corrective action is required.

In certain cases, the auditors are also given the authority of intervention, which includes commands and orders of immediate force and which can lead to the immediate closing of particularly risky production units. That is an element of their role that (in view of the destructive power of a single error triggering fires, explosions, or heavy emissions of particularly toxic substances into the environment) deserves to be judged as inevitable: 'As auditors we do that, too', as was stated in one of the interviews, 'when we go someplace and see anything of immediate danger we say "please stop that at once"!' (Interview, 13 December 2000). From this, however, it does not necessarily follow that direct intervention is the most frequent case, it is only on the table when the local managers in particular points have utterly failed, that is, the auditors in such cases function as a sort of 'supplementary' decision-maker.

Finally, a third background of comparison concerns the relationship between the monitoring instruments under research (which have not been formalised by any international organisation as yet) on the one hand, and the existing standardised testing procedures such as those described as 'quality management' and 'environmental management system' in ISO-Norm 9000 and in Norm Series 14000, on the other. The ISO instruments also pretend to be a type of 'meta control', but without being able to reach that goal – they attach too much importance to formal organisational elements such as internal documents, procedures, and handbooks and neglect most of the substantive aspects of actual practice. As a result, the accuracy and the concrete usefulness of these tools is in a rather bad shape: 'The audit process becomes a world to itself, self-referentially creating auditable images of performance'.[30] Thus, in a test

---

[30] Power, M., *The audit society: rituals of verification*, Oxford (Clarendon Press) 1997, p. 96; further: Rieker, J., ISO 9000-Norm ohne Nutzen?, in *Manager-Magazin*, December 1995: 'ISO has turned into a piece of junk. Mid-sized enterprises all report that not a single week passes in which no self-proclaimed ISO counselor shows up to promise them the quick and easy way to the ISO rubber stamp. There are plenty of ready-made handbooks, in which the company's name is the only thing missing' (at 204).

according to the ISO 14000 norm, neither the state of the protective equipment on the spot nor the quantity of the emitted pollutants are included, the only issue is whether the environmentally relevant processes were regularly measured and documented. This shortcoming can lead to the curious situation that an enterprise which pollutes the environment excessively can be classified as in full compliance.[31] Even if this assessment of the current ISO audits may seem too pessimistic to some readers, it is important to see that the environmental practitioners under research share this assessment. The danger of bureaucratic paralysis, as it is almost prejudiced in the ISO norms, has often been a topic during the interviews, as a negative background of comparison (in German: *negativer Gegenhorizont*) to the direction of their own activities. The following passage was the answer to the question whether it is at all possible during the audits to gain a realistic image of the state of affairs at the foreign establishment:

Interviewee 1: This is simply a matter of experience, since we are a mix of operational and strategic actors, actually everybody for himself, and do not have this split: 'there is an audit division doing something theoretical'. And the more you do this the more experience you acquire.
Interviewee 2: That is our concept, we are gaining information from different sources. That we do not become specialised in only one area, losing our grip on reality – that is my biggest fear, that we lose our grip on reality, instead we always seek to find out what's really going on at the site (Interview, 15 January 2001).

An effective audit demands both an overview of the organisational structure including competencies and procedures, as well as an investigation of the factual practices concerning the daily operations, maintenance, and renovation of plant equipment. The complementarity of both dimensions requires that each auditor has a double qualification as 'strategist' (organiser, manager) and as practitioner with the necessary 'grip on reality' (engineer, technician), being able to interconnect both dimensions in a sensible way. The phrasing 'there is an audit division doing something theoretical' is a caricature of an approach which, instead of controlling self-control in the subdivisions, only produces descriptions of self-descriptions. It signifies an approach which is also unlikely to be taken seriously by those being audited. From the cited statements, it can be derived that a formalistic regime such as that of ISO 14000 will not be adopted by the practitioners under research and, should they still take some of the elements of ISO 14000, these aspects will, in all events,

---

[31] For criticism see Krut, R. and Gleckman, H., *ISO 14000: a missed opportunity*, London (Earthscan) 1998.

be complemented through other, more substantial and well-founded tools of investigation.[32]

2. Instruments and methods of corporate governance: inquiry, counsel, instruction

For a more exact analysis of transnational environmental management in the chemical branch, it must be reconstructed which role techniques, framing strategies,[33] and governance tools the relevant non-state actors employ in order to reach a realistic assessment of the on-site situation during inspections and to maintain an appropriate balance between local operational responsibility and global company-wide governance. In principle, irrespective of the location being monitored and irrespective of the person conducting the checks, the sequence of proceedings remains the same in every audit. Before the auditors departure for their visit, they have a look through various documents, such as the descriptions of production processes and plant types at the factory under examination or documents concerning the modifications and renovations carried out over the last years. This step fulfils the function of getting a first overview and finding provisional clues as a starting point for further inquiry. If an audit of the location has already been undertaken in the past, one examines the earlier audit report for the deficiencies that were recognised and the corrective measures that were imposed on the subsidiary (which again demonstrates that environmental reviews, despite the temporal intervals, are directed towards a long-term integration of the various subunits into the corporate structure).

Before the auditors proceed to their on-site inspections, an intense preliminary meeting with the personnel in place is conducted as an intermediary step. This step fulfils an important function as an 'opening bracket' (Goffman) and requires on average half a day. 'Everybody is a bit scared of strangers, people there are a bit scared, and we are a bit scared too. To overcome that, we don't just start by discussing the issues, we also try to break the ice on the first afternoon' (Interview, 15 January 2001). The emphasis on 'ice breaking' indicates a distinctive awareness that the investigation can cause a certain uncertainty, a considerable degree of distrust, and various strategies of dissimulation and evasion on the part of the audited. At the preliminary meeting, the participants will be told what is coming towards them during the field work and they are assured that acceptable and appropriate solutions for any problems revealed will be found. This serves to assure the collaboration of the local personnel

---

[32] Such additional initiatives to substantiate ISO 14000 are not, sociologically speaking, an indirect outcome of the ISO standards, instead, they must be seen as further proof of ISO 14000's dysfunctionality. But see Meidinger, E., 'Private' environmental regulation, human rights and community, *Buffalo Env. L. J.* 7 (1999/2000), pp. 125–237, at 202.

[33] On the concept of 'frame' in interpretative sociology, see Goffman, E., *Frame analysis: an essay on the organization of experience*, Cambridge (Harvard University Press) 1974.

as an important precondition for conducting the audit in a trouble-free and frictionless manner: 'in the past, cover-ups would certainly take place – that is actually now only the exception, because they know there is a fair treatment' (Interview, 13 December 2000). The tendency of employees (or some employees) to treat unpleasant information as an internal secret of the foreign subsidiary necessitates particular efforts for the creation of trust, and the corporate environmental and safety managers address this problem by seeking to transform the loyalty of the local personnel to the local firm into a loyal and engaged attitude toward the demands of the corporate group.

When the frame of interaction is established and the staff's most important reservations are dispelled, the substantial field work can begin, starting with an evaluation of the formal organisational structure, internal programmes and competencies, and moving on to an inspection of the physical devices on the ground. Each of these steps takes an entire day. The particular sequence, starting with a review of the present management system, refers to the fact that significant organisational deficits can often be revealed simply by a pure textual analysis of the relevant internal regulations. Existing gaps in the structure of competencies and missing procedures for certain problems represent deficiencies of such structural significance that they can under no circumstances be compensated by the talents and the improvisation of the personnel on the shop-floor; but, at the same time, it is important to see that even the most convincing and graceful formal structure is no real assurance against defective applications and forms of negligence and failure. Investigating the formal structures fulfils the function to find out, 'is a closer inspection on the ground needed, or are the results already such that one can say, "I'm sorry, but you are no hero here"' (Interview, 13 December 2000). System failures (i.e. gaps in the formal structure) which reveal themselves during the textual analysis often give cause for immediate complaints, while the inspections on the following day fulfil the goal of putting those parts of the enterprise's management system to the test which at first seem unproblematic.

This second part of the process, on-site inspections, represents an important step towards the 'three dimensionality' of the object under investigation. Many technical and organisational shortcomings can even be discovered with the naked eye, if one only takes the step of going in the field: for example, open containers of chemicals standing about the work-place, mislabelled or unlabelled containers, leaking gas and liquids, or workers without adequate protective clothing.[34] Many of the hidden and, at first glance, invisible problems

---

[34] For an overview of the dramatic failings which can arise in the realm of labour and health protection even in the German parent company, see the examples provided by Hien, W., *Chemische Industrie und Krebs: Zur Soziologie des wissenschaft-lichen und sozialen Umgangs mit arbeitsbedingten Krebserkrankungen in Deutschland*, Bremerhaven (Wirtschaftsverlag) 1994.

can also be identified on site, if a special perceptual structure is employed – an open analysis and a deciphering mode of investigation, inferring indirectly the critical aspects and possible sources of error from both, the visible elements of a plant and the explanations of the operational personnel. This implies a nearly criminological attitude on the part of the auditors, some 'competent scepticism' and the readiness to concentrate also on inconspicuous aspects, to analyse them in depth, and to question the taken-for-granted procedures of daily plant operation:

> You see it through questions. You go through the location and things become quite obvious. And you ask, right then, can you give me a rough idea how this functions, and how is it handled and what happens, if it fails. And you immediately note whether your partner really has it together or whether he is somehow evasive. And then you go on, so now I have the feeling that – look here, we're doing that, in this case we do it so and so. Is that a possible path in order to help you? And then it gets worked out. (Interview, 15 January 2001).

The local practitioners will be confronted with the request for details, with possible and hypothetical technical alternatives ('look here, we are doing that so, and so') and with the question why this concept and not some other was chosen. Presenting himself in a markedly jovial manner, the just cited practitioner still is conducting a test. Sociologically, the emphasis on a free and easy style does not contradict the classification of the audit as an oral examination, in fact it even confirms that interpretation. The local representatives are forced to mobilise good reasons why a particular solution was chosen. They must clarify whether all possible alternatives were taken into consideration, and they must prove that all hypothetical sources of disturbance are covered ('what happens if it fails?'). Evasive answers are an indicator that the addressed problem has apparently not been sufficiently considered. At the same time, the playing field for omissions, evasions, and euphemisms is further restricted by the auditor's possibility to scrutinise the information at any time on the basis of the visible parts of the present technical devices.

Thus far, some remarks on the corporate managers' methods and techniques to create an independent and reliable database for the assessment. As outlined above, the concepts of private governance, of paralegal orders, or transnational self-regulatory systems (in German: *transnationale Regulative*) should be reserved for situations where breaches and violations lead to effective counter-measures. Now the simple definition and indication of deficiencies by acknowledged technical experts also have their own persuasive and binding authority: practices which had been overlooked or pushed into the background are thereby made visible and drawn back into the centre of attention. Those in positions of responsibility are instructed as to the concrete risks, dangers, and damages resulting from the identified omissions, and this cuts off their strategic possibility of exculpating themselves on the basis of surprise, inexperience, or problems in the transfer of knowledge. In the description of one of the interview partners: 'Well, there are situations in which it is often repeated, "No, I did not know this or that, not at all". Assuming that this is true, it is a reasonable result of the review to be able to say "well, please do that then"' (Interview, 13 December 2000). Even if the auditors abstain from presenting their critique as formally binding commands, their instructions bear a significant degree of obligation, since the auditors are exponents of reliable expert knowledge and raise well-founded objections which the addressee cannot ignore without thereby putting his own technical competence at stake.

However, the governance tools and 'authoritative resources' (Giddens) of the corporate managers clearly reach far beyond the execution of their technical competence. As outlined above, violations of the basic rules of plant operation trigger direct intervention and commands of immediate force. In certain particularly dangerous fields, one could say, the operative autonomy of the foreign subsidiary turns out to be an 'operative autonomy under reservation' – the reservation being that the auditors will, in the case of significant failure on the spot, act as direct representatives of the corporate headquarters, reaching through the subdivisions' autonomy. This interventionist element is to be found in all companies in the sample, irrespective of the fact that many of the interviewees tend to put the accent on the cooperative and persuasive aspects of their task. In the present case, as in every form of norm enforcement, an appropriate combination of intrinsic and extrinsic leadership elements is necessary: undoubtedly, stimulating the employees' commitment to the internal norms and rules, improving their diligence by instruction and training, and the creation of an integrated system of values, are important preconditions for a frictionless coordination, but without the flanking effect of hierarchical tangible tools, voluntary means alone would remain a mostly unreliable and inconsistent mode of governance. From today's perspective, the installation of the appropriate steering mechanisms represents an indispensable element of the existing state of common sense in the branch. When the parent company becomes aware of serious errors in its subdivisions, it cannot limit itself to internal suggestions and warnings, particularly when these turn out to have no effect. Acting as a mere consultant in the face of threatening disasters and damages, the parent company would take the role of someone who already has accepted these damages and who gives his warnings simply pro forma, as an immunisation against later inculpation.[35]

---

[35] This seems to have been exactly the attitude of Union Carbide with regard to the chaotic factory in Bhopal. From today's perspective, the scandal is above all the fact that the site's problems were well known to the directors but effective counter-measures were not taken. See Bogard, W., *The Bhopal tragedy: language, logic and politics in the production of a hazard*, Boulder (Westview Press) 1989, p. 5.

For the large amount of 'middle-range' problems, problems which require correction but are not so severe as to trigger direct intervention, the major governance tool consists in the audit reports, which at the same time represent the concluding point of each individual audit. These documents contain a list of the identified shortcomings, often weighted according to their potential for causing damages. The reports also describe the concrete counter-measures defined by the auditors. Those are often presented in the style of non-binding recommendations. However, their non-binding character is restricted to the choice of means, while the cure of the defects in a reasonable time span is obligatory. Deficiencies which had already been criticised in the context of an earlier audit, but which remained uncured in the meantime, are labelled as such and particularly emphasised. The fulfilment of the stated duties is guaranteed through the corporate hierarchy as an important backing for the internal auditors: the findings are passed over to the leaders of the concerned divisions so that these can exert influence on the responsible site managers. At the same time, the leaders of the subdivisions must themselves give account to the board of directors. In all enterprises of the sample, the board holds special meetings on company-wide environmental and safety issues once a year, where the basic results of internal monitoring are discussed and evaluated.

In sum, corporate environmental managers serve as the driving force in a complex apparatus of observation, reporting, and implementation. Even where their competencies seem to be only preparatory to decision-making, they are of significant influence. Instead of creating additional units restricted to counselling and other supportive functions, well-integrated new task forces with a considerable basis of authoritative resources were installed, thereby reorganising the division of responsibilities between the parent company and the various subsidiaries in a more adequate way.

3. Some reflections on the reach of the analysed self-regulatory systems; goals for further research

The preceding reflections were intended to reveal a layer of practices by which the separate subsidiaries of a multinational company are embedded in an integrated regulatory framework. These practices try to maintain a single minimum standard of environmental protection and safety throughout the various subdivisions of the multinational. Elements such as substantial inspections on the ground, strategies for the discovery of latent and subtle problems, the obligatory definition of violations, the empowerment to intervene, and the backing from the board of directors supply the system with a striking degree of sharpness, problem proximity, and effectiveness. At the same time, this does not imply that this instrument is not in some regards capable of further improvement and modification. A more precise analysis of the capacities and restrictions of internal monitoring would require more detailed insights into the firm and branch-specific meshwork of concrete technical and organisational standards. Those standards constitute the operative core of self-regulatory action and can be reconstructed with the same methods applied here – a task that must be left for further research.

However, even at this stage of analysis some of the difficulties and structural shortcomings which limit the reach of the described governance mechanisms can be determined. Some indicators point to the fact that the audits often follow the principle of 'safety first'. On the one hand, that can be an adequate response to the limited personal and time resources. On the other, it can lead to a rather superficial test of genuine environmental aspects. This especially concerns locations where serious deficiencies in the dimension of disaster prevention and factory safety predominate. Accordingly, the on-site inspection occasionally is simply called a 'safety inspection', and sometimes the interviewees state that the most crucial motivation for internal monitoring is that 'no enterprise wants to find itself on the front page of the news when an accident happens' (Interview, 30 June 2000). Another indicator for this bias is the auditors' emphasis on their skills as safety engineers as the most important basis for their work, as was often observed in the interviews. The chances to overcome this one-sidedness in the long run and to reach a more balanced relation between environmental and safety aspects are not marginal. But at this early stage, the entire system indicates that is a rather temporally remote development (at the moment, the majority of enterprises find themselves between the second and the third wave of audits).

A further objection against the audits in their present form refers to their limited reliability and objectivity. Although most of the interviews contain statements highlighting the precision of internal monitoring (e.g. 'we audit according to a systematic unitary method'), one also finds descriptions emphasising the openness of the process and the auditors' considerable discretion: 'each auditor necessarily has a single field of specialisation because of his education. Thus he will employ a very rough rasp on everything first, and then according to his background and that which is found at the site go deeper into particular points' (Interview, 20 February 2001). A flexible and open style of investigation is an important precondition for the accuracy and the substantive content of the audit, but if the subjective view of the individual auditor is as influential as described in the quotation, only an increase of available time and size of the auditors' team would help to overcome possible distortions. The question of reliability also concerns the formalisation of internal technical and organisational standards. At the present stage, as several statements in the interviews show, the internal norms and rules do not at all represent a codified or systematic order. As to the results of the audits, continual efforts for the formulation and further development of company-wide standards are taking place in all enterprises under research. However, because of the variety of the technical devices in use and due to disagreement between the environmental representatives and business managers in the firms, those efforts seem to be making only slow progress.

A third problematic aspect is the examination of legal compliance in the course of auditing. In fact, an intense examination of the various subunits on the basis of the prevailing local legal standards is desirable, since these might in several points exceed the company-wide basic rules and internal standards. Further, a neglect of formal legal requirements seriously reduces the power of the local administrative authorities and their ability to plan and supervise the industry. However, this step of internal monitoring turns out to be extremely difficult, partly due to the complex variety of the different national law systems, their specific procedures, the different duties imposed on the employer, and the patchiness of concretising standards, partly due to the auditors' inability to overcome language barriers (for example, in the context of auditing a location in China). Normally, the auditors content themselves with a quick look-through of the legally required official documents that the foreign establishment has on hand. They then ask the local managers questions as to the completeness of these documents and whether they are all up to date. This proceeding, often designated as a 'systematic approach', on closer examination turns out to be a mere prothesis since the auditors neither possess the necessary knowledge of the local legal requirements nor can they detect whether the conditions defined in the official certificates are observed by those responsible – to do so they would first have to be able to read and decode the documents.

Despite the described restrictions, environmental governance systems in the transnational chemical branch represent a striking example of the present private regulatory structures on the global scale. A closer reconstruction in depth would be a matter of investigating in more detail the internal rules and standards in the various dimensions of environmental protection, first as a cross-section, systematising the different norms and rules regarding their problem proximity, their level of aspiration, and their functional interplay, and secondly as a longitudinal study, considering further development and adaptation to existing or newly arising regulatory necessities. The latter is a process of refined adjudication depending on various 'micropolitical'[36] negotiations and discussions inside the companies' headquarters. In this context, the environmental and safety managers take the role of programme initiators who try to push through new standards against the reservations of top management: 'Depending on whom you are talking to, standards are always connected with money... Standards are always such a hot topic – do we need a new standard for this? No, that costs money, and so on' (Interview, 5 December 2001). It is the task of the corporate environmental units to combat these objections, for example by referring to the costs of possible accidents, the benefit of more efficient

---

[36] See Burns, T., Micropolitics: mechanisms of institutional change, *Administ. Science Q.* 1 (1961), pp. 257–281.

processes, or the public image of the enterprise – aspects which are also given great importance in the business management and environmental economics literature.[37]

These motivations might, in fact, play an important role for the fine-tuning of corporate governance. However, the genesis of the self-regulatory systems as such is to be illuminated from a more fundamental and 'holistic' sociological perspective. Here too, there is a great need of further research. However, sufficient evidence exists to apply a model of crises and response as the crucial driving force for the emergence of transnational self-regulatory structures.[38] Thus, environmental protection and safety in multinational enterprises are not merely a question of separate, isolated purposes. They are also a matter of broader learning processes triggered in situations where the predominating self-definitions, mental maps, and points of reference which are the basis for the concrete organisational structure turn out to be wrong.

The background of the crisis was partly the result of the Bhopal disaster of 1984. As a consequence, many enterprises learned the lesson that similar accidents could also occur in their activities. Although a certain degree of diligence and responsibility for the situation at the foreign factories might also have been employed before, it seems that all the activities of the headquarters were then crystallised around the old, decentralised model with the idea that taking the role of a technical adviser would suffice for an orderly state of affairs at any location – a view that can since be regarded as obsolete. Considerations of the enterprise's image or the attractiveness for clients and associates are in no events irrelevant to this development. But, from a realistic point of view, their significance appears to be restricted to the function of an additional 'sounding board', further intensifying the collapse of the old model. The crucial motivation consists in the tendency of the enterprises to seek an exit from the crisis, as any other organised form of social practice would tend to do, to regain control over its own affairs, and thereby regain a minimum of certainty and normality.

IV. Transnational self-regulatory systems and interlegality: building blocks for a theory of company-level organisational failure

Transnational governance mechanisms (*transnationale Regulative*) emerge out of the prevailing legal porosity, filling the gaps in the state-centric regulatory structure. They are equipped with their own sources of normative validity, establishing far-reaching binding effects without having to rely on the generative patterns of positive law. It would, however, be false to conclude from

---

[37] See Brodel, op. cit.; Fichter and Schneidewind, op. cit.
[38] See Oevermann, U., Genetischer Strukturalismus und das sozialwissenschaftliche Problem der Erklärung der Entstehung des Neuen, in Müller-Doohm, S. (ed.), *Jenseits der Utopie: Theoriekritik der Gegenwart*, Frankfurt (Suhrkamp) 1991.

this that both orders stand separately from each other, without any intersections. Instead, the emerging normative structures of world society lead towards 'a complicated mesh of "inter-legal" relations between various layers of law, a field with hierarchies, crossings, and mutual references, but most probably also with contradictions and imbalances'.[39] Under the conditions of globalisation, formal law is increasingly compelled to take into account the extra-legal rules of the social and economic world. For the maintenance of its own functions, positive law has to scrutinise in concrete individual cases whether the paralegal norms of world society represent consolidated forms of common practice in certain fields of action, whether they are adequate instruments for problem-solving, and whether they are to be regarded as sources of legitimate expectations. For a more precise definition of what might be called 'interlegal research' (in German: *Interlegalitaetsforschung*), it is crucial to understand that this programme is only practicable as an interdisciplinary project in which social and legal science mutually complement each other.

As to the sociological part, this demands above all a strict regard for the professional standards of reconstructive qualitative research: a strong commitment to the principle of value-free scientific analysis, since otherwise the results cannot be used as a reliable empirical expert's report by the various recipients in justice and jurisprudence. However, the postulate of value-free analysis implies in no way that the particular criteria which in the various fields of action prevail as rules of practical common sense should not be designated as such. On the contrary, the analysis of private governance is a matter of precisely defining what constitutes the normality of the relevant field of practice, which general rules are in force, and where these have their normative foundations. The sociological interpreter is facing the task to reconstruct normality, without employing a normative view himself, and without reducing normality to aspects of the average factual behaviour. Where breaches of the existing rules, defaults, or tendencies to fall behind the present stage of development are found, these must be classified as deviations.[40]

As concluding remarks, some of the legal 'resonances' (Luhmann), implications, and interconnections resulting from the above described private governance structures will be outlined. The following considerations stand outside

---

[39] Winter, op. cit. p. 245. On the concept of interlegality, see further Santos, op. cit.

[40] That the initially mentioned procedures of reconstructive social research accomplish exactly this (see n. 13 above), cannot be discussed here in closer detail. For the juristic reader is thereto added, that in view of the contemporary stage of qualitative methodology, many of the conflict points of the debate over value judgements, which were fiercely fought over in the 1970s (see Adorno, T. W. *et al.* (ed.), *Der Positivismusstreit in der deutschen Soziologie*, Neuwied (Luchterhand) 1969) have shown themselves to be outdated. Exactly because the researcher abstains from individual value judgements, he is in the position to diagnose the suitability, the problem proximity and the substantive rationality (or, on the contrary, the failure, the deformations or restrictions) of a given form of practice in an objective and empirically valid manner.

the essential sociological analysis and are only mentioned under the reservation of a more detailed juridical examination. Under strictly formal aspects, multinational enterprises represent, as ever, extremely fragmented entities, since the foreign subsidiaries are founded as legally independent companies according to local law (these are, first and foremost, public limited companies and limited liability companies). The legal separation of parent and subsidiary implies extensive protections for the parent company against liability for tortious practices in the foreign subsidiaries. Appropriate criteria for the diligent coordination and leadership of the various subdivisions are at best to be found in international 'soft law'.[41] The duties of the headquarters are generally absent in the contemporary national laws. Juridical preoccupation with the problems resulting from the multinational character of the companies often leads to the confusion of extra-territorial jurisdiction. A jungle of jurisdictional problems and possible conflicts of laws, the precarious recognition of judgments from foreign courts, and many other uncertainties seriously hinder access to law and can have a restrictive effect on the readiness of the legal institutions to even accept such cases.[42]

But even where procedural questions like these are clarified, the most crucial problem remains the possibility to assign the local damages to the wrongful decisions or failure of the company's headquarters. This difficulty in principle is nothing new, since it also impresses itself on most questions of organisational liability in the national context. Any legal regulation of complex and highly differentiated enterprises, be it tort or criminal regulation, faces the problem of finding special techniques and legal forms in order to reduce the problem of unclear internal decision structures. In transnational relations, these problems of accountability are generally analogous, but of a higher intensity. That fact has at times led to descriptions of the multinational as an 'amorphous' phenomenon with no fixed form, wherein power and domination appear as free floating elements with no clear anchorage: a flexible network of 'semi-autonomous action centres' without any superior or inferior relationships,[43] a 'horizontal organisation,'[44] and a 'heterarchy' of subsystems mutually coordinating themselves and each other.[45]

---

[41] For an overview of the existing codes of conduct, see Böttger, K., *Die Umweltpflichtigkeit von Auslandsdirektinvestitionen im Völkerrecht*, Baden-Baden (Nomos) 2002; Horn, N., *Legal problems of codes of conduct for multinational enterprises*, Deventer (Kluwer) 1980.

[42] An overview of the pitfalls of the transnational penetrations can be found in Muchlinski, op. cit. p. 123; also see Otto, M., *Der prozessuale Durchgriff*, München (Beck) 1993.

[43] Teubner, op. cit. p. 194.

[44] White, R. and Poynter, T. A., Achieving worldwide advantage with the horizontal organization, *Business Q*. 54 (1989), pp. 55–61, at 55.

[45] Hedlund, G., The hypermodern MNC: a heterarchy, *Human Resource Manag*. 25 (1986), pp. 9–35, at 9.

That these estimations by no means correspond to reality – at least not to the reality of corporate governance in the chemical branch – is evident given the above background of empirical results. Exactly because the multinationals do not in their internal relations represent a monolithic block, numerous instances of control and oversight can be installed to the point of a literal 'microjustice' (Foucault) of surveillance and correction. If the multinationals have to be regarded, at least in certain aspects of internal coordination, as well-integrated organisations, the central concepts and patterns of contemporary corporate liability law deserve to be reconsidered too. At the moment, liability of the parent company is limited to cases where local damages are provoked through direct and clearly identifiable interventions of the parent company into the autonomous sphere of the subsidiary (for example, where a factory is instructed to continue operation despite significant disturbances). In fact, that pattern in practice seems to be rather seldom the case. In order to modernise company liability law, it might be helpful to transfer specific criteria from analogous legal constellations in the national context to the transnational scale, especially the concept of organisational and managerial failure (in German: *Organisations- und Managementversagen*).[46] The one-sided concentration on direct, wrongful intervention could thereby be transformed into a broader and more realistic approach, which would also take into account aspects of negligence or violations against branch-specific duties of diligence on part of the parent company. It would be worth a separate study to investigate the legal orders of the different countries as well as recent court decisions to see whether these already show signs of an emerging concept of organisational failure in multinational companies, and to which extent criteria of diligence are included that informally arose from the common practice in the different branches of transnational activity. The auditing procedures of ISO 9000 and ISO 14000 often receive an astonishing amount of attention in legal sciences, but, compared with other, less visible forms of private governance, the regulatory effect of these procedures is rather small, since practice, as shown, goes well beyond the formal routines of these norms.[47]

In the interlegal mesh of transnational self-regulation and formal law, the latter could serve to impose additional incentives on the corporations, to make them obey the existing criteria of diligence, supervision, and protection as precisely as possible. The juridical adaptation of rules and norms constituting

---

[46] See Bosch, N., *Organisationsverschulden in Unternehmen*, Baden-Baden (Nomos) 2002; Matusche-Beckmann, A., *Das Organisationsverschulden*, Tübingen (Mohr-Siebeck) 2001; Heine, G., *Die strafrechtliche Verantwortlichkeit von Unternehmen*, Baden-Baden (Nomos) 1995.

[47] On the integration of the ISO scheme in formal law, see Meidinger, op. cit. p. 202; Brüggemeier, G., Enterprise liability for environmental damage: German and European law, in Teubner, G. et al. (ed.), *Environmental law and ecological responsibility*, Chichester (Wiley) 1994, p. 75.

common practice in a branch will also put the late-comers under pressure, and to some extent the expectations of third parties, if they are based on empirically valid assumptions about the stage of diligence in the concerned branch, will gain better legal protection. Of course, all of this can be attained only with great care: the juridification of the emergent normative structures should neither lead to discouraging organisational responsibility nor should it degenerate into an undifferentiated automatism, assigning liability for any problem at the foreign locations without further examination to the parent company. To avoid this, a company where appropriate governance mechanisms are installed must be given the chance to exculpate itself. Looking back to recent losses and damages, it is always possible (but also rather cheap) to make the point that, had the parent company paid more attention, the accident would never have happened. Thus, the appropriate standard for corporate diligence is not an illusory all-embracing responsibility of the headquarters, it can only be found in the existing stage of self-regulation, the prevailing common sense, and the criteria of practical rationality that characterise the concerned field of practice in general.

The present analysis is restricted to one selected case, namely large multinational companies from the German chemical branch. Further inquiries into the issues of private self-regulation, interlegality, and global governance will expand the approach step by step to other branches and to companies from other home countries. As one of several concepts interconnecting both disciplines (sociological research and juridical evaluation), the figure of 'transnational fields of practice' (in German: *transnationale Verkehrskreise*) might help to raise awareness for the existing criteria of diligence in the separate branches. According to this model the multinational enterprises of a particular branch represent a specific, distinguishable category of actors, a certain milieu or sector, and thus stand apart from the average domestic firm in developing countries. Their considerable stock of specialised technical knowledge, extraordinary steering capacities, and the variety of voluntary governance mechanisms in the corporate world are an important resource to compensate for gaps of positive law. Thus, to some extent, imposing a higher degree of diligence on the multinationals than on the local firms in the various African, Asian, or Latin American regions seems to be justified, at least within the limits of the normative structures already prevailing in the different transnational fields of practice.

7

Responsibility of transnational corporations in international environmental law: three perspectives

ANDRÉ NOLLKAEMPER

I. Introduction

This chapter examines recent developments pertaining to the international responsibility of transnational corporations for activities that may cause harm to the environment.[1] While the position of transnational corporations in international law has been subjected to previous analyses,[2] also in regard to

---

The author would like to thank Janneke Nijman, Erika de Wet, and Gerd Winter for their helpful comments on an earlier draft of this article and Elizabeth Perel for research assistance. This chapter was written as part of the Pioneer programme on the Interactions between Public International Law and National Law, sponsored by the Netherlands Organization for Scientific Research (NWO).

[1] The chapter uses the definition of transnational corporations that is contained in the *Draft Norms on the Responsibilities of Transnational Corporations and Other Business Enterprises with regard to Human Rights* (hereafter: '*Draft Norms on the Responsibilities*'). The term 'transnational corporation' refers to 'an economic entity operating in more than one country or a cluster of economic entities operating in two or more countries – whatever their legal form, whether in their home country or country of activity, and whether taken individually or collectively'. The *Draft Norms on the Responsibilities* are annexed to UN Doc. E/CN.4/Sub.2/2002/13, 15 August 2002. Much of what will be said in this chapter applies equally to other corporations. However, because of the transnational nature of their activities, transnational corporations pose particular challenges for international environmental law.

[2] e.g. Fatouros, A. A., *Transnational corporations: the international legal framework*, London (Routledge) 1994; Rigaux, F., Transnational corporations, in Bedjaoui, M. (ed.), *International law: achievements and prospects*, Boston (Nijhoff) 1991; United Nations Conference on Trade and Development, Division on Transnational Corporations and Investment, *Companies without borders: transnational corporations in the 1990s*, London (International Thomson Business Press) 1996. Many of these analyses are inspired by problems of social rights or human rights; see e.g Branson, M.A., The social responsibility of large multinational corporations, *Transnational Lawyer* 16 (2002), pp. 121–139; Addo, M. K.(ed.), *Human rights standards and the responsibility of transnational corporations*, The Hague (Kluwer) 1999; Kamminga, M. T. and Zia-Zarifa, S. (eds.), *Liability of multinational corporations under international law*, The Hague (Kluwer) 2000.

international environmental law,[3] there are reasons for a new consideration of the topic.

First, transnational corporations substantially contribute to the worldwide stress on the environment. Many acts that deplete natural resources, contribute to the depletion of the ozone layer and to climate change, deplete fish stocks, clear-cut forests, move waste across boundaries, and so on, are not performed by states, but rather by economic entities operating in more than one state. Recent data indicate that the detrimental effects of the activities of transnational corporations on the worldwide environment are substantial.[4] In the perspective of the book of which this chapter is a part, it can be said that transnational corporations pose a considerable challenge to global environmental governance.

Secondly, there is a variety of recent initiatives of a political and/or legal nature that seek to improve international regulation of transnational corporations. Noteworthy is the work of the ILC on international liability,[5] the adoption of the *Norms on the Responsibilities of Transnational Corporations and Other Business Enterprises with regard to Human Rights* by the UN Subcommission on the Promotion and Protection of Human Rights,[6] and the United Nations Global Compact.[7]

This chapter will examine and comment on these recent developments and, more broadly, analyse the responsibility of transnational corporations from the perspective of general international law. It does not examine in detail the various principles and rules that have been applied to transnational corporations in codes of conduct, through self-regulation, or otherwise. On these issues ample literature exists.[8] Rather, this chapter seeks to assess what these principles and rules tell us about the way in which the international legal order addresses activities of transnational corporations that result in environmental problems of international concern.

---

[3] e.g. Sands, P., *International environmental law: emerging trends and implications for transnational corporations*, New York (United Nations Publications) 1993; Hamilton, D. T., Regulation of corporations under international environmental law, in Canadian Council of International Law, *Preserving the global environment*, Proceedings of the Annual Conference of the Canadian Council on International Law, Ottawa (CCIL) 1989, pp. 72–92; Anderson, M., Transnational corporations and environmental damage: is tort law the answer? *Washburn L. J.* 41 (2002), pp. 399–425; Hansen, M. W., Managing the environment across borders: a survey of environmental management in transnational corporations in Asia, *Transnational Corporations* 12 (Transnational Corporations and Management Division, Department of Economic and Social Development, United Nations) (2003), pp. 27–52.

[4] UNEP overview report 10 years after Rio: the UNEP assessment, available at www.uneptie.org/outreach/wssd/docs/global/UNEP_report- english.pdf

[5] ILC, *First report on the legal regime for allocation of loss in case of transboundary harm arising out of hazardous activities by Mr. Pemmaraju Sreenivasa Rao*, Special Rapporteur, UN Doc. A/CN.4/531, 2003.

[6] See n. 2 above.

[7] The United Nations Global Compact, available at www.unglobalcompact.org/Portal/

[8] See, with further references, Jonas Ebbesson, Chapter 8.

Apart from certain conceptual clarifications relating to the different use of the term 'responsibility' in public international law, on the one hand, and the discourse on 'corporate responsibility', on the other (section II), the chapter makes essentially three arguments. First, it argues that the responsibility of corporations is largely determined by a normative order that operates separately and largely independently from public international law and indeed from any other legal order (section III). Secondly, it argues that as far as the legal dimension of responsibility of corporations is concerned, international law relies heavily on responsibility defined and effectuated via the national legal order (section IV). Thirdly, it argues that as far as it is envisaged that international law itself would directly regulate the responsibility of corporations, the forms and modalities have as yet hardly been thought through; in any case, they cannot simply be transplanted from the law of responsibility as that applies to states and international organisations (section V).

II. The term 'responsibility'

Documents and literature dealing with the international responsibility of transnational corporations use the term 'responsibility' in at least two different meanings.

First, the term 'responsibility' is used to refer to the legal consequences that arise out of a breach of international law. This use of the term is consistent with the meaning of the term in the work of the ILC on responsibility of states[9] and of international organisations.[10] In this meaning, the term does not refer to particular standards of conduct (so-called 'primary rules'), but rather to obligations that result from a breach of the standards of conduct that apply to them ('secondary rules'). It is in this meaning that the term is used, for instance, by Crawford and Olleson when they write (after having discussed the relatively clear secondary rules applicable to states and international organisations) '[t]he position so far as ... corporations ... are concerned is far less clear: just as it is doubtful whether they are in any meaningful sense 'subjects' of international law, so it is doubtful whether any *general* regime of responsibility has developed to cover them'.[11]

Secondly, the term 'responsibility' is used as shorthand to refer to the obligations applicable to transnational corporations. In the terminology used by the ILC, the term then refers to primary rules of conduct. The term 'responsibility' has in this meaning occasionally been applied to states. For instance, Principle

---

[9] See Articles 1 and 2 of the ILC's *Draft Articles on Responsibility of states for Internationally Wrongful Acts*, Annex to UN Doc. A/RES/56/83, 28 January 2002.

[10] See Article 3 of the ILC's *Draft Articles on the Responsibility of International Organizations*, UN Doc. A/CN.4/L.632, adopted on 4 June 2003.

[11] Crawford, J. and Olleson, S., The nature and forms of international responsibility, in Evans, M.D., *International law*, Oxford (Oxford University Press) 2003, p. 447.

21 of the 1972 Stockholm Declaration provided that states have the *responsibility* to ensure that activities within their jurisdiction or control do not cause damage to the environment of other states or of areas beyond the limits of national jurisdiction. However, in regard to states, the term is not often used in this meaning. It is noteworthy that the ICJ referred to the rule that states must ensure that activities within their jurisdiction or control do not cause damage to the environment of other states (which in the 1972 Stockholm Declaration was referred to as a 'responsibility') as an obligation,[12] rather than as a responsibility. In contrast, in regard to transnational corporations, this use of the term 'responsibility' is more common. It is, for instance, in this meaning that the term appears to be used in the concept of 'corporate responsibility' adopted by the International Chamber of Commerce[13] and in the *Norms on the Responsibilities of Transnational Corporations and Other Business Enterprises with regard to Human Rights*. These documents speak of obligations, not of the consequence of the breach of obligations. It also is in this meaning that the term is used in much of the literature.[14]

Sometimes it is not really clear in which of the two meanings the term responsibility is used[15] and the analysis may become somewhat confused. Though there is an obvious relationship between responsibility in the meaning of obligations and responsibility in the meaning of consequences arising out of a breach of an obligation, the difference between the two concepts is significant and they should be clearly distinguished in any discussion on the position of transnational corporations in international law.

III. Private responsibility

The responsibility of corporations is largely determined by a normative order that operates separately and largely independently from public international

---

[12] ICJ, *Legality of the threat or use of nuclear weapons*, Advisory Opinion, ICJ Reports 1996, para. 29.

[13] The ICC proposed as a definition of corporate responsibility: 'the voluntary commitment by business to manage its activities in a responsible way': Business in society: making a positive and responsible contribution, available at www.iccwbo.org/home/news_archives/2002/businsocdoc.asp

[14] e.g. Muschlinski, P., Human rights, social responsibility and the regulation of international business: the development of international standards by intergovernmental organisations, *Non-state Actors and International Law* 3 (2003), pp. 23–152, at 130–131; Westfield, E., Globalization, governance, and multinational enterprise responsibility, *Virginia J. Int'l L.* 42 (2002), pp. 1075–1108.

[15] For instance in Addo, M. (ed.), *Human rights standards and the responsibility of international organizations*, The Hague (Kluwer) 1999; Paust, J. J., Human rights responsibilities of private corporations, *Vand. J. Transnat' l L.* 35 (2002), p. 801.

law and indeed from any other legal order. In part as a response to shortcomings perceived in the second and third model to be discussed below, private responsibility has become increasingly relevant for environmental policies of transnational corporations. It encompasses the various modes of self-regulation adopted by individual transnational corporations[16] and more collective arrangements within the private sector.[17] This form of responsibility is often discussed under the heading of corporate responsibility.[18] Responsibility in this meaning is an ambiguous term, but primarily appears to relate to obligations assumed by corporations (primary rules), rather than to rules that define that corporations that violate rules of conduct should be accountable and face the consequences for their actions (secondary rules).

Although corporate responsibility is often discussed in one breath with the position of transnational corporations in international law, this form of 'responsibility' has nothing to do with responsibility in international law. It is neither based on the violation of norms that according to the sources of international law are binding on transnational corporations, nor are the consequences of a violation of standards of conduct in any way determined by international law. Of course, this does not mean that this form is not or cannot be of much relevance for the actual operation of corporations: it simply means that public international law has a limited domain and that there are other normative orders operating outside that domain – normative orders that may, moreover, use their own concepts and terminology.

From the perspective of general international law, this form of private regulation can be construed in two ways. First, one can take the position that the international legal order is an all-encompassing legal order that necessarily regulates all behaviour in international society. It then may be said that international law regulates transnational corporations by granting them a liberty to determine their own responsibilities. This does not mean that corporations can do whatever they want: their liberty coexists with the liberty of states to regulate corporations. Since international law also protects the power of the

---

[16] See e.g. the overview in Ong, D. M., The impact of environmental law on corporate governance: international and comparative perspectives, *EJIL* 12(4) (2001), pp. 685–726; Gleckman, H., Transnational corporations strategic responses to 'sustainable development', *Green Globe Yearbook* (1995), pp. 93–106.

[17] e.g. ICC Business Charter for Sustainable Development, available at, www.iccwbo.org/home/environment_and_energy/sdcharter/charter/about_charter/about_charter.asp

[18] Westfield, op. cit.; Scriven, J. G., Corporate responsibility and regulating the global enterprise, *Transnational Lawyer* 16(1) (2002), pp. 153–168; Venkata Raman, K., Corporate responsibility to protect the global environment: emerging issues of law and equity, in Bouthillier, Y. L., McRae, D. M., and Pharand, D. (eds.), *Selected papers in international law: contribution of the Canadian Council of International Law*, The Hague (Kluwer) 1999; Ong, op. cit.

state to regulate and control corporations, the liberty it leaves to corporations may have limited effects.[19]

This first construction of the position of transnational corporations in the international legal order is, however, somewhat odd, as it assumes that international law regulates (by granting a liberty) persons that it recognises only to a limited extent as legal persons.

Secondly and more plausibly, one can take the position that, in contrast to the national legal order, the international legal order is not an all-encompassing legal order. This situation has been explained in constitutional terms: the international legal order does not possess a '*Gesamtverfassung*' that grasps the entire community.[20] Rather, it is a limited order that governs only part of international transactions, in particular those of entities exercising public authority. This model recognises that the political domain of the international legal order is, compared to other systems, relatively undeveloped. International law determines the scope of public authority of states and international governmental organisations, but these do not fully reflect and organise a global community.[21] It may be true that, as Teubner writes, 'wo sich autonome Gesellschaftsektoren entwickeln, werden zugleich eigenständige Mechanismen der Rechtsprodukion herausgebildet', but these would not necessarily have to be integrated or linked to the political public order system.[22] Private norms that are adopted to steer corporate behaviour, such as corporate responsibility or '*lex mercatoria*',[23] could be said to constitute a private subsystem[24] that is not subjected to international law.[25]

In certain respects, one could say that the deference of the international legal order to the private sector is a political choice and not a necessary consequence of the limits of the legal system. Nonetheless, it is to be recognised that the interventions of the public sphere are limited due to the political structure of representation of the common interest and the power of corporations. The allocation of power within the global system supports a pluralistic legal structure, whereby persons and entities that are not incorporated in and regulated

---

[19] The failed attempt to negotiate a multilateral agreement on investment was in part an attempt to limit that power and to enhance the liberties of the private sector. See Stern, B., How to regulate globalization, in Byers, M. (ed.), *The role of law in international politics*, Oxford (Oxford University Press) 2000, pp. 247–268, at 249.

[20] Teubner, G., Globale Zivilverfassungen: Alternativen zur staatszentrierten Verfassungstheorie, *ZaöRV* 63 (2003), pp. 1–28, at 5.

[21] Ibid., p. 12.   [22] Ibid, p. 14.

[23] Robé, J., Multinational enterprises: the constitution of a pluralistic legal order, in Teubner, G. (ed.), *Global law without a state*, Aldershot (Dartmouth) 2003, pp. 45–77, at 50–52; Virally, M., *Un tiers droit? Réflexions théoretiques, le droit des relations economiques internationales: études offertes à Berthold Goldmann*, Paris (Litec) 1982, pp. 374–385.

[24] See Teubner, op. cit. p. 6; Robé, op. cit. pp. 68–71; Stern, op. cit. p. 261 nn: 'Law, as a creation of states, has to compete with other, private means of regulation.'

[25] Stern, op. cit. pp. 262–263.

by the public international legal order may form their own normative system.[26] That perspective helps in part to explain why direct regulation of transnational corporations has as yet not really been achieved.

Even though formally corporate responsibility is not a part of the international legal order, it is not necessarily isolated from international environmental law. It is a plausible hypothesis, though one in need of more empirical research, that principles of international environmental law have had a large measure of 'persuasive'[27] or 'influential' authority[28] on the development of corporate responsibility.

Private norms adopted by way of self-regulation may also in other ways be legally relevant for international law. An assessment of the contents and effect of principles of corporate responsibility is helpful for understanding the possibility of development of international law in this area. Because the main principles of international environmental law are written for public rather than for private entities, they need to be 'translated' to the private sector (see further section V). An assessment of experiences in self-regulation and corporate responsibility seems greatly helpful in understanding the possibility to apply particular primary international rules to corporations.[29]

Also, private rules may be relevant for the application of international environmental law in judicial practice. For example, it has been reported that norms of corporate responsibility have been invoked before and applied as principles of interpretation in domestic cases.[30]

The fact that corporate responsibility regulation can be legally relevant for international environmental law, of course, does not change its legal status. As noted in a different context by Prosper Weil, between showing due interest in normative developments not based on the sources of international law 'and integrating them into the normative system under the cover of a sliding scale of normativity, there is a gap that can be bridged only at the cost of denying the specific nature of the legal phenomenon'.[31]

The role played by corporate responsibility serves as a useful reminder of the limited domain of responsibility in public international law and indeed of public international law itself. The regulation of responsibility of corporations beyond the national legal order need not take place in the international legal

---

[26] Robé, op. cit. pp. 70–71. See more generally Hall, R. B. and Biersteker, T. J. (eds.), *The emergence of private authority in global governance*, Cambridge (Cambridge University Press) 2002.
[27] Knop, K., Here and there: international law in domestic courts, *New York University J. Int'l Law and Politics* 32(2) (2000), pp. 501–535.
[28] Moran, M., Authority, influence and persuasion: Baker, Charter values and the puzzle of method, in Dyzenhaus, D. (ed.), *The unity of public law*, Oxford (Hart Publishing) 2004, p. 389.
[29] Ong, op. cit.   [30] Muschlinski, op. cit. p. 129.
[31] Weil, P., Towards relative normativity in international law?, *AJIL* 77 (1983), p. 413, at 417.

order. Much of the debate on international legal personality of transnational of corporations (that usually serves as a stepping stone towards a discussion of international legal responsibility or liability) is rather abstract and may be of little help in an actual understanding of the form and scope of responsibility that guide the operation of transnational corporations.[32]

IV. Responsibility under national law

The second model for responsibility of transnational corporations is responsibility under national law. This has long been the dominant model for regulation of responsibility of transnational corporations. For many decades, international law has attempted to resolve any problems that the activities of transnational corporations may pose for public values, by strengthening national legal orders. International law has to some extent clarified the obligations of states (both 'host states' and 'home states') to control private entities, and has confirmed that failure to impose and enforce obligations on corporations may, in terms of secondary rules, result in the responsibility of the state.[33]

In this model, international law does not directly address the responsibility of transnational corporations. Rather, it addresses the obligations of states vis-à-vis private corporations. Following Kelsen, one can say that most parts of international environmental law oblige the state, and that the state subsequently determines in its own legal order the rules by which corporations have to comply, and the responsibilities they incur if they fail to do so, in order to ensure that the state can comply with its own obligations under international law.[34]

The dominance of this model of regulation at the same time explains and is a result of the limited status of transnational corporations in international law. It is true that in certain narrow respects, transnational corporations have acquired a legal status that is independent from the national legal order of the state in which they are incorporated and/or of the state in which they are active. That holds true in particular for the position of transnational corporations under regional or bilateral investment treaties that grant corporations certain rights of protection and sometimes the right to bring legal action before

---

[32] See, for a discussion of the concept of international legal personality, also applied to transnational corporations: Nijman, J., *The concept of international legal personality: an inquiry into the history and theory of international law*, The Hague (TMC Asser Press) 2004.

[33] Joseph, S., Taming the Leviathans: multinational enterprises and human rights, *NILR* 46 (1999), pp. 171–203; Franchioni, F., Exporting environmental hazard through multinational enterprises: can the state of origin be held responsible?, in Francioni, F. and Scovazzi, T. (ed.), *International responsibility for environmental harm*, The Hague (Kluwer) 1991, pp. 275–298.

[34] Kelsen, H., *Law and peace in international relations, the Oliver Wendell Holmes Lectures*, 1940–41, Cambridge, Mass. (Harvard University Press) 1942, p. 96.

international arbitral tribunals.[35] Some writers allow on this basis for the possibility of some form of international legal personality. For instance, Friedmann stated that corporations acquire a 'limited *ad hoc* subjectivity to the extent that their transactions are controlled by the norms of public rather than private international law'.[36] Yet, the status of transnational corporations is a limited one. The international legal order has overwhelmingly made use of political rather than legal instruments to influence the activities of transnational corporations.[37] Malanczuk writes that while writers and governments in Western countries are usually 'prepared to admit that ... companies have some degree of [limited] international legal personality',[38] even the most influential global multinational corporations such as IBM and Unilever 'have not been upgraded by states to international subjects proper'.[39] Brownlie notes that '[i]n principle, corporations of municipal law do not have international legal personality'.[40]

Even though we can accept that the concept of legal personality is a compound concept and that transnational corporations do not need to possess *all* rights and duties that are possessed by states in order to be recognised as legal persons,[41] one has to acknowledge that the position of transnational corporations in the international legal order is weak. Their lack of full international legal personality leaves transnational corporations in principle subjected to the national legal order of one or more states.

All this is reflected in international environmental law, which directs its rights and duties at the state and relies on the way in which the state in its national law controls corporations. Illustrative of the reliance of general international law on national law is the current work of the International Law Commission (ILC) on transboundary harm. It was widely recognised in the ILC as well as in the United Nations General Assembly that the 'operator' (that is 'any person in command or control of the activity at the time the incident

---

[35] Weil, P., The state, the foreign investor and international law: the no longer stormy relationship of a ménage à trois, in Schlemmer-Schulte, S. and Tung, K. (eds.), *Liber amicorum Ibrahim F. I. Shihata: international finance and development law*, The Hague (Kluwer) 2001, pp. 839–856.

[36] Friedmann, W., *The changing structure of international law*, New York (Colombia University Press) 1964, p. 223.

[37] See section IV.

[38] Malanczuk, P. (ed.), *Akehurst's modern introduction to international law*, London (Routledge) 1997, p. 100.

[39] Ibid., p. 102.

[40] See Brownlie, I., *Principles of public international law*, Oxford (Oxford University Press) 2003, p. 65. See for other negative views the references in Kokkini-Iatridou, D. and de Waart, P. J. I. M., Foreign investments in developing countries: legal personality of multinationals in international law, *Netherlands Yearbook of International Law* 14 (1983), pp. 87–131.

[41] The ICJ noted: 'The subjects of law in any legal system are not necessarily identical in their nature or in the extent of their rights': ICJ, *Reparations for injuries*, Advisory Opinion, ICJ Reports 1949, p. 178.

causing transboundary damage occurs'),[42] should bear primary responsibility for environmentally harmful activities. Special Rapporteur Rao, having reviewed the comments in the Sixth Committee, noted:

> Any scheme of allocation of loss should place the duty of compensation first on the operator. The operator is in control of the activity and is also its direct beneficiary. This approach would adequately reflect the 'polluter pays' principle, in particular the policy of internalizing the costs of operation. Accordingly, the operator is required to obtain the necessary insurance coverage and show appropriate financial guarantees.[43]

However, the text adopted by the ILC[44] envisaged that the obligations of prevention and compensation are imposed on the state, not directly on the operator. The Draft Articles on International Liability in case of Loss from Transboundary Harm arising out of Hazardous Activities provide, for instance, that each state should take necessary measures to ensure that prompt and adequate compensation is available for victims of transboundary damage caused by hazardous activities located within its territory or otherwise under its jurisdiction or control.[45] This principle will require measures in the national legal order.

Only in a few instances, international environmental law determines in detail the responsibilities to be applied to private operators. The best examples in this category are the liability conventions that determine, for those states that accept them, the detailed contents of national law and more particularly the rules of liability that apply to private operators who cause damage to the environment.[46] To a certain extent, these types of obligations also rely on the national legal order. For instance, they rely for their application on national courts that have jurisdiction in regard to the claim.[47]

---

[42] Principle 2(e); UN Doc. A/CN.4/L.662, 20 July 2004.

[43] ILC, *International liability for injurious consequences arising out of acts not prohibited by international law (international liability in case of loss from transboundary harm arising out of hazardous activities), Second report on the legal regime for the allocation of loss in case of transboundary harm arising out of hazardous activities by Pemmaraju Sreenivasa Rao*, Special Rapporteur, UN Doc. A/CN.4/540, 15 March 2004, p. 14.

[44] *Draft Articles on Prevention of Transboundary Harm from Hazardous Activities, Report of the ILC on the work of its fifty-third session*, Official Records of the General Assembly, Fifty–sixth session, Supplement No. 10 (A/56/10), chp.V.E.1), e.g. Articles 3 and 6.

[45] ILC, UN Doc. A/CN.4/L.662, 20 July 2004, Principle 4.

[46] e.g. Convention on Civil Liability for Damage Resulting from Activities Dangerous to the Environment, 21 June 1993, ETS no. 150. See discussion by Churchill, R. R., Facilitating (transnational) civil liability litigation for environmental damage by means of treaties: progress, problems, and prospects, *Y. B. Int'l Env'l L.* 12 (2001), p. 3.

[47] e.g. Article 19 of the Convention on Civil Liability for Damage Resulting from Activities Dangerous to the Environment 1993.

One might also construe this latter type of treaties as direct regulation of corporations by international law.[48] The liability conventions impose direct liability on operators.[49] Hyde noted that, in light of the fact that national courts would exercise jurisdiction in regard to acts that international law criminalises (but the argument can be applied by analogy to liability of corporations), it is:

> not unscientific to declare that [the individual] is guilty of conduct which the law of nations itself brands as internationally illegal. For it is by virtue of that law that such sovereign acquires the right to punish and is also burdened with the duty to prevent or prosecute.[50]

If one adopts this perspective, one can say that this form of regulation and responsibility straddles indirect responsibility under national law and direct responsibility under international law, to be discussed in section V.

Another way in which international law could be relevant for responsibility or liability at national level, is that states may choose to make international environmental law directly applicable to transnational corporations in the national legal order. If they do, it might be said that in those states, international environmental law directly controls the activities of corporations.[51] However, there is very limited evidence that this has been done. It has often been discussed whether this could apply to the Alien Tort Claims Act (ATCA) of the USA. Through application of national tort law, combined with a liberal reading of international law, corporations could be held liable for environmental damage. However, lower courts have been reluctant to accept the position that environmental harm would be a violation of international law in the meaning of the ATCA.[52] The decision of the US Supreme Court in *Sosa* v. *Alvarez Machain* appears for all practical purposes to have blocked the way to an application

---

[48] Ratner, S. R., Corporations and human rights: a theory of international responsibility, *Yale L. J.* 111 (2001), pp. 443–545, at 480–481 (stating that to hold otherwise would be to confuse the existence of responsibility with the mode of implementing it).
[49] e.g. Article 6 of the Convention on Civil Liability for Damage Resulting from Activities Dangerous to the Environment 1993: 'The operator in respect of a dangerous activity mentioned under Article 2, paragraph 1, sub-paragraphs a to c shall be liable for the damage caused by the activity as a result of incidents at the time or during the period when he was exercising the control of that activity.'
[50] Hyde, C. C., *International law, chiefly as interpreted and applied by the United States*, Boston (Little, Brown and Company) 2nd rev. edn. 1947, p. 33.
[51] Hongju Koh, H., Separating myth from reality about corporate responsibility litigation, *J. Int'l Economic L.* 7 (2004), pp. 263–274, at 267 (referring to 'domestic legislative internationalization of an international norm'); Nollkaemper, A., Public international law in transnational litigation against multinational corporations: prospects and problems in the courts of the Netherlands, in Kamminga and Zia-Zarifa, op. cit. pp. 265–281.
[52] *Beanal* v. *Freeport-McMoran, Inc.*, 197 F.3d 161, 167 (5th Cir. 1999). Environmental claims were also discussed in *Aguinda* v. *Texaco, Inc.*, dismissed on *forum non conveniens*, 303 F.3d 470. See in general Herz, R. L., Litigating environmental abuses under the Alien Tort Claims Act: a practical assessment, *Virginia J. Int'l L.* 40 (2000), p. 545.

of the ATCA to environmental law. It was held that 'courts should require any claim based on the present-day law of nations to rest on a norm of international character accepted by the civilized world and defined with a specificity comparable to the features of the 18th-century paradigms'.[53] This makes it very unlikely that any international environmental norm would be a basis of jurisdiction or a cause of action. In other jurisdictions the situation is not much different.[54] For these reasons, the direct role of international law in regulation and responsibility of corporations is likely to remain limited.

Apart from the limited possibilities that international law would directly determine either the obligations (primary norms) or responsibility/liability (secondary norms), international law operates through and is dependent on national law. This does not mean that responsibility under national law is of limited relevance for a proper regulation of transnational corporations. It has often been said that, because of the transnational nature of transnational corporations, reliance on national law would be of relatively limited use for the regulation of transnational corporations and that regulation of transnational corporations should be strengthened by lifting corporations from the national to the international legal order. Though there may be cases where the national legal order is unreliable because the state is unable or unwilling to enforce laws against transnational corporations, for instance in cases of collusion between states and corporations or in cases of weak or failing states, there is something odd about that argument. In general, the regulatory power of the national legal order is superior to the power of the international legal order. Also, when subjects are regulated by international law, it commonly is appreciated that the effectiveness of regulation is contingent on national rather than international law.[55] International regulation as such will at best be the beginning of an answer to the practical problems of environmental degradation caused by transnational corporations and will eventually have to rely on the national legal order.

Rather than denying the potential for reliance on national law and embracing the international legal order, the better and perhaps more realistic approach would seem to be to strengthen the responsibilities of both home states and host states, to strengthen the regulatory power of states, and to improve coordination of national legal systems, for instance by clarifying rules on jurisdiction, applicable law, enforcement, transboundary access to decision-making, participation in impact assessment procedures, and access to courts. This is at least in part the route that also has been advocated for the ILC.[56] In this respect, the

---

[53] See http://supct.law.cornell.edu/supct/html/03-339.ZO.html
[54] Anderson. M. and Galizzi, P., *International environmental law in national courts*, London (British Institute of International and Comparative Law) 2002.
[55] Conforti, B., *International law and the role of domestic legal systems*, Dordrecht (Martinus Nijhoff Publishers) 1993.
[56] See A.E. Boyle, Chapter 23.

second paradigm is not only the traditional paradigm of international law, but also the paradigm that holds the most prospects for improving regulation and effective environmental performance by transnational corporations.

Apart from the interaction between international law and national legal orders, there may also be an interaction between corporate responsibility (which, as noted above, functions largely in separation from international law) and the national legal order. However, like international law, principles of corporate responsibility in general seem to operate independently from national law. Determinations of responsibility and liability of corporations in the national legal order will proceed on the basis of national law, both in terms of obligations and principles of liability. In legal terms, corporate responsibility not only is separated from the international legal domain but also from the national legal order. However, this is an area where more research in the practice of courts may be useful.

V. Direct responsibility in international law

In addition to the development of corporate responsibility and responsibility under national law, we have seen cautious steps for the development of a third model: direct responsibility of transnational corporations in the international legal order. This development is based on the premise that, on the one hand, corporate responsibility would provide insufficient guarantees for proper environmental policies and, on the other hand, national legal orders would be incapable of providing sufficient degrees of protection. Subjecting transnational corporations directly to international law has been thought to be able to fill these lacuna.[57]

The policy arguments for such a development are particularly strong when multinational corporations are beyond the control of both the home and the host state. There is an analogy here with the development of international human rights law and of international law on individual criminal responsibility – two areas where, because of the inadequacy of national law, international law addresses private persons directly.

As yet, the international legal order has largely confined its approach to transnational corporations to normative instruments that rely on political rather than legal authority. States and international organisations have adopted a variety of texts that call on transnational corporations to adopt and implement certain policies, without imposing legal obligations or responsibilities. The best example is the OECD *Guidelines for Multinational Enterprises*, as revised in 2000.[58] These provide, inter alia, that:

---

[57] e.g. Kokkini-Iatridou and de Waart, op. cit. pp. 101–102; Ratner, op. cit. pp. 461–465.
[58] See www.oecd.org/dataoecd/56/36/1922428.pdf

> Enterprises should, within the framework of laws, regulations and administrative practices in the countries in which they operate, *and in consideration of relevant international agreements, principles, objectives, and standards,* take due account of the need to protect the environment, public health and safety, and generally to conduct their activities in a manner contributing to the wider goal of sustainable development (emphasis added).

The document lists a range of particular actions that should be undertaken by enterprises, including the establishment of a system of environmental management that would provide for collection of data regarding the environmental impacts of their activities, the establishment of measurable objectives and targets for improved environmental performance, and monitoring and verification of progress toward environmental objectives or targets.

Another recent political initiative is the adoption, in August 2003, by the UN Subcommission on the Promotion and Protection of Human Rights of the *Norms on the Responsibilities of Transnational Corporations and Other Business Enterprises with regard to Human Rights.*[59] The document applies international principles related to human rights (pertaining to such diverse areas as labour, health, non-discrimination, and safety), including a provision on environmental protection, to transnational corporations and other business enterprises:

> Transnational corporations and other business enterprises shall carry out their activities in accordance with national laws, regulations, administrative practices and policies relating to the preservation of the environment of the countries in which they operate, as well as in accordance with relevant international agreements, principles, objectives, responsibilities and standards with regard to the environment as well as human rights, public health and safety, bioethics and the precautionary principle, and shall generally conduct their activities in a manner contributing to the wider goal of sustainable development.

A third development at the political level is the Global Compact, launched in 2000. This is a mechanism that brings companies together with UN agencies: the Office of the High Commissioner for Human Rights, the International Labour Organisation, the United Nations Environment Programme, the United Nations Development Programme, and the United Nations Industrial Development Organisation. The involvement of the UN in this collaborative effort with the private sector is authorised and supported by the General Assembly[60]

---

[59] *Norms on the Responsibilities of Transnational Corporations and Other Business Enterprises with regard to Human Rights,* UN Doc. E/CN.4/Sub.2/2003/12/Rev. 2 (2003), approved 13 August 2003, by UN Subcommission on the Promotion and Protection of Human Rights, Res. 2003/16, UN Doc. E/CN.4/Sub.2/2003/L.11, 2003, p. 52. See also Weissbrodt, D. and Kruger, M., Norms on the responsibilities of transnational corporations and other business enterprises with regard to human rights, *AJIL* 97(4) (2003), pp. 901–922.

[60] A/RES/55/215; A/RES/56/76; A/RES/58/129.

and also on that basis can be considered as a means for the organised international community to further sustainable development by cooperating with the private sector.[61]

Finally, the 2002 World Summit on Sustainable Development recognised that 'in pursuit of its legitimate activities the private sector, including both large and small companies, has a duty to contribute to the evolution of equitable and sustainable communities and societies'.[62]

These developments are noteworthy because they indicate that the international community (organised in the Commission on Human Rights, the World Summit on Sustainable Development or other forums), has recognised a responsibility to protect international public (environmental) values by influencing the private sector directly, not only through states.

However, these developments do not carry direct legal consequences for transnational corporations, neither in terms of primary or secondary rules. To the extent that they envisage the need that corporations answer for the consequences of their policies, for instance through monitoring processes in the framework of the OECD[63] or possible processes that may be developed in conjunction with the *Norms on the Responsibilities of Transnational Corporations and Other Business Enterprises with regard to Human Rights*,[64] that would be a political and not a legal 'responsibility'. In fact, the documents largely seem to rely on private forms of responsibility and, as such, defer to the first model of responsibility (section II). For instance, the World Summit on Sustainable Development agreed that 'there is a need for private sector corporations to enforce corporate accountability, which should take place within a transparent and stable regulatory environment'.[65]

In legal scholarship there has been some support for the proposition that the actions at the political level should be transformed into direct international legal regulation and possibly also responsibility of transnational corporations.[66] Various scholars have proposed international conventions that would impose direct obligations on corporations.[67] One could say that such legal development would partly integrate the free-standing private order in, or at least link it with, the public international legal domain. In the words of Teubner, such

---

[61] See generally Kell, G. and Ruggie, J. G., Global markets and social legitimacy: the case for the 'Global Compact', *Transnational Corporations* 8 (1999), pp. 101–120.

[62] A/CONF.199/20, para. 27.

[63] See Tully, S., The 2000 review of the OECD Guidelines for Multinational Enterprises, *ICQL* 50 (2001), pp. 394–404.

[64] Para. 16 states: 'Transnational corporations and other business enterprises shall be subject to periodic monitoring and verification by United Nations, other international and national mechanisms already in existence or yet to be created, regarding application of the Norms.'

[65] A/CONF.199/20, para. 29.   [66] Joseph, op. cit.

[67] See Jonas Ebbesson, Chapter 8; Hongju Koh, op. cit. p. 273.

developments would create a '*Mischungsverfassung*' between the public and the private domain.[68]

There is no theoretical or conceptual barrier to such a development. The argument that transnational corporations do not possess international legal personality does not impede the direct imposition of international environmental principles. In fact, personality would simply follow such an imposition.[69]

At the same time, it is clear that, as noted above, the organisation of political power at the global level is not conducive to such a legal development. Also, it is clear that many states may have political objections to such a development and also fear potential legal consequences. One pertinent objection may be that an international procedure against a corporation may implicate the home state or the host state, when the corporation would take the position that it complies with the (defunct) legislation of the state in question. Another objection may be that granting transnational corporations the status of legal persons in the international legal order might reduce the controlling power of the national legal order.

Probably caused by such more or less plausible objections, the state of the law is not encouraging. There are no indications that the types of principles presently contained in the OECD Guidelines or the draft UN Norms of the Global Compact would be made legally binding on corporations, let alone that a system of secondary rules would emerge. Indeed, it has been suggested that the move towards public-private partnerships in the United Nations may, in fact, discourage a development of the law.[70] Present international law also does not provide for a general principle of direct civil responsibility (or liability) or criminal responsibility of corporations in international law. There is no treaty or state practice that allows us to identify a general principle to that effect.[71] As to criminal responsibility, while one can accept that in areas where individuals can be held responsible, such responsibility can be extended to corporations, this is of little relevance for violations of environmental law since an act that causes harm to the environment in principle will not entail individual responsibility.[72] It also seems very doubtful whether, outside the category of

---

[68] Teubner, G., see n. 20 above; cf. Hongju Koh, op. cit. p. 273 (referring to 'private-public regimes').

[69] Cf. Ratner, op. cit. pp. 474–476.

[70] Utting, P., Why all the fuss?, *UN Chronicle* 40(1) (2003), available at www.un.org/Pubs/chronicle/2003/issue1/0103p65.html

[71] But see Ratner, op. cit. p. 497 (arguing that in cases where the state is responsible for certain acts of private actors, 'those actors can also be held responsible for that same conduct under international law').

[72] Hongju Koh, op. cit. p. 265; Ratner, op. cit. p. 494. It is to be taken into account, though, that the jurisdiction of the International Criminal Court does not extend to corporations.

crimes for which international individual responsibility exists,[73] international law contains a general principle on corporate complicity with wrongs under public international law.[74]

The absence of substantial legal development in this area is matched by an absence of fundamental legal thinking on the question of what the responsibility of transnational corporations, if it were to be developed, would look like. It is to be recalled that corporate responsibility has little, if anything, to do with responsibility of corporations under international law. If we are to see a development towards responsibility of corporations in international law, there are several fundamental issues to be considered. The four most pertinent issues appear to be the way in which such norms would be made binding on corporations; the way in which the legal obligations and responsibilities would be lifted into the public order; the translation of public (primary) norms to private entities, and the application of responsibility norms to private entities.

The first question is how the objective to make rules of international law binding on corporations is to be achieved. This problem is somewhat comparable to similar questions that have arisen in the past with regard to the application of international law to international organisations and de facto regimes or rebel movements. For organisations, the problem is solved by allowing international organisations to become a party to treaties. For de facto regimes, the problem (at least as far as international humanitarian law is concerned) is solved, in principle, by the understanding that when a state becomes party to a humanitarian law treaty that provides obligations for rebel groups, rebel groups within its territory also are bound to the rules contained in that treaty. The second approach appears more relevant for transnational corporations than the first one. However, the situation differs because transnational corporations are characterised by the fact that they, at least to some extent, escape the control of the national legal order. A treaty which would meaningfully regulate obligations and responsibilities of corporations would be in need of substantial ratification.

The second and closely related question is whether and how such a treaty would actually achieve its purpose of directly regulating the obligations and responsibilities of corporations. It would primarily bind states. Imposing direct obligations and responsibilities on corporations most likely would remain dependent on effectuation of the obligations and responsibilities in national law – much like human rights law or much of international criminal law. But in that case we will not actually be speaking of international responsibility of corporations, just as the responsibility of most of international criminal law that is effected in national courts is based on national law. The other alternative would

---

[73] Hongju Koh, op. cit. p. 267.
[74] See for the argument in support of a principle of complicity Clapham, A., On complicity, in Henzelin, M. and Roth, R. (eds.), *Le droit penal à l'épreuve de l'internationalisation*, Paris (Brulant) 2002, pp. 241–275; Ratner, op. cit. pp. 500–502.

be to create an international forum, somewhat comparable to international criminal tribunals, that in fact would effectuate an international responsibility. While this need not necessarily be of a criminal nature, it is, however, a very unlikely prospect.

The third question is whether and how norms of public law can be applied to private entities. Principles of public international law are drafted as public law norms applying to public authorities.[75] Can norms that were developed to apply to states be applied to private entities? The nature and purpose of state authority is widely different from the nature and purpose of authority exercised by corporations. As a consequence, the principles and underpinnings of public international law and corporate responsibility are also different. It may not be possible to solve the legal problems created by a shift in authority from the public to the private sphere by a wholesale and non-discriminate transfer of public international law norms to the private sphere.

The *Draft Norms on the Responsibilities of Transnational Corporations and Other Business Enterprises with regard to Human Rights* illustrate the problem. They consider that transnational corporations are obligated to respect generally recognised responsibilities and norms in a long list of over thirty treaties and other instruments. This includes some treaties that pertain to private actors, including civil liability treaties (such as the Convention on Civil Liability for Damage Resulting from Activities Dangerous to the Environment) and criminal law treaties (such as the Torture Convention). But, it also includes a wide variety of treaties that can be characterised as public law instruments: the addressees are states, and they require state action for their application. They oblige transnational corporations to 'carry out their activities in accordance with relevant international agreements, principles, objectives, responsibilities, and standards with regard to the environment'. However, many of these agreements, principles, objectives, responsibilities, and standards require political decisions, as well as a reordering of governmental priorities and legislation. Can these principles, which often rely on balancing private rights with the public interest, really be applied without substantial adjustment to private entities? Such standards will provide insufficient guidance to the courts and will be of little or no use in determinations of corporate liability. A blanket transfer of public norms to the private sphere may fail to recognise that while public law norms may need to be translated to the private sphere, they cannot simply be transplanted without adjustment.[76]

---

[75] Ratner, op. cit., pp. 492–493.
[76] But see Ratner, op. cit., pp. 513–514, suggesting that the balancing of interests between individual rights and state interests could be replaced by a balancing of interests between individual rights and the interests of an enterprise. Arguably, the same reasoning could be applied to the balancing of interests that is part of international environmental obligations.

In the translation of public to private standards, one also will have to take into account the nature of the corporation. The Draft Norms on the Responsibilities raise the question of whether one set of public international law principles can, without discrimination, be applied to all corporations. As they are presently formulated, they apply to all 'transnational corporations and other business enterprises'. That may not be a problem for principles that require corporations to refrain from ordering killings. But is it possible to apply principles that require more positive action, for instance in the sphere of labour rights or environmental protection, to all corporations? The possibility to comply with certain norms may be dependent on power, resources, capabilities, and factual situations and these norms will have to be subject to some form of due diligence standard.

The OECD Guidelines and the Global Compact are more attuned to the specific position of transnational corporations. The Global Compact contains three principles pertaining to the environment: businesses should (1) support a precautionary approach to environmental challenges; (2) undertake initiatives to promote greater environmental responsibility; and (3) encourage the development and diffusion of environmentally friendly technologies. In this respect, these non-legally binding norms, just as the norms adopted voluntarily by the private sector, offer a better model for legal regulation of transnational corporations than a large part of state-oriented public international law.

The fourth question concerns the application of secondary rules to transnational corporations. It has already been noted that it is not immediately obvious what role an international responsibility of corporations would actually play, given its reliance on national law. Nonetheless, in assessing the options for legal development, the question of the nature of responsibility of corporations may need to be considered.

It is a plausible proposition that once international law would directly impose primary norms on transnational corporations, secondary rules would also become applicable.[77] However, the question then arises as to the nature and scope of such responsibilities. Several authors have considered that the secondary rules of state responsibility may be applied to responsibility of corporations.[78] The Draft Norms on the Responsibilities state, somewhat confusingly:

> Transnational corporations and other business enterprises shall provide prompt, effective and adequate reparation to those persons, entities and communities that have been adversely affected by failures to comply with

---

[77] It is to be noted, though, that there is no general acceptance that rebel groups, who are bound by primary norms, are responsible for their acts under international law; see Zegveld, L., *Accountability of armed opposition groups in international law*, Cambridge (Cambridge University Press) 2002.

[78] Hongju Koh, op. cit. p. 268 (applying the rule of state 'complicity' to corporations); Ratner, op. cit. pp. 495–496.

these Norms through, inter alia, reparations, restitution, compensation and rehabilitation for any damage done or property taken. In connection with determining damages in regard to criminal sanctions, and in all other respects, these Norms shall be applied by national courts and/or international tribunals, pursuant to national and international law.[79]

The last words seem to suggest that international law contains principles of responsibility that are attuned to the specific characteristics of transnational corporations. While there may be parallels between responsibility of states and responsibility of corporations (not surprising since state responsibility law in part is derived from national law analogies that as such are applicable to corporations), there can be no automatic transposition. The nature of the organisation of states, the rules that apply to them, as well as the nature of the defences that states may invoke, cannot automatically be applied to corporations.[80]

The application of public international law norms also raises the question of the relationship between obligations and responsibilities of private entities on the one hand and of states on the other. If one accepts a set of independent obligations of transnational corporations with accompanying responsibilities, these will most likely coexist with the obligations and responsibility of states. The Draft Norms on the Responsibilities recognise that states have the primary responsibility in regard to the protection of human rights (one must presume that that also applies to the provision dealing with environmental protection). The coexistence of such responsibilities would raise questions of joint and several liability, primary and subsidiary responsibility, etc. On such issues, little work has been done.

VI. Conclusion

Responsibility of transnational corporations for activities that cause harm to the environment is a multidimensional problem. Relevant norms are scattered among different levels of regulation: between national and international levels and between public and private spheres of regulation. In this sense, responsibility of transnational corporations is a preeminent example of 'multilevel governance'.

In this complex group of forms of regulation, the role of public international law is modest. It leaves matters of responsibility to the private sectors and national law – perhaps because that is most efficient, perhaps also because, given the position of states, there is no real alternative. There appears to be limited support to develop rules that would directly regulate transnational corporations in the international legal order, and even less to develop international enforcement mechanisms. It seems that the role of international law will continue to be an indirect one that exerts its influence through the obligations

---

[79] At para. 18.   [80] Ratner, op. cit. pp. 495, 519.

and policies of states. Beyond this, the modest role of the international legal order is best seen as providing a somewhat incoherent framework for political decision-making that influences both national laws and policies and private arrangements within the private sector.

If international law were to develop in the direction of direct responsibilities of transnational corporations, critical questions need to be faced. These relate to the conditions of responsibility, the nature of responsibility (civil, criminal, or 'international'), reparation, and its relationship to the responsibility of states. In literature, one senses an overestimation of the possibility to translate the law as it applies to states and other public entities to transnational corporations. As yet, there is a certain imbalance between the expanding literature on the topic of responsibility of transnational corporations on the one hand, and the embryonic understanding of the nature of such responsibility on the other.

Whether or not it is worthwhile to spend much time on developing proper concepts of international responsibility for corporations remains to be seen. The better approach would seem to be to strengthen the responsibilities of both home states and host states, to strengthen the regulatory power of such states, and to improve coordination of national legal systems, for instance by clarifying rules on jurisdiction, applicable law, enforcement, transboundary access to decision-making, participation in impact assessment procedures, and access to courts. In that respect, it is national rules on responsibility and liability (although possibly guided by international law) that offer the best prospects to contribute to improved environmental performance of transnational corporations.

8

Transboundary corporate responsibility in environmental matters: fragments and foundations for a future framework

JONAS EBBESSON

I. Transboundary subjectivity rather than effects

Corporations, just like pollution, are becoming increasingly transboundary, and they spread in increasingly complex structures. Economists and sociologists debate whether corporations, for the most part, operate as *multinational enterprises* (MNEs) with some national base, as *transnational corporations* (TNCs) active in many countries but without a particular link to any country, or through even more diffused *international networks* or clusters of firms, subunits, suppliers, and subcontractors.[1] There is no general agreement on how to label the various forms of transboundary economic organisation,[2] and neither does the given distinction reveal the diversity of corporate structures. Rather, the

---

This chapter is part of a project on responsibility of transnational corporations for environmental harm in international law, supported by the Bank of Sweden Tercentenary Foundation.

[1] E.g. Castells, M., *The rise of the network society, the information age*, vol. I, Oxford (Blackwell) 1996, pp. 190–195.

[2] The Subcommission on the Promotion and Protection of Human Rights, *Norms on the Responsibilities of Transnational Corporations and Other Business Enterprises with regard to Human Rights*, UN Doc. E/CN.4/Sub.2/2003/12/Rev.2, 2003, para. 20, defines 'transnational corporation' as 'an economic entity operating in more than one country or a cluster of economic entities operating in two or more countries – whatever their legal form, whether in their home country or country of activity, and whether taken individually or collectively'. According to the OECD, *Guidelines for Multinational Enterprises 2001*, reprinted in OECD, *Annual report 2001: Guidelines for multinational enterprises: global instruments for corporate responsibility*, Paris (OECD) 2001, also available at www.oecd.org, '[a] precise definition of *multinational enterprise* is not required for the purpose of the Guidelines. These usually comprise companies or other entities established in more than one country and so linked that they may co-ordinate their operations in various ways. While one or more of these entities may be able to exercise a significant influence over the activities of others, their degree of autonomy within the enterprise may vary widely from one multinational enterprise to another. Ownership may be private, state or mixed' (emphasis added).

difficulty in terming and defining them reflects the multitude of structures and relationships.

A significant factor when allocating responsibility for environmentally harmful activities is whether one corporate unit is wholly or partly owned or controlled by another, or formally a unit within a well-defined enterprise. Yet, new corporate relations and modes of economic organisation may influence the legal conceptions of responsibility and corporate governance, so as also to make a corporate entity responsible for the conduct of another entity that is formally autonomous but actually dependent on the former.

It is a truism that corporations – whether active in one, two, or more countries – cause harm to health and the environment, and that the adverse effects may extend beyond the borders of the state of the activity. When such effects occur, the course fits with the current paradigm of international environmental law, which is particularly focused on transboundary *effects* on health and the environment, and transboundary *fluxes* of harmful substances. However, the main concern of this chapter is rather the mentioned transboundary *subjectivity and structure* of the corporations themselves, when acting in several states and jurisdictions, and the possibility of abusing this structure so as to escape from responsibility.

While the bulk of international environmental law is prompted by the immediate or potential transboundary fluxes of pollution or by physical or biological effects across state borders, these are not the only rationales. Problems related to health and the environment may call for 'larger than national conceptions' also in other cases. One example is where national law, because of its bound nature, cannot cover all the conduct harmful to the nation's citizens, and where multiple national legal systems tend to clash.[3] Such conceptions are relevant to the control of MNEs/TNCs.

So far, though, the development of international law through various multilateral and bilateral trade and investment agreements has been limited to promoting corporate *interests* and improving the protection of corporate *rights*, without a corresponding development to define the transboundary *duties and responsibilities* of these same corporations. In addition, the national deregulation of capital markets, strict policies of the International Monetary Foundation,[4] and a general integration of the international economy has facilitated the expansion of corporations across state borders, and complicated state control of corporate activities – thus creating a new 'geography of power'.[5] In all, the

---

[3] See Fox, E. M., 'Global markets, national law, and the regulation of business: a view from the top', in Likosky, M. (ed.), *Transnational legal processes: Globalisation and power disparaties*, London (Butterworths) 2002, pp. 135–147.

[4] For a critical account of the International Monetary Foundation, see Stiglitz, J., *Globalization and its discontents*, London (Penguin) 2002.

[5] Sassen, S., *Losing control?: Sovereignty in an age of globalization*, New York (Columbia University Press) 1996.

rights bestowed on corporations when transcending state borders are further developed than international rules and institutions to control them or make them responsible for damage to health and the environment.[6]

By juridical cunning, corporations active in different countries can therefore abuse the inadequacy of national institutions and jurisdictional borders to avoid taking appropriate protective measures and accepting responsibility, including liability.[7] For instance, by splitting the corporation into several bodies in different jurisdictions, a parent company may circumvent responsibility and liability over its subsidiaries, even though it maintains full de facto control of the activities. A similar case arises when a foreign company imposes overwhelming de facto control on a subcontractor, making the latter virtually dependent upon the former. The situation is even more complicated when a subunit or subcontractor, strongly pushed by other actors in the network, causes harm to health or the environment, without there being a single parent company or easily identifiable corporate unit on which responsibility can be transferred. In all, this waning responsibility may have detrimental effects to health and the environment, and may also complicate or even bar the pursuit of environmental justice.[8]

Despite the call for larger than national conceptions and for changes in international law, e.g. at the 2002 World Summit on Sustainable Development,[9] the control of MNEs/TNCs essentially remains a domestic legal issue for the state where the harmful activity takes place. There is no general international legal framework devoted to the issue. What exist, though, are uncoordinated *fragments* that define corporate responsibility in international law, in various national laws of extra-territorial application, and in 'non-legal' arrangements. It is the intention of this chapter to identify such fragments and consider whether

---

[6] Kamminga, M. and Zia-Zarafi, S., Liability of multinational corporations under international law, in Kamminga, M. and Zia-Zarafi, S. (eds.), *Liability of multinational corporations under international law*, The Hague (Kluwer) 2000, pp. 5–7.

[7] Unless specified, I use the term 'responsibility' in a generic sense, thus comprising the duty to take preventive measures and to restore and compensate for damage, but also so as to include criminal liability.

[8] As pointed out by Muchlinski, P., Corporations in international litigation: problems of jurisdiction and the United Kingdom asbestos cases, *Int'l and Comparative L. Q.* 50 (2001), p. 1, lawyers have also tended to rely on legal concepts which lead them to often unsatisfactory results rather than considering the economic realities of the cases and developing new doctrines.

[9] See Cordonier Segger, M.-C., Sustainability and corporate accountability regimes: implementing the Johannesburg Summit agenda, *RECIEL* 12 (2003), pp. 295–309. For historical accounts on the international discussions and arrangements concerning transnational corporations, see Tiewul, S., Transnational corporations and emerging international legal standards, in de Waart, P., Peters, P., and Denters, E. (eds.), *International law and development*, Dordrecht (Martin Nijhoff) 1988, pp. 105–113; and, with respect to foreign direct investment, Wallace, C. D., *The multinational enterprise and legal control: host state sovereignty in an era of economic globalization*, The Hague (Nijhoff) 2002, p. 1074.

they may provide any foundation for a future legal framework for controlling corporations that are active across state borders.

II. Founding a framework on fragments

Fragments found in any of the hundreds of treaties and also in non-binding instruments on environmental matters, form patterns and develop the patchwork of international law. When new notions, and generally accepted environmental standards and principles, have been internationally expressed, e.g. through such treaties, they may provide a legal basis to examine corporate governance in a transboundary context even outside the narrow scope of each particular convention.[10] If so, there may be some acceptance for bringing them into a more comprehensive legal framework. This is particularly the case if the principles and concepts have received some recognition outside industrial countries in Europe and North America. As illustrated below, however, some of the most advanced instruments of international law relating to corporate responsibility in environmental matters are limited to the Northern regions, in particular to Europe, and do not include Africa, Asia, or Latin America.

Other areas of international law – investment regimes,[11] arrangements to combat bribery, and international human rights law – may also contribute relevant fragments, either because they influence the protection of health and the environment, or because they apply to similar or related matters. The fact that environmental and other international agreements are formally addressed to states and only indirectly to other subjects does not as such prevent them from providing concepts and principles for a legal framework on corporate responsibility (whether applied in practice through implementing national legislation, as a self-executing treaty, or even as a framework that defines corporations as the subjects directly addressed).[12]

The survey of normative fragments for controlling MNEs/TNCs should also include national laws and unilateral measures of extra-territorial reach. So far, though, there is no common approach to extra-territoriality. Therefore, until some extra-territorial competence becomes generally accepted and applied (and thus potentially a part of customary international law), access to

---

[10] Ong, D. M., The impact of environmental law on corporate governance: international and comparative perspectives, *European J. Int'l L.* 12 (2001), pp. 685, 694; Choucri, N., 'Corporate strategies towards sustainability', in Lang, W. (ed.), *Sustainable development and international law*, Dordrecht (Nijhoff) 1995, pp. 189, 195.

[11] A brief survey of environment protection provisions in investment treaties is provided by United Nations Conference on Trade and Development, *Environment: UNCTAD series on issues in international investment agreements*, Geneva (United Nations) 2001.

[12] This is discussed further in André Nollkaemper, Chapter 7. Also Ebbesson, J., *Compatibility of international and national environmental law*, London/The Hague/Boston (Kluwer) 1996.

these national procedures will remain dependent on the nationality and 'home country' (if any) of the corporation in question.

Finally, existing 'non-legal' arrangements, such as international policy documents, guidelines, and codes of conduct, are relevant for the establishment of a transboundary legal framework. Some codes are adopted by intergovernmental organisations (e.g. the United Nations,[13] OECD,[14] and the ILO[15]) others by business associations, individual corporations, or third parties such as environmental associations, trade unions, and citizens' organisations. An increasing number of corporations, particularly firms of high environmental impact, make policy statements and codes of conduct with commitments to environmental performance.[16] These codes differ considerably from one to another in defining the commitment to health and the environment.[17] Some only mention environmental protection briefly, others set higher commitments, e.g. to comply with and exceed legal requirements, and to use 'best practice'. Many companies also establish environmental management systems, either self-designed or based on EMAS or ISO 14001, and routines for environmental reporting.[18]

Being formally 'voluntary and not legally enforceable',[19] and not intended to imply legal commitments, does not prevent the codes of conduct from affecting the legal conceptions and development. First, codes of conduct may be seen as part of the contract with consumers or business parties, or reflect what consumers and contract parties could reasonably have expected when entering into agreements with the company. Secondly, governments (including the European Union) have explicitly incorporated various voluntary initiatives into their regulatory strategy.[20] Thirdly, environmental management schemes and

---

[13] Agenda 21, UN Doc. A/CONF.151/26; UN Global Compact, available at www.unglobalcompact.org/Portal/Default.asp; Subcommission on the Promotion and Protection of Human Rights, *Norms on the Responsibilities of Transnational Corporations and Other Business Enterprises with regard to Human Rights*, UN Doc. E/CN.4/Sub.2/2003/12/Rev.2, 2003.

[14] OECD, *Guidelines for Multinational Enterprises 2001*, reprinted in OECD, *Annual report 2001: Guidelines for multinational enterprises: Global instruments for corporate responsibility*, Paris (OECD) 2001; also available at www.oecd.org.

[15] ILO, Tripartite Declaration of Principles Concerning Multinational Enterprises and Social Policy, 3rd edn. 2001; available at www.ilo.org/public/english/employment/multi/download/english.pdf

[16] The OECD Guidelines, pp. 57–75, provide a brief comparison of some such codes of different foundations.

[17] OECD, *Corporate responsibility: private initiatives and public goals*, Paris (OECD) 2001, pp 40–44.

[18] Ibid., pp. 97–105.

[19] OECD Guidelines, section I:1.

[20] OECD, *Corporate responsibility: private initiatives and public goals*, Paris (OECD) 2001, p. 43. One example is the environmental management and auditing systems. European Community Regulation 761/2001/EC Allowing Voluntary Participation by Organisations in a Community Eco-management and Audit Scheme (EMAS), [2001] OJ L114/1,

certain parts of policy statements may be transformed to legal criteria even without codification. By setting the standard of corporate conduct in relation to health and the environment and thus reflecting expected behaviour and common practice, codes of conduct and management systems are highly relevant when examining whether a company has acted with due care, established an adequate management system and, possibly, when determining which subject (parent company or subsidiary) is responsible for the harm caused. Yet, this only works where the national legal system is adequately developed to provide such links. One way to also make these concepts applicable when corporations operate in countries with inadequate legal infrastructure is to draw on them when drafting a transboundary legal framework.

III. Three dimensions for a responsibility scheme

The very rationale for a transboundary legal framework on corporate responsibility would be to relax the impact of state borders when holding corporations responsible for harm to health and the environment, and when pursuing environmental justice. To this end, any transboundary arrangement based on an international accord will have to include traditional institutional and cooperative arrangements, and, possibly, monitoring and reporting systems as well as instruments for financial aid. As to the core legal issues, however, defining corporate responsibility involves three dimensions of law: substance, procedure, and subjectivity.

The first dimension, *substance*, comprises basic legal principles on environmental protection, performance requirements and standards, and liability criteria. Here, an international agreement may set out norms of preventive action and/or norms defining the consequences of violating performance standards and of causing harm to health or the environment. Performance requirements and liability criteria define, in more or less precise terms, the expected/accepted conduct of corporations in relation to health and the environment, and the consequences of non-compliance. Examples of such requirements are technical standards, emission standards, production standards, complete prohibitions, principles on preventive and precautionary measures, compulsory environmental impact assessments, and management systems.

An alternative to agreeing on common performance standards or liability criteria would be to define common norms of conflict that prescribe the national law to be applied by domestic courts in a specific transboundary case. Such an

considerably draws on the ISO system, and is maintained as a voluntary management and auditing scheme. In Swedish law, parts of the non-binding managment schemes (e.g. record keeping on the allocation of responsibility and on the use of chemicals, and routines for continuous risk assessment) have been transformed into mandatory legal requirements on 'self-control' of environmentally harmful activities.

agreement may stipulate whether a court in the home country of a MNE, when examining acts by subsidiaries abroad, should apply its national rules, the rules of the state of the activity, or the rules of the state where the harm occurred. An agreement of this kind would not define the criteria for responsibility or liability, but rather coordinate national laws and allow each state to regulate on its own accord.

The second dimension is *procedure*, i.e. the means, procedures, and remedies available for having performance requirements and liability criteria applied, enforced, and implemented. In a transboundary context, jurisdictional allocation and coordination is decisive. Without passable transboundary procedures for enforcement and implementation and without adequate remedies, performance requirements and liability criteria set out in legal texts remain of limited value. For the most part, in terms of participation, effectiveness, and efficiency, it makes sense that the procedures to remedy harm and violations of performance standards are available in the country of the activity/harm. If the procedures are too remote, geographically, economically or socially, it is difficult, if not impossible, for most people to participate in, let alone initiate, proceedings.[21] Yet procedures outside the state of the activity/harm are worthwhile for the plaintiff in situations where domestic procedures and institutions are absent or completely unreliable. In cases involving multinational enterprises, the main alternative to procedures and remedies in the state of the activity/harm is recourse to national courts or administrative authorities in the corporation's home country or in a third country. Today, recourse to such procedures depends on the 'home state' of the corporation, since national laws on corporate responsibility differ with regard to extra-territorial jurisdiction, and also with respect to the choice of laws and the perception of parent company – subsidiary relations.[22]

When MNEs/TNCs are held responsible for harm to health or the environment, an alternative (or additional) option to procedures before national courts and institutions would be to establish an international forum to deal with such disputes. Which procedure is the most suitable would depend on the remedy sought and whether the matter is one of civil liability, compliance with administrative regulations, or a criminal case.

The third dimension, corporate *subjectivity*, refers to the corporate organisation, and to who is legally responsible for violations of performance requirements and for harm to health or the environment. Relevant factors determining subjectivity are whether the corporation is perceived as one or several legal units and whether the responsibility for acts and omissions by a subsidiary in the

---

[21] Hey, E., *Reflections on an international environmental court*, The Hague (Kluwer) 2000, pp. 20–21.
[22] See e.g. Kamminga, M. and Zia-Zarafi, S., op. cit. *passim*.

state of the harmful activity can somehow be channelled to the parent company, with its main office, registered seat, and assets outside that state.[23]

IV. Substance

Performance requirements and liability criteria in national and international (and European Community) law affect corporations as part of criminal, administrative, and/or civil responsibility/liability schemes. As such they may be applied when supervisory agencies and permit authorities decide on the safety measures to be taken or to stop unlawful activities completely, when defining a criminal offence, and when deciding on a claim for injunction or compensation for damage in private litigation.

In search of some global definition of unacceptable activities that harm the environment, the 1998 Rome Statute of the International Criminal Court provides a very special case. The definition of war crimes includes intentionally launched attacks, clearly excessive in relation to the military advantage, that cause 'long-term and severe damage to the natural environment'.[24] MNEs/TNCs, or rather persons acting on behalf of the corporations, can be held criminally responsible and liable for punishment if involved in ordering, soliciting, or inducing the acts or aiding or otherwise assisting or contributing to such a crime.[25] Whilst including corporate activities within its parameters, the Rome Statute and the definition of war crimes still do not cover the more conventional cases of corporate misconduct.

International restrictions on corporate conduct are also found in environmental treaties of global reach, which prohibit different harmful activities. Examples of such activities are the dumping of wastes at sea, transboundary shipment in hazardous wastes, releases of oil drainage, dirty ballast, and tank-washing water from oil tankers when sailing in 'special areas', hunting of and trading in endangered species, and uses of various hazardous and ozone-depleting substances (e.g. DDT, PCBs, and CFCs).[26] For some activities, where a complete prohibition has not been desired or agreed, treaties of global application prescribe restrictions in terms of safety measures and precautions to be

---

[23] In the context of international law, the subjectivity issue also pertains to the status of corporations under international law and to what extent they can be held directly liable in transboundary contexts. See André Nollkaemper, Chapter 7; and Tiewul, op. cit.
[24] Rome Statute of the International Criminal Court 1998, 37 I.L.M. (1998) 999, Article 8.
[25] Article 25.
[26] Convention on Persistent Organic Compounds 2001 (POP Convention), 40 I.L.M. (2001) 532; Convention on the Control of Transboundary Movements of Hazardous Wastes and their Disposal 1989, 28 I.L.M. (1989) 657; Convention on International Trade in Endangered Species of Wild Fauna and Flora 1973 (CITES), 993 U.N.T.S. 243; International Convention for the Prevention of Pollution by Ships 1973 (1973/78 MARPOL Convention), 12 I.L.M. (1973) 1319, as amended by the 1978 Protocol; Protocol to the London Dumping Convention 1996, 26 I.L.M. (1996) 1415.

taken.[27] It is possible to deduce from these treaties the legally expected performance of every operator under the jurisdiction of the parties.[28] Still, they only apply to specific fields of activities, where the legal position of operators is defined, and neither complete prohibitions nor detailed performance standards can be used in responsibility schemes intended for a broader scope of application. More suitable to this end are the general concepts, principles, and policies set out in environmental treaties and international policy documents (e.g. the Stockholm, Rio, and Johannesburg Declarations,[29] Agenda 21, the Johannesburg Plan of Implementation,[30] and the OECD *Guidelines for Multinational Enterprises*),[31] such as:

- the precautionary principle (or 'precautionary approach');
- the polluter pays principle;
- the principle of best practical means, implied also by concepts such as best available technology and best environmental practice;
- environmental impact assessments;
- environmental management systems; and
- transparency.

Even though not all notions listed reflect general international law,[32] they have been endorsed in many contexts and documents; in some treaties of global application, e.g. the UN Convention on the Law of the Sea 1982,[33] in regional treaties and in policy documents adopted by various international organisations. Some concepts also find their support in the International Law Commission (ILC) Articles on Prevention of Transboundary Harm from Hazardous Activities, submitted to the UN General Assembly in 2001.[34] Despite the focus of the ILC Articles on the responsibility of states rather than corporations, if

---

[27] Such performance standards are found e.g. in the 2001 POP Convention with respect to the use of chemicals; and the 1973/78 MARPOL Convention for oil tankers and other vessels.

[28] Ebbesson, op. cit. pp. 46–76.

[29] *Report of the World Summit on Sustainable Development*, Johannesburg, South Africa, 26 August–4 September 2002, UN Doc. A/CONF.199/20. For references to the Stockholm and Rio Declarations, see n. 3 above.

[30] Ibid.

[31] See n. 14 above. Although the OECD Guidelines are not globally endorsed, they have a global reach since they comprise most industrial countries, and most home countries to multinational enterprises.

[32] For such a discussion with respect to some of these concepts and principles, see Birnie, P. and Boyle, A., *International Law and the Environment*, Oxford (Oxford University Press) 2nd edn. 2002, pp. 104–152.

[33] 21 I.L.M. (1982) 1261.

[34] International Liability for Injurious Consequences arising out of Acts not Prohibited by International Law (Prevention of Transboundary Harm from Hazardous Activities); see ILC, *Report on the Work of its Fifty-third Session*, UN Doc. A/56/10/SUPPL.10, 2001, pp. 366–436.

transformed into a convention as proposed by the ILC, they will entail duties on corporations as well, e.g. with respect to information and impact assessment.

Some more advanced attempts to define generally applicable performance standards can be found at the regional level. European Community environmental law on, for instance, impact assessments, access to environmental information, and performance standards, applies to corporations.[35] Legal frameworks of a horizontal character have also been adopted by the UN Economic Commission for Europe (UNECE) concerning environmental impact assessments, public participation, and industrial accidents;[36] and, less successfully, by the Council of Europe with respect to criminal responsibility and civil liability.[37] The implementation of these conventions affects the duties and responsibilities of corporations, and they all include transboundary aspects. As such they add relevant fragments towards a broader framework.

The increasing demand for transparency of corporations with high environmental impact also reflects an element of responsibility, i.e. a duty to make relevant information about the activity and its possible impact on health and the environment available. Most environmental treaties require that states gather, exchange, and disseminate environmental information. However, the duty of states to make specific environmental information accessible to the public is not yet as well established. In transboundary contexts, the mentioned ILC Articles define a general duty for states to provide environmental information to the public. Combined with the non-discrimination principle, also found in the ILC Articles, this duty of states mirrors a transboundary right, albeit of a general character, to access environmental information.[38]

Regionally, a transboundary right of access to environmental information has been greatly clarified by the Aarhus Convention 1998.[39] In order to comply

---

[35] Most European Community environmental legislation is laid down in directives addressed to the Member States, rather than 'directly applicable' to private subjects. Still, several directives define the legal positions of corporations to be reflected in the Member States. Moreover, the European judicature has developed doctrines on legal (rather than factual) implementation as well as on conformist interpretation and application of directives in the light of the EC Treaty, Article 10, thus making some directives effective on private subjects even when not satisfactory implemented.

[36] See www.unece.org/env.

[37] The Convention on the Protection of the Environment through Criminal Law 1998, CETS no. 172, Article 2, prescribes that 'discharge, emission or introduction of a quantity of substances or ionising radiation into air, soil or water' should be criminalised if it '(i) causes death or serious injury to any person, or (ii) creates a significant risk of causing death or serious injury to any person . . . when committed intentionally'. Also, other activities that are likely to cause substantial harm to persons, property, animals, and plants should be criminalised; see www.coe.int At the time of writing, however, the Convention has not entered into force due to being ratified by too few states.

[38] ILC, op. cit. Articles 13 and 15.

[39] Convention on Access to Information, Public Participation in Decision-making and Access to Justice in Environmental Matters 1998, 38 I.L.M. (1999) 515, and see www.unece.org

with the Aarhus Convention, each party must ensure that domestic systems for information-gathering are in place. Indirectly, this amounts to a duty for each corporation to provide the needed information. The Protocol on Pollutant Release and Transfer Register 2003,[40] related to the Aarhus Convention, makes this duty explicit and prescribes in detail the reporting requirements of operators. Apart from the Aarhus Convention, the case law of the European Court of Human Rights also pushes for higher standards of transparency. In *Guerra and others* v. *Italy*,[41] the Court held that access to 'essential information' that makes it possible to assess the risks one might run due to corporate activities is a fundamental human right.[42] While phrased as a right against the state, to be complied with by the parties, it nonetheless entails two kinds of duties. First, the parties are obliged to ensure that such information is made available to members of the public. Secondly, each party must make sure that every corporation in its territory is in fact obliged to report to authorities or to the public directly about their activities involving releases and transfers of hazardous chemicals; if not, the first obligation can hardly be met.

In addition to performance standards and transparency, various international agreements provide fragments for a civil liability scheme. Existing civil liability treaties of global application are limited to certain kinds of activities (e.g. pollution by oil and hazardous substances from ships, nuclear installations, and transboundary movements of hazardous wastes). They have in common that they are designed for hazardous activities, that liability is strict and not based on negligence, and that the maximum level of compensation is fixed. The early civil liability conventions were limited to injuries to persons and property, but more recent treaties have broadened the scope so as also to embrace harm to environmental interests in a wider sense.[43] Despite the slow expansion of liability institutions and their potential as models for more generally applicable schemes, they still apply only to a limited scope of activities.

Again, the more advanced sections of transboundary schemes are found at the regional level. Attempts have been made by the European Union and the Council of Europe to establish generally applicable rules on liability for

---

[40] See www.unece.org/env

[41] *Guerra and others* v. *Italy*, 116/1996/735/932 (ECtHR), 19 February 1988, paras 50–54.

[42] For accounts of this decision, see e.g. Handl, G., 'Human rights and protection of the environment', in Eide, A., Kraus, C., and Rosas, A. (eds.), *Economic, social and cultural rights: a textbook*, Dordrecht (Kluwer) 2000, p. 303; and Déjeant-Pons, M. and Pallemaerts, M., *Human rights and the environment*, Strasbourg (Council of Europe) 2002, pp. 35–38.

[43] Boyle, A., 'Environmental damage in international law', in Bowman, M. and Boyle, A. (eds.), *Environmental damage in international and comparative law*, Oxford (Oxford University Press) 2002, pp. 17, 19. For a comparison between different international (and national) liability schemes, see also Larsson, M., *The law of environmental damage*, Stockholm (Juristförlaget) 2000, pp. 172–212.

environmental harm.[44] Experience shows that it is already difficult to agree on common liability criteria at this level,[45] and adopting globally applicable liability rules will not be easier, unless the legal framework is limited to a general agreement, e.g. that reparation is to be made by full compensation. If agreed upon, however, even such a general statement, that in principle reparation or compensation be made wherever harm occur, could make national courts less reluctant to decide transboundary cases.

Failing agreement on international substantive standards or liability criteria, an alternative would be to agree internationally on norms of conflict that stipulate the national law to be applied by national courts or authorities in a specific case. Such an agreement may state whether *lex delicti*, *lex fori*, or even the most favourable law for the plaintiff should be applied against the defending corporation.[46] While there is no such international agreement on environmental matters today, at least one treaty, applicable in a rather different transboundary situation, sets out that a case of compensation for environmental harm must not be decided by rules less favourable to the plaintiff than those in the state of the activity.[47]

A case for applying *lex loci delicti* outside the state of the activity/harm would be when that state has laws in place, but it lacks adequate remedies or institutions to enforce the laws. When no such law exists in the state of the activity, an alternative for the court/authority outside the state of the activity would be to apply *lex fori*. This would have the effect of imposing, from abroad, restrictions or safety measures to be taken in the state of the activity. While extra-territoriality is controversial in particular with respect to enforcing performance requirements, the alternative to extra-territoriality may be no means at all for those affected, to have the activity stopped.[48] Still, some investment treaties prohibit such extra-territorial application of 'home country regulations',[49] while the OECD Guidelines call on governments to cooperate in

---

[44] Directive 2004/35/EC of the European Parliament and of the Council on Environmental Liability with regard to the Prevention and Remedying of Environmental Damage, [2004] OJ L143/56; Convention on Civil Liability for Damage Resulting from Activities Dangerous to the Environment, 32 I.L.M. (1993) 1228.

[45] Boyle, op. cit. p. 17.

[46] Another approach far less attractive to the plaintiffs would be to agree internationally that the lowest common denominator of two or more states involved in the specific case constitutes the substance for determining responsibility in a transboundary context. While resembling the principle of criminal law, that extra-territorial jurisdiction requires 'dual criminality'; this would indeed be a too modest approach for transboundary civil liability.

[47] Nordic Environment Protection Convention, 1974 13 I.L.M. (1974) 1421, Article 3.

[48] See n. 61 below for a reference to Dutch law where this is possible in some cases.

[49] UNCTAD, *Home country measures: UNCTAD series on issues in international investment agreements*, Geneva (United Nations) 2001, pp. 44–48.

good faith with a view to resolving possible conflicting requirements; thus not excluding extra-territorial application of performance requirements.[50]

In terms of substance, if there are no internationally accepted performance requirements or liability criteria at all, the court of the home state would still have to decide on which substantive law to apply; whether found in *lex fori* or *lex loci delicti*. The difference is that failing an international agreement, the norms of conflict would be defined unilaterally, without international coordination.

V. Procedure

The previous paragraphs presume that some extra-territorial jurisdiction exists, and there are some signs in international law for expanding jurisdiction outside the state of the activity/harm, at least in cases concerning *compensation*. The development of international civil liability treaties is one such sign. While the earlier liability treaties grant jurisdiction to the state of the activity/incident,[51] some treaties of more recent origin provide for alternative jurisdictions, including the court of the state where the defendant has its habitual residence or principal place of business.[52] This may establish a transboundary remedy where the domestic institutions fail in the country where the harm occurred.

Despite these signs of increasing acceptance of alternative jurisdictions, no general principle of international law has been developed for alternative jurisdictions in environmental cases, and no treaty of global reach generally defines jurisdiction in cases of corporate responsibility. Nor can a common approach by national laws be found to jurisdiction in these cases.

At the regional level, the principal European treaty on jurisdiction in civil and commercial matters, the Brussels Convention 1968,[53] places jurisdiction

---

[50] OECD Guidelines, op. cit.
[51] International Convention on Civil Liability for Oil Pollution Damage 1969, 9 I.L.M. (1970) 45, Article IX; Convention on Third Party Liability in the Field of Nuclear Energy 1960, *American J. Int'l L.* 55 (1961), p. 1082, Article 13; Convention on Civil Liability for Nuclear Damage 1963, 2 I.L.M. (1963) 727.
[52] Convention on Civil Liability for Damage Resulting from Activities Dangerous to the Environment 1993, 32 I.L.M. (1993) 1228, Article 19; Protocol on Liability and Compensation for Damage Resulting from the Transboundary Movements of Hazardous Wastes 1999, Article 17; and 2003 Protocol on Civil Liability and Compensation for Damage Caused by the Transboundary Effects of Industrial Accidents on Transboundary Waters to the Convention on the Protection and Use of Transboundary Watercourses and International Lakes 1992 and to the Convention on the Transboundary Effects of Industrial Accident 1992, www.unece.org, Article 13.
[53] Brussels Convention on Jurisdiction and the Enforcement of Judgments in Civil and Commercial Matters 1968 (consolidated version), [1998] OJ C271/1. The Convention is still in force, although for most EU Member States it has been replaced by Regulation 44/2001/EC, [2001] OJ L12/1. The 1988 Lugano Convention on Jurisdiction and the Enforcement of Judgments in Civil and Commercial Matters 1988, [1988] OJ L319/5, extends the principles to EFTA members.

with the domicile of the defendant.[54] In the case of a multinational enterprise, this is the state where it has its seat (which in turn will be decided by national law). The Brussels Convention harmonises the laws in Europe in cases where the defendant is domiciled in a state party, but the situation remains different in most common law systems.[55] Although it is held that the principle of service – *forum conveniens* – may be declining as the principle for defining jurisdiction in most common law systems in favour of more generous criteria,[56] courts in these systems may still dismiss cases against multinational enterprises for harm caused abroad on the ground of *forum non conveniens*. Hence, while there is no formal bar for courts in common law countries to try a case, there is no general acceptance either that suing the defendant in its home state is the most convenient route for litigation.[57] For that reason, a case concerning activities/harm abroad may be dismissed.

Alternative remedies in environmental cases are *injunctions* and *mandamus actions*, e.g. claims for having activities banned, precautionary measures imposed, or the environment reinstated. To date, however, no environmental treaty defines transboundary jurisdiction in such cases,[58] and there are only minor, if any, signs in treaty law for increasing acceptance of extra-territorial jurisdiction for other claims than compensation.[59] Some investment treaties regulate 'home country measures', but instead of acknowledging such transboundary jurisdiction and enforcement of rules of the home state, they intend

---

[54] See the different contributions in McLachlan, C. and Nygh, P. (eds.), *Transnational tort litigation: jurisdictional principles*, Oxford (Oxford University Press) 1996.
[55] Including the United Kingdom and Ireland when the Brussels/Lugano Conventions do not apply.
[56] Nygh, P., The common law approach, p. 21, at 36–37; and Juenger, F. K., An addendum on the United States approach, p. 40, both in McLachlan and Nygh, op. cit.
[57] An illustrative case is the US Alien Tort Claims Act, 28 USC s. 1350 (1994). While granting federal courts jurisdiction in cases where an alien sues for a tort committed abroad in violation of the law of nations, the courts may – and do – dismiss cases on ground of *forum non conveniens*. See Juenger, F. K., Environmental damage, in McLachlan and Nygh, op. cit. pp. 201, 203–209; Birnie and Boyle, op. cit. pp. 273–274.
[58] Again, the Civil Liability Convention 1993 is most relevant, since Article 19 sets out a right for environmental organisations to request a prohibition of a dangerous activity or an order for measures to be taken by the operator. However, as far as jurisdiction is concerned, these claims can only be made before the court or administrative authority in the state of the activity or the state 'where the measures are to be taken.' Although this seems to preclude suing the corporation in its home state rather than where the activity takes place, one may argue that the measures needed to prevent harm must be taken where the corporation has its seat or domicile.
[59] According to Article 1 of the Brussels Convention 1968, n. 53 above, it does not apply to 'administrative matters'. Yet, the line between civil and administrative matters is not easy to draw. While in one jurisdiction claims for injunction and mandamus action in environmental matters may amount to an administrative matter, in another they are perceived as civil matters.

to avoid expansive jurisdiction.[60] Yet, in some cases, national courts have been prepared to decide on injunctions in order to enforce obligations to be complied with abroad.[61]

Criminal sanctions against corporations are mostly intended for physical persons, even when the act took place in the corporate environment. Extra-territorial criminal jurisdiction, as defined by various national laws, usually requires that the person charged has close ties with the state of the court (citizenship, residence, etc.). Moreover, dual criminality is a common prerequisite for extra-territorial jurisdiction in criminal cases, i.e. the act should be a criminal offence in the state of the court as well as the state where the act was committed. Finally, some qualification as to the latitude of the criminal act is often required in order to spare distant courts from dealing with minor offences.

Several environmental agreements oblige the parties to *penalise* violations of prescribed performance requirements,[62] either in the state of the activity or in the state where the person is resident. Despite these cases of potential extra-territoriality, however, no environmental treaty addresses the issue of extra-territorial jurisdiction to the same extent as the OECD Bribery Convention 1997.[63] Applicable to bribery of foreign officials, the OECD Bribery Convention amounts to a transboundary legal framework that defines responsibility in corporate activities. The state parties are not only obliged to make bribery of foreign officials a criminal offence, but also to establish jurisdiction for prosecuting nationals for offences committed abroad.[64]

The OECD *Guidelines for Multinational Enterprises* do not deal with jurisdiction at all, but establish National Contact Points in each member state for the purpose of overseeing the implementation. If an 'issue' concerns a multinational enterprise with its home country in the OECD, active in another OECD country, the issue can be raised before the National Contact Point in either country, and they are expected to consult each other. Rather than allocating jurisdiction, the National Contact Points are intended to further the effectiveness of the Guidelines, by e.g. contributing to 'the resolution of issues that arise

---

[60] UNCTAD, *Home country measures: UNCTAD series on issues in international investment agreements*, Geneva (United Nations) 2001, pp. 44–48.

[61] One such country is the Netherlands. See Betlem, G., Transnational litigation against multinational corporations before Dutch courts, in Kamminga, M. T. and Zia-Zarifi, S., op. cit. pp. 283, 292–293, referring to the *Interlas* judgment, where the Dutch Hoge Raad recognised that injunctive relief is an available remedy in the Netherlands to enforce an obligation to be complied with abroad. The court also argued that it did not matter whether the obligation is imposed by Dutch or foreign law.

[62] See e.g. the 1973/78 MARPOL Convention, n. 26 above, Article 4; CITES, n. 26 above, Article VIII; and the Convention on the Control of Transboundary Movements of Hazardous Wastes and their Disposal 1989, n. 26 above, Article 4.

[63] OECD Convention on Combating Bribery of Foreign Public Officials in International Business Transactions 1997, www.oecd.org

[64] Article 4.

relating to implementation of the Guidelines in specific instances', and to 'offer a forum for discussion and assist' in dealing with the issues raised.[65] They are neither supposed strictly to enforce the Guidelines nor to make legally binding decisions. Instead, they may make softer means of dispute resolution available, such as good offices, consultations, conciliation, and mediation. If no agreement is reached by the parties involved in the 'issue', the Contact Point may make recommendations on the implementation of the Guidelines. While this seems to refer mainly to future conduct, there is nothing in the Guidelines that prevent a National Contact Point, in a specific case, from resolving the issue by recommending the multinational enterprise to pay compensation for damage.

An alternative to remedies and procedures before national courts and administrations (inside or outside the state of the activity/harm) is to establish an *international forum* and procedure for disputes between non-state actors; a tribunal (court or arbitration board) with the capacity to make binding decisions, or some quasi-legal arrangements, such as inspection panels, compliance committees, or mediating organs. Thus far, though, no adequate remedy before an international forum is available for claims by individuals against MNEs/TNCs. As argued, one of the few cases where an international forum (the International Criminal Court) could decide on criminal responsibility for harm to health and the environment is when the act is a part of a war crime (or of complicity to such a crime). Again, while important in principle this procedure is not available to more conventional cases of corporate conduct. In theory, the Permanent Court of International Arbitration would be competent to try a case on compensation where the plaintiffs and the defending corporation accepted its jurisdiction, but it is of little use in most environmental, non-contractual disputes against MNEs/TNCs, unless the defendant (quite unlikely) *ex post facto* accepts the court's competence to settle the dispute.[66]

VI. Subjectivity

The final dimension, subjectivity, refers to the perception of the corporate structure and organisation. As far as multinational enterprises are concerned, the legal issue is whether the parent corporation can be held responsible for activities in other countries, carried out by subsidiaries in its corporate structure (or in other ways under its control) although, legally speaking, they are considered separate subjects. If international law only provides limited fragments on substance and procedure for a transboundary responsibility scheme, it provides even less on corporate subjectivity and organisation. Despite the concern about MNEs/TNCs in the last thirty years or so, and despite the expansion of commercial activities and direct investments across state

---

[65] Procedural Guidance to the OECD Guidelines, n. 14 above.
[66] Hey, op. cit.

borders, there are still no international rules governing the organisation of corporations which are active in different countries.

As argued in the introduction, such corporations organise in heterogeneous ways; the relationships differ between the units/subjects concerned and so does the degree of central control within the corporations. First, compared with portfolio investments, direct investments involve more control over the investment and activity.[67] Thus, the issue of parent company responsibility refers in particular to cases of foreign direct investments. Secondly, there are numerous possible relationships between the different units in a corporation organised across state borders; subsidiary, associate, joint venture, subaffiliation, and affiliation by contract or licence. Still, the formal relation between the different units does not provide the full picture of the organisation or of where the decisions on policies, measures, and omissions are actually made. What matters most from an organisational viewpoint is rather the element of de facto control.

While maybe 'no two [international multinationals (transnationals)] share exactly the same organizational form',[68] many multinational enterprises have centralised their environmental policy-making and established corporate headquarters to deal with safety, health, and environmental issues.[69] Thereby, the internal, organisational responsibility for implementing and controlling the corporation's environmental performance has moved closer to the parent company. These codes of conduct are means for avoiding bad publicity and minimising the effect on the environment. However, the adoption of such standards and implementation programmes also implies more active involvement and de facto control of the parent company. Therefore, the parent company also incurs a greater share of responsibility for activities carried out by its subsidiaries, and in some cases its subcontractors. The situation is more complex where one or several units/actors use their economic dominance and influence on another unit without acting as a parent company, but through informal network (as 'network enterprises').[70] In these cases, as in portfolio investments, responsibility may be diluted to the extent that no one subject can be said to maintain de facto (let alone de jure) control.

Although there is no international legal framework setting out the principles for placing responsibility within corporate organisations (of whatever

---

[67] Wallace, C. D., *The multinational enterprise and legal control: host state sovereignty in an era of economic globalization*, The Hague (Nijhoff) 2002, pp. 137–153.

[68] Wallace, op. cit. p. 153; also Ratner, S. R., Corporations and human rights: a theory of legal responsibility, *Yale L. J.* 111 (2001), pp. 443, 518–522.

[69] See Martin Herberg, Chapter 6.

[70] Castells, op. cit. p. 192 argues that such network enterprises are increasingly international (not transnational), and their conduct will result from the interaction between the global strategy of the network and the nationally/regionally rooted interests of their components.

form) across state borders, the shift of internal responsibility is reflected in and supported by some international policy documents. Agenda 21, for instance, encourages business and industry to

> establish world-wide corporate policies on sustainable development, arrange for environmentally sound technologies to be available to affiliates owned substantially by their parent company in developing countries without extra external charges, encourage overseas affiliates to modify procedures in order to reflect local ecological conditions and share experiences with local authorities, Governments and international organizations.[71]

Agenda 21 does not set out in detail the measures to be taken or how corporations are to be organised, but the passage confirms the responsibility of the parent company or head unit to adopt policies and control overseas affiliates. Whereas Agenda 21 refers to affiliates substantially owned by the parent company, the UN Subcommission on Human Rights, in its *Draft Norms on the Responsibilities of Transnational Corporations*, goes a step further by urging transnational corporations to apply and incorporate the principles even in their contracts or other arrangements and dealings with contractors, subcontractors, suppliers, and licensees.[72] Neither Agenda 21 nor the Subcommission on Human Rights' Norms reflect international law, but they support the notion that corporate responsibility should be linked to the operational control, and in this respect, they also provide for lowering the corporate veil.

While corporate organisation and the allocation of responsibility has not been subject to global treaty-making, the issue has been raised in the (again European) context of the UNECE Convention on Transboundary Effects of Industrial Accidents.[73] The Convention parties must, inter alia, ensure that the operator is obliged to take all measures necessary for the safe performance of the hazardous activity and for the prevention of industrial activities.[74] The Convention defines 'operator' as any natural or legal person 'in charge of an activity, e.g. supervising, planning to carry out or carrying out the activity'.[75] The question then is what is meant by being in charge of the activity. This could be interpreted in a strict legalistic sense, following a formal divide between the corporate units, or understood as keeping control de facto. The latter interpretation is supported by the European Community's (a party to the Convention)

---

[71] Agenda 21, n. 13 above, Ch. 30.22.
[72] Subcommission on the Promotion and Protection of Human Rights, in its *Draft Norms on the Responsibilities*, n. 2 above, para. 15.
[73] 31 I.L.M. (1992) 1330.
[74] Article 3. The same definition applies for the 2003 Liability Protocol to the 1992 Convention; see n. 52 above.
[75] Article 1(e).

legislation intended to implement the Convention,[76] where 'operator' is defined as:

> any individual or corporate body who operates or holds an establishment or installation or, if provided for by national legislation, *has been given decisive economic power in the technical operation thereof*.[77]

This is one of few legislative acts on environmental matters above national level where it is recognised that someone else than the subject directly carrying out the activity is in charge. The corporate divide is thus slightly relaxed and de facto control ('decisive economic power') is made a factor determining responsibility.

While international law is still indifferent to the issue, the notion of de facto control when allocating corporate responsibility also seems to have implicit support in some of the most famous cases of environmental harm caused by multinational enterprises (Seveso, Bhopal, Amoco Cadiz, and Cape). At least, according to one author, the national courts did not make the corporate veil 'an insurmountable obstacle.'[78] Even so, one cannot derive from them a common position in national laws (civil law systems and common law systems) in general.[79] Such a position requires further efforts of coordination and harmonisation.

VII. Outlines for a future framework

In this final section, drawing on the previous survey, I will outline options for a future transboundary framework on corporate responsibility. Yet, it would be premature to insist on specific elements. Any such arrangement is a result of drafting, bargaining, and negotiations, and there is no short-cut to create a binding instrument with a claim to be legitimate. Before a global treaty on corporate responsibility materialises, a likely step would be some kind of intergovernmental (UN) conference particularly devoted to the issue, where all interests and perspectives involved could be confronted and considered.

Leaving aside the cooperative elements and institutional structures of a treaty (including capacity-building, financial arrangements, and related aspects), I

---

[76] Directive 96/82/EC of 9 December 1996 on the Control of Major Accident Hazards Involving Dangerous Substances, [1997] OJ L10/13.
[77] Article 3(3). Emphasis added.
[78] Scovazzi, T., Industrial accidents and the veil of transnational corporations, in Francioni, F. and Scovazzi, T., *International responsibility for environmental harm*, London (Graham & Trotman) 1991, p. 395, analysing the legal proceedings in the 1976 Seveso, 1984 Bhopal, and 1978 Amoco Cadiz cases. For an analysis of the Cape case, see e.g. Muchlinski, op. cit.
[79] As Muchlinski, op. cit. p. 4 *et seq.*, argues, even the British courts ruled in different ways in the different Cape cases.

shall concentrate on the three dimensions surveyed in previous sections.[80] The establishment of a treaty on corporate responsibility in environmental matters challenges the strict reading of state sovereignty. State sovereignty will remain a cornerstone in the legislative process towards a binding transboundary framework as well, but states' control of activities within their territories will have to be balanced against the need to provide remedies for those adversely affected by corporate activities. In this sense, such a framework would be less state-centred than existing environmental agreements.

The drafting of a treaty on corporate responsibility resembles drafting other international treaties: the broader the scope in terms of activities, states, situations, and environmental effects, the more general and abstract the substance tends to be. For many cases, however, even general provisions could provide a firm legal basis to review conduct in a specific case, and to determine whether the corporation should be held responsible and liable for remedying the situation. Moreover, it may make national courts less hesitant in trying cases concerning corporate activities abroad.

More specifically, a treaty on corporate responsibility could either be drafted so as to address the duties and responsibilities of corporations directly or through intermediate phrases, like 'the Parties should ensure that . . .'. There are already plenty of international treaties, e.g. some human rights conventions and the Rome Statute of the International Criminal Court 1998, where direct language is used in order to define the rights and responsibilities of private subjects. If established as a transboundary framework with the intention actually to define corporate responsibilities, it makes sense that it be drafted with such direct language as well.

1. Substance: preventive principles, performance requirements, and liability criteria

The general concepts and principles listed in section IV are relatively imprecise and 'open-textured', but this does not prevent them from being applicable in specific cases. For instance, the precautionary principle and the principle of best practicable means – in particular the reference to best available technology – can be employed when assessing the performance of corporations active in different countries.[81] Despite their flexibility, they provide benchmarks for determining

---

[80] While jurisdictional issues have been discussed in this chapter, *transboundary recognition and enforcement* of legal decisions has been ignored. This is, however, still relevant, e.g. when a decision on compensation is made in the state of the activity and the corporation does not have sufficient assets in that state. The liability conventions and the Brussels Convention, mentioned in section V, all provide for some recognition and enforcement of foreign judgments.

[81] This argument also gains support from the fact that the precautionary principle is addressed directly to MNEs by various codes of conduct and policy documents.

whether a corporation has paid due account to risks and uncertainties, and whether the safety measures taken somehow correspond to the technological development. If included in a responsibility scheme, supported by the notion of polluter pays, these principles would set a standard while placing the burden on the corporation to justify any deviation to the detriment of health or the environment. In a rather similar way, environmental impact assessments can be part of a responsibility scheme for MNEs/TNCs. If such assessments are made compulsory for certain activities, lack of an adequate assessment would be a relevant factor when deciding on liability for harm caused.

As far as civil liability criteria are concerned, existing environmental agreements provide foundations to draw on. In addition to a general statement that damage be compensated for, a liability scheme will have to define whether liability is strict or based on negligence, what defences exist to liability, whether liability is joint, and if there is a minimum threshold of significance, a maximum limit for compensation, or a time limitation.

Moreover, some requirement on transparency, reporting, and making information about the activities public is a conceivable element of a legal framework. Such information includes indicators of material used, waste production, energy consumption, location of activities, precautionary measures, and descriptions of the impact of activities (on biodiversity, air, water, soil, etc.). There are already reporting requirements for corporations established internationally (albeit not in a general legal framework) to draw on.[82] In addition to making information publicly available, reporting duties may include sending these reports to a national or international body for review. Failure to provide adequate information may affect decisions concerning claims for damage.

If norms of conflict instead of common standards are opted for, it should be decided whether preventive principles or liability criteria of *lex delicti* or *lex fori* apply in a specific case (given that the case is tried outside the state of the activity). A special situation arises when activities are carried out in areas where there is no law on environment or health protection. To be of any use in such situations, the treaty should set out that cases be resolved either on the basis of *lex fori* (or equivalent) or international principles.

2. *Procedure: jurisdiction and remedies*

Since hiding behind state borders is a prime issue in controlling corporations, it is essential that a legal framework deals with this by providing for transboundary jurisdiction. The possibility of bringing the procedure to the corporation's home country would be advantageous from the viewpoint of the plaintiff when local remedies are not satisfactory. Still, the split subjectivity of the corporation and the corporate veil remain problematic hurdles, if it is not

---

[82] In particular the Global Reporting Initiative, see www.globalreporting.org/

clear which unit(s) – subsidiary, parent company, etc. – can be made responsible in a given case.

Compensation for damage is the most likely remedy in transboundary cases, and the most common claim in the known transboundary cases on corporate responsibility. For a transboundary legal framework, jurisdiction of the corporation's home state should at least be made a secondary option in such cases, if there is no adequate forum in the state of the activity/harm.

If national fora are relied upon, the most adequate solution would be to give the plaintiff alternative routes to initiate the case. This would fit the more recent civil liability treaties in the field of environment protection, where optional fora are provided for. In particular, the plaintiff should have the option of choosing between the state of the incident, the damage, and the defendant's residence.

Where there is no functioning system of environmental control in the state of the activity, transboundary injunctions or mandamus actions would also be useful remedies for those harmed or likely to be harmed by corporate activities. From the viewpoint of these persons, the possibility to sue for injunction or mandamus action in the home state of the corporation rather than in the state of the activity/harm would provide a more preventive remedy than compensation. Today, transboundary claims for injunction and mandamus action are being increasingly accepted in cases where *affected persons outside* the state of the activity bring claims to a *court in* the state of the activity.[83] However, the rather different situation of *persons in* the state of the activity bringing a suit for injunction or mandamus action before a *court or administration outside* the state of the activity/harm remains more controversial, even contentious, as it is perceived as interfering in another state's sphere of sovereign action. Yet, in cases where there is no functioning state where the activity took place or the harm occurred, where the state is too weak or where it is even hostile to the plaintiffs' cause, referring to state sovereignty without duly balancing other interests amounts to *Begriffsjurisprudenz*, the effect being that the 'state' appears only pro forma and as an obstacle for justice. If all injunction or mandamus action procedures outside the state of the activity are precluded in such cases, those exposed to severe harm would lack any remedy against unacceptable activities of multinational enterprises (and transnational corporations).

A similar argument is valid in cases of criminal responsibility. If this aspect is included in the treaty on corporate responsibility, dual criminality should

---

[83] Most notable is the Aarhus Convention 1998, n. 39 above, which provides for minimum procedural rights and equal access to environmental procedures in transboundary cases. Less advanced are the Nordic Environmental Protection Convention 1974, n. 47 above, and the OECD Recommendation on Equal Right to Access and Non-Discrimination in relation to Transfrontier Pollution 1974, C(77)28Final(1977), 16 I.L.M. (1977) 977, which only provide for equal access. See Ebbesson, J., The notion of public participation in international environmental law, *Yearbook of Int'l Environmental Law 1997* 8 (1998), pp. 51, 81–87; and Birnie and Boyle, op. cit. pp. 269–275.

not be a prerequisite for jurisdiction in cases where the crime is committed in areas without national environmental or penal laws.

An international legal framework on corporate responsibility should also include an organisation to oversee the implementation. In addition, it is possible to set up an institution for dispute settlement. The issues to be negotiated when drafting such a forum are, e.g. its mandate and competence, the status of its decisions (legally binding only recommendatory), and whether some sort of financial aid should be available. Today, there is no transnational arrangement functionally equivalent to existing arrangements to settle commercial or investment disputes, for trying cases where individuals have been affected by corporate misdeeds. Still, there is hardly any difference of principle (but of finance) explaining why international dispute settlement procedures should not be available for torts, where persons who are adversely affected claim compensation from MNEs/TNCs.

3. Subjectivity: corporate structures and organisation

Transboundary rules or procedures to impose corporate responsibility would not be of much use unless the responsibility for acts and omissions of one unit in the corporate web can be linked to another unit. In clear-cut cases this means making a parent company responsible for harm caused by its subsidiary. There are two possible ways to construct the liability scheme for parent companies. One is to hold the parent company liable for negligence of the daughter simply because it exercises control of the daughter (i.e. piercing the corporate veil). The other is to make the parent company liable because of *its own* negligence in controlling the activities of the daughter. In the yet more complex situations, the question arises whether one company should be made responsible for the conduct of another, because the former maintains considerable economic influence or dominance on the latter even without any formal power.

As pointed out, there is no principle of international law on how to place the responsibility within a corporate structure. In contract law, the notion of 'responsibility of control' is debated, meaning that the corporation breaching a contract can be exculpated only if it can show that the breach was due to circumstances beyond its control. It is possible to expand this notion to cases of non-contractual responsibility and liability in corporate activities, e.g. when harm is caused to health and the environment.[84] The decisive factor, then, regarding responsibility would be whether the harm caused was beyond the control of the corporation rather than sheer negligence.

Drawing on the notion of responsibility of control, responsibility based on de facto control could also be developed as an operational principle and a decisive

---

[84] Wilhelmsson, T., *Senmodern ansvarsrätt: privaträtt som redskap för mikropolitik*, Uppsala (Iustus) 2001, p. 248.

criterion of corporate responsibility in international law. Thus, rather than explaining the allocation of responsibility to the parent company as piercing the corporate veil, the rationale for making it responsible would be its own negligence in controlling its daughters. To the extent the parent company exercised or should have exercised control over the unit that caused harm to health or the environment, the former, one may argue, has been negligent in maintaining de facto control. Theoretically and maybe practically, this scheme could also be applied to other relationships than parent company – subsidiary. If a dominant actor (a contractor), which did not actually carry out the harmful activity, nonetheless exercised such dominance that the subcontractor did not have much say in a case, the former could be made responsible for the harm.

De facto control is a possible criterion when defining a liability scheme for corporations, but it needs further analysis, e.g. on how to avoid too farfetched chains of liability. If established as a factor for placing responsibility, the institution resolving the dispute would still have to decide in each case whether a sufficient degree of control was (or should have been) maintained to claim responsibility on this ground. As an element of a legal principle on corporate responsibility, de facto control can be a decisive factor both in cases concerning compensation for damage and when transboundary injunctions are asked for.

If established as a part of international law, some leeway would still be left to each state to regulate the constructions of corporations, and for corporations to organise themselves. The aim, though, would be to avoid situations where a company with de facto control or expected control hides behind the veil of corporate subjectivity.[85] In many cases it would remain difficult to identify the subject(s) responsible for certain harm. Even so, this construction would fit better also with the notion of network enterprises, where the influence and control of one or several actors over another is not defined by formal ownership.

4. So: is all this unrealistic?

Considering the many aspects of a transboundary legal framework, the diverse interests and views among stakeholders (states, business community, NGOs, and members of the public) on such a development, the sketch above can of course be challenged as unrealistic, but also be criticised for being too modest. In the recent history of international law, many new issues and approaches appeared unrealistic until they were actually brought to the table, seriously discussed, accepted, and implemented (the Aarhus Convention 1998, the Ottawa Convention 1997 prohibiting certain types of landmines, and the Rome Statute 1998 being some examples), and it is not unlikely that corporate responsibility may become yet another such case.

---

[85] See e.g. Muchlinski, op. cit. p. 4.

It may take some time to establish. Still, the underlying problems related to harm caused by transboundary corporations cannot be ignored, and they will have to be dealt with in one way or the other, ways that are more or less coordinated. One alternative is to pursue multilaterally; to convene an intergovernmental conference on the topic, assess the possibilities of improving the coordination and cooperation in this field (e.g. by way of a declaratory document, the establishment of an intergovernmental body, or a decision to commence negotiations of a framework treaty). Another alternative is to hope for unilateral measures and a more 'spontaneous' legal development, through national legislation or case law, whenever courts are confronted with these issues. Yet another alternative is to rely solely on voluntary measures and 'market-based' instruments.

However, it would be more than naïve to assume that effective control of MNEs/TNCs, etc. could be achieved merely by uncoordinated extra-territorial jurisdiction of national laws or by 'non-legal', voluntary means. It will *also* require legal coordination, harmonisation, and cooperation that transcends state borders. The fragments explored may be used for this purpose, but a lot remains to be invented.

PART IV

The potential of the state

9

The diffusion of environmental policy innovations

KERSTIN TEWS

I. Introduction

This chapter explores which factors drive the diffusion of environmental policy innovations. Some central assumptions made by diffusion research to date will be challenged by empirical findings taken mainly from an exploratory research project.[1] Empirical data related to the adoption of twenty-one basic environmental policy innovations in forty-eight countries over a time period of fifty years[2] was collected and discussed in the context of theoretical considerations[3] and various case studies.[4]

I would like to thank Manfred Binder, Klaus Jacob, and the editor of this volume for their very helpful comments.

[1] The project on The Diffusion of Environmental Policy Innovations as an Aspect of Globalisation was conducted at the Environmental Policy Research Centre at the Freie Universität Berlin and financed by the Volkswagen Foundation. Research findings of the various researchers of the team (Busch, P.-O., Binder, M., Jörgens, H., Kern, K., Tews, K.) can be downloaded from our website at www.fu-berlin.de/ffu

[2] The term 'basic environmental innovations' indicates those environmental instruments or institutions that describe basic trajectories of environmental policy development, in contrast to only incremental innovations which follow the path of those basic trajectories. The twenty-one basic environmental policy innovations were selected in a discursive process among environmental experts. The data covers all OECD countries and the remaining European countries of Central and Eastern Europe. Excluded are developing countries, mainly due to insufficient availability of data. See Busch, P.-O. and Jörgens, H., *Globale Diffusionsmuster umweltpolitischer Innovationen*, Berlin (Environmental Policy Research Centre) forthcoming, available at www.fu-berlin.de/ffu; Binder, M., *Umweltpolitische Basisinnovationen im Industrieländervergleich: Ein grafisch-statistischer Überblick*, Berlin (Environmental Policy Research Centre) 2002, ffu report 06–2002, available at www.fu-berlin.de/ffu,

[3] See Tews, K., *Der Diffusionsansatz für die Vergleichende Policy-Analyse: Wurzeln und Potenziale eines Konzepts: Eine Literaturstudie*, Berlin (Environmental Policy Research Centre) 2002, ffu report 02–2002, available at www.fu-berlin.de/ffu/

[4] See Kern, K. and Kissling-Näf, I., *Politikkonvergenz und Politikdiffusion durch Regierungs- und Nichtregierungs-organisationen: Ein internationaler Vergleich von Umweltzeichen*, Berlin (Social Science Centre) 2002, Discussion Paper FS II 02–302, available at www.wz-berlin.de; Tews, K., *Die Ausbreitung von Energie/CO$_2$-Steuern: Internationale Stimuli und nationale Restriktionen*, Berlin (Environmental Policy Research Centre) 2002, ffu report

The chapter begins with a discussion of the conceptual distinction between diffusion and other mechanisms of convergence. There then follows a discussion of factors that may have a crucial impact on the patterns of diffusion. Within this section, interrelations with other types of global or regional governance are discussed. This includes both special features of the EU framework as well as the impact of global norms. The chapter proceeds to discuss the restrictions in the diffusion process, which heavily depend on innovation characteristics and national capacities to innovate. The chapter's main intention is to shed some light on the complex interplay of factors affecting diffusion patterns. In doing so it provides several points of departure for new research questions that are hoped to inspire the scientific debate on globalisation and policy convergence.

II. Diffusion as distinct mechanism of convergence

Comparative policy analysis has revealed the phenomenon that national environmental policy patterns are becoming similar. This observation immediately evokes the question of the nature of these similarities. Are they similarities resulting purely from idiosyncratic domestic factors and/or 'similar modernisation forces having the same, but separate, effects'?[5] Or are they more than purely similar but a result of processes interlinking national policy decisions to those beyond national jurisdiction?

For the latter processes, the literature available offers a variety of mechanisms assumed to be responsible for the fact that national policy-making is related to policy-making elsewhere – which leads to the observable phenomenon of convergence.

There are processes in which national decision-making is consciously directed towards gaining a convergent pattern of regulatory policy. This mechanism is sometimes labelled as 'harmonisation'[6] or 'obligated policy transfer'.[7] The common notion of all these terms is that national policies move consciously towards a jointly agreed standard – most commonly in the form of a multinational agreement.

08–2002, available at www.fu-berlin.de/ffu/; Busch, P.-O., *Die Diffusion von Einspeisevergütungen und Quotenmodellen: Konkurrenz der Modelle in Europa*, Berlin (Environmental Policy Research Centre) 2003, ffu report 03–2003, available at www.fu-berlin.de/ffu/

[5] Bennett, C. J., Understanding ripple effects: the cross-national adoption of policy instruments for bureaucratic accountability, *Governance* 10(3) (1997), pp. 213–233, at 215.

[6] Bennett, C. J., What is policy convergence and what causes it?, *British J. Political Science* 25(3) (1991), pp. 215–233.

[7] Dolowitz, D. P. and Marsh, D., Learning from abroad: the role of policy transfer in contemporary policy making, *Governance* 13(1) (2000), pp. 5–24.

A further mechanism is called 'hierarchical imposition',[8] 'coercive policy transfer',[9] or 'domination'.[10] The joint notion is that there exists an asymmetric power relation between the importer and exporter of policies, usually in the form that the 'weaker' one wishes to gain resources from the 'stronger' one who imposes conditions on access to its resources by making the 'weaker' one import a policy.

A third mechanism of convergence singled out in the literature is policy diffusion.[11] The driving forces of this mechanism are to be addressed in this chapter. Diffusion is the spreading of innovations due to communication instead of hierarchy and/or collective decision-making between actors across national borders. Theoretical considerations suggest that the analysis of diffusion processes is a challenging endeavour since it has to consider a complex interplay of three factors: international and transnational factors, which horizontally and vertically interlink jurisdictions and enable the transfer of policy content; national factors, which filter experiences from abroad and determine national responsiveness to external stimuli; and the characteristics of the policy innovation, which may indicate its 'diffusability'.[12]

Thus, the term 'policy diffusion' is used in the notion of a spreading process of policy innovations among the countries of the international system driven by different mechanisms comprising all voluntary types of policy adoptions ranging from policy learning to copying or mimetic emulation. The domestic implementation of international binding law as well as coercive policy transfers should be singled out from the diffusion concept. Making the focus of diffusion research so narrow is motivated by analytical considerations: as all horizontal policy diffusion may result in policy convergence even in the absence of strong international regimes – for a long time assumed to be the only means of global governance – that narrow notion of diffusion may sharpen our research focus and add *new* questions and perspectives for prospective research on mechanisms of global governance.

To avoid misunderstandings, it should be stated that each 'program, idea or practice that is new *to the government adopting it*'[13] is called a 'policy innovation',

---

[8] Caddy, J., Harmonization and asymmetry: environmental policy co-ordination between the European Union and Central Europe, *J. European Public Policy* 4(3) (1997), pp. 318–336; Tews, K., *EU-Erweiterung und Umweltschutz: Umweltpolitische Koordination zwischen EU und Polen*, Leipzig (Leipziger Universitätsverlag) 1999.
[9] Dolowitz and Marsh, op. cit. [10] Bennett (1991), op. cit.
[11] For summaries of the state of the art in policy diffusion research, see Kern, K., *Die Diffusion von Politikinnovationen: Umweltpolitische Innovationen im Mehrebenensystem der USA*, Opladen (Leske + Budrich) 2000; Tews, K., *Der Diffusionsansatz*, op. cit.
[12] Tews, K., Busch, P.-O., and Jörgens, H., The diffusion of new environmental policy instruments, *European J. Political Research* 42(4) (2003), pp. 569–600.
[13] Walker, J. L., The diffusion of innovations among American states, *American Political Science Review* 63 (1969), pp. 880–899, at 881.

which neither implies that it has not been done before elsewhere nor that is a good thing to do. The merits of this approach are: first, we can also learn from cases we do not like (e.g. spreading of roll-back tendencies in environmental policy); secondly, it opens up the concept by preventing systematic bias owing to implicit assumptions concerning the motivation to adopt an innovation. Thus, it may include mechanisms labelled in literature as 'isomorphism',[14] 'legitimacy',[15] 'policy bandwagoning',[16] or 'norm cascades'.[17] The joint notion is that uncertainty may even result in 'the blind leading the blind'[18] – relying on reputation instead of demonstrating good or best practice on how to tackle a problem, which can be *learned* from.

The analytical approach, when defining diffusion as the dependent variable, focuses on detecting factors facilitating or hampering the spread of policy innovations within the international system. The overwhelming majority of diffusion studies approach their research question concerning drivers and restriction of policy diffusion from a macrolevel perspective. This is due to the definition of diffusion, which only becomes manifest through sequences of individual cases of policy transfer from abroad. Diffusion studies in political science typically intend to detect patterns in these sequences of national policy adoptions, which might allow for the deduction of underlying mechanisms and motivations. It is evident that a policy adoption alone (output level) can neither tell us whether the imported policy has an impact, nor whether the imported policy is intended to have an impact at the domestic level at all. Nevertheless, the very focus on sequences of policy outputs, especially when it is based on a broad empirical data set, might provide us with patterns suggesting hypotheses which inform and may serve as a guide for subsequent micro- and mesolevel studies.

III. Basic findings

The previous decades have seen a remarkable spread of environmental policy innovations right from the beginning of the establishment of environmental

---

[14] Di Maggio, P. and Powell, W. W., The iron cage revisited: institutional isomorphism and collective rationality in organizational fields, in Di Maggio, P. and Powell, W.W. (eds.), *The new institutionalism in organizational analysis*, Chicago (University of Chicago Press) 1991, pp. 63-82.
[15] Bennett (1997), op. cit.
[16] Ikenberry, J. G., The international spread of privatization policies: inducements, learning, and 'policy bandwagoning', in Suleiman, E. and Waterbury, J. eds.), *The political economy of public sector reform and privatization*, Boulder (Westview Press) 1990, pp. 88–110.
[17] Finnemore, M. and Sikkink, K., International norm dynamics and political change, *International Organization* 52(4) (1998), pp. 887–917.
[18] Hirshleifer, D., The blind leading the blind: social influence, fads, and informational cascades, in Tommasi, M. and Ierulli, K. (eds.), *The new economics of human behavior*, Cambridge (Cambridge University Press) 1995, pp. 188–215.

policy as a distinct competence of state regulation (Figure 9.1). This can hardly be explained by national compliance with common standards agreed on a multinational level. As the empirical data illustrates, the more integrated measures, especially the 'softer' informational and planning measures such as eco- and energy-efficiency labels, access to environmental information laws, environmental plans and strategies, environmental reporting, and certain new institutions (e.g. councils for sustainable development and other types of governmental environmental advisory councils), have succeeded adoptions of policy instruments, which pursue a fragmented and largely command-and-control-based regulatory approach. Another insight drawn from the large-N observation of the innovations' expansion reveals varying speeds of an innovation's expansion. A higher frequency of innovation adoptions is evident, in particular, with respect to the softer instruments. On the one hand, this higher rate of adoption might be deduced from certain innovation characteristics, which further their 'diffusability' (see section V). On the other hand, this more rapid spread may also be facilitated by a higher level of international communication and directed dissemination of information about these instruments by transnational and international actors. The latter assumption gains additional weight by another pattern revealed in Figure 9.1: innovation activities accumulate at certain points in time. These points in time correspond to high level international communication of environmental issues. This first occurred around 1972, before a second even more obvious jump in adoption frequency around 1992 – both years are cornerstones in the international debate on environmental protection at UN conferences.

A tentative conclusion to be reached is that national innovation decisions are considerably influenced by policy choices elsewhere, and international sources play an important role for domestic policy change.

IV. Factors driving environmental policy diffusion

In the following section, central assumptions of diffusion literature will be confronted with empirical findings. As communication is assumed to be the most basic mechanism of diffusion, diffusion studies typically analyse the patterns of how innovations spread from one country to another over time, in order to detect those communication channels which seem to further policy diffusion. Communication research has produced empirical findings and mathematical models demonstrating that innovations disseminated by third parties into an adopter population spread more quickly than innovations communicated through direct interaction between the members of the social system.[19] Kristine Kern has applied this hypothesis to political science diffusion research,

---

[19] Mahajan, V. and Peterson, R. H., *Models for innovation diffusion*, Beverley Hills (Sage) 1985.

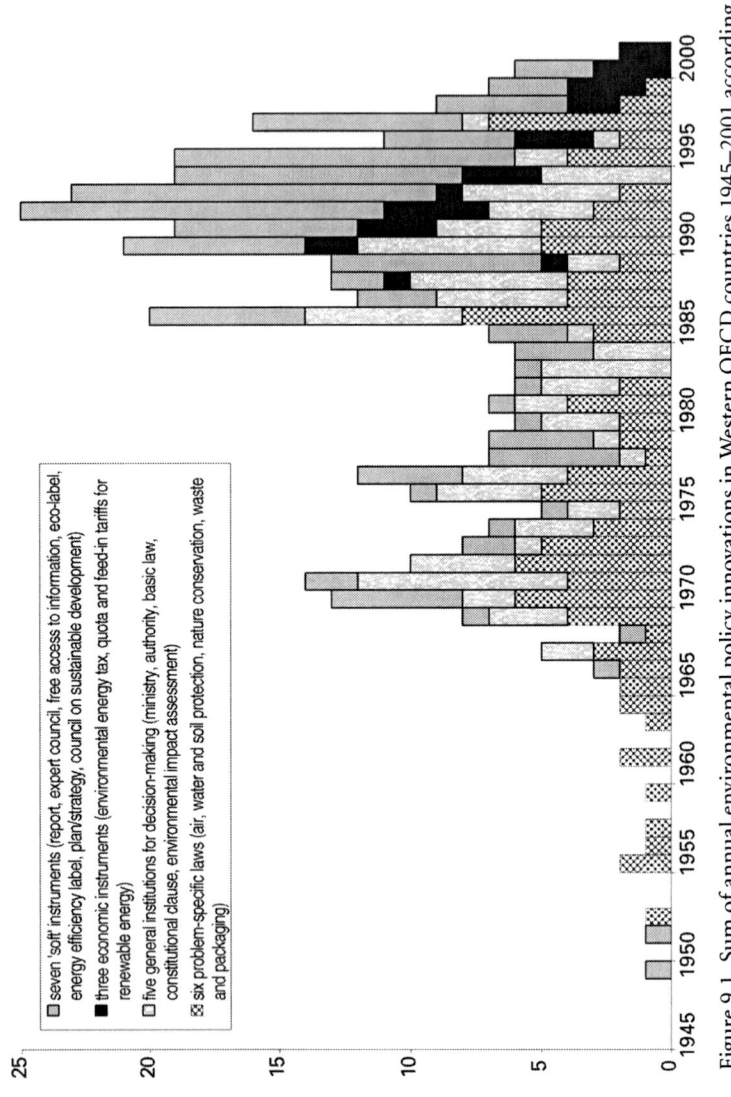

Figure 9.1 Sum of annual environmental policy innovations in Western OECD countries 1945–2001 according to innovation type

Source: Binder, M., *Umweltpolitische Basisinnovationem im Industrieländervergleich: Ein grafisch – statistischer Überblick*, Berlin (Environmental Policy Research Centre) 2002.

proposing to call the two modes of transfer 'institutionalised' and 'direct policy transfer'. While direct policy transfer is dominated by horizontal and bilateral communication patterns between countries, institutionalised policy transfers can comprise both multilateral communication patterns mediated by certain institutions established at the international level, as well as vertical communication patterns between these superior institutions and national political jurisdictions. It is assumed that institutionalised policy transfer induces a more rapid spread, i.e. a higher rate of adoption at the beginning of the process, due to the fact that the information on the policy innovation is available for all countries from the very beginning.[20] In contrast, direct policy transfer is assumed to cause a diffusion pattern comparable to concentric circles starting from the innovation centre (first adopter country), as the information necessary to adopt the policy innovation initially is only available to neighbouring countries.[21]

The large-N scope of our study allows to look for such patterns across innovations, across time, and across countries, which might indicate those communication channels which foster policy diffusion. Thus, we have to search for typical patterns in the sequences of distinct national policy adoptions, which might indicate horizontal or bilateral communication channels between countries, and for 'anomalous' higher adoption frequency across all innovations, which might indicate vertical or mediated multilateral communication channels.

1. *Proximity of states*

When looking for the impact of horizontal communication channels on adoption decisions, there are no clear patterns in the sequences of national policy adoptions. It is assumed in literature that policy innovations spread more quickly among countries with dense interaction and communication linkages due to spatial proximity[22] or joint history. However, apart from certain timely successive adoptions in the Scandinavian countries (concerning waste

---

[20] Kern, op. cit. p. 143.
[21] Although one could assume that the increase of political and economic integration of states within the international system in the last century and (not to forget) the development and massive spread of new information technologies will cause such regional diffusion patterns to decline, studies show that they still occur. In fact, the regional diffusion patterns that have been observed among US states, such as in tax policies, do have more to do with the characteristics of the innovation rather than the regionally limited communication patterns: Berry and Berry argue, 'when policy adoptions are attempts to compete with other states ... the likelihood of regionally focussed, rather than nationally based, diffusion seems greatest': Berry, F. S. and Berry, W. D., Innovation and diffusion models in policy research, in Sabatier, P. A. (ed.), *Theories of the policy process*, Boulder/Oxford (Westview Press) 1999, pp. 169–200, at 175.
[22] Lutz, J. M., Regional leadership patterns in the diffusion of public policies, American Politics Q.15 (1987), pp. 387–398.

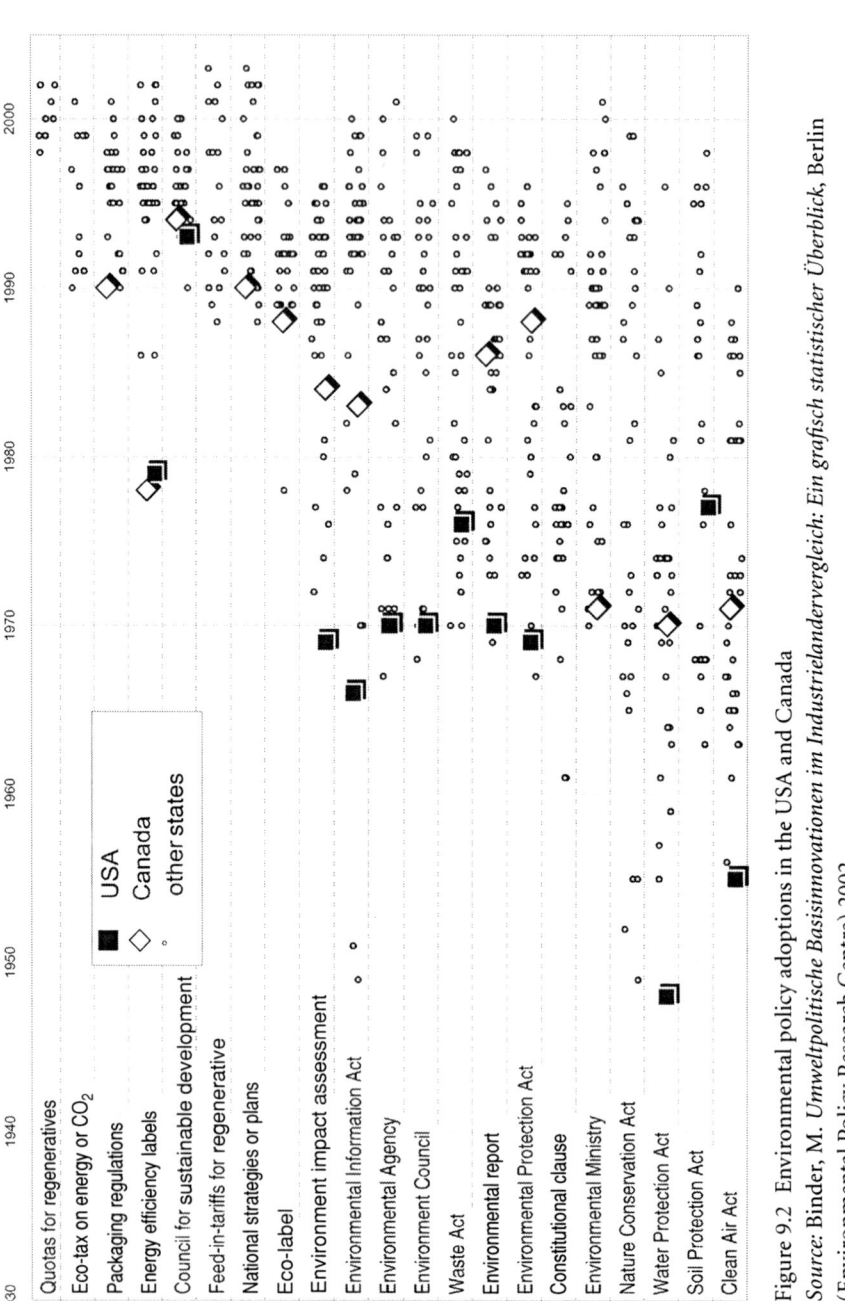

Figure 9.2 Environmental policy adoptions in the USA and Canada
Source: Binder, M. *Umweltpolitische Basisinnovationen im Industrieländervergleich: Ein grafisch statistischer Überblick*, Berlin (Environmental Policy Research Centre) 2002.

regulations, energy efficiency standards, and energy/carbon taxes), there exists hardly any evidence for the assertion that proximity might account for diffusion patterns.[23] Surprisingly, even between the USA and Canada, where US influence on Canadian environmental regulations is presumed in the relevant literature,[24] we cannot detect typical patterns in our data (Figure 9.2).[25] Not only did both countries not adopt the same set of basic environmental innovations, more astonishingly, there are up to twenty years between the US and Canadian adoptions seen in the air and water protection laws, basic environmental framework laws, free access to environmental information provisions, and laws on environmental impact assessment. Only with respect to energy efficiency labels and council for sustainable development are there policy adoptions within a close time frame of one another.

These findings can be interpreted as the relatively unsurprising result of increased global communication, through international organisations and transnational actor networks, as well as technological progress in communication technologies. Lessons can not necessarily be learnt from the pattern of regionally fixed communication channels. The content of transfer activities (ideas, approaches, instruments) within such bilateral and/or regional networks is increasingly shaped by information disseminated by the superior, open, and more comprehensive internationalised communication networks.

2. *Institutionalised policy transfer*

The term 'institutionalised policy transfer' describes the communicative activities of transnational non-state advocacy or knowledge networks as well as international intergovernmental organisations, in the organisation, mediation, and stimulation of transnational discourses of environmental problems, ideas, and policy instruments. These different actors are the links between the national and the international level. They differ with respect to resources and capabilities to influence diffusion processes. What they share is their involvement in the 'idea game', which entails 'formulating, transferring, selling and teaching not formal regulations but principled or causal beliefs helping to constrain or enable certain types of social behaviour'.[26] While certain international organisations use the lever of asymmetric power relations to impose policies,[27] these international and transnational actors cannot and/or do not want to apply such

---

[23] See Binder (2002), op. cit.
[24] Hoberg, G., Sleeping with an elephant: the American influence on Canadian environmental regulation, *J. of Public Policy* 11 (1991), pp. 107–132.
[25] Each data point in Figure 9.2 is a national adoption of the respective policy innovation.
[26] Marcussen, M., The OECD in search of a role: playing the idea game, paper prepared for presentation at the ECPR 29th Joint Session of Workshops, 6–11 April 2001, Grenoble, France.
[27] Dolowitz and Marsh, op. cit.

resources. Instead, environmental think tanks – be it non-state actors or international organisations such as the OECD – are weak in terms of decision-making power but strong in providing the intellectual matter and/or legitimacy that might underpin these decisions. Institutionalised policy transfer works through various mechanisms.

(a) Multilateral environmental discourses organised and mediated by international and transnational agents of transfer

The boom of national environmental policy activities in the shadow of international environmental events around 1972 and 1992 (see Figure 9.1) indicates that certain sources for change in national policy can be found at the international level. These high profile events serve as platforms for a multistakeholder discourse in which experiences can be shared, networks created, national performances awarded or reproached due to the high public and political attention paid to the issue under consideration. In particular the latter may explain the higher adoption frequencies of environmental policy innovations just before and shortly after these UN conferences on the environment in 1972 and 1992. The former director of the OECD's environmental directorate, Bill Long, argues that the number of high profile, environmentally related international events between the late 1980s and the mid-1990s 'commanded the attention of OECD governments . . . As a result "environment" was very high on the OECD's agenda . . . with initiatives and support emanating from the OECD Council and the Secretary General's Office; and proposals for new work and approaches being brought by member country experts into a wide array of OECD committees and technical groups'.[28]

Beside such global events, environmental protection is internationally established through various legally binding or non-binding environmental regimes, within intergovernmental organisations, and through various transnational environmental advocacy networks. International institutions might serve as platforms for protagonists of new ideas – policy entrepreneurs, ranging from individuals and other non-state actors to (pioneer) countries' representatives. Intergovernmental organisations, such as the OECD, do not act only by member state mandate. Instead, they have a varying but definite degree of discretion beyond the control of member states. In this function as broker or seller of ideas and potential multipliers of innovative policy solutions, international bureaucracies may become an access point for actors that are usually perceived as weak in terms of power in international relations, ranging from non-state actors to small states. Such international bureaucracies are a favourable institutional precondition for political entrepreneurship, pioneer behaviour, and horizontal diffusion dynamics. A fitting example of such interplay can be found in

---

[28] Long, B. L., *International environmental issues and the OECD 1950–2000: an historical perspective*, Paris (OECD) 2000, p. 80.

the OECD programme activities on new energy/carbon taxes, which started to accelerate simultaneously with the first national adoptions of carbon taxes in the Scandinavian member states in the early 1990s. These activities aimed not only at coordinated actions among OECD members but also provided policy guidance drawn from national experiences in first mover countries.[29]

These international institutions and/or organisations dealing with environmental issues may 'encourage actors to adopt extended time horizons and norms'[30] and 'make unilateral adjustments in behaviour – even in the absence of any legal obligation to do so',[31] which may result in competitive dynamics on the horizontal level in the attempt to gain advantages or avoid losses. States are embedded in dense networks of transnational and international social relations, this is assumed to shape their perceptions of the world and their role in that world.[32] This normative or ideational pressure to converge causes states to 'alter institutions and regulations because a set of beliefs has developed sufficient normative power that leaders fear looking like laggards if they do not adopt similar policies'.[33]

(b) Benchmarking activities by international and transnational agents of transfer

Activities of actors engaged in the 'idea game' are quite relevant for the inducement of competitive diffusion dynamics. They systematically spur on 'benchmarking' by regularly comparing national performances in specific issue areas such as environmental policies. Referring their evaluations to a mutually agreed target serves as an instrument 'in the exercise of "shaming" and peer pressure'.[34] At the 1991 G-7 Economic Summit in London, the heads of government commended the OECD for launching the Country Environmental Performance Review Programme. In doing so, national governments voluntarily committed themselves to increasing their accountability with respect to their domestic and international environmental objectives. The OECD's environmental performance review programme, launched in 1992, is the main instrument of this organisation to provide information on member countries' performances concerning the OECD's largely non-obligatory policy recommendations. The

---

[29] See Tews, *Die Ausbreitung*, op. cit.
[30] Underdal, A., Conclusions: patterns of regime effectiveness, in Miles., E. L., Underdal, A., Andresen, S., Wettestad, J., Skjærseth, J. B., and Carlin, E. M. (eds.), *Environmental regime effectiveness: confronting theory with evidence*, Cambridge/London (MIT Press) 2002, pp. 435–465, at 460.
[31] Underdal, A., One question, two answers, in Miles *et al.*, op. cit. pp. 3–45, at 5.
[32] Finnemore, M., *National interests and international society*, Ithaka (Cornell University Press) 1996, p. 2.
[33] Drezner, D. D., Globalization and policy convergence, *Int'l Studies Review* 3 (2001), pp. 53–78, at 57.
[34] Botcheva, L. and Martin, L. L., Institutional effects on state behaviour: convergence and divergence, *Int'l Studies Q.* 45 (2001), pp. 1–26, at 15.

publicity of these reports ensures that national governments, their opposition, and national and transnational non-state actors, utilise this information to *legitimise* decisions and/or demands. A comparably bad national performance may stimulate a national government to be oriented towards 'good practices' provided by other countries and/or promoted by international organisations, either due to internal 'public pressure' or external 'peer pressure'.

(c) Model production by international and transnational agents of transfer

What kind of advantages are there to an institutionalised type of knowledge transfer beyond purely its overall availability? Why should policy-makers be more motivated to adopt a policy promoted by international and transnational agents? One possible answer might be that the politicians' needs and the provisions of these transfer institutions complement each other. Concerning the politicians' needs, the main reason for policy-makers to look at and orient towards what others do is uncertainty, which forces mimetism.[35] In this situation, international organisations provide meta-standards based on scientific considerations and/or 'models' based on national 'best practices'. However, a national policy innovation does not automatically evolve into a model. A national policy can only gain the status of a model if others award the policy innovation this attribute. The informational and benchmarking activities of international organisations provide exactly that service. For policy-makers acting under uncertainty, these models offered by reputable transfer institutions:

- allow for short-cuts in the *search for solutions*, thus, reducing transaction costs;
- otherwise, adopting policies, which have been promoted by transfer institutions may also be motivated by the *search for legitimacy* within the international system.

3. Effects of institutionalised policy transfer: qualification of the hypothesis

The hypothesis that institutionalised policy transfer accelerates the diffusion process gained only minimal support through empirical findings. First, an acceleration effect cannot be observed for all types of instruments promoted internationally. Secondly, the hypothesis must additionally be reconsidered in

---

[35] Di Maggio and Powell, op. cit. p. 69. Di Maggio and Powell state that organisations do not only compete for material resources and customers, but also for political power and institutional legitimacy. Therefore, they orient towards the behaviour/practices of those who are perceived as most prestigious or legitimated within the organisational field in order to be regarded in the same manner as legitimate and reputable.

the light of cases where international institutions hinder rather than promote the diffusion process.

(a) Type of instruments

If we compare the patterns of expansion for the early media-related environmental instruments with the younger horizontal environmental instruments, it is relatively easy to detect an acceleration process in the expansion of the softer horizontal informational and planning measures, starting in the late 1980s (Figure 9.3). In contrast, media-related environmental regulations do not feature such obvious unsteadiness in their expansion. Additionally, new energy/carbon taxes do not feature such accelerations, either. They start to spread at the very moment an avalanche of national adoptions of the softer environmental instruments is triggered. Evidently, the factors triggering the spread of soft environmental instruments are insufficient also to accelerate the spread of these market-based environmental instruments.

The virtually upright course of the curve of environmental plans (Figure 9.3) can best be interpreted as an example of a 'norm cascade' as assumed by the constructivist school in international relations theory, where adopting a certain policy (environmental plan) becomes a means to exhibit the country's 'identity' as a legitimate member of the global society. The avalanche of national adoptions of softer environmental instruments in the early 1990s can be ascribed to their high ranking on agendas of international conferences and the work of international organisations such as the OECD or UNEP. Apart from climate protection and biodiversity as the core issues of the Second UN Conference on Environment and Development in Rio, it was precisely these new horizontal approaches in environmental governance – ranging from integrative planning to informational measures and participatory approaches – that dominated the discussions at the time.

One of the OECD's most substantive contributions to help diffuse these UNCED recommendations was the creation of a non-governmental international network of individuals sharing experiences on and promoting good practice in national environmental planning – the Green Planners Network.[36]

However, institutionalised policy transfer via expert networks and intergovernmental organisations did not affect the speed at which distinct innovations spread in the same way. We see, for example, no accelerating effect with respect to energy/carbon taxes (Figure 9.3) although these instruments have been promoted by scientific networks, as well as the most reputable international organisations, for decades, later enhanced by activities of non-state environmental organisations. Furthermore, the obvious decline in national innovation

---

[36] Jörgens, H., *Governance by diffusion: implementing global norms through cross-national imitation and learning*, Berlin (Environmental Policy Research Centre) 2003, ffu report 07–2003, available at www.fu-berlin.de/ffu/

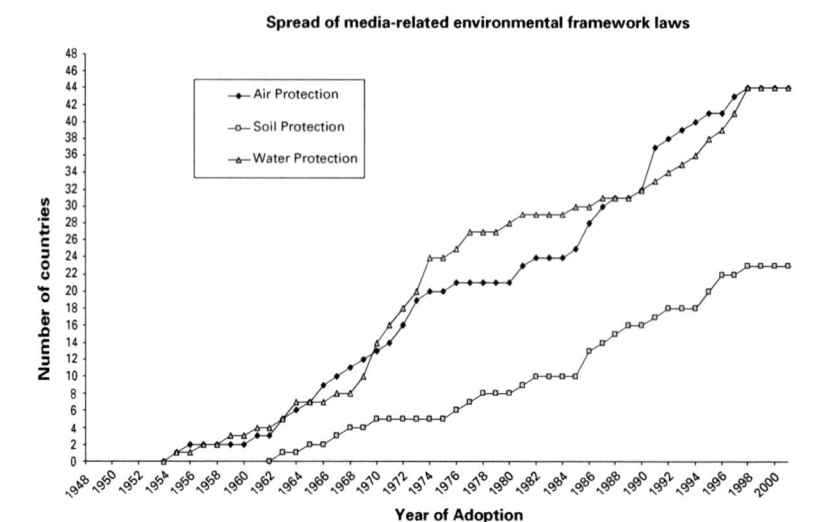

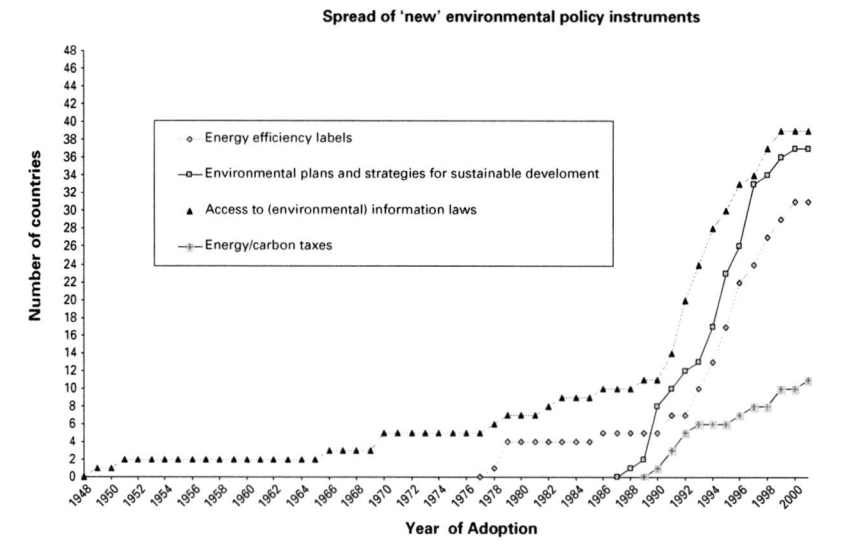

Figure 9.3 Comparison of the patterns of spread of media-related and 'new' environmental policy innovations
Source: based on data from Busch, P.-O. and Jörgens, H., *Globale Diffusionmuster umweltpolitischer Innovationen*, Berlin (Environmental Policy Research Centre) forthcoming, available at www.fu-berlin.de/ffu

activities in the late 1990s requires an explanation (see Figure 9.1). This decline cannot be explained by a decrease in the international institutionalisation of environmental policy transfer activities.

Summing up, the assumption that institutionalised policy transfer would accelerate diffusion processes does not hold true in general. Communication by international organisations or transnational actor networks is relevant to the understanding that the respective knowledge is available almost everywhere, that certain knowledge becomes more obvious, more relevant, and more awarded by recipients – but policy diffusion can only be assumed if these communicated ideas circulating in the international sphere intersect with a government's desire to adopt related policies. In fact, the international drivers and the national governments' desire to adopt occurred more or less simultaneously in a variety of countries – an acceleration of diffusion did indeed happen. However, this effect is only observed with respect to certain environmental policy innovations. As a tentative conclusion, which will be discussed later in this chapter in more detail, one could argue that innovation characteristics are the most relevant tie between international communication activities and national factors where adoption decisions have to be made (see section IV. 5).

(b) Hampering horizontal policy diffusion

Diffusion researchers expect a special catalysing effect on the spread of policy innovations when models are provided by agents of diffusion compatible with heterogeneous national institutional settings. However, this assumption requires development. First, competing international organisations might offer competing models – model competition increases uncertainty.[37] Secondly, the model construction by transfer institutions might contradict preferences of those countries that have already adopted an alternative model of the innovation, causing them to challenge the promoted model for fear of costs resulting from a prospective obligatory national adjustment.

The latter consideration has been drawn from observations in the EU context. The European Commission as central transfer institution does not only *offer* models but is able to transform them into *blueprints for obliged transfers*. Models presented by the European Commission are therefore objects of Member States' and interest groups' lobbying. In literature we find the argument that prospective harmonisation within the EU sets incentives for pioneer policy in order to demonstrate and provide a feasible model for the EU as a whole. Providing one's own approach first aims at protecting the domestic administration from costly adjustments to European policies, which do not

---

[37] Kern, K., Konvergenz umweltpolitischer Regulierungsmuster durch Globalisierung: Ursachen und Gegentendenzen, in Röller, L.-H. and Wey, C. (eds.), *Die Soziale Marktwirtschaft in der neuen Weltwirtschaft*, Berlin (Edition Sigma) 2001, pp. 327–350, at 344.

fit in with national administrative practices and traditions.[38] However, there is empirical evidence which indicates that the anticipation of prospective harmonisation tends to hamper pioneer policy and horizontal diffusion processes. The regulatory competition between Member States predominantly induced 'wait and see behaviour' instead of 'going ahead behaviour' in order to prevent a readjustment to the prospective EU solution which is potentially deviant to the national practice. This was seen in cases of energy efficiency labels for certain household devices,[39] feed-in tariffs vs. quota regulations for electricity from renewables,[40] and to a certain degree also during the eleven-year-long struggle over a common energy/carbon tax.[41] What all these cases had in common was that European harmonisation was anticipated, but not the criteria or standards of the prospective joint solution – a kind of model.

(i) The energy efficiency label case The unilateral development and the spread of energy efficiency labels were mainly hindered by the 1979 EU Framework Directive regulating the labelling of energy efficiency of household devices (79/530/EEC). This directive only allowed for unilateral adoptions if they conformed to a (not yet existing) prospective EU directive. It was not until the early 1990s that certain Member States decided to jump over this barrier by announcing unilateral action in order to provoke Commission activities. However, in 1990 Denmark was forced by the Commission to postpone the introduction of its own national efficiency label. In 1991, facilitated by announcements from Italy, the Netherlands, France, and Great Britain to do the same, Denmark was allowed to introduce a national energy efficiency label in close cooperation with the European Commission. The EU Directive from 1994 is consequently based on the Danish model. Thus, it took thirteen years from the first introduction of an energy efficiency label in Canada in 1978 until the first adoption by an EU Member State, despite the fact that the EU Framework Directive from 1979, which announced such labels, had quite rapidly followed this early mover. With the exception of Denmark, the spread of energy efficiency labels within the EU was therefore hindered by the harmonisation announcement. However, after 1994 the spread was facilitated by the harmonisation mechanism even beyond the EU within the Central and Eastern European region due to adjustment requirements with the *acquis communautaire*.[42]

---

[38] Heritier, A., Knill, C., and Mingers, S., *Ringing the changes in Europe: regulatory competition and the transformation of the state*, Berlin (de Gruyter) 1996; Andersen, M. S. and Liefferink, D., Introduction: the impact of the pioneers on EU environmental policy, in Andersen, M. S. and Liefferink, D. (eds.), *European environmental policy: the pioneers*, Manchester/New York (Manchester University Press) 1997, pp. 1–39.
[39] See Busch and Jörgens, op. cit.   [40] See Busch (2003), op. cit.
[41] See Tews, *Die Ausbreitung*, op. cit.
[42] For more details see Busch and Jörgens, op. cit.

THE DIFFUSION OF ENVIRONMENTAL POLICY INNOVATIONS 243

(ii) The case of energy/carbon taxes In the case of energy/carbon taxes the harmonisation process took eleven years (1992–2003). Within this time, seven European Member States unilaterally introduced such taxes. This already indicates that the barrier of prospective harmonisation was not as high as in the case of energy efficiency labels. Nevertheless, with the exception of Denmark and the Netherlands, which announced and unilaterally introduced such a tax to push a joint EU tax in 1992, the struggle over the joint measure – first proposed in 1992 by the European Commission – prevented other Member States from following the example of the European pioneers for a long time.[43] The prospect of a joint EU solution even weakened the proposal of the then German environment minister Töpfer to adopt a carbon dioxide levy in Germany, for fear of conflicts with the prospective EU model.[44] In an amended draft directive from 1994, unilateral adoptions by Member States were explicitly allowed by the Commission. This reanimated the debate in Germany and other countries, but it took a further five years before such energy tax measures were adopted in other European Member States: Italy (1999), Germany (1999), and Great Britain (2001).[45]

(iii) The case of feed-in tariffs v. tradable quotas for electricity from renewables The case study by Busch[46] illustrates how the European Commission as a transfer institution can induce model competition. It describes the diffusion process of market introduction programmes for renewable energy. This diffusion process has to struggle with the presence of two models in the guarantee of market access for renewable energy: feed-in tariffs and tradable quotas. Whereas feed-in tariffs had already diffused among eight Member States by 1994, the European Commission began contemplating harmonisation in 1995 by suspecting fixed tariffs of hindering competition. In 1998 the Commission proposed harmonisation based on the tradable quota model. Surprisingly, until 1998 no single Member State had adopted such a quota regulation, while the German feed-in tariff law had already become a model for others. The preference of the European Commission for the quota regulation to become the European solution created uncertainty for those who had already adopted, intended to adopt or amend existing feed-in tariff regulations. Although feed-in tariffs proceeded to spread worldwide (after a short break between 1995–1997), since 1998 only two of the states which have adopted them have been European Member States. However, five European Member

---

[43] With the exception of Denmark and the Netherlands, these countries were at that time not members of the EU: Finland, Norway, Sweden.
[44] Reiche, D. T. and Krebs, C., *Der Einstieg in die Ökologische Steuerreform: Aufstieg, Restriktionen und Durchsetzung eines umweltpolitischen Themas*, Frankfurt (Peter Lang) 1999.
[45] For more details see Tews, *Die Ausbreitung*, op. cit.
[46] Busch (2003), op. cit.

States did adopt quota regulations partly in addition to existing feed-in tariffs (until 2002). Some countries plan to phase out feed-in tariffs. In 2002, the Spanish Minister for Energy announced the phasing out of feed-in tariffs and its replacement by a system based on quota regulation.[47] If both instruments were mere functional equivalents (this is also contested) this would not be a matter of concern. However, EU harmonisation is still intended (although postponed by the new Commission in 2000 until 2012) and a joint model is still envisaged. Thus, one of the groups of countries will have to pay the costs of adapting to the other model. If the preferences of the Commission persist ('the move from a fixed tariff approach towards one based on trade and competition is at some stage inevitable')[48] the countries that have gone ahead with this environmental innovation will bear the costs. Bearing these considerations in mind, the question as to whether a strategic 'second move' would be more promising arises. The potential inducement of such first mover costs by transfer institutions, which favour models – irrespective of an ongoing 'success story' – need to be considered in more detail, as without pioneers there will be no followers, and thus, no diffusion.

4. Interplay with other convergence mechanisms

The spread of a few of the environmental policy innovations was influenced by an interplay of various convergence mechanisms. With the exception of the previously mentioned regulatory harmonisation within the EU, the EU effect can also be observed beyond its Member States. Countries attempting to become (meanwhile having become) Member States had to adopt the whole *acquis communautaire* before accession. This type of 'conditioned transfer'[49] accounts, to a certain degree, for a higher level of environmental activities in Central and Eastern Europe.

However, from a diffusion perspective focussing on voluntary policy adoptions, the observation that there seem to be diffusion dynamics either in the run-up phase of multilateral negotiations, parallel to them, or even as an alternative to such governance by international cooperation, is much more interesting. International cooperation is perceived as one central mechanism causing convergence. However, as empirical findings suggest, trends to adopt similar policies are even observable when negotiations about the joint target are still in progress or the target and the institutions created to control adequate state behaviour are perceived to be too weak to guarantee compliance.

---

[47] Ibid.
[48] European Commission, *Electricity from renewable energy sources and the internal electricity market*, Working Paper of the European Commission, Brussels (European Commission) 1998, p. 17 quoted in Busch (2003), op. cit.
[49] Dolowitz and Marsh, op. cit.

(a) Diffusion in the run-up and shadow of intergovernmental negotiation ('hard law')

The establishment of negotiation arenas and/or issue-specific international bureaucracies to develop environmental regimes intended to oblige parties to the prospective agreement to comply, build important institutional framework conditions for unilateral actions of pioneer countries and possibly foster diffusion dynamics.

An interesting example of this interplay between attempts to cooperate internationally and unilateral actions is presented by the development of the climate change regime (Figure 9.4). It is quite interesting to see that a majority of industrialised countries voluntarily adopted national targets to reduce greenhouse gas emissions in the early stage of the international norm-building process (1988–1992). Most of the early mover countries explicitly expressed their ambition to be among the front-runners in the establishment of an international climate change regime. They made a point of unilaterally adopting national targets in order to set standards to be followed by others. In particular, the Netherlands and Norway demonstrated this type of leadership in international processes referring to domestic policy development. Their form of leadership is distinct from other types that refer directly to the international level[50] insofar as it consists of demonstrative *national front-runner policy*. In contrast to structural leadership, which relies heavily on asymmetric power relations, this type depends heavily on a certain degree of attribution by others. Soft factors such as reputation and credibility play an important role. In literature it is sometimes referred to as 'environmental leadership'[51] or 'directional leadership'.[52] This early period of the establishment of the climate change regime was framed by a variety of international conferences, which put the climate change challenge onto the international political agenda. The cornerstones were the Toronto Conference in June 1988, the Second World Climate Conference in October/November 1990 in Geneva, and the Rio Conference in June 1992 where the UNFCCC was signed by 154 countries. In 1990 alone, an avalanche of twelve national adoptions of unilateral emission targets increased the number

---

[50] Young, O. R., Political leadership and regime formation: on the development of institutions in international society, *International Organization* 45(3) (1991), pp. 281–308. Young made a distinction between structural, entrepreneurial, and intellectual leadership: all refer to the international regime formation process but are based on distinct sources – power for structural leadership, diplomatic skills as a broker for entrepreneurial leadership, and the production and use of innovative ideas for intellectual leadership.

[51] Andersson, M. and Mol, a.P. J., The Netherlands in the UNFCCC process: leadership between ambition and reality, *International Environmental Agreements: Politics, Law and Economics* 2 (2002), pp. 49–68, at 50.

[52] Gupta, J. and Ringius, L., The EU's climate leadership: reconciling ambition and reality, *International Environmental Agreements: Politics, Law and Economics* 1 (2001), pp. 281–299, at 282.

of countries with domestic goals to fourteen (plus Norway and the Netherlands in 1989). By the year 1992, eighteen countries had announced voluntary targets. Thus, the national goals set by the early adopters were effective in terms of their signal effect to other countries to keep pace with the emerging trend in the early phase of the issue's evolution.[53] Furthermore, all of the Scandinavian early mover countries adopted one of the most challenging policy measures related to climate change protection: they all introduced new energy/carbon taxes, explicitly referring to the fulfilment of their *voluntary* domestic target, which was also meant to increase their credibility as directional leaders.

Furthermore, empirical studies provide evidence that diffusion processes might even provide alternatives to governance by international cooperation. A case study investigating the spread of environmental labels identifies one of the factors forcing non-state actors to develop and spread the FSC label policy innovation certifying the quality of forests – the failure to create an International Forest Convention.[54]

(b) Diffusion effects of 'soft law' agreements

International harmonisation and diffusion dynamics also interact where only international soft law agreements are involved. Such types of negotiated standards define principles and rules of state behaviour without strong sanction mechanisms to guarantee compliance.[55] They are often contracted in the form of declarations or charters and define guidelines for state behaviour. These types of international agreements are increasingly used as flexible instruments in global environmental policy – complementary or as specific precursors of so-called 'hard law'. These institutions might also matter, if transnational advocacy networks and domestic pressure groups use the international norm to generate pressure on their governments for policy change.

Agenda 21, which reflects 'global consensus and political commitment at the highest level on development and environmental co-operation',[56] and the Rio Declaration, are examples of such soft law agreements. Agenda 21 pushed the spread of national environmental plans and strategies for sustainable development.[57] Principle 10 of the Rio Declaration stimulated additional actors to advocate national legal provisions for free access to environmental information. In 1993, the UN Economic Commission for Europe (UNECE) was called upon by the participating environmental ministers to set up a task force on environmental rights and obligations. At the Fourth Ministerial Conference in the

---

[53] Binder, M. and Tews, K., Goal formulation and goal achievement in national climate change policies, Berlin (Environmental Policy Research Centre) 2004, ffu report 02–2004, available at www.fu-berlin.de/ffu/

[54] Kern and Kissling-Näf, op. cit.

[55] Sand, P. H., *Lessons learned in global environmental governance*, Washington, DC (World Resource Institute) 1990; Botcheva and Martin, op. cit.

[56] Quoted from the Preamble of Agenda 21. [57] Jörgens, op. cit.

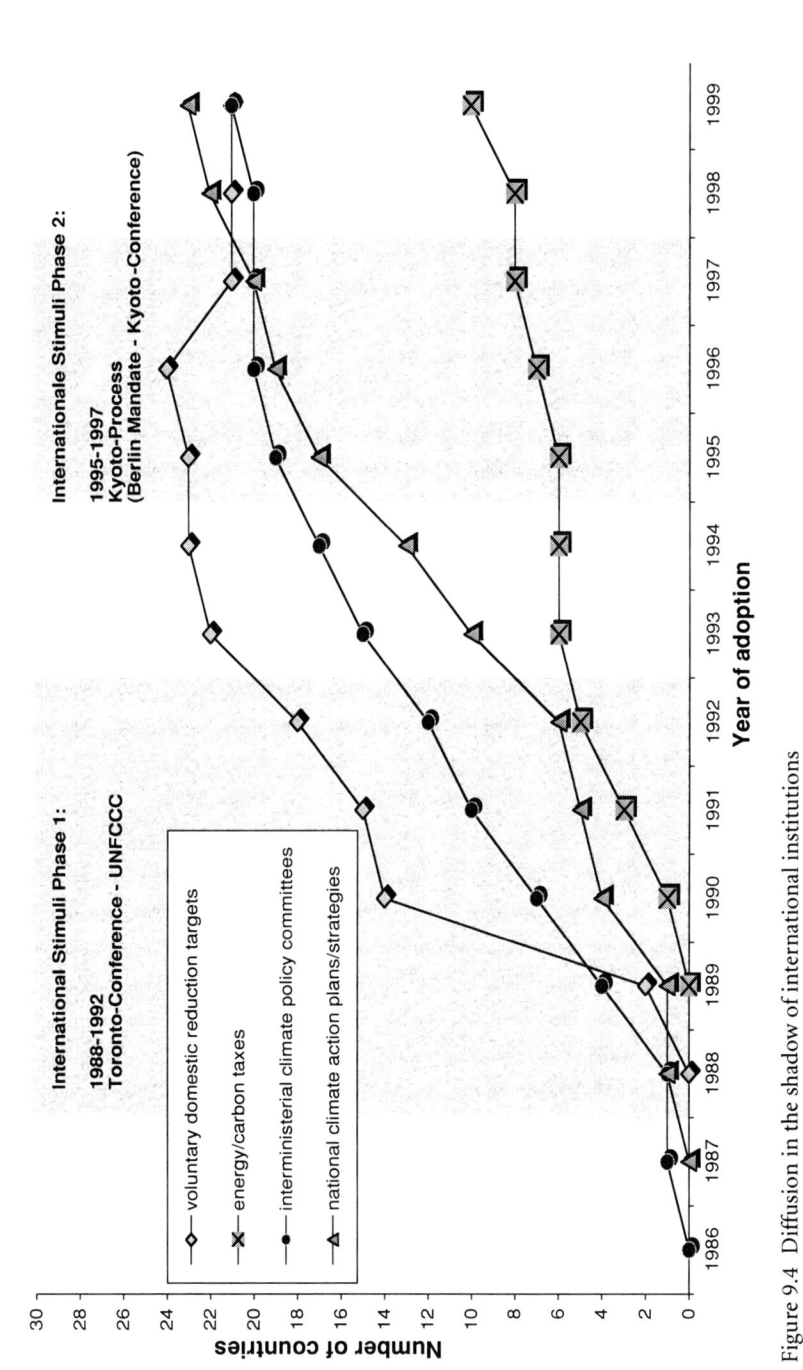

Figure 9.4 Diffusion in the shadow of international institutions

Source: own data collection, energy/carbon taxes adapted from Busch, P.-O. and Jörgens H., *Globale Diffusionmuster umweltpolitischer Innovationen*, Berlin (Environmental Policy Research Centre) forthcoming, available at www.fu-berlin.de/ffu

Environment for Europe series in 1998, this appeal culminated in the adoption of the UNECE Convention on Access to Information, Public Participation and Justice, the so-called Aarhus Convention. At the beginning of the twenty-first century, the issue of free access to environmental information (FAI) captured the political agenda of almost all international organisations.[58] Summing up, we can observe that the diffusion of FAI provisions began to accelerate when the issue entered the agendas of supranational bodies and international organisations. They served as international platforms for the original promoters of these legal provisions – citizens and environmental organisations. Hence, this process can be partially referred to as a mechanism of convergence coming 'from below', driven mainly by non-governmental actor networks that effectively used international platforms as catalysts and multipliers. Later it became a 'top down-driven' mechanism. With respect to the perspective of global convergence in FAI provisions, it can be assumed that the high prominence of that issue in international declarations and conventions may facilitate a future international policy output. UN Secretary-General Kofi Annan interpreted the adoption of the Aarhus Convention as 'a giant step forward in the development of international law in this field'.[59]

5. Policy characteristics as the major variable

There is no automatism in the spread of policy innovations, which can simply be derived from certain diffusion mechanisms. Even among countries which are closely linked in terms of dense cultural, economic and/or political relations or feature similar structural determinants of environmental capacity, we observe differing propensities to innovate. Hence, there is no single relationship between diffusion patterns and influencing factors. We have observed that international drivers do matter, however, they alone do not account for diffusion patterns. National factors matter, yet – analogically to international drivers – they do not suffice as an explanation of diffusion patterns. International stimuli to adopt a certain innovation nationally meet *heterogeneous national capacities and actor configurations*, which function as filters or, in other words, determine national responsiveness to experiences from abroad.

Therefore, in order to understand and influence the interplay between the various factors, the most suitable approach would be to look at innovation characteristics since they are the most relevant tie between international and national factors. Innovation characteristics affect:

---

[58] See e.g. OECD Council Recommendation on Environmental Information, adopted in Paris by the Environmental Ministers and the OECD Council in 1998, or the Free Access Provisions within the Environmental Side Agreement to the North American Free Trade Agreement from August 1993.

[59] OECD, *Public access to environmental information proceedings*, Athens 5–7 June, ENV/EPOC/GEP(2000)8, Paris (OECD) 2000, p. 13.

- the impact of institutionalised policy transfer;
- capacity requirements at national level; and
- the impact of other countries' behaviour on domestic action.

Innovations have to pass an adoption decision process. A policy adoption depends on the internal demand for solutions and a capacity to adopt. However, the hurdles to adopting an innovation additionally seem to differ according to innovation characteristics.

Thus, the 'diffusibility' of a policy innovation is indicated by its characteristics in terms of its administrative implications and/or its political feasibility. Although this phenomenon is mentioned in early diffusion literature,[60] it is often neglected in contemporary empirical research.

However, defining properties of policy innovations is a challenging task. Policy innovations have to pass through the whole national policy cycle. At each stage, the decision process can break off due to the underlying problem structure or problems of compatibility or political feasibility, which might differ between countries. It is difficult to find general items for these raw categories without considering diverse national contexts that can significantly influence compatibility and feasibility of a policy innovation. Bearing in mind these heterogeneous national contexts, only minimum criteria are defined in the generalisation of the properties of policy innovations, which may affect the rate of adoption in the international system.[61]

It is to be assumed that the *problem structure* influences the rate of adoption. It has been observed empirically that policies related to problems of long-term degeneration, whose effects are not directly visible and which, therefore, cannot easily be placed on the political agenda, diffuse rather slowly. The same applies to policies aimed at problems for which standard technical solutions are not available, such as land use, groundwater pollution, or loss of biodiversity.[62]

Regarding the *compatibility* of policy innovations with existing regulatory styles and structures, it seems likely that the extent of policy change induced by a regulatory innovation is decisive for its diffusion. Given the filtering effect of national institutions, it is assumed that an innovation's ability to diffuse will depend on how easily it can pass through these filters. The spread of innovations that can easily be added to existing structures and induce only incremental change can be expected to be faster than the spread of innovations that conflict with traditional regulative structures and policy styles. Certain empirical

---

[60] Rogers, E. M., *Diffusion of innovations*, New York (Free Press) 4th edn 1995.
[61] Tews, Busch, and Jörgens, op. cit.
[62] Kern, K., Jörgens, H., and Jänicke, M., *The diffusion of environmental policy innovations: a contribution to the globalisation of environmental policy*, Discussion Paper FS II 01–302, Berlin (Social Science Centre) 2001; Jänicke, M. and Jörgens, H., Strategic environmental planning and uncertainty: a cross-national comparison of green plans in industrialised countries, *Policy Studies J.* 28(3) (2000), pp. 612–632.

findings verify these assumptions. The comparison of the patterns of expansion of twenty-one environmental policy innovations revealed that the 'softer' policy innovations developed in recent years, such as environmental plans and strategies for sustainable development, councils for sustainable development, and access to environmental information laws,[63] exhibit the speediest spreading rate.[64] On the one hand, this rapidity could be ascribed to promotion activities of international and transnational actors. Yet, on the other hand, these instruments feature some characteristics that seem to make it easier to adopt them nationally. As studies of new environmental instruments show, these softer, open, and flexible instruments are characterised by the 'possibility of escaping policy obligation'.[65] These instruments assume some necessary preconditions in order to induce change. They assume the presence of motivated and capable actors, 'who are willing to work with the policy instrument . . . towards the intended goal'.[66] Thus, the potential weakness of these soft instruments may foster their widespread adoption, as national political agendas may be strongly influenced by external international drivers. The spread of free access to environmental information provisions seems to be a suitable example for such international 'norm cascades,'[67] as the global spread of this innovation accelerated immediately after having captured global policy arenas and the agenda of influential international organisations. It is interesting to note that access to environmental information provisions was adopted even by countries[68] with little public capacity to gather, organise, or provide these types of information, and where NGOs were very weak. This leads to the conclusion that policy adoption may not always be motivated by the expected impact of policy instruments (in this case more efficient participatory environmental management). Instead, the relative importance of a policy norm on the global environmental agenda and the perceived appropriateness of FAI provisions to respond instrumentally to this norm has proved sufficient to motivate the adoption of these regulations

---

[63] The spread of this innovation as shown in Figure 9.2 includes general provisions for free access to information, i.e. not restricted to *environmental* information, as they were first adopted in Sweden, Finland, and fifteen years later in the USA. Up to 1991, all adoptions concerned general provisions. However, they should be included as they served as benchmarks for the most active agents of the diffusion of the environmental innovation – transnational environmental NGOs. Only in 1991 did free access to environmental information as an instrument of environmental policy start to diffuse with the adoption of the Resource Management Act in New Zealand and an adoption in Latvia (Tews, Busch, and Jörgens, op. cit. pp. 588–592).

[64] See Binder (2002), op. cit.; Busch and Jörgens, op. cit.

[65] Knill, C. and Lenschow, A., On deficient implementation and deficient theories: the need for an institutional perspective in implementation research, in Knill, C. and Lenschow, A. (eds.), *Implementing EU environmental policy: new directions and old problems*, Manchester/New York (Manchester University Press) 2000, pp. 9–35.

[66] Ibid., p. 26.   [67] Finnemore and Sikkink, op. cit.

[68] For example, Albania in 1998 and Macedonia in 1996.

in nation states intending to be legitimate members within the international society. However, such adoption cascades are only likely with respect to policy innovations that can be easily added and require certain preconditions to be fulfilled in order to be effective.

The *political feasibility* of an innovation is assumed to depend on its potential to provoke conflicts with powerful actor groups. In particular, the instruments' fiscal effects influence the potential amount of conflict that could be induced by the innovation. Redistributive policies, which affect powerful interests, especially those that are internationally mobile, are less likely to diffuse rapidly. Therefore, the policy innovation's exposure to regulatory competition can be characterised as a raw criterion for the prospect of its rate of adoption. Advancing this assumption even further, Scharpf suggests that the political feasibility of an innovation encountering regulatory competition depends on whether the underlying economic competition concerns either the quality of products or costs of production.[69] The former are assumed to spread more quickly than the latter. These assumptions have been verified in empirical research. Whereas those policy instruments informing about and regulating the quality of products, such as eco-labels and energy efficiency labels, show the second fastest spread among the twenty-one environmental policy innovations, the spread of energy/carbon taxes is comparably slow. Thus, international trade can be both a conduit as well as a brake for the diffusion of market-based environmental policy instruments. It can work as a conduit for the diffusion of product-related environmental regulations if consumer behaviour is at least to some extent influenced by environmental concerns. These environmental preferences are strongly shaped by the activities of non-state environmental organisations.[70] As environmental concerns increase among consumers in the OECD, and increasingly within the Central and Eastern European region, governments adopt voluntary labelling schemes and suppliers participate as this is considered a rationale for ensuring sales opportunities and a market share. Furthermore, such product-related measures concern the logic of a coordination game rather than a Prisoner's Dilemma: conflict is about the type of joint solution and not about the joint solution itself. Thus, at least within the EU, their spread was also caused by positive coordination among Member States. Accordingly, as these national labelling instruments award environmentally sound products, which are globally traded, international organisations and

---

[69] However, under certain circumstances production-related measures can transform into product qualities: on international markets for high quality goods regulative measures affecting product qualities in terms of lower consumption and production externalities may result in competitive advantages for domestic producers – the so-called 'certification effect' of national regulative measures. Scharpf, F. W., *Regieren in Europa: Effektiv und demokratisch?*, Frankfurt/New York (Campus) 1999.

[70] Kern and Kissling-Näf, op. cit.

networks which were hardly involved in the initial phase of the spreading process increasingly try to play a part.

International trade works more as a brake when these market-based instruments are related to production costs. The slowing effect of redistributive market-based environmental instruments upon its expansion is caused by their exposure to concerns regarding competitiveness. These concerns then interfere with the political feasibility. Consequently, in the case of energy/carbon taxes, the innovation's characteristics have even proved sufficiently strong to almost overrule what are usually the quickening effects of international promotional activities that many of the most influential international organisations have been putting forward for many years. They were, however, adopted by a limited group of countries. Thus, we have to assume that their expansion is determined more by national factors. A case study comparing successful and unsuccessful national efforts to introduce an energy/carbon tax revealed that policy process factors, such as elite consensus, strategy management, and coalition-building, determine an adoption, much more than structural politico-institutional and economic variables.[71]

V. Conclusions

The central lesson we have learnt from environmental policy diffusion research is that national environmental policy development may, under certain circumstances, become the point of departure for an internationalisation of environmental policy. From the perspective of global environmental governance even more important is the fact that national patterns in environmental policy-making converge beyond coordinated collective action of nation states. Thus:

- diffusion may become a substitute for negotiated harmonisation in global environmental governance.

In contrast to harmonisation as a mechanism of convergence, diffusion processes do not begin with a jointly agreed standard that national policies have to cope with. Instead, via knowledge diffusion, dissemination best practice, and benchmarking activities of actors engaging in the 'idea game', a national policy innovation might become the model for policy developments in other countries. This finding has two further interesting aspects:

- diffusion processes are mainly influenced by actors generally perceived to be weak, in terms of decision-making power.

Transnational advocacy networks and environmental think tanks draw attention to policy developments overseas. Thus, they build the main linkage between national jurisdictions, which enables policy experiences from abroad to be

[71] Tews, *Die Ausbreitung*, op. cit.

included in national decisions. They do not dispose of power to make decisions; they provide the intellectual matter and legitimacy that underpin these decisions. Thus, they act as agents of policy diffusion:

- the existence of such agents of diffusion offers opportunities for even small states to define global environmental developments.

In particular, the Netherlands and the Scandinavian countries have acquired notable reputations as environmental pace-setters. In our data they belong to the group of countries that were either first or early movers in adopting the environmental policy innovation, but they are never to be found in the group of the later adopters.

To sum up, despite increasingly being faced with influences from abroad, nation states' capability to act is – contrary to any pessimistic assumption – not just restricted; indeed, opportunities to govern have also been broadened. The existence of diffusion dynamics within the international system has been found to offer opportunities for innovative national policy-making.

10

Process-related measures and global environmental governance

CHRISTIAN TIETJE

I. Introduction

There is hardly any other subject in the broad area of trade and environment subject to so much political and academic discussion than the legality of process-related measures. Even though the problem of so-called processes and production measures (PPMs) is certainly not new in the international economic and environmental system,[1] it was not until the WTO Panel decision in the *Tuna I* case[2] that it attracted intense scrutiny. However, even though extensive material on the legality of PPMs has been produced in recent years,[3] the overall complexity of the problem still appears to lack thorough analysis. This is mainly due to the fact that most scholars are hesitant to present arguments that reach further than making a statement on the (more or less) illegality of PPMs under the current law of the World Trade Organization (WTO). Based

---

[1] See e.g., GATT, *Industrial pollution control and international trade*, GATT studies in international trade, no. 1, Geneva (GATT) 1971.

[2] *United States – Restrictions on Imports of Tuna* (*Tuna I*), Report of the Panel, 3 September 1991, DS21/R – 39S/155 (not adopted).

[3] See e.g., Charnovitz, S., The law of environmental 'PPMs' in the WTO: debunking the myth of illegality, *Yale J. Int'l L.* 27 (2002), pp. 59–110; Puth, S., *WTO und Umwelt – Die Produkt-Prozess-Doktrin*, Berlin (Duncker & Humblot) 2003, passim; Howse, R. and Regan, D., The product/process distinction: an illusory basis for disciplining 'unilateralism' in trade policy, *EJIL* 11 (2000), pp. 249–289; Gaines, S. E., Processes and production methods: how to produce sound policy for environmental PPM based trade measures?, *Columbia J. Environmental L.* 27 (2002), pp. 383–432; Schlagenhof, M., Trade measures based on environmental process and production methods, *J. World Trade* 29 (1995), pp. 123–155; Hudec, R. E., The product-process doctrine in GATT/WTO jurisprudence, in Bronckers, M. and Quick, R. (eds.), *New directions in international economic law: essays in honour of John H. Jackson*, The Hague/London/Boston (Kluwer Law International) 2000, pp. 187–217; Peel, J., Confusing product with process: a critique of the application of product-based test to environmental process standards in the WTO, *New York University Environmental L. J.* 10 (2002), pp. 217–244; Zreczny, A. I., The process/product distinction and the tuna/dolphin controversy: greening the GATT through international agreement, *Buffalo J. Int'l L.* 1 (1994), pp. 79–133; Jackson, J. H., Comments on shrimp/turtle and the product/process distinction, *EJIL* 11 (2000), pp. 303–307.

on this legal assessment, the environmental civil society, namely environmental NGOs, overwhelmingly see WTO law as an enemy to environmental protection because trade measures based on environmental PPMs are prohibited. Recently, Steve Charnovitz presented a comprehensive study arguing that 'PPMs affecting trade are not prohibited per se'.[4] A similar conclusion has been put forward by Robert Howse and Donald Regan.[5] Moreover, only more recent studies make an explicit connection between PPMs and environmental governance.[6]

It is not the aim of this contribution to analyse all legal and policy arguments in favour and against the use of PPMs in international economic law in detail. Rather, after an overview of the basic theoretical and practical problems of PPMs, and the current legal situation under WTO law, a broader perspective on PPMs and global environmental governance will be given.

II. Theoretical and practical problems of PPMs

In the most general form, the notion 'PPMs' describes governmental or private measures that are related to the process and production methods of a product and not to the physical characteristics of the end products as such. That is to say, regulated by whatever measure is not the product itself – the way it is actually 'on the market' – but rather the way it is made, its process and production.

1. Examples of environmental PPMs

Examples of PPMs cover a wide range of different cases such as regulations on workers' safety during the production process, environmental standards concerning the production process, e.g. maximum air pollution, and the prohibition of the use of certain materials such as asbestos while producing a product. Probably the best known current example of a PPM that has led to much controversy in international economic law is the *Shrimp* case. It concerned a US import prohibition on shrimp products made out of shrimps which were caught without using a certain technique ensuring that sea turtles were not affected by fishing the shrimps.[7]

As the *Shrimp* case indicates, one very important area of the use of PPMs relates to measures taken with regard to the protection of the environment. An example of this is seen in EU Council Regulation 1036/2001 'prohibiting imports of Atlantic big eye tuna (Thunnus obesus) originating in Belize, Cambodia, Equatorial Guinea, Saint Vincent and the Grenadines and Honduras'

---

[4] Charnovitz, op. cit.   [5] Howse and Regan, op. cit.
[6] See Charnovitz, op. cit., p. 70 *et seq.*; Trüeb, H. R., *Umweltrecht der WTO*, Zürich (Schulthess) 2001, p. 130.
[7] See *United States – Import Prohibition of Certain Shrimp and Shrimp Products*, Report of the Appellate Body, 6 November 1998, WT/DS58/AB/R.

because vessels from those countries fish big eye tuna in a manner which diminishes the effectiveness of tuna conservation measures as recommended by the International Commission for the Conservation of Atlantic Tuna (ICCAT).[8] Another example is the import prohibitions on tropical timber that does not come from sustainable managed forests based on respected recommendations of the International Tropical Timber Organization (ITTO).[9] A related case occurred in 1992 when Austria introduced a mandatory labelling requirement for tropical timber and timber products.[10] A similar example is that of the EU eco-labelling scheme which is based on the so-called lifecycle approach.[11]

2. The problematic distinction between product-related and non-product-related PPMs

Even though it seems to be clear what PPMs are, a distinction is usually made in academic literature between two different types of PPMs: product-related and non-product-related PPMs. Product-related PPMs are those that are 'used to assure the functionality of the product, or to safeguard the consumer who uses the product'.[12] In contrast, a 'non-product-related PPM is designed to achieve a social purpose that may or may not matter to a consumer'.[13] This distinction between product-related and non-product-related PPMs seems to be included in the Agreement on Technical Barriers to Trade ('TBT Agreement'). In paragraph 1 of Annex 1 to the TBT Agreement, a technical regulation is defined as a '[d]ocument which lays down product characteristics or their related processes and production methods'. This definition seems to indicate that only product-related PPMs are covered by the TBT Agreement. From this perspective it is thus rational to argue that product-related PPMs might find some justification under WTO law, whereas non-product-related PPMs have a more severe problem of legality under WTO law.[14]

It is obvious that the distinction between product-related and non-product-related PPMs has the clear advantage of being straightforward and fairly simple. However, taking a closer look at the distinction leads to the question of whether it is really that easy to differentiate between the two categories. Thus,

---

[8] [2001] OJ L145/10, 31 May 2001. [9] For details see e.g., Puth, op. cit., p. 39.

[10] For details see Sucharipa-Behrmann, L., Austrian legislative efforts to regulate trade in tropical timber and tropical timber products, *Austrian J. Public and Int'l L.* 46 (1993/94), pp. 283–292.

[11] For details see Tietje, C., Voluntary eco-labelling programmes and questions of state responsibility in the WTO/GATT legal system, *J. World Trade* 29 (1995), pp. 123–158.

[12] Charnovitz, op. cit., p. 65.

[13] Ibid.; for further details see Puth, op. cit., p. 44 *et seq.*; OECD, *Processes and production methods (PPMs): conceptual framework and considerations on use of PPM based trade measures*, OECD Doc. OCDE/GD(97)137, p. 12.

[14] For details on the discussion see Puth, op. cit., p. 59 *et seq.*; Howse and Regan, op. cit., p. 251.

Charnovitz has convincingly pointed out that any PPM is product-related at least in international trade relations because the 'sanction' imposed on non-compliance with a PPM will always be a trade measure which is by definition product-related.[15] Moreover, it is questionable whether the consumer – who is actually the one who is directly or indirectly affected by any PPM or who is the one executing a PPM measure on the market – is able to differentiate between product-related and non-product-related PPMs. In this context, the said differentiation is, of course, impossible to apply in cases in which a certain regulatory measure has multiple purposes. Finally, in cases such as measures requiring a minimum amount of recycled content of a product, the process is actually the product. This again makes it impossible to apply the product-related/non-product-related doctrine.[16]

In conclusion, the distinction between product-related and non-product related PPMs is hardly convincing. On the contrary, this distinction is to a large degree artificial. It actually hides the underlying problem of PPMs, because of its underlying assumption that PPMs must have a product relation in order to fit into the product-related rules of world trade law. This, however, begs the question of if and how world trade law deals and should deal with PPMs as a reality, and perhaps also as a necessity, in today's international system. Thus, rather than strictly focusing on the distinction of product-related and non-product-related PPMs, this chapter will deal with PPMs as such. However, it is, of course, evident that environmentally motivated PPMs, being those PPMs that are of central interest in this chapter, are generally non-product-related. Thus, disregarding the question of whether one follows the above distinction or not, the legal problem with regard to WTO law remains the same.

3. Basic arguments against and in favour of PPMs

Arguments in favour and against PPMs in the international trading system have been exchanged over and over again, even more so since the *Tuna* cases. However, if one takes a closer look at the debate it becomes obvious that at least the central arguments in favour of the PPM/product distinction date back to the GATT study on Industrial Pollution Control and International Trade from 1971.[17]

The first – and probably most important – argument against the legality of PPMs is based on the strict application of the theory of comparative advantages.[18] As PPMs are related to production factors that are different in countries

---

[15] Charnovitz, op. cit., p. 66.   [16] Ibid., p. 66.
[17] GATT, op. cit.; see also Puth, op. cit., p. 72.
[18] See e.g., Jackson, J. H., World trade rules and environmental policies: congruence or conflicts?, *Washington and Lee L. Rev.* 49 (1992), pp. 1227–1275, at 1243; Tietje, C., *Normative Grundstrukturen der Behandlung nichttarifärer Handelshemmnisse in der WTO/GATT Rechtsordnung*, Berlin (Duncker & Humblot) 1998, p. 210.

and have to be different in order to gain optimal economic welfare, their regulation runs counter to the theory of international division of labour. Thus, different environmental standards have to be accepted. This argument certainly is persuasive – whether certain exceptions to the validity of the argument exist will be discussed later on in this contribution.[19]

The second argument against PPMs concerns the issue of extra-territoriality.[20] Disregarding the fact that most of the extra-territoriality arguments have more or less the same rationale as the ones put forward under the heading of comparative advantages, it is clear that under general public international law, reference to extra-territoriality is not convincing. Public international law recognises several ways to establish jurisdiction by a state beyond a strict application of the principle of territoriality, namely the effects doctrine, which provides firmly established guidelines justifying state measures that are not exclusively concerned with a factual situation entirely within a certain territorial jurisdiction.[21] Moreover, one may even argue that PPMs are applied to products that are about to enter the market (or have already entered the market) of the regulating state, and thus, that a territorial jurisdictional link is always present.[22] Therefore, it is clear that the issue of extra-territoriality no longer plays a role in the more recent jurisprudence of the WTO Appellate Body.[23]

A third argument against PPMs focuses mainly on their unilateral nature.[24] Similar arguments are made under the headings of the fear of beginning on a 'slippery slope' and opening 'Pandora's box'.[25] However, in order to analyse how a coherent approach towards PPMs in the international system is possible in more detail, simply referring to the 'danger' of unilateralism is not sufficient. Such an argument disregards the fact that international environmental regulatory efforts are not always successful, and – at least in certain instances – need additional support by individual states. The question is thus not unilateralism versus multilateralism, but rather where exactly regulatory efforts to protect the environment should be undertaken in order to be in accordance with international trade law. The following sections of this chapter will come back to this question in more detail.

---

[19] See section IV.3.
[20] See e.g., Jackson, (1992), op. cit., p. 1240 *et seq.*; for further references see Puth, op. cit., p. 72 *et seq.*
[21] See e.g., Brownlie, I., *Principles of public international law*, Oxford (Oxford University Press) 6th edn. 2003, p. 306.
[22] For details on the discussion see Trüeb, op. cit., p. 354 *et seq.*   [23] See section III.3.
[24] See e.g., Strauss, A. L., From GATTzilla to the green giant: winning the environmental battle for the soul of the World Trade Organization, *University of Pennsylvania J. Int'l Economic L.* 19 (1998), pp. 69–820, p. 796.
[25] Jackson (1992), op. cit., pp. 1240 and 1243; for further details see Puth, op. cit., p. 74 *et seq.*

III. PPMs and WTO/GATT law

The legal debate on the legality or illegality of PPMs under WTO/GATT law[26] concentrates on three main issues: (1) whether PPMs (especially non-product-related PPMs) per se are in violation of obligations under the GATT 1994 and can thus only be justified by Article XX GATT; (2) whether PPMs, if not considered as being per se in violation of GATT obligations, can be used in order to make an assessment on the like product issue of Article III GATT; and (3) whether trade-restricting measures in the form of PPMs, being prima facie in violation of GATT obligations, can be justified under Article XX GATT – and if so, under what conditions.

1. PPMs are not per se in violation of obligations under the GATT

Under the GATT 1994, a strict differentiation has to be made between trade measures being executed at the border (Article XI(1) GATT) and trade measures affecting products once they have entered the internal market of a WTO member (Article III GATT).[27] Moreover, according to the note to Article III GATT, a governmental regulation which applies both to an imported product and to the like domestic product and is enforced upon the imported product at the time or point of importation, is nevertheless being legally treated under Article III GATT. Taking this basic setting of GATT law into account makes it necessary to first decide whether a governmental regulation applies to imported and domestic like products. The Panel in the *Tuna I* case strictly followed this approach and held:

> The text of Article III:1 refers to the application to imported or domestic products of 'laws, regulations and requirements affecting the internal sale . . . of products' and 'internal quantitative regulations requiring the mixture, processing or use of products'; it sets forth the principle that such regulations on products not be applied so as to afford protection to domestic production. Article III:4 refers solely to laws, regulations and requirements affecting the internal sale, etc. of products. This suggests that Article III covers only measures affecting products as such. Furthermore, the text of the Note Ad Article III refers to a measure 'which applies to an imported product and the like domestic product and is collected or enforced in the case of the imported product at the time or point of importation'. This suggests that this Note covers only measures applied to imported products that are of the same nature as those applied to the domestic products, such

---

[26] In this contribution, only those legal aspects of PPMs that relate to GATT law are discussed. Thus, the specific aspects of PPMs under the SPS and the TBT Agreement will not be analysed.

[27] For details see Tietje (1998), op. cit., p. 225 *et seq.*

as a prohibition on importation of a product which enforces at the border an internal sales prohibition applied to both imported and like domestic products.[28]

On the basis of this holding, the Panel consequently concluded that the relevant US measures applied to:

the domestic harvesting of yellowfin tuna to reduce the incidental taking of dolphin, but that these regulations could not be regarded as being applied to tuna products as such because they would not directly regulate the sale of tuna and could not possibly affect tuna as a product.[29]

Thus, in the view of the Panel, the US measure could not be analysed under Article III GATT. Instead, as it did have a trade restrictive impact, it was, in the view of the Panel, a violation of Article XI(1) GATT.

This reasoning of the Panel in the *Tuna I* case was also more or less applied by the Panels in the *Tuna II* and in the *Shrimp* case.[30] As a consequence it is largely argued, at least on the basis of the above-mentioned decisions, that any non-product-related PPM would never be subject to Article III GATT, but always to Article XI(1) GATT. As such, if these PPMs have trade restrictive effects that are enforced at the border, they would prima facie violate this provision.[31]

However, one must strongly object to the conclusion that non-product-related PPMs are per se in violation of obligations under the GATT. The main argument against the logic of the Panels in the above-mentioned cases is that their reasoning could lead to the absurd situation that certain trade measures are not regulated by GATT law at all, even though they directly have a protectionist purpose: this would be the case if a PPM that clearly discriminates against foreign products, exclusively applies on the internal market. In this case, according to the Panels, neither Article III GATT nor Article XI(1) GATT would be applicable, due to there being no regulation concerning a product and no trade restricting border measure given. It is obvious that WTO/GATT law is not designed to give governments the explicit freedom to imply trade restrictive measures with a clear protectionist purpose just because the respective government chose to enact a PPM and not a regulation directly concerned with a product.[32]

Even though it is clear that the Panel reports so far cannot be taken as convincing jurisprudence on PPMs, they are still on the record as applicable decisions. This is because the Appellate Body has not yet had a chance to correct

---

[28] *Tuna I*, Panel Report, op. cit. para. 5.11.   [29] Ibid., para. 5.14.
[30] *United States – Restrictions on Imports of Tuna* (*Tuna II*), Report of the Panel, 16 June 1994, DS29/R (not adopted), para. 5.8; *United States – Import Prohibition of Certain Shrimp and Shrimp Products*, Report of the Panel, 15 May 1998, WT/DS58/R, para. 7.11 *et seq.*
[31] For details on conclusions by scholars and NGOs, see Puth, op. cit., p. 237; Howse and Regan, op. cit. p. 251.
[32] For details see Howse and Regan, op. cit. p. 256.

the Panel's decisions due to procedural reasons. In the *Shrimp* case, the one case in which an overruling of the Panel would have been possible, the USA did not challenge the relevant passages in the Panel report.[33]

2. The question of PPMs is a question of 'like products' and 'treatment no less favourable' under Article III GATT

Before turning to the question of under which conditions PPMs constituting a prima facie violation of GATT law can be justified under Article XX GATT, the question, of course, remains in which cases Article III GATT applies to PPMs. As the fact that a measure does not directly regulate a product or its characteristics as such is not sufficient to determine the applicability of Article III GATT, additional criteria have to be applied. Suggestions in this direction have been put forward for some time[34] and have now been made more specific by other authors[35] and the Appellate Body. The main point in this regard becomes clear if one applies a principle-oriented perspective on Article III GATT. The national treatment obligation under GATT together with the most-favoured nation clause of Article I(1) GATT are both concrete expressions of the principle of non-discrimination.[36] Thus, the rationale of Article III GATT as an obligation of non-discrimination is to provide equality of market opportunities, not to guarantee market access as such.[37] Market access is only granted and protected by tariff bindings (Article II(1) GATT) and the prohibition of non-tariff trade barriers (Article XI(1)).

Thus, if Article III GATT is not a rule on market access, the question of whether the provision applies to PPMs cannot be answered simply by asking whether a restriction on market access occurred. Rather, the question must be whether a discrimination between foreign and like domestic products is applied. In this regard, the first aspect that must always be analysed is whether 'like products' are available. This logically follows from the structure of Article III GATT as an equal treatment clause. An equal treatment clause can only be applied, if it is clear that 'equal' situations are being considered. However, it is clear that, at least in legal terms, no two persons or things are actually 'equal'. They can only be substantially equal. In order to decide whether persons or things are substantially equal, they have to be comparable. Comparability in legal terms under any equal treatment clause is only given if the persons or things in question can be related to a common reference point, a *tertium comparationis*,

---

[33] Howse and Regan, op. cit. p. 256.
[34] See extensively, Tietje (1998), op. cit. p. 234 *et seq.*; Tietje, C., Das Übereinkommen über technische Handelshemmnisse in Prieß, H. and Berrisch, G. M. (eds.), *WTO-Handbuch*, München (C. H. Beck) 2003, pp. 273–325, p. 294.
[35] Most prominently by Howse and Regan, op. cit.
[36] Comprehensively Tietje (1998), op. cit., p. 189 *et seq.*
[37] Tietje (1998), op. cit., p. 192 *et seq.*; Howse and Regan, op. cit., p. 257.

which, in turn, is the common generic term (the *genus proximum*) that is applicable to the persons and things in question.[38]

It is important to understand this general theoretical structure of Article III GATT, because otherwise it is not possible to appreciate that the determination of 'like products' is essentially a value judgement. The determination of likeness under Article III GATT – just as any determination on the question whether persons or things are 'equal' – cannot be made under strict logical considerations. Rather, it has to be decided on a case-by-case basis. This has been explicitly recognised by the Appellate Body with regard to Article III GATT. The Appellate Body held in the *Asbestos* case:

> We turn to consideration of how a treaty interpreter should proceed in determining whether products are 'like' under Article III:4. As in Article III:2, in this determination, '[n]o one approach . . . will be appropriate for all cases'.[39] Rather, an assessment utilizing 'an unavoidable element of individual, discretionary judgement'[40] has to be made on a case-by-case basis.[41]

Such a case-by-case determination, however, cannot be made without taking into account the basic legal values that determine the respective legal order in which the decision about equality is made. Otherwise, contradictory legal statements within one legal order would be possible.[42] Applying this theoretical approach to Article III GATT means that any assessment on likeness under Article III(4) GATT has to be made with regard to the overall rationale of the provision. This directly refers to Article III(1) GATT and the general prohibition of protectionism therein.[43] The Appellate Body thus correctly held in the *Asbestos* case that:

---

[38] For details on this structure of Article III GATT, see Tietje (1998), op. cit., p. 237 *et seq.*; see also now extensively Regan, D., Regulatory purpose and 'like products' in Article III:4 of the GATT (with additional remarks on Article III:2), *J. World Trade* 36 (2002), pp. 443–478, p. 443.

[39] See *Japan – Alcoholic Beverages*, Appellate Body Report, 1 November 1996, WT/DS8/AB/R, WT/DS10/AB/R, WT/DS11/AB, p. 114.

[40] See ibid., p. 113.

[41] *European Communities – Measures Affecting Asbestos and Asbestos Containing Products*, Appellate Body Report, 12 March 2001, WT/DS135/AB/R, para. 101; for details on the *Asbestos* case see Howse, R. and Tuerk, E., WTO impact on internal regulations: a case study of the Canada–EC asbestos dispute, in de Búrca, G. and Scott, J. (eds.), *The EU and the WTO: Legal and constitutional issues*, Oxford (Hart Publishing) 2001, pp. 283–328, at 283.

[42] For details see Tietje (1998), op. cit. p. 237 *et seq.*

[43] See Japan – Alcoholic Beverages, Appellate Body Report, op. cit. pp. 109 and 110: 'The broad and fundamental purpose of Article III is to avoid protectionism in the application of internal tax and regulatory measures. More specifically, the purpose of Article III 'is to ensure that internal measures 'not be applied to imported and domestic products so as to afford protection to domestic production''. Toward this end, Article III obliges Members of the WTO to provide equality of competitive conditions for imported products in relation to domestic products . . . Article III protects expectations not of any particular trade volume but rather of the equal competitive relationship between imported and domestic

although this 'general principle' is not explicitly invoked in Article III:4, nevertheless, it 'informs' that provision. Therefore, the term 'like product' in Article III:4 must be interpreted to give proper scope and meaning to this principle. In short, there must be consonance between the objective pursued by Article III, as enunciated in the 'general principle' articulated in Article III:1, and the interpretation of the specific expression of this principle in the text of Article III:4. This interpretation must, therefore, reflect that, in endeavouring to ensure 'equality of competitive conditions', the 'general principle' in Article III seeks to prevent Members from applying internal taxes and regulations in a manner which affects the competitive relationship, in the marketplace, between the domestic and imported products involved, 'so as to afford protection to domestic production'.[44]

Furthermore, once it is established that the general principle of Article III(1) GATT has to be taken into account while making a determination on the question of 'like products', it is only logical that 'a determination of "likeness" under Article III:4 is, fundamentally, a determination of the nature and extent of a competitive relationship between and among products'.[45] As demonstrated, this holding of the Appellate Body is fully in line with basic theoretical consideration. In addition as Howse and Regan have convincingly argued, taking the prohibition on protectionism into account is also in accordance with further legal and policy aims of GATT law. Their argument that Article III GATT essentially contains an implicit prerequisite in the sense that 'like' in Article III(4) GATT means 'not differing in any respect relevant to an actual non-protectionist regulatory policy'[46] is consequent within the theoretical logic of the provision, and has been argued elsewhere for some years already.[47]

Thus, PPMs under Article III GATT have to be analysed in a first step with regard to the question of 'like products'. The determination of likeness under Article III GATT can only be a value judgement in light of the general rationale of the provision to guarantee fair market conditions for foreign and domestic like products. Therefore, the existence of a competitive relationship between the products in question is central to the determination of likeness. In this regard, the Appellate Body in the *Asbestos* case made clear that an assessment of a competitive relationship has to be made not only with regard to the physical characteristics of the end-product, but also with regard to the attitude of consumers towards the respective products. As the Appellate Body held, there are:

---

products'; see also *Asbestos*, Appellate Body Report, op. cit., para. 97; Tietje (2003), op. cit., p. 296 *et seq.*; Regan, op. cit.

[44] *Asbestos*, Appellate Body Report, op. cit. para. 98.
[45] Ibid., para. 99.
[46] Howse and Regan, op. cit. p. 260 *et seq.*
[47] Comprehensively Tietje (1998), op. cit. p. 236 *et seq.*; Tietje (2003), op. cit. p. 295 *et seq.*; different, however, Quick, R. and Lau, C., Environmental motivated tax distinctions and WTO law, *JIEL* 6 (2003), pp. 419–458, p. 434.

four categories of 'characteristics' that the products involved might share: (i) the physical properties of the products; (ii) the extent to which the products are capable of serving the same or similar end-uses; (iii) the extent to which consumers perceive and treat the products as alternative means of performing particular functions in order to satisfy a particular want or demand; and (iv) the international classification of the products for tariff purposes.[48]

At this point of the analysis it becomes clear that PPMs can be considered in the determination of likeness in the sense of Article III GATT, i.e. the health and environmental aspects of the process and production of a product are of significance for consumers today (at least in developed countries). Thus, products that have been produced using an environmentally friendly process might have a totally different (more favourable) position on the market than products which have similar product characteristics as such, but which are produced in a way that is harmful for the environment. If this is the case – and can be proven – the products at stake would not be considered as being 'like products' in the sense of Article III GATT, provided no protectionist intent of the respective PPM is given.[49] As a consequence, in such a case an internal regulation of a WTO member on PPMs would not be subject to WTO/GATT restrictions, as it would apply to products that are 'unlike' in the sense of Article III GATT.[50]

Moreover, even in a case in which the influence of a PPM-related regulatory intent would not be strong enough on consumer perspectives in order to regard the products at issue as being 'unlike', according to the jurisprudence of the Appellate Body it would still be possible to uphold a respective PPM as being in conformity with Article III GATT. The Appellate Body in *Asbestos* clarified that a two-step approach in applying Article III GATT is necessary: first, the detailed analysis of likeness has to be conducted; secondly, if a positive determination on likeness is possible, it has to be assessed whether the PPM at issue provides 'less favourable treatment' in the sense of Article III GATT.[51] The Appellate Body observed:

> that there is a second element that must be established before a measure can be held to be inconsistent with Article III:4. Thus, even if two products are 'like', that does not mean that a measure is inconsistent with Article III:4. A complaining Member must still establish that the measure accords to the group of 'like' imported products 'less favourable treatment' than it

---

[48] *Asbestos*, Appellate Body, op. cit. para. 101.
[49] On the consequences of the Appellate Body decision in *Asbestos* on the PPM doctrine, see also Howse and Tuerk, op. cit., p. 297: 'This in effect blunts, without explicitly repudiating, the product/process distinction'.
[50] Tietje (2003), op. cit. p. 298; a more restrictive and hesitant interpretation of the *Asbestos* decision of the Appellate Body is given by Charnovitz, op. cit. p. 90 *et seq.*
[51] *Asbestos*, Appellate Body, para. 100.

accords to the group of 'like' domestic products. The term 'less favourable treatment' expresses the general principle, in Article III:1, that internal regulations 'should not be applied . . . so as to afford protection to domestic production'. If there is 'less favourable treatment' of the group of 'like' imported products, there is, conversely, 'protection' of the group of 'like' domestic products. However, a Member may draw distinctions between products which have been found to be 'like', without, for this reason alone, according to the group of 'like' imported products 'less favourable treatment' than that accorded to the group of 'like' domestic products.[52]

In sum, a closer look on the regulatory structure of GATT law – both from a theoretical perspective and with regard to the jurisprudence of the Appellate Body – demonstrates that PPMs are by no means per se in violation of GATT/WTO law. On the contrary, it is a central element of GATT/WTO law to give governments explicit freedom for regulatory measures on processes and production which are related to environmental or similar concerns.[53] It is only essential to bear in mind that PPMs, first, must be connected to a legitimate regulatory purpose, and, secondly, may not be applied so as to afford (economic) protection to the domestic industry.

3. PPMs and Article XX GATT

A prima facie violation of Article III GATT can occur in the case of a PPM being applied that does not relate to criteria sufficiently strong enough to distinguish similar products in terms of 'likeness'. The question then, of course, is whether such a PPM, namely one that is applied for environmental purposes, can be justified under Article XX GATT. Article XX GATT is a very complex, and until recently, highly disputed provision. However, recent jurisprudence of the Appellate Body gives precise guidelines on how to understand and apply this provision. Two aspects relevant to interpreting Article XX GATT with regard to PPMs will be highlighted below.

The first problem emerging in the application of Article XX GATT to PPMs dates back to the first *Tuna* case in which the Panel rejected any possibility of justifying PPMs that have an extra-territorial scope under Article XX GATT.[54] This highly controversial opinion of the Panel has been corrected in the *Shrimp* case. The Appellate Body explicitly held that '[i]t is not necessary to assume that

---

[52] Ibid., para. 100.
[53] For a detailed analysis of those regulatory freedoms within the legal structure of WTO/GATT law see Tietje (1998), op. cit., p. 291 *et seq.*; see also most prominently *United States – Measures Affecting Alcoholic and Malt Beverages*, Report of the Panel, 19 June 1992, DS23/R, 39S/206, para. 5.25: '[T]he purpose of Article III is not to prevent contracting parties from differentiating between different product categories for policy purposes unrelated to the protection of domestic production'.
[54] *Tuna I*, Panel Report, op. cit. para. 5.25.

requiring from exporting countries compliance with, or adoption of, certain policies (although covered in principle by one or another of the exceptions) prescribed by the importing country, renders a measure a priori incapable of justification under Article XX'.[55] Three main arguments have been put forward by the Appellate Body to support its holding: first, the wording of Article XX GATT does not contain language requiring an a priori exclusion of PPMs as justifiable measures; secondly, 'conditioning access to a Member's domestic market on whether exporting Members comply with, or adopt, a policy or policies unilaterally prescribed by the importing Member may, to some degree, be a common aspect of measures falling within the scope of one or another of the exceptions (a) to (j) of Article XX';[56] and, thirdly, any a priori exclusion of PPMs from the scope of application of Article XX GATT would – contrary to accepted rules of treaty interpretation – 'rende[r] most, if not all, of the specific exceptions of Article XX inutile'.[57]

If one accepts the convincing decision of the Appellate Body in Shrimp,[58] the question, of course, is under which conditions a PPM can be justified under Article XX GATT. Disregarding specific interpretative problems, namely those under Article XX lit. (b) and (g) GATT,[59] the main point in this regard concerns the correct interpretation of the chapeau of Article XX GATT. It is settled jurisprudence of the Appellate Body today that the chapeau of Article XX GATT is an expression of the general prohibition of abuse of rights.[60] Moreover, in Shrimp, the Appellate Body further clarified that the chapeau requires a balancing of rights and duties under WTO/GATT law.[61]

Applying the jurisprudence of the Appellate Body to PPMs leads directly to the question of under which conditions a country may enact regulatory measures that impose burdens on the processes and production of products in other countries. In order to decide upon the fulfilment of the requirements of

---

[55] Shrimp, Appellate Body, op. cit. para. 121.   [56] Ibid.   [57] Ibid.
[58] See also United States – Import Prohibition of Certain Shrimp and Shrimp Products, Report of the Panel, 15 June 2001, Recourse to Article 21.5 of the DSU by Malaysia, WT/DS58/RW, para. 5.43.
[59] For details see Matsushita, M., Schoenbaum, T. J., and Mavroidis, P. C., The World Trade Organization: law, practice, and policy, Oxford (Oxford University Press) 2003, p. 451.
[60] United States – Standards for Reformulated and Conventional Gasoline, Report of the Appellate Body, 15 May 1996, WT/DS2/AB/R, p. 20; Shrimp, Appellate Body, op. cit. para. 151.
[61] Shrimp, Appellate Body, op. cit. para. 159: 'The task of interpreting and applying the chapeau is, hence, essentially the delicate one of locating and marking out a line of equilibrium between the right of a Member to invoke an exception under Article XX and the rights of the other Members under varying substantive provisions (e.g., Article XI) of the GATT 1994, so that neither of the competing rights will cancel out the other and thereby distort and nullify or impair the balance of rights and obligations constructed by the Members themselves in that Agreement. The location of the line of equilibrium, as expressed in the chapeau, is not fixed and unchanging; the line moves as the kind and the shape of the measures at stake vary and as the facts making up specific cases differ'.

the chapeau of Article XX GATT in such a case, a distinction must be drawn between PPMs based on multilateral efforts to solve a given environmental or similar problem, and those being of a unilateral nature. In *Shrimp*, the Appellate Body correctly pointed out that unilateral measures of one state with extra-territorial effect are not justifiable under the chapeau of Article XX GATT in cases where it is impossible to take 'into consideration different conditions which may occur in the territories of those other Members'.[62] Moreover, the Appellate Body established the rule that in order to be able to justify an extra-territorial PPM aimed at protecting the environment, states first have to try to solve the underlying global environmental problem through efforts of global negotiations.[63] The Appellate Body based this assumption on several international instruments of a binding and a prima facie non-binding character, such as Principle 21 of the Rio Declaration on Environment and Development, which states (in part): 'Unilateral actions to deal with environmental challenges outside the jurisdiction of the importing country should be avoided. Environmental measures addressing transboundary or global environmental problems should, as far as possible, be based on international consensus'.[64]

It thus becomes clear that the problem of PPMs and Article XX GATT is essentially an issue of balancing the legitimate interest of one state to enact environmental regulations, on the one hand, and the interest of the international community to restrict the use of unilateral measures in favour of multilateral approaches towards problems that affect more than one country, on the other. One way to find the right balance in this regard is to apply the principle of international cooperation as in the *Shrimp* case. This is not only convincing from a legal point of view,[65] but brought about positive results for the environment in the *Shrimp* case itself.[66] We will discuss this approach and other policy means to solve the problems of PPMs in more detail in the next section.

IV. PPMs and global environmental governance

The current interpretation of WTO/GATT law, namely by the Appellate Body, already indicates that the entire issue of PPMs is closely related to global environmental governance. Indeed, quite a few political and legal problems of PPMs that occur regularly could possibly be solved if effective multilateral environmental treaties were in force. This, however, is not the case with regard to many

---

[62] *Shrimp*, Appellate Body, op. cit. para. 164.   [63] Ibid., para. 166 *et seq.*
[64] Reprinted in Johnson, S. P. (ed.), *The earth summit: the United Nations Conference on Environment and Development* (UNCED), London/Dordrecht/Boston (Kluwer Law International) 1993, p. 120.
[65] For details see Tietje, C., The duty to cooperate in international economic law and related areas in Delbrück, J. (ed.), *International law of cooperation and state sovereignty*, Berlin (Duncker & Humblot) 2002, p. 45.
[66] For details see Charnovitz, op. cit. p. 95 *et seq.*

environmentally motivated PPMs.[67] Moreover, the constant problem of international environmental treaties that touch upon PPMs is, of course, that they – at least to a certain degree – lack efficiency.[68] In addition, the modern approach of environmental policy to take the whole lifecycle of products into account is not yet fully implemented in the relevant international environmental treaties. Thus, an obvious gap exists between the necessities of modern environmental policy, on the one hand and the scope and efficiency of international legal forms of cooperation, on the other hand. A good example of the problems thus occurring is the far-reaching integrated product policy of the European Union.[69]

The task of global environmental governance is to provide an analytical and practical framework on an efficient allocation of environmental resources within the complex settings of the national, European, and international level.[70] Thus, one has to ask by which institutions (norms) PPMs serving the interest of optimal environmental resources allocation should be managed. Three basic possibilities exist: (1) international cooperation in the already indicated sense; (2) standard-setting in international organisations; (3) unilateral measures.

1. International cooperation

The obligation to solve global environmental problems by interstate cooperation has been an important aspect of the application of Article XX GATT by the Appellate Body in the *Shrimp* case.[71] This corresponds to a general duty of cooperation in international environmental law.[72] Moreover, there are additional arguments in favour of an obligation to cooperate before using PPMs on a unilateral basis. These arguments basically relate to the fact that, in most cases, PPMs have a certain extra-territorial reach. Processes and products methods regulate technical aspects of a process that takes place at any location, and thus not only within the territory of the regulating state. This situation has the following consequences.

First, unilateral trade measures, in response to problems at least partly beyond the reach of a national jurisdiction, are never the best solution.

---

[67] For further details see Matsushita, Schoenbaum, and Mavroidis, op. cit. p. 465 *et seq.*
[68] For details, see e.g., Ott, H., *Umweltregime im Völkerrecht*, Baden-Baden (Nomos Verlagsgesellschaft) 1998.
[69] See the detailed analysis by Quick and Lau, op. cit., p. 419 *et seq.*
[70] On environmental governance, see e.g., Trüeb, op. cit., p. 130 et seq.
[71] See section III.3.
[72] For a comprehensive analysis see Stoll, P. T., The international environmental law of cooperation, in Wolfrum, R. (ed.), *Enforcing environmental standards: economic mechanisms as viable means?*, Berlin (Springer) 1996, pp. 39–93 at 39; Ott, op. cit. p. 273 *et seq.*; Odendahl, K., *Die Umweltpflichtigkeit der Souveränität*, Berlin (Duncker & Humblot) 1998, p. 211.

According to the economic theory of optimal intervention,[73] interference of governments in the spontaneous order of the market[74] can only be justified if it directly, and therefore efficiently, addresses the market problem concerned. With regard to global problems, i.e. issues concerning the protection, conservation, and distribution of global public goods, only a multilateral solution has the capacity directly to solve the problem.[75] Secondly, it is well recognised in general public international law that the legality of extra-territorial measures is – at least to a certain degree – a question of balancing the competing state interests concerned.[76] In this regard, the phenomenon of overlapping jurisdiction is not new in public international law. An extensive discussion on these problems exists with regard to the extra-territorial application of anti-trust law. International legal doctrine and practice apply criteria of reasonableness or balancing of interests, more or less uniformly, in order to solve problems that occur in cases of the application of extra-territorial measures.[77] The same approach should be applied to conflicts on trade and environment,[78] namely with regard to PPMs. The Appellate Body in *Shrimp* in fact did exactly this.

Moreover, it is worth recognising that general public international law has several examples of the need to balance competing interests, especially in cases involving global public goods, and therefore a reciprocal duty to cooperate. The most prominent example can probably be taken from the law of the sea. As the ICJ has made clear in its decision in the *Fisheries Jurisdiction Case (United Kingdom v. Iceland)* of 1974, problems of overlapping jurisdiction between two states have to be solved by balancing the competing interests concerned. The process of balancing has to be conducted in the form of negotiations between the states concerned.[79] Such negotiations are the typical form of inter-state cooperation. They have to be conducted with a view to fulfilling good faith obligations deriving from the basic obligation of a peaceful settlement of

---

[73] Corden, W. M., Policies towards market disturbance, in Snape, R. H. (ed.), *Issues in world trade policy*, London (Macmillan Press) 1986, pp. 121–139, at 121; Corden, W. M., *Trade policy and economic welfare*, Oxford (Clarendon Press) 1974, pp. 9–41.

[74] For this concept see Hayek, F. A., *Recht, Gesetzgebung und Freiheit*, Band 1, Landsberg (Verlag Moderne Industrie) 1980, p. 33.

[75] For this approach with regard to the *Tuna* cases, see Tietje (1998), op. cit. p. 324; see also Trüeb, op. cit., p. 362.

[76] For a detailed discussion on the legal nature of this duty of balancing the interests concerned, see Meng, W., *Extraterritoriale Jurisdiktion im öffentlichen Wirtschaftsrecht*, Berlin/Heidelberg (Springer) 1994, p. 595.

[77] Ibid.

[78] Hansen, P. I., Transparency, standards of review, and the use of trade measures to protect the global environment, *Virginia J. Int'l L.* 39 (1999), pp. 1017–1068, at 1038 with further references.

[79] ICJ, *Fisheries Jurisdiction Case (United Kingdom v. Iceland)*, ICJ Reports 1974, p. 1 (para. 69 et seq.).

disputes, as provided for in Article 33 of the UN Charter.[80] Explicit provisions on balancing competing interests in cases of overlapping jurisdiction can be found today, for example, in Articles 56(2), 58(2), 87(2), and 142(1) of the United Nations Convention on the Law of the Sea (UNCLOS).

The duty to cooperate can thus be seen as stemming from the necessity to balance competing interests in areas of overlapping jurisdiction. As the whole issue of PPMs demonstrates, it becomes more and more difficult to make clear-cut distinctions between different regulatory international and national legal regimes. Thus, the duty to cooperate is of increasing importance in order to be able to balance competing interests. With regard to extra-territorial measures concerning the protection of global public goods, i.e. in the environmental field, not only the interests of the individual states concerned but also the interests of the international community as a whole[81] have to be taken into account. Consequently, this requires states to undertake efforts for a multilateral solution of the relevant environmental problems.

The question, of course, remains whether international law provides clear and explicit criteria that determine the process of cooperation. Following the proposed approach that the duty to cooperate in international economic law and related areas essentially derives from the necessity of balancing interests in areas of overlapping jurisdiction, the answer seems to be 'no'. Whether a given duty to cooperate has been fulfilled can only be decided on a case-by-case basis. Even though it is precisely this that has been criticised, in particular by US scholars arguing that the notion of balancing interests would delegate 'extraordinary discretion' to international tribunals, and would thus enable 'unacceptable abuses',[82] such fears seem to be unfounded. They strongly remind one of the debate between H. L. A. Hart and Ronald Dworkin on legal rules and principles.[83] Only if one takes a strictly positivistic point of view, arguing that any legal problem has to be resolved by strict positive rules, may one fear the openness of the given duty to cooperate. Following a more principle-oriented approach, however, leads to the conclusion that the international judicial system gains

---

[80] Ibid., para. 75 *et seq.*; see also *North Sea Continental Shelf Cases*, ICJ Reports 1969, p. 1 (para. 85 *et seq.*).

[81] See *Barcelona Traction Case*, ICJ Reports 1970, p. 32; Frowein, J. A., Die Verpflichtungen erga omnes im Völkerrecht und ihre Durchsetzung, in Bernhardt, R, Geck, W. K. *et al.* (eds.), *Festschrift für Hermann Mosler*, Berlin/Heidelberg (Springer) 1983, pp. 247–273, at 241; Delbrück, J., 'Laws in the public interest': some observations on the foundations and identification of erga omnes norms in international law, in Götz, V., Selmer, P., and Wolfrum, R. (eds.), *Liber amicorum Günther Jaenicke*, Berlin/Heidelberg (Springer) 1998, pp. 17–36, p. 17; Ragazzi, M., *The concept of international obligations erga omnes*, Oxford (Clarendon Press) 1997, passim.

[82] Schoenbaum, T. J., International trade and protection of the environment: the continuing search for reconciliation, *Am. J. Int'l L.* 91 (1997), pp. 268–313, p. 291.

[83] Hart, H. L. A., *The concept of law*, Oxford (Clarendon Press) 2nd edn. 1994, p. 259 (Postscript 3. (ii) Rules and Principles).

increasing importance in the case-by-case process of developing criteria for the duty to cooperate. The Appellate Body in its recent jurisprudence on trade and environment, i.e. in its Article 21.5 DSU review in the *Shrimp* case,[84] took up this challenge and 'cut the Gordian knot – to permit certain environmental PPMs without creating an exception that would swallow other GATT rules'.[85]

2. International standardisation

Particularly in the European Union, several of the legal, economic, and political problems of PPMs have sought solution through the harmonisation of the administrative procedures and laws of the Member States.[86] However, the ECJ recently made clear that harmonisation under the general rules of Article 95 EC Treaty is only possible under restrictive conditions.[87] This is a strong indication that harmonisation is not by itself the one and only solution for the whole PPM issue. Rather, the concept of harmonisation always has to been seen in light of the competing concept of regulatory competition. Indeed, regulatory competition is currently a central element in the jurisprudence of the ECJ.[88]

The advantages of regulatory competition also have to be taken into account with regard to PPMs and the international trading system. Currently, it is widely accepted that the market provides for a whole range of incentives having a positive effect on the environment.[89] Thus, different environmental standards in different countries are not per se an enemy to global environmental protection.[90] Harmonisation of environmental standards, therefore, needs justification that goes beyond the mere fact of diverging regulatory concepts.

---

[84] *United States – Import Prohibition of Certain Shrimp and Shrimp Products*, Appellate Body Report, 22 October 2001, Recourse to Article 21.5 of the DSU by Malaysia, WT/DS58/AB/RW.
[85] Matsushita, Schoenbaum, and Mavroidis, op. cit., p. 464.
[86] For details on harmonisation under Article 94 *et seq*. EC Treaty, see Tietje, C., Art 94 *et seq.*, in Grabitz, E. and Hilf, M. (eds.), *Das Recht der Europäischen Union*, München (C. H. Beck) 2003, Article 94 *et seq*.
[87] Case C-376/98, *Germany v. European Parliament and Council of the European Union* [2000] ECR I-8419, ECJ.
[88] See recently, e.g., Case C-208/00, *Überseering BV v. Nordic Construction Company Baumanagement GmbH (NCC)* [2002] ECR I-9919, ECJ; Case C-167/01, *Kamer van Koophandel en Fabrieken voor Amsterdam v. Inspire Art Ltd* [2003] ECR I-10155, for further details see Tietje, in Grabitz and Hilf, op. cit., Vor Art. 94–97 EGV marginal note 25; Barnard, C. and Deakin, S., *Market access and regulatory competition*, Jean Monnet Working Paper 9/01, available at www.jeanmonnetprogram.org/papers/01/012701.html.
[89] For a comprehensive analysis, see e.g., Stewart, R., Environmental regulation and international competitiveness, *Yale L. J.* 102 (1993), pp. 2039–2106, at 2051.
[90] Classic reading in this regard is Oates, W. E. and Schwab, R. M., Economic competition among jurisdictions: efficiency enhancing or distortion inducing?, *J. Public Economics* 35 (1988), pp. 333–354, at 335; for further details see also Trüeb, op. cit. p. 163 *et seq*.

One way for a reasonable balance between regulatory competition, on the one hand and international harmonisation of PPM standards in order to prevent political and legal disputes among jurisdictions, on the other hand, is to apply voluntary standards. The most prominent and successful example in this regard is the ISO 14000 series. It is today widely used by private enterprises to implement an environmental management system in accordance with the lifecycle approach of modern environmental policy.[91] Even though ISO 14000 does not establish specific standards for PPMs, its approach to improve environmental management clearly affects a wide range of non-product-related environmental aspects in a positive way.[92] Moreover, as a voluntary standard it leaves all possibilities for additional regulatory measures open. Thus, it does not prevent the positive effects of regulatory competition.

However, voluntary international standardisation and the concept of regulatory competition may have their limits once international externalities occur which could lead to the necessity of internalisation of those international externalities by regulatory measures on the international or the national level; we will return to this point in the next section. Another situation that requires stronger legal reference to international standardisation occurs if a PPM, because of its nature and scope of application, might be inherently more trade restrictive than necessary to fulfil a legitimate objective (see Article 2.2. TBT Agreement). Such cases are specifically dealt with by the Agreement on the Application of Sanitary and Phytosanitary measures (SPS Agreement) and the TBT Agreement and the obligations therein to take international standards into account while dealing with PPMs and similar measures on the national level.[93]

3. Unilateral measures

Finally, we have to address the issue of unilateral PPMs. The possibility already demonstrated for a legality of unilateral PPMs under WTO law needs some more

---

[91] For details see Roht-Arriaza, N., Compliance with private voluntary agreements: the example of the International Organization for Standardisation's ISO 14000 environmental management and related standards, in Brown Weiss, E. (ed.), *International compliance with nonbinding accords*, Washington (American Society of International Law) 1997, pp. 205–218, at 205.

[92] On the importance of ISO for global environmental governance in general, see Roht-Arriaza, N., Shifting the point of regulation: the International Organization for Standardisation and global lawmaking on trade and the environment, *Ecology L. Q.* 22(3) (1995), pp. 479–539.

[93] See Article 2.4 TBT, Agreement and *European Communities – Trade Description of Sardines*, Report of the Appellate Body, 26 September 2002, WT/DS231/AB/R, para. 196; and Article 3 SPS, Agreement and, e.g., *European Communities – Measures Concerning Meat and Meat Products (Hormones)*, Report of the Appellate Body 16 January 1998, WT/DS47/AB/R, para. 162; Quick, R. and Blüthner, A., Has the Appellate Body erred? An appraisal and criticism of the ruling in the WTO hormones case, *JIEL* 2 (1999), pp. 603–639.

clarification from a policy perspective. Even though the obligation to cooperate is an important argument while discussing PPMs and WTO law, it does not answer the question of whether unilateral PPMs might be justified in economic terms and in light of global environmental governance considerations.

First of all, it is important to remember that not all PPM issues can and should be regulated on the international regulatory level. The factual and theoretical limits of international regulations on PPMs thus logically call for making sure the possibility of unilateral measures remains. This conclusion is also justified from a broader economic perspective. It is widely recognised in economic theory that externalities are to be classified as market failures that justify state intervention.[94] According to the theory of environmental externalities, state intervention is justified if physical or psychological externalities occur. However, as the WTO legal system is only concerned with trade in physical goods, unilateral state intervention in international free trade may not be justified purely because of psychological externalities (e.g. the cruel killing of animals), at least not with regard to economic considerations.[95] The only way to justify PPMs based on psychological externalities would be to apply Article XX GATT to the obligation to cooperate.

Physical externalities may have a cross-border effect which could justify unilateral PPMs. This is the case if processes and production methods in one state affect the environment located in another state. A classic example in this regard would be air pollution caused by the production in one state and causing damage to trees in the neighbouring state. Externalities of this kind are always international externalities that justify unilateral state intervention in the freedom of international trade.[96]

The situation is more complicated in the case of global environmental goods and shared resources. In theses cases the externalities that occur can not be clearly related to property rights of individual states. However, in order to apply the theory of externalities, a clear cut distinction on rights of usage of a specific good (property rights) is necessary.[97] Otherwise it is impossible to decide on whether the usage of an (environmental) good is exceeding the property holder's sphere. Thus, one may not say that the processes and products methods in one state are only possible because of the usage of another state's environmental goods. Hence, the theory of international externalities does not provide an answer as to whether unilateral PPMs are justified in a case of global

---

[94] See e.g., Bhagwati, J. T. and Srinivasan, T. N., Trade and the environment: does environmental diversity detract from the case for free trade?, in Bhagwati, J. T. and Hudec, R. E. (eds.), *Fair trade and harmonisation*, vol. I, Cambridge (MIT Press) 1996, pp. 159–223.

[95] For further details, see Bhagwati and Srinivasan, op. cit., p. 160 *et seq.*; see Puth, op. cit. p. 111 with further references.

[96] Bhagwati and Srinivasan, op. cit. p. 196 *et seq.*

[97] Dunoff, J. L. and Trachtman, J. P., Economic analysis of international law, *Yale J. Int'l L.* 24 (1999), pp. 1–59, at 15.

public goods or shared recourses.[98] This conclusion again directly leads to the importance of the obligation to cooperate as elaborated on above.

V. Conclusion

The case of PPMs is a complex one. As demonstrated, no clear-cut answer on the question of their legality or illegality can be given. Rather, in order to make a convincing analysis and decision on PPMs, different legal and policy arguments and economic considerations have to be taken into account on a case-by-case basis. This may not be very satisfying for some readers. However, this is an inevitable consequence of the complex multilevel setting in the international environmental and international trading system. As regulations which are able to cope with current environmental problems cannot merely be enacted either on the international or the national level, supplementary regulatory efforts in different regulatory regimes are necessary. This is, indeed, the main idea of global governance.[99] PPMs are a prime example of the necessity of understanding global governance, i.e. global environmental governance, and to find legal and political solutions for the problems that occur in today's complex multilevel governance architecture.

---

[98] Puth, op. cit. p. 113 *et seq.*

[99] See the famous definition by the Commission on Global Governance: '[T]he sum of the many ways individuals and institutions, public and private, manage their common affairs. It is a continuing process through which conflicting or diverse interests may be accommodated and co-operative actions may be taken. It includes formal institutions and regimes empowered to enforce compliance, as well as informal arrangements that people and institutions either have agreed to or perceive to be in their interest': *Our global neighbourhood, the report of the Commission on Global Governance*, Oxford (Oxford University Press) 1995, p. 2.

11

The impact of the USA on regime formation and implementation

THOMAS GIEGERICH

I. The US attitude towards international regimes in general

1. Isolationism, unilateralism, and multilateralism as ever competing trends in US foreign policy-making

Three general approaches to foreign policy have struggled to gain control over the US decision-making process in the past: isolationism, unilateralism, and multilateralism. Each of these approaches has prevailed at one time or another but never dominated this process unchallenged. Foreign policy decisions are therefore usually based on a compromise which includes elements of all three of these trends to a varying degree. The fact that the President and Congress represent a variety of different opinions with regard to the formulation of foreign policy goals, and the fact that the President as well as Congress is involved in the formulation of policy goals, guarantees the inclusion of the three approaches mentioned in the decision-making process. Usually, the President will lean towards either unilateralism or multilateralism, while Congress will introduce a counter-balance of either multilateralism or unilateralism, and also an element of isolationism. This applies to international regimes of any kind, not only to environmental law, but conflicts between the President and Congress have prevented the USA from ratifying major international environmental agreements. One example is the Basle Convention on the Control of Transboundary Movements of Hazardous Wastes and their Disposal.[1] This Convention, which had been negotiated under the auspices of the United Nations Environmental Program with the active participation of the USA, was sent to the Senate in 1991 by President George Bush Sr. At the same time, the President submitted to Congress proposals for implementing legislation.[2] His successor, President Clinton, also supported the Basle Convention although his support weakened with the 1995 amendment to ban all movements of waste from OECD states to

---

I am indebted to Nora Janssen for her valuable research and linguistic assistance.
[1] 22 March 1989, 28 I.L.M. (1989) 652.
[2] See the report in *AJIL* 85 (1991), p. 674.

developing states and the 1999 Liability Protocol. But as Congress has not yet taken the necessary action due to industry and environmental group opposition, the USA has so far been unable to ratify the Convention.[3]

Isolationism dates back to the eighteenth century. In his Farewell Address of 1796, President George Washington advised his countrymen to engage in foreign commerce but to refrain from excessive political entanglements. Instead, the American people were to concentrate on a strong government able to defend its neutrality.[4] Ever since, isolationism has been an undercurrent of American foreign policy. It last figured prominently in the 1920s and 1930s when the USA was struggling to overcome the Great Depression. These days it plays only a secondary role.

The USA later became capable of and willing to use its growing political and military power to enforce national interests at an international level. This unilateral approach reached its peak during the administration of Theodore Roosevelt. It was kept in check during the Cold War by the confrontation with another superpower but gained importance during the Reagan administration, and certainly dominates the current administration of George W. Bush, at a time when the USA is the sole remaining superpower. Advocates of unilateralism consider international regimes as no more than a method of realising national interests more easily and effectively. The preservation of sovereignty in the sense of freedom to pursue national interests is their most important concern.[5] They are also usually sceptical about the role of law and legal institutions in international relations in general, a scepticism more common in the USA than in Europe.[6] And they are more inclined to use legal rules as tools and less to accept them as constraints.[7] A scepticism towards rules and the willingness to preserve national sovereignty are usually also the underlying causes for the USA's reluctance to participate in international environmental regimes, even where they reflect US domestic law.[8]

Multilateralism, i.e. the willingness to integrate oneself into an international community of equals to solve the world's problems jointly, found its way into the US foreign policy decision-making process after the US intervention in the Second World War. The building of multilateral institutions and regimes ease

---

[3] Choksi, S., The Basel Convention on the Control of Transboundary Movements of Hazardous Wastes and their Disposal, *ELQ* 28 (2001), pp. 509, 526. Brunnée, J., The United States and international environmental law, *EJIL* 15 (2004), pp. 617, 624.

[4] Padover, S. K. (ed.), *The Washington papers: basic selection*, New York, 1955, p. 309.

[5] Bolton, J. R., Should we take global governance seriously?, *Chicago J. Int'l L.* 1 (2000), p. 205. See also Rice, C., Promoting the national interest, *Foreign Affairs* 79 (2000), p. 45.

[6] Cf. Pildes, R. H., Conflicts between American and European views of law, *VJIL* 44 (2003), p. 145.

[7] Krisch, N., Weak as constraint, strong as tool, in Malone, D. M. and Khong, Y. F. (eds.), *Unilateralism and US foreign policy*, 2003, p. 41.

[8] See Anderson, T. L. and Grewell, J. B., It isn't easy being green, *Chicago J. Int'l L.* 2 (2001), p. 427; Lutter, R., Sovereignty, federalism, and the identification of local environmental problems, *Chicago J. Int'l L.* 2 (2001), p. 447; Brunnée, op. cit. pp. 622, *et seq.* 641.

the making of decisions, enhance their effective implementation, and lead to burden-sharing. President Woodrow Wilson wanted to secure world peace and democracy by establishing the League of Nations as a partnership of democratic states.[9] Wilson's multilateralism was, however, defeated by isolationist tendencies in the Senate which failed to ratify the Versailles Treaty. After its decisive contribution to the allied victory over the Axis powers in the Second World War, the USA, under the leadership of President Franklin D. Roosevelt, became one of the founders of the United Nations Organisation which established a new system of collective security.

2. The USA and the United Nations: veto power as an insurance policy

The United Nations, from the USA's point of view, is not a truly multilateral regime. As a permanent member of the Security Council, the USA has the power to veto a decision taken by this UN organ (Articles 23(1), 27(3) of the UN Charter). Initially, Stalin had demanded such a veto power while Roosevelt had rejected it.[10] For Roosevelt, it had apparently been so important to establish an effective international regime for the maintenance of peace and security and so unlikely that the USA could become the addressee of enforcement measures that he did not consider the veto as indispensable.

The USA would nevertheless have been unable to ratify the UN Charter without this veto power because it would otherwise have been impossible to secure the necessary two-thirds majority in the Senate.[11] The USA had thus initiated the establishment of a regime governed by a multilateral decision-making body for the sake of world peace – but ultimately made sure that it would never be able to restrict the USA's freedom of action. The USA later came to appreciate its veto power after UN membership had grown and diversified and produced an increasing number of instances in which US interests clashed with the interests of a majority of the other UN members. After the Cold War, the hegemonistic temptation temporarily prevailed over multilateral prudence but has not entirely defeated it. In the aftermath of the Iraq invasion of 2003, the USA is now trying to utilise the legitimising and nation-building capacities of the United Nations – because that is what a large majority of the US public favours.[12]

---

[9] Wilson's speech for declaration of war against Germany (2 April 1917); The fourteen points (8 January 1918), both in Commager, H. S. and Cantor, M. (eds.), *Documents of American history*, vol. II, 10th edn. 1988, pp. 130, 137.

[10] Grewe, W. G. and Khan, D.-E., History MN 39 *et seq.*, in Simma, B. (ed.), *The Charter of the United Nations*, 2nd edn. 2002.

[11] Cf. Telman, D. A. J., The instance of collective security regimes, in Franck, T. M. (ed.), *Delegating state powers*, 2000, pp. 133, 157.

[12] Cf. Kwakwa, E., The international community, international law, and the US, in Nolte, G. and Byers, M. (eds.), *US hegemony and the foundations of international law*, 2003, pp. 25, 38.

3. The USA and international human rights regimes: attractive force on a distant observer

After the Second World War, in an attempt to internationalise its own Bill of Rights to save the world from barbarism, the USA advocated the introduction of human rights norms into international law as minimum standards binding states even with regard to their own citizens. Eleanor Roosevelt, the widow of F. D. Roosevelt, became the 'mother' of the Universal Declaration of Human Rights which in 1948 was solemnly proclaimed by the UN General Assembly as a common standard of achievement for all peoples. The USA also played a key role in the negotiating process that led up to the subsequent human rights treaties which form the 'International Bill of Rights'.

Resistance in the Senate against this 'International Bill of Rights', which was based on the concern for federalism and the separation of powers, then, however, compelled the USA to take an isolationist course for decades. When it started to ratify human rights treaties in 1988, the USA was ultimately succumbing to the attractive force such treaties inevitably exert on a nation eager to maintain its credibility as the protagonist of human rights in the international arena. It has, however, ratified only some of these treaties and has in each case added reservations, understandings, and declarations so as to ensure it not being obliged to amend any of its domestic laws. This approach has been described as 'à la carte multilateralism'[13] or 'pick'n mix'.[14] Nor has the USA submitted to any individual complaint procedure.

4. The USA and the international court system

(a) The USA and the International Court of Justice: disappointed father

The UN Charter establishes the International Court of Justice as the principal judicial organ of the Organisation (Article 92 *et seq.* of the UN Charter). The idea to set up a permanent international court for the peaceful settlement of disputes in accordance with international law was first raised unsuccessfully by the US delegation to the Second Hague Peace Conference in 1907. This project was pursued without US participation by the League of Nations until the Statute of the Permanent Court of International Justice was adopted by the League's Assembly in 1920. US plans to accede to the Statute never materialised.[15]

---

[13] Cf. Kwakwa, op. cit. p. 53.
[14] Redgwell, C., US reservations to human rights treaties, in Nolte and Byers, op. cit. pp. 392, 394. See also Schou, N., Instances of human rights regimes, in Franck, op. cit. p. 209 *et seq.*
[15] Schlochauer, H.-J., Permanent Court of International Justice, in Bernhardt, R. (ed.), *Encyclopedia of public international law*, vol. III, 1997, p. 988.

But the USA became the driving force behind the plan to include an International Court of Justice in the new United Nations Organisation which would help to establish the rule of law in international relations.[16] As a founding member of the United Nations, the USA was automatically bound by the ICJ Statute (Article 93(1) UN Charter). It was even prepared to recognise the Court's jurisdiction in legal disputes according to Article 36(2) of the ICJ Statute as compulsory, but only upon attaching several reservations. The most important was the 'Connally reservation' stating that the ICJ would not be issued with the competence to adjudicate 'disputes with regard to matters essentially within the domestic jurisdiction of the United States as determined by the United States of America'. This attempt to reserve the power of unilaterally determining the bounds of the ICJ's jurisdiction in each individual case was strongly criticised and considered void by some.[17]

The USA did not hesitate to make use of the World Court whenever it seemed to further its national interests, the most prominent example being the Hostages case it won against Iran during the Carter administration.[18] But not even at that time did it refrain from unilateral action, trying to rescue its hostages by a military commando operation that ultimately failed. When Nicaragua later sued the USA in view of the support the Reagan administration provided to the Contra rebels in Nicaragua, the USA did not invoke the Connally reservation but tried to deny the ICJ's jurisdiction on other grounds. After the ICJ had confirmed its jurisdiction over the case,[19] the USA boycotted the further proceedings and terminated its recognition of the ICJ's compulsory jurisdiction. When the Court later found that the USA had violated international law in supporting the Contras,[20] the USA repudiated its judgment.

More recently, in the LaGrand death penalty case, the USA ignored a restraining order issued by the ICJ pursuant to Article 41 of the Statute[21] when LaGrand was executed by the State of Arizona before the ICJ decided on the merits. The Clinton administration, out of respect for the federal system, did not exhaust all legal and political avenues available against Arizona. The ICJ later determined that this had violated the ICJ Statute.[22]

(b) The USA and the International Criminal Court: sorcerer's apprentice?

The Nuremberg and Tokyo Trials were devised by the USA as a means of demonstrating that the rule of law could prevail over the atrocities committed by the Nazi and Japanese political and military leaders. In the early 1950s, the

---

[16] Ibid., vol. II, 1995, p. 1084.
[17] Cf. Dolzer, R., Connally reservation, in Bernhardt, R. (ed.), *Encyclopedia of public international law*, vol. I, 1992, p. 755 *et seq.*
[18] ICJ Reports 1980, p. 3. [19] ICJ Reports 1984, p. 392. [20] ICJ Reports 1986, p. 14.
[21] ICJ Reports 1999, p. 9. [22] ICJ Reports 2001, pp. 104, 109 *et seq.*

USA initiated work on the statute of an international criminal court but the project was postponed until the triable offences were defined.[23] In the wake of the atrocities committed in Yugoslavia and Rwanda in the 1990s, the USA was one of the protagonists of the two ad hoc international criminal tribunals set up by the UN Security Council. The USA also actively worked for a general and permanent international criminal court (ICCt) to deal with large-scale crimes against the international community as a whole. But it was clear from the outset that the USA was unwilling to subject its own citizens to the jurisdiction of this multilateral court unless it could control the initiation of proceedings.[24]

When this attempt failed due to the negotiating process having developed its own dynamics which the USA could no longer control, it not only withdrew from the project but actively tried to prevent it. After the entry into force of the Rome Statute the USA pressurised the UN Security Council as well as dozens of states into granting US officials an exemption from their treaty obligation to extradite suspects to the ICCt.[25] In essence, the USA considers the international criminal court system as an appropriate and even necessary tool to help enforce the most basic human rights and humanitarian law standards against others, while it believes it neither necessary nor appropriate to submit itself to a system which could, it believes, be abused by its enemies.[26]

5. The USA and the Chemical Weapons Convention

The Convention on the Prohibition of the Development, Production, Stockpiling and Use of Chemical Weapons and on their Destruction[27] establishes the most intrusive verification mechanism of any arms control treaty to date, authorising inspections of chemical plants in the territory of states party to such a treaty by an international Organization for the Prohibition of Chemical Weapons. It was the USA that had proposed these on-site inspections to ensure compliance.[28] The USA was ultimately prepared to submit to these inspections although they bear the danger of industrial espionage. The US Senate's Resolution of Ratification, however, contains many conditions, and the Chemical Weapons Convention Implementation Act of 1998[29] does not faithfully transpose the provisions of the convention but deviates from it in some respects.[30]

---

[23] Ferencz, B. International Criminal Court, in Bernhardt, op. cit. pp. 1123, 1124.
[24] See generally Nolte, G., The US and the International Criminal Court, in Malone and Khong, op. cit. p. 71.
[25] Cf. Murphy, S., Contemporary practice of the US, AJIL 96 (2002), p. 725; id., AJIL 97 (2003), p. 710.
[26] Boon, K., Instances of International Criminal Courts, in Franck, op. cit. p. 171.
[27] 13 January 1993, 32 I.L.M. (1993) 800.
[28] Zucker, J. B., The instance of chemical weapons control, in Franck, op. cit. pp. 95, 96.
[29] 21 October 1998 (Pub. L. No. 105–277).
[30] For the details, cf. Zucker, op. cit. p. 99 *et seq.*

The USA has still gone remarkably far because it has understood that it can only prevent the future use of chemical weapons against itself and its allies by adhering to such an inspection regime. In this instance, the President and Congress agreed that there was no viable alternative to the multilateral implementation regime and that thus a waiver of sovereign rights was indispensable for the long-term preservation of national security. In contrast to its attitude toward the chemical weapons inspection regime, the USA has so far not been ready to support a Protocol which would add a reliable verification scheme to the Convention on the Prohibition of the Development, Production and Stockpiling of Bacteriological (Biological) and Toxin Weapons and on their Destruction of 1972.

6. *The USA and the World Trade Organization*

The USA does, however, participate in multilateral regimes that show some affinity with a supranational system based on the delegation of national sovereignty in one specific field of international cooperation: international trade, more specifically the World Trade Organization[31] and, to a lesser extent, the North American Free Trade Agreement.[32] Both at the universal and the regional level, the USA is a member of international organisations that implement treaty-based legal commitments with regard to international trade. While the political decision-making process in the WTO (Ministerial Conference and General Council) and NAFTA (Free Trade Commission), e.g., concerning the binding interpretation of the treaty, is based on consensus,[33] state parties retain the right of veto in the NAFTA but not in the WTO. For if a party prevents a consensus in the WTO by raising a formal objection, the Ministerial Conference or the General Council can in many cases decide by a majority vote. The WTO system, and again to a lesser extent NAFTA, also establishes an automatic dispute settlement mechanism leading to binding quasi-judicial decisions which no party can block.[34]

Against this backdrop it is no surprise that the participation in both the WTO and NAFTA was fiercely contested in the USA. The forces of multilateralism prevailed because the US economy was expected to gain tremendously from the liberalisation of trade only if it was coupled with an effective implementation mechanism. But the Uruguay Round Agreements Act of 1994 (URAA)[35] on which the USA's participation in the WTO is based, tries to mitigate the effects of

---

[31] Agreement Establishing the World Trade Organization, 15 April 1994, 33 ILM (1994) 1125.
[32] Rahimi-Laridjani, E., The instance of commercial regimes, in Franck, op. cit. pp. 61, 63 *et seq.*
[33] Article IX(1) WTO; Article 2001(4) NAFTA.
[34] Article 16(4), 17(14) of the Dispute Settlement Understanding; Chapters 19 and 20 of the NAFTA.
[35] Pub. L. No. 103–465 (19 US Code §§ 3511 *et seq.*).

WTO law on the US legal system as far as possible.[36] Ultimately, the WTO system was only considered acceptable to Congress in view of the right of unilateral withdrawal.[37] The URAA stipulates that Congress is to review the effects of the WTO Agreement on the interests of the USA, the costs and benefits to the USA of its participation in the WTO, and the value of its continued participation in the WTO every five years. Depending on the outcome of the review, Congress may compel the President to terminate US membership in the WTO.[38]

7. Political heritage and constitutional constraints: national sovereignty, separation of powers, and federalism concerns shaping foreign policy decisions

It is not only the political heritage of isolationism and unilateralism which prevents the USA from wholeheartedly adopting a multilateralist attitude. There are also constitutional constraints to multilateralism: the US Constitution of 1787 was intended to provide a framework for the development of an effective federal system on the American continent entirely different and distinct from the European monarchies. Three hallmarks of this eighteenth century Constitution are relevant in this context: the national sovereignty of the (then) newly independent USA, the separation of powers first among the different branches of the federal government, and secondly among the federal government and the preexisting states (federalism).

The Constitution requires a two-thirds majority in the Senate before the President can conclude a treaty with a foreign power. It has long been controversial if and to what extent the federal government may use its treaty-making power to set legal standards in areas where legislative power is reserved to the states. It has also been controversial to what extent the 'treaty route' may be used to enact what for all practical purposes is federal statutory law in the absence of a constitutional delegation of legislative powers to Congress, despite the House of Representatives' lack of involvement in the treaty-making process. The USA therefore frequently adds a declaration to its ratification denying the self-executory character of treaty provisions, and also tries to ensure that the formulation of, for example, environmental agreements leaves enough leeway to the state parties to ensure that they cannot be directly enforced in national courts.[39]

There have been attempts to modify the rigours and systemic breaks of this constitutional scheme of treaty-making in practice. One attempt has been the extra-constitutional invention of the Congressional-Executive agreement that is concluded by the President with the consent of a simple majority in both Houses

---

[36] Rahimi-Laridjani, op. cit. p. 73 *et seq.*   [37] Article XV WTO.   [38] 19 US Code § 3535.
[39] Rabkin, J., American constitutional sovereignty vs. international law, in Wilson, B. P. and Masugi, K. (eds.), *The Supreme Court and American constitutionalism*, 1998, pp. 255, 276.

of Congress.[40] Another attempt has been the so-called 'fast track authority' which Congress reluctantly, infrequently, and only temporarily bestows on the President who then negotiates an international agreement according to Congressional guidelines and under the constant supervision of a Congressional committee. The result is subsequently presented to Congress which can either accept or reject it as a whole but cannot make changes or enter reservations. Both devices have primarily been used with international trade agreements, in view of the foreign commerce power given by the Constitution to Congress as a whole and not the Senate alone, but not with international environmental agreements, and it is hard to imagine that they would.

The Constitution does not give the federal government the competence to transfer any power to international organisations nor to integrate the USA into a supranational regime that has the competence to enact laws or take decisions with direct effects within the US legal system. Today, the legitimacy of international regimes, including international environmental regimes, is generally called into question inside and outside the USA.[41] Specifically, it would be incompatible with American conceptions of democracy to transfer decision-making authority to bodies not politically responsible to the US electorate – sovereignty and democracy are considered as twins.[42] This constitutional interpretation, that is perhaps not absolutely compelling but nonetheless very widely shared, renders US participation in international regimes, which are true instances of global governance and beyond US control, impossible.[43] The US attitude seems quite natural although not necessarily entirely honest for a superpower whose decisions will affect the lives of many people in many parts of the world, while decisions taken by others will not affect it to the same extent. One may even call this attitude self-righteous, taking into consideration that the USA has not infrequently promoted the establishment of (quasi-) supra-national regimes by other states, e.g., the European states, whose continuing sovereignty it believed would run counter to regional or universal stability.

II. The USA and international environmental law

The same trends which characterise the US decision-making process with regard to international law and foreign policy in general can also be detected in the

---

[40] Henkin, L., *Foreign affairs and the Constitution*, 2nd edn. 1996, p. 215 *et seq.*
[41] See Bodansky, D., The legitimacy of international governance, *AJIL* 93 (1999), p. 596.
[42] Cf. Franck, T. M., Can the US delegate aspects of sovereignty to international regimes?, in Franck, op. cit. p. 1 *et seq.*
[43] In recent years, a growing amount of legal and political science literature has been devoted to proving this point: Rabkin, op. cit.; Bolton, op. cit.; Kahn, P. W., Speaking law to power, *Chicago J. Int'l L.* 1 (2000), p. 1. For a more moderate view, see Stephan, P. B., International governance and American democracy, *Chicago J. Int'l L.* 1 (2000), p. 237. See also the address by then Senate Foreign Relations Committee Chairman Jesse Helms to the UN Security Council on 20 January 2000 (Murphy, S. D., *US practice in international law*, vol. I, 2002, p. 4 *et seq.*).

area of international environmental law and policy: leadership coupled with a sense of mission, on the one hand, preservation of sovereignty and of the vertical and horizontal balance of powers within the US federal system, on the other.

1. Environmental law in the USA: the protagonist regulator and market power

Earlier than most other states, the USA enacted laws for the preservation of its natural heritage (establishment of the Yellowstone National Park in 1872) and for the protection of the environment. Since the National Environmental Policy Act of 1969 (NEPA) was enacted, environmental impact assessments are required whenever the federal government or its agencies act in ways which affect the quality of the human environment.[44] Several US federal courts have accorded the NEPA extra-territorial effects in that US governmental agencies are required to file an environmental impact statement for every major action affecting the quality of the human environment outside the territorial jurisdiction of the USA, such as the USA's Exclusive Economic Zone and in particular the global commons such as Antarctica.[45] In 1970, the Environmental Protection Agency was founded as an independent agency to coordinate efforts on the federal level to reduce pollution of the air, soil, and water, repair damage already done, and help to protect the environment in the future. The USA thus proved to be a pioneer in this respect, setting an example for the international community, including the EC whose 1985 Directive on environmental impact assessment is modelled on NEPA. The standard-setting role of the USA becomes even more obvious if one takes the environmental legislation passed by the states into account, which sometimes by far exceed the federal standards.

The US federal and state environmental standards also have indirect extraterritorial effects because of the market power of the world's largest economy. Foreign producers who want to sell their goods on the vast US market will have to abide by US or state environmental standards. To give just one example: it is the Californian legislature which in fact determines the current emission standards for the automobile industry around the world due to the sheer extent of the Californian demand for automobiles. These standards are then later copied by other legislatures in states whose industry has already adapted to them 'voluntarily'. As we will see later, the liberty of states to prescribe environmental standards unilaterally is not unlimited in the free trade era of the WTO.[46]

---

[44] 42 US Code §§ 4321 et seq.
[45] Murphy, S. D., Contemporary practice of the US, AJIL 97 (2003), p. 962.
[46] See section II. 4(a).

2. The US role in the formation of international environmental law: pursuit of national interests with a sense of mission

As in all other policy areas, the USA is usually pursuing national interests with a sense of mission when it participates in the formation of international environmental norms: if it tries to internationalise its own environmental standards this will not only serve the interests of the US economy but also be intended to serve the interests of the international community as a whole, as determined by the USA. Sometimes economic interests may dominate but in other instances the environmental interests will be more important. However, even when environmental interests prevail one must distinguish between the pursuit of national environmental interests and the pursuit of global environmental protection interests.

(a) Pursuit of national environmental interests: *Trail Smelter Arbitration*

The first international environmental law case to be adjudicated by an international arbitral tribunal arose from the determination by the USA to protect the environment within its borders from industrial air pollution originating in the Canadian province of British Columbia that was causing extensive damage, with serious economic consequences for agricultural businesses across the border in Washington State. The arbitral tribunal held that Canada had violated its international obligations towards the USA.[47] Although the value of the Trail Smelter Arbitration as a precedent is sometimes questioned, the award is often cited for the proposition that a state must not use or permit the use of its territory in a manner that causes serious environmental damage in a neighbouring state. Such actions will incur international responsibility and be liable to payment of damages.[48] By espousing the claims of US farmers suffering economic losses, the USA provided an international tribunal with the opportunity to venture into a yet uncharted area of public international law. For selfish environmental and economic reasons it helped bring the first, and yet imperfect, international judicial pronouncement of a general rule of international environmental law into existence.

(b) Pursuit of national economic interests: NAFTA Supplemental Agreement on Environmental Cooperation

Environmental concerns are not always the driving force behind US advances to conclude environmental agreements. Sometimes such concerns are only

---

[47] RIAA 3 (1949), p. 1903. On recent developments concerning the still existing smelter, cf. Brunnée, op. cit. p. 632 *et seq.*
[48] Cf. Madders, K. J., Trail Smelter Arbitration, in Bernhardt, R. (ed.), *Encyclopedia of public international law*, vol. IV, 2000, p. 900.

secondary to economic interests which call for the protection of US producers from eco-dumping. The term 'eco-dumping' is used by industrial nations, in which production is expensive due to high environmental standards, to label what they consider as unfair competition from developing or threshold countries, where production is cheaper because of lower environmental standards. From this perspective, an advanced environmental law puts a state at a competitive disadvantage. As import restrictions for goods based on the neglect of environmental protection in the countries of origin are hard to justify under the GATT,[49] the only legal path to avert eco-dumping is to raise the environmental standards in those countries by concluding agreements with them which prescribe a minimum level of environmental protection. As the industrialised nation will usually have already reached a much higher level of environmental protection, the obligatory effect of such agreements with regard to environmental norms is practically one-sided. The developing country will accept its treaty obligations only with the view to being granted access to the developed nation's market. Agreements of this kind are not necessarily only concerned with eco-dumping but often also foster the protection of the environment, especially if the parties to the treaty are situated in the same region.

One important example for this mechanism is the North American Free Trade Agreement (NAFTA) of 1992 between Canada, Mexico, and the USA.[50] The NAFTA itself, which was concluded during the administration of President George Bush Sr., already includes a limited number of provisions dealing with environmental concerns. Article 104 of the NAFTA provides that (only) 'specific trade obligations' set out in certain exhaustively enumerated 'environmental and conservation agreements' will prevail over inconsistent provisions of the NAFTA. Article 2101 of the NAFTA permits the states parties to this agreement to make exceptions with regard to Part 2 (Trade in Goods) and Part 3 (Technical Barriers to Trade). For this purpose, they may employ Article XX GATT which is incorporated into the NAFTA. It is further clarified that the measures referred to in Article XX(b) GATT include environmental measures necessary to protect human, animal, or plant life or health, and that Article XX(g) GATT applies to measures relating to the conservation of living and non-living exhaustible natural resources.

As these provisions alone seemed insufficient to protect the USA from eco-dumping primarily by Mexico and at the same time to improve the environmental situation in North America, the NAFTA was supplemented by a specific environmental agreement after only one year: the North American Agreement on Environmental Cooperation (NAAEC) of 1993[51] that tries to raise the

---

[49] See also Section II.4(a).   [50] 32 I.L.M. (1993) 289, 605.

[51] Ibid., p. 1480. Block, G., Trade and environment in the Western hemisphere, *Env. L.* 33 (2003), p. 501.

environmental standards to an acceptable level.[52] It was negotiated by the Clinton administration after Clinton – whose running mate and later Vice President Albert Gore was a spokesman for the environmental cause – had made a campaign promise to this effect.[53] Upon closer inspection one can easily discern that the quite general clauses of the NAAEC do not commit the USA in any way to change its own environmental laws. Article 3 of the NAAEC provides:

> Recognizing the right of each Party to establish its own level of domestic environmental protection and environmental development policies and priorities, and to adopt or modify accordingly its environmental laws and regulations, each Party shall ensure that its laws and regulations provide for high levels of environmental protection and shall strive to continue to improve those laws and regulations.

Exceeding these very general substantive obligations, the NAAEC takes a further step towards an international regime by establishing a Commission for Environmental Cooperation. The Commission is to oversee the implementation of the agreement and develop recommendations for its further elaboration.[54] However, the main decision-making body of this Commission, the Council, consisting of cabinet level representatives of the parties, decides by consensus,[55] and its recommendations only have a precatory character and do not entail any legal obligations.

In the ongoing negotiations of a Free Trade Area of the Americas, i.e., an extension of NAFTA to the whole American continent, the USA is also striving to include environmental provisions. This is one of the negotiating objectives of the administration prescribed by the Bipartisan Trade Promotion Authority Act of 2002.[56]

(c) Pursuit of international agreements to save the world's nature and environment

(i) UNEP But the US attitude towards the protection of the international environment is by no means entirely selfish. The Nixon administration played a major role in initiating and financing the UN Conference on the Human Environment in June 1972 which produced the Stockholm Declaration,[57] a

---

[52] The analogous and concurrent treaty dealing with the problem of social dumping is the North American Agreement on Labor Cooperation, 32 I.L.M. (1993) 1499.
[53] Muffett, W. C., Environmental cooperation in North America, in Morrison, F. L. and Wolfrum, R. (eds.), *International, regional and national environmental law*, 2000, pp. 505, 527 *et seq.*
[54] Article 8 *et seq.*, Article 10(1)(b), (2) of the NAAEC.   [55] Article 9(6) of the NAAEC.
[56] §§ 2101 *et seq.* of Publ. L. No. 107–210 (Trade Act of 2002), 116 Stat. 993, codified in 19 US Code § 3802(a)(7), (b)(11).
[57] 11 I.L.M. (1972) 1416.

political document containing clearly formulated principles and recommendations which constitute a milestone in the development of international environmental law. Six months later, the UN General Assembly, with the support of the USA, created the United Nations Environment Programme (UNEP).[58] The USA has been the single largest contributor to UNEP's Environment Fund, donating almost US$300 million from 1973–2003. For lack of a founding treaty, UNEP has never been able to develop into an international organisation with a legal personality of its own and a specialised agency of the United Nations, neither has it obtained the power to enact legally binding norms. It has, however, contributed to the development of soft law and sponsored international negotiations leading to several environmental agreements.

(ii) CITES   The USA often promotes and accedes to environmental agreements also out of idealistic motives, namely a general concern for the conservation of the world's nature and environment outside US borders (the global commons). One example is the Convention on International Trade in Endangered Species of Wild Fauna and Flora of 1973 (CITES)[59] which was signed in Washington, DC, four years after the US Congress had passed the Endangered Species Act that had served as a primer.[60] CITES restricts the import and export of animal and plant specimens belonging to the tens of thousands of endangered species listed in the appendices to the Convention. The Convention obliges the states parties to prohibit trade in these endangered species and punish violators. The USA has accepted these obligations without reservation.

CITES has no international implementation machinery apart from the obligation of the states parties to report regularly to the Secretariat provided by the Executive Director of UNEP. In practice, however, an implementation regime has developed with US consent since the 1980s, culminating in the imposition of trade sanctions, i.e. the suspension of trade in CITES-listed species with treaty violators.[61] Amendments to the Appendices to CITES are adopted by a two-thirds majority vote at the Conference of the Parties but states can contract out of such amendments by making a reservation within ninety days. Amendments to the text of the Convention will enter into force for those states only which have deposited an instrument of acceptance. The USA has accepted the amendment of 1979 but not the amendment of 1983.

(iii) **Protection of the ozone layer**   The USA was the driving force in the relatively short negotiations leading to the Vienna Convention for the Protection

---

[58] Resolution 2997, 15 December 1972.   [59] 12 I.L.M. (1973) 1055.
[60] Dorsey, K., Environment, in Jentleson, B. W. and Paterson, T. G. (eds.), *Encyclopedia of US foreign relations*, vol. II, 1997, pp. 84, 91.
[61] Reeves, R., *Policing international trade in endangered species*, 2002, p. 91 *et seq.*

of the Ozone Layer[62] and the Montreal Protocol on Substances that Deplete the Ozone Layer,[63] and quickly ratified both treaties. It did so, first, because obviously only a multilateral approach could save the world's vital ozone layer, and, secondly, because the US industry was more advanced regarding the phasing out of ozone-depleting substances compared to its competitors in Western Europe and Japan and wanted to avoid the competitive disadvantage of unilateral US restrictions instead of multilateral restrictions.[64] In this instance, the national interests of the USA perfectly coincided with the interests of the international community in the protection of the environment.

(iv) Protection of the Antarctic and Arctic environment With regard to the protection of the extremely vulnerable Antarctic environment, the USA also proved to be a pioneer when it enacted the Antarctic Conservation Act of 1978. At the time, relevant international legal norms were rare. The Antarctic Treaty of 1959[65] does not specifically deal with environmental protection,[66] and the Convention on the Conservation of Antarctic Seals of 1972[67] is limited in scope. Intensive efforts toward comprehensive protection of the Antarctic environment began with the Convention on the Conservation of Antarctic Marine Living Resources of 1980,[68] and the Protocol on Environmental Protection to the Antarctic Treaty of 1991.[69] The USA has ratified the Antarctic Treaty, the Convention on the Conservation of Antarctic Seals, and the Convention on the Conservation of Antarctic Marine Living Resources and signed (but not ratified) the Protocol on Environmental Protection to the Antarctic Treaty, and enacted the Antarctic Science, Tourism, and Conservation Act of 1996[70] to implement the Environmental Protocol. Article 16 of the Protocol envisages the creation of an annex concerning liability for environmental damage caused by human activities, something essential for the effectiveness of the environmental regime.[71] A draft proposed by a group of legal experts in 1998 was rejected

---

[62] 22 March 1985, 26 I.L.M. (1987) 1529. On the US decision-making process, cf. Sitaraman, S., Evolution of the ozone regime, in Harris, P. G. (ed.), *The environment, international relations, and US foreign policy*, 2001, pp. 111, 120.

[63] 16 September 1987, 26 I.L.M. (1987) 1550. Sitaraman, op. cit. p. 123 *et seq.*

[64] Dorsey, op. cit. p. 94; Bui, D., The instance of environmental regimes, in Franck, op. cit. pp. 33, 35 *et seq.*; Falkner, R., Business conflict and US international environmental policy, in Harris, op. cit. pp. 157, 163 *et seq.*

[65] 19 I.L.M. (1980) 860.

[66] But see Article IX lit. f of the Antarctic Treaty which has been the basis for numerous measures to protect the Antarctic environment (Bastmeijer, K., *The Antarctic Environmental Protocol and its domestic implementation*, 2003, p. 38).

[67] 11 I.L.M. (1972) 251.   [68] 19 I.L.M. (1980) 841.

[69] 30 I.L.M. (1991) 1460. Bastmeijer, op. cit.

[70] Pub. L. No. 104–227, 2 October 1996, 110 Stat. 3034.

[71] Wolfrum, R., Environmental protection of ice-covered regions, in Morrison and Wolfrum, op. cit. pp. 329, 336 *et seq.*

by the USA and other states as too far-reaching because it could jeopardise scientific exploration activities. The USA's counter-proposals were considered as too restrictive by more environmentally-minded states. As a result, the negotiations on the liability annex which started in 1992 have so far been fruitless. The USA is generally reluctant to enter into treaties assigning liability.[72]

There is no treaty mechanism in place to protect the Arctic environment. The eight states exercising territorial sovereignty over parts of the Arctic, including the USA, announced the Arctic Environmental Protection Strategy as a political (not a legal) commitment to a comprehensive cooperation in 1991.[73] One of their major objectives was the internationalisation of efforts to clean up toxic waste in the Russian Arctic. On the basis of this common strategy, the Arctic Council was established in 1996.[74] It has been designed as a high level political forum for informal cooperation, and not as a treaty-based international organisation with legal personality, due to the reluctance of the USA. The Arctic Council is intended to 'provide a means for promoting cooperation, coordination and interaction among the Arctic States, with the involvement of the Arctic indigenous communities and other Arctic inhabitants on common Arctic issues, in particular issues of sustainable development and environmental protection in the Arctic'.[75] The Ottawa Declaration moves from environmental protection to the broader concept of sustainable development but does not define it because of disagreement among the Arctic states.

3. The US unwillingness to submit to international regimes: 'splendid isolationism?'

(a) The UN Convention on the Law of the Sea

The modern international law of the sea regime is embedded in the comprehensive 1982 UN Convention on the Law of the Sea (UNCLOS).[76] Its extensive Title XII (Articles 192–237) deals with the protection and preservation of the marine environment. While the USA has always accepted most parts of UNCLOS, including its Title XII, it has, for economic reasons, consistently rejected the restrictive and bureaucratic deep seabed regime of Title XI,[77] as have other Western industrialised states. Title XI was modified by an Implementation Agreement of 1994 so as to enable universal ratification of UNCLOS. However, the USA, contrary to most of its allies, has not yet done so, although former President Clinton transmitted UNCLOS and the Implementation Agreement to

---

[72] Choksi, op. cit. p. 530.   [73] *Yb. Int'l Env. L.* 2 (1991), p. 585.
[74] Ottawa Declaration on the Establishment of the Arctic Council, 19 September 1996, 35 I.L.M. (1996) 1382. See Bloom, E. T., Establishment of the Arctic Council, *AJIL* 93 (1999), p. 712.
[75] See s. 1(a) of the Ottawa Declaration (footnote omitted).   [76] 21 I.L.M. (1982) 1261.
[77] Klein, P., The effects of US predominance, in Nolte and Byers, op. cit. pp. 363, 365 *et seq.*

the Senate in 1994 and the current Bush administration announced its support for UNCLOS in 2001, citing national security, economic, and environmental interests. But there still is opposition from Republicans in the Senate who object to the 'United Nations bureaucracy' created by the Convention.[78] The USA has in the meantime abided by the rules of UNCLOS outside Title XI which to a large extent codifies customary international law.

The USA proposed a ban on dumping oil at sea by ships as early as 1926,[79] and it promoted and quickly ratified the International Convention for the Prevention of Pollution from Ships (MARPOL) 1973[80] and the 1978 Protocol.[81] The most recent 1997 Protocol to amend MARPOL in regulating the prevention of air pollution from ships was signed by the USA in 1998 and submitted to the Senate in 2003 for advice and consent. A major US concern with regard to this Protocol has been whether a party may impose more stringent national standards on vessels calling at its ports than those provided by the Protocol. In his Letter of Submittal the Secretary of State certified that states parties to the Protocol retained this power.[82]

(b) Biodiversity and biosafety

The Convention on Biological Diversity (CBD)[83] was one of the major results of the 1992 Rio Conference on Environment and Development of the United Nations ('Earth Summit'). It attempts not only to conserve the variety of plants, animals, and micro-organisms as a common heritage of mankind but also to regulate the access to and the sustainable use of the existing species' genetic resources, and the fair and equitable sharing of the benefits from this use between the developed states and their (agricultural and pharmaceutical) enterprises as the principal users, on the one hand and the developing states as the principal states of origin of these resources, on the other.[84] In this respect, the CBD presents itself as a compromise between the interests of the developed and the developing part of the world. While the USA started out as the world's leading environmentalist at the Earth Summit, it became apparent in the course of the conference that it pursued not only environmental but also other conflicting interests. The USA had originally proposed a convention on the preservation of biological diversity but President Bush Sr. eventually refused

---

[78] Reed, C. and Pinsker, L. M., New US support for the Law of the Sea, *Geotimes*, January 2002 (www.geotimes.org/jan02/NN_los.html). The Senate Foreign Relations Committee began hearings on UNCLOS in October 2003 (Murphy, S. D., Contemporary practice of the US, *AJIL* 98 (2004), pp. 169, 173).

[79] Dorsey, op. cit. p. 93.

[80] 12 I.L.M. (1973) 1319. See Barkdull, J., US foreign policy and the ocean environment, in Harris, op. cit. p. 134 *et seq.*

[81] 17 I.L.M. (1978) 546.

[82] Murphy, S. D., Contemporary practice of the US, *AJIL* 97 (2003) pp. 962, 979 *et seq.*

[83] 31 I.L.M. (1992) 818. [84] For a survey see www.biodiv.org

to sign the actual 1992 Convention because of its vague language on property rights and restrictions of biotechnology. The President also mentioned in this context that the USA was already doing more than any other country to protect biodiversity and that it was therefore unnecessary to join the CBD.[85] Shortly after his inauguration, the newly elected President Clinton signed the CBD in 1993 after an interpretive statement had been drafted that satisfied some of the business community's concerns, but no steps have been taken so far by the USA to ratify it because of opposition in the Senate.[86]

The 2000 Cartagena Protocol on Biosafety to the Convention on Biological Diversity[87] aims at:

> ensuring an adequate level of protection in the field of the safe transfer, handling and use of living modified organisms resulting from modern biotechnology that may have adverse effects on the conservation and sustainable use of biological diversity, taking also into account risks to human health, and specifically focusing on transboundary movements (Article 1).

It has so far not even been signed by the USA, for much the same reasons as for not ratifying the CBD. The USA did, however, actively participate in the negotiations which brought forth the Protocol, unsuccessfully trying to limit its scope in the interest of US exporters of agricultural products.[88]

(c) UN Framework Convention and Kyoto Protocol on Climate Change

The other major result of the Rio Earth Summit was the signing of the UN Framework Convention on Climate Change (UNFCCC).[89] Its objective is to stabilise greenhouse gas concentrations in the atmosphere at a level that would prevent dangerous anthropogenic interference with the climate system.[90] Again, the USA had taken the lead in instigating scientific studies, raising international awareness, and countering the adverse climate impacts of these emissions.[91] It immediately signed the Framework Convention and ratified it within little more than four months. But this Convention only establishes general principles (Article 3) and the obligation to devise national policies of fact-finding,

---

[85] Dorsey, op. cit. p. 96.
[86] Dorsey, K., Environmental Protection Agency, in Jentleson and Paterson, op. cit. pp. 97, 98; Bui, D., The instance of environmental regimes, in Franck, op. cit. pp. 33, 38; Falkner, op. cit. p. 168 *et seq.*; Blomquist, R. F., Ratification resisted: understanding America's response to the Convention on Biological Diversity, 1989–2002, *Golden Gate Univ. L. Rev.* 32 (2002) p. 493.
[87] 39 I.L.M. (2000) 1027. Entered into force 11 September 2003.
[88] Boisson de Chazournes, L., Unilateralism and environmental protection, *EJIL* 11 (2000) pp. 315, 327.
[89] 31 I.L.M. (1992) 849.   [90] Article 2.
[91] Assunção, L., Turning its back to the world?, in Malone and Khong, op. cit. pp. 297, 299, 301. See generally Harris, P. G. (ed.), *Climate change and American foreign policy*, 2000.

research and development of technological capabilities, education etc.[92] While the developed countries assumed an obligation to return to the 1990 level of greenhouse gas emissions[93] it was the USA that prevented the inclusion of a specific timetable in this respect because it wanted to maintain national sovereignty over its economy.[94]

While it was soon recognised that the mere stabilisation of greenhouse gas emissions at the level of 1990 was insufficient to prevent climate change and that therefore a significant reduction of emission levels was called for, it was years before an agreement on the necessary concrete obligations concerning targets and timetables was reached by the parties to the UNFCCC. The USA took an active part in the negotiations but could not realise all its objectives. It successfully pushed for the inclusion of emission trading which enables states overfulfilling the agreed standards to sell emission certificates to others that lag behind. It was, however, unsuccessful as far as its demands to impose obligations to reduce emissions also on the developing states are concerned. The Kyoto Protocol to the UNFCCC, which was ultimately signed in December 1997,[95] elaborates on the principle of common but differentiated responsibilities in that it obliges only the developed states, but not the developing states, to go beyond the UNFCCC: only they assume a commitment to reduce their greenhouse gas emissions by a certain percentage compared to the level of 1990 until 2012.[96]

In July 1997, in the final phase of the negotiations, the US Senate had passed a resolution by a margin of 95:0 that it would not ratify any treaty which imposed excessive costs on the US economy and exempted the developing states from the obligation to reduce their emissions. The key sponsors of this bipartisan resolution were Democratic Senator Byrd of West Virginia (with an important coal sector) and Republican Senator Hagel of Nebraska (dependent on mechanised agriculture sensitive to fuel prices). Both feared the negative impact an obligation to reduce greenhouse gases would have on the economies of their home states as this was expected to decrease the demand for coal[97] and raise fuel prices.[98] A further problem of the negotiations concerned the reduction margin the USA was prepared to assume. Only at a late stage of the negotiations and largely due to the personal initiative of then Vice-President Gore did it accept a 7 per cent reduction with regard to 1990 emission levels

---

[92] Article 4(1).   [93] Article 4(2)(b).
[94] Dorsey, op. cit. p. 96; Beyerlin, U., *Umweltvölkerrecht*, 2000, p. 175 n. 462.
[95] 37 I.L.M. (1998) 22.
[96] Bothe, M., The United Nations Framework Convention on Climate Change, *ZaöRV* 63 (2003), pp. 239, 241; Brunnée, J., The Kyoto Protocol, *ZaöRV* 63 (2003) 255, 265.
[97] Coal-burning power plants account for more than 50 per cent of the electricity generated in the USA (Murphy, S. D., *US practice in international law*, vol. I: 1999–2001, 2002, p. 176).
[98] Assunção, op. cit. p. 315 n. 1.

while the EU members opted for an 8 per cent reduction.[99] The USA signed the Kyoto Protocol in November 1998 so as to be able to participate actively in the negotiations on the operational rules for implementing it. But already then-President Clinton announced that he would not submit the Protocol to the Senate for ratification unless key developing states voluntarily took on binding commitments to reduce emissions.[100] This referred to major Third World emitters such as Brazil, China, and India.[101] The condition pursued not only an environmental but also an economic agenda by protecting US industries from a competitive disadvantage.[102]

While the newly-elected President George W. Bush had made a campaign pledge to reduce carbon dioxide emissions, he assured Republican Senators in a letter from March 2001 that he would not seek to restrict the emission of carbon dioxide by power plants because that would increase energy prices.[103] He opposed the Kyoto Protocol because it exempted the developing states and would cause serious harm to the US economy as it would increase production costs in energy-intensive sectors. In this context, the administration usually also refers to remaining scientific uncertainties as to how exactly man-made greenhouse gas emissions affect the world's climate. The USA has nevertheless continued to participate in follow-up negotiations of the Conference of the Parties to the UNFCCC concerning rules to elaborate the Kyoto Protocol, and emphasised that it would not stop others from moving ahead as long as legitimate US interests were protected. But the USA has also made clear that its intention not to ratify the Kyoto Protocol was final.[104]

This withdrawal by the world's largest emitter of greenhouse gases from a multilateral project to save the planet from the consequences of what many people consider 'its waste of energy' provoked an international outcry – not the least because it coincided with the USA's withdrawal from another common project, the International Criminal Court. But while it withdrew its signature from the Rome Statute and actively tries to undermine the functioning of this court, it has assumed a position of benevolent neutrality toward the Kyoto Protocol which still carries its signature. It remains yet to be seen in both cases whether the USA's withdrawal will ultimately kill the two multilateral projects or actually promote them by generating an attitude of defiance against the hegemon in the other states.[105]

---

[99] Annex B of the Kyoto Protocol. See Assunção, op. cit. p. 304.
[100] Murphy, S. D., Contemporary practice of the US, *AJIL* 93 (1999), pp. 470, 491.
[101] Bothe, op. cit. p. 254.
[102] On the influence of the US business community on the US international environmental policy-making process with regard to climate change, cf. Falkner, op. cit. pp. 157, 166 *et seq.*
[103] Murphy, op. cit. p. 176.   [104] Ibid., p. 176 *et seq.*
[105] Cf. Brunnée, op. cit. p. 266 *et seq.*

It is true that the current Bush administration has a particularly close relationship with the energy industry, primarily in the person of Vice-President Cheney who played a leading role in shaping the administration's energy policy.[106] But given the energy crisis persisting in parts of the USA (e.g., power outages in California) and the dependency of the 'American way of life' on an abundant supply of cheap energy, it would be difficult for any President to convince Congress and the US public that it is in the USA's own medium- and long-term interests to reverse current emission trends.[107] In any event, it is estimated that the USA would need to cut current greenhouse gas emissions by more than 20 per cent to meet its Kyoto target by 2012.[108] According to some commentators, the President's strategy may just be to gain time and prepare the US private sector for the 'Kyoto shock'.[109] The Bush administration has not abandoned the objective of reducing emissions unilaterally but is pursuing it primarily on the basis of voluntary commitments by US industry and only to a much smaller extent than envisioned by the Kyoto Protocol.[110] By fostering technological progress, becoming more energy-efficient, and increasing spending on research projects,[111] the Bush administration tries to underline its commitment to a leadership role on the issue of climate change, recognising its responsibility in the world.[112] However, at the Johannesburg World Summit on Sustainable Development of 2002, it was again primarily the USA which, together with OPEC, blocked attempts to incorporate concrete targets or a timetable with regard to an increase in the use of renewable energy resources into the Johannesburg Plan of Implementation.[113]

Whether the USA returns to a multilateral approach, reversing its recent climate policy shift, will depend on the outcome of the next Presidential elections in November 2004. According to an Associated Press report of 3 February 2004, most Democratic contenders in the presidential campaign of 2004 have publicly announced that they would reengage in multilateral negotiations but refrained

---

[106] Cf. the US Supreme Court decision of 24 June 2004 in *Cheney v. US District Court for the District of Columbia* (No. 03–475).
[107] See Assunção, op. cit. p. 309 *et seq.*   [108] Ibid., p. 306.   [109] Ibid., p. 314.
[110] According to the US Climate Action Report 2002 (third national communication of the USA under the UNFCCC, submitted 28 May 2002 (http://unfccc.int/resource/docs/natc/usnc3.pdf)), President Bush made a commitment of a 4.5 per cent reduction from forecast emissions in 2012 – which means only a deceleration of a rise in emissions not a reduction in absolute figures (p. 3). And the commitment apparently covers only industrial emissions while leaving aside emissions from the transportation sector etc. (see Statement by the President, 12 February 2003 (www.whitehouse.gov/news/releases/2003/02/20030212.html)).
[111] In this respect, cf. the Strategic Plan for the US Climate Change Science Program (July 2003).
[112] Ibid., p. 1.
[113] Beyerlin, U. and Reichard, M., The Johannesburg Summit, *ZaöRV* 63 (2003), pp. 213, 219.

from specific promises to seek ratification of the Kyoto Protocol from the Senate, presumably because the necessary two-thirds majority will be hard to come by for any future President. Following the example of UNCLOS, it could in the end prove necessary to start multilateral negotiations with a view to developing alternatives to the Kyoto Protocol, not least because it is unclear if the European states that have already ratified it will be able to reach their reduction targets.[114] In this context, a Declaration on Transatlantic Relations annexed to the Presidency Conclusions of the December 2003 Brussels European Council calls upon the EU and its transatlantic partners to defend a common agenda based on the promotion of the rule of law, democracy, and human rights, poverty reduction, health and environmental protection. It advocates an international order based on effective multilateralism.[115]

4. Unilateral prescription and enforcement of environmental standards by the USA

The USA has not hesitated to use its political and economic power for the purpose of unilaterally prescribing environmental standards and imposing them on other states as well as their nationals and enterprises. In some cases, it has unilaterally defined these standards in its national law, in other cases it has taken them from international treaties and turned them against states which were not parties to these treaties.

(a) Prescription of national standards provoking GATT troubles: gasoline, dolphins, and turtles

The USA's prescription of environmental standards via import restrictions for non-conforming foreign goods has on several occasions been found to violate its WTO commitments (Articles I, III, XI, XIII GATT).[116] One such instance concerned US import restrictions on gasoline. In an effort to prevent a rise in air pollution levels in the USA, the Environmental Protection Agency, based on the Clean Air Act of 1990, promulgated the 'Gasoline Rule' setting quality standards for domestic refiners and importers of gasoline. This attempt to protect the 'national' environment was held to be incompatible with Article III(4) GATT because the Gasoline Rule treated imported gasoline less favourably than domestic gasoline and this discrimination could not be justified under Article XX GATT because it was unnecessary for achieving the goal of countering a rise in pollution levels.[117]

---

[114] Tänzler, D. and Carius, A., Perspektiven einer transatlantischen Klimapolitik, *Aus Politik und Zeitgeschichte* B27(2003), pp. 12, 17.
[115] Section 4 of the Declaration.   [116] See Christian Tietje, Chapter 10.
[117] The Appellate Body Report is reprinted in 35 I.L.M. (1996) 603. See also Cho, S., Gasoline, *EJIL* 9 (1998), p. 182.

Other instances concerned US attempts unilaterally to protect the global commons. The USA had placed restrictions on imports of tuna and shrimp from states which did not impose on their fishermen the use of dolphin-safe or turtle-safe catching methods essentially identical to the ones in force for US fishermen. While these import requirements undoubtedly promoted the universal interest in the preservation of endangered species, they had economic side-effects in that they favoured US producers and placed external competitors, which were subject to the different environmental regulations of their flag-state, at a disadvantage.[118] In the two *Tuna* cases which were adjudicated under the GATT 1947 before the entry into force of the WTO Agreement, the Panels came to the conclusion that the USA had violated its GATT obligations when, for the sake of protecting the environment outside its own jurisdiction (the global commons), it enforced national or international environmental standards against other states that were not bound by these standards. The USA's unilateral trade measures could not be justified under Article XX GATT.[119] Due to US objections, however, these two Panel Reports of 1991 and 1994 were not adopted by the GATT Council under the then-existing positive unanimity rule.[120]

The *Shrimp* case arose after the entry into force of the Dispute Settlement Understanding in the Annex to the WTO Agreement of 1994[121] which introduced the new rule of negative unanimity. This meant that the USA could no longer block the adoption of a Panel or Appellate Body Report by the Dispute Settlement Body (DSB).[122] The Appellate Body Report was therefore adopted by the DSB in this case. It held that a WTO member could rely on Article XX(g) of the GATT to protect endangered species as parts of the global commons if there was a sufficient nexus with its own territorial jurisdiction, i.e., if the species also existed on the territory of the respective WTO member. It further held that the prohibition of arbitrary discrimination and disguised restriction on international trade in the chapeau of Article XX GATT prevented the USA from unilaterally imposing its own specific regulatory programme to protect endangered species on other states without examining the adequacy of the latters' protection methods and without entering into prior good faith negotiations with these states for the purpose of reaching a multilateral agreement

---

[118] On the origins of the import restrictions which as a matter of fact had tried to internationalise restrictions already imposed on US fishermen, cf. DeSombre, E. R., Environmental sanctions in US foreign policy, in Harris, op. cit. p. 197 *et seq.*

[119] The first Panel Report is reprinted in 30 I.L.M. (1991) 1594, the second in 33 I.L.M. (1994) 839.

[120] Hudec, R. E., The GATT/WTO Dispute Settlement Process: can it reconcile trade rules and environmental needs?, in Wolfrum, R. (ed.), *Enforcing environmental standards: economic mechanisms as viable means?*, 1996, pp. 123, 143.

[121] 33 I.L.M. (1994) 1226.   [122] Articles 16(4), 17(14) DSU.

on species protection.[123] The failure of a good faith attempt to solve a common environmental concern multilaterally was thereby held to be a precondition for unilateral trade measures.

While the USA has occasionally given environmental interests priority over trade interests it was among a group of major trading powers (including the EC) which unsuccessfully tried to obtain recognition of the supremacy of the multilateral trading system over multilateral environmental agreements at the Johannesburg World Summit on Sustainable Development of 2002.[124]

(b) External enforcement of international standards: trade sanctions to protect whales

One instance in which the USA has used its power as the world's leading trading nation to enforce international standards concerns the protection of whales. The International Convention for the Regulation of Whaling strives 'to establish a system of international regulation for the whale fisheries to ensure proper and effective conservation and development of whale stocks'.[125] It has created an International Whaling Commission (IWC) which can set harvest quotas by a three-quarters majority vote that become binding upon all parties to the Convention unless they formally object within ninety days. The IWC has no power to enforce even binding quotas. When the IWC decided in 1982 to phase out commercial whaling completely, several states, including Japan and Norway, objected, thus contracting out of the whaling moratorium. The Convention combines precise legal rules with a decentralised system of implementation and dispute resolution.[126]

To improve the implementation of whale conservation, the USA, a founding member of the IWC regime, on the initiative of individual Congressmen and Senators, established a unilateral enforcement mechanism by Congressional legislation, in the 1970s. The 1971 Pelly Amendment to the Fishermen's Protective Act of 1967[127] directs the Secretary of Commerce to certify to the President if 'nationals of a foreign country, directly or indirectly, are conducting fishing operations in a manner or under circumstances which diminish the effectiveness of an international fishery conservation program'.[128] The President may then, in his discretion, direct the Secretary of the Treasury to prohibit the importation of fish products from the certified state. He must report to

---

[123] Report of the Appellate Body, 12 October 1998, reprinted in 38 I.L.M. (1999) 118. See also the further Report of 22 October 2001, reprinted in 41 I.L.M. (2002) 149.
[124] Beyerlin and Reichard, op. cit. p. 224 *et seq.* See generally Böckenförde, M., Zwischen Sein und Wollen, *ZaöRV* 63 (2003), p. 971.
[125] 2 December 1946, 161 UNTS 72. The quotation is taken from the Convention's Preamble.
[126] Setear, J. K., Can legalization last?, *VJIL* 44 (2004), p. 711.
[127] The amendment is codified in 22 US Code §1978.
[128] 22 US Code § 1978 extends beyond whaling to fisheries in general. It was later amended to cover also violations of international programmes for endangered or threatened species.

Congress within sixty days following certification on any action taken and give reasons if he fails to impose sanctions. Whether import sanctions under the Pelly Amendment would be compatible with WTO law remains to be tested.[129] The same holds true of the Marine Mammal Protection Act of 1972,[130] which prohibits the importation into the USA of marine mammals and marine mammal products, with certain exceptions.

Because of the Presidential reluctance to impose such sanctions under the Pelly Amendment, Congress in 1979 enacted the Packwood-Magnuson Amendment to the Fishery Conservation and Management Act of 1976[131] which requires the Secretary of State to impose sanctions on a certified state in the form of an at least 50 per cent reduction of this state's fishing quota in the US fishery-conservation zone, leaving no room for the exercise of discretion. But there still is discretion with regard to the certification.[132] Usually the threat of a certification by the Secretary or of the imposition of sanction following such certification will induce the state concerned to make a commitment of future compliance with the relevant international fishery conservation programme.[133]

(c) Promoting the environmental awareness of multilateral development banks

Multilateral development banks on universal and regional levels,[134] whose capital is mostly provided by developed countries often grant loans to developing countries which are used to finance large-scale projects. Some of these projects have had disastrous environmental consequences. Thus, in the 1980s, environmental NGOs in the USA successfully lobbied Congress to enact legislation promoting the environmental awareness of the banks. The Pelosi Amendment of 1989 required the US Secretary of the Treasury to direct the US-appointed executive directors in the directorates of the banks to vote against loans for projects which could have a major environmental impact unless either the borrowing country or the bank made an environmental impact assessment available to the board members and to affected local groups and NGOs at least 120 days in advance. In view of the importance of US funding to the multilateral development banks, all of them quickly introduced this requirement into their internal operating procedures.[135]

---

[129] See above. [130] 16 US Code §§1361–1407.
[131] The amendment is codified in 16 US Code § 1821(e)(2).
[132] *Japan Whaling Association* v. *American Cetacean Society*, 478 US 221 (1986).
[133] On US sanctions against Japan, cf. *AJIL* 95 (2001), p. 149.
[134] The International Bank for Reconstruction and Development (World Bank), the Asian Development Bank, the African Development Bank, and the Inter-American Development Bank.
[135] Bøås, M., Multilateral development banks, in Harris, op. cit. pp. 178, 184.

(d) Internal enforcement of international standards: damages for victims of 'international environmental torts' under the Alien Tort Claims Act?

One special feature of US unilateralism in environmental matters introduces the US federal courts which can be used for the internal enforcement of international environmental standards. Under the Alien Tort Claims Act (ATCA) of 1789, the US district courts have jurisdiction of any civil action by an alien for a tort only, committed in violation of the law of nations or a treaty of the USA.[136] Since 1980, numerous civil actions have been based on the ATCA, usually against persons responsible for violations of elementary human rights such as the freedom from torture, hostage-taking, extra-judicial killings, and forced disappearances.[137] With the ATCA, the USA provides a forum to victims of human rights violations seeking just satisfaction to whom no other appropriate forum is available.

More recently, the ATCA has also served as a basis for damage claims against corporations for torts allegedly committed in violation of international environmental law standards.[138] So far, none of these environmental tort claims has been successful, partly because the US courts considered themselves a *forum non conveniens*, partly because they found that the alleged interferences of defendants with the environment did not violate customary international law. The most recent case in point is *Flores v. Southern Peru Copper Corp.* in which Peruvians sought damages from the defendant US corporation claiming that the latter's copper mining operations in Peru had caused asthma and lung disease. The action was dismissed for lack of subject matter jurisdiction and failure to state a claim because the US Court of Appeals for the Second Circuit found that environmental pollution, within a nation's borders, that adversely affects human life or health did not violate any binding rules of international law, expressly leaving open the question whether international law prohibited transnational pollution.[139]

In spite of the current reluctance of US courts to award damages to individuals for environmental torts, the ATCA remains available to provide the necessary enforcement mechanism if international law develops further in this respect. The current Bush administration has, however, tried to induce federal courts

---

[136] 28 US Code § 1350.
[137] Stephens, B. and Ratner, M., *International human rights litigation in U.S. courts*, 1996, p. 7; Rau, M., Domestic adjudication of international human rights abuses, *ZaöRV* 61 (2001), p. 177.
[138] Cf. e.g., *Amlon Metals, Inc. v. FMC Corp.*, 775 F. Supp. 668 (SDNY 1991); *Beanal v. Freeport-McMoran, Inc.*, 969 F. Supp 362 (E.D. La. 1997), 197 F.3d 161 (CA5 1999); *Jota v. Texaco, Inc.*, 157 F.3d 153 (CA2 1998); *Aguinda v. Texaco, Inc.*, 142 F. Supp.2d 534 (SDNY 2001), 303 F.3d 470 (CA2 2002); *Ken Wiwa v. Royal Dutch Petroleum Co.* (CA2 2000), 40 ILM (2001) 481; *Flores v. Southern Peru Copper Corp.* (CA2 2003), 43 I.L.M. (2003) 196.
[139] See n. 138 above.

THE IMPACT OF THE USA ON REGIME FORMATION   301

to limit the scope of the ATCA and to exercise restraint in adjudicating aliens' claims to the extent that they should enforce only those norms of international law which had been 'affirmatively incorporated into the laws of the United States' by Congress.[140] In view of the reluctance of the USA to incorporate norms of international environmental law, environmental torts could hardly ever be adjudicated if this stance were to be accepted by the federal courts. The US Supreme Court has recently restricted the scope of the ATCA to violations of international law norms with definite content and universal acceptance among civilised nations.[141] It has thus left the door open to a certain extent for US courts to adjudicate environmental torts but at the same time advised them to exercise great caution.

III. Current disputes between the USA and the EU: European protectionism or precautionary principle?

The USA and the EU have often been at odds over environmental issues, with the EU calling for the definition and implementation of multilateral standards and the USA stalling multilateral solutions and preferring unilateral ones. But the picture is not all black and white – as usual, some instances actually show a shade of grey, because from the US perspective, European environmental concerns appear to be a pretext concealing protectionist objectives. This impression has led to several disputes within the WTO system concerning European 'green' protectionism.[142]

1. Use of growth hormones in the production of US beef

The most important case in point concerns the ban by the EC on the importation of beef with traces of certain growth hormones used in the USA and Canada but prohibited in the EC. Although there was no scientific proof that the consumption of beef with hormone residues below the levels allowed by the *Codex Alimentarius* was detrimental to human health, the EC referred to the precautionary principle to justify the import ban. The Appellate Body found that the risk assessment by the EC was insufficient and therefore declared the ban incompatible with Article 5 of the SPS Agreement[143] which meant that the

---

[140] Amicus curiae brief submitted by the Department of Justice on 8 May 2003 to the US Court of Appeals for the Ninth Circuit (excerpts reprinted in *AJIL* 97 (2003), p. 703).
[141] *Sosa v. Alvarez-Machain*, Slip Opinion p. 38, 542 US _ (29 June 2004), available at www.supremecourtus.gov/opinions/opinions.html.
[142] Cf. the overview by Mavroidis, P. C., The trade disputes concerning health policy, in Petersmann, E.-U. and Pollack, M. A. (eds.), *Transatlantic economic disputes*, 2003, p. 233.
[143] Agreement on the Application of Sanitary and Phytosanitary Measures in Annex 1A to the 1994 WTO Agreement.

EC retained the chance to improve its risk assessment with further scientific studies.[144] As the EC failed to do so within the fifteen-month period, it was granted that the USA was authorised to impose counter-measures. The dispute has not yet been resolved.[145]

2. Use of genetically modified organisms in US agricultural and food products

A similar dispute is currently unfolding between the USA and the EC. It concerns the use of genetically modified organisms in food production, which is now common in the USA but technically banned in the EC because the latter has not considered any applications for approval of biotech products since 1998 in view of widespread popular objections. This approvals moratorium has restricted imports of US agricultural and food products. In addition, several EC Member States have maintained national marketing and import bans. Therefore, the USA requested the establishment of a WTO Panel on 'measures affecting the approval and marketing of biotech products' on 8 August 2003.[146] Even if the approval procedures are resumed, a further issue remains – the strict EC labelling rules for food products and animal feed which require the disclosure of any genetically-modified ingredients. This will compel the US agricultural industry to separate harvests of genetically-modified and natural products which it has not done so far, leading to a considerable increase in production costs and an ensuing loss of market shares, thus effectively restricting imports. In view of the negative attitude of many European consumers to novel food, it may also have a stigmatising effect.

The dispute over genetically-modified organisms provides a fine example of the different attitudes concerning technological advances on both sides of the Atlantic: while most Americans will emphasise their promise, most Europeans tend to concentrate on their dangers. Europeans will therefore generally demand a high level of precaution in the face of yet uncertain impacts of new technologies, whereas Americans will be more anxious not to stifle progress by overregulation.[147]

---

[144] *EC – Measures Concerning Meat and Meat Products (Hormones)* Report of the Appellate Body, 16 January 1998, WT/DS26/AB/R and WT/DS48/AB/R (www.worldtradelaw.net/reports/wtoab/ec-hormones(ab).pdf).

[145] Ford, R. A., The Beef Hormone dispute and carousel sanctions, *Brooklyn J. Int'l L.* 27 (2002), p. 543.

[146] WT/DS291/23. Lell, O., Die neue Kennzeichnungspflicht für gentechnisch hergestellte Lebensmittel – ein Verstoß gegen das Welthandelsrecht?, *EuZW* (2004), p. 108. See also Scott, J., European regulation of GMOs and the WTO, *Col. J. Eur. L.* 9 (2003), p. 213.

[147] Esty, D. C., Strengthening the international environmental regime, in Petersmann and Pollack, op. cit. pp. 371, 373.

IV. Conclusion: will the hegemon lead or be led the way?

The USA has been a driving force behind the protection of the international environment over the decades. More recently, other nations have overtaken it in their readiness to build effective international regimes to save the planet through law. This bears testimony to the growing perception that there is an international community with certain fundamental common values and interests, one being the protection of the environment. The unilateral pursuit of national interests by the USA outside or even in defiance of international regimes is not unique to environmental regimes, nor is it unique to the USA. But being the current economic and political hegemon, the USA's approach has much more serious factual consequences and a much greater impact on the international rule of law.[148] Instead of exercising leadership by example, the USA has increasingly assumed the role of a nay-sayer, and even a gravedigger, to concerted efforts of the international community. It has thereby seriously damaged its international credibility as a responsible and law-abiding nation.

In view of its powerful position in political, economic, and military terms, the rest of the world has no means of compelling the USA to participate in multilateral regimes, environmental or other, which its current political leaders consider as detrimental to the USA's national interests. Nor can the success of international efforts at environmental protection be secured by somehow passing over or actively excluding the USA. The international community's only chance consists in including the USA and convincing it (and this ultimately means the US public opinion representing the majority of the US voters) that the protection of the international environment (the global commons) is in its own (long-term) national interest and that effective protection can be guaranteed only on a multilateral basis. It must also be made clear that multilateralism does not mean the unconditional surrender of the USA to the rule of its anti-American foes, but a partnership of mutual trust among equals necessary to achieve a common goal – a partnership in which the *primus inter pares* position will quite easily fall to the USA as the foremost political and economic power.

As important segments of the US public and of Congress will be receptive to the notions of leadership by example, international credibility, the special responsibility of the world's largest polluter, international community, and the salvation of the planet from environmental nightmare, this 'soft approach' towards bringing the giant back on the multilateral course may after all prove successful. Intensifying the lobbying efforts by NGOs in Congress and attempts to influence US public opinion may help in this respect.[149] It would be particularly important to emphasise that international environmental regimes do

---

[148] Cf. Kwakwa, op. cit. p. 26.
[149] See Harris, P. G., International environmental affairs and US foreign policy, in Kwakwa, op. cit. pp. 3, 22.

not necessarily hurt the US economy but that they will create new markets for advanced environmental technology. It should also be stressed that the state of the world environment is affecting the national security of the USA in manifold ways, with environmental security gradually gaining in importance.[150]

The world outside the USA could contribute to the success of such a 'soft approach' by recognising that US proposals on environmental and other matters are not always selfish mechanisms of an incorrigibly imperialist nation eager to dominate and exploit others, but usually sincere attempts at reaching a compromise which could be safely steered through the isolationist and unilateralist shallows of the US Senate. These shallows are an important reason why the USA often prefers informal cooperative structures over legally binding international treaty regimes, let alone international organisations with an independent legal personality and implementation powers. Informal cooperation mechanisms remain within the foreign affairs power of the President and can still be quite effective. Sometimes they can be a first step towards a legal regime. If a well-functioning multilateral informal cooperation in environmental matters that includes the USA later needs to be upgraded to a multilateral legal regime so as to enhance its effectiveness, the USA will be more likely to join.

---

[150] Allenby, B., New priorities in US foreign policy, in Harris, op. cit. p. 45.; Barnett, J., Environmental security and US foreign policy, in Harris, op. cit. p. 68.; Brunnée, op. cit. p. 643 *et seq.*

12

Transnational bureaucracy networks: a resource of global environmental governance?
The case of chemical safety

MICHAEL WARNING

I. Introduction

Chemicals are ubiquitous. They are virtually used everywhere; pesticides and fertilisers help to increase agricultural production and biocides assist in the combat of transmittable diseases, to name just two of the most important uses of chemicals. The economic importance of chemicals becomes obvious if a few facts are considered. Approximately 8,100,000 substances are commercially available;[1] annually, the chemical industry manufactures goods worth US $1,600 billion;[2] in 2002, trade in chemicals accounted for 10.5 per cent of world merchandise trade.[3] But the ubiquitous use has a downside. The complex production processes and the unwanted harmful effects on the environment and human and animal health lead to a 'control problem'.[4]

Catastrophes such as the accidents in Seveso, Bhopal, and Schweizerhalle are rather drastic examples of the dangers arising from the production of chemicals.[5] The hazards of incremental pollution become clear in the case of the Minamata disease. Methyl mercury was discharged by a chemical plant

---

[1] Cf. Chemical Abstract Service's CHEMCATS (www.cas.org/cgi-bin/regreport.pl).
[2] OECD, Brochure: OECD's environmental health and safety programme, available at www.oecd.org/dataoecd/18/0/1900785.pdf, at 3.
[3] WTO, *International trade statistics 2003*, Table IV.35.
[4] Schneider, V., Transnationale Chemikalienkontrolle: Internationale Technikentwicklung in einer Kontroll-Lücke? in Albrecht, U. (ed.), *Technikkontrolle und Internationale Politik, Die internationale Steuerung von Technologietransfers und ihre Folgen*, Leviathan Sonderheft 10, Opladen (Westdeutscher Verlag) 1989, pp. 195–219, at 199.
[5] Cf. Nanda, V. P. and Bailey, B. C., Nature and scope of the problem, in Handel, G. and Lutz, R. E. (eds.), *Transferring hazardous technologies and substances: the international legal challenge*, London (Graham and Trotman) 1989, pp. 3–39 , at 3–11 and 17–19; Heil, K.-H., Die Auswirkungen des Sandoz Unfalls auf die Biozönose des Rheins, in Kinzelbach, R. and Friedrich, G. (eds.), *Biologie des Rheins*, Stuttgart (Fischer) 1990, pp. 11–26.

into Minamata Bay and accumulated in fish which later was consumed by fishermen and their families.[6] However, serious as such accidents and incremental pollution as results of the production processes certainly are, the bulk of environmental risks from chemicals is related to the placing on the market, the use, and the disposal of chemicals in the form of products.[7] Whilst risks from production processes widely are of local or regional concern, risks from products have created a truly global problem.[8] One example is the long-range transport of persistent organic pollutants (POPs). Many POPs, i.e. substances like DDT, Lindan (γ-HCH), or PCB, do not remain local but are transported across long distances through the atmosphere. They have even been found in the bodies of the indigenous Arctic population as a result of bio-accumulation in the food chain.[9] Another example are chlorofluorocarbons (CFCs). First considered a safe and cheap refrigerant because of their low toxicity and thermodynamic properties, their effects on the ozone layer became known only after large amounts had been released into the atmosphere.[10]

These examples illustrate the need for early and reliable information about the chemicals, sound risk assessment, and expedient risk management. For new substances, regulation in industrialised countries – the EU, the USA, and Japan in particular – requires more or less extensive tests for new substances.[11] Therefore, information about risks is available. But as far as existing substances are concerned, a rather huge knowledge gap (aptly labelled 'toxic ignorance') exists.[12] Legislation to gather information on existing substances

---

[6] National Institute for Minamata Disease (www.nimd.go.jp/archives/english/tenji/e_corner.html).

[7] Scheringer, M., *Persistenz und Reichweite von Umweltchemikalien*, Weinheim (Wiley-VCH) 1999, p. 2.

[8] Wissenschaftlicher Beirat der Bundesregierung Globale Umweltveränderungen (WBGU), *Welt im Wandel: Neue Strukturen globaler Umweltpolitik*, Berlin (Springer) 2001, p. 28.

[9] Kallenborn, R. and Herzke, D., Schadstoff-Ferntransport in die Arktis, *UWSF – Z Umweltchem Ökotox* 13 (2001), pp. 216–226, at 216; WBGU, *Welt im Wandel: Strategien zur Bewältigung globaler Umweltrisiken*, Berlin (Springer) 1998, p. 128.

[10] WBGU (2001), op. cit., pp. 28–31.

[11] EU: Council Directive 67/548/EEC, 27 June 1967, on the approximation of laws, regulations, and administrative provisions relating to the classification, packaging, and labelling of dangerous substances; USA: Toxic Substances Control Act (TSCA); Japan: Chemical Control Law (Law No. 117); these laws are extensively analysed by Johnson, L. A., Fujie, T., and Aalders, M., New chemical notification laws in Japan, the United States, and the European Union, in Kagan, R. A. and Axelrad, L. (eds.), *Regulatory encounters: multinational corporations and American adversarial legalism*, Berkeley (University of California Press) 2000, pp. 341–371.

[12] EC Joint Research Center, *Public availability of data*, Ispra (IRC) 1999; Environmental Defense Fund, *Toxic ignorance*, New York (EDF) 1997; EPA, *Chemical hazard data availability study*, 1998; cf. also White Paper, '*Strategy for a future chemicals policy*', COM(2001)88 final, p. 6.

has been introduced rather lately[13] and has proven to be widely ineffective.[14] Moreover, the very divergent national approaches of gathering information and assessing risks results in duplication of work and requires time-consuming compatibilisation.

Therefore, it becomes obvious that solving these problems is an international challenge and chemical safety is an international task.[15] But international conventions that address the problem have remained scarce.[16]

Instead, transnational networks of national governmental experts have stepped in. This chapter will explore to what extent these networks have been able to solve the problem, thereby showing that they can complement formal international law.[17] The informal law and management produced by these networks can be understood as an increasingly important element of the broader multilevel system of international, regional, and national formal and informal law and management.[18]

In the following, the transnational chemicals network will first be described and then analysed as a transnational informal institution. A normative reflection about the legitimacy of the phenomenon will conclude the chapter.

II. Description

1. Actors

Chemical safety is not entrusted to one particular and leading international organisation. Instead, a large number of international organisations,

---

[13] Council Regulation (EEC) 793/93, 23 March 1993, on the evaluation and control of the risks of existing substances.

[14] Cf. Spieker gen. Döhmann, I., US-amerikanisches Chemikalienrecht im Vergleich, in Rengeling, H.-W. (ed.), *Umgestaltung des deutschen Chemikalienrechts durch europäische Chemikalienpolitik*, Cologne (Heymanns) 2003, pp. 151–198, at 165–168; US General Accounting Office (GAO), Testimony before the subcommittee on toxic substances, research and development, Committee on environment and public works, US Senate, Toxic Substances Control Act: preliminary observations on legislative changes to make TSCA more effective, p. 6.

[15] Hildebrandt, B.-U. and Schlottmann, U., Chemikaliensicherheit – eine internationale Herausforderung, *Angew. Chemie* 110 (1998), pp. 1382–1393, at 1386; Alston, P., International regulation of toxic chemicals, *Ecology L. Q.* 7 (1978), pp. 397–456, at 398.

[16] A list of relevant treaties can be found at Warning, M. and Winter, G., Ansätze zu einer globalen Chemikalienregulierung, in Rengerling, H.-W. (ed.), *Umgestaltung des deutschen Chemikalienrechts durch europäische Chemikalienpolitik*, Cologne (Heymanns) 2003, pp. 241–274, at 263 and Pallemaerts, M., Toxics and transnational law: international and European regulation of toxic substances as legal symbolism, Oxford (Hart Publishing) 2003, pp. xxi–xxiii.

[17] Slaughter, A.-M., Government networks: the heart of the liberal democratic order, in Fox, G. H. and Roth, B. R., Democratic governance and international law, Cambridge (Cambridge University Press) 2000, pp. 199–235, at 203 and 220.

[18] See Warning and Winter, op. cit. p. 242.

associations of international organisations, and non-governmental organisations (NGOs) are concerned with chemical safety.

(a) International organisations

The International Labour Organization (ILO) has been engaged in chemical safety since its foundation in 1919, when it adopted recommendations on white phosphorous[19] and lead.[20] In 1921, a Convention on the use of lead in paint followed.[21] To date, the ILO has adopted further conventions and recommendations.[22]

The World Health Organization (WHO) has been concerned with the effects of hazardous substances (particularly pesticides) since the 1950s. It has a long history of cooperation with the Food and Agriculture Organization (FAO) and the ILO.[23]

The United Nations Environmental Programme (UNEP) was founded by a Resolution of the United Nations General Assembly in 1972.[24] As a result of Recommendation 74(e) of the Action Plan for the Human Environment adopted in 1972 by the United Nations Conference on the Human Environment (UNCHE), the International Register of Potentially Toxic Substances (IRPTC) was installed at the UNEP.[25]

Other organisations have a more specialised approach to chemical safety. The FAO focuses on pesticides. The United Nations Industrial Development Organization (UNIDO) and the United Nations Institute for Training and Research (UNITAR) engage in capacity-building. The United Nations Economic Commission for Europe (UNECE), the International Maritime Organization (IMO), the International Civil Aviation Organization (ICAO), and the

---

[19] White Phosphorus Recommendation, 1919 (no. 6).
[20] Lead Poisoning (Women and Children) Recommendation, 1919 (no. 4).
[21] White Lead (Painting) Convention, 1921 (no. 13).
[22] Convention concerning Safety in the Use of Chemicals at Work (C170), 1990; Recommendation concerning Safety in the Use of Chemicals at Work (R177), 1990; Convention concerning Safety in the Use of Asbestos (C162), 1986; Convention concerning Protection against Hazards of Poisoning arising from Benzene (C136), 1971; Recommendation concerning Protection against Hazards of Poisoning arising from Benzene (R144), 1971.
[23] Schneider, V., *Politiknetzwerke der Chemikalienkontrolle: eine Analyse einer transnationalen Politikentwicklung*, Berlin (de Gruyter) 1988, pp. 97 and 189; Mercier, M., Present and planned activities of the International Programme on Chemical Safety (IPCS) on existing chemicals, in Umweltbundesamt (UBA) (ed.), *Proceedings of the workshop on the control of existing chemicals under the patronage of the Organisation for Economic Co-operation and Development*, Berlin (UBA) 1981, pp. 39–44, at 39.
[24] UNGA Res. 2997 (XXVII), 15 December 1972.
[25] Further information on IRPTC: Wagner, B., Das neue Chemikalienprogramm von UNEP Chemicals, *UWSF– Z Umweltchem Ökotox* 10 (1998), pp. 245–253, at 245; Huismans, J. W., The international register of potentially toxic chemicals (IRPTC), *Ecotoxicology and Environmental Safety* 4 (1980), pp. 393–403; see Alston, op. cit. p. 418 *et seq*.

Intergovernmental Organisation for International Carriage by Rail (OTIF) are concerned with the transport of hazardous substances.

The Organisation for Economic Cooperation and Development (OECD) maintains a programme on chemical safety (Environment Health and Safety Programme) since 1971.[26] It is considered to be an actor in covering both economic and environmental aspects.[27]

(b) Interorganisational agreements

Some of these international organisations have agreed to set up the International Programme on Chemical Safety (IPCS), the International Forum on Chemical Safety (IFCS), and the Inter-Organization Programme for the Sound Management of Chemicals (IOMC).

IPCS was established in 1980 by the WHO, ILO, and UNEP in order to bundle and coordinate their efforts in the field of chemical safety.[28] Thirty-six countries participate in IPCS.[29] IPCS is based on a Memorandum of Understanding between the cooperating organisations. It has two tasks: establishing the scientific health and environmental risk assessment basis for safe use of chemicals (normative function) and strengthening national capabilities for chemical safety (technical cooperation). IPCS is regarded as the nucleus of international cooperation by Agenda 21, Chapter 19, section 6.

The organisational structure of IPCS is composed of the Central Unit (CU), the Intersecretariat Coordinating Committee (ICC), the Programme Advisory Committee (PAC), Task Groups, and Working Groups. The WHO Programme for the Promotion of Chemical Safety (PCS) acts as the CU and is responsible for the management and coherence of the IPCS. Scientific or technical activities are either undertaken by PCS or the relevant units of the cooperating organisations. The ICC is chaired by the manager of the CU, the cooperating organisations delegate representatives. It decides on activities of IPCS and provides guidance for the Director of IPCS on the budget. The PAC is an advisory body and consists of no more than twenty experts. Working Groups and Task Groups are convened by the Director of IPCS and function as an informal advisory mechanism. National Focal Points in the participating countries are supposed to disseminate information from IPCS in the country and relay the country's views to IPCS. Participating institutions (PIs) are governmental or non-governmental institutions outside IPCS that participate in and conduct IPCS activities.[30]

---

[26] See OECD, op. cit. p. 13; the Council addressed the issue for the first time with Recommendation of the Council of the determination of the biodegradability of anionic synthetic surface active agents, C(71)83/Final, 13 July 1971.
[27] See Hildebrandt and Schlottmann, op. cit. p. 1390.
[28] See Schneider, op. cit. p. 98; see Mercier, op. cit. p. 39.
[29] See Hildebrandt and Schlottmann, op. cit. p. 1389.
[30] IPCS, Redesigning IPCS, 2003; About IPCS, available at www.who.int/ipcs/about_ipcs/en; Redesigning IPCS, available at www.who. int/ipcs/about_ipcs/redesign/en

The IFCS was initiated as a response to Chapter 19, section 76 of Agenda 21, where reference is made to a meeting of government experts in London in 1991.[31] The WHO, ILO, and UNEP initiated the International Conference on Chemical Safety (ICCS) which was finally held in Stockholm in 1994.[32] The ICCS was attended by representatives from 114 countries, United Nations bodies, specialised agencies from the United Nations, other intergovernmental and non-governmental organisations, and adopted a resolution on the establishment of an IFCS and its Terms of Reference (ToR).[33]

The IFCS is a worldwide conference convened about every four years with the purpose to develop strategies and priorities for the implementation of Agenda 21, Chapter 19 and promote coordination and collaboration among the actors (s. 1. ToR). Participation is open to 'governmental participants',[34] 'intergovernmental participants',[35] and 'non-governmental participants'.[36] Only the govermental participants have the right to vote. Forum sessions – which take place biennially or triennially[37] – are managed by certain organs, including a President and five Vice-Presidents elected at each session as well as the Forum Standing Committee (s. 6 ToR, Annexes 2 and 3). The Forum or the Forum Standing Committee may establish ad hoc Working Groups for specific tasks (s. 8 ToR). Working Groups are made up of government representatives; however, they may be open to other participants, who do not have the right to vote. National Focal Points have to be established in each country. The WHO provides a Secretariat.

The IOMC was established by the UNEP, WHO, ILO, FAO, UNIDO, and OECD in 1995 in order to coordinate their activities to implement Agenda 21,

---

[31] The London meeting was held to discuss the enhancement of international cooperation on chemical safety and recommended among other things the establishment of an intergovernmental forum on chemical risk assessment and management. Cf. Carpenter, C. and Krueger, J., A brief history of IFCS, *Earth Negotiations Bulletin*, 15(1) (1997), available at www.iisd.ca/linkages/ chemical/ifcs/enb1501e.pdf, p. 2.

[32] See Carpenter and Krueger, op. cit. p. 2.

[33] Resolution on the Establishment of an Intergovernmental Forum on Chemical Safety, IPCS/ IFCS/ 94.Res.1, Stockholm, 29 April 1994; changed and amended on Forum III, third session of the Intergovernmental Forum on Chemical Safety, Final Report, IFCS/ Forum III/ 23w.

[34] Member States of the United Nations, its specialised agencies, and the International Atomic Energy Agency (IAEA), and the associate members of these organisations.

[35] Relevant UN bodies and specialised agencies and subregional or regional, political, and economic groups of countries that are concerned with chemical safety – organisations such as the European Community (EC) or the Organization for Economic Co-operation and Development (OECD).

[36] International non-governmental organisations concerned with science, health, workers' interests, the environment, consumers, and industry, involved in the field of chemical safety.

[37] IFCS I: 1994 Stockholm; IFCS II: 1997 Ottawa; IFCS III: 2000 Salvador da Bahía; IFCS IV: 2003 Bangkok; IFCS V: 2005 or 2006 Hungary.

Chapter 19.[38] UNITAR joined the IOMC in 1997.[39] The IOMC is based on a Memorandum of Understanding (MoU).[40] According to the MoU, it has the task to coordinate the common or individual policies and activities of the participating organisations (s. 2.2 MoU). The activities match the six programme areas of Agenda 21, Chapter 19, but are not limited to them (s. 3 MoU).

The IOMC has two organs: the Inter-Organization Coordinating Committee (IOCC) and a Secretariat. The IOCC is composed of one representative from each of the seven participating organisations. It adopts its own rules of procedure and elects a Chairperson and if necessary a Vice-Chairperson. The IOCC may invite observers, set up advisory bodies (s. 3 MoU) and meets at least twice a year (s. 4 MoU). The functions of the IOCC are mainly to enable the participating organisations to coordinate and to align their individual activities, to prevent overlapping work, and to promote joint programmes (s. 5 MoU).

A Secretariat is set up to provide the IOCC with organisational services (s. 7 MoU). It is located at the WHO which serves as the administering organisation.

Technical Coordinating Groups (TCG) have been set up on the technical level.[41] These groups aim at enabling consultation between the participating organisations. The IOCC has issued Standard Operating Procedures (SOP) for the TCGs. According to the SOP, depending on the agreement of the IOCC, the groups may invite representatives from intergovernmental organisations, governments, and international industry, labour, and public interest non-governmental organisations (NGOs), if they are active in the relevant area. The TCG on the Assessment of Existing Industrial Chemicals and Pollutants serves a special purpose, as it helps to coordinate the IPCS and OECD programmes in this area and thus contributes to the prevention of duplication of work, though this may never be completely avoided.[42]

(c) Private actors

In particular, the IFCS is open to non-governmental actors. International associations of trade unions such as the International Union of Food, Agricultural, Hotel, Restaurant, Catering, Tobacco and Allied Workers' Associations (IUF) and the International Federation of Chemical, Energy, Mine and General Workers' Unions (ICEM), environmental interest groups such as the Pesticide Action Network (PAN) and Greenpeace International, and scientific factions such as

---

[38] See Hildebrandt and Schlottmann, op. cit. p. 1387.
[39] The World Bank and the United Nations Development Programme (UNDP) may join in the near future: IOMC/IOCC, Summary Record of the Eighteenth Meeting, IOMC/IOCC/03.44.
[40] Memorandum of Understanding concerning Establishment of the Inter-Organization Programme for the Sound Management of Chemicals.
[41] IOMC, Technical coordinating groups (www.who.int/iomc/groups/en/).
[42] See IPCS, op. cit. p. 12 s. 50.

the International Union for Pure and Applied Chemistry (IUPAC), participate in the IFCS.

The International Council of Chemical Associations (ICCA) was founded in 1989 and is of great importance as it represents twelve regional and national chemical associations and therefore the chemical manufacturers worldwide. The main purpose of the ICCA is to enable the chemical industry to coordinate its efforts in chemical safety ('responsible care'), to discuss policies, and to present a single view to international governmental organisations such as the WTO, OECD, or UNEP, and international private organisations such as the International Standards Organization (ISO).[43]

The ICCA has set up working groups that are composed of experts from the member organisations. The Working Groups perform and coordinate research in specific areas.[44]

2. Activities

The organisations listed above unfold a broad range of activities in the field of chemical safety that often extend to the national level and involve the specialised bureaucracy on the national level.

The activities can be divided into three groups: agenda-setting, collection of information and risk assessment, and the preparation of risk management.

(a) Agenda-setting

Agenda-setting means identifying and discussing problems and setting goals to solve these problems. It is the major function of the IFCS. The first ICCS/IFCS identified 'priorities for action' for each of the six programme areas of Chapter 19 of Agenda 21.[45] Some of the priorities for action are formulated in very general terms (e.g. Programme Area A, no. 4: 'Industry should be encouraged to generate and supply data required for risk assessment to the greatest possible extent'), others are rather detailed and almost authoritative (e.g. Programme Area A, no. 6, 7: '200 additional chemicals should be evaluated by 1997'... 'If the target in item 7 is met, another 300 chemicals should be evaluated by 2000').

The second IFCS made a number of recommendations for the implementation of the programme areas in Chapter 19 and monitored the status of the priorities for action identified by the ICCS/IFCS I.[46]

The Bahía Declaration on Chemical Safety and priorities for action beyond 2000 were the result of the third IFCS.[47] The Declaration reaffirms the participants' commitment to Agenda 21, Chapter 19. Article III specifies six priorities

---

[43] ICCA, *A global voice for the chemical industry* (ICCA) 2002, p. 1.
[44] Ibid., p. 2.   [45] ICCS/IFCS I: Final Report, IPCS/ICCS/94.8, p. 14.
[46] IFCS II: Final Report, IFCS/FORUM II/97.25w, p. 5; Annexes 15 and 16.
[47] IFCS: Final Report, IFCS/ Forum III/23w, Bahía Declaration and Annex 6.

that are set for review at Forum IV, Forum V, and beyond. Article V lists rather authoritatively the key goals of the priorities for action beyond 2000 (e.g. 'By 2001: the Convention on Persistent Organic Pollutants will have been adopted', 'By Forum IV in 2003: the Rotterdam Convention will have entered into force'). The priorities for action beyond 2000 refer to the Programme Areas of Agenda 21, Chapter 19 in a similar manner as the priorities for action identified by ICCS/IFCS I did. Again, clear deadlines for activities are given while the activities are clearly defined (e.g. 'through the industry initiative an additional 1,000 chemicals hazard assessments will be provided by 2004'). The Bahía Declaration and Priorities for Action gain more weight as they have been endorsed by the UNEP Governing Council and considered to be the foundation of a Strategic Approach to International Chemicals Management (SAICM).[48]

SAICM became the main issue of Forum IV. A 'thought starter' identifies obstacles, gaps, and omissions in the Bahía Declaration and priorities for action beyond 2000 and indicates potential actions.[49]

(b) Information-gathering and risk assessment

Activities concerning the collection of risk information and the assessment of risks have mainly been undertaken by the OECD and IPCS networks. They include:

- the drafting of Principles of Good Laboratory Practice (GLP) and Test Guidelines;
- the elaboration of Screening Information Data Sets (SIDS);
- the various activities of the IPCS;
- the establishment of a Globally Harmonized System for Hazard Classification and Labelling of Chemicals (GHS).

(i) Principles of GLP and Test Guidelines Since the late 1970s, Principles of GLP and Test Guidelines have been a preoccupation of the OECD. OECD Council Decision C(81)30[50] stipulated the principle of mutual acceptance of data (MAD): data which has been generated in accordance with the Test Guidelines and under observation of the Principles of GLP in one member state have to be accepted by other member states.

Test Guidelines have been adopted for tests concerning physical-chemical properties, effects on biotic systems, degradation and accumulation, and health

---

[48] Decision adopted by the Governing Council at its Seventh Special Session/ Global Ministerial Environment Forum, SS.VII/3, 15 February 2002.
[49] Forum IV Thought Starter Report to SAICM PrepCom1, IFCS/ FORUM IV/13w Rev 2, 9–13 November 2003.
[50] OECD Council Decision concerning the Mutual Acceptance of Data in the Assessment of Chemicals, C(81)30/FINAL.

effects.[51] They are complemented by the Principles of GLP.[52] The Principles cover the organisational aspects of testing (e.g. organisation of the facility and its personnel; the apparatus, material, and reagents used for testing).

The OECD's Test Guidelines and GLP principles are referred to by EC legislation and in this way become binding law.[53] The international importance of the Test Guidelines and Principles of GLP can be partially attributed to MAD. MAD enables the international comparability and exchange of data, thereby helping to avoid the duplication of tests. The benefits are a reduction of animal testing and expenses for tests.

(ii) SIDS The OECD's SIDS programme attempts to close the knowledge gap by way of collecting and if necessary generating data.

According to OECD Council Decision-Recommendation C(90)163/Final,[54] the OECD's member countries cooperate to investigate HPV chemicals. The aim is to compile data for SIDS dossiers either by gathering existing data or generating new data through tests, evaluate the data, conduct an initial hazard assessment, prepare a SIDS Initial Assessment Report (SIAR) and a SIDS Profile, and if necessary undertake so-called 'post-SIDS' work.

The investigation begins with the selection of a chemical from the HPV list[55] by a so-called sponsor country.[56] Its obligation is to collect the data and prepare the SIAR. The SIAR summarises the substance's identity and its physical-chemical properties, general information on exposure, human health hazards and initial assessment for human health, hazards to the environment and initial assessment for the environment, and conclusions and recommendations.[57] Only two recommendations are possible: either 'the chemical is currently of low priority for further work' or 'the chemical is a candidate for further work'.[58]

The SIAR is discussed at a Screening Initial Assessment Meeting (SIAM). The SIAM is attended by representatives from the sponsor countries, other member countries, and the EC, experts from non-member countries nominated by IPCS

---

[51] OECD Guidelines for the Testing of Chemicals, Overview of currently available test guidelines, Version 20 October 2003.

[52] See OECD, op. cit. p. 19. See n. 2 above.

[53] Cf. Introduction to Annex V to Directive 67/548/EEC on the classification, packaging, and labelling of dangerous substances; Article 1(1) of Council Directive 87/18/EEC, 18 December 1986, on the harmonisation of laws, regulations, and administrative provisions relating to the application of the principles of good laboratory practice and the verification of their applications for tests on chemical substances.

[54] Decision-Recommendation of the Council on the cooperative investigation and risk reduction of existing chemicals, C(90)163.

[55] OECD Environment Directorate, *The 2000 OECD list of high production volume chemicals*, Paris (OECD) 2001.

[56] OECD Secretariat, *Manual for investigation of HPV chemicals*, Paris (OECD), 2003, ch. 1, 5.3; list of sponsored chemicals and sponsor countries is available at http://cs3-hq.oecd.org/scripts/hpv/index.asp

[57] See ibid., ch. 5, s. 5.2.1.   [58] See ibid., ch. 5, s. 5.3.2.

and/or IFCS, the BIAC, the TUAC, and NGOs, representatives from companies which produce the substance that has been screened, and Secretarial staff from the OECD, IPCS, and UNEP Chemicals. The participants have to reach a consensual agreement on the assessment of the chemical.[59] The outcome of the SIAM is a SIDS profile which summarises the SIAR and contains the recommendations and conclusions of the SIAM.[60]

The sponsor country finalises the SIAR in consideration of the comments made at the SIAM and submits it along with the SIDS dossier to the OECD Secretariat.[61] The SIDS dossier and SIAR are made publicly available through UNEP Chemicals.[62]

The ICCA HPV Chemicals Initiative is a separate programme; however, it is interlinked with the OECD SIDS Programme. The HPV Chemicals Initiative was initiated in 1998 by the ICCA Board of Directors and calls upon companies to prepare SIDS, SIAR, and SIDS profiles for HPV chemicals.[63] For this purpose, the ICCA has taken the OECD List of High Production Volume Chemicals as a basis for a Working List of currently 1,325 chemicals whose investigation is considered to deserve priority treatment.[64] To facilitate the work, companies form consortia and share the costs of the investigation.[65] The documents prepared in the HPV Initiative are brought forward into the OECD SIDS Programme via a sponsor country and is the subject of a SIAM.[66]

(iii) **Activities undertaken by the IPCS** The IPCS maintains a number of activities to collect and evaluate data on chemicals. The outcomes of these activities are the product of a close cooperation between the competent authorities of those countries involved in the IPCS and internationally accepted experts and usually are the subject of peer reviews.[67] The content of the respective document is determined by an intended target group and its purpose.

---

[59] See ibid., Description of OECD work on investigation of high production volume chemicals.
[60] See ibid., ch. 5, s. 5.1 and Figure 5.1.
[61] See ibid., Description of OECD work on investigation of high production volume chemicals.
[62] SIDS for around 180 substances are available at www.chem.unep.ch/irptc /sids/oecdsids/sidspub.html
[63] ICCA, What is the ICCA HPV chemicals initiative? available at www.cefic.org /activities/hse/mgt/hpv/hpvinit.htm
[64] Latest list (August 2003) available at www.cefic.org/activities/hse/mgt/hpv/ICCA%20Working%20List%20-%20August%202003.xls
[65] List of consortia available at www.hpvchallenge.com/reports/ReportsMain.cfm; 2,904 chemicals in programme, 1,600 commitments, www.hpvchallenge.com/reports/hpv_stats.cfm.
[66] See OECD Secretariat, op. cit., Description of OECD work on investigation of high production volume chemicals; 120 substances have thus far been assessed by SIAM, cf. ICCA, Progress, at www.cefic.org/activities /hse/mgt/hpv/progress.htm
[67] See Hildebrandt and Schlottmann, op. cit. p. 1389.

Environmental health criteria (EHC) monographs are prepared for scientists and administrators who are engaged in the establishment of safety standards and regulations. The information summarised in EHCs is drawn from scientific sources and focuses on the physical-chemical properties of a substance, sources of exposure, and the effects on animals (carcinogenicity, mutagenicity, and teratogenicity). EHCs also include a risk evaluation for human health and the environment.

Concise international chemical assessment documents (CICAD) briefly sum up the relevant information on a substance drawn from evaluation documents or EHCs. CICADs provide hazard information, dose-response relationship, and a risk characterisation.

International chemical safety cards (ICSC) are prepared cooperatively by the IPCS and the EC. Their purpose is to provide workers on the 'shop floor level' with critical information about health and safety issues concerning a specific substance. They exclude exposition data.

Poison information monographs (PIM) summarise the physical-chemical and toxicological properties, medical features caused by various ways of exposure, patient management, and laboratory investigation. In this regard, they constitute the international consensus on the diagnosis, management, and prevention of poisonings.[68]

(iv) Globally Harmonized System for Hazard Classification and Labelling of Chemicals (GHS) Regulation on the classification and labelling of chemicals – i.e. the assignment of a hazard category like toxic or corrosive to a substance and the communication of the classification – belongs to the cornerstones of chemical safety legislation. The multitude of divergent national classification and labelling has proved to be cost inefficient as well as ineffective regarding the protection of workers and consumers. For example, one system may classify a substance as 'very toxic' if LD_{50} is less than 25mg/kg if administered orally, while another system will consider it 'very toxic' if LD_{50} is less than 50mg/kg.

As a first step, the Coordination Group for the Harmonization of Chemical Classification Systems (CG/HCCS) was established by ILO, WHO, UNEP, the United Nations Committee of Experts on the Transport of Dangerous Goods (UNCETDG), and OECD. It was endorsed in 1992 by the IPCS and operated since 1995 under the umbrella of the IOMC.[69] Apart from the organisations participating in the IOMC, the CG/HCCS was joined by representatives from

---

[68] See ibid., p. 1389; Gärtner, S., Küllmer, J., and Schlottmann, U., Chemikaliensicherheit in einer verletzlichen Welt, *Angew. Chem* 115 (2003), pp. 4594–4607, at 4604; all mentioned documents are available at www.inchem.org

[69] ILO, Background, available at www.ilo.org/public/english/protection/safework/ghs/back.htm; examples for international systems are the UN Recommendations on the Transport of Dangerous Goods (UNRTDG) and the WHO recommended classification of pesticides by hazard.

several countries, IMO, ICAO, the EC Commission, and several NGOs (e.g. WWF, ICEM); ILO provided the Secretariat.[70]

The CG/HCCS devised ten general principles to guide the development of the globally harmonised system of classification and labelling of chemicals (GHS) and define its scope and purpose.[71] One principle stated that harmonisation must not lead to a lower level of protection for human health and the environment.

The document agreed on after long and comprehensive deliberations – the actual GHS – includes two elements: harmonised criteria for classifying substances and mixtures according to their health, environmental, and physical hazards and harmonised hazard communication elements, including elements for labelling and safety data sheets.[72]

The GHS is supported by an organisational structure that is supposed to guarantee the further development of the GHS and support its worldwide implementation. UN ECOSOC reconfigured UNCETDG in 1996 in order to create such a structure.[73] The UN Committee of Experts on the Transport of Dangerous Goods and on the Globally Harmonized System of Classification and Labelling of Chemicals (UNCETDG/GHS) operates on the strategic level and coordinates the activities, while its Subcommittee of Experts on the Transport of Dangerous Goods (UNSCETDG) and Subcommittee of Experts on the Globally Harmonized System of Classification and Labelling of Chemicals (UNSCEGHS) are responsible for the technical level. UNSCEGHS has the task to implement, maintain, and if necessary update the GHS.[74] Delegates from various countries, international organisations (WHO, ILO, IMO, OECD), and NGOs (e.g. ICCA) participate in UNSCEGHS.

The GHS was adopted by UNSCEGHS in December 2002; this decision was endorsed by UNCETDG/GHS in February 2003.[75] ECOSOC requested the UN Secretary-General to publish and disseminate the GHS.[76]

---

[70] ILO, Participation in the IOMC CG/HCCS, available at www.ilo.org/public/english/protection/safework/ghs/particip.htm

[71] Pfeil, N., Gerner, I., and Vormann, K., Stand und Auswirkungen der globalen Harmonisierung der Einstufung und Kennzeichnung gefährlicher Stoffe und Güter, *Chemie Ingenieur Technik* 72 (2000), pp. 305–312, at 306; United Nations, *Globally harmonized system of classification and labelling of chemicals* (GHS), New York and Geneva (United Nations) 2003, ch. 1, s. 1.1.1.6.

[72] See ibid., ch. 1, s. 1.1.2.1.

[73] UN ECOSOC Res. 1999/65, Reconfiguration of the committee of experts on the transport of dangerous goods into a committee of experts on the transport of dangerous goods and on the globally harmonized system of classification and labelling of chemicals.

[74] See GHS, ch. 1, s. 1.1.3.2.1.

[75] UNCETDG/GHS, *Report of the committee of experts on its first session*, ST/SG/AC.10/29, 11–12 December 2002.

[76] UN ECOSOC Res. 2003/64, Work of the committee of experts on the transport of dangerous goods and on the globally harmonized system of classification and labelling of chemicals.

(c) Risk management

Measures aiming at the reduction of risks arising from the exposure to the hazards of chemicals (risk management) are almost exclusively regulated by international treaties.

A number of international treaties or Annexes to international treaties govern the transport of dangerous goods. The European Agreement Concerning the International Carriage of Dangerous Goods by Road (ADR), the European Agreement Concerning the International Carriage of Dangerous Goods by Inland Waterways (ADN), and the Regulations Concerning the International Carriage of Dangerous Goods by Rail (RID)[77] contain provisions concerning the nature of substances that may be transported and the appropriate safety measures. They have their basis in the UN Recommendations on the Transport of Dangerous Goods (UNRTDG) and are therefore closely harmonised.[78] The transport of dangerous goods by sea is covered by the International Maritime Dangerous Goods (IMDG) Code, the ICAO maintains the Instructions on the Safe Transport of Dangerous Substances by Air (TI) which are similar provisions for transport by air.

Another group of treaties governs the international trade in hazardous substances. The scope of the Basel Convention on the Control of Transboundary Movements of Hazardous Wastes and their Disposal, which entered into force in 1992, is limited to wastes. However, this includes waste from the manufacture of chemicals or waste that contains specific hazardous chemicals. The Basel Convention distinguishes three categories of waste and requires a Prior Informed Consent (PIC) procedure for specific wastes; PIC means that prior to the export, the consent of the designated national authority of the import country is required.

The Rotterdam Convention on the Prior Informed Consent Procedure for Certain Hazardous Chemicals and Pesticides in International Trade entered into force in February 2004. The Rotterdam Convention emanated from the London Guidelines for the Exchange of Information on Chemicals in International Trade and the International Code of Conduct on the Distribution and Use of Pesticides.[79] The London Guidelines were adopted by the UNEP Governing Council in 1987;[80] the Code of Conduct was adopted by the FAO Conference in

---

[77] Attachment I to Annex B (Articles 4 and 5) Uniform rules concerning the contract for international carriage of goods by rail (CIM) of the Convention concerning International Carriage by Rail (COTIF).

[78] Jones, W. F. and Yeater, M. D., Hazardous substances, in Sand, P. (ed.) *The effectiveness of international environmental agreements: a survey of existing legal instruments*, Cambridge (Cambridge University Press) 1992, pp. 309–338, at 314.

[79] For an exhaustive analysis of the development, see Pallemaerts, op. cit. pp. 511–594.

[80] UNEP Decision 14/27, Environmentally safe management of chemicals, in particular those that are banned and severely restricted in international trade.

1985.[81] Both are legally non-binding instruments that a large number of countries voluntarily adhere to.[82] The necessity for a PIC procedure for chemicals and pesticides arises from the fact that developed countries export substances that are restricted or banned in their countries of origin to less developed countries that often lack the capacities properly to assess the hazards and risks their use implicates.[83] The voluntary PIC procedure, therefore, was a step to address this problem. However, the voluntary PIC procedure brings about a number of problems. First and foremost, compliance is not effectively guaranteed, an enforcement mechanism does not exist.[84] Therefore, Agenda 21 formulated in Programme Area C of its Chapter 19 the objective to develop a legally binding PIC mechanism. The Rotterdam Convention attempts to mend the flaws of the voluntary PIC procedure and requires PIC for certain chemicals and pesticides listed in its Annex III.

The third group of treaties imposes bans and restrictions on the use, marketing, and sometimes even manufacture of certain chemicals. The Stockholm Convention on Persistent Organic Pollutants was adopted in 2001 and entered into force in May 2004. As noted above, POPs pose a global problem. Thus, the Stockholm Convention calls upon its signatories to eliminate or restrict the intentional or unintentional production and use of twelve POPs (Articles 3 *et seq.* and Annexes A–C). Furthermore, it makes provision for technical assistance to ensure the implementation of the Convention in developing countries (Article 12). The Stockholm Convention is designed as a framework convention with an opting-out mechanism in Article 25(4). Annexes A–C list the substances that are to be restricted or eliminated and may be amended in accordance with Article 8 and Annex D. Countries may abstain from the ratification of amendments.[85]

Within the framework of the Vienna Convention for the Protection of the Ozone Layer from 1985, the Montreal Protocol on Substances that Deplete the Ozone Layer obliges the parties to reduce the production or consumption of

---

[81] FAO Conference 10/85, International Code of Conduct on the distribution and use of pesticides.

[82] The implementation and compliance is detailed in Mekouar, M. A., Pesticides and chemicals: the requirement of prior informed consent, in Shelton, D. (ed.), Commitment and compliance: the role of non-binding norms in the international legal system, Oxford (Oxford University Press) 2000, pp. 146–163, at 156 and See Pallemaerts, op. cit. p. 549.

[83] Ross, J., Legally binding prior informed consent, *Colorado J. Int'l Law and Policy* 10 (1999), pp. 499–529, at 501.

[84] See Ross, op. cit. p. 515.

[85] Comments on the Stockholm Convention at Lallas, P. L., The Stockholm Convention on persistent organic pollutants, *Am. J. Int'l L.* 95 (2001), pp. 692–708, at 695–708; Chen, C. S., Persistent organic pollutants: regime formation and norm selection, *Connecticut J. of Int'l L.* 13 (1998), pp. 119–148.

certain substances. The ultimate goal is the cessation of the consumption of these substances.[86]

The International Convention on the Control of Harmful Anti-fouling Systems on Ships was prepared by the IMO and adopted in 2001. It prohibits the use of paints that contain organtins on certain ships. These paints are being used to prevent algae or molluscs growing on the hull, their components (e.g. Tributyltin/TBT) are persistent and may cause harm to marine life (deformation, sex changes due to endocrine effects). Ultimately, they may enter the food chain and affect human health.[87]

III. Analysis

In the following section, the phenomenon of informal rule-making and networking described above will be analysed with a view to understanding its rationale and putting it into context with other forms of governance.

1. The structure of networks and their rule-making

In the field of chemical safety, the instrument of an international treaty has mostly been chosen for risk management measures such as the regulation of the transportation of dangerous goods, transboundary trade in goods, and restrictions on manufacture, marketing, and use, but not for the harmonisation and acceleration of information-gathering and risk assessment.

Treaties restricting the manufacture, marketing, or use of a substance are the most difficult to achieve because they have the greatest economic and environmental impact. They struggle with tensions between national sovereignty and the responsibility of each state and the international community to protect the global environment in an environment which is already loaded with conflicting interests of environmental protection and economic development.[88] Lawmaking techniques which have been developed to cope with such difficulties are to go from framework conventions to more detailed Protocols, and to empower international bodies to make binding 'secondary' law without requiring ratification or accession but only reserving to the contracting parties the right to

---

[86] The Vienna Convention and the Montreal Protocol are briefly described and assessed at Birnie, P. and Boyle, A., *International law and the environment*, Oxford (Oxford University Press) 2nd edn. 2002, pp. 517–523.

[87] Further information available at IMO, Anti-fouling systems, www.imo.org /Environment/mainframe.asp?topic_id = 223

[88] See Pallemaerts, op. cit. p. 712.

opt out.[89] Both techniques have been employed, e.g. in the Stockholm POP Convention.[90]

However, although framework conventions and the opting-out mechanism are innovative ways to ensure the conclusion and implementation of a treaty, 'positive integration' in the sense of proactive harmonisation of national product-related risk management is still sparse.[91] One reason, certainly, is that, in order effectively to manage a risk, the risk has to be known, which is not the case. Another reason may be that states protect their chemical industry and are generally defending their sovereign rights.

Therefore, the relevant actors in the field have committed themselves to create informal or soft law. In particular, intergovernmental organisations (IGOs) conclude agreements with other IGOs or states to coordinate activities and/or stipulate cooperation. This is the case with the Memoranda of Understanding that form the basis of the IPCS and the IOMC.[92] Especially in the case of the formation of the IOMC, the MoU well served its purpose to coordinate relations between the participating organisations as overlapping activities were indeed reduced and resources pooled.

Agreements between IGOs are complemented by rules that govern the internal organisation of the network formed on their basis. This is the case with the IFCS ToR and the IOMC MoU. Those rules determine the purpose of the relevant institution, lay down process regulations, and set an institutional framework (e.g. establishment of Secretariats).

A third kind of soft law sets the agenda and establishes the basic goals and assumptions of the policy field. Chapter 19 of Agenda 21 has played this role very effectively. It was repeatedly referred to by the various actors when initiating or stabilising their activities, for instance in the setting up of IPCS, the formation

---

[89] Sommer, J., Environmental law-making by international organisations, *Zeitschrift für ausländisches öffentliches Recht und Völkerrecht* 56 (1996), pp. 628–667, at 644.

[90] For a description of the opting-out mechanism of the Stockholm Convention, See Lallas, op. cit. p. 708.

[91] Godt, C., The need for and unavailability of international 'positive integration', in Winter, G. (ed.), *Risk assessment and risk management of toxic chemicals in the European Community, experiences and reform*, Baden-Baden (Nomos) 2000, pp. 236–261, at 256.

[92] Generally, the law regulating the internal organisational affairs of an IGO (the primary law, i.e. the founding treaty, and secondary law, rules derived from the treaty, the principle of implied powers, or its organisational power (*Organisationsgewalt*)) is part of international law, cf. Seidl-Hohenveldern, I. and Loibl, G., *Das Recht der internationalen Organisationen einschließlich der supranationalen Gemeinschaften*, Cologne (Heymanns) 7th edn. 2000, pp. 219 and 226–229; however, Memoranda of Understanding are rather politically than legally binding and thus can be counted as 'soft' law, cf. Wolfrum, R. and Matz, N., *Conflicts in international environmental law*, Berlin (Springer) 2003, pp. 164 (n. 354), 173 *et seq.*

of the IFCS,[93] the creation of the GHS,[94] and the elaboration of the Conventions of Rotterdam[95] and Stockholm.[96]

The most important kind of soft law is made for the working level. It contains technical standards such as the OECD Test Guidelines and the Principles of GLP. Only in rare cases the standards have the quality of binding decisions, an instance being the OECD Decision C(81)30/Final on Mutual Acceptance of Data (MAD).[97] In the normal case they receive the quality of a recommendation, like the OECD Test Guidelines and the Principles of GLP.[98]

The last group of 'soft' law can be characterised as proto-law preceding 'hard' law. This is the case with the UNEP London Guidelines, the FAO Code of Conduct, and the GHS. The UNEP London Guidelines and the FAO Code of Conduct introduced a voluntary PIC procedure for chemicals and pesticides. The Rotterdam Convention emanated from these two 'soft' law instruments stipulating a compulsory PIC procedure. Ironically, this 'hardening' of the legal character of the rules has come at the cost of making the content softer at some points, a development which has aptly been called 'from "hard" soft law to "soft" hard law'.[99] GHS is supposed to fulfil a recommendatory function as the UNRTDG does. In a similar fashion to UNRTDG, which has served as the basis for numerous 'hard' laws on the transport of dangerous goods, GHS will be a model for regulations concerning classification and labelling of substances. After all, the success and efficacy of a harmonised system still depends on an accurate incorporation into national law.

The kinds of soft law just described are both the products of transnational networks and their basis of operation. Networks are characterised by a certain degree of non-hierarchical interconnection of actors and a commonly understood task, i.e. problem-solving.[100] Sometimes networks reach a high degree of institutional solidification, as e.g. in the case of IFCS, IOMC, or IPCS. Then the design of the networks very much resembles the one of an IGO, but for their informal and more flexible character: a set of basic rules governs the creation

---

[93] Recital no. 6, Preamble to the Resolution on the Establishment of an Intergovernmental Forum on Chemical Safety.
[94] See United Nations, op. cit., Foreword, para. 3.
[95] Recital no. 2, Preamble to the Rotterdam Convention.
[96] Recital no. 7, Preamble to the Stockholm Convention.
[97] According to Article 5 lit (a) OECD Convention, Council decisions are legally binding, as opposed to recommendations (cf. Article 5 lit b).
[98] Cf. C(81)30/Final, Pt II, s. 1.   [99] See Pallemaerts, op. cit. pp. 551–594.
[100] F. Scharpf, Positive und negative Koordination in Verhandlungssystemen, in Hértier, A. (ed.), Policy-Analyse, Politische Vierteljahresschrift Sonderheft 24, Opladen (Westdeutscher Verlag) 1993, pp. 57–83, at 72; Picciotto, S., Networks in international economic integration: fragmented states and the dilemmas of neo-liberalism, Northwestern J. Int'l Law and Business 17 (1996–1997), pp. 1014–1056, at 1020 and 1035; Börzel, T., Organizing Babylon: on the different conceptions of policy networks, Public Administration 76 (1998), pp. 253–273, at 260.

of the system, different organs are set up and endowed with specific tasks, Secretariats take administrative duties, etc.

As regards membership, networks may consist of persons representing different IGOs and acting with the aim of coordinating their activities. They may also involve persons acting for those states which play an important role in the field and must be integrated from the outset. A case in point is the setting up of IOMC; another is the establishment of CGHCCS. In these cases, IGOs found informal means to align their activities and to pool resources. Networks may further provide interconnections between actors on the national level and an IGO which provides some kind of loose institutional framework, such as Secretarial assistance and the possibility to enact a more formal (although not legally binding) resolution of the IGO's bodies. For example, the competent national authorities have cooperated on issues like GLP, Test Guidelines, SIDS, or GHS. Finally, networks cross-cut the public and the private sphere, allowing industry and non-economic NGOs to participate in the deliberations, such as in the cases of both IPCS and IFCS.

As to their functions, three types of networks may be distinguished. 'Agenda-setting networks' are dedicated to the formulation of agendas, or rather 'to do lists', as in the case of the Bahía Declaration. 'Rule-making networks' can be called those which are convened in order to develop rules such as the Test Guidelines, GLP, or the GHS. 'Administrative networks' may be termed those which actually work on individual cases, such as, in the chemicals field, the generation, dissemination, and assessment of information in the SIDS procedure.

As to the internal organisation of networks a certain division of functions can be observed. Persons representing IGOs usually initiate activities, offer a basis for other actors to exchange their views and cooperate, and provide Secretarial assistance. Persons representing states do most of the actual work that has to be done. They can base their input on the expertise of their national sectoral administrative agencies. Those which take the task most seriously and provide the most elaborated assistance tend to be most influential. Industrial and non-economic NGOs represent the various interests that play a role in the field of chemical safety like occupational safety, health, environmental safety, and the economy. They offer expertise and promote their political goals. Sometimes, they even provide organisational assistance such as the generation and collection of information on HPV substances by ICCA.

In any case, however, the networks are dominated by public actors. If decisions are to be taken, only representatives from IGOs and states have a vote. The networks must therefore be called public networks – transnational bureaucracy networks, to be more precise – and are to be distinguished from private networks as in the case of self-organisation of multinational corporations. Although the members of networks acting for the states are mostly public servants in their states' service, they do normally not see themselves as representatives of their state and do not behave as such. They regard themselves rather as experts who have to solve an objective problem, thus claiming a kind of transnational professionalism in the transnational public interest beyond private and state egoisms.

2. Networks and their soft law in context

Institutionalised forms of international administrative cooperation as a measure to address global, and therefore common, problems date back to the nineteenth century when administrative unions (AUs) were established as nonpolitical international entities to compensate for the insufficiencies of the individual state and harmonise technical standards, such as for telecommunications or the postal system.[101] Along with the foundation of the League of Nations came the creation of IGOs (e.g. the ILO, founded in 1919) with more extensive political tasks.[102] The efficacy of an IGO is highly dependent on its member states' commitment. If a member state participates in an obstructive manner or does not participate at all in the IGO's activities, the rule of consensual decision-making will lead to a blockade of the IGO's activities. Thus, the process of decision-making within IGOs becomes cumbersome and inflexible.

This problem also appears within the international legal order. The negotiation of international treaties is tedious and the outcome is sometimes doubtful. Like a mimosa that closes its petals upon a slight touch, some states retreat and cite their sovereignty if the content of a treaty imposes unwanted restrictions. Once established, treaty regimes can only be changed unanimously, which again leads to inflexibility. It has already been pointed out that innovative ways have been conceived to make international treaties more effective and balance the states' sovereignty and the need for flexible legal solutions to global problems. Framework conventions and stepwise amendments bring about the possibility to respond quickly and adapt the treaty to new challenges.[103] However, the framework convention itself does not contain obligations; its success depends on the adoption of amendments.[104] Accordingly, framework conventions cannot fulfil their purpose if the parties to the convention are not willing to adopt amendments or if important parties choose to opt out (e.g. the USA in the

---

[101] Cf. Tietje, C., *Internationalisiertes Verwaltungshandeln*, Berlin (Duncker & Humblot) 2001, pp. 124–130; Delbrück, J., Prospects for a 'World (internal) law?': legal developments in a changing international system, *Indiana J. Global Studies* 10 (2002), pp. 401–431, at 405.

[102] Seidl-Hohenveldern, I. and Stein, T., *Völkerrecht*, Cologne (Heymanns) 10th edn 2000, p. 28; for a distinction between AUs and IGOs, cf. Delbrück, J., Internationale und nationale Verwaltung, Inhaltliche und institutionelle Aspekte, in Jeserich, K. G. A. and Pohl, H. (eds.), *Deutsche Verwaltungsgeschichte Band 5*, Stuttgart (DVA) 1987, pp. 386–403, at 391–393.

[103] See Tietje, op. cit. pp. 245–255.

[104] Beyerlin, U., *Umweltvölkerrecht*, Munich (Beck) 2000, p. 42.

case of the Kyoto Protocol to the UN Framework Convention on Climate Change).

Network-based soft law has the potential to meet the demands for flexibility and effectiveness required by the globalisation of environmental problems and given the wearisome and unwieldy procedures of international law and its inherent problems of compliance.[105] The members of a network can benefit from each other's expertise.[106] Power does not have to be transferred to a supranational entity and thus, sovereignty remains intact.[107] States can effectively cooperate on common problems while avoiding centralised bureaucracies of IGOs.[108] However, IGOs do not become obsolete. The formation of transnational networks of bureaucracies (TNBs) relies on IGOs, as they provide the framework. Like a 'spider's web', networks take advantage of the existence of IGOs and use them as points of attachment.[109] Thus, networks complement the traditional international system.

Some scholars speak of legal pluralism in order to give network-based soft law a place in the legal system as a whole.[110] This may be a good start in order to raise awareness for the very phenomenon. The term, however, does not alert us to look more closely at the interrelations between the informal and the formal. Although networks are basically self-governing, they nevertheless depend on the formal institutional framework of international and national law. This is often the case in relation to the foundation of a network, and in relation to the implementation of the soft law produced by it. More fundamentally, networks and their soft law can be seen to be based on, and even demanded by, the principle of cooperation among states which is a principle of international customary law within the meaning of Article 38 of the ICJ Statute.[111] The cooperation principle must, however, be reshaped in order to cope with the declining role and disaggregation of states. It must be understood to invite the direct and horizontal interaction of state bodies across the border, where the formal interaction by diplomatic means does not work. This kind of cooperation can better benefit from the expertise of the participants, while still maintaining attributes of statehood such as the link to a territory, a nation, and the monopoly on the legitimate use of force.[112]

---

[105] See Tietje, op. cit. p. 264; Dupuy, P.-M., Soft law and the international law of the environment, *Michigan J. Int'l Law* 12 (1991), pp. 420–435, at 421.

[106] See Slaughter (2000), op. cit. p. 200.   [107] See Slaughter (2000), op. cit. p. 220.

[108] Slaughter, A.-M., Globalization, accountability, and the future of administrative law, *Indiana J. Global Studies* 8 (2000), pp. 347–365, at 347.

[109] See Picciotto, op. cit. pp. 1020 and 1039.

[110] For the case of *lex mercatoria*, cf. Teubner, G., 'Global Bukowina': legal pluralism in the world society, in Teubner, G. (ed.), *Global law without a state*, Aldershot (Dartmouth) 1997, pp. 3–30.

[111] See Matz and Wolfrum, op. cit. p. 161, with further references; see Tietje, op. cit. p. 223, with further references.

[112] See Slaughter (2000), op. cit. p. 200.

The success of informal approaches to global problems like soft law and TNBs are a proof of the willingness of states to cooperate in spite of their reluctance to submit themselves to binding regimes. The inclusion of NGOs into these networks connotes their increased valuation as international actors.[113] However, the description of TNBs presented above makes clear that the state as an actor is not displaced by new actors within the international system, but rather finds its place within a multilevel system.[114]

IV. Evaluation

Evaluating the TNB networks in the chemicals field, we will apply criteria of efficacy, legitimacy, respect for basic rights and values, and legal protection against misuse of powers.

1. Efficacy

As the networks often formulate quantified targets themselves, it is possible to measure their effectiveness. It seems to be a common pattern that the targets are set high but are never reached. For example, in 1999 the OECD SIDS Initiative set the target to produce SIARs for 1,000 priority HPV chemicals within about five years. So far, only a small fraction has been completed.[115] The limited resources which the participating national authorities can commit to international activities are the reason for the slow process. Of course, this problem is not exclusive to TNBs. On the other hand, burdens accruing to national authorities can be alleviated because the inclusion of so many participants in one network allows for a global division of labour, and all the more so, if the self-regulatory potential of industry is integrated into the network. A participant observer once compared the system of international chemical safety to a train that took long to start rolling. Now it is rolling, slowly, but nevertheless rolling.

2. Legitimacy

Despite their problem-solving capacity, TNBs may come to false conclusions. Although what they do appears to be more or less technical in nature, political

---

[113] For an overview of the argumentation of actors in international affairs, cf. Hobe, S., Die Zukunft des Völkerrechts im Zeitalter der Globalisierung, Perspektiven der Völkerrechtsentwicklung im 21. Jahrhundert, *Archiv des Völkerrechts* 37 (1999), pp. 253–282, at 261–264; Delbrück, J., Structural changes in the international system and its legal order: international law in the era of globalization, *Schweizerische Zeitschrift für internationales und europäisches Recht* 11 (2001), pp. 1–36, at 21–26; Tietje, op. cit. p. 410.
[114] See Godt, op. cit. p. 34.
[115] For information on the performance, see Warning and Winter, op. cit. p. 266.

values are also involved, such as the acceptance or not of the precautionary principle: for example, what parameter and concentration thresholds that define toxicity may be fixed in a way that substances are not labelled as toxic although in fact they do cause health damage? How can it be secured that this does not occur?

The question is related to the legitimation of what the network elaborates. Within a state, democratic legitimacy of executive rule-making is based on parliamentary empowerment, flanked by participatory rule-making procedures. This source is not available for transnational informal rule-making. The chain of legitimation from the electorate via the Parliament up to the appointed ministers, 'down' to their bureaucrats and 'up' again to the networks of the same, is just too long to make sense. Decisions emanating from TNBs, therefore, suffer from a 'chronic lack of legitimacy'.[116] The same is true for the transformation of the networks' 'products' into domestic practice. Many states simply apply the soft law derived from TNBs in their administrative practice without even noticing that what they apply has an extra-constitutional origin. Others, like Germany, have constitutional prerequisites demanding that a binding effect of soft law standards can only be achieved if a parliamentary law makes reference to the particular standard. This is then regarded as providing legitimacy for the standard. But if legitimacy is to be understood as going beyond sheer legal constructions, this is by no means satisfactory. For example, to achieve the goal of the GHS to harmonise hazard classifications, the national legislature must transform a decision made by public authorities almost verbatim.

No matter, if states underestimate the legitimacy question by directly applying the standards, or if they overestimate the potential of formal procedures (as in the case of Germany), the quest for more effective legitimacy can hardly be answered on the national level, for the simple fact that in the global dimension there are just too many national legal systems involved. The cure can only be found on the transnational level itself.

One possibility to mend the legitimacy deficit is the establishment of transnational networks of national legislatory bodies.[117] However, transnational chemical safety regulation is too limited a matter to be suitable for parliamentary interlinkage.

We are therefore left with quests for NGO participation in, and transparency of, transnational decision-making. The standard should be set high in this regard. It may even be considered that international customary principles are emerging, qualifying the necessary degree of legitimacy of transnational networks. Alternatively, requirements for transnational rule-making may be derived from national constitutions where they are concerned about opening

---

[116] See Picciotto, op. cit. p. 1047.
[117] Slaughter, A.-M., The real new world order, *Foreign Affairs* 76 (no. 5) (1997), pp. 183–197, at 197.

up internal law for external soft law. Under certain conditions, democratisation of transnational networks may be taken as a substitute for internal democratic control.[118]

For NGOs this means that their access must be extended beyond the representation of business interests and embrace civil NGOs representing civil society. Participation must include the right to be informed and the right to be heard. On the other hand, it should be considered to require some kind of inner democracy of NGOs in order to prevent closed corporatist shops.

Transparency is a necessary complement to NGO participation because it reaches the public at large, including the unorganised parts of civil society. For instance, the activities of networks dealing with the globalisation of financial markets are to a great extent hidden from the public.[119] The field of chemical safety is a striking example to the opposite. A wealth of information is available via the Internet. The public reflection on the achievements and the identification of goals through the IFCS also adds to the transparency of TNBs.

There are, nevertheless, minor flaws. For example, the consultations of the CGHCCS[120] or the discussions at the SIAMs are not available to the public. These might prove to be important for a comprehensive assessment of the development of GHS or the evaluation of the SIAR. Thus, TNBs should be as transparent as possible. Business secrets, etc., should not be revealed, but any information that allows the reconstruction of the decision process should be made available. This will allow the public to monitor the TNBs' activities.

3. Legal protection

Judicial protection of legal rights rests on the principle that courts should have jurisdiction on the same level on which the contested decision was made, or on higher levels than that of decision-making. For instance, recourse against EC legal acts is possible at the European courts, be it directly in case of individual and direct effect, be it indirectly via the preliminary ruling procedure. Recourse against national laws is likewise available with ordinary national and constitutional courts.

By contrast, things are different in relation to international law. There, national courts are competent to decide about the validity of law which was made at superior levels. This also applies to transnational soft law. For example, if a SIAR comes to the conclusion that a substance is harmful or harmless, there is no extra-national forum where an individual impaired by the substance may

---

[118] See Godt, op. cit. p. 241; Kamminga, M. T., The evolving status of NGOs under international law: a threat to the inter-state system?, in Kreijen, G. (ed.), *State sovereignty and international governance*, Oxford (Oxford University Press) 2002, pp. 387–406, at 404.
[119] See Slaughter (2000), op. cit. p. 215.
[120] See www.ilo.org/public/english/protection/safework/ghs/ cghccs.htm

complain. It is true that the SIAR serves as a basis for national binding regulation which may be challenged in national courts. But the SIAR that underpins the national regulation reflects transnational consensus which transcends the particular state. This will also be understood by the national judge, who will therefore think twice before contesting the consensus.[121] The consequence of this observation is that court-like procedures should also be established at the transnational level. This means that a dispute resolution procedure should be envisaged for relevant network-based soft law. For instance, in the case of chemicals safety, it is imaginable that an arbitration body could be created which receives complaints about decisions of the network by relevant companies, states, or NGOs.

V. Conclusion

In the case of international chemical safety, TNBs developed because the global scale of the problem demanded transnational administrative cooperation. Their development is 'work in progress' and there certainly is potential for improvements. The example of the OECD SIDS Initiative illustrates how slow the process of global risk assessment and how difficult cooperation actually is. But the task cannot be mastered by one state alone. On the whole, TNBs are at least getting something done.

Therefore, TNBs should be regarded as a new mode of governance, joining experts from the public and the private sphere and offering the flexibility needed to tackle complex environmental problems. The discussion should focus on how to improve them and to ensure the legitimacy of their decisions.

---

[121] See Warning and Winter, op. cit. p. 268.

PART V

The potential of world regions

13

The EU: a regional model?

LUDWIG KRÄMER

The present contribution will examine whether global environmental law and policy can profit from the experience of the European Union (EU) in this field. In the first section, EU environmental policy and law will be presented. In section II, some aspects are discussed which show deficiencies or gaps in global environmental policy and law. Section III discusses the possibility of transferring some experience from the EU scene to the international level. The chapter ends with some concluding remarks.

I. The European Union's environmental policy and law

The European Union is a regional integration organisation, consisting at present of twenty-five nation states and more than 450 million people. It is established by the Treaty on European Union which enshrines several other Treaties.[1] One of its objectives is the achievement of a balanced and sustainable development:

> The Union's sustainable development strategy is based on the principle that the economic, social and environmental effects of all policies should be examined in a coordinated way and taken into account in decision-making.[2]

Since the beginning of the 1970s, the European Union has developed an environmental policy which has been, over the years, extended and fine-tuned, and presently covers practically all areas of environmental concern. Some 350 sets of provisions[3] – in the EU terminology, Regulations or Directives – deal with environmental issues, in particular water and air pollution, waste management,

---

[1] Treaty on European Union (consolidated version) [2002] OJ C325/5. The EC Treaty, on which most legal measures are based, is an integrated part of the Treaty on European Union. At present, a process has started to replace the Treaty on European Union by a Constitution.
[2] Goeteborg European Council, June 2001, Presidency's Conclusions, para. 22.
[3] The exact number cannot be precisely determined, since all depends on the definition of 'environmental provisions'. Thus, e.g., provisions on exhaust emission from cars might be classified as environmental provisions, but also (as the EU did) as trade-related provisions. Similar examples could be found for numerous trade, transport, energy, competition, consumer protection, food, or agricultural provisions.

nature conservation and biodiversity protection, products and noise, permits, ozone layer and climate change issues.[4] These provisions are binding for all EU Member States and oblige them to adapt their national, regional, and local legislation to the provisions of EU environmental law.

The following will not describe in detail the procedural or substantive European environmental policy law. It will rather try to elaborate on the specificity of EU institutions, policies and procedures, compared to the numerous international environmental conventions, and to institutions, policies, and procedures under public international environmental law.

1. Institutions

Environmental decisions within the European Union are adopted jointly by the European Parliament and the Council.[5] However, decisions may only be taken on proposals by the European Commission. The Commission is a body that consists of twenty-five members – one from each Member State – who are appointed by the Council. These twenty-five members must act 'in the general interest' of the European Union and are supported by the Commission staff, which consists of some 22,000 officials; these officials are equally obliged to act in the general interest of the European Union. Thus, although the members of the Commission and the officials come from Member States, they act independently from their national governments. A number of legal guarantees such as recruitment procedures, lifelong employment, salary, pension, etc., are intended to ensure this loyalty to the common interest, rather than to the state of origin.

The European Parliament consists of representatives of the peoples of the EU Member States; its members are elected by direct universal suffrage. There are political parties formed at European level in order to organise the political participation of the European Parliament. Their policy is more or less obliged to consider the impact of policies on the whole of the European Union. In legislative procedures, the European Parliament decides by simple majority in a first reading, and in the second reading with the absolute majority of its members.

The Council is composed of representatives of EU Member States' governments. Where the Council has to take decisions by a qualified majority (this being the rule in environmental matters),[6] the votes of the Member States are

---

[4] For an overview, see Jans, J., *European environmental law*, Groningen (Europa Law Publishing) 2nd edn. 2000; Krämer, L., *EC environmental law*, London (Sweet & Maxwell) 5th edn 2003.

[5] In exceptional, expressly enumerated cases, the Council alone decides, by unanimity. These cases concern eco-taxes, town and country planning, quantitative management of water resources, land use and important energy-related measures; see Article 175(2) EC Treaty.

[6] See n. 5 above.

weighed according to their size. Majority decisions require the agreement of the majority of Member States and about two-thirds of the votes in favour of the decision.[7]

The European Court of Justice (ECJ) has the task to ensure that, in the interpretation and application of EU law, 'the law is observed'.[8] The ECJ is thus the highest arbiter in disputes on EU environmental law, especially because Member States have committed themselves not to subject a dispute concerning the interpretation or application of EU law to any methods of settlement other than those provided for in the EU Treaty[9] (Article 292). There is one judge from each Member State. However, the different cases are attributed to the Court's chambers or judges according to objective criteria; it is thus the rule that a case is heard by the ECJ, without a judge from the Member State which the case concerns taking part.

2. Policy development

When the EU environmental policy was initiated, there was no mandate by the Council or by the EU Member States to tackle this or that aspect or to protect this or that part of the environment. In order to eliminate this vacuum, the European Commission suggested to elaborate the European Environmental Action Programme which would fix, for a period of four to five years, objectives, principles, and priorities for action at EU level. After some hesitation, this proposal was accepted. The Action Programme was extensively discussed by all EU institutions and then the Commission was allowed to go ahead with the implementation of the programme.[10]

Following the first Action Programme of 1973, the Commission regularly elaborated and proposed new Environmental Action Programmes, which were all amply discussed and finally approved.[11] In 1993, this procedure was institutionalised and the participation of the European Parliament strengthened. At present, the Sixth Environmental Action programme is running. It extends till 2012 and provides overall 156 environmental actions at EU level.[12]

---

[7] See Article 205 EC Treaty.   [8] See Article 220 EC Treaty.
[9] See Article 292 EC Treaty. It is under this provision that the European Commission recently took legal action against Ireland before the ECJ, because Ireland had applied to the International Maritime Court, which was set up under the Convention on the Law of the Sea. The Commission is arguing that this Convention had been ratified by the EU which, under Article 300 (7) EC Treaty, makes it part of EC law.
[10] See First Environmental Action Programme [1973] OJ C112/1.
[11] See Second Environmental Action Programme [1977] OJ C139/1; Third Environmental Action Programme [1983] OJ C46/1; Fourth Environmental Action Programme [1987] OJ C328/1; Fifth Environmental Action Programme [1993] OJ C138/5.
[12] Decision 1600/2002 laying down the Sixth Community Environmental Action Programme [2002] OJ L242/1.

The advantage of this approach of working with action programmes is that it made all interested groups – Member States, the European Parliament, stakeholders, and non-governmental organisations – reflect and advise on priority action, on the necessities of research, and on considering short-term, medium-term and long-term objectives. To a considerable extent, the obligation to discuss priorities and measures at European level led to the establishment of environmental structures, such as the creation of environmental departments within national governments, an environmental committee within the European Parliament, or European environmental protection organisations. Also, the discussion of a programme led the way to the consideration of environmental objectives and priorities in all parts of the European Union, and in particular in those regions where environmental concerns were less a political priority. Furthermore, the discussion on environmental issues was streamlined and organised by the programmes: while no region or no Member State was prevented from fixing supplementary priorities and deciding on other actions, the establishment of a written programme made it possible to concentrate discussions, to catch the attention of media and of public opinion, and to politically determine that, according to the decision of the European Parliament and the Council, this or that measure had to be taken in the environmental sector within the next coming years. In this way, the environment received a voice: governments, parliamentarians, and stakeholders were, to a certain extent, politically committed to implement the action programme.

At the level of the EU Member States, the joint elaboration and adoption of an Environmental Action Programme had the advantage of integrating also those EU Member States which did not have an elaborate environmental policy. Such Member States existed and exist at present within the EU. The joint discussion on a programme obliged them to think over priorities, address regional concerns, or reflect on gaps or omissions in their national policy.

Of course, the Environmental Action Programmes are of a flexible nature. In the past, there have always been environmental measures which were adopted at EU level, without having been mentioned in a specific programme. Other measures were announced in the action programmes, but were not realised. Such a flexibility is normal in the European Union, where the responsibility on environmental matters is shared between EU Member States and the European Union. The control of the Council and the Commission by the European Parliament, the watchdog position of environmental organisations and, above all, a very attentive public opinion in the EU Member States which is mindful of an appropriate protection of the environment, do not make it politically too easy to explain, why this or that measure that had been announced in an Environment Action Programme is not implemented. Flexibility of the action programmes is also furthered by the fact that regular mid-term reviews are carried out which allow the adaptation of priorities and actions to changed political, economic, or environmental circumstances.

3. Decision-making[13]

The exclusive right of initiative for a legislative measure lies, as mentioned, with the European Commission. The draft text is elaborated by the Commission staff and extensively discussed with Member States, professional and environmental organisations, and all interested groups. Such discussions sometimes take years,[14] but enable the original draft to be reviewed, adapted, and fine-tuned. Since 2003, the text's economic, social, and environmental impact is in addition assessed. This assessment is published, together with the finally adopted Commission proposal.

The proposal is then discussed by the European Parliament which normally charges its influential environmental committee to prepare its opinion; by the Council which charges a Working Group, composed of officials from Member States; and by two other EU institutions, i.e., the Economic and Social Committee and the Committee of the Regions. The Commission is always present in the discussions and defends its proposal.

Once the other institutions have adopted their opinions, the Council fixes a Common Position on the proposal. This Common Position is discussed for a second time by the European Parliament, which may suggest amendments. If divergencies with the Council exist, a conciliation procedure is set up which has to find a compromise text within a fixed time period. Where a compromise text is found, it becomes legislation; otherwise, the legislation is rejected. The final text of the legislative measure is published in all languages of the EU Member States.

A very important element of EU environmental legislation is the fact that any Member State may maintain or introduce more stringent protective measures than those that were adopted at EU level, provided that they comply with the general provisions of EU law.[15] This possibility is, however, severely restricted for trade-related environmental measures, where far more restrictive possibilities exist for Member States to maintain existing, or introduce new, national legislation.[16]

4. Implementation

Once a piece of environmental legislation is adopted, the EU Member States are obliged to adapt their national environmental legislation accordingly. The European Commission has the obligation 'to ensure that . . . the measures

---

[13] For details see Articles 175(1) and 251 EC Treaty.
[14] Thus, EC legislation on the marketing of plant protection products, Directive 91/414/EC [1991] OJ L230/1, was adopted fifteen years after the Commission had made a proposal; Directive 85/337/EC on the assessment of the environmental impact of certain projects [1985] OJ L175/40, was adopted after eight years of preparatory work.
[15] See Article 176 EC Treaty.   [16] For details see Article 95 EC Treaty.

taken by the institutions... are applied'.[17] Thus, the Commission has an active role to play in the implementation process. This provision is the key to the understanding of the specificity of the EU implementation system.

Member States have to send to the Commission all legislative measures which they have adopted in compliance with adopted EU measures. These measures are examined to see whether they completely and correctly transpose the EU measure: where the Commission has doubts, it discusses with Member States (in writing or in bilateral meetings) the different interpretations and tries thus to ensure a complete and correct legislative alignment of national law. Occasionally, the Commission also assembles all Member States in a meeting, in order to discuss the meaning of certain EU provisions, clarify misunderstandings, or otherwise, as well as promote a consistent and coherent interpretation and application of the EU provisions.

Since the Commission has to ensure the application of the EU provisions, it does not limit itself in ensuring the transposition of the EU provisions into the national legislative system. EU Member States have regularly to report, not only on this legislative transposition, but also on the application of these provisions in practice. It is true, though, that these national reports mostly deal with the formal transposition of EU provisions rather than their practical application.

To obtain better information on the actual state of the environment, an Environment Agency was set up with the task of collecting, processing, and distributing, together with EU Member States, information on the state of the European environment.[18] Its findings also provide valuable information on the state of application of the different EU environmental provisions which were adopted. Other sources on the practical application of EU provisions are media reports, information by stakeholders, or complaints from private persons, which are sent to the European Commission. This last source developed quite remarkably[19] over the years; generally, the different complaints give a relatively good assessment of the practical application of EU provisions in a Member State. The authors of such complaints are individual persons, but also industrial or commercial undertakings, local councils, political parties, members of local, regional, national, or European Parliaments, scholars, lawyers, regional or national governmental ministers, ambassadors etc. The Commission has only committed itself to look into each individual complaint, take the matter up with the EU Member State, and keep the name of the complainant confidential, if that is wished. Otherwise, the informing person or body has no procedural or substantive guarantee in the subsequent procedure, which is

---

[17] Article 211 EC Treaty.
[18] Decision 1210/90 on the Establishment of the European Environment Agency and the European Environment Information and Observation Network [1990] OJ L120/1.
[19] In 1982, the Commission received ten environmental complaints, in 2002, 697; for details see Krämer, op. cit., p. 383 *et seq.*

organised entirely between the European Commission and the Member State in question.[20]

5. Dispute prevention and settlement

Where the Commission finds that a specific provision or even a whole set of provisions of EU environmental law is not incorporated into the national law of an EU Member State or not effectively applied in practice, it takes the matter up with the Member State in question. This normally happens in writing and no formalised procedures exist in this regard. The Member State is informed about the problem as it is perceived by the Commission and is invited to comment on it within a specific time limit. This exchange of correspondence makes it possible to clarify factual elements, eliminate misunderstandings about the meaning of EU or national legal provisions or other measures, and to settle other factual or legal aspects. If the Commission is satisfied with the explanations and clarifications submitted, the issue is settled. Where this is not the case, a formal letter is sent to the Member State in question which elaborates once more the points which are of factual and legal concern to the Commission. The Member State has a specific limit to provide an answer. In addition, one or more meetings may take place to discuss and solve the issues at stake.

Where the discrepancy is not solved, the Commission has the possibility of writing a second formal letter (the so-called reasoned opinion), where it summarises the factual and legal situation and invites the EU Member State to comply with its EU law obligations. Again, the Member State has to react within a specific time limit and, once more, one or more scientific, technical, legal, or political meetings may take place, depending on the requests from either side. In case these efforts fail, the Commission may appeal to the ECJ and ask for a declaratory judgment which states whether the Member State in question is in breach of EU environmental law.

The whole procedure is time-consuming and takes approximately four to five years from the letter of formal notice to the judgment of ECJ. However, the procedure, which remains non-public prior to the application to the Court, ensures that most cases concerning non-compliance are solved out of court. During the pre-court procedure, the Commission repeatedly resorts, at its discretion, to press releases and other means of informing the public concerning the dispute, in order to ensure better compliance.

Where the ECJ has decided a case, a Member State is obliged to take the necessary measures to comply with that judgment. If it does not do so, the Commission may start fresh proceedings against the Member State, as described above. This time, however, it may ask the ECJ in its application to oblige the Member State to pay a lump sum or a penalty payment as a result of

---

[20] See the complaint form published by the Commission [1999] OJ C119/5.

non-compliance with the first judgment. The ECJ determines the payment at its discretion, depending on the circumstances and taking into account the duration of the non-compliance, the severity of the infringement, and the ability of the Member State to pay the penalty.[21] Until the end of 2003, this procedure was used two times against Member States, both times in environmental matters.[22]

An EU Member State may also appeal to the ECJ, if another Member State has not complied with its obligations under environmental law. Such an application is not limited to cases where the environment or other assets of the applying Member State are impaired. This possibility is used only in very exceptional cases and has, until now, never been used in an environmental case.[23]

The EU has basically no income of its own, but receives a specific amount of financial contributions from Member States. Therefore, the policy that financial assistance should be granted, only if there is compliance with EU environmental provisions, is of limited application. However, it is not completely irrelevant. Indeed, in the framework of its regional policy, the EU distributes considerable amounts of money, in particular via the Structural Funds (agricultural, social, and regional programmes) and the Cohesion Fund (environmental and transport projects). The implementation of these policies is shared between the Commission and the Member States. However, no project receives EU financial support if it is not in compliance with existing EU legal requirements. Funding in the context of regional policy support is also refused by the Commission, where a Member State has failed to comply with its obligations to designate natural habitats. In contrast to that, EC regional policy funding could not be refused where obligations are not complied with which concern, for example, waste water treatment or air pollution.

Where it becomes evident at a later stage that a specific project has breached EU environmental provisions, the EU may require that the money granted be refunded.

6. The involvement of the public

When the EU was founded at the end of the 1950s, it was almost entirely a classical regional organisation, where non-state actors almost had no possibility of participation. Over the years, however, the EU progressively opened to the public, in particular in environmental matters, which has become a pace-setter for other policy sectors. In 1990, an individual right of access to environmental information – that is in the hands of public authorities – was introduced at the

---

[21] See Commission Communications [1996] OJ C242/6 and [1997] OJ C63/2.
[22] See ECJ, Case C-387/97 *Commission v. Greece* [2000] ECR I-369; Case C-278/01 *Commission v. Spain* [2003] ECR I-1416 7.
[23] Article 227 EC Treaty; see also n. 9 above.

level of Member States and later also at the level of the European Union.[24] The first measures intended to give individuals and environmental organisations the right to participate in decision-making affecting the environment date from 1985; they have been progressively extended since then.[25] Access to national courts is the subject of a proposal for legislation. Access of environmental organisations to the ECJ will equally be possible, once a recent Commission proposal is adopted.[26] The process of introducing environmental rights for individuals and/or environmental organisations received very considerable support from the UNECE 'Convention on Access to Information, Participation in Decision-making and Access to Justice in Environmental Matters' (Aarhus Convention), which was signed in 1998 by all EU Member States, and by the EU itself.

Transparency and consultation of stakeholders and improved participation rules played a particular role in EU policy, where EU decision-making not only added to or completed, but completely replaced national decision-making procedures. This trend was particularly visible in product-related standard setting, such as for biotechnology, pesticides, or chemicals. In these sectors, though, environmental concerns were often put in the second or third rank of priority while economic considerations prevailed at EU level.

7. Integration

The EU recognised relatively early that a serious protection of the environment would not be possible through mere adoption of provisions for the different sectors of the environment such as water and air, nature, waste, or noise. It therefore decided that all other policies had to take environmental requirements into consideration.[27] It is difficult to make this requirement operational; a number of political steps were taken in the past in an attempt to apply this provision, without much success. However, politically, this requirement offers the greatest potential for ensuring economic development that takes into consideration environmental concerns. The above-mentioned requirement of an impact assessment for legislative proposal is but the most recent example

---

[24] Directive 90/313/EC on the freedom of access to information on the environment [1990] OJ L156/58; Regulation (EEC) 1049/2001 regarding public access to European Parliament, Council and Commission documents [2001] OJ L145/43; Directive 2003/4/EC on public access to environmental information and repealing Directive 90/313/EC [2003] OJ L41/26.

[25] Directive 85/337, Article 6; Directive 2001/42 on the assessment of the effects of certain plans and programmes on the environment [2001] OJ L197/30; Directive 2003/35/EC providing for public participation in respect of the drawing up of certain plans and programmes relating to the environment [2003] OJ L156/17.

[26] See COM(2003) 622 and 624, 24 October 2003 on the two legislative proposals.

[27] Article 6 EC Treaty: 'Environmental protection requirements must be integrated into the definition and implementation of the Community policies and activities .., in particular with a view to promoting sustainable development'.

of introduction of environmental concerns to measures in the transport and energy, agriculture, fishery, regional, or other policy areas.

II. Problems of global environmental law and policy

Is there anything in this, rather sketchily, described system that could be taken into consideration for application elsewhere on this planet? The question already implies that the present system of environmental governance is capable of improving. Not being a specialist of either public international law or international environmental law, I would not dare to make a negative judgment of the structures, institutions, Conventions, and enforcement mechanisms which exist at present at the global or international level. I am too well aware of the observation which my colleague Veit Koester so often made in his contributions to international environmental law:[28] where would the environment be without all the Conventions and the endless efforts of so many environmental persons all over the world to elaborate and negotiate them and, subsequently, ensure their monitoring and application?

Nevertheless, it would be wrong to assume that the present state of world environmental governance is necessarily the best. The following difficulties and problems regarding global environmental governance appear to exist.

1. The existing global conventions

With time, it becomes progressively more and more difficult to set up effective global standards for the protection of the environment. The different global environmental Conventions which have been elaborated in the last thirty years demonstrate the difficulties of drafting provisions that are meaningful, enforceable, and capable of ensuring protection. A look into the different sectors demonstrates this with sufficient clarity.

In the water sector, there are Conventions on dumping of wastes and other matters,[29] on the prevention of pollution from ships,[30] and on the law of the sea, which contain a number of environmental provisions.[31] The Dumping Convention limits itself to the deliberate release of wastes from ships, platforms, aircraft, etc. and is thus not considerably larger in its field of application than the Convention on the Prevention of Pollution from Ships. The Convention on the Law of the Sea largely refers to the states and requires them to regulate

---

[28] See, e.g., Köster, V., The five global biodiversity-related conventions: a stock-taking, *RECIEL* 11 (2000), p. 96.
[29] Convention on the Prevention of Marine Pollution by Dumping of Wastes and other Matters, 19 December 1972, London.
[30] International Convention for the Prevention of Pollution from Ships, 2 November 1973, London.
[31] United Nations Convention on the Law of the Sea, 10 December 1982, Montego Bay.

pollution from land-based sources, seabed and other activities, vessels, and the atmosphere. In view of this, the requirement in Article 192 that 'States have the obligation to protect and preserve the marine environment' is rather void of content. Overall, it cannot really be argued that the main pollution to coastal and other marine waters, the slow and progressive deterioration of the marine environment in general, is adequately adressed by the existing global Conventions, though some regional Conventions are more specific. The numerous exceptions contained in these Conventions for offshore petrol exploration and for the transport of petrol by sea only add to this conclusion.

There are, as far as can be seen, no global provisions on the protection of fresh water.

In the area of atmospheric issues, the 1987 Montreal Protocol on Substances that Deplete the Ozone Layer[32] with its subsequent amendments is, up to now, a success story and might progressively restore the damaged ozone layer by 2050, if the present efforts are continued. In contrast to that, the New York Climate Change Convention 1992[33] is a model of a convention as it should not be: it contains an enormous amount of 'greenspeak', but very few concrete legal obligations. Even the cautiously expressed commitment to limit CO_2 emissions by 2000 to the 1990 levels was neither respected nor enforced; the wording is so vague that it leaves doubt whether there is any legal obligation to this effect at all. It is true that the 1997 Kyoto Protocol to the Climate Change Convention[34] is more concrete. However, it only contains obligations for industrialised countries – it is thus not global!

In the area of biological diversity there are the Ramsar Convention on Wetlands 1971,[35] the Paris Convention for the Protection of the World Cultural and Natural Heritage 1972,[36] the Washington Convention on Trade in Endangered Species of Wild Fauna and Flora (CITES) 1972,[37] and the Rio Convention on Biological Diversity 1992.[38] The first two Conventions leave it to the contracting parties to designate areas which should come under the protective shield of the Conventions. The CITES Convention does not protect endangered species as such, but only the trade therein. And the Convention

---

[32] Convention on the Protection of the Ozone Layer, 22 March 1985, Vienna, and Protocol on Substances that Deplete the Ozone Layer, 16 September 1987, Montreal.
[33] UN Framework Convention on climate change, 9 May 1992, New York.
[34] Protocol to the United Nations Framework Convention on Climate Change, 21 December 1997, Kyoto.
[35] Convention on Wetlands of International Importance especially as Waterfowl Habitat, 2 February 1971, Ramsar.
[36] Convention for the Protection of the World Cultural and Natural Heritage, 16 November 1972, Paris.
[37] Convention on International Trade in Endangered Species of Wild Fauna and Flora, 3 March 1973, Washington.
[38] Convention on Biological Diversity, 5 June 1992, Rio de Janeiro.

on Biological Diversity lists a large number of objectives and principles, but is short in containing precise legal obligations which could be legally enforced.

In the area of products and waste, the Rotterdam Convention on Prior Informed Consent 1988[39] covers information issues of certain hazardous chemicals and pesticides which are banned or severely restricted in use. The Stockholm Convention 2001 bans trade in a dozen chemicals, a very short list of all chemicals on the market.[40] The Basel Convention 1989 on the shipment of hazardous waste[41] finally tried to apply the system of prior informed consent to waste shipments, before an amendment of 1997 prohibited the export of hazardous waste from industrialised countries to developing countries.[42] The application of this Convention is severely hampered by the fact that the core notion of 'environmentally sound waste management', used by the Convention, is not defined and leaves a very large discretion to all contracting parties. Also, the Convention was not ratified by the USA, which deployed considerable efforts so as to hinder it from becoming really effective.

This short and necessarily incomplete[43] overview of global environmental Conventions makes obvious their scattered nature and their inconsistent and incomplete character. This becomes obvious, when one tries to imagine that all these different Conventions were fully implemented and applied by all contracting parties. It is submitted that the environment on this planet would even then still not be in a sustainable state, i.e. in a state where the progressive deterioration is stopped and gradually reversed. The impression is that the wording of the international Conventions has, in the latter years, become more general, imprecise, and non-committal, rather than becoming more precise.

2. The USA and global environmental protection

The USA exercises a very considerable influence in all international environmental discussions, amongst other things, through their financial contributions which are normally substantial, their ability to influence the distribution of posts in the Secretariats of Conventions, as well as of the UNEP itself, their close cooperation with economic non-governmental organisations, the fact that English is the only language which is used internationally, and the fact that their diplomatic network is very effectively spread over the world, which

---

[39] Convention on Prior Informed Consent Procedure for Certain Hazardous Chemicals and Pesticides in International Trade, 11 September 1998, Rotterdam.
[40] Convention on Persistent Organic Pollutants, 2001, Stockholm.
[41] Convention on the Control of Transboundary Movements of Hazardous Wastes and their Disposal, 22 March 1989, Basel.
[42] Amendment of 1995.
[43] The enumeration leaves out, e.g. the Conventions on nuclear energy, on transport issues, as well as the numerous regional environmental Conventions.

helps them to find like-minded countries in order to ensure that they are never in an isolated position. In the last twenty-five years, the USA has approached environmental issues more or less exclusively under trade and/or foreign policy auspices. Its contribution to the establishment of global environmental provisions was rather limited. Whenever one reads documents on international negotiations, be they on the discussion of the Climate Change Convention, the Basel Convention on waste shipments or the Convention on Biodiversity, be they on the discussions at the Rio 1992 or Johannesburg 2002 global UN Conferences, or even when the WTO negotiations Protocols are considered, the USA's attempts to prevent the promotion and adoption of progressive global environmental provisions or even of the fixing of targets runs like a red thread through all reports, minutes, or statements. This attitude started with the Reagan administration in the early 1980s, when the conservative Congress majority (which has continued to exist throughout) reoriented the international attitude of that country with regard to the environment.

Apart from the 1987 Montreal Protocol on the Protection of the Ozone Layer, there appears to be not one single global Convention or Protocol where the USA used its overridingly strong position in international environmental negotiations to press for better, more stringent, and more protective measures. They used their position in the driver's seat to step on the brakes rather than advance the spaceship (Earth) in its environmental dimension.

This US policy is deliberate and, from the point of view of the USA, certainly legitimate and is not to be questioned. However, the discussion here is on the global environment. And it is not really logical that persons, bodies, and institutions all over the world who care for the environment, should take the US policy as a *fait accompli* and allow the efforts to ensure an environmentally sustainable development of this planet to be slowed down, reduced to the minimum, or even completely paralysed, just because the three priorities for the USA at the international level are free trade, free trade, and free trade.

3. Global economic and social standards

Within the WTO provisions and discussions, a slow but progressive development of common, worldwide standards for economic exchanges and trade, which begin to include investment issues, financial and other capital questions, and which give a structural background of provisions for trade-related issues, is noticeable. The International Labour Organization (ILO) has been developing, over decades, labour standards which gradually become applicable, worldwide at least in the form of 'core labour standards'; examples are the ban on apartheid, child work, prisoners' work, the guarantee of trade union rights, etc. However, when a European or North American undertaking is doing business in the Third World, there is no environmental standard which applies, except the national environmental legislation of the developing country.[44] However, would it not be normal practice, for example, for an industry, wherever it might be operational on this planet, to discharge its waste water into rivers, lakes, or coastal waters only after cleaning them? Would it not be normal practice for solid waste not to be discharged into waters or at non-authorised places, but rather only on authorised landfills? These examples could be applied to all sectors of environmental policy. Generally, states relatively easily agree on international economic and (within the ILO) social standards, but are, driven by the USA, reluctant to agree on precise environmental standards.

4. Implementation of environmental Conventions

Compliance and implementation are the biggest problems for any environment policy; global environmental Conventions likewise are not an exception to this. The techniques for implementing international environmental principles and provisions are very insufficient. They basically consist of provisions on environmental information and liability as well as compensation for environmental damage – this latter aspect can be left aside, since it is really of no significant relevance in environmental matters. Most Conventions require the contracting parties to report on measures which they have taken in order to comply with the Convention's requirements. There is a lack of mechanisms such as inspections or fact-finding surveys. The above-mentioned imprecise drafting of Conventions facilitates incomplete or inadequate implementation. Overall, it is not exaggerated to state that environmental Conventions constitute a good framework within which contracting parties may take measures for the protection of the environment – if they so wish. Where a contracting party for one reason or the other does not wish to take the necessary compliance measures, there is hardly any mechanism to ensure such compliance.

The implementation gap is basically a result of the fact that the environment is an interest without a group. In other words, it has no voice. In the daily bargaining of different vested interests in society, it is relatively easy to put the environmental interests in second or third place. This leads to another observation which is true for almost all states, though one which is rarely expressed, since it touches a taboo: the biggest cause of environmental degradation is the state, either by virtue of its actions, such as permits, licences, economic measures such as infrastructure development; or by virtue of its omissions to adopt and enforce appropriate protection measures, despite the fact that the state authorities in any state have the task of ensuring that the existing legal provisions are applied.

---

[44] Efforts on developing an instrument on 'corporate social responsibility' which would include environmental issues, started after the Johannesburg Conference, but have so far not given any concrete results.

5. State of the global environment

The consequences for environmental policies are obvious. There is (leaving aside the ozone layer issue) practically no environmental area where one can state with confidence that the environment is, globally speaking, on a good path: climate change issues, forest protection, waste management, the protection of endangered species (and not just the trade in these!), biodiversity, the urban environment, drinking water and waste water management, the omnipresence of chemicals in the environment, the threat to the natural environment by genetically modified plants and animals.

The list is long and could easily be prolonged. Just to mention again, the situation would be much worse without the considerable efforts of many persons, networks of scientists and researchers, officials and public bodies all over the world. However, this observation is not a reason to be satisfied with the state of the environment on this planet.

It seems almost impossible to reach meaningful global environmental agreements against the will of the USA. Indeed, there are hardly any driving forces to push seriously for energetic, meaningful, and determined initiatives in order to improve the present situation. A number of developed countries (Australia and New Zealand, Japan and South Korea) are more or less directly aligned to the USA. Russia and other countries in Eastern Europe implicitly seem to continue the old doctrine of Socialism and act as if no environmental problems exist, neither at home or globally. Latin American countries concentrate on the fight against economic hardships and do not seem prepared to give some priority to environmental concerns *over* economic issues. A similar observation can be made as regards the threshold countries from the developing world: China, India, Malaysia, Indonesia, and Mexico see, like many African countries, stringent environmental provisions and medium- or long-term environmental strategies and their implementation as an impediment to economic development and as a rather dirty trick of environmental protagonists from industrialised countries to prevent developing countries from improving their economic development and their wealth.

This situation appeared clearly at the Rio Conference of 1992 and became more evident at the Johannesburg Conference of 2002: environmental organisations, UNEP representatives, and some other representatives pleaded for sustainable development which included economic development and adequate environmental protection. Most developing countries were mainly interested in talking about economic development, access to world markets, and other economic or financial subjects. Despite the demonstrations in Seattle and elsewhere, this situation has not changed.

Environmental policy is hence in a similar situation as human rights: the need to protect the environment is globally recognised, as is the need to protect human rights. However, there are no global binding instruments to ensure this protection. At national level, the need to protect human rights (the environment) has found its way into many constitutions and numerous political and legal statements. Nevertheless, the protection often remains at the level of words and good intentions. The difference between environmental protection and human rights lies in the physical situation: human rights do not disappear, even if some or all of them are not respected in parts of the world for a certain period of time. As long as there are human beings, there will be the aspirations to ensure human rights for them. As regards the environment, however, there is but one environment. Once the tropical forests have disappeared, it will not be possible to restore them or the impact they had on the global environment. The great number of disappearing species makes it impossible to replenish the Earth. Once the Maldives disappear into the ocean, due to climatic change and rising waters, they will not reappear.

III. A way forward shown by the European Union?

Looking again at the question, where could progressive ways be found, it might be worthwhile to examine more closely the example of the European Union. In my opinion, the EU is the only region in the world where combining economic growth, social development, and environmental protection is a declared policy, and where efforts are made to put this policy into institutional, political, and societal reality. The description of the EU environmental policy and law in the first section above hopefully made it clear that this is not to try to paint a rosy picture of the state of sustainable development affairs in the EU. Here, too, there is political rhetoric on the environment, there is environmental placebo legislation, and there is a continuous tension between economic interests and (social and) environmental concerns. The struggle to protect the environment through day-to-day decisions is not different from trying to ensure, for example, equality of men and women in daily life or the practical application of other human rights. Yet, with all existing shortcomings, the European Union might be a worthwhile subject of consideration for looking ahead.

1. Institutions

(a) As regards the institutions, the EU has a body – the European Commission – which is required to take care of the general European interests. These interests certainly include the environment. Since the environment has no frontiers – what a common place! – it means that the European body examines the state of the environment within the European region, independently from the different Member States' frontiers. Indeed, one of the big problems of international environmental law is that the nation states are the principal source of information about the state of the environment in their countries. The European Commission has, in addition, surrounded itself with a European

Environmental Agency which collects, processes, and distributes information on the environment, together with a number of scientific committees or bodies. These 'satellites', together with the Commission, contribute towards the progressive establishment of a European-wide consensus on data, on scientific standards and evaluations, and slowly penetrate into technical-industrial sectors.[45]

These activities gradually lead to the understanding that the environment, in the same way as human rights, is not a purely national issue. They also lead to the acceptance that the European institutions do not limit themselves to looking into transboundary environmental problems, but tackle environmental problems as a whole, whether it be drinking water, bathing water, used water, domestic waste, natural habitats, incineration of waste, environmental impact assessment, or many other items.

It would be presumptuous to suggest that in other regions of the world, a body similar to the European Commission should be instituted. This institution, as well as the European Union, is the result of a long political, economic, and cultural evolution in Western Europe. Although Western European experience so far shows that the European integration has clear economic, social, and environmental advantages for all countries that participate in this integration process, the European Union does not even consider to try to export the EU model. Whereas the question of exporting the institution of the European Commission does not exist, it might be worthwhile questioning whether regional environmental agencies under the auspices of the United Nations could not be instituted. Such an agency may take over some of the European level functions which are handled by the European Commission (such as will be discussed in the next section). What would be essential is that such a regional environmental agency be, as far as possible, independent from the governments of the nation states in the region. This suggests that officials in such an agency be employed by the United Nations and not employed nor directly paid by their state of origin.

(b) The second institutional element to be mentioned is the existence of the ECJ. Up to now, it has given some 400 judgments in environmental matters. The most interesting aspect of that fact, in comparison to international law, is perhaps that none of those cases was brought by one EU Member State against another; about 80 per cent of the cases were brought to the Court by the European Commission. Some emanated from national courts. It is therefore not surprising to note that almost none of the environmental cases deals with transboundary disputes; transboundary disputes, it must be concluded are extremely rare in reality. In contrast, the majority of disputes submitted to

---

[45] Through these satellites, the EU is progressively developing common standards on genetically modified organisms and products, on the testing of chemicals, industrial safety, the licensing of pesticides and food, etc.

dispute settlement bodies or courts in international environmental law are mainly transboundary.

The ECJ is well accepted as the supreme authority in the interpretation of environmental law. It has issued a number of landmark decisions which had legal effects reaching far beyond the environmental sector. On frequent occasions, its judgments clarified unclear or contradictory wording within specific pieces of legislation or between different texts.

The ideologically motivated – 'US citizens may only be judged by a US court' – objection of the USA against international courts is well known and this means that for a foreseeable time, there is no chance of an international court that could deal with environmental matters. The question is, however, whether regional environmental courts could not be set up, with the consent of the regional states, on the basis of regional Conventions. In a legal contribution like this, there is no need to make reference to the pacifying effects of dispute settlement by independent courts. What is relevant is for the court jurisprudence to be accepted by all countries in the region. This is achievable only when the necessary institutional steps are taken in order to ensure judicial independence. This would probably also mean that the court can only hear a case when the state where the case is located agrees to the judicial process.

2. Policy development

It has already been mentioned that the environmental degradation would not be reversed, even if all the global environmental Conventions were fully implemented. This statement probably remains true also, if one includes the numerous regional environmental Conventions. In any event, following the European Union considerations, it might be worthwhile to consider whether there should not be regional environmental action programmes which would be drafted by either the regional environmental agency, mentioned above, or by the United Nations. Such programmes would then be discussed by the states of the regions and finally approved. Their implementation would be in the hands of the regional environmental agency and the regional states in question.

Such regional environmental action programmes have several advantages. First, they get away from the point-by-point discussion of some environmental problems, as they are presently discussed under the global and regional environmental Conventions; they rather allow the raising of the specific environmental problems of the region. Secondly, regional environmental programmes focus public attention on priorities, and allow the transmission of the message that it is the public's environment which is at stake. This may facilitate the search, and the finding of solutions, for environmental problems which are region-specific. Thirdly, regional environmental action programmes and their joint implementation may have cumulative effects that spring from joint action, have confidence-building consequences, and exercise domino effects that could spring from successful action. Finally, the continuous discussions which necessarily accompany the putting into operation and monitoring of the action programme are susceptible to create a network spirit among those that are charged with these tasks.

3. Decision-making

The elaboration of regional binding provisions is certainly the most delicate issue. There is a tradition that international Conventions – global as well as regional – are adopted by general consent, which is normally perceived as an expression of the sovereignty of nation state. International declarations on the environment hasten to stress the sovereign right of each state to use, exploit, and destroy its own environment.[46]

The time might have come to start serious discussions on the validity of this concept in the twenty-first century. The sovereign right of a state to destroy the ozone layer, tropical forests, to pollute the oceans or to deplete all the fish in the seas, to provoke by its individual action a climate change for the whole Earth, is already questionable under existing rules of law – and is indeed questioned. Furthermore, the discussion on human rights and their worldwide respect, or the 'sovereign' right of each state to have nuclear or other weapons of mass destruction, demonstrate the shallowness of the arguments on national sovereign rights. Recent history is full of examples where sovereign rights of states have been disregarded in the name of whatever international principles, be it the fight against Communism, the right of states to take preventive warfare action, the need of some states to protect their citizens within another state, or the fight against terrorism or other objective or subjective concerns.

Being the way it is, environmental protection is neither a hidden aggression nor an attempt to interfere with internal governments' business. Regional environmental provisions try to pool human and financial experience, avoid 'a race to the bottom' for fear that the neighbour might have a competitive advantage, and help to improve the environmental as well as the economic situation of those concerned. If it is correct that economic progress, in the long run, cannot be achieved without accompanying environmental protection – and I am certainly of the opinion that this is a correct statement – then it might well be worthwhile for researchers and scientists to demonstrate this interrelationship between economic growth and environmental concern with a conviction that is sufficiently convincing for governments.

---

[46] See Stockholm Declaration of the United Nations Conference on the Human Environment, Principle 21: 'states have, in accordance with the Charter of the United Nations and the principles of international law, the sovereign right to exploit their own resources pursuant to their own environmental policies'. To the same effect, see Principle 2 of the Rio de Janeiro Declaration on Environment and Development.

I do believe that cool reflection on advantages and disadvantages could motivate governments all over the world to accept majority decisions in environmental matters – perhaps with the exception of the USA. Obviously, though, no serious attempt has yet been made to initiate such reactions. This means that, in any regional environmental cooperation, there would have to be a period where decisions on measures to be taken would have to require a general consent. This period will be more or less long and depends on the time needed until enough confidence is built among the states participating in the regional environmental cooperation. They need to understand that common environmental measures are 'win-win' situations for all of them and not a hidden form of political, economic, or other means of gaining dominance in the region. The regional environmental agency could do a lot to contribute in progressively building such confidence.

4. Implementation

There are several specific features which mark the implementation process in the European Union. The first is that the facts on implementation or non-implementation are not assembled by the EU Member States alone, but that the European Commission itself plays a very active role in monitoring implementation. In international regional environmental cooperation, the regional environmental agency could request the transmission of legislative, administrative, and other measures which serve to implement those measures that had been decided on in the different states. The agency could also use other sources to find out about implementation measures, use meetings with the public authorities of the state, scientific findings, its own data, information from citizens or journalists, for this purpose. The important lesson to learn from the European Union's experience is that the agency must be allowed to play an active role in implementation monitoring and not be reduced to a passive receiver of information which member states might gracefully wish to transmit with more or less reluctance.

OECD countries agreed among themselves to send inspection delegations, composed of experts from OECD member states, in turn to OECD member countries. These inspect environmental performance of a specific state and submit a report to the OECD, which is subsequently published.[47] During the inspection, the team closely cooperates with the authorities of the state where the inspection is being carried out. This often leads to the drafting of reports in a rather diplomatic language without daring to point fingers at cases of insufficient implementation or omissions, or going into details regarding specific issues. Despite these shortcomings, the reports are valuable since they

---

[47] See e.g., OECD, Environmental performance reviews: Germany (1993); Norway (1993); Portugal (1993); United Kingdom (1994); Italy (1994), all in Paris.

override the idea of national sovereignty in the implementation of environmental measures. These inspection reports might well serve as an example for other regions.

Just for the sake of being complete, it should be mentioned that the European Commission publishes an annual report on the monitoring of application of EU law which contains a comprehensive chapter on environmental law.[48] The Commission also conducts inspections in Member States, though on a case-by-case basis. However, this is irregularly done due to lack of resources.

5. Dispute prevention and settlement

The first lesson to learn from the EU experience in this area is the fact that the disputes which are really of relevance are not between two or more states, but rather between human activity, on the one hand and the environment, on the other. It is the environment which is constantly damaged by human activity, and since the environment has no voice, any dispute prevention and settlement procedure should see the giving of such a voice to the environment as its foremost task. Obviously, it would be helpful if a regional environmental agency assumed this task.

Furthermore, it is obvious from the EU experience that any monitoring activity in a region should not be limited to transboundary environmental issues. Indeed, from an environmental point of view, the number of such cases is negligible and it is not really worthwhile to set up a regional machinery to deal with them. What matters much more is the respect of the regional and international provisions on environmental protection which exist. Once more, a regional environmental agency which earnestly monitors implementation of the regional environmental legal provisions would be able to prevent a considerable amount of environmental damage through this activity, by forcing the states in the region to stop illegal practices or activities.

It is a question of maturity for a state to be ready to go to court if a body such as a regional environmental agency would be allowed to sue it for violation of environmental law. Without doubt, there would have to be an elaborate pre-court procedure between the agency and the state in question, during which an out-of-court settlement of the problem may be found. In the European Union, the pre-court procedure in environmental matters is twice as long as the court procedure.[49] From 100 cases involving the pre-court procedure, only approximately 7 per cent actually reach the ECJ. Again, in all this institution-building at regional level, much will depend on the determination and readiness

---

[48] See, e.g., *Nineteenth report on monitoring application of Community law*, COM (2002) 324, 28 June 2002.
[49] See Krämer, L., Die Rechtsprechung der EG-Gerichte zum Umweltrecht 2000–2001, *EuGRZ* (2002), pp. 483–498.

of the regional states to practise an environmental policy that is worth its name and goes beyond, rhetoric.

Any judgment from a court at the present state of international environmental law would only be of a declaratory nature. Nowhere in the world do states seem ready to pay a penalty or compensation for breach of their environmental obligations. This may, however, be enforceable if, after the court's judgment, the regional environmental agency makes a follow-up to ensure that the court's declaration is followed by remedial action.

6. The involvement of the public

Knowledge gives power. It is therefore understandable that the concept of a 'global Aarhus Convention' on the right of access by citizens to information held by public authorities, participation in decision-making, and access to the courts in environmental matters, did not find much support in UNEP discussions, incidentally, neither from the USA. Sharing data on environmental deterioration with citizens, journalists, scholars, and persons from other states as well, sounds like heresy to many governments and states which prefer secrecy, closed societies, and mechanisms which leave their power structures untouched.

The lesson to learn from the European Union is that it is possible to ensure access to information by citizens and to help them participate in decisions that affect the environment without (a) questioning the whole system of the citizens' involvement in public affairs, which might be revealed not to be entirely democratic in all states; or (b) provoking a mass of aspirations from citizens which might shatter traditional administrative structures. Indeed, the European experience shows that in the majority of cases, citizens ask for environmental information when the information is of direct and individual interest to them. The same applies to requests for participating in administrative decision-making: persons normally ask to participate when the measure affects their personal or professional interests. Environmental organisations have a tendency to be somehow more general in their requests. However, the huge number of environmental issues, the scarcity of staff and financial resources create limits to the number of their requests. Finally, competitors and professional organisations constitute a specific group of potential applicants. Again, here the application is normally made where there is a competitive interest in the project.

In contrast to that, there are many political and societal advantages for opening access to information and decision-making in environmental matters; they need not all be described here. Openness and transparency increase acceptability of decisions. They lead to decision-making which is more readily accepted by the population. They have at least a tendency to reduce corruption. They make the knowhow of persons and groups available to the administration and thus exercise a long-term influence on administrative decision-making. They also allow a more continuous public discussion of environmental issues and problems.

Since there is a clear win-win situation in a more open and transparent environmental administration, the first phrase of this section should be repeated: knowledge gives power. And the readiness to share power is not prevalent anywhere. From an environmental point of view, one might add that power tends to corrupt, and absolute power tends to corrupt absolutely. However, those who hold the power will neither like to hear this word nor to listen to it.

7. Integration

The integration of environmental requirements into other policies such as agriculture and fishery, transport and energy, trade and economic policy, remains, in the European Union and elsewhere, one of the main challenges for the future. The efforts of the European Union still are not such that they could be presented as a success story. Nevertheless, lessons may also be learned from the less successful experiences. The first lesson is that the requirement of 'integrating' or of a political objective such as 'sustainable development' is meaningless. It is hardly possible to find any person in the world that is opposed to a sustainable development and to the necessity of integrating environmental and other requirements. The devil is always in the detail.

This means that the integration process needs to be laid down in detail in – once more – action programmes which specify which individual measures are to be taken for each individual policy sector, in order progressively to align environmental and agricultural (transport, energy, etc.) needs. In doing this, it should not be forgotten that integrating environmental requirements is a continuous process and cannot be achieved within a duration of four, five, or even ten years.[50] Consequently, what is necessary is a continuous monitoring of such action programmes, since in daily policy, good intentions are easily forgotten.

In this regard, a regional environmental agency could play a useful coordinating and monitoring function. Indeed, if one would want to make agricultural and fishery, transport, energy, and other policies 'greener', a profound analysis and careful assessment of technological, economic, and sociological conditions and possibilities is required, including the financing of any eventual measure that is taken. One should be aware, however, that in whatever way the integration of environmental concerns in other policies is organised, the objective remains difficult to achieve.

---

[50] Also in this aspect, the parallel with human rights, such as the equality between men and women, is obvious.

IV. Towards a regionalised environmental policy

The point of departure of this contribution was the criticism with regard to the international legal and political efforts in the environmental area. I argued that the USA has been, for the last twenty years, opposed and sometimes even hostile to any serious global effort to preserve, protect, and improve the quality of the environment. In view of its overriding political and economic influence on global affairs, and the state of its internal political and social structure, it is not foreseeable that this paralysing of environmental global efforts will end soon.

Since a global policy which leads to an improvement of the present environmental situation, and not just to slowing down of environmental deterioration, is not possible at present, it is suggested that some consideration be given to regionalisation of environmental issues. In most regions of the world, the social, economic, and political structures are not too different. Hence, regional measures for environmental protection may be easily adaptable to the specific situations of the different regions.

For the last thirty years, the European Union has pursued a European environmental policy which is, in law, complementary to the environmental policies of the EU Member States. However, it has served as a de facto innovating and progressive policy for a number of sectors, and for a number of EU Member States. Its merits have been gradually recognised by all EU Member States. Though the environment in the European Union is still not in a state which allows it to be called a model for other regions, the environmental infrastructure which the European Union set up over the last thirty years might serve as a solution to environmental problems in other regions of this planet.

Since there is only one planet, Earth, and the environment has no national frontiers, it seems very old-fashioned to organise transboundary environmental protection in the twenty-first century along lines of environmental Conventions and nation states' frontiers. What is needed is a transboundary body which takes up the regional environmental issues in a more organised and systematic way. In other words, the plea is for a regional transboundary environmental policy, not only for – regional or global – environmental Conventions.

In organising such a policy (this means the conceiving, drafting, discussing, negotiating, and adopting of a political framework and the necessary individual measures), two instruments which were borrowed from the EU environmental policy system were put to discussion: an environmental driving force such as a regional environmental agency, which is not dependent on the regional states' pressure and which could initiate, form, and negotiate, and decide on environmental policy together with the regional states. And then the laying down of objectives, principles, and priorities of such regional environmental policy in a regional environmental action programme. Of course, it is thought that in such regional settings, the United Nations Environmental Programme might play the role of a driving force for environmental improvement which is so regularly hindered at the global level.

This chapter discusses a number of relevant aspects for such regionalised environmental policies, taking lessons from the EU environmental policy. It is obvious that the different existing regional organisations, in particular NAFTA,[51] Mercosur,[52] SADC,[53] and ASEAN,[54] have neither institutions nor structures nor policies to offer for environmental policies that follow the EU model. Their environmental activities correspond to the classical intergovernmental cooperation: cooperation is agreed upon, or policies, strategies, or action plans concerted, at different administrative and policy levels. The execution of all – non-binding – decisions in full conformity with the principle of national sovereignty is an issue for each contracting state. There is no institution or body which has the task of taking care of the general (environmental) territorial interests of the member states of the organisation; there is neither a common court of justice or a guarantee of uniform enforcement of the agreed (environmental) provisions within the whole organisation.

It is obvious that one might well argue about the possibility of extending this or that aspect of EU environmental policy to other regions of the world. The essential question, however, still remains whether the present form of global environmental policy has not led into an impasse where environmental measures are often not more than simply placebo measures, meant to placate the concerned world public, and to allow other objectives to be pursued with greater determination. From an environmental point of view, the Seattle and Cancun demonstrations may seem as signs that the present state of global development is not at all sustainable. Since this is obviously a deliberate strategy by some, it might be worthwhile to reflect on alternatives to the present state of affairs. Hopefully, this chapter contributes to such a reflection.

---

[51] North American Free Trade Agreement (NAFTA) and its side agreement the North American Agreement on Environmental Cooperation (NAAEC) to which Canada, Mexico, and the USA belong, came into effect in 1994. The latter agreement expressly provides for 'the right of each party to establish its own levels of domestic environmental protection ... and to adopt or modify accordingly its environmental laws and regulations' (Article 3).

[52] Mercosur, the Mercado Común del Sur, has Argentina, Brazil, Paraguay, and Uruguay as members; Bolivia and Chile are associated.

[53] Southern African Development Community (SADC), membership consists of fourteen states.

[54] Association of South-East Asian Nations (ASEAN).

14

Transition and governance: the case of post-communist states

STEPHEN STEC, ALEXIOS ANTYPAS, AND TAMARA STEGER

I. Introduction

Taken as a whole, the experience of European countries in transition (CITs) represents a unique contribution to the sustainable development discourse, globally and regionally.[1] At one historical moment, transition redefined the context for sustainable development discourse in Europe.[2] Yet, surprisingly, the lessons learned in human, technical, and governance terms are rarely expressed or applied by CIT governments in international forums. The opportunity for doing so with one voice rapidly gave way to divergent perspectives as the forces unleashed following the fall of Communism took sway. CIT governments set differing social, economic, and environmental priorities on the basis of reemergent national consciousness, local conflicts, urgent restructuring, and regional integration into new blocs. Nevertheless, a common ecological consciousness of transition has persisted.[3] It emerges occasionally on the political level but more significantly is embodied in special regional institutions and the new civil society. Simultaneously, the relevant international forums have undergone a perceptible shift towards more inclusive mechanisms in international law- and policy-making. It is through this shift from government to governance that some voice has been given to the lessons learned from transition in the sustainable development discourse.

---

[1] Stec, S., Do two wrongs make a right? Adjudicating sustainable development in the Danube dam case, *Golden Gate University L. Rev.* 29 (1999), pp. 326–328, at 317.

[2] United Nations, Sustainable development in Europe, North America and Central Asia: Progress since Rio, ECE/CEP/84, 2002.

[3] See Stec, S., Ecological rights advancing the rule of law in Eastern Europe, *Env'l L. and Litigation* 13 (1998), pp. 275–358, at 278. See also Starzewska, A., The legislative framework for EIA in centrally planned economies, in Walthern, P. (ed.), *Environmental impact assessment: theory and practice*, London and New York (Routledge) 2nd edn 1992, pp. 210–224, at 221; Feshbach, M. and Friendly, A., *Ecocide in the USSR*, New York (Basic Books) 1992, pp. 237–238. Compare Genov, N., Environmental risks in a society in transition: perceptions and reactions, in Vari, A. and Tamas, P. (eds.), *Environment and democratic transition: policy and politics in Central Eastern Europe*, Dordrecht (Kluwer Academic Publishers) 1993.

II. Convergence and divergence

1. Convergence

(a) Shared ecological consciousness

The late 1980s and early 1990s was a time when ecological consciousness erupted throughout Europe to such an extent that borders no longer mattered and those systems reliant upon strong artificial borders disintegrated. The role of environmentalism in the politics of transformation, revolution, and transition in Eastern Europe is well established.[4] Environmental organisations led the civil society explosion, as both NGOs and even political parties.[5] When Vaclav Havel became President of the Czech and Slovak Federal Republic in 1990, he brought attention to the state of the environment in his acceptance speech and made environmental appointments a priority in his government.[6] Environment Minister Jozef Vavrousek proposed a national policy for integrating environmental protection as a primary goal in the shift to a market economy, even at the cost of slower economic growth.

Bulgaria's new government declared that it was an 'ecological market economy'. The new Hungarian government gave ample credit to the environmental movement as a force for democratisation, claiming that a 'historical opportunity' had opened for environmental protection[7] as it backed out of building a 'gigomaniacal' scheme to divert the Danube.[8] Poland cancelled construction of its first nuclear power plant, already 40 per cent complete, and Germany quickly closed its only Communist-era RBMK Chernobyl-type reactor. On 19 August 1991, when Boris Yeltsin scrambled atop the tank in front of the Parliament

---

[4] See e.g., Stec (1999), op. cit. pp. 329–346 and references cited therein; Vari and Tamas, op. cit.; Barbara, H., *Environmental politics in Poland: a social movement between regime and opposition*, New York (Columbia University Press) 1996; Jancar-Webster, B., Eastern Europe and the former Soviet Union, in Sheldon, K. (ed.), *Environmental politics in the international arena: movements, parties, organizations and policy*, Albany (State University of New York Press) 1993; Jancar-Webster, B. (ed.), *Environmental action in Eastern Europe: response to crisis*, Armonk, NY (M. E. Sharpe) 1993.

[5] Szirmai, V., The structural mechanisms of the organization of ecological-social movements in Hungary, in Vari, and Tamas, op. cit. p. 153; French, H. F., *Green revolutions: environmental reconstruction in Eastern Europe and the Soviet Union*, Washington (Worldwatch) 1990, p. 29.

[6] French, op. cit. p. 38.

[7] Hungary's National Renewal Program 1990–1992, Budapest, 1990, quoted in Lehoczki, Z. and Balogh, Z., Hungary, in Klarer, J. and Moldan, B., *The environmental challenge for Central and Eastern European economies in transition*, Chichester (John Wiley & Sons) 1997, p. 131.

[8] See Czechoslovak President on security cooperation and Nagymaros Barrage, BBC summary of world broadcasts, 18 February 1991, Pt. 2, Eastern Europe: A. International Affairs, 2 USSR – Eastern European Relations, EE/0999/A2/1, quoted in Stec (1999), op. cit. p. 319, n. 10.

building in Moscow, the next person to climb the tank was Soviet Environment Minister Nikolai Vorontsov – the first non-Communist appointed to the Soviet government in seven decades – who denounced the assumption of power by the 'coup-plotters' as 'illegal'.[9] Green parties took up posts in Bulgaria, Romania, Lithuania, Estonia, Latvia, and the Slovak Republic.

(b) 'Ecological euphoria' stage of constitution and law drafting

During the green revolutions of 1989–91, even law-making was subject to 'ecological euphoria'. In November 1990, Hilary French could state:

> Given the important role that environmental protest played in the recent upheavals in Eastern Europe and the Soviet Union, environmentalists can fairly claim a mandate for strong environmental controls.[10]

Eight days after signing the agreement dissolving the USSR, the first legal act passed by an independent Russian Federation was the Environmental Law.[11] Ukraine, the site of the Chernobyl accident that sent shock-waves through Soviet society, had passed its own environmental law even earlier.[12] In 1991, the Union of Democratic Forces government of Bulgaria passed one of the most advanced environmental laws in the region.[13] One particularly impressive example can be found in the Czech and Slovak Federal Republic,[14] where individuals such as Josef Vavrousek and Bedrich Moldan moved quickly to pass new environmental legislation. Four major pieces of environmental legislation were adopted on the federal level in 1991.[15] Events were mirrored in the break-up of the former Yugoslavia, where Slovenia moved quickly to adopt a state-of-the-art environmental law following independence.

Constitutions of this era included core environmentally sound and sustainable development principles: the right to a healthy environment,[16] access to environmental information, and compensation for environmental harm. Article 42 of the Russian Federation Constitution of 1993, for example, provided: 'Everyone has the right to a decent environment, reliable information about

---

[9] Yeltsin becomes the focus of Russian opposition in coup, *Washington Post*, 20 August 1991, p. A17.
[10] French, op. cit. p. 10.
[11] Law No. 2060-1 passed in December 1991, *Rossiiskaia gazeta*, 3 March 1992.
[12] Law of Ukraine on Environmental Protection, 28 November 1991, Vidomosti Verkhovnoi Radi Ukrainy, 4(1991), item 546.
[13] Law No. 86/1991.
[14] The Czech and Slovak Federal Republic succeeded Czechoslovakia in 1990. On 1 January 1993 the two constituent republics became independent states.
[15] Air Law, Waste Law, Environmental Protection Act, and EIA Law.
[16] The course of the development of the right in Europe has been described in Stec, S. (ed.), *Handbook on access to justice under the Aarhus Convention*, Szentendre (Regional Environmental Center) 2003, pp. 73–75.

the state of the environment, and compensation for harm caused to his health or property by ecological breaches of the law.'[17] In the course of revising the Constitution of the German Federal Republic following reunification, a new Article 20a was adopted which stated the general aim *(staatszielbestimmung)* of a clean and healthy environment.[18]

Several laws also made reference to responsibility towards future generations. For example, the Law on Environmental Protection of Moldova[19] includes among its main purposes ensuring 'the supreme responsibility of every generation to protect the environment for future generations'.[20] Furthermore, among the basic principles of environmental protection in Moldova is the 'priority of scopes and activities for environmental protection in the frame of economic, social and personal interests of the society for present and future'.[21] The Constitution of Ukraine incorporates 'the general rule that natural resources of the Ukraine constitute a heritage of its people'.[22] This characterisation acknowledges intergenerational responsibility for maintaining such heritage.

2. Convergence to divergence

The period of ecological euphoria was short-lived. Divergences among countries evident even before 1989 increased dramatically following the removal of Moscow's heavy domination.[23] Almost immediately following the collapse of Communism, the consensus based on common ecological consciousness began to fade as centrifugal forces, some dormant for many years, emerged to

---

[17] Commentators have described the Russian conception of the right to a decent environment as a social right that at times may serve as a legal basis for private subjective rights against polluting enterprises: Van den Berg, G. P., Russia's Constitutional Court: a decade of legal reforms, P. 2, The Constitution of the Russian Federation annotated, *Review of Central and East European Law* 28 (2002–03), pp. 273–654, at 400–401. 'Decent' is not defined specifically, but has been linked to the comprehensive system of quantitative norms based on science and risk assessment. Ibid.

[18] See Meyer-Teschendorf, K. G., Verfassungsmäßiger Schutz der natürlichen Lebensgrundlagen, *Zeitschrift für Rechtspolitik* (1994), p. 73; Rohn, St. and Sannwald, R., Die Ergebnisse der Gemeinsamen Verfassungskommission, *Zeitschrift für Rechtspolitik* (1994), p. 65; Vogel, H.-J., Aus dem Westen nichts Neues – Kritische Stellungnahme zu den Ergebnissen der Gemeinsamen Verfassungskommission, *Neue Justiz* (1994), p. 145.

[19] 17 June 1993.

[20] Law Environmental Protection (Moldova), Article 2.   [21] Ibid., Article 3(1).

[22] Shemshuchenko, Y., Human rights in the field of environmental protection, in the Draft of the new Constitution of the Ukraine, in Diemann, S. and Dyssli, B. (eds.), *Environmental rights: law, litigation and access to justice*, London (Cameron May) 1996, p. 37.

[23] See statement of Vladimir Solonari, Chairman of the Helsinki Citizens' Assembly, Moldova: Helsinki Citizens' Assembly, Civil peace and democracy in multi-ethnic societies, in *Proceedings of International Series of Seminars and Round-Table Discussions, Bender, September 9–12, 1993*, Chisinau (Helsinki Citizens' Assembly) 1995, p. 7.

play a major role in the transition of Eastern Europe.[24] The causes of divergence were many and the shape of divergence varied measurably from country to country. Shifts were evident as soon as the old regimes had fallen. A key distinction developed between two sets of legal, administrative, and social traditions along the lines of the age-old division between the Eastern and Western Roman Empires.[25] Agreements on the subregional level to enhance environmental security became a priority. Gradually, new groupings began to coalesce, as reflected in developments in environmental movements and in legislative drafting. The major historical shift of European Union enlargement played a major role in the latter process.

In the mid-1990s, shifts in the East-West sustainable development dialogue began to take place. The first was a reassertion of Eastern partnership through recognition that certain values and capacities from the CITs should be preserved and could even play a role in finding solutions on the pan-European level. This found partial expression in the Sofia Initiatives at the 1995 Sofia EfE Conference. A second shift was the development of civil society in the CITs and the correspondingly greater role NGOs from the CITs played in law- and policy-making on the national and international levels. The period 1996–1998 saw unprecedented input from non-governmental actors from CITs during the negotiation of the Convention on Access to Information, Public Participation in Decision-making and Access to Justice in Environmental Matters (Aarhus Convention, 1998).[26] This 'ambitious venture in the area of "environmental democracy"'[27] was also the first international agreement in Europe that derived substantially from the circumstances of transition. The third shift was

---

[24] In Slovakia, economic considerations replaced environmental considerations at the top of the list of problems identified in public opinion polls between May and October 1990. See Huba, M. in Klarer and Moldan, op. cit. p. 257. By 1992, a Bulgarian Prime Minister who himself was a member of a Green party, announced that the environment had been dropped to last on the Bulgarian government's list of priorities. See Georgieva, K., Environmental policy in a transition economy: the Bulgarian example, in Vari and Tamas, op. cit. pp. 67–87, at 67.

[25] See Stec, S., Access to information and public participation in environmental decision-making in the Commonwealth of Independent States, *Review of Central and East European Law* 23 (1997), pp. 355–529, at 366–371; Stec (1998), op. cit. p. 279 (analogising the legal and administrative tradition of the Eastern parts of Europe as a 'Byzantine Wheel' of paternalism, statism, and vertical control).

[26] See Wates, J., The public participation convention: progress report on the negotiation, *ELNI* 1 (1997), pp. 29–32, at 30. See generally ch. 4, Power to the people: convention on access to information, public participation in decision-making and access to justice in environmental matters, in Agarwal, A. *et al.* (eds.), *Poles apart*, New Delhi (Centre for Science and Environment) 2001; Toth Nagy, M., Drafting the Aarhus Convention: a case study on the role of civil society organizations in international policy-making, OECD study (informal document, on file with authors).

[27] Annan, K., Foreword, in United Nations Economic Commission for Europe, *The Aarhus Convention: an implementation guide*, New York and Geneva (United Nations), 2000, p. v.

the coalescence of CITs into two major blocs based on prospects for integration into Euro-Atlantic structures, in particular the EU.

The Aarhus Convention represents perhaps the most significant contribution of common ecological consciousness to the sustainable development discourse and is unlikely to be paralleled. It has had a comparatively bigger impact on the legislation of Western Europe than that of Eastern Europe. Several EC Directives have had to be amended to be brought into conformity with it. The open standing rules common in CITs will soon be applicable throughout the EU. The pace of ratifications has confirmed the greater difficulty of Western states to adjust their legislation to the Convention requirements.[28] On the international level, the Aarhus Convention, through its clear connection between environment and human rights, has extended the general recognition of NGOs as international legal persons in the field of international human rights law[29] to the environment as well. The Aarhus Convention Compliance Committee, in which members serve in their personal capacity, is the first environmental compliance mechanism based on human rights models.

3. Divergence I: regionalisation and selective integration

(a) Divergence, environment, and security

The OSCE has considered environment and security since the Lisbon Summit in December 1996, where heads of state called on the OSCE to focus on ways of identifying the risks to security arising from economic, social, and environmental problems. The OSCE's Economic Forum addressed 'Security Aspects in the Field of the Environment' at its 1999 annual meeting, giving rise to an international initiative on environment and security. A major focus of international efforts in this arena is in conflict reduction concerning shared natural resources that now must be managed by numerous states. Consequently, the period of transition has seen the development of a large number of specialised regional agreements, institutional arrangements, bodies for coordinating financial assistance and other initiatives, sponsored by international organisations such as UNEP,[30] UNDP,[31] the REC,[32] the Council of Europe,[33] or the Stability Pact for South Eastern Europe.[34] UNEP in particular has tackled harmonisation initiatives in the Russian Far East, the Caucasus, and Central Asia.[35] Many such subregional processes have been either created or influenced by transition. The

---

[28] See www.aarhusconvention.org
[29] See Philippe, S., Enforcing environmental security, in Philippe, S. (ed.), *Greening international law*, London (Earthscan) 1993, pp. 50–64, at 55.
[30] See e.g., Conventions on the Carpathian Mountains, Caspian Sea, and Black Sea.
[31] Tisza River Basin Sustainable Development Programme, in cooperation with the REC.
[32] Regional Environmental Reconstruction Programme for South Eastern Europe (REReP).
[33] Initiative on Sustainable Spatial Development of the Tisza River Basin.
[34] International Framework Agreement on the Sava River Basin.   [35] See www.unep.ch/

Sava River Framework Agreement was inconceivable when the river fell within the borders of one state. The Aral Sea was similarly situated. The Caspian Sea was formerly surrounded by two countries; now there are five. The independence of the Baltic states fundamentally changed international relations concerning the Baltic Sea,[36] resulting in the adoption of the Convention on the Protection of the Marine Environment of the Baltic Sea Area (Helsinki, 1992). Although regional arrangements have some common characteristics, there are also stark differences based upon the constellations of states involved. Thus, the International Framework Agreement for the Sava River Basin could be negotiated by states with a common language and a recent identity of institutions. The Tisza River Basin presents a more complex picture with respect to the legal, policy, and institutional frameworks[37] of the countries, not to mention language, culture, level of development, and integration into regional economic integration organisations. A regional MEA on the Tisza is unlikely before the end of the decade.

(b) European Union enlargement

Although the environmental/democratic movement in Eastern Europe did not originate with a vague, idealistic goal of integration into Euro-Atlantic structures, this became the only political and security option for many CITs. CITs have thus coalesced into two distinct groups: those who have entered or have prospects for entering the European Union, and those who do not. For the former group, harmonisation, approximation, transposition, and implementation of the *acquis communautaire* has been an overriding goal. For the latter group, EU enlargement has not greatly influenced law and policy.

After a period of general assistance aimed at stabilisation, financial and technical assistance became increasingly tied to accession to the EU and NATO. European Union assistance towards CITs has played a critical role in their orientation. Major shifts in EU assistance policy took place in 1996 and 2000. In 1996, the EC shifted the focus of reform under the PHARE programme from demand-driven to accession-driven assistance. As a part of the reform, a two-prong approach to assistance was adopted. An institution-building component focused primarily on adoption and implementation of the *acquis communautaire*, including the development of relevant structures, human resources, and management skills, and an investment component was aimed at helping the candidate countries bring their industries and major infrastructure up to Community standards. Assistance to the ten candidate countries was further

---

[36] The Soviet environmental authorities' plans for an integrated system for monitoring the Baltic Sea were halted by the declarations of independence of the Baltic states in 1991. See Feshbach and Friendly, op. cit. pp. 245–46.

[37] See REC, Regional assessment of legal, policy and institutional frameworks related to sustainable water management issues in Tisza riparian countries, Szentendre (Regional Environmental Center) 2004 (on file with authors).

refocused and reoriented in 2000 towards preparation for EU membership. Several support mechanisms were brought together within a single framework, called an Accession Partnership, drawn up with each candidate country, which outlined the priority areas in which each country needed to make progress in order to prepare for accession. Bilateral development assistance from EU Member States has generally, although not exclusively, followed the course of assistance from the Commission. Significant EU donors in the environmental field have included the Scandinavian countries, the Netherlands, the United Kingdom, Germany, and Austria.

Meanwhile, EU support to the non-accession countries was unchanged by the reorganisation, and continued to provide support in their transition to democracy and a market economy. Technical Assistance to the Commonwealth of Independent States (TACIS), established in 1991, is the European Commission's technical assistance programme for economic reforms in the Commonwealth of Independent States and Mongolia.[38] TACIS financing has been used primarily for technical assistance that transfers know-how from the EU (in the form of policy advice, consultancy teams, studies, and training) by developing and reforming legal and regulatory frameworks, institutions, and organisations, and by setting up partnerships, networks, twinning and pilot projects. It also provides limited support for investment projects. Since 1996, TACIS has also focused on the EU border regions, through the TACIS Cross-Border Cooperation (CBC) programme.

(c) Compatible pan-European responses

Significant non-EU bilateral donors have included Switzerland, Norway, Japan, and the USA. These donor countries also changed the focus of assistance around 1996–1997. The USA shifted from broadly supporting transition through ad hoc projects with an emphasis on grant-making to a more focused, programme-oriented, institution-building approach supporting the extension of successful pilot projects throughout a larger geographical region. For example, US AID funded eight further Public Environmental Review Centers in NIS/EECCA[39] based on a successful original centre. Japan, one of the largest providers of international assistance globally, plays a substantial role in Eastern Europe. The Japan Special Fund (JSF) was established in 1992 by the Ministry of Foreign Affairs, Europe and Asia Bureau, as a means of managing certain earmarked contributions of Japan to the REC. As European Union expansion became the dominant force in the Central and Eastern European (CEE) region, the pan-European context for assistance made a compatible shift, as the focus of international processes gradually moved further east to NIS/EECCA.

---

[38] Regulation (EEC) 2053/93.
[39] Newly independent states, or East Europe, Caucasus and Central Asia.

4. Divergence II: The development of environmental law and practice in Eastern Europe

(a) Early model applicability trends in CITs

Substantial environmental law reform had taken place as a last-gasp effort of Soviet authorities.[40] Far from being relics of history, the laws passed during that period are still the basis of a substantial part of the environmental legislation in the NIS/EECCA region. They are based on the system of state administration and social organisation referred to as the Byzantine Wheel,[41] consistent with the circumstances of partially reformed Eastern countries. Environmental impact assessment (EIA) and ecological expertise (sometimes collectively referred to as biosphere reflection) were a major focus of environmental law drafting in CITs in this period.[42] The NIS/EECCA countries have retained the ecological expertise form for the most part, some of them in a rather undeveloped state. In some cases this is tempered by greater public participation opportunities during the process of a *state ecological expertise* (EE), sometimes contained in a procedure called OVOS.[43] In fact, attempts to introduce EIA-type multi-stakeholder processes into decision-making have been modified to remove any doubt that EE and OVOS are for the sole purpose of checking compliance of projects with existing environmental legal norms.[44]

Already during the period of 'ecological euphoria' a divergence among CITs arose as a consequence of the rapid turning westward of a part of the CEE region. Countries such as Czech Republic based environmental law drafting on broader international, in particular Western, experience.[45] This divergence

---

[40] See Stec, S., EIA and EE in CEE and CIS: convergence or evolution?, in Nespor, S. (ed.), A world survey of environmental law, Special issue *Rivista Giuridica dell' Ambiente* (1996), pp. 343–358 (surveying late Soviet ecological expertise laws). Numerous regional protection schemes were abandoned upon the break-up of the Soviet Union. See Feshbach and Friendly, op. cit. pp. 245–246.

[41] See n. 25 above.

[42] For distinctions between various models of biosphere reflection, see Stec (1996), op. cit. pp. 343–358. For a survey of EIA/EE laws and policies in CITs, see Cherp, A., EA legislation and practice in Central and Eastern Europe and the former USSR: a comparative analysis, *Env. Impact Assessment Rev.* 21 (2001), pp. 335–361.

[43] 'OVOS' is the Russian abbreviation for 'assessment of environmental impacts', although the term refers to a document within the ecological expertise process rather than an EIA in the Western sense. See Cherp, A. and Lee, N., Evolution of SER and OVOS in the Soviet Union and Russia (1985–1996), *EIA Rev.* 17(3) (1997), pp. 177–204; Cherp, A. and Golubeva, S., Environmental assessment in the Russian Federation: evolution through capacity-building, *Impact Assessment and Project Appraisal* 22 (2004), pp. 121–130.

[44] See discussion of 1994 modifications to Ministry of Environment's draft OVOS Regulations in response to comments of officials of other ministries in Cherp and Lee, op. cit. p. 7. These modifications clarified the role of the public in OVOS as assisting in the enforcement of existing legislation, rather than representing pluralistic interests in the context of a multidisciplinary, holistic decision-making process.

[45] There were exceptions, however. See e.g., Environmental protection law of Bulgaria, no. 86, 18 October 1991, Articles 19–23b.

widened in the following years. As an implementable legal framework was the priority throughout CITs, the particular choice of model was driven by fundamental characteristics of state and administration, including decentralisation, separation of powers, pluralism, acceptance of the rule of law, inclusion, transparency and participation, paternalism, and security concerns.

The law-drafting processes after the period of 'ecological euphoria' illuminate whether shedding the Byzantine Wheel involves revolutionary change or is merely difficult. Hungary and Bulgaria provide interesting examples. The project to replace Hungary's 1976 Law on the Protection of the Human Environment began in the 1980s during the late Communist phase. In 1991, the Parliament took drafting out of the hands of the government and set up an independent expert commission. The commission took ecological euphoria to an extreme, presenting an impressive but unworkable magnum opus in Spring 1992 that attempted to correct democratic deficiencies in many areas of law.[46] Responsibility for drafting was thereafter returned to the governmental environmental authority, which basically ignored the commission draft. Over the course of 1993–1994, the government received PHARE technical assistance to review the draft from the point of view of European Union approximation, which included criticism by a larger group of experts via a 'public participation process' coordinated by a private foundation. In 1995, the law was finally passed.[47] Despite the comprehensiveness of the process, certain deficiencies remained that had to be corrected through later law-making.[48]

In Bulgaria, a euphoric post-Communist law was based in part on late Soviet models. Political changes that brought a return to government of former Communists led to the first case of 'legislative backsliding on the environment'[49] in the CITs. Originally, Articles 19–23b of the Environmental Protection Act of Bulgaria[50] provided for mandatory environmental impact assessment for a wide range of activities and plans.[51] In 1995, the Parliament, at the urging of the Council of Ministers but without the support of the Ministry of Environment, amended the Environmental Protection Act to allow the government to avoid EIA in certain cases involving 'objects which have particular importance for the vital needs of the population of the country (or a part of it), which involves their urgent construction'.[52] Only the statement of a single expert approved

---

[46] See Environment Protection Code of Hungary, Tentative Draft, February 1992, draft translation (on file with authors).

[47] Act on Environmental Protection of Hungary, no. LIII, 1995.

[48] For example, the law stopped short of requiring decision-makers to respond with reasons to EIA comments, requiring authorities only to investigate 'essential' comments. In later versions, all comments were required to be addressed factually and legally.

[49] *Environmental Advocacy* 1(2) (Summer 1995), p. 4.   [50] No. 86, 18 October 1991.

[51] See Article 19. EIAs were obligatory for national and regional development programmes; territory–structuring and urban development plans and their amendments, and projects for reconstruction and enlargement of existing enterprises included therein; and specific types of projects enumerated and registered pursuant to an Appendix to the Law.

[52] Official Journal no. 31/ 4 April 1995.

by the Ministry of Environment evaluating environmental impacts was needed to begin construction. 'Vital needs' was vaguely defined as 'those connected with the safety and security of the health and life of the population'.[53] The amendments were challenged before the Constitutional Court, which declined to consider the case.[54] EIA Regulations issued in August 1995[55] somewhat tempered the amendments by requiring consent of competent environmental authorities of the applicable territorial development or urban development plan in order to invoke Article 23bis. In 2002, Bulgaria adopted a new Environmental Protection Law[56] whose EIA provisions are in compliance with the corresponding EC Directive and which does not provide for abridged EIA in the case of 'vital needs'.

It was remarkable that, four years after their adoption, certain elementary EIA provisions involving rights of the public to participate in decision-making were abridged so that cases of 'vital needs' could be determined according to (controllable) expert-based evaluations. The Hungarian example evinces a slow and bumpy but steady process of approximation and harmonisation. The Bulgarian example is a swinging pendulum, demonstrating a fundamental conflict in the underlying values of political and societal blocs.

In the NIS/EECCA region, early horizontal information laws were relatively weak and even those placed a theoretical emphasis on access to environmental information.[57] Some NIS/EECCA countries adopted ambiguous laws providing a right to information on the *state* of the environment only, or in some cases to information *about* the environment or *on* EIA documentation.[58] The NIS/EECCA laws demonstrate an understanding of access to information as a means of validating the performance of environmental protection authorities. In Russia, the Law on Sanitary-Epidemiological Well-Being of the Population,[59] the main vehicle for access to information concerning specific polluters, is couched in terms of gaining access to such information in order to discover whether authorities are properly controlling them. One of the more significant laws in Eastern Europe particularly dedicated to the right to information could be found in Russia: the Federal Law on Information, Informatisation,

---

[53] See Article 23bis.
[54] Decision N1, 10 July 1995.   [55] Regulation no. 1, 7 August 1995.
[56] See State Gazette no. 02/91, 25 September 2002, amended State Gazette no. 02/98, 28 October 2002.
[57] The provisions of information laws in the NIS region have been summarised up to 1996. See Stec (1997), op. cit. p. 355.
[58] See, e.g., Law on Environmental Protection (Belarus), Article 5 (providing for the right of persons 'to demand and receive complete and authoritative information about the state of the environment and measures intended to protect it'); Law on Environmental Impact Assessment 1995 (Armenia), Article 8.1 (providing that the public can 'obtain information . . . on the [EIA] documentation').
[59] Vedomosti S'ezda narodnykh deputatov RSFSR i Verkhovnogo Soveta 20 RSFSR (1991), Item 641.

and Information Protection.[60] Environmental information and 'other information necessary to provide for safe functioning of settlements, industrial objects, general citizens and population safety'[61] enjoys a special status among the categories of information that cannot be the subject of classification on the basis of secrecy.

NIS/EECCA governments showed an appreciation of governance issues since the changes began, e.g., the Ministry for Environmental Protection and Nuclear Safety of Ukraine in its 1994 *Report on the state of the environment and activities in Ukraine* lauded the role of 'green movements' in constructive opposition to find a way out of 'ecological crisis'.[62] But after a period of remarkable openness, the NIS/EECCA region saw a resurgence of state power, with state security laws and apparatuses becoming reestablished in the mid-1990s. In this atmosphere, even modern, far-reaching information laws could not prevent the notorious *Nikitin* case from going forward,[63] in which an anti-nuclear activist became the first person charged with high treason in Russia since the fall of the Soviet Union. Upon Nikitin's release, his lawyer was quoted by Reuters as saying, 'This is the first case in the history of Soviet-Russian state security that social pressure has succeeded in forcing the Federal Security Service to observe the laws and stop its trampling of human rights.'[64]

(b) Innovative environmental legislation and jurisprudence

Certain innovations can be found from the organic phase of environmental legislative drafting, particularly prior to the preeminence of the EU *acquis communautaire* in CEE and the reestablishment of state security as a priority in the NIS/EECCA. Unique factors, such as the transition from planning to decision-making, played a role, but the predominant theme was innovations relating to issues of governance and the assertion of rights of the public,[65] including 'citizen initiative' provisions in the Czech Republic, Slovakia, and Poland, citizen enforcement,[66] and well-developed information and participation

---

[60] No. 8/607, 20 February 1995.
[61] Russian Federation Law on Information, Informatisation and Information Protection, no. 8/607, 20 February 1995, Article 10.
[62] At p. 36, quoted in Stec (1997), op. cit. pp. 518–519.
[63] The facts and procedure of the case are summarised in Stec (2003), op. cit. pp. 177–179; see also Stec (1997), op. cit. pp. 491–492.
[64] See www.grida.no/ngo/bellona/nikitin.htm
[65] Other innovations can be found in the areas of emissions trading (Poland), economic instruments (Armenia), personal liability for decision-makers (Russia), self-monitoring and self-reporting (FYR Macedonia, Romania) and environmental funds (throughout).
[66] See Law on Environmental Protection (Georgia), Article 6 ('Environmental NGOs and citizens have the right to appeal to the Court in the case of violation against this Act and other environmental laws'); Hungarian Act on Environmental Protection, no. LIII, June 1995, Articles 1(f), 97(2). The latter provides that authorities whose attention is brought to environmental violations by the public shall, in addition to taking enforcement measures,

provisions.[67] Governance tools contributing to the sustainable development discourse have included the establishment of multistakeholder advisory bodies to government[68] and the involvement of NGO representatives in governmental delegations in international processes. Many of these developments related to EIA, an important innovation during periods of rapid redevelopment. Civil society has played a substantial role in legislative development. Hungarian law has long included a provision whereby interested NGOs can be placed on a list for notification and participation with respect to law drafting. An NGO drafted a complete legislative act on access to environmental information in Moldova that was considered by the Parliament.

With comparatively strong social bonds, an educated populace, and a consensual style of decision-making, the CITs are relatively less concerned with the prospect of public organisations representing relevant societal interests in administrative and judicial proceedings. Even though its historical basis is in scientific Socialism and syndicalism, there has been no great move away from 'open' or 'organisational' standing. On the contrary, on a pan-European level, Western Europe has moved towards the East on this issue.[69] Under the

---

'be obliged to make a full response within the period stipulated in the law to the written notice' from the public concerning the violations. Citizen participation in enforcement is formulated as a duty in Moldova under its Law on Environmental Protection, Article 31. The environmental inspectorates on all levels have the right to invite citizens and officials to make written statements on violations of the environmental protection legislation according to Article 28(h) of the Law.

[67] e.g., the Russian Law on Sanitary and Epidemiological Well-Being of the Population includes the right of members of the public to receive environmental information directly from enterprises. See Stec (1997), op. cit. p. 470. Romania introduced relatively strong provisions on self-reporting and self-monitoring, including notification of the public: Law on Environmental Protection, no. 137, 29 December 1995, Articles 21, 79(f).

[68] e.g., Hungary's National Environmental Protection Council established as an advisory body to the government under the Environmental Protection Act, Article 45. One-third of the members of the NEPC are made up of representatives of environmental NGOs.

[69] Although open standing can be found in many places, it has been relatively rare in Western Europe. Germany and the United Kingdom, for example, have been called 'the most backward, the least developed' in this area. Ormond, T., Access to justice for environmental NGOs in the European Union, in Diemann, S. and Dyssli, B. (eds.), *Environmental rights: law, litigation and access to justice*, London (Cameron May) 1996, p. 72. Yet in Germany, where such rules are established on the level of the *Länder*, there is a greater acceptance of open standing in the former East Germany: four out of five of the former East German states have adopted such rules, whereas only seven of eleven Western states have done the same. For a discussion of the legal basis for deciding such issues on the *Länder* level, see Van der Zwiep, K., and Backes, C., *Integrated system for conservation of marine environments*, Baden (Nomos Verlagsgesellschaft) 1994, pp. 117–119. Van der Zwiep and Backes cite Bizer, Internationale Fachtagung, 'Verbandsbeteiligung im europäischen Vergleich', *NVwZ* (1990), p. 1053 for an examination of the relative isolation of Germany in Europe with respect to this regime. The Netherlands and some Latin countries have several decades of experience in granting special status to environmental organisations. Italy, for example, allows environmental NGOs to intervene in civil cases brought by the state or local authorities for environmental damages, but only the latter are permitted to initiate

Environmental Protection Act of Slovenia,[70] professional and other associations and other non-governmental organisations for the protection of the environment may undertake environmental protection activities in the context of their competencies and rights and obligations.[71] This rule has been used by an environmental NGO to establish standing to bring an action before the Constitutional Court complaining against the legality of decrees adopting building plans for certain localities.[72]

Because the development of EIA as a law and policy tool was a priority in the CITs, several interesting variations could be found. These included:

- triggering mechanisms including change of ownership (privatisation, restitution) or petition of members of the public;[73]
- periodic EIA for ongoing enterprises;[74]
- public participation in the screening phase of EIA;[75]
- public ecological expertise (an alternative full-blown environmental assessment undertaken by a public organisation);[76]
- different levels of binding legal effect of the final determination (recommendation or permit);
- NGO drafting of EIA Regulations;[77]
- EIA commissions;[78]
- EIA of draft legislation.[79]

---

such cases. See Nespor, S., Liability litigation in Italy, in Diemann and Dyssli, op. cit. p. 259. The Aarhus Convention has accelerated the acceptance of open standing in Western Europe.

[70] Official Gazette RS, no. 32/93.
[71] Environmental Protection Act (Slovenia), Article 4(3).
[72] See Decision of the Constitutional Court of Slovenia, Doc. AN01045, 21 December 1995, Official Gazette RS3:96, (1995).
[73] Environmental Protection Act (Bulgaria), no. 86/91, Articles 19, 20 as amended; see also Cherp, O., EIA in the Republic of Belarus, in Bellinger, E. et al., Environmental assessment in countries in transition, Budapest (CEU Press) 2000.
[74] Environmental Protection Act (Bulgaria), Article 20 (requiring certain enterprises to undergo EIA every five years).
[75] See Act on Environmental Impact Assessment (Slovakia), no. 127/94, 1 September 1994, Article 10.
[76] See e.g., Ministries of Environment, Territorial Development and Construction, Health, and Agriculture and Food Industry of Bulgaria, Regulation no. 1 on Environmental Impact Assessment, 7 August 1995, Article 4.4.
[77] For example, the Estonian Green Movement participated in the drafting of EIA Regulations as early as 1996: Estonian Green Movement, Advising citizens, Szentendre (Regional Environmental Center for Central and Eastern Europe) September 1996, p. 16.
[78] Erik, M., Commissions for environmental impact assessment, Delft (Delft University Press) 1995 (examining the Polish, Hungarian, and Dutch EIA Commissions).
[79] See e.g., Law on Environmental Protection (Moldova), Article 30.3; Act on Environmental Protection (Hungary), no. LIII, 1995, Article 98(2); Law on Ecological Expertise (Russia), Article 7(4); Law on Environmental Protection (Ukraine), Article 9; Law on Environmental Protection (Romania), no. 137, 29 December 1995, Article 5.

Other valuable experience from CITs related to EIA came in areas of impact prediction methods, scope of impact, cumulative impacts, qualitative indicators, risk assessment, uncertainty and timing of procedures, bearing the costs of procedures,[80] responding to comments received,[81] and expanded or integrated assessments such as sustainability impact assessment, social impact assessment, etc. Moreover, EIA in the development of plans, policies, and programmes – later known as strategic environmental assessment, or SEA – could be found to a much greater extent in CITs than in the West at the same time.[82]

Environmental jurisprudence in CITs has developed along with the legislation. Cases have concerned the content and application of constitutional rights for a healthy environment,[83] standing for environmental NGOs, validity of particular EIAs, access to environmental information, failure to carry out administrative duties, and compensation for harm to health and environment.[84] The *Nikitin* case alone[85] has been one of the single most influential cases in determining basic rights of the accused in Russia. On the international level, the first sustainable development case decided by the International Court of Justice arose out of the circumstances of transition.[86] Cases brought by environmental advocates in CITs are also making their way to the European Court

---

[80] In some countries the costs of EIA are borne by authorities because of fear of loss of independence if the costs would be borne by the proponent. See e.g., Ministries of Environment, Territorial Development and Construction, Health, and Agriculture and Food Industry of Bulgaria Regulation no. 1 on Environmental Impact Assessment, Sofia, 7 August 1995, Article 12.

[81] e.g., Law of the Russian Federation on State Ecological Expertise, Article 8(3); Law on Environmental Impact Assessment (Armenia), Article 9.7; Law on Environmental Protection (Romania), no. 137, 29 December 1995, Article 11(h). Compare Act on Environmental Protection 1995 (Hungary), Article 93(6) (authorities need only investigate comments that are 'essential').

[82] e.g., Russian Federal Law 4556, Law on Ecological Expertise, accepted by State Duma, 19 July 1995, approved by Federation Council, 15 November 1995; Law on Environmental Impact Assessment of 1995 (Armenia), Article 15; Law on State Ecological Expertise (Belarus); Ministries of Environment, Territorial Development and Construction, Health, and Agriculture and Food Industry of Bulgaria, Regulation no. 1 on Environmental Impact Assessment, 7 August 1995, Article 5.2.1; Law on Environmental Protection (Romania), no. 137, 29 December 1995, Article 63; Order of the Ministry of Water, Forests and Environmental Protection of Romania on the approval of the procedure for the settlement of environmental impact assessment of economic and social units, 11 April 1996.

[83] Decision of the Constitutional Court of Slovenia, Doc. AN01045, 21 December 1995, Official Gazette RS, no. 3/96 (holding that the constitutional right to a healthy environment includes a duty and interest in preventing environmental damage that can serve as a basis for legal standing); *Protected Forests* case (Hungary), see Stec (1998), op. cit. pp. 320–321. Both cases are described in Appendix B, Stec (2003), op. cit. pp. 235–236, 239.

[84] See generally Table of Cases in Stec (2003), op. cit. pp. 87–90, with keywords.

[85] See also *Nikitin v. Russia*, ECHR, Appl. 00050178/99, decided 20 July 2004.

[86] See *Gabcikovo-Nagymaros Project (Hungary v. Slovakia)*, 37 I.L.M. (1998) 162, esp. separate opinion of Vice-President Weeramantrys.

of Human Rights. A recent decision of the Court found in favour of an environmental NGO in Latvia that had been sued for defamation for criticising the environmental record of a mayor.[87]

(c) The impact of accession on law drafting

By the time of the first real assessment of progress in approximation of CIT law drafting to the environmental *acquis communautaire* in 1996, a great deal of environmental law drafting had taken place, organically arising out of the circumstances of transition, and including a number of innovations. Yet there is no evidence that the innovations made through the organic development of environmental law drafting in the CITs were recognised, much less taken into account in the further elaboration of the EU *acquis communautaire*. In contrast, at the time of the previous enlargement in 1995, the German Federal Minister of the Environment, Nature Conservation, and Nuclear Safety said that a goal of the EU should be to come up to the standards of the new members.[88] It appeared inadmissible at the time that the experience of CITs could produce relevant results. This attitude pervaded the Aarhus Convention negotiations, even while EU Member States were among those taking a conservative attitude towards the Convention, and CITs were at least as advanced concerning relevant legislation as the existing Member States.[89] Statements at the time equated the attitude of CITs towards the Convention as an indication of their commitment to accession. The main finding of the European Commission was that approximation of environmental legislation was poorly advanced. This is indicative of two things: first, that the goal of approximation did not have a great influence on legislative drafting until after the EC adjusted its assistance policy; secondly, that the innovations in environmental law were considered a nullity by the EC since they did not meet the strict criteria of the *acquis communautaire*.

EU standards are objectively high and internationally progressive, and Member States are free to provide additional environmental safeguards consistent

---

[87] *Vides Aizsardzibas Klubs* v. *Latvia*, Application no. 57829/00, decided 27 May 2004.

[88] Experiences with the EU Treaty from a national perspective: why a strengthening of the concept of sustainability is necessary, Speech by Angela Merkel, German Federal Minister of Environment, Nature Conservation and Nuclear Safety, on the occasion of the Conference on Europe's Common Future, Berlin, 5 October 1995. The new members were Austria, Finland, and Sweden.

[89] See Hallo, R. E, Directive 90/313/EEC on the freedom of access to information on the environment: its implementation and implications, in Hallo, R. E. (ed.), *Access to environmental information in Europe*, The Hague (Kluwer Academic Publishers) 1996, pp. 5–7, 20–21 (classifying European Union Member States in three categories with respect to implementation of the EU Directive 90/313/EEC on access to environmental information, with the first group consisting of countries that made formal transposition on time and completely). In an interview with one of the authors in 1997, Hallo expressed the opinion that the Czech Republic, Hungary, and Poland would even then have qualified for the middle group.

with other provisions of the EU Treaty.[90] The EU emphasises practical implementation, a major advancement over the prior practice of existing Member States regardless of whether they were CITs. The positive effects have included the introduction of requirements for advanced pollution abatement technology on new plants and large investments in cleaning up pollution hot spots. Because of the emphasis placed by the Commission on certain criteria and the reorientation of assistance, the accession process itself became an exercise in priority-setting. Those matters concerning which the applicants showed comparatively little 'achievement,' including in many cases environmental legislation, consequently moved up on the domestic agenda.

At the same time, due to the overarching goal of Euro-Atlantic integration as a means for prosperity, peace, and security, EU standards were accepted uncritically without leverage for dialogue. International institutions were reinforcing in this regard.[91] Domestic environmental priorities were ignored if they did not rate high in the accession process, and all attempts at innovation were forgotten. Governments sacrificed their creativity and initiative to the overriding, and overwhelming, task of readying their countries for entry into the EU. Additionally, as in other policy areas, the environmental *acquis communautaire* was negotiated between old Member States whose priorities are reflected in the final legislation. Having no opportunity to amend the *acquis* during the accession period, the new Member States were stuck with accepting legal frameworks that did not necessarily fit well with their institutional, legal, or cultural systems, or their environmental priorities.

Moreover, concern has been expressed about the ability of the candidate countries to resist economic pressures for unsustainable development, and the prospects for preserving the more sustainable aspects of CIT societies, for example those pertaining to packaging, transport, agriculture, and biodiversity. At the same time that the EU is struggling internally with the challenges of achieving environmentally sound and sustainable development, it presents its *acquis communautaire* as an immutable and non-negotiable iconography.

For example, the absence of a broad horizontal access to information law in the *acquis communautaire*, combined with the presence of EC Directive 90/313 on access to environmental information, had a major impact on the rate at which accession CITs have adopted horizontal information laws. Meanwhile, CITs outside the accession process were less driven to focus on environmental information laws and could dedicate resources towards fashioning horizontal information laws. Arguably, EU accession has had a negative impact, since

---

[90] [2002]OJ C 325/01, 24 December 2002.
[91] e.g., European Bank for Reconstruction and Development (EBRD), *Environmental policy*, London (EBRD) 1996 ('The Bank will work through the EU to assist its countries of operations in the adoption of sound environmental policies as delineated in Article 130R (Environment) in the Treaty on European Union').

the piecemeal environmental approach is inadequate to address endemic problems and the need for fundamental restructuring that can be addressed through horizontal information laws. Notably, the EU has recently moved forward on horizontal information legislation as far as access to EU institutions is concerned.

III. Beyond EU accession

Now that the accession process has been completed for some CITs, the new Member States have entered a new phase in the development of their environmental governance regimes. The opportunities for this part of the region are great, and we can expect significant development in this area in the coming years. Among the highest priority areas are:

- a prolonged focus on domestic environmental priorities by all relevant domestic environmental actors;
- a concerted initiative by the new Member States to have their priorities reflected in the development of EU level environmental law;
- a strong push to develop administrative capacity in the environment ministries and inspectorates;
- a stronger commitment on the part of governments to support financially NGO sectors that are still struggling to develop professional skills and participate in policy-making;
- a greater commitment by the citizenry to support financially NGO work;
- a commitment on the part of governments to demonstrate transparently that they are taking the necessary steps to implement the environmental *acquis communautaire*.

On the latter point, the European Commission was well aware of the implementation gap that was certain to ensue as the countries of Central and Eastern Europe transposed the *acquis*, noting in the Agenda 2000 report that 'full compliance with the acquis could only be expected in the long to very long term and would necessitate increased levels of public expenditure'.[92] Nevertheless, governments will be held accountable for meeting their commitments. This will require not only monitoring by the European Commission, which it hardly has the resources to do with great rigor, but also active participation on the part of NGOs. Fulfilling this function and participating professionally at the EU level will prove to be a challenge to civil society organisations in the region.

For those CITs that are candidates to join the EU (Bulgaria, Croatia, Romania), the dominant environmental governance priority will remain

---

[92] Agenda 2000, Summary and conclusions of the opinions of the Commission concerning the applications for membership to the European Union presented by the candidate countries, COM (97) 2000.

readying themselves for accession. An emphasis should be placed on implementation, however. Given the relatively low capacity for environmental governance in these states, improved implementation of environment law would constitute significant progress for the environment. In countries that are part of the Stabilization and Association Process, capacities are so low and the need for reform is so profound that harmonisation with the *acquis communautaire* must be treated as a long-term prospect and urgent priorities such as municipal waste must be addressed through whatever means are available.

While EU accession has fostered legislation but dampened innovation in the CEE countries, the amount of legislative innovation in the NIS/EECCA and South-Eastern European countries has not been very high either. One major reason is the lack of interest in such laws in the face of heightened security concerns and the reestablishment of the 'octopus of state power and the Byzantine Wheel.'[93] In addition, democratisation represented, at least in some places, a challenging shift in control out of the hands of the few and into the hands of the many. Where inefficient and corrupt governments are deeply entrenched, the withering away of the state does not take place without a fight.

For countries for whom EU membership is at best a remote prospect, EU standards may represent 'good practice' from a highly developed region, but the aura of the magic formula for prosperity, peace, and security does not apply. In some sense this is beneficial, since these countries are freer to examine EU environmental legislation and the requirements of implementation with a critical eye. They are not restricted in considering solutions to the grave environmental problems they face by pressures resulting from the rush to 'enter Europe.' On the other hand, these countries have not had the influence or support of accession-based assistance to increase capacities and fundamentally rewrite the whole body of environmental legislation. Thus, the second stage of environmental law-drafting in CEE has been largely missed in the NIS/EECCA region.

IV. The Russian Federation

The shocking revelations of 'ecocide' that followed the collapse of the Soviet Union[94] were followed by high public expectations that a new era of democracy would lead to rapid environmental improvements. Neither democracy nor effective environmental governance structures have taken root in the Russian Federation. Instead, environmental protection has become a low priority issue for local, regional, and national political elites; governance institutions

---

[93] Stec (1998), op. cit. pp. 290–294; Stec (1997), op. cit. pp. 369–371.
[94] Feshbach and Friendly, op. cit. See also Demosthenes., P., *Troubled lands: the legacy of Soviet environmental destruction*, Boulder (Westview Press) 1993.

are fragmented and underfunded, and environmental and resource quality continue to decline in many instances. Some 15 per cent of Russia's territory and 20 per cent of the population live within government declared environmental disaster zones, and up to 66 million people may live in areas where the air pollution levels exceed permissible levels.[95] Furthermore, illegal exploitation of natural resources such as wildlife (including endangered species) and timber has risen dramatically since 1991.[96] The government itself is hostile to environmental concerns, and the FSB (successor to the KGB) has waged a campaign against environmental activists who have challenged the government's policies on radioactive waste disposal. Some have been charged with espionage and others have been harassed in order to impede their work.[97]

As a clear indication of its intention to relegate environmental protection to the margins, the Russian government eliminated the State Committee for Environmental Protection in May 2000. The Committee had previously in 1997 been downgraded from ministry status and had suffered from a chronic lack of resources and a weak political mandate. The functions of the Committee have been moved to the Ministry of Natural Resources, which is responsible for licensing the development of Russia's oil, gas, and mineral resources. The Ministry of Natural Resources is widely known to have retained the dominant ethic of resource exploitation with little concern for environmental protection or mitigation.[98] Responsibility for environmental protection has to a great extent been devolved to Russia's regions and local authorities, which are still largely dominated by the former nomenclatura, or Communist elite, and suffer from extensive corruption that entails illegal natural resource concessions.[99]

Western aid to the Russian Federation has focussed extensively on the development of sophisticated economic instruments for environmental protection as well as on the provision of information to communities and capacity building to influence government and private enterprises. Wernstedt[100] identifies

---

[95] Mnatsakanian, R., A poisoned legacy, *Our Planet* 8(6) (1997), pp. 8–12.

[96] Kotsov, V., and Nikitina, E., Russia in transition: obstacles to environmental protection, *Environment* 35(10) (1993), pp. 10–20.

[97] Amnesty International and other human rights organisations have extensively documented these abuses. See e.g., Amnesty International, AI Index: EUR 46/009/2001, 30 March 2001, Russian Federation FSB v. environmental activist Grigory Pasko – punishment without a crime, available at http://web.amnesty.org/library/Index/engEUR460092001

[98] See Zakharov, V., Timber business is friendlier to the forest than Ministry of Natural Resources, *Russian Forest Bulletin* 20 (2002), available at www.forest.ru/eng/bulletin/20/1.html

[99] Kosov, op. cit. See also WWF, Quick overview facts on illegal logging in Russia available at www.panda.org/about_wwf/where_we_work/europe/problems/illegal_logging/Downloads/ ILLEGAL%20LOGGING%20RUSSIA.pdf

[100] Wernstedt, K., Environmental protection in the Russian Federation: lessons and opportunities, *J. Environmental Planning and Management* 45(4) (2002), pp. 493–516.

three fundamental conditions that these instruments and approaches require in order to be effective: functioning markets; formal and informal institutions that include a well developed legal framework and a 'culture of compliance'[101] within the society; and functioning environmental information and information dissemination systems to support a culture of public participation. Not one of these conditions has been well developed in the Russian Federation. In some cases the opposite of what is needed is more evident – a culture of evasion instead of a culture of compliance, a culture of secretiveness instead of a culture of information provision. Consequently, some authors have concluded that the approach that many environmental aid programmes have taken have not been sensitive to Russian conditions and have done precious little to improve the quality of environmental management in the Russian Federation.[102]

Foremost among the challenges for improving environmental governance in the Russian Federation that Western and domestic actors can help address are:

- further developing the institutional framework to support the rule of law in general;
- promoting a culture of respect for the law and compliance;
- promoting transparency and government accountability, and combating corruption;
- providing strong financial support to the Russian environmental NGO sector;
- holding the federal government accountable for meeting its international legal commitments in the area of the environment.

V. The Caucasus and Central Asia

The Caucasian states of Azerbaijan, Armenia, and Georgia, and the Central Asian States of Turkmenistan, Kazakhstan, Kyrgyzstan, Uzbekistan, and Tajikistan face many of the same governance problems as the Russian Federation and in some cases even more serious ones. Lagging behind the Russian Federation in economic and political reforms, most countries in these regions are beleaguered with autocratic governments, deeply embedded corruption, and extraordinary rates of poverty and unemployment. Some of the countries are listed by Freedom House as among the least free in the world, with Turkmenistan and Uzbekistan being named as among 'the worst of the worst' in the world.[103]

---

[101] Bell, R. G., Building trust: laying a foundation for environmental regulation in the former Soviet bloc, *Environment* 42(2) (2000), pp. 20–32.
[102] Bell, R. G. and Russell, C., Ill-considered experiments: the environmental consensus and the developing world, *Harvard Int'l Rev.* (Winter 2003, pp. 20–25). See also Stec (1998), op. cit. pp. 337–358 (on designing effective environmental advocacy programmes in the NIS).
[103] Freedom House, *The worst of the worst: the world's most repressive societies, a special report to the 60th session of the United Nations Commission on Human*

Though mostly autocratic,[104] these states have, like the Russian Federation, also seen a decline in central control over environmental management and natural resources, leading to widespread neglect of the environment and illegal and unsustainable exploitation of resources.[105] Complicating matters, oil and gas exploitation in the Caspian Sea region bodes ill for the development of stable and sustainable economies free of corruption, in spite of the unprecedented financial opportunities that these natural resources represent.

Environmental governance cannot be separated from the abject poverty of South Caucasus and Central Asia, or from the misgovernment and corruption that became endemic after 1991. Nor can the environment be considered in isolation from the several armed conflicts that have plagued these regions, including an Islamic insurgency in Uzbekistan, a civil war in Tajikistan, and wars in Karabakh (between Armenia and Azerbaijan), Chechnya, and Abkhazia. These latter conflicts, while occurring on Russian soil, have had extensive ripple effects throughout the Caucasus, as has the war in Afghanistan throughout Central Asia. In addition to the direct environmental destruction caused by war, the resulting instability has severely damaged infrastructure and limited the capacity for environmental monitoring.

Further instability is caused by competition over water resources in Central Asia, where water is scarce and has been severely mismanaged for decades. Soviet development planners opted for a massive water diversion scheme that made it possible to turn parts of Central Asia into a great cotton production centre. Towards this end, the Amu-Daria and Syr-Daria Rivers, which account for about 90 per cent of the region's surface waters, were diverted to supply water to massive cotton plantations, resulting in a catastrophic shrinkage of the Aral Sea and pesticide contamination of many tens of thousands of hectares of land under cotton cultivation. Water shortages have raised tensions among the countries of the region that share the two major rivers, with the downstream countries of Uzbekistan and Turkmenistan enjoying a greatly disproportionate share of water to support their agricultural sectors, more or less as under the Soviet system. Moreover, rural people with little political influence have suffered the most from water shortages and all of the hardships and risks involved therein.[106]

The more generic governance issues in Central Asia and the Caucasus supersede environmental governance issues. Consequently, environmental

---

Rights, Geneva (Freedom House Press) 2004, available at www.freedomhouse.org/research/mrr2004.pdf

[104] The recent democratic revolution in Georgia is a regional anomaly.

[105] Regional Environmental Centers for Central Asia, the Caucasus, and Moldova, 2002, proposals for transition to sustainable development for countries covered by New Regional Environmental Centers' activities, available at www.carec.kz/english/Archive/archive.htm

[106] O' Hara, S., Central Asians divided over use of dwindling water supply, *Local Government Brief* (Summer 2004), pp. 18–23.

governance reform must be closely attached to general governance reform and development, though this does not imply that environmental projects should be scrapped or marginalised in the near term. Rather, environmental projects, especially those funded by international donors, must build in good governance components from the start, and must aim as much at economic and political reform as at environmental performance. Clean-up funds for dealing with the toxic consequences of the Aral Sea disaster, for instance, will be mismanaged and squandered unless the institutional frameworks necessary to ensure transparency and accountability are in place. The international community should exert pressure upon the Central Asian and Caucasian states to implement fully the Aarhus Convention, which all of these states but Uzbekistan are parties to.

The assumption that there is a 'development curve' – that countries that are further east are merely a few to several years behind the new Member States in terms of development, and that therefore initiatives that were successful in those countries may be applied universally – is wrong. In some countries, development of civil society is a matter of generational change that may never occur. It would be a mistake, therefore, to expect results in these countries from initiatives that may have worked in other CITs. In terms of effective environmental protection, moreover, the prognosis is not good. A whole set of enforcement tools that depend on citizen empowerment will work to a much lesser degree in these countries. While surely an imperfect solution, there is currently no meaningful alternative to prolonging strict command-and-control regimes, while strengthening enforcement capabilities by skilled professionals.

Does this therefore lead to the conclusion that citizen empowerment in environmental protection should not be promoted in certain countries? Quite the contrary. The high level of passive environmental awareness in these same countries reveals an untapped source of motivating energy for the empowerment of citizens in the field of environmental protection that has had an impact on the development of civil society generally. These situations are not contradictory. From the point of view of optimising the development of civil society in these same countries, specific initiatives to support citizen empowerment in environmental protection have a strong demonstrative capability. There are many examples where environmental protection proved to be a factor strong enough to motivate citizens to take part in various procedures to achieve their goals. For the foreseeable future, however, civil society organisations, if they are to survive, will depend upon foreign funding and training.

VI. From government to governance: environmental governance challenges in CITs

The historic political divergences among the CITs have left these nations with significantly different environmental governance challenges, even while they have all shared in some converging trends such as the formal adoption of environmental laws and the development of a civil society sector. The environmental crisis inherited from the Communist era is not over. For countries where democracy is declining, such as the Russian Federation, or has failed altogether, such as the Central Asian states, the environmental outlook from today's standpoint is bleak, and getting worse. For the states that have entered or will enter the European Union, great challenges remain – in implementing laws, developing administrative capacity, updating technology, and cleaning up hot spots – but gradual though uneven progress is being made. The Caucasus is highly vulnerable due to the rapid exploitation of fossil resources in the Caspian Sea, and the Balkan states are only now beginning to recover from war and social dislocation, and the environment remains low on the political agenda.

Environmental movements and professional and grass-root environmental organisations are widely acknowledged to play essential environmental governance functions.[107] Environmental movements rally public support for environmental protection. Professional environmental organisations provide input into policy-making processes, represent the public interest in siting and other decisions, and provide the public with accurate technical and non-technical information on the environment. Grass-root environmental organisations mobilise community members to seek solutions to specific local environmental problems, thereby stimulating community consciousness, cohesion, and capacity for collective action.

Important factors in relation to the success or failure of environmental NGOs more than ten years after the period of ecological euphoria are often related to resources (personnel, grants, expertise, etc.), relationship to government, information access and sharing, and dealing with differences within the movements themselves. The development of civil society has been a major focus of international assistance. Consequently, many NGOs are comparatively well-off and have high capacities in relation to underfunded and crisis-ridden ministries, governments, and Parliaments. As a result, certain NGOs have been targeted by authorities in the NIS/EECCA through control measures including reregistration, tax control, and other schemes,[108] often citing the foreign influence over such organisations, while selected 'professional' NGOs have

---

[107] Janicke, M. and Weidner, H. (eds.), National environmental policies: a comparative study of capacity-building, Berlin (Springer) 1997.
[108] Provisions to protect NGO activity from state or private interference are generally toothless. See Law on Public Associations (Moldova), Article 13.1 (right of citizens to bring judicial or administrative action against acts, by the state or its officials, which 'hamper the foundation of public associations of citizens and the realization of their legal and charter activity'); Law on Environmental Protection (Russian Federation), Articles 12 and 13; Law on Environmental Protection (Belarus), Article 8 (right of action against those who deliberately interfere with the exercise of the rights of public associations for environmental protection).

been coopted as partners into state structures to make use of the funding web of international assistance. Some within the environmental community have complained that the latter environmental groups are falling prey to 'doing the Ministry's work'.[109] Information access and sharing are also either facilitated or hampered depending on relations with the state as well as with other NGOs who compete for funding.

The environmental movement in CITs evolved as the regions evolved. A more professionalised, urban-based stream of environmentalism emerged alongside community-based, predominantly rural, culturally-based efforts.[110] Environmentalism has reemerged most effectively in these new forms in those CITs where a certain measure of economic and social stability returned in the late 1990s.[111] Tensions based on these two streams, however, have begun to pose an obstacle to cooperation among environmental organisations, which have come to reflect typical urban-rural and ideological and cultural splits.

Despite these increasingly apparent divergences among environmental NGOs during the transition period, environmental organisations face common challenges. First, the NGOs – whether rurally based and culturally focused or urban-based and professionally focused – can and should develop a broader social base of support in order to be sustainable and relevant to their societies. Governance studies show that the public in CITs has more confidence in environmentalists and experts than in authorities' ability to solve environmental problems.[112] Secondly, NGOs must more clearly define their relationship to the state, preserving their autonomy while at the same time increasing the environmental governance capacity of the system as a whole. Generally throughout the region, there need to be more watchdog NGOs and perhaps fewer NGOs performing essentially consulting work for governments. Securing a steady

---

[109] These phenomena were noted as early as 1998. Stec (1998), op. cit. p. 280. The phenomenon of 'absorption' of new institutions into state structures was also noticed as early as 1998. See Pastukhov, V., The end of post-Communism: perspectives on Russian reformers, 7(3) *East Europe Const. Rev.* (Summer 1998), pp. 64–70, at 64.

[110] Steger, T., Environmentalism and democracy in Hungary and Latvia, Ph.D. Dissertation, Syracuse University, 2004.

[111] See Stec (1998), op. cit. pp. 278–279. By 1998, although economic pressures were still strong, a European Commission survey confirmed a dormant, but high 'ecological consciousness' had reawakened or continued. The *International Herald Tribune* reported on 12 December 1997 that the Czech Republic's environmental expenditures had risen by 50 per cent between 1993 and 1996, to about 3 per cent of GDP, while Hungary's expenditures had more than tripled during the same period to 3.9 per cent of GDP. These increases were partly due to the desire to meet EU accession goals.

[112] Ibid. See also Genov, N., Environmental risks in a society in transition: perceptions and reactions, in Vari and Tamas, op. cit.; Kravchenko, S., Environmental legislation and enforcement in Ukraine, in Nespor, op. cit. p. 438 (88 per cent of respondents in a social science study in Ukraine did not know anything about their environmental law).

funding base for watchdog and related activities is going to be the most serious challenge facing the NGO community.

VII. Conclusions

The process of transition represents the convergence of a number of important trends. The first involves the concept of sustainability as a paradigm for solutions to environmental problems, in which the role of legislative formulations to promote sustainability is significant. Next is the transition towards greater democracy, which has two relevant aspects: the ascendancy of the rule of law over arbitrary rule by men, and the 'withering away of the state' accompanied by an increasing role in society for voluntary organisations. Finally these trends are accompanied by new economic relationships and shifts in economic values. Legislative solutions for protecting the environment and achieving sustainability have had to take into account the trend towards greater definition of spheres of rights and a diminishing ability of governments to control effectively human activity.

Divergences in the region have, however, also clearly established themselves, for good and bad. The fundamental division between those countries that have gained or can realistically aspire to EU membership and those who are not on course to membership is already wide and growing wider. While democratisation, liberalisation, and environmental modernisation are key elements of the transition period in the EU accession states, the NIS/EECCA countries are either drifting back or, as in the case of the Central Asian states, have fully reverted to some degree of authoritarian rule, constricted markets, and command-and-control style environmental regulation that is often hampered by corruption and lack of administrative capacity. The common ecological consciousness rooted in the downfall of scientific Socialism, embodied predominantly in civil society organisations, represents a factor of continuity contributing to the resolution of diverse governance challenges in all CITS.

The changes in Eastern Europe are relevant to processes outside the region, for 'Western' values are being tested with basic questions running deeper than any corresponding dialogue could in the stable West. The result ought to illuminate the discourse in the West about its own course of environmental law reform. This process will take place both within the expanded EU and on the pan-European level. New developments throughout the CITs ought to be able to take into account the strengths and weaknesses of both the 'old' East and the 'old' West – a compromise that might lead at least part of the way towards real sustainability. While we may always be peering through the looking glass darkly when attempting to predict the future, it seems a certainty that at least in much of the formerly scientific Socialist region the development of environmental law will present many fascinating and challenging turns in the years and decades ahead.

PART VI

Formation and implementation of international regimes

15

Multilateral environmental agreements and the compliance continuum

JUTTA BRUNNÉE

I. Introduction

The promotion of compliance with international environmental commitments is among the most challenging issues of global environmental governance. Compliance is an issue that straddles various arenas and disciplinary debates. Not only has the issue received much attention in both the practice and the theory of global governance, it is also a genuine 'governance' issue in that it demands engagement of international lawyers with the insights of international relations experts, and vice versa.

In the context of multilateral environmental agreements (MEAs), the topic of compliance has come to be synonymous with the design of non-compliance procedures and other strategies specifically geared to promoting compliance. Six MEA-based non-compliance procedures are in effect,[1] several others are at

In articulating the idea of the 'compliance continuum', this chapter draws together ideas developed in previous work on law-making under multilateral environmental agreements (MEAs) and on compliance with MEAs, respectively. See Brunnée, J., COPing with consent: lawmaking under multilateral environmental agreements, *Leiden J. Int'l L.* 15 (2002) pp. 1–52; Brunnée, J., The Kyoto Protocol: testing ground for compliance theories, *ZaöRV* 63(3) (2003), pp. 255–280. See also Brunnée, J. and Toope, S. J., Persuasion and enforcement: explaining compliance with international law, *Finnish Y. B. Int'l L.* 13 (2002), pp. 273–295.

[1] The paradigm example remains the non-compliance procedure developed under the Montreal Protocol on Substances that Deplete the Ozone Layer, 26 I.L.M. (1987) 1550; adjusted and amended 29 June 1990, 30 I.L.M. (1990) 539; adjusted and amended 25 November 1992, 32 I.L.M. (1993) 875 ('Montreal Protocol'). For the non-compliance procedure (NCP) see *Report of the Fourth Meeting of the Parties*, UN Doc. UNEP/OzL.Pro.4/15, 1992, Decision IV/5, Annexes IV, V, 32 I.L.M. (1993) 874 ('*MOP-4 Report*'); and *Report of the Tenth Meeting of the Parties*, UN Doc. UNEP/OzL.Pro.10/9, 1998, Decision X/10, Annex II. A compliance procedure was also adopted under the Protocol to the Convention on Long-Range Transboundary Air Pollution on Further Reduction of Sulphur Emissions 1979, on 14 June 1994. See 33 I.L.M. (1994) 1540, 1545. In 1997, that Convention's Executive Body extended the application of the procedure to all Protocols to the Convention. See *Concerning the Implementation Committee, its Structure and Functions and Procedures for Review of Compliance*, UN Doc. ECE/EB.AIR/53, 1998, Decision 1997/2, Annex III; see also ibid., Decision 1997/3, Annex IV; *Concerning the Implementation Committee, its Structure and Functions*

various stages of negotiation.² Indeed, the inclusion of a compliance regime appears to have become a routine agenda item for MEA negotiations. Often, the main question is not so much whether a compliance procedure should be developed but what its approach should be: should it be largely 'soft' and facilitative, or should it include 'hard', enforcement-oriented features?³ In this respect, the debates about the design of MEA-based compliance regimes have much overlap with the prominent theoretical debate about whether compliance is best promoted through managerial or enforcement-oriented approaches.⁴

The rapid evolution of MEA-specific compliance procedures illustrates that the practice of international environmental law has come a long way in a relatively short period of time. A little over ten years ago, MEAs contained only limited compliance-related elements. Typically, these elements consisted

and Procedures for Review of Compliance, U.N. Economic Commission for Europe, Executive Body, UN Doc. ECE/EB.AIR/59, 1998, Decision 1998/6, Annex II, in Brown Weiss, E. et al., *International environmental law: basic instruments and references*, Ardsley, NY (Transnational Publishers) supp. 1999. Under the Espoo Convention on Environmental Impact Assessment in a Transboundary Context, 30 I.L.M. (1991) 1461, a compliance procedure was established in Feburary 2001. See *Report of the Second Meeting of the Parties*, UN Doc. ECE/MP.EIA/4, Decision II/4, revised as Decision III/2, in *Report of the Third Meeting of the Parties*, UN Doc. ECE/MP.EIA/6. In April 2002, a non-compliance regime was adopted under the Aarhus Convention on Access to Information, Public Participation in Decision-Making and Access to Justice in Environmental Matters, 38 I.L.M. (1999) 517. See *Report of the First Meeting of the Parties*, UN Doc. ECE/MP.PP/2/Add. 8, 2 April 2002, Decision I/7. On 12 December 2002, a compliance regime was established under the Basel Convention on the Control of Transboundary Movements of Hazardous Wastes and their Disposal, 18 I.L.M. (1999) 657. See Decision IV/12 (Appendix), Establishment of a mechanism from promoting implementation and compliance, in *Report of the Sixth Meeting of the Parties*, UN Doc. UNEP/CHW.6/40 ('Basel Convention NCP'). Finally, in February 2004, a compliance regime was adopted under the Cartagena Protocol on Biosafety to the Convention on Biological Diversity, 39 I.L.M. (2000) 1027. See *Report of the First Meeting of the Parties*, UN Doc. UNEP/CBD/BS/COP-MOP/1/15 (Report of the First COP-MOP), Decision BS-I/7, Annex ('Biosafety Protocol NCP').

[2] Under the Kyoto Protocol to the United Nations Framework Convention on Climate Change, 37 I.L.M. (1998) 22, a compliance regime was adopted in the November 2001 Marrakech Accords. See Decision 24/CP.7, *Report of the Conference of the Parties to the United Nations Framework Convention on Climate Change on its Seventh Session*, UN Doc. FCCC/CP/2001/13/ Add.1-3. The compliance regime awaits entry into force of the Protocol. Compliance regimes are under consideration under the Convention to Combat Desertification, 33 I.L.M. (1994) 1016; the Rotterdam Convention on Hazardous Chemicals, text available at www.pic.int/en/ViewPage.asp?id = 104; and the Stockholm Convention on Persistent Organic Pollutants, text available at www.pops.int/documents/convtext/convtext_en.pdf

[3] See Brunnée, J., A fine balance: facilitation and enforcement in the design of a compliance regime for the Kyoto Protocol, *Tulane Env. L. J.* 13 (2000), pp. 223–270.

[4] On the 'managerial' approach, see Chayes, A. and Handler Chayes, A., *The new sovereignty: compliance with international regulatory agreements*, Cambridge, Mass. (Harvard University Press) 1995. On the 'enforcement' approach, see Downs, G. W., Enforcement and the evolution of cooperation, *Mich. J. Int'l L.* 18 (1998), p. 319.

in requirements for reporting by parties on their performance, and compilation and publication of information on parties' performance through treaty bodies.[5] In addition, MEAs generally made provision for the resolution of disputes related to the interpretation or application of the agreement.[6] However, in international environmental affairs, neither binding dispute settlement nor the traditional 'rule-breach-sanction' model of international law have played a significant role.[7]

The evolution of compliance procedures notwithstanding, the MEA compliance debate has remained relatively narrow, and shaped by the assumption that states' compliance decisions are mainly driven by interest assessments.[8] Interest-based accounts seem so commonsense as to obscure the fact that they not only represent a theory about how states behave, but also imply a theory about the 'nature and operation' of international law.[9] Specifically, the implication is that international law is binding merely in a thin, formal sense, derived from particular sources of law and formal state consent.

However, the twin ideas that international law binds only in a formal sense and that, for its strength, it depends upon enforcement or other external factors, have potentially damaging effects, particularly for international environmental law. At one level, international environmental law is often 'soft' law, either in terms of the formal status of norms, or in terms of the broad-meshed principles

---

[5] For an overview, see United Nations Environment Programme (UNEP), *Study on dispute avoidance and dispute settlement in international environmental law*, UN Doc. UNEP/GC.20/INF/16, 1999, pp. 18–25. See also Sachariev, K., Promoting compliance with international environmental legal standards: reflections on monitoring and reporting mechanisms, *Y.B. Int'l Env'l L.* 2 (1991), pp. 31–52.

[6] See UNEP, op. cit. pp. 54–56. And see Koskenniemi, M., Peaceful settlement of environmental disputes, *Nordic J. Int'l L.* 61 (1991), pp. 73–92, at 82.

[7] Brown Weiss, E., Understanding compliance with international environmental agreements: the baker's dozen myths, *University of Richmond L. R.* 32 (1999), p. 1555, at 1582 (noting that dispute settlement options under MEAs have remained unused). Fitzmaurice, M. A. and Redgwell, C., Environmental non-compliance procedures and international law, *Netherlands Y. B. Int'l L.* 31 (2000), pp. 35–65, at 37 (on the problems of 'fit' between remedies of the law of state responsibility and treaty law compliance problems in the MEA context).

[8] Note that another limitation of many contributions to the MEA compliance debate is their focus on interstate dynamics, leaving aside domestic processes that may affect state compliance. Given its focus on compliance regimes within MEAs, this chapter also confines itself to compliance theories that are centred on interstate processes. On the need to account for both international and domestic compliance factors, see Hathaway, O. A., Between power and principle: a political theory of international law, *U. Chi. L. Rev.* 72 (2005), pp. 469–536. For an extensive empirical assessment of national implementation and compliance with key MEAs, see Brown Weiss, E. and Jacobsen, H. K. (eds.), *Engaging countries: strengthening compliance with international environmental accords*, Cambridge, Mass. (MIT Press) 1998.

[9] See Kingsbury, B., The concept of compliance as a function of competing conceptions of international law, *Michigan Int'l L. J.* 19 (1998), pp. 345–372, at 346.

it furnishes. Where it is formally binding, international environmental law is rarely enforced through binding dispute settlement or sanctions. Therefore, in the eyes of many observers, international environmental law is simply weak. At another level, the '*couple diabolique* obligation-sanction', as Prosper Weil aptly described it,[10] diverts attention from other ways to understand the binding effect of international law, and thus from potentially significant facets of the compliance picture.[11] From the standpoint of international law, the most regrettable casualties of this attention deficit have been some of the very questions that international lawyers should be uniquely placed to elucidate: questions about the distinctive features that enable legal norms and processes themselves – without assistance from external inducements – to exert influence on actors.[12]

This chapter aims to broaden the MEA compliance debate, and suggests that the debate would be most usefully framed in terms of a 'compliance continuum'. I will begin with a sketch of the dominant theoretical perspectives on compliance with MEAs, the managerial and enforcement approaches. I will then outline an alternative theoretical framework. Drawing on constructivist international relations theory, I will suggest that an 'interactional' understanding of international law can complement the managerial and enforcement-oriented accounts. Through examples from the Kyoto Protocol to the United Nations Framework Convention on Climate Change (UNFCCC), I will illustrate that the interactional account has several significant implications for international environmental law. By focussing attention on the legitimacy of law and law-making, it looks beyond formal legal status as the sole indicator of the strength of given norms. By focussing attention on specific features that enable legal norms to exert influence, it speaks directly to compliance questions. It suggests that the continuum of means to promote compliance begins at the law-making stage, and points to specific strategies for strengthening MEA-based norms' legitimacy and thus ability to exert compliance pull. But the interactional framework also illuminates the other end of the compliance continuum, highlighting

---

[10] Weil, P., Le droit international en quête de son identité, *RCADI* 237 (1992), pp. 9–370, at 53.
[11] See also Johnston, D. M., *Consent and commitment in the world community: the classification and analysis of international instruments*, Irvington-on-Hudson (Transnational Publishers) 1997, p. 62 (noting that the '[r]estriction to formal, legally binding instruments has limited the traditional scholar's interest to those instruments that are accepted as creating obligations enforceable by an international tribunal, as if the amenability of international disputes to settlement were the only concern for international lawyers').
[12] See also Bodansky, D., Customary (and not so customary) international environmental law, *Indiana J. Global Leg. Stud.* 3 (1995), pp. 105–119, at 116–119 (arguing that, given the rarity of third party dispute settlement, more attention should be paid to the independent ability of norms to exert compliance pull ('first party control') or to shape interactions among international actors ('second party control').

options for the enhancement of both managerial and enforcement-oriented responses to non-compliance.

II. Theoretical perspectives on compliance with MEAs

Until relatively recently, compliance issues were primarily the domain of international relations scholars and their inquiries into the causes of state behaviour. Only in the last ten to fifteen years have international lawyers focussed more explicitly on matters of compliance, prompting a lively exchange between the two disciplines.[13] In the context of MEAs, compliance scholarship has been dominated by a debate between proponents of managerial and enforcement-oriented models.[14] While the latter tends towards the realist end of the institutionalist spectrum, the former draws upon norm-focussed, process-oriented, explanations of compliance. The MEA debate has paid less attention to explicitly constructivist frameworks,[15] and to the features that may enable legal norms to influence states in distinctive ways. As will be argued below, such approaches offer important additional insights and would help strengthen efforts to promote compliance with MEAs.[16]

1. The managerial and enforcement-oriented accounts

The managerial approach finds its origins in the work of Abram Chayes and Antonia Handler Chayes, which argues for a 'cooperative, problem-solving approach' to promoting compliance with international regulatory agreements such as MEAs.[17] The Chayes challenge the pessimistic realist assumption that states' compliance or non-compliance decisions are driven solely by interests and power balances.[18] Instead, they assume that states generally enter into commitments with an intention to comply and that non-compliance more often

---

[13] For overviews on the recent theoretical debates, see Kingsbury, op. cit. Raustiala, K. and Slaughter, A. M., International law, international relations and compliance, in Carlsnaes et al. (eds.), *Handbook of international relations*, London (Sage) 2002, pp. 541–558; Brunnée, J. and Toope, S. J., Persuasion and enforcement: explaining compliance with international law, *Finnish Y. B. Int'l L.* 13 (2002), pp. 273–295.

[14] For an overview on the debate between managerial and enforcement-oriented approaches, see Danish, K., Management v. enforcement: the new debate on promoting treaty compliance, *Va. J. Int'l L.* 37 (1997), pp. 789–810.

[15] But see Raustiala, K., Compliance and effectiveness in international regulatory cooperation, *Case W. Res. J. Int'l L.* 32 (2000), pp. 387–440, at 405–409; Downs, G. W., Danish, K. W., and Barsoom, P. N., The transformational model of international regime design: triumph of hope or experience?, *Col. J. Transnat'l L.* 38 (2000), pp. 465–514, at 468 and 493 (suggesting that constructivist ideas underpin many recent efforts at regime design).

[16] In this section, I draw on Brunnée, J., The Kyoto Protocol: testing ground for compliance theories, *ZaöRV* 63(3) (2003), pp. 255–280.

[17] Chayes and Chayes, op. cit. p. 3. [18] Ibid.

results from norm ambiguities or capacity limitations than from deliberate disregard.[19] Therefore, apart from the fact that 'sanctioning authority is rarely granted by treaty, rarely used when granted', the Chayes argue that sanctions are 'likely to be ineffective when used'.[20] Rather than adopt an 'enforcement model',[21] compliance strategies should direct attention to the actual causes of non-compliance and 'manage' these through positive means.

Managerial prescriptions consist in a blend of transparency (regarding both the regime's norms and procedures and the parties' performance), dispute settlement, and capacity-building.[22] The main engines of managerialism are continuous processes of argument and persuasion, 'justificatory discourse' that ultimately 'jawbones' states into compliance.[23] The Chayes highlight the role of international law in framing such discourse, noting that states' justifications of their conduct tend to be more compelling when in keeping with a legal rule.[24] The compliance strategy builds upon treaty parties' 'general sense of obligation to comply with a legally binding prescription'.[25] But the condition of the 'new sovereignty' provides the ultimate underpinning for managerial strategies.[26] Given growing interdependence, most states can only realise their sovereignty through participation in various international regimes. The need to remain a 'member in good standing of the international system',[27] therefore, is more likely to explain compliance than costs or benefits in the context of an individual regime.[28]

The main rival theory on treaty compliance is advanced by George Downs and colleagues and is grounded in rational choice and game theoretical models.[29] Downs *et al.* do not embrace the 'enforcement model' label but prefer to call themselves political economists. Indeed, they are not necessarily arguing for enforcement in the sense of genuine sanctions. Their concept of 'sanction' encompasses a broad range of measures that create costs or remove benefits.[30] Downs *et al.* emphasise that the relative need for incentives and disincentives, and their feasibility, depend upon the type of 'game' and the incentive structures that underlie a given regime.[31] In brief, the claim is not that sanctions are always required to ensure cooperation, but only that they are needed where strong incentives exist for non-compliance. This is the case where treaties require states to depart significantly from what they would have done in the absence of the treaty ('deep cooperation').[32]

---

[19] Ibid., pp. 10–5.   [20] Ibid., pp. 32–33.
[21] The Chayes positioned their 'managerial model' as an alternative to what they labelled the 'enforcement model' of compliance, thus coining the terms that have framed much of the compliance debate: ibid., p. 3.
[22] Ibid., pp. 22–25.   [23] Ibid., pp. 25–26.   [24] Ibid., p. 119.   [25] Ibid., p. 110.
[26] Ibid., pp. 26, 28.   [27] Ibid., p. 28.   [28] Ibid., p. 27.
[29] Downs, G. W., Rocke, D. M., and Barsoom, P. N., Is the good news about compliance good news about cooperation?, *Int'l Org.* 50 (1996), pp. 379–406, at 382–387.
[30] Ibid., pp. 320–321.   [31] Ibid., p. 322.   [32] Ibid., pp. 382–383.

According to Downs *et al.*, the most significant weakness of the managerial approach is that it provides policy advice without sufficient attention to context, and without sufficient evidence.[33] The Chayes do assert that empirical evidence supports managerialism.[34] But Downs *et al.* claim that managerial 'policy inferences are dangerously contaminated by selection problems',[35] and build upon many treaty examples that involve merely 'shallow' cooperation. Therefore, the patterns of compliance and absence of sanctions that were reported by the Chayes do not justify the conclusion that sanctions are never required or appropriate to ensure cooperation.[36] It is equally possible and, according to Downs *et al.*, even likely that 'there is little need for enforcement because there is little deep cooperation'.[37]

Aside from the differences in their policy prescriptions for compliance strategies, the managerial and enforcement schools place significantly different emphasis on the role of international law. Downs *et al.*'s approach casts states as rational, egoistic actors and thus as primarily motivated by incentives and disincentives. In this framework, then, international law's impact is at best indirect; it is a tool to create, structure, or stabilise incentives and disincentives. By contrast, for the Chayes, law and legal processes play central roles as drivers of the compliance strategy. Much emphasis is placed upon the ways in which international law influences state behaviour by framing the boundaries of persuasion and argument. Drawing on Thomas Franck, the Chayes stress the importance of procedural legitimacy and basic substantive fairness in giving legal norms distinctive power – 'compliance pull'.[38] And yet, ultimately, the Chayes too rely on an interest-based explanation for compliance. It is the impact of the 'new sovereignty', not international law, that accounts for the success of managerialism: 'The need to be a member in good standing of the international system ensures that most compliance problems will yield to the managerial process we describe'.[39]

By falling back on an interest-based explanation, the Chayes do not fully exploit the norm focus of their account. They do not explain precisely how the

---

[33] Ibid., p. 397
[34] Chayes and Chayes, op. cit. pp. 32–33, and chs. 2 (Treaty-based military and economic sanctions), 3 (Membership sanction), and 4 (Unilateral sanctions).
[35] Downs *et al.* (1996), op. cit. p. 380.   [36] Ibid., p. 391.
[37] Ibid., p. 388. See also Victor, D. G., Enforcing international law: implications for an effective global warming regime, *Duke Envt'l L. and Pol'y F.* 10 (1999), pp. 147–184, at 152–157. Of course, this complaint must be seen against the background of the often noted difficulties in demonstrating conclusively that a commitment as such, rather than sanctions or incentives, influenced state behaviour. These difficulties complicate countering the 'selection problem' argument. See, e.g., Simmons, B., Compliance with international agreements, *Annu. Rev. Polit. Sci.* 1 (1998), pp. 75–93, at 89–90.
[38] Chayes and Chayes, op. cit. pp. 127–134. And see Franck, T. M., The power of legitimacy among nations, Oxford (Oxford University Press) 1990, p. 26, at 493.
[39] Chayes and Chayes, op. cit., p. 28.

processes they describe come to influence actors, or why legitimacy enhances the compliance pull of legal norms.[40] These gaps can be narrowed by drawing on the insights of constructivist international relations (IR) theory. Given the Chayes' focus on processes of interaction and persuasion, constructivism provides a natural complement to managerialism.[41] As I will suggest later in this chapter, it may also speak in important ways to Downs *et al.*'s enforcement-oriented compliance prescriptions.

2. Constructivism and interactional international law

Like institutionalists, constructivists focus on interaction and discourse among actors. However, constructivist theory questions the assumptions that interests are separate from interaction, and that state action is largely driven by strategic pursuit of interests. Constructivism focuses on identity formation through social interaction and on the identities of states as generators of interests.[42] Constructivists describe how institutions and norms foster 'shared understandings', which can then shape both the identity of the actors and the further evolution of the institutions and norms themselves.[43] This emphasis on the shaping of identities has important implications: ideas, shared understandings, or norms are seen not as direct causes of behaviour but as structures that both constrain and enable choices.[44] In this framework, international law can be understood as neither imposed social control nor as completely subordinate to the interests of states. Rather, law is generated and shaped through interaction and, in turn, affects behaviour by influencing actor identity, thereby reconstructing interests.

While constructivism provides a more norm-friendly account of international relations, it too does not fully illuminate the distinctive impact of legal norms on state compliance. In previous work with Stephen Toope, I suggested that the work of Lon Fuller holds particular promise for understanding the role of law in international society.[45] Fuller outlines an interactional view of law

---

[40] Koh, H. K., Why do nations obey international law?, Book Review of *The new sovereignty: compliance with international regulatory agreements* by Chayes, A. and Handler Chayes, A. and of *Fairness in international law and institutions* by Franck, T. M., *Yale L. J.* 106 (1997), pp. 2599–2659, at 2640–2641.

[41] See also Downs *et al.* (2000), op. cit. Raustiala and Slaughter, op. cit. p. 544; Raustiala, op. cit. p. 407 (all noting managerialism's constructivist leanings).

[42] Wendt, A., Anarchy is what states make of it: the social construction of power politics, *Int'l Org.* 46 (1992), pp. 391–425, at 397–398.

[43] See Ruggie, J. G., What makes the world hang together? Neo-utilitarianism and the social constructivist challenge, *Int'l Org.* 52 (1998), pp. 855–885, at 869–870; Wendt, op. cit. pp. 396–397.

[44] Ruggie, op. cit.

[45] For a more detailed discussion of the framework sketched in this paragraph, see Brunnée, J. and Toope, S. J., International law and constructivism: elements of an interactional theory of international law, *Col. J. Trans. L.* 39 (2000), pp. 19–74, at 43–64. See also Brunnée, J. and Toope, S. J., Interactional international law, *International Law FORUM de droit international* 3 (2001), pp. 186–192.

that has a good deal in common with constructivism.[46] Through interaction, relatively stable patterns of expectation must emerge to allow the application of norms in specific contexts. Rules are persuasive and legal systems are perceived as legitimate when they are broadly congruent with the practices and shared understandings in society.[47]

At the core of Fuller's explanation of the specific influence of legal norms are certain internal characteristics that distinguish law from other forms of social ordering. Fuller outlined eight criteria: generality of rules; promulgation; limiting cases of retroactivity; clarity; avoidance of contradiction; not asking the impossible; consistency over time; and congruence of official action with the underlying rules.[48] Most lawyers would likely recognise these criteria as describing important features of 'good' law. What makes Fuller's account provocative is the claim that the distinctiveness of law rests on these features, rather than primarily on external factors such as the validity of sources, hierarchical authority, or the ability to enforce. Indeed, it is these internal characteristics that produce the 'binding' quality of law.[49] The greater the extent to which the internal characteristics are present, the greater the legitimacy of the norms or legal system and the greater the power of law to promote adherence. While these internal characteristics imply some basic substantive requirements,[50] they are most closely connected to processes of law-making and to processes of application, such as interpretation or implementation.

Of course, the interactional account is not alone in its focus on internal features of law and attendant legal legitimacy. Most notably, it finds support in Thomas Franck's influential theory on 'the power of legitimacy' in international society.[51] Franck's work stands out for its explicit focus on compliance questions, and his effort to develop a *legal* theory on why states comply with 'powerless rules'.[52] Franck's work stands out also because it challenges conventional (rationalist) wisdom, and builds on the fact that states frequently comply with international law when this may not correspond to their immediate interests.[53] Since there is no systematic enforcement that could explain the pattern of compliance, argues Franck, it must be certain features of international law itself that account for its ability to exert 'compliance pull'.[54] Franck's hypothesis is

---

[46] Fuller, L. L., *The morality of law*, New Haven, Conn. (Yale University Press) rev. ed. 1969.
[47] Postema, G. J., Implicit law, *L. and Phil.* 13 (1994), pp. 361–387.
[48] See Fuller, op. cit. pp. 33–94, 152–186.
[49] '[T]he internal morality of the law is not something added to, or imposed on, the power of law, but is an essential condition of that power itself': Fuller, op. cit. pp. 46–91, 155.
[50] Fuller's internal tests of legality remained deliberately neutral to substantive goals pursued through the legal system. However, he argued that, to the extent that legal systems meet the internal requirements, they likely will also meet external standards of legitimacy, such as fairness or equality: Brunnée and Toope (2000), op. cit. pp. 56–57.
[51] Franck (1990), op. cit.   [52] Ibid., p. 3.
[53] Various examples are provided in Franck, T. M., Legitimacy in the international system, *Am. J. Int'l L.* 82 (1988), pp. 705–759.
[54] Franck (1990), op. cit. p. 493.

pushed further by the interactional account, for which the internal legitimacy of international law, its binding force, and its compliance pull are all inextricably linked. These linkages are at the heart of the idea of the compliance continuum and will be examined more closely in the next two sections of this chapter.

III. Reflections on the binding effect of international environmental law

From the vantage point of the interactional account, the strength of international environmental law can be appreciated in more nuanced fashion than through a purely formal lens. The interactional understanding acknowledges that the boundaries between legal norms and other social norms are fluid.[55] Since all norms have the potential to shape the identities of states, both formal legal norms and other norms can be influential. Indeed, this is a phenomenon that international environmental lawyers frequently take advantage of through resort to 'soft law'.[56] Most observers would agree that 'soft law' is influential,[57] that it is often difficult to distinguish 'soft' and 'hard' law,[58] and that 'soft law' can evolve into 'hard' law.[59] However, a purely formal conception of law has trouble with the category of soft law,[60] and with explaining exactly why it is influential.

By contrast, the interactional perspective embraces the entire normative spectrum and helps explain why the notions of 'soft' and 'hard' alone do

---

[55] See also Fuller, op. cit. p. 122 ('[B]oth rules of law and legal systems can and do half exist. This condition results when the purposive effort necessary to bring them into full being has been, as it were, only half successful.').

[56] See, generally, Shelton, D. (ed.), Commitment and compliance: the role of non-binding norms in the international legal system, Oxford (Oxford University Press) 2000. In the context of treaty law, see also Boyle, A. E., Some reflections on the relationship of treaties and soft law, *Int'l and Comp. L. Q.* 48 (1999), pp. 901–913.

[57] See e.g., Charney, J., Compliance with soft law, in Shelton, op. cit. p. 114; Joyner, C., Recommended measures under the Antarctic Treaty: hardening compliance with soft international law, *Mich. J. Int'l L.* 19 (1998), pp. 401–444; Dupuy, P.-M., Soft law and the international law of the environment, *Mich. J. Int'l L.* 12 (1991), pp. 420–435, at 434–435; Boyle, op. cit (examining different types of legal effects exerted by soft law).

[58] See e.g., Dupuy, op. cit. pp. 428–431; Joyner, op. cit. pp. 406–414.

[59] See e.g., Chinkin, C., The challenge of soft law: development and change in international law,' *Int'l and Comp. L. Q.* 38 (1989), pp. 850–866, at 856–859; Dupuy, op. cit. pp. 431–434; Joyner, op. cit. p. 425.

[60] See Dupuy, op. cit. p. 420 (beginning his article with the observation that '"[s]oft" law is a paradoxical term for defining an ambiguous phenomenon. Paradoxical because, from a general and classical point of view, the rule of law is usually considered "hard", . . . or it simply does not exist. Ambiguous because the reality thus designated, considering its legal effects as well as its manifestations, is often difficult to identify clearly.'). See also Klabbers, J., The redundancy of soft law, *Nordic J. Int'l L.* 65 (1996), pp. 167–182, at 168 (charging that soft law 'lacks plausible theoretical underpinnings, and . . . finds little support in . . . state practice and judicial practice').

not furnish sufficient descriptors of legal normativity.[61] As suggested above, any inherent ability of international law to bind derives from the extent to which internal characteristics guide processes of law-making and application, generating distinctive legal legitimacy and persuasiveness. Importantly, in an interactional framework, law-making and application can be appreciated as not strictly separate, but as constituting a continuum of activities.[62] Through interpretative processes, or processes designed to promote compliance, law is remade as the scope or content of norms shift and give rise to new normative understandings. This account has particular salience for MEAs, and for the law-making through Conferences of the Parties (COPs).

1. Law-making pursuant to MEAs

The framework–Protocol model is designed to foster conditions under which common understandings regarding the problem at hand, and legal commitments, can develop.[63] Typically, an initial framework agreement contains general commitments of the parties to address the problem, provides for information-gathering, establishes a COP or other plenary body for regular exchange among the parties, and creates basic decision-making procedures. In subsequent arrangements, parties can develop specific commitments, dealing with all or part of the underlying concern. Indeed, the bulk of law-making activity now usually takes place not with respect to an MEA's initial adoption, but in the subsequent process of expansion and adaptation of which the original treaty is only the starting point.

Three broad types of approaches are employed to expand or modify parties' commitments under MEAs. First, parties can adopt a new Protocol,[64] or they can opt for an amendment to the original treaty or to an existing Protocol.[65]

---

[61] See also Brunnée, J. and Toope, S. J., Environmental security and freshwater resources: ecosystem regime building, Am. J. Int'l L. 91 (1997), pp. 26–59, at 31–37, 58 (arguing that prelegal norms have independent value in framing 'contextual regimes' that shape patterns of interaction, and that law emerges on a continuum from mere interaction to an acceptance of binding obligation).

[62] This follows necessarily from the interactional conception of law as mutually constructed. See Brunnée and Toope (2000), op. cit. pp. 51–52.

[63] See e.g, Beyerlin, U. and Marauhn, T., Law-making and law-enforcement in international environmental law after the 1992 Rio Conference, Berlin (Erich Schmidt Verlag) 1997, pp. 28–33. For a critical perspective on the framework Protocol model see e.g., Downs et al., op. cit. pp. 471–488 (offering a survey of the arguments that have been made to suggest that regimes can be designed so as to induce 'a mutually reinforcing series of normative and cognitive shifts among member states because states in effect are socialized by the regime').

[64] In the present context, a Protocol is an agreement designed to complement an earlier framework treaty. See, e.g., Article 17 of the United Nations Framework Convention on Climate Change (UNFCCC), reprinted in 31 I.L.M. (1992) 849.

[65] See e.g., Article 15 UNFCCC; Article 20 of the Kyoto Protocol to the UNFCCC.

Further, parties can adopt or amend Annexes that provide operational detail to flesh out the terms of the treaty.[66] In each of these scenarios, law-making conforms to the formalities of treaty law. While the relevant instruments are developed through meetings of the COP, legal commitment is effected separately from adoption by the COP – through either express (Protocols; amendments) or presumed (Annexes) consent by individual states to be bound.[67] However, thirdly, there are also cases where a treaty or Protocol simply stipulates that additional rules are to be elaborated and adopted by COP decision. It is in this context that a practice is evolving that, beyond participation in a consensus decision of the COP, does not seem to envisage a subsequent, separate consent step by individual states. Measured against the standard framework of treaty law, it is not clear whether the relevant decisions are formally binding or constitute soft law. Limited examples of this phenomenon can be found under a variety of MEAs.[68] Suffice it for present purposes to consider the Kyoto Protocol to the UN Framework Convention on Climate Change, where standard setting by COP decision appears to have reached new levels.

2. The Kyoto Protocol example

The Kyoto Protocol stipulates an emission reduction commitment for developed countries and countries with economies in transition listed in Annex I to the UNFCCC. Under Article 3.1, Annex I parties must ensure that their collective greenhouse gas emissions are reduced by at least 5 per cent below 1990 levels in an initial commitment period from 2008 to 2012. Individual targets are listed in Annex B to the Protocol; they range from 8 per cent reductions to 10 per cent increases.[69] However, in negotiating the Kyoto Protocol, parties did not finalise the details required to implement the regime. Instead, the Protocol asks the UNFCCC COP and its counterpart, the 'Conference of the Parties serving as the Meeting of the Parties' to the Protocol (COP/MOP), to elaborate and adopt the guidelines, rules, or procedures that are needed to flesh out several of the Protocol's most important elements.[70]

---

[66] See e.g., Article 16 UNFCCC; Article 21 Kyoto Protocol.
[67] For a detailed discussion, see Brunnée, J., COPing with consent: lawmaking under multilateral environmental agreements, *Leiden J. Int'l L.* 15 (2002), pp. 1–52, at 15–21.
[68] For a detailed review, see Brunnée (2002), op. cit. pp. 30–33.
[69] Annex B inscribes percentages of greenhouse gas emissions in 1990 for each Annex I party and the party's assigned amount is determined by multiplying this percentage by five, i.e. the number of years in the commitment period (Article 3.7).
[70] See Articles 3.4, 5.1, 6.2, 7.4, 8.4, 12.7, 16, 17, and 18 Kyoto Protocol. Indeed, much of what the Kyoto Protocol delegates to COP decisions pertains to the types of terms that have tended to be added to a treaty through Protocols, amendments, or Annexes – and thus through the requisite formal or simplified consent procedures.

For example, Articles 6, 12, and 17 of the Kyoto Protocol call upon the COP or COP/MOP to develop the details of the so-called Kyoto mechanisms. These mechanisms are intended to give parties flexibility in meeting their emission reduction commitments under the Kyoto Protocol by allowing them to acquire emission rights or reduction credits from other parties.[71] In view of the potentially significant difficulties that some parties will face in achieving domestic emission reductions, the Kyoto mechanisms were among the most important, and most hotly contested, aspects of the Protocol.[72] The significance of the mechanism decisions notwithstanding, neither these nor the other above-mentioned Kyoto Protocol provisions, explicitly authorise binding decision-making by the COP or COP/MOP. The provisions use terms that have no connotation of binding rule-making at all,[73] or no necessary connotation of binding effect.[74]

Whatever the correct interpretation of these Kyoto Protocol provisions with respect to the COP's or COP/MOP's law-making powers,[75] the draft decisions that emerged from COP-7 in July 2001 use language that is normally reserved for legally binding commitments ('shall'). For example, under the draft umbrella decision on the Kyoto mechanisms, an Annex I party is eligible to participate in emissions trading only if it is in compliance with its emissions inventory and reporting obligations under the Protocol.[76] The draft decisions on the individual Kyoto mechanisms set out various additional 'eligibility' requirements.[77]

---

[71] See Articles 6 (joint implementation), 12 (clean development mechanism), and 17 (international emissions trading) Kyoto Protocol. For an overview, see Brunnée (2000), op. cit., pp. 232–236.

[72] See Wirth, D. A., The sixth session (Part two) and seventh session of the Conference of the Parties to the Framework Convention on Climate Change, *Am. J. Int'l L.* 96 (2002), pp. 648–660, at 651–653.

[73] Articles 5.1, 6.2, 7.4, 8.4 Kyoto Protocol ask the COP or COP/MOP to adopt 'guidelines'.

[74] Articles 12.7 and 18 Kyoto Protocol call for the elaboration of 'procedures'; Articles 3.4 and 17 for the adoption of 'rules'. Procedures and rules *can*, but need not, be binding. Given the exceptional nature of binding COP decisions, stronger language would arguably be required to so authorise the COP or COP/MOP.

[75] There has been some debate on this point. See e.g., Röben, V., Institutional developments under modern international environmental agreements, *Max Planck Y. B. of United Nations Law* 4 (2000), pp. 363–443, at 371–372, 383–384 (referring to decisions under Articles 6, 8 or 12 Kyoto Protocol as 'implementing legislation'). Some conclude that the relevant decisions could be legally binding. See, e.g., Churchill, R. and Ulfstein, G., Autonomous institutional arrangements in multilateral environmental agreements: a little-noticed phenomenon in international law, *Am. J. Int'l L.* 94 (2000), pp. 623–659, at 639 (referring to 'rules' adopted pursuant to Article 17 Kyoto Protocol).

[76] See Decision 15/CP.7, Draft Decision (Mechanisms), ¶5, in *Report of the Conference of the Parties to the United Nations Framework Convention on Climate Change on its Seventh Session*, UN Doc. FCCC/CP/2001/13/Add.1-3, 21 January 2002 ('Marrakech Accords').

[77] See Marrakech Accords, op. cit., Decision 16/CP.7, Draft Decision (Article 6), 21–29; Decision 16/CP.7, Draft Decision (Article 12), 31–34; Decision 16/CP.7, Draft Decision (Article 17), 2–4.

Thus, whether or not the mechanism rules are formally binding, they will significantly affect the legal position of a party under the agreement.

Questions of formal legal status also arise with respect to the Kyoto Protocol's compliance regime. According to Article 18 of the Protocol, the compliance procedures are to be adopted through a decision of the first meeting of the parties to the Protocol. However, '[a]ny procedures and mechanisms... entailing binding consequences shall be adopted by means of an amendment to [the] Protocol'. This requirement confronts the parties with a dilemma. An amendment can be adopted only once the Protocol is in force and it will bind only those parties that ratify it.[78] The Protocol will thus enter into force without a compliance regime that includes 'binding consequences', and without any guarantee that all parties will be exposed to binding consequences.

The decisions adopted at COP-7 in Marrakech reflect the continuing disagreements among parties regarding the legal status of the compliance regime and leave the issue unresolved. In the decision on the compliance regime, COP-7 adopted the 'text containing the procedures and mechanisms relating to compliance under the Kyoto Protocol' (annexed to the decision).[79] It recommends to the meeting of the parties to the Protocol that, at its first session, it adopt the Procedures and Mechanisms on Compliance under the Kyoto Protocol ('Procedures and Mechanisms') 'in terms of Article 18'.[80] In addition, the decision's Preamble notes that it is the meeting's prerogative 'to decide on the legal form' of the compliance regime.[81]

Nothing would prevent the COP/MOP from adopting the Procedures and Mechanisms by simple decision. Since, absent explicit authorisation, decisions of meetings of parties are not legally binding, this would mean that the consequences outlined in the Procedures and Mechanisms could not be considered to be binding strictly speaking.[82] But would their adoption in legally binding form really make a significant difference to their effectiveness? If a party truly wished to resist the imposition of non-compliance consequences, it would likely do so whether they are formally binding or not. Insistence on adoption of the Procedures and Mechanisms by amendment merely allows parties to opt out of the compliance regime. Thus, adoption by simple decision, applicable to all parties, may well be more likely to create a successful compliance regime.[83]

---

[78] Article 20.4 Kyoto Protocol. Note that Russia deposited its ratification of the Kyoto Protocol on 18 November 2004. According to its Article 25, the Protocol will enter into force on 16 February 2005.

[79] Procedures and Mechanisms on Compliance under the Kyoto Protocol are contained in an Annex to Decision 24/CP.7, in Marrakech Accords, op. cit. ('Procedures and Mechanisms').

[80] Ibid., p. 2.   [81] Ibid., Preamble.

[82] See Wang, X. and Wiser, G., The implementation and compliance regimes under the Climate Change Convention and its Kyoto Protocol, *RECIEL* 11 (2002), pp. 181–198, at 197.

[83] See Ott, H. E., Climate policy after the Marrakesh Accords: from legislation to implementation, 2001, pp. 7–8, available at www.wupperinst.org/download/Ott-after-

In sum, from a formal standpoint, and pending further clarification, the legal situation is at best ambiguous. To the extent that parties understand some of the rules contained in the relevant decisions as mandatory and agree to subject themselves to their terms, the distinction between COP decisions that are, technically speaking, legally binding and those that are not may well be more apparent than real.

3. Applying the interactional framework

It is at this point that the interactional framework provides additional guidance, precisely because it looks beyond exclusively formal criteria. It helps explain why it is incomplete to say that international environmental law is weak because it is largely non-binding, or that it would be stronger if only it were formally binding. And, in offering an alternative explanation of the strength of international law, the interactional framework draws attention to the linkages between law-making and compliance. Specifically, in highlighting characteristics that enable legal norms and processes to mobilise compliance pull, it provides guidance for law-making that is sensitive to the compliance continuum.

In brief terms, international environmental law-making, whether formally binding or not, must keep law's internal legitimacy criteria in constant reference and strive for rules that ask reasonable things (e.g. commitments that are achievable), that actually guide the application of norms in the MEA regime (e.g. in interpretative decisions, or the work of compliance bodies) and the development of new norms (e.g. in Protocols, amendments, or COP decisions), and that are transparent and relatively predictable (e.g. as to required conduct or decision criteria and processes).[84] Further, law-makers must ensure that law-making processes are inclusive, so as to expose all relevant actors to the mutual construction of norms and identities. Inclusiveness, in turn, demands that actors are included, or excluded, on principled grounds. In the case of COPs, this means that law-making processes, as a general matter, have to be open to all parties to the agreement. To the extent possible, parties must also be enabled to participate on a level playing field, a requirement that is particularly important for the involvement of developing country parties.[85]

---

marrakesh.pdf; and Wiser, G., Report on the compliance section of the Marrakech Accords to the Kyoto Protocol, 2001, p. 4, available at www.ciel.org/Publications/ Marrakech_Accords_Dec01.pdf. But see Ulfstein, G. and Werksman, J. The Kyoto Compliance system: towards hard enforcement, in Hovi, J., Stokke, O. S., and Kefstein, G. (eds.), *Implementing the climate change regime: international compliance*, London (Earthscan) 2005, pp. 39–65.

[84] For a detailed discussion of the requirements of interactional law-making in the MEA context, see Brunnée (2002), op. cit. pp. 33–50.

[85] For example, in the case of some developing countries, genuine participation may be contingent upon financial and legal capacity. Aside from financial constraints, human

IV. The compliance continuum

An interactional understanding of international law implies the idea of the compliance continuum. Questions about the binding effect – the strength – of international environmental law and questions about compliance lead to the same point: to the extent that law has an inherent ability to promote compliance, it is rooted in internal characteristics that give norms distinctive legal legitimacy. When the underlying norms are generated with attention to these factors they are more likely to support meaningful compliance strategies. It is this aspect of the compliance continuum, the interlinkages between the processes and substance of law-making and the potential for success of various compliance strategies, that remains to be explored. Both of the most commonly promoted compliance strategies, the managerial and enforcement-oriented approaches, could be enriched by the insights of the interactional account.

1. The Kyoto Protocol compliance regime

Again, the Kyoto Protocol and, in particular, its Procedures and Mechanisms on compliance, furnish an excellent setting in which to examine the attendant questions.[86] The declared goals of the Kyoto Protocol's Procedures and Mechanisms are to 'facilitate, promote and enforce compliance' with the Protocol.[87] This set of goals takes the procedures and mechanisms beyond the largely facilitative range of approaches of existing non-compliance regimes.[88] The Kyoto compliance regime also sets itself apart through institutional and procedural arrangements that reflect the broader range of its goals. One of the regime's most notable features is its institutional core, a Compliance Committee that will have a 'facilitative branch' and an 'enforcement branch'.[89]

The task of the facilitative branch is to promote compliance with Protocol commitments through advice and assistance, 'taking into account the

---

resource constraints can be a significant factor. For example, small developing country delegations may comprise negotiators with only limited experience or legal knowledge. See Gupta, J., North-South aspects of the climate change issue: towards a negotiating theory and strategy for developing countries, *Int'l J. Sustainable Development* 3(2) (2000), pp. 115–135. Lack of understanding of procedural or substantive issues can prompt obstructionist attitudes, or can lead to the adoption of rules on the basis of misunderstandings. In either case, outcomes are unlikely to be persuasive.

[86] In this discussion, I draw on Brunnée (2002), op. cit. pp. 16–27. A detailed review of the Kyoto compliance regime is also provided in Wang and Wiser, op. cit, pp. 186–198.

[87] Procedures and Mechanisms, I.

[88] For example, the Implementation Committee under the Montreal Protocol is to secure 'amicable solutions' to compliance problems. See *MOP-4 Report*, op. cit., Annex IV, para 8.

[89] Procedures and Mechanisms, II.2.

principle of common but differentiated responsibilities and respective capabilities' enshrined in the UNFCCC.[90] The facilitative branch is responsible for questions concerning the implementation of Protocol commitments other than those related to Annex I parties' emission reduction commitments.[91] Emission reduction commitments under Article 3.1 of the Protocol, and inventory and reporting commitments under Articles 5 and 7, are within the purview of the facilitative branch only when referred to it by the enforcement branch, or prior to and during the commitment period.[92] In keeping with the role of the facilitative branch, the means at its disposal in addressing compliance problems include: advice and facilitation of assistance to individual parties, facilitation of financial and technical assistance, and recommendations to the party concerned.[93]

While the facilitative branch resembles existing compliance mechanisms, the enforcement branch displays a series of features that are unprecedented in the MEA context. The enforcement branch is tasked with the resolution of all compliance questions relating to Annex I parties' emission target-related commitments: the reduction commitment under Article 3.1, relevant inventory and reporting commitments under Articles 5 and 7, and eligibility requirements for use of the Kyoto mechanisms.[94] Unlike compliance bodies under other MEAs,[95] the enforcement branch not only determines whether a party is in compliance with its commitments but also applies 'consequences' to non-compliance.[96] These consequences are cast not as punitive but as providing for 'the restoration of compliance to ensure environmental integrity', and 'for an incentive to comply'.[97]

In terms of intrusiveness, the range of consequences contemplated under the enforcement branch of the Kyoto Protocol procedures begins roughly where the

---

[90] Ibid., IV.4, XIV.   [91] Ibid., IV.5.
[92] Ibid., IV.6; IX.12. Compliance with the emission reduction commitment can be assessed only at the end of the 2008–2012 commitment period set up by Article 3.1. However, there is room for 'promoting compliance and providing for early warning of potential non-compliance' during the commitment period (IV.6).
[93] Ibid., XIV(a)–(d).
[94] Ibid., V.4. With respect to the eligibility requirements, the Procedures and Mechanisms are complemented by the rules governing the Kyoto mechanisms. These rules provide that the eligibility of an Annex I party for participation in the mechanisms is contingent upon their compliance with the inventory and reporting commitments under Articles 5 and 7 of the Protocol. The enforcement branch is tasked with eligibility assessments. See Marrakech Accords, op. cit., Decision 15/CP.7, Draft Decision (Mechanisms), 5; Decision 16/CP.7, Draft Decision (Article 6), 21–29; Decision 16/CP.7, Draft Decision (Article 12), 31–34; Decision 16/CP.7, Draft Decision (Article 17), 2–4.
[95] See e.g., *MOP-4 Report*, op.cit., Annex IV, para. 9.
[96] Procedures and Mechanisms, I, V.6, and XV. For a detailed discussion of the role and powers of the enforcement branch, see Ulfstein and Werksman, op. cit.
[97] Procedures and Mechanisms, V.6.

spectrum of consequences under existing non-compliance procedures tends to end.[98] The consequences that can be applied under the Procedures and Mechanisms differ depending on the underlying commitment. In cases of non-compliance with inventory or reporting commitments, consequences will consist in a declaration of non-compliance and in the requirement that the party concerned prepare a 'compliance action plan'.[99] That plan must include an analysis of the causes of non-compliance, the measures that the party intends to take to remedy the non-compliance, and a timetable for their implementation. Progress in the implementation of the plan must be reported to the enforcement branch.[100] Where the enforcement branch has determined that a party has not met one or more of the eligibility requirements for the Kyoto mechanisms, the consequence will be suspension of the party from participation in the mechanisms.[101] Finally, in the case of the emission reduction commitments under Article 3.1, there will be a grace period during which parties can acquire emission rights or credits to bring themselves within their assigned amounts.[102] Where a party nonetheless exceeds its emission entitlement, it will suffer suspension from eligibility to sell emission rights, and it will be required to develop a compliance action plan.[103] In addition, the excess emissions will be deducted, at penalty rate of 1.3, from that party's allowable emissions for the next commitment period.[104] The penalty rate is intended to discourage parties from simply postponing their emission reductions to the subsequent commitment period.[105]

In comparison to existing non-compliance procedures, the Kyoto Protocol's Procedures and Mechanisms bring an array of innovations. In part, these innovations are likely the result of the experience gained under other MEAs, and the growing degree of comfort with the operation of non-compliance procedures. For example, while the role of the Montreal Protocol's non-compliance procedure is to 'secure an amicable solution . . . on the basis of respect for the provisions of the Protocol',[106] observers have noted a gradual 'hardening' of its practice, including increasing resort to 'sticks' to address persistent patterns of non-compliance.[107] The Kyoto Protocol builds on this tentative move towards

---

[98] For the non-compliance procedure under the Montreal Protocol, possible responses to non-compliance are set out in an 'indicative list of measures' and include appropriate assistance, cautions, and suspension of rights and privileges under the Protocol. See *MOP-4 Report*, op. cit., Annex IV. And see Marauhn, T., Towards a procedural law of compliance control in international environmental law, *ZaöRV* 56 (1996), pp. 696–731, at 718–720.

[99] Procedures and Mechanisms, XV.1.
[100] Ibid., XV.2 and 3.   [101] Ibid., XV.4.
[102] Ibid., XIII, XV.5.   [103] Ibid., XV.5(a), (b), 6, 7.   [104] Ibid., XV.5(c).
[105] During the negotiations, various 'penalty' options, including deduction of excess emissions and payments into a 'compliance fund' were under discussion. See Brunnée (2000), pp. 248–249.
[106] See *MOP-4 Report*, op. cit., Annex IV, para 8.   [107] See Victor, op. cit. pp. 166–170.

more enforcement-oriented approaches.[108] In this context it is worth noting that the Protocol will require 'deep cooperation' from Annex I parties: they must reduce their greenhouse gas emissions significantly below 'business as usual' levels;[109] these reductions will require significant action in a broad swath of economic sectors and will impact on a wide range of commercial and private activities; compliance with Kyoto commitments has significant economic implications; non-compliance by some parties is likely to raise significant competitiveness concerns for others. Therefore, it may be tempting to see the Protocol as a test case for the claims of the 'enforcement' school. At first blush, one may even be inclined to see that school's assumptions confirmed in the very design of the Procedures and Mechanisms. After all, it is precisely the Protocol's most challenging commitments that would attract enforcement-oriented non-compliance consequences. However, it is important to note that, at least in part, the innovations of the Procedures and Mechanisms are responses to the unique features of the Protocol itself, such as its reliance on emissions trading mechanisms. It is arguable that, in view of the mechanisms' explicit reliance on market dynamics, a clear set of disincentives against non-compliance – 'consequences' in Kyoto terms – are needed to ensure the success of this part of the Kyoto regime.[110]

---

[108] But note that there does not seem to be an overarching trend towards 'harder' compliance mechanisms. Two of the compliance regimes adopted after the Kyoto Protocol procedures are primarily facilitative and discursive in approach. The Basel Convention NCP is described as a 'facilitation procedure' and prioritises technical assistance, capacity-building and access to financial resources to promote compliance. Similarly, the 'measures to promote compliance and address cases of non-compliance' under the Biosafety Protocol NCP are primarily designed to assist parties in coming into compliance. See Biosafety Protocol NCP, III, 1(a).

[109] Given emission trends since the adoption of the Protocol, the actual reductions required from parties would be far greater than the percentages stipulated in the Protocol. For example, the USA would have been required to make reductions of 30–35 per cent from business-as-usual projections for the 2008–2012 period. See Bodansky, D., Bonn voyage: Kyoto's uncertain revival, *The National Interest* 65 (Fall 2001), pp. 45–55, at 47. Canada's situation is similar. See Rolfe, C., Opportunities and liabilities from greenhouse gas emissions and greenhouse gas emission reductions, March 1999, p. 4, available at www.wcel.org/wcelpub/1999/12753.html

[110] Note that the European Emissions Trading System (ETS), which is to take effect for a range of industrial sectors in January 2005, is backed by an automatic, stringent penalty regime. Emissions in excess of a company's allowance incur a penalty rate of 40 Euro/CO2t during 2005–2007, and 100 Euro/CO2t during 2008–2012. In addition, the excess emissions must be made up in the following compliance period. Finally, under a 'naming and shaming' provision, the names of operators that are not in compliance will be publicised. See Directive 2003/87/EC of the European Parliament and of the Council of 13 October 2003 establishing a scheme for greenhouse gas emission allowance trading within the Community and amending Council Directive 96/61/EC, [2003] OJ L275/32, Articles 16, 17.

2. Persuasion, facilitation, and enforcement

The design of the Procedures and Mechanisms combines facilitative, normative-discursive, and enforcement-oriented approaches. As just noted, given the Kyoto Protocol's strong reliance on the market-based Kyoto mechanisms, interest-based compliance decisions and (dis)incentives will clearly matter. But this prediction is not inconsistent with the theoretical arguments advanced in this chapter. Only time, and actual practice under the regime, will tell which approach is most conducive to promoting compliance with the Protocol – or whether it is in fact a combination of approaches that is required.[111] In any case, stressing the importance of constructivist-normative explanations of state behaviour is not to deny the relevance of rationalist explanations. As others have observed, cost-benefit calculations and normative socialisation each explain important aspects of compliance processes.[112]

It is the potential for the two dynamics – and attendant reliance upon 'sanctions' or 'persuasion' – to complement one another that has not received sufficient attention. The assertion that 'sanctioning authority is rarely granted by treaty, rarely used when granted, and likely to be ineffective when used' is incomplete. It does not sufficiently consider the conditions under which it may be possible both to agree upon sanctions and to make effective use of sanctions. Equally incomplete is the argument that sanctions will be needed to ensure compliance with 'deep cooperation' commitments. Even if that assumption as such is correct, it does not elucidate how a regime would get to the point at which the adoption and imposition of effective sanctions is possible.

It is precisely these gaps that attention to the insights provided by an interactional understanding of international law can help fill. Arguably, the very processes that this chapter highlighted as important to the formation and persuasive power of legal norms are also crucial to enabling a regime to use enforcement-oriented approaches effectively. The promotion of compliance does not begin with the use of mechanisms for the application of preestablished rules. Nor can non-compliance mechanisms, simply through their creation within treaty regimes, be expected to ensure compliance. Incentives and disincentives, formal dispute settlement, and enforcement through sanctions all have a role to play in influencing international actors. But these means to promote compliance are more likely to be acceptable, and effective, when a sufficiently strong body of shared understandings and legitimate processes has developed within

---

[111] See also Raustiala, op. cit. p. 420 (highlighting the interaction between managerial and enforcement-focused elements in the context of the Montreal Protocol NCP).

[112] See e.g., Finnemore, M. and Sikkink, K., International norm dynamics and political change, *Int'l Org.* 52 (1998), pp. 887–918, at 909–915; Abbott, K. W. and Snidal, D., Hard and soft law in international governance, *Int'l Org.* 54 (2000), pp. 401–420, at 422; Downs *et al.* (2000), op. cit. p. 468.

a regime.[113] It is already in the processes through which norms are created that the foundations for ultimate compliance, and compliance strategies, must be built.

These observations relate directly to how one might assess the promise of the Kyoto Protocol's compliance regime. The Procedures and Mechanisms have been heralded by various commentators as ground-breaking, notably because they would create the first compliance regime to include enforcement-oriented features.[114] There is some irony in the fact that this 'hardening' of approaches to compliance with MEAs may well end up being accomplished in legally 'soft' form. If so, the interactional account suggests that the Procedures and Mechanisms' non-binding form should not automatically be seen as indicative of its weakness. The regime's ability to operate and to impose consequences will likely depend at least as much on its perceived legitimacy as on its legal form. Indeed, the interactional understanding of law cautions that adoption in binding form may create a false sense of assurance, diverting attention from the need to develop the persuasive power of the climate change regime.

V. Conclusion

I have outlined an alternative, broader approach to compliance issues. The purpose of this discussion was not to suggest that the managerial or enforcement-oriented theories of compliance are wrong. Rather, my goal was to illustrate that they may miss or at least undervalue important parts of the compliance picture. The constructivist-inspired interactional theory of international law, by opening up the vista of the compliance continuum, illuminates a wider range of options – and, arguably, prerequisites – for effective compliance strategies.

The interactional account suggests that some answers to the compliance challenge can be found by looking to legitimacy factors rather than simply to formal indicators to explain the binding force of international law. This lens not only helps counter the stereotyping of international environmental law as weak. It also highlights opportunities for cultivating the compliance pull of international environmental norms already at the law-making stage. Procedurally, law-making must provide for interactional processes that involve all relevant actors in the mutual construction of identities and norms. Substantively, law-making must be sensitive to the internal characteristics that give norms distinctive legal legitimacy. Crucially, when the underlying norms are

---

[113] See also Brunnée and Toope (2000), op. cit. p. 47.
[114] See e.g., Wiser, G., Kyoto Protocol packs powerful compliance punch, *International Environment Report* 25 (2002), p. 86, available at www.ciel.org/Publications/INER_Compliance.pdf; Ott, op. cit. p. 6. But see also Vespa, M., Kyoto at Bonn and Marrakech, *Ecology L. Q.* 29 (2002), pp. 395–421, at 414–416 (arguing that the Kyoto penalties are inadequate to deter non-compliance).

generated with attention to these factors, when they are seen as legitimate, they are also more likely to support meaningful compliance strategies.

Clearly, managerial or enforcement approaches capture important parts of the compliance process. For example, when non-compliance results primarily from technical or financial capacity limitations, the causes of non-compliance must be addressed through concrete managerial measures. Similarly, when non-compliance results from deliberate disregard of treaty commitments, sanctions could serve both to deter non-compliance and express the collective disapproval of the parties to an MEA. However, the interactional account can enhance these approaches in important ways. It helps explain why managerial processes come to influence actors and can help increase their potential to do so. Equally, it can help create the conditions in which an enforcement-oriented strategy could develop and operate effectively.

16

On clustering international environmental agreements

KONRAD VON MOLTKE

I. Introduction

Even as consensus emerges that creating a World Enviroment Organisation (WEO) is not possible, never mind whether it is desirable, there is widespread consensus that the existing structure of international environmental management needs reform and strengthening. The impetus for this consensus is fourfold:

- the creation of the Commission on Sustainable Development (CSD) at the 1992 United Nations Conference on Environment and Development (UNCED) did not result in a strengthening of international environmental regimes;
- the World Summit on Sustainable Development (WSSD) to mark the tenth anniversary of UNCED, did nothing to further this debate;
- the continuing need to develop international responses to the challenges of sustainable development has resulted in a structure that is increasingly complex and widely viewed as inadequate to the growing needs that are associated with it;
- the nexus between international economic and environmental policy has grown increasingly powerful, and threatens to result in a deadlock unless some of the organisational issues are resolved in a satisfactory manner.

This growing consensus that international environmental management needs reform and strengthening found its expression in Decision 21–21 of the Governing Council of the United Nations Environment Programme (UNEP).[1] Yet, while this decision launched a process, there remains a remarkable scarcity of realistic proposals on measures that can be adopted. Based on the documents from the UNEP process, one of the issues that will be important in this debate is that of 'clustering', that is grouping a number of international environmental

---

[1] International environmental governance, available at www.unep.org. See also the reports of the *Earth Negotiations Bulletin* at www.iisd.org

regimes together so as to make them more efficient and effective.[2] Whether international environmental regimes are effective has attracted a broad stream of research, resulting in a mixed assessment but not leading to any clear conclusions as to what should be done to increase effectiveness.[3] Clustering is one possible approach.[4]

II. Clustering

The current number of international environmental regimes is clearly too large. This plethora of agreements is rooted in the fact that structural differences exist between many environmental problems, thus requiring separate institutional responses.[5] The institutions required to manage biodiversity are obviously different from those needed for hazardous wastes, and the institutions for climate change differ in many respects from those for water management, or ocean governance for that matter. Nevertheless, it is clear that the actual number of international environmental agreements – in excess of 300 by some counts – is not the appropriate number from the perspective of effectiveness.

The actual merger of existing international environmental agreements is a daunting task. It has been accomplished but once, when the Oslo and Paris Conventions were merged.[6] Yet despite the manifest advantages of a merger and despite the fact that the membership of both agreements was identical and involved a limited number of highly developed states, the process of merger

---

[2] The views on existing arrangements according to the responses to the questionnaire provided by the Secretariats, include the following: (a) clustering provides opportunities for synergies, particularly within each cluster, where agreements have much in common in terms of issues to be addressed; (b) issues of common interest also cut across clusters, for example, trade, capacity-building, and the development of national legislation that supports the implementation of Conventions and Protocols at the country level; (c) opportunities exist for closer cooperation among the scientific bodies of the agreements; (d) an increase is occurring in arrangements which enable Conventions to work together in a more integrated manner, leading to the development of joint programmes of work in areas of common interest. From *International environmental governmental governance, Report of the Executive Director*, UNEP/IGM/1/2, 4 April 2001, para. 69.

[3] Miles, E. et al., *Environmental regime effectiveness: confronting theory with practice*, Cambridge, Mass. (MIT Press) 2002; Brown Weiss, E. and Jacobson, H., *Engaging countries: strengthening compliance with international environmental accords*, Cambridge, Mass. (MIT Press) 1998; Victor, D. et al. (eds.), *The implementation and effectiveness of international environmental commitments: theory and practice*, Cambridge, Mass. (MIT Press) 1998.

[4] von Moltke, K., *Whither MEA's? The role of international environmental management in the trade and environment agenda*, Report for Environment Canada, available at www.iisd1.iisd.pubs.html

[5] von Moltke, K., Institutional interactions: the structure of regimes for trade and environment, in Young, O. (ed.), *Global Governance: drawing insights from the environmental experience*, Cambridge, Mass. (MIT Press) 1997, pp. 247–272.

[6] Skjaersteth, J. B., Toward the end of dumping in the North Sea: the case of the Oslo Commission, in Miles et al., op. cit. pp. 63–86.

took many years to accomplish. The reasons why such a merger does not appear feasible except in singular cases are numerous:

- The reasons to negotiate new agreements despite the existence of older ones must have been compelling at the time, so a subsequent change needs to address these reasons, and show why they are no longer compelling – this creates an additional barrier to change.
- Membership of related or overlapping agreements is rarely identical. Thus, key countries party to the Convention on International Trade in Endangered Species (CITES) are not party to the Convention on Biodiversity (CBD). Their merger entails the risk of losing parties in one regime without gaining more penetration in others.
- Even where membership is identical, the domestic constituencies supporting related or overlapping regimes may differ. This is most frequently expressed by differences in bureaucratic responsibilities. Thus, the agency responsible for the Basel Convention on the International Transport of Hazardous Wastes may not be responsible for the management of toxic substances and consequently plays a minor role in the Convention on Prior Informed Consent (PIC) or Persistent Organic Pollutants (POPS).
- The existence of an international environmental regime frequently gives rise to congruent structures in international civil society, for example, scientific groups, commercial interests, or advocacy organisations, resulting in a committed constituency whose very existence may be threatened by proposals to merge, move, or abolish a regime.
- In several instances, later conventions represent an evolution in thinking about certain environmental problems. Despite addressing related or overlapping problems they may exhibit quite different institutional structures and pursue distinct priorities that a merged regime would have difficulty in balancing.
- Decisions concerning the location of Secretariats are often highly competitive; some countries have shown an active interest in attracting the permanent organisation associated with a given regime. Having expended effort to obtain the location of a Secretariat in their country, having generally been required to support that Secretariat in a variety of ways, the countries concerned have strong stakes of ownership in the Secretariat.

In practice, any attempt to negotiate all the factors that obstruct merger, even when it seems logically unimpeachable, will require extraordinary effort while possibly producing modest results in terms of greater effectiveness or efficiency. At the very least, it risks the misallocation of one of the scarcest of resources: the negotiation effort of the constituencies involved and the attention of senior policy-makers.

Under these circumstances, it may be appropriate to seek a variety of institutional and organisational arrangements short of merger that will increase the efficiency and effectiveness of existing agreements without requiring elaborate changes in legal or administrative arrangements. This is what is meant by 'clustering'. It is important to view clustering as a process and not as a single act, so the immediate task is to create conditions that are conducive to fostering a process of clustering.

III. The tools of clustering

The notion of clustering assumes that there are ways to promote closer integration of related or overlapping international environmental regimes, short of merging organisations. It is worth listing the tools of clustering, even though not all may be applicable to every cluster, and certain clusters may have additional tools that can be utilised.

1. The Conference of the Parties

The Conference of the Parties (COP) or some similar institution meets periodically in locations that are determined from one meeting to the next. Several options are available with regard to the COP, precisely because no permanent commitments have been made thus far concerning timing and location.

(a) Colocation

The COP of clustered agreements can be held simultaneously in a changing location. This would facilitate coordination between the regimes while leaving a range of options open concerning the relationship between these simultaneous meetings, for example consecutive scheduling, joint bureaus, or joint activities relating to civil society. It would, of course, also reduce the number of conferences that need to be hosted.

(b) Permanent location

In addition to deciding to hold COPs simultaneously, it is possible to always hold them in the same location, whether simultaneously or not. This permits the development of an infrastructure to support the COPs, including the possible creation of specialised missions from member states. One lesson from the experience of the WTO that may be applicable to environmental regimes is the advantage of a single location and the importance of permanent missions devoted to the WTO agenda. These missions have in fact become an integral part of the organisational structure of the WTO, and explain in large measure how the organisation manages to cover a wide agenda with a relatively small Secretariat. Of course, this raises the issue of UNEP and the desirability of holding these meetings in Nairobi, an option that is unlikely to be appealing to many countries.

The advantages of holding simultaneous meetings are clear. This would bring the additional benefit of facilitating developing country participation in the environmental regimes. It would also tend to strengthen the role of member states.

(c) Executive and subsidiary bodies

Many COPs have executive and subsidiary bodies that meet between sessions of the COP. The scheduling of these meetings can occur according to a variety of conventions, alternating between a permanent location and a flexible one (as in the case of the World Bank and International Monetary Fund annual meetings), always in alternating locations, or in some rotating pattern with the COP itself.

There are numerous permutations that can evolve on the basis of the above variables. While it is theoretically desirable to have COP meetings occur at the location of the regime Secretariat(s), it is certainly not indispensable. Most international environmental regimes currently hold COPs at locations remote from their Secretariat. Given that the Secretariats of clustered regimes may actually be in several locations, there is no reason to assume that holding the COPs at the seat of one of them will exhibit particular advantages.

It is, of course, striking that there has been no move towards clustering COPs or subsidiary bodies, despite the fact that this is in some sense a 'free good', controlled by the parties and not requiring any form of payment or recompense to achieve. This suggests that the desire actually to do something about international environmental governance is in fact less pronounced than one might assume from official declarations.

2. Subsidiary bodies

Most international environmental regimes have a number of subsidiary bodies concerned with scientific and financial matters. It may prove possible to move beyond colocation to a more permanent form of coordination between these bodies. This measure can precede coordination of COPs or follow it, depending on priorities of the particular cluster. Delay in holding simultaneous meetings or identifying a permanent location for the subsidiary bodies (which can, but need not, be identical to the location of the COP) can help to ease the transition and contribute to maintaining the presence of international environmental regimes in a wide range of locations.

To a certain extent, the emergence of the Millenium Ecosystem Assessment represents an initiative in this direction. While not explicitly described as such, the Millenium Assessment is in many respects designed to provide the conservation regimes with the kind of scientific grounding that the climate regime derives from the Intergovernmental Panel on Climate Change (IPCC).

3. Secretariats

All major international environmental regimes have a Secretariat to ensure continuity and coordination. These Secretariats are often the most visible manifestation of the regime so that efforts at strengthening and coordination tend to focus on them. At the same time, moving a Secretariat requires extraordinary effort.

The specific role of the Secretariats can differ from one regime to another, reflecting both different legal authority and the result of a dynamic development of the regime itself. The organisational arrangements for individual Secretariats also differ widely, even among quite small organisations, depending on whether it is an independent body, located within some larger international organisation, revolving between states (like the Antarctic Secretariat) or based on a non-governmental organisation. Finally, leadership plays a significant role in Secretariats, which can acquire certain characteristics as a consequence of the personality of the person responsible for them.[7]

Given all these constraints, the prospects for dramatic reorganisation of Secretariats appear remote. In practice, such reorganisation is not as vital as it may appear. Regime Secretariats are responsive to a range of factors, including the COP, domestic and international constituencies, financial arrangements, sources of scientific advice and media pressure, which are more amenable to change than the Secretariats themselves.

In practice, every cluster is liable to involve several existing regimes with separate Secretariats, which will only rarely be in the same location. Consequently, solutions need to be found that permit these Secretariats to work more closely together, short of actually moving them. Staff exchanges, the use of common staff under certain circumstances, and the aggressive adoption of communications technologies, all can serve to alleviate what might otherwise appear as an insuperable problem.

4. Financial matters

Purposeful use of financial incentives represents a significant factor in clustering. Like most other measures to promote clustering, the use of financial tools is promising only if it is undertaken consistently by all key parties to an agreement. Nevertheless, individual parties may find that it is possible to make appropriate adjustments in their own approach to financial issues relating to regime clusters. While this may not produce the desired changes in the regime as a whole, it can increase the efficiency in the allocation of that party's resources and create incentives for other parties to act in a complementary manner.

---

[7] von Moltke, K. *et al.*, Secretariats: background note for the Pocantico Meeting on International Secretariats, June 1995.

Most international environmental regimes are supported by voluntary contributions. The power of the purse represents an important tool in situations where a significant group of parties agrees on the need to promote clustering.

(a) Regime budgets

The budgets for the operation of individual environmental regimes are generally quite modest, with the signal exception of the climate regime. Yet taken together, the budgets of all regimes in a cluster can be substantial. These include the resources required to ensure the participation of developing countries. All regimes struggle to obtain adequate resources to ensure their operations, with voluntary contributions predominating. Any move to cluster resources for groups of regimes would create powerful incentives for coordination between those responsible for the regimes' finances.

(b) Development assistance

Many international environmental agreements call for the provision of new and additional funds for development assistance. Indeed, UNCED involved an implied bargain that developing countries would participate more actively in international efforts to protect the environment, and developed countries would contribute more vigorously to the funding of relevant activities. Developed country performance in this area leaves much to be desired. Close tracking and active coordination of development assistance funding for certain clusters should generate incentives to ensure the more effective and efficient use of the scarce resources that are available.

(c) Subsidies

Subsidies are an integral part of the environmental policies of any country. Most countries have found that in the early stages of creating essential environmental infrastructure, subsidies are necessary to accelerate the process and to drive it beyond the relatively modest parameters that have been set. Such subsidies involve the risks associated with any programme of subsidy – that they become self-defeating, subject to capture by interest groups, and ultimately represent an obstacle to the achievement of market-based environmental objectives. Despite these drawbacks, subsidy programmes are an integral part of any environmental strategy, whether open or disguised in a variety of ways. In effect, they represent a way to finance environmental conservation that does not have an identifiable market value.

The Global Environment Facility (GEF) is an institution for international subsidies. With its role in several regimes, the GEF already represents an institution of clustering. Its role in a more clustered system needs to be considered carefully. In practice, each cluster involves quite distinct types of activities that require international support. It appears desirable to ensure a closer link between the substantive authority and the project activity than has been accomplished under the current structure.

5. Electronic clustering

At least theoretically, modern communications technology offers a range of opportunities for reinforcing the relationship of related and overlapping environmental regimes. In practice, modern technology relies on personal relationships as much as previous technologies so that electronic activities on their own entail few substantive benefits. They can, however, provide a powerful tool to support other kinds of clustering activities and facilitate linkages over distance.

6. Communications

The public image of international regimes is formed to a significant degree by their communications strategy. Clusters can develop a joint communications strategy, including publications and an Internet strategy, that can help to strengthen the internal links of the cluster.

7. Cluster coordinator

No cluster can function without clear assignment of roles and responsibilities. In many respects this assignment – and the likely conflicts surrounding it – form the heart of any clustering activity. It is critical to ensure that an individual, or a group of individuals, are given clear responsibility for the work of a cluster. Cluster coordination can occur at the site of one of the Secretariats, at the site of joint COPs, or at a site that offers particular advantages from the perspective of the UN system, New York or Geneva in particular.

In theory, international Secretariats are the servants of the member states and the COP. Yet in practice, the need to articulate underlying issues in a continuous manner has given Secretariats – and in some instances their respective leadership – roles that transcend this fairly limited notion. Clustering of COPs will tend to reinforce the role of states in the regimes, in particular if a system of permanent representatives at a location of COPs emerges. Clusters will, however, have need of leadership and a visible public presence, particularly where issues of great public saliency are concerned. Striking the right balance in this regard is one of the major challenges of any clustering process.

8. Implementation review

International environmental regimes are characterised by a high degree of subsidiarity. In other words, the activities of several levels of governance must work together. From this perspective, an active policy of implementation review that encompasses both the national and the subnational levels appears particularly important.

One option is to focus on groups of related or overlapping agreements, permitting a more detailed and specific review. In this instance it becomes possible to articulate quite specific performance goals for the period between reviews in relation to a given cluster.

Reviews could proceed along the lines established by the WTO and the Organisation for Economic Cooperation and Development (OECD). This involves the preparation of a country report, either by the authorities of the country in question or by the relevant Secretariats, or by an agency such as the United Nations Environment Programme (UNEP), followed by a country visit by a team of 'reviewers'. The reviewers are chosen in consultation with the country involved and should be given an opportunity to travel as necessary and to meet with any person or groups in the country that they find necessary. The country report, together with the reviewers' findings, are subsequently discussed in a forum of member states established for this purpose.

9. Capacity-building

Environmental management is institutionally demanding. It requires a large number of effective institutions at the domestic level, and it requires administrative structures that promote cooperation. Many international environmental agreements contain provisions concerning capacity-building. Yet these promises have proven hard to keep, for lack of financial resources as well as for a lack of human resources. Properly conceived, capacity-building initiatives can become powerful tools for clustering, conveying the necessary skills and providing a more coherent and effective international environmental management structure to interact with.

IV. Creating clusters

It is common practice to group international environmental agreements by topic, since this is preferable to the only alternative – chronological order – to create some structure in a universe of several hundred agreements. Like any system imposed on a structure that evolved without systematic intent, this requires a certain degree of arbitrary assignment. It is not the purpose of the following grouping to achieve a perfect system to categorise all international environmental agreements. Its intent is to form clusters of agreements not by subject area but by problem structure. The concept of 'problem structure' has not received systematic treatment. Yet it is central to a discussion of effectiveness of international (environmental) regimes based on the fit between institutional design and problem structure.[8] The approach chosen here is largely pragmatic and intuitive; indeed, to some extent it works back from institutional design to problem structure, assuming that regimes with similar institutions must address problems that exhibit similar structure. While this is self-evidently a case of circular reasoning, it suffices for the present purpose, namely to suggest certain regime clusters for further discussion.

While some clusters remain quite predictable, it emerges that some agreements that apparently deal with the same issue – the atmosphere or conservation, for example – do not belong together because of major institutional differences that are rooted in differences in problem definition. Other agreements that appear to deal with institutional issues relevant to most problem clusters – the PIC Agreement, for example – in fact address only the institutional needs of a single cluster.

The formation of clusters is clearly a matter for broad discussion, careful consideration, and full negotiation. It is not the kind of issue that is amenable to analytical approaches alone since only the process of negotiation can ensure that all important stakeholders are heard and all significant issues are given due consideration.

1. The conservation complex[9]

The conservation complex is characterised by two major global Conventions whose relationship remains a matter for discussion, and a number of other global and regional agreements that are at present poorly integrated. Three of the Conventions mark the evolution of international approaches to conservation. The Ramsar Convention is largely devoid of substantive international obligations and sees its primary focus at the national level. CITES addresses the most obviously international dimension of conservation – trade in endangered species. At the same time, it has become the focus of an extraordinary scientific effort to identify and assess potentially endangered species of all kinds. The CBD seeks to achieve a fully integrated approach to conservation, recognising both human use and the need to protect entire ecosystems, addressing both in situ and ex situ conservation techniques.

While the complex would clearly benefit from a significant organisational overhaul, each regime has developed its own constituency, which defends its independence. Integration requires a comprehensive understanding of the

---

[8] Young, O., *The institutional dimensions of environmental change: fit, interplay, and scale*, Cambridge, Mass. (MIT Press) 2002.

[9] World Heritage Convention; Convention on Biological Diversity; Convention on the Conservation of Migratory Species; CITES; Ramsar; Convention to Combat Desertification; FAO International Treaty on Plant Genetic Resources; and the International Tropical Timber Agreement.

issues and of the role each of the regimes can play in developing an international response to the imperative of conservation.

To represent a significant step forward, a Global Conservation Regime would need to provide additional institutional support to the protection of wetlands and other critical habitat and incorporate most regional conservation activities, several of which deal with migratory species that are not covered by the global agreements.[10] An initial step towards clustering could be the identification of critical conservation areas that are of importance to all or most of the conservation regimes and to focus resources on these areas.[11] The Millenium Ecosystem Assessment can serve as a science-based input for this cluster.

2. The global atmosphere[12]

The two agreements in this cluster involve complex institutional arrangements. Indeed, one of the burdens on the climate regime is the tendency of some observers to assume that the ozone regime represents a template on which to build. In practice, the ozone regime is based on a relatively traditional agreement that identifies pollutants and then takes steps to reduce their production, use, and emission to levels that are deemed acceptable. The climate regime deals with several 'pollutants' that are ubiquitous, indeed that are an integral part of life. Control of these substances requires structural change at all levels of the economy. The resulting regime is essentially an investment regime that seeks to reduce emissions by shifting the focus of public, corporate, and private investment.[13]

Despite these differences, the two global atmospheric regimes represent an obvious clustering. Yet the prospects for achieving significant progress are burdened by the historical decision to set up the United Nations Framework Convention on Climate Change (UNFCCC) as an essentially independent organisation within the UN system, rather than assign it to one of the competing claimants, primarily UNEP and WMO. The UNFCCC is already one of the largest Convention Secretariats in the United Nations, and the complexity of the issues it faces suggest it will grow further in importance.

---

[10] The Bonn Convention on the Conservation of Migratory Species has not evolved into the universal framework that its drafters envisaged, lacking some key members and without a strong civil society constituency.

[11] There are currently competing definitions of 'critical area'. These differences would need to be negotiated so as to arrive at a single operational definition.

[12] UNFCCC; Vienna Convention and Montreal Protocol; the Convention on long-range transboundary air pollution exhibits a significantly different problem structure.

[13] von Moltke, K., *An international investment agreement? Implications for sustainable development*, Winnipeg (International Institute for Sustainable Development) 2000. Also available at www.iisd.org/publications/publication_list.asp?themeid = 7

3. The hazardous substances complex[14]

All of the agreements in this cluster are managed by UNEP, so that it already exhibits some coherence. The control of hazardous substances is essentially the control of the products of a few industries, primarily chemicals and minerals. A preponderant portion of these industries is located in or controlled from OECD countries. Consequently, ways must be found to better integrate the OECD work in this area into a broader global framework.

The recently concluded Convention on Prior Informed Consent and the Convention on Persistent Organic Pollutants represent essential building blocks of this cluster. With these in place it should be possible to move towards greater integration, but for the obstacles outlined above. In many countries, the agencies responsible for hazardous wastes are not identical to those responsible for the control of toxic substances. Frequently, waste management is the responsibility of federal subunits while toxic substances control is invariably the responsibility of national authorities.

4. The marine environment complex[15]

There are a large number of agreements that deal with the marine environment involving several organisations, including the International Maritime Organization (IMO), UNEP, and International Tribunal on the Law of the Sea (ITLOS). The IMO manages agreements concerning pollution from ships; UNEP manages the regional seas programme; and the ITLOS Secretariat handles the broader legal framework. The approach of each group of agreements is markedly different.

The law of the sea is the most classic of all fields of international law, carrying the encrustation of several centuries. While it represents the framework within which all other marine activities are undertaken, it has a mixed record of effectiveness with regard to matters that concern the environment. It has, however, given rise to the ITLOS, a unique institution in that it parallels the work of the WTO dispute settlement process but with a higher degree of predictability and transparency.

Over a period of several decades, the IMO has succeeded in bringing the problem of intentional discharges of oil from ships into a management structure that holds out the prospect of being effective. It has reduced the pollution risks

---

[14] Bamako Convention; Basel Convention; Convention on Civil Liability for Damage Caused During Carriage of Dangerous Goods by Road, Rail, and Inland Navigation Vessels; PIC Convention; Convention on Transboundary Effects of Industrial Accidents; Waigani Convention; POPS Convention. The FAO Code of Conduct on the Distribution and Use of Pesticides could be included since it has a similar problem structure. Its institutional approach is, however, hardly comparable.

[15] IMO Conventions; Regional Seas Conventions; OSPAR Convention; Helsinki Convention.

associated with marine accidents by steadily improving the design of the ships carrying the most hazardous cargoes. It has established rules concerning the intentional discharge of oil from ships, in particular for deballastage, that can address what is the largest source of oil pollution from ships, even though enforcement can be difficult. The IMO has always struggled with the problems posed by flag state jurisdiction, and some of its advances are due to innovations limiting the reach of this principle, for example by permitting the introduction of port state jurisdiction over certain activities.

UNEP's regional seas programme addresses the broader environmental agenda, including the dumping of waste at sea – an activity that has largely been stopped – and the exceedingly difficult challenge of controlling land-based pollution so as to protect the marine environment. In principle, the regional seas programme also addresses issues of coastal zone management, an area that is particularly burdened in most countries by the existence of numerous competing jurisdictions. The UNEP programme is hampered by its technical complexity and the fact that it imposes demanding requirements on national governments that are not always willing or able to live up to them. For this reason, it is the most ambitious, and presumably the least effective, of the three sets of agreements.

The current effectiveness of the agreements in this complex is mixed. Further strengthening of port state jurisdiction and of the rights of states to control their exclusive economic zones (EEZ) may prove helpful. The creation of an effective cluster in this area is likely to prove exceedingly difficult.

5. The extractive resources complex[16]

This is the most difficult of all environmental issues, and the one with the largest potential impact on the trade regime. At present, international commodity regimes are largely mixed public/private structures designed to extract natural resources and to distribute them globally, for example, the banana regime, the aluminium regime, the cotton regime, or the forest products regimes. Attempts to introduce environmental criteria, let alone sustainable development criteria, into these regimes have met with limited success. Yet all of these regimes have a significant sustainable development dimension. The environmental impacts are largely focused at the extractive end, while funding for each regime, including for sustainable development, needs to come from the consumer rather than from public sources. Consequently, the problems of these regimes relate as much

---

[16] This complex includes most forestry agreements and public/private initiatives such as the Forest Stewardship Council or the Marine Stewardship Council. It also encompasses fisheries and agreements concerned with the environmental impacts of agriculture. For a theoretical background, see von Moltke, K. *et al.*, *Global product chains: northern consumers, southern producers, and sustainability*, Trade and Environment 15, Geneva (United Nations Environment Programme) 1998.

to the functioning of international markets as to the possibility for developing international agreements covering their sustainability.

V. Joint institutions

Several institutions[17] recur throughout the structure of international environmental management. International environmental regimes are characterised by a large variety of institutions. The reasons are to be found in the structure of environmental problems that require social and economic institutions to address a phenomenon that is governed by the laws of nature.[18] As a consequence, international environmental regimes have exhibited a remarkable degree of innovation as they have struggled to match their institutional arsenal to the structure of the problem they attempt to address.

Some institutions, in particular those that translate science into policy and that seek to assess environmental conditions in a systematic manner, are pervasive throughout international environmental regimes. Even when not every regime utilises a particular institution, it is worth considering the options for creating cross-cutting rules to ensure consistent application and to develop new organisational structures to promote greater efficiency and effectiveness. This is an area of activity for a broadly based organisation, such as UNEP.

1. Science assessment

Science assessment is the interpretation of research for policy purposes. Most countries use science assessment institutions to mediate the complex relationship between scientific research and public policy. Arguably the most characteristic institution of all environmental regimes – because without scientific research there can be no environmental management – science assessment offers a range of options for the clustering process at a universal level.

Few international environmental regimes have the necessary resources to undertake science assessments of their own or even to review science assessments undertaken at national level with a view to identifying the specifically international interest. Apart from the IPCC, there are no fully developed science assessment mechanisms at the international level. The resources required to undertake full-scale science assessment on a major issue of international environmental concern are very significant. It makes much more sense to focus the necessary resources on one or two regimes at any one time rather than

---

[17] The term 'institutions' is used here in its strict technical sense to denote the rules of the game that characterise a regime. Thus, 'property' is an institution but UNEP is an organisation.

[18] Young, Oran (ed.), *Global governance: drawing insights from the environmental experience*, Cambridge, Mass. (MIT Press) 1997.

distributing them widely, as now occurs. Consequently, a structure needs to be devised that can draw on the best scientists worldwide in changing fields of research. The model would be the US National Research Council (a branch of the National Academy of Science), which is required by charter to provide government with advisory services (for pay) yet manages to maintain its independence and its ability to identify appropriate participants in its panels from a range of disciplines. The Millenium Ecosystem Assessment represents a step in this direction.

2. Monitoring and environmental assessment

Specific environmental measures are based on numerous assumptions about environmental conditions, the need to adopt measures, and the impact of these measures on environmental conditions. These assumptions are fraught with uncertainties, attributable in particular to lack of scientific knowledge or lack of information about actual environmental conditions. Responsible policy-making will ensure that these assumptions are tested on a continuous basis, primarily through further research and through an appropriate programme of monitoring and environmental assessment.

Monitoring and environmental assessment are also required for international environmental policy. In practice, much of the monitoring will be undertaken at national or subnational levels, but it is important to ensure comparability of data and coordination of monitoring schedules to ensure that international concerns can also be addressed. Some countries may require assistance in setting up and funding monitoring systems. The actual assessment process needs to have an independent international component.

Monitoring and assessment are cross-cutting activities. It does not make sense to engage in separate monitoring for each cluster since many of the pollutants of concern, in particular, heavy metals and persistent organic pollutants, migrate from one environmental medium to the next and must be monitored on an integrated environmental basis. Consequently, this represents an institution that is best entrusted to a universal organisation. The current system of monitoring and assessment needs to be significantly strengthened. This requires both additional funding and a process to set priorities and to eliminate duplication of effort.

3. Transparency and participation

Transparency and participation have emerged as central institutions for all environmental regimes, a reflection of both scientific uncertainty and subsidiarity: public authorities, even local authorities, cannot have detailed knowledge about environmental conditions in specific locations, and some environmental phenomena emerge in the field before they become apparent in the laboratory.

The institutions of transparency and participation have become the standard response to this dilemma. Indeed, most concerned with environmental issues have come to expect certain levels of information and access as an integral part of all environmental regimes.

An attempt to develop a broader international agreement applicable to all international environmental regimes is necessarily fraught with risk: if asked to codify current practice, some countries are likely to seek to limit it. The Aarhus Convention outlines a number of practices that are widely accepted in Europe. The fact that neither Canada nor the USA subscribed to this agreement even though they are members of the United Nations Economic Commission of Europe (UNECE) where it was developed, suggests just how difficult it will be to generate consensus on these institutions on a broader basis.[19]

4. *Implementation review*

In most international environmental agreements, implementation review is the responsibility of the COP. One instrument to promote greater coherence among these regimes, and within their member states, in matters of international environmental management, is to institute joint implementation review of individual countries. Such a review process would require some level of cooperation between the regimes involved and at the same time foster greater coherence in the implementation efforts of the countries that are being reviewed.

This is an area where the example of the GATT/WTO may be helpful. The Trade Policy Review Mechanism (TPRM) has evolved patterns of work that appear to be acceptable to member states while still generating information that can be useful to other states and at the international level.

5. *Dispute settlement*

Dispute settlement (based on legally binding rules) is the issue most frequently mentioned as distinguishing trade regimes from environmental ones. It is also frequently mentioned as an area where environmental regimes could benefit from further institutional strengthening. Yet there is no evidence from environmental regimes themselves that this is an area of great current concern. In practice, the International Court of Justice (ICJ) serves as a dispute settlement mechanism of last resort. Not only has it not been used, there are some cases where it has been explicitly avoided and in those instances alternative forms of dispute settlement have emerged.

The assumption that stronger dispute settlement in environmental agreements will relieve pressure from the trade dispute settlement process assumes a parallelism between trade and environment that does not exist. In the trade

---

[19] See www.unece.org/env/pp/

regime, dispute settlement is the premier implementation tool – and to a significant degree the pathway by which interpretation of the agreements can be adjusted[20] – and consequently the place to which issues such as the environment must migrate. There is no process for the multilateral implementation of trade rules, resulting in a structure that may be termed 'multiunilateral'. Each country can interpret the trade rules as it sees fit, and that interpretation stands unless it is challenged by some other country in a dispute.

Environmental regimes pursue effectiveness and implementation through different institutions and there is no reason to assume that the availability of a reinforced environmental dispute settlement mechanism will change that in any way. Most importantly, environmental regimes ultimately seek to change human behaviour, and the implementation of international obligations by states is but one step in that process. States can implement international environmental agreements perfectly and there may still be no change in human behaviours, let alone any improvement in environmental conditions. Consequently, it makes little sense to focus too much effort on state implementation by attempting to institute a more robust dispute settlement process in international environmental regimes.

The nature of the legal obligations entailed in MEAs – and the structure of the ensuing regime – is such that environmental regimes rarely generate the kind of state–state dispute that is characteristic of the WTO system. Appropriate remedies would be difficult or impossible to craft. When such disputes arise, they tend to migrate directly to the Conference of the Parties of the relevant agreement since they require a process of negotiation rather than adjudication. It is certainly possible to interpret the long and arduous process on listing, relisting, and possibly delisting the African elephant in CITES, which several times worked its way through the institutions of the regime to the COP and back, as a process of dispute settlement.

The disputes that can arise in international environmental regimes concern lack of implementation of domestic environmental law, whether or not it implements international obligations. One state can hardly launch a complaint about such non-compliance against another. No state is flawless in this regard. The adequacy of domestic implementation is a matter that requires careful assessment. It is not a matter of interpreting international legal obligations and the remedy is not a change in the rules, domestic or international, but a change in the functioning of domestic institutions. The Commission on Environmental

---

[20] This is an area in which theory and practice diverge in the trade regime. Theoretically, dispute settlement should not be a vehicle for interpretation of the WTO agreements. In practice, this has repeatedly occurred, for example in the evolving interpretation of Articles XXb and XXg. See Jackson, J., 'The legal meaning of a GATT dispute settlement report: some reflections', in Jackson, J. (ed.), *The jurisprudence of GATT and WTO: insights on treaty law and economic relations*, Cambridge (Cambridge University Press) 2000, pp. 118–132.

Cooperation (CEC) created by a side agreement to the North American Free Trade Agreement (NAFTA) has a unique approach to this problem, permitting citizen complaints about non-compliance.[21] Yet it is the very difference in approach represented by the CEC that is most eloquent in underlining the differences in approach of the trade and the environment regime.

Another possible example for dispute settlement is to be found in international investment agreements (IIAs). More than 2,300 bilateral and regional IIAs exist but only two multilateral agreements within the WTO.[22] Most bilateral and regional IIAs include investor–state dispute settlement, together with state–state procedures. The number of investor–state disputes has been burgeoning, and many of them have environmental implications. Unfortunately, the institutional arrangements for investor–state investment dispute settlement are deeply flawed and in urgent need of reform.[23] That is not to say that improved investor–state dispute settlement procedures could not become an effective tool for the implementation of environmental obligations by both states and investors.

VI. National coordination

For many years, observers have decried the lack of national coordination of positions in different international regimes. Certainly, an increase in national coordination holds the promise of promoting clustering; and without increased coordination clustering is unlikely to advance. Yet the obstacles are significant, and are not accessible to international negotiations. The one international instrument that may be able to promote national coordination is an integrated process of implementation review.[24]

There are essentially three obstacles to greater national coordination: domestic distribution of responsibilities; development of constituencies; and the politics of coordination. Greater national coordination can only be expected if all three factors are addressed at the same time.

1. Domestic distribution of responsibilities

The greatest obstacle to coordination is the domestic distribution of environmental responsibilities. One of the paradoxes of the debate about a WEO is that

---

[21] See www.cecmtl.org

[22] The General Agreement on Trade in Services (GATS), in particular with respect to services delivered by commercial presence (mode 4), and the Agreement on Trade Related Investment Measures (TRIMs).

[23] See in this regard the body of work by the International Institute for Sustainable Development (IISD), at www.iisd.org/investment/

[24] See section III.8.

it occurs despite the fact that no country has established a domestic agency that covers all the issues that would be addressed by a WEO.[25]

The reasons for this state of affairs are manifold. 'Environmental management' in practice involves a significant number of policy areas that share a concern for impacting the environment through changing human behaviour but which exhibit widely differing problem structures. It is consequently reasonable to assign responsibility for biodiversity to one agency and for waste management to another. Indeed, even when both are undertaken from the same agency, they may in practice have little routine overlap, except in agency leadership.

In addition to exhibiting different problem structures at the national level, environmental issues are subject to different levels of subsidiarity. Some issues such as land use are deeply rooted in local governance. Other issues, such as the management of watershed, exhibit regional structures. Yet other issues, such as the control of hazardous chemicals, are typically of national concern. Finally some issues, such as atmospheric pollution, can be addressed in a variety of ways depending on the degree of centralisation or decentralisation that is typically preferred by a country. With such a variety of possible approaches, it is hardly surprising that every country has an essentially unique pattern of environmental responsibilities.

The environmental agenda grew incrementally, sometimes over a period of decades. In most developed countries, the roots of water pollution control and the management of industrial facilities reaches back into the nineteenth century. Biodiversity protection, on the other hand, is an issue of the last decade of the twentieth century. The notion that 'the environment' as a whole requires integrated management did not emerge until the 1970s. Countries responded differently to these changing perceptions. While most countries, with the signal exception of the USA and Russia, have cabinet level environment ministries, none has one that encompasses all aspects of the environment as it is now understood.

The traditional approach to a need for coordination of national positions in international fora is to assign responsibility to the foreign affairs agency. This is possible where the issues concerned do not involve changes in domestic legislation and the responsibilities of subnational units in a federal system. When domestic interests are directly affected, foreign affairs agencies have few of the needed skills to balance international needs against domestic regulations and priorities. In many countries, this has led to wholesale delegation of international responsibilities to the various environmental agencies. Coordination

---

[25] This paradox is also reflected in the European Union, where the Environment Council covers an agenda that is typically much broader than the ministerial responsibilities of its members.

may be better in countries where that has not occurred but at the price of poor integration with domestic policies.

2. Constituencies

The adoption of an international environmental agreement almost always engenders the emergence of a complex regime that includes many actors beyond the states parties to the agreement. Several groups from civil society are typically involved, including scientists, industry, and commerce, and advocacy groups of all kinds. Even government agencies other than those primarily responsible for an issue can find themselves involved. This phenomenon is one of the most important sources of effectiveness of international environmental agreements, since it permits the regime to establish deep roots within countries.

The existence of these constituencies can, however, become a significant obstacle once there is a call for coordination. Moreover, these constituencies are not readily influenced by international negotiation and are frequently in a position to create roadblocks to the process.

In some instances, there are also phenomena of bureaucratic clientism, in the sense that each bureaucracy has a commitment to 'its' international regime, which it views as a vehicle to advance its own agenda, both internationally and domestically. Frequently, it is the international dimension that enables the agency in question to attract policy attention from the highest levels of government, and the prestige and resources that can flow from that.

3. Politics of coordination

Domestic coordination carries a price. A government that engages in a domestic process of coordination must make hard decisions, at least in the sense of decisions that may displease some constituency or another. Such decisions carry an immediate political price since it involves a clear declaration of government policy in one form or another.

Once the government in question reaches the international level with its carefully coordinated position, it finds that it is but one voice among many. Only very few international actors are able to impose their domestically established compromise on the international process. The USA is able to do so in many areas but not when it comes to environmental policy. Moreover, such actors are the most unwelcome of negotiating partners, since they are liable to present their domestic positions on a 'take it or leave it' basis, being unwilling or unable to engage in real negotiation. In other words, governments that have carefully coordinated positions are less likely to engage in productive negotiations.

VII. How to begin

The first – and the last – step are the hardest parts of any policy process. The risks are greatest when the first step is taken; and the negotiation process will typically leave the most difficult decisions to last. For this reason, every international negotiation – and clustering is unquestionably first and foremost a negotiation process – needs 'champions', countries that have an interest in promoting a certain outcome and are willing to invest some political capital in achieving it. Only the existence of such champions enables international negotiation to lead to outcomes that represent not simply the lowest common denominator of the countries involved. Clusters will also need champions.

The burdens of being champion are such that most processes require no more than a single champion. When more than one appear, it is mostly due to domestic considerations that more than one government feel a need to appear as a champion in an issue at the international level, than of the negotiation itself. Within most negotiations, countries are willing to ally themselves with a champion once he has been identified. This reduces the burden of leadership.

Traditionally, the country where a Secretariat is located has been viewed as the natural champion of a given regime, with the exception of Geneva and New York, which are seats of the United Nations and are viewed as relatively neutral in character.

The essential first step in clustering is consequently the identification of champions for various clusters. The existence of several potential clusters suggests that several opportunities exist for championing a cluster. Without such champions, none of the clusters is likely to become a reality.

Institutions, knowledge, and change: findings from the quantitative study of environmental regimes

HELMUT BREITMEIER

I. Introduction

States create international institutions with the aim of facilitating the exchange of data, coordinating and strengthening scientific monitoring and national research efforts, and aiding the implementation of international research programmes. Examples of such goals are seen in various Articles of the 1979 ECE Convention on Long-Range Transboundary Air Pollution in Europe. These provide that member states 'shall by means of exchange of information, consultation, research and monitoring, develop... policies and strategies which shall serve as a means for combating the discharge of air pollutants' (Article 3), or that member states should 'exchange information on and review their policies, scientific activities and technical measures' (Article 4). Similar provisions are included in many other international framework conventions.[1] The role of international institutions as arenas which contribute to changing the cognitive foundations of governance beyond the nation state has been one of the central topics addressed by the study of regime effectiveness.[2] Regime

---

[1] There are numerous examples illustrating the inclusion within international agreements/institutions of functional goals aimed at improving the knowledge base. The Vienna Convention for the Protection of the Ozone Layer 1985 includes such regulations as well as the United Nations Framework Convention on Climate Change 1992 (UNFCCC) and the 1994 United Nations Convention to Combat Desertification 1994 (UNCCD). The broad majority of bi-, multilateral, and global environmental regimes establish institutional mechanisms for the production of consensual knowledge in the issue area.

[2] On the reflective role of regimes, see Keohane, R. O., International regimes: two approaches, in *Int'l Studies Q.* 32 (1988), pp. 379–396; Adler, E. and Haas, P. M., Conclusion: epistemic communities, world order, and the creation of a reflective research program, in *Int'l Organization* 46 (1992), pp. 367–390. On the study of regime effectiveness, see Haas, P. M., Keohane, R. O. and Levy, M. A. (eds.), *Institutions for the Earth: sources of effective international environmental protection*, Cambridge Mass. (MIT Press) 1st edn 1993; Miles, E. L., Underdal, A., Andresen, S., Wettestad, J., Skjaerseth, J. B., and Carlin, E. M. (eds.), *Environmental regime effectiveness: confronting theory with evidence*, Cambridge Mass. (MIT Press) 1st edn 2002; Young, O. R. (ed.), *The effectiveness of international environmental regimes: causal connections and behavioral mechanisms*, Cambridge Mass. (MIT Press) 1st edn 1999; Young, O. R., *International governance: protecting the environment in a stateless society*, Ithaca (Cornell University Press) 1st edn 1994.

analysts have paid special attention to exploring the role of the institutional design in the evolution of consensual knowledge.[3] This impact of institutions has mainly been studied in individual regimes – comparative or quantitative studies remain absent. In the following chapter, an effort will be made to explore the impact of international regimes on those components of consensual knowledge relevant to policy-making in transboundary environmental issue areas. Empirical measurements are based on data collected for the International Regimes Database (IRD). The IRD is a research tool designed by a German-American research team in collaboration with forty-six case study experts who coded twenty-three international environmental regimes.[4] This quantitative analysis of regimes tests the validity of theories arguing that regimes have an effect on the consensual knowledge that determines decision-making by states or influences discussion in the transnational public about the appropriateness of regime policies.

First, the twenty-three regimes used for empirical analysis will be described briefly. It is impossible to describe the guidelines for the development of case designs that were used for the coding of regimes comprehensively. However, a few issues will be clarified pertaining to the design of the IRD and to the kind of data analysis to be applied by empirical analysis.

Secondly, the degree to which consensual knowledge changed in issue areas where these regimes have been established will be explored. The causal impact ascribed to regimes by coding experts for observed changes will be described. In addition, the question of whether changes observed in cognitive foundations correspond with the existence and operation of institutional mechanisms that were established in regimes for scientific research, monitoring, and the review of implementation or the adequacy of commitments will be explored. In this context, the consequences arising from the finding that consensual knowledge is not as far established in some regimes as is required for the development of effective policies will also be briefly discussed.

II. Case design and the coding of regimes

The IRD is a tool which combines data on various aspects related to the formation, attributes, consequences, and dynamics of regimes.[5] The coding of

---

[3] There are a large number of studies dealing with the institutional design as a factor that accounts for the effectiveness of institutions on various levels (e.g., local or global). Seminal contributions on the topic have been made by Ostrom, E., *Governing the commons: the evolution of institutions for collective action*, Cambridge (Cambridge University Press) 1st edn 1990, or by Young, O. R., *The institutional dimensions of environmental change: fit, interplay, and scale*, Cambridge Mass. (MIT Press) 1st edn. 2002.

[4] A list of experts who participated in the coding can be obtained from the IRD homepage, http://cms.ifs.tu-darmstadt.de/ib/ for schung.

[5] For an in-depth description of the architecture of the IRD, or of development of case designs for the coding of single regimes, or of empirical findings, see Breitmeier, H., *The legitimacy*

regimes has been carried out through use of a comprehensive data protocol.[6] The different sections of the codebook consider a large number of theoretical concepts that emerged in the context of regime analysis. The codebook consists of 136 questions which were developed for the measurement of variables belonging to these approaches. Various drafts of this codebook have been tested in trial runs. Environmental and non-environmental regimes were coded by case study experts on an experimental basis in these trial runs. This led to further improvements in the content of the codebook and to the expansion and refinement of rules used for the structuring of a regime. The trial runs were used to test whether the questions posed in the codebook are comprehensible to coding experts, whether operationalisation methods which translate theoretical concepts into nominal or ordinal scales were plausible, and whether the explanations and examples used for illustrating the meaning of single questions were useful. For example, questions in the codebook which deal with the cognitive setting of a regime were designed for measuring the degree to which (i) the nature of the problem was understood, or (ii) information on the possible methods of dealing with a problem was complete. These variables were described in the codebook in such a way that they were understandable to coding experts. Ordinal scales were used for the measurement of these cognitive variables.

The database combines data on twenty-three environmental regimes that were established in global, multilateral, regional, and bilateral contexts. The broad majority of these regimes were coded by two experts independently of one another so that an assessment could be made in regard to whether coders using the same coding instrument come to the same results regarding the coding of single variables for a regime. Experts well known for their knowledge on these regimes within the scientific community were chosen to complete the coding. The coding of these experts is based on the empirical knowledge they gained from many years of case study research. One could object that the involvement of regime experts in such a coding project can lead to biased judgements, on the basis that experts can be biased towards institutions. This can lead them to overestimate the impact of institutions on observed improvements. These concerns were met by taking measures during the development of the data protocol and the selection of case study experts for the coding. For example, separate measurements were made for the level of consensual knowledge that could be reached in an issue area and the causal role that could be ascribed to a regime for observed developments. Coding experts were aware from the beginning of this coding project that the data they delivered would be made available to the broader scientific community for review.

of international regimes, findings from the international regimes database, forthcoming. For another comprehensive description of the design and findings of this project, see Breitmeier, H., Young, O. R., and Zürn, M., Analyzing international environmental regimes: from case study to database, Cambridge, Mass. (MIT Press) 2005.

[6] See Breitmeier, H., Levy, M. A., Young, O. R., and Zürn, M., *International regimes database (IRD): data protocol*, IIASA working paper no. 154, Laxenburg (IIASA) 1996.

The regimes have all been coded from their formation to the year 1998. This common end-point allows the exploration of various aspects related to the performance of these regimes by the end of the twentieth century. Regimes were subdivided into several components that reflect the legal-institutional complexity of governance systems. The development of the case structures used for the coding took place in so-called 'pre-coding negotiations'. These negotiations were carried out between the project team and regime experts. The coding did not focus on the macro-level of a regime but took into account the existence of different legal and institutional forms which make up a regime as a whole. For example, the Antarctic regime has been subdivided into components such as the Antarctic Treaty, the Convention on the Conservation of Flora and Fauna, the Convention on the Conservation of Antarctic Marine Living Resources, the Convention on the Conservation of Seals, or the Protocol on Environmental Protection.[7] This distinction between institutional forms allows the determination of whether the level of consensual knowledge varies for different issues in a regime (e.g., the conservation of seals, conservation of flora and fauna).

Regime components were frequently divided into several time periods if events or so-called 'watersheds' occurred in the issue area that justified such division. Watersheds were identified if regimes experienced a significant restructuring of principles or key norms, significant changes in the composition of membership, or an expansion in the functional scope and deepening of regime rules. Under the circumstances, the so-called 'regime element' that reflects a time period of a distinct regime component emerged as the smallest unit of analysis. The twenty-three regimes have been subdivided into a total of ninety-two regime elements. A set of data comprising 184 regime elements would have emerged if all regimes were coded by two experts independently of one another. Because double coding exists for only twenty-one of the total of twenty-three regimes, the IRD includes data on 172 regime elements.[8] It should be noted that stark differences were found pertaining to the legal-institutional complexity that determined these regimes (see Table 17.1). Complex legal-institutional frameworks based on five regime components were identified for cases like the Antarctic regime, the ozone regime, or the LRTAP regime. On the other hand, only one regime component was identified for various resource

---

[7] On the evolution and effectiveness of the Antarctic regime, see Stokke, O. S. and Vidas, D. (eds.), *The effectiveness and legitimacy of the Antarctic treaty system*, Cambridge (Cambridge University Press) 1st edn 1996; Joyner, C. C., *Governing the frozen commons: the Antarctic regime and environmental protection*, Columbia, S.C. (University of South Carolina Press) 1st edn 1998; Peterson, M. J., *Managing the frozen south: the creation and evolution of the Antarctic treaty system*, Berkeley (University of California Press) 1st edn 1988.

[8] For the two regimes on long-range transboundary air pollution in Europe and on fisheries in the South Pacific region, codings were delivered by one expert each. This explains why only twenty-one of the twenty-three regimes were coded by two experts independently of one another.

Table 17.1 *International regimes database: regime elements*

Regime	Regime elements (components and periods)
Antarctic Regime 1959–1998	Antarctic Treaty (1959–1980) (1980s) (1989/91–1998) • Conservation of Flora and Fauna (1964–1980) (1980s) (1989/91–1998) • Conservation of Seals (1972–1980) (1980s) (1989/91–1998) • CCAMLR (1980s) (1989/91–1998) • Protocol on Environmental Protection (1989/91–1998)
Baltic Sea Regime 1974–1998	Principles of Co-operation (1974–1992) (1992–1998) • Environment Protection Principles (1974–1992) (1992–1998) • Regulations for all Sources of Marine Pollution (1974–1992) (1992–1998) • Nature Conservation (1992–1998)
Barents Sea Fisheries Regime 1975–1998	Norwegian-Russian Cooperation on Fisheries in the Barents Sea Region (1975–1998)
Biodiversity Regime 1992–1998	Convention on Biological Diversity (1992–1998)
CITES Regime (Trade in Endangered Species) 1973–1998	CITES Convention (1973–1989) (1989–1998) • TRAFFIC Network on Monitoring and Compliance (1978–1989) (1989–1998)
Climate Change Regime 1992–1998	UNFCCC (1992–1997) (1997–1998) • UNFCCC Financial Mechanism (1992–1997) (1997–1998) • Kyoto Protocol (1997–1998)
Danube River Protection Regime 1985–1998	Danube River Protection (1985–1991) (1991–1994) (1994–1998)
Desertification Regime 1994–1998	UNCCD (1994–1998)
Great Lakes Management Regime 1972–1998	Great Lakes Water Quality (1972–1978) (1978–1998) • Great Lakes Water Quantity (1972–1978) (1978–1998) • Great Lakes Ecosystem Management (1978–1998)
Hazardous Waste Regime 1989–1998	Basel Convention (1989–1995) (1995–1998) • Amendment to the Basel Convention (1995–1998) • OECD/EU/Lome IV Regulations (1989–1995) (1995–1998) • Bamako Convention (1991–1995) • Bamako/Waigani Conventions (1995–1998)
IATTC Regime (Inter-American Tropical Tuna Convention) 1949–1998	Conservation and Management of Tunas and Tuna-Like Fishes (1949–1976) (1976–1998) • Conservation and Management of Dolphins (1976–1998)

ICCAT Regime (Conservation of Atlantic Tunas) 1966–1998	ICCAT Convention (1966–1998)
Regime for the International Regulation of Whaling 1948–1998	Whaling Regime (1946–1982) (1982–1998)
London Convention Regime 1972–1998	Wastes and Substances the Dumping of which is Prohibited (1972–1991) (1991–1998) • Wastes and Substances which, in Principle, may be Dumped (1972–1991) (1991–1998) • Regulation of Incineration at Sea (1978–1991) (1991–1998)
ECE Regime on Long-Range Transboundary Air Pollution 1979–1998	LRTAP Convention (1979–1982) (1982–1998) • First Sulphur Protocol (1985–1998) • NOX Protocol (1988–1998) • VOCs Protocol (1991–1998) • Second Sulphur Protocol (1994–1998)
North Sea Regime 1972/74–1998	OSCOM/PARCOM (1972/74–1984) • OSCOM/PARCOM/OSPAR (1984/92–1998) • North Sea Conferences (1984–1998)
Oil Pollution Regime 1954–1998	Oilpol (1954–1978) • MARPOL (1973/78–1998) • Regional Memoranda of Understanding (1982–1998)
Regime for Protection of the Rhine Against Pollution 1963–1998	Berne Convention (1963–1998) • Chloride Pollution Convention (1976–1998) • Chemical Pollution Convention (1976–1998) •
Ramsar Regime on Wetlands 1971–1998	Ramsar Convention (1971–1987) (1987–1998)
Regime for Protection of the Black Sea 1992–1998	Bucharest Convention and Protocols (1992–1998) • Black Sea Strategic Action Plan (1996–1998)
South Pacific Fisheries Forum Agency Regime 1979–1998	General Management of Fisheries (1979–1982) (1982–1995/97) (1995/97–1998) • Compliance of Fisheries Management (1979–1982) (1982–1995/97) (1995/97–1998)
Stratospheric Ozone Regime 1985–1998	Vienna Convention (1985–1990) (1990–1998) • Montreal Protocol (1987–1990) 1990–1998) • London Amendment (1990–1998) Copenhagen Amendment (1992–1998) • Multilateral Fund (1990–1998)
Tropical Timber Trade Regime 1983–1998	International Tropical Timber Agreement (1983–1998)

regimes dealing with fisheries in the Barents Sea region, with the conservation and management of tuna in the Atlantic, or whaling – to mention only a few. The number of watersheds determined in these regimes had a significant impact on the final number of so-called regime elements for which data was collected. The most comprehensive case structure emerged for the Antarctic regime for which five regime components and two watersheds were identified. Three of these components existed before the two watersheds occurred so all of them have been divided into three regime elements. This also had consequences for the number of regime elements that were analysed for single regimes. Since the Antarctic regime consists of twelve regime elements, it is the most complex case in this database. The question remains whether equal importance should be attached to all of the twenty-three regimes by quantitative data analysis. Admittedly, regimes for the conservation and management of tuna in the Atlantic or in the Eastern Pacific are less complex and have a lower impact on the global ecosystem than far-reaching measures in global regimes can have for the protection of stratospheric ozone or the global climate. The presentation of data on developments at a single regime level can illustrate how far consensual knowledge has advanced in complex and less complex issue areas.

III. Changing cognitive foundations and the impact of regimes

The evolution of consensual knowledge in environmental issue areas will be measured by a first measurement determining the level of consensual knowledge on the nature of the problem within the issue area and a second measurement identifying the completeness of information on policy options. The knowledge of cause-effect relationships or possible policies for political management relates to problems in issue areas. Before one can determine the extent of knowledge available about an environmental problem or about potential political management policies, the problem itself has to be identified. Regimes can be conceived as problem-driven arrangements. For each regime that has been explored, the basic problem that existed in the issue area has been identified by the research team together with coding experts. For example, 'coordination of fisheries management among the members of the South Pacific Forum in order to 1) regulate tuna harvest by distant water fishing nations and 2) maximize the returns to the Pacific Island Countries' has been identified as the problem that has been managed by the South Pacific fisheries regime. The definition of the problem that determined the Black Sea regime involved 'ongoing degradation of the ecosystem of the Black Sea and unsustainable use of its natural resources'. It should be noted that for a few regimes, coding experts found it necessary to identify more than one basic problem in the issue area. This occurred in the coding of the Antarctic regime for which 'growth of interest in managing exploitation of resources in and around Antarctica' has been defined as the basic environmental problem. Nevertheless, two additional subproblems relating to jurisdictional differences or conflicts among claimant states, or between claimant states and major non-claimant states were identified.

Some of the problems coded for single regimes changed so fundamentally during the course of a regime that their definition was expanded by member states. A good example of this expansion can be seen in the regime established in the Inter-American Tropical Tuna Convention 1949. The initial focus on the management and conservation of tuna, baitfish, and other kinds of fish taken by tuna vessels in the Eastern Pacific Ocean was broadened in the mid-1970s. Increasing dolphin mortality rates due to the use of purse seine fishing led states to expand this initial definition to include the conservation of dolphins.[9] The basic problem that existed in the issue area has been coded for each regime element. In some regimes, more than one basic problem was determined by coding case study experts. One basic problem existed in 133 regime elements. Two separate problems were coded for fifteen regime elements. In twenty-four regime elements, three problems determined the issue area. A total of 235 problems exist in the database. Case study experts occasionally avoided the coding of regime elements they felt were lacking the information necessary for the coding of single variables. Thus, the total amount of data describing the level of knowledge on the type of problem or about policy options lies below this potential maximum.

1. Knowledge of the nature of the problem

A consensus regarding the nature, causes, and consequences of the problem, solutions, or which factors should be maximised in the issue area, often only emerges after a lengthy epistemic process combining efforts by national and international agencies and various types of non-state actors. This knowledge must have reached a certain level before policy-makers will finally agree to implement far-reaching policies. States often disagree on whether this kind of knowledge is already established to the extent that it calls for the implementation of international policies. Some European states were dubious during the first half of the 1980s that emissions of CFCs and other chlorine-containing compounds are damaging to the stratospheric ozone layer.[10] In the second

---

[9] On the evolution of this regime, see Peterson, C. L. and Bayliff, W. H., *Organization, functions, and achievements of the Interamerican Tropical Tuna Commission*, Special Report no. 5, La Jolla/California (Interamerican Tropical Tuna Commission) 1st edn 1985; Joseph, J., The tuna-dolphin controversy in the eastern Pacific Ocean: biological, economic and political impacts, *Ocean Development and Int'l Law* 25 (1994), pp. 1–30.

[10] On changes in the consensual knowledge on the causes of stratospheric ozone depletion or the evolution of policy options, see Benedick, R. E., *Ozone diplomacy: new directions in safeguarding the planet*, Cambridge Mass. (Harvard University Press) 1991; Haas, P. M., Banning chlorofluorocarbons: epistemic community efforts to protect stratospheric ozone, in *Int'l Organization* 46 (1992), pp. 187–224; Litfin, K. T., *Ozone discourses: science*

half of the 1980s, the combined efforts of national agencies like NASA and international organisations like WMO or UNEP produced proof of large-scale depletion of stratospheric ozone and the causal role of chlorine-containing compounds in this depletion. This led European countries and the chemical industry to withdraw their opposition to the implementation of policies for the phasing-out of ozone-depleting substances. In the late 1970s, Scandinavian countries complained about the acidification of lakes and forests on their territories. While some European countries had initially denied their part in the causation of these environmental problems, subsequent monitoring and research efforts confirmed that transboundary dispersion of air pollutants was damaging the environment beyond as well as inside polluter countries.[11] International institutions were considered one of several factors contributing to social learning at a domestic level.[12] Political awareness about the impact of air pollutants on forests, lakes, and public health changed in Europe in the 1980s and the availability of technical options led to the implementation of international policies for the reduction of air pollutants in European countries.

Which findings are included in the IRD regarding the level of understanding about the nature of the problem that could be found in regimes? For every problem that received political management in a regime element, a measurement was made with respect to whether the nature of the problem was well understood in the issue area. This variable was intended to demonstrate the degree of consensus established regarding the nature, causes, and consequences of a problem, solutions to the problem, or which factors should be maximised in the issue area. Some progress has to be made with the level of this knowledge before policy-makers will take measures for the reduction of environmental pollution or the conservation of natural resources. The ordinal scale used in

---

and politics in international environmental cooperation, Columbia (Columbia University Press) 1st edn 1994; Parson, E. A., Protecting the ozone layer: science and strategy, New York (Oxford University Press) 1st edn 2003; Roan, S., Ozone crisis: the 15-year evolution of a sudden global emergency, New York (Wiley & Sons) 1st edn. 1989.

[11] On the evolution of the LRTAP regime, see Gehring, T., Dynamic international regimes: institutions for international environmental governance, Berlin (Peter Lang) 1994; Levy, M. A., International cooperation to combat acid rain, in Bergesen, H. O., Parmann, G., and Thommessen, O. B. (eds.), Green globe yearbook of international co-operation on environment and development, Oxford (Oxford University Press) 1st edn 1995; pp. 59–68; Wettestad, J., Clearing the air: European advances in tackling acid rain and atmospheric pollution, Aldershot (Ashgate) 1st edn 2002.

[12] The factors that account for social learning in domestic societies were studied comprehensively by an interdisciplinary research project. The findings of this project are reported in Social Learning Group, Learning to manage environmental risks, vol. I, A comparative history of social responses to climate change, ozone depletion, and acid rain, Cambridge Mass. (MIT Press) 1st edn 2001 and Social Learning Group, Learning to manage environmental risks, vol. II, A functional analysis of social responses to climate change, ozone depletion, and acid rain, Cambridge Mass. (MIT Press) 1st edn 2001.

measurement distinguished between five different levels of consensual knowledge that has been achieved in the issue area as a result of the activities of the scientific community, policy experts, or discourse among policy-makers and the broader political public. The spectrum of the scale was between understandings established very strongly and those not at all established. Partially established understandings were positioned between these upper and lower limits. Strongly or weakly established understandings were positioned above or below the middle of the scale. The data available from the coding of this variable consists of a total of 221 problems within 168 regime elements. These regime elements cover all twenty-three regimes. A further subsection of data details developments in those regime elements ending in 1998. This subsection indicates the level of understanding of the nature of the problem found more recently in regimes.

For more than two-thirds of the problems that were strongly or very strongly established, some degree of understanding was identified by coding experts (see Table 17.2). Data suggests that a minimum of strongly established understandings have emerged for the majority of regimes. On the other hand, partially or weakly established understandings have been identified for around one-third of these problems. This relatively positive finding is partly brought about by the broad number of very strongly established understandings indicated for problems coded for the Antarctic regime. In fourteen regimes, either strongly or very strongly established understandings were identified for more than half of the problems coded for regime elements ending in 1998. This illustrates that by the end of the twentieth century, the nature of the problem was at least strongly understood for the majority of regimes. Obviously, the potential level of consensual knowledge which could be reached in these regimes is dependent upon the identification of the major causes and effects of a problem. While understandings that are at least strongly established predominate in this subsection of fourteen regimes, findings also reveal that very strongly established understandings only developed in some of these issue areas. This illustrates that despite the improvements that could be made, the consensual knowledge of the problem type remains incomplete in many of these issue areas. In a number of cases where the existence of watersheds allows the investigation of different time periods within a regime, data reveals that understanding of the nature of the problem improved over time. The Baltic Sea regime is such a case, where the problem type was partially understood during the first period of between 1972 and 1992. But during the second period leading up to 1998, this understanding improved further and consensual knowledge on the nature of the problem became strongly established. Efforts towards research, scientific monitoring, and the development of policy options have been intensified by members of the Baltic Sea regime in the past two decades. The Helsinki Commission expanded its institutional framework just as the single regime members intensified their

Table 17.2 Level of understanding of the nature of the problem

Regimes	Problems coded for a regime[a] (Total/regime elements ending in 1998)	1 = Very strongly established understanding (Total/regime elements ending in 1998)	2 = Strongly established understanding (Total/regime elements ending in 1998)	3 = Partially established understanding (Total/regime elements ending in 1998)	4 = Weakly established understanding (Total/regime elements ending in 1998)	5 = Not at all established understanding (Total/regime elements ending in 1998)
Antarctic Regime	63/26	40/16	17/8	2/0	4/2	0
Baltic Sea Regime	14/8	0	8/8	6/0	0	0
Barents Sea Fisheries	2/2	1/1	1/1	0	0	0
Biodiversity Regime	3/3	1/1	1/1	0	1/1	0
CITES Regime	12/6	0	5/5	5/1	2/0	0
Climate Change Regime	10/6	0	6/6	4/0	0	0
Danube Regime	6/2	1/1	2/1	2/0	1/0	0
Desertification Regime	2/2	0	1/1	1/1	0	0
Great Lakes Regime	10/6	0	6/3	2/2	2/1	0
Hazardous Waste Regime	14/8	0	9/4	2/2	3/2	0
IATTC Regime	6/4	2/1	3/2	1/1	0	0
ICCAT Regime	2/2	0	1/1	0	1/1	0
Whaling Regime	8/4	0	6/4	2/0	0	0

Regime			
London Convention[b]	12/6	2/0	7/6	3/0	0
LRTAP Regime	7/5	0	1/1	3/3	3/1
North Sea Regime	6/4	0	0	4/4	2/0
Oil Pollution Regime	6/4	6/4	0	0	0
Rhine Regime	8/8	3/3	2/2	2/2	1/1
Ramsar Regime	4/2	2/1	0	2/1	0
Black Sea Regime	4/4	0	4/4	0	0
South Pacific Fisheries	6/2	0	2/0	2/1	2/1
Stratospheric Ozone Regime	14/10	0	12/10	2/0	0
Tropical Timber Trade Regime	4/4	0	0	2/2	2/2	0

[a] Data before the oblique stroke belongs to the total number of elements coded for a regime. Data after indicates developments in elements of regimes ending in 1998.

[b] One expert indicated for two regime elements in the London Convention regime that, in comparison with earlier periods, understanding about the type of problem has developed less during latter periods ending in 1998. This finding reflects that the levels of understanding of the nature of a problem can partly decrease over time if new forms of pollution arise which demand that further effort is made to detect their causes and effects on the state of the environment.

research and monitoring activities at a national level.[13] The end of the East-West conflict established a new political climate which facilitates cooperation among countries bordering the Baltic Sea, improving the exchange of data. Similar improvements could be achieved in regimes dealing with climate change, the conservation and management of whaling, or the prevention of pollution by the dumping of waste and other matter (London Convention regime). The climate change regime illustrates that the understanding of the causes and effects of the greenhouse effect emerged from close collaboration between global research programmes and national activities. Besides the climate change regime's institutional framework for assessing the causes and effects of the climate problem, the regime itself also relies on the capacities established in international organisations such as WMO for the development of consensual knowledge, which emerged in many member states of UNFCCC long before the regime was established, or that are provided by service-oriented non-governmental scientific organisations. In a few cases, understanding had reached a high level already before a regime was established. A case in point is the Antarctic regime, where problems concerning overlapping claims by claimant states or between claimants and non-claimants were already strongly understood during regime formation. Developments in a few regimes also indicate that knowledge of the nature of the problem has advanced less quickly in the period leading up to the end of the twentieth century. Good examples of this are the regimes dealing with trade in tropical timber, hazardous waste, or the protection of the North Sea. Potential levels of knowledge in these regimes lead us to conclude that further efforts will be necessary to improve consensual knowledge in these issue areas.

Whilst the findings described above indicate the evolution of the understanding of the type of the problem, another measurement focussed on identifying whether this understanding has been determined by change during the time periods that delimit regime elements. A binary distinction between little or no change and significant change has been used for identifying this change. This set of data consists of 204 problems belonging to 155 regime elements. It covers changes in understanding of the nature of a problem that could be identified for all regime members. Theoretically, change can be understood as merely a development, i.e., both a regression as well as a deepening of understanding. However, regressions in less well-established understanding were not detected when different time periods were compared in regimes. Over half the data indicates that the understanding of the nature of the problem in a regime element changed significantly. This change did not only affect problems where strongly

---

[13] For further information on the impact of the work of the Helsinki Commission and its collaboration with national institutions, see Auer, M. and Nilenders, E., Verifying environmental cleanup: lessons from the Baltic Sea Joint Comprehensive Action Programme, *Environment and Planning C: Governmental Policy*, 19 (2001), pp. 881–901.

or very strongly established understanding of cause-effect relationships had emerged, but also for problems where this understanding was less developed. The first conclusion that can be drawn from this finding is that even if strongly or very strongly established understandings are found, environmental issue areas can still be determined by change in the consensual knowledge. This suggests that research and monitoring efforts should also be maintained in those issue areas where strongly or very strongly established understandings have emerged. Secondly, there can be changes in the understanding of the nature of the problem which are not far-reaching enough to bring about improved levels of consensual knowledge. One should also take into account that regimes have to cope with new challenges arising from changing socio-economic behavioural patterns or technical developments which negatively impact on the environment. For example, the use of new fishing technologies or the emergence of new fishing nations can increase the pressure on fish resources. The ability to avoid a regression in the level of consensual knowledge can in some instances be itself considered as an achievement if one takes into account new cause-effect relationships which were not previously relevant but have gained relevance in later periods.

For a large number of regimes the understanding of the type of problem has been determined by significant change in observation periods ending in 1998. Some regimes, among them the CITES regime, the ozone regime, the Great Lakes regime, or the Baltic Sea regime, were determined by such change during the various time periods, whereas other regimes experienced such change during earlier periods during the 1970s or 1980s. A case in point is the whaling regime which was primarily determined by significant change in the understanding of the conservation of whale stocks during its early period between 1946 and 1982. These findings suggest that the understanding of the type of problem was affected by significant change in a broad number of regime elements. They also illustrate that this understanding could be improved in several regimes.

The understanding of the nature of the problem has also been affected by change in a number of important nations. For example, countries like the USA, Germany, or Russia (including the former Soviet Union) experienced significant change in their understanding of the problem type in several regimes. Sixty-eight of a total of 161 sets of data indicate that understanding of the nature of environmental problems in the USA has changed significantly. In some regimes, the findings derived from this data are very clear. The understanding in the USA in regard to five regimes has significantly changed. Furthermore, coding experts ascribed between a modest and significant causal influence of this change to some of these regimes (e.g., the Great Lakes Management regime, the ozone regime, the London Convention regime). Over the years, collaboration between the USA and Canada has led to significant improvements in the understanding within both countries relating to the sources and impact of pollution in the Great Lakes area. The Boundary Waters Treaty concluded between the USA and Canada in 1909 focussed primarily on resolving conflicts between the countries over the use of water. The International Joint Commission (IJC) has been given various functions to fulfil the goals of this Treaty. While both states agreed to prevent pollution of boundary waters in Article IV of the Treaty, it was not until the Great Lakes Water Quality Agreements of 1972 and 1978 that a regime was established for the environmental management of the Great Lakes. This regime emerged partly as a result of the IJC's work in the 1960s and early 1970s, which revealed that water pollution issues had become more relevant in the Great Lakes region and that they were not appraised adequately by the legal institutions governing the use of water between the two countries at that time.[14] This finding should not lead to an underestimation of the capacity of the USA to improve its knowledge of cause-effect relationships independently of other states; but in some respects, this finding also highlights that even those countries with comprehensive research and monitoring facilities have to rely partly on international institutions or other national agencies to improve consensual knowledge of the nature of the problem.

2. Policy options

A second measurement determined the completeness of information on various policy options. Policy-makers must be convinced that the use of available policy options will improve the state of the environment. Effective problem-solving can require implementation of policies in a number of different industrial sectors and can affect the behaviour of a large number of consumers.[15] Detailed information on policy options must be available in order to enable policy-makers to identify possible obstacles to implementation. Political decision-making requires consideration of whether implementation of proposed solutions will provoke resistance by interest groups that could endanger a state's ability to comply with international commitments or worsen a government's

[14] On the evolution of this regime from a historical perspective, see Kehoe, T., *Cleaning up the Great Lakes: from cooperation to confrontation*, Dekalb (Northern Illinois University Press) 1st edn 1997. See also Valiante, M., Muldoon, P., and Botts, L., Ecosystem governance: lessons from the Great Lakes, in Young, O. R. (ed.), *Global governance: drawing insights from the environmental experience*, Cambridge Mass. (MIT Press) 1st edn 1997, pp. 197–225; Klinke, A., Regieren jenseits des Staates durch deliberative Politik: Das deliberative Handlungs- und Strukturpotential im nordamerikanischen Große-Seen-Regime, Dissertation, forthcoming.

[15] On the implementation of international environmental commitments, see Victor D. G., Raustiala, K., and Skolnikoff, E. B. (eds.), *The implementation and effectiveness of international environmental commitments: theory and practice*, Cambridge Mass. (MIT Press) 1st edn 1998.

prospects for reelection. Incomplete knowledge can cause states to postpone the implementation of international policies or can be used by single states as an excuse to prevent the broadening or deepening of international norms and rules. The debate between industrialised countries concerning the implementation of the Kyoto Protocol is partly determined by a lack of consensus about feasible policy options. Considering the substantial costs which arise from the implementation of the Kyoto Protocol, whether in relation to the economic and financial burden for private and public sectors or to political costs for securing ratification and domestic implementation, it is questionable whether the USA will remove its opposition to this Protocol in the near future. On the other hand, consensus among regime members about alternative policy options to the Kyoto Protocol is currently beyond reach.

The completeness of information on policy options has been measured for every regime element problem. Policy options for tackling a problem may focus on measures which have to be taken in different sectors. These options are based on information on the most important variables for solving the problem. An ordinal scale from one to three has been used for measurement: very high level of completeness referred to a situation where all necessary information on the different options was available; a medium level of completeness to a situation where despite information on options available, certain kinds of information for some or all options were still lacking; a low level of completeness described a situation where information on most of the possible options was not available or options themselves may not yet have been identified. Again, a distinction will be made between our data from a subsection describing developments in regime elements ending in 1998.

The results of the coding reflect that most of the problems had a medium level of completeness of information on policy options (see Table 17.3). For 133 of the total 207 problems coded for 166 regime elements, a medium level of completeness of information on policy options emerged. Very high level of completeness were identified for only thirty-seven problems. This suggests that information on policy options has reached a medium level in most regimes. This data suggests that there is a strong demand for the further improvement of information available on policy options. This is understandable in light of the complexity of many transboundary environmental problems. Global regimes for climate change, the conservation of biodiversity, or the combat of desertification have to implement a broad range of policies on different levels. Since the main causes of environmental problems can change significantly, it is questionable whether even a very high level of information on policy options can be achieved in complex issue areas. Nevertheless, one of the implications of this data is that information on feasibly implemented policies is insufficient and must be improved in most of the regimes.

Table 17.3 Completeness of information on policy options

Regime	Problems coded for a regime[a] (Total/regime elements ending in 1998)	1 = Very high completeness (Total/regime elements ending in 1998)	2 = Medium completeness (Total/regime elements ending in 1998)	3 = Low completeness (Total/regime elements ending in 1998)
Antarctic Regime	55/24	13/6	34/15	8/3
Baltic Sea Regime	14/8	0	14/8	0
Barents Sea Fisheries	2/2	2/2	0	0
Biodiversity Regime	2/2	1/1	1/1	0
CITES Regime	12/6	3/3	5/3	4/0
Climate Change Regime	10/6	0	6/5	4/1
Danube Regime	6/2	0	4/2	2/0
Desertification Regime	2/2	1/1	1/1	0
Great Lakes Regime	10/6	0	7/4	3/2
Hazardous Waste Regime	14/8	0	14/8	0
IATTC Regime	3/2	0	2/2	1/0
ICCAT Regime	2/2	1/1	0	1/1
Whaling Regime	8/4	3/2	4/2	1/0
London Convention	12/6	1/1	11/5	0
LRTAP Regime	7/5	0	7/5	0
North Sea Regime	6/4	0	4/4	2/0
Oil Pollution Regime	3/2	2/2	0	1/0
Rhine Regime	8/8	4/4	3/3	1/1
Ramsar Regime	4/2	1/0	2/2	1/0
Black Sea Regime	4/4	0	4/4	0
South Pacific Fisheries	6/2	0	4/2	2/0
Stratospheric Ozone Regime	13/9	5/5	4/2	4/2
Tropical Timber Trade Regime	4/4	0	2/2	2/2

[a] Data before the oblique stroke relates to the total number of elements coded for a regime. Data after indicates developments in elements of a regime ending in 1998.

A second measurement indicates that this knowledge has been affected by significant change in many regimes. For a total of 195 problems, there is data available which shows whether policy option information has been affected by change during the lifecycle of a regime element. For about half of these problems, a significant change in the completeness of information on policy options has been identified. This change has not led to the regression of consensual knowledge, but it can instead be understood as a development that reflects a dynamic increase in this knowledge. For the other half, little or no change has been detected. In some respects, the finding that half of the problems were determined by significant change seems to contradict the previous result that knowledge on policy options has frequently been much less established than is required for the development of effective policies. This leads us to conclude that the change affected the consensual knowledge of policy options only to an extent that allowed the achievement of medium completeness in this knowledge.

A third factor measures those changes that occurred relating to information on policy options within important states. A number of examples illustrate that such change has in fact occurred in some countries. Sixty-nine of a total of 159 sets of data indicate that information on policy options in the USA has changed significantly. In thirty-six instances in this group/subsection, the regime was seen to have had a significant causal influence on change in this country. In addition, twenty sets of data within this group indicate that the regime had at least a modest causal impact. The changes identified in the USA or other countries predominantly involved possible improvements that could be made towards the completeness of information on policy options. For example, coding experts identified significant changes to the information on policy options which could be used by the USA or Canada for the management of water quality and quantity in the Great Lakes. Similar improvements to information on policy options occurred in relation to the ozone regime. The ozone regime has been ascribed a modest causal influence in the significant changes to the information on policy options identified in the USA. A similar picture emerges from the sixty-two sets of data on changes that affected Germany's knowledge on policy options. Thirty-nine sets of data from this subset indicate that Germany has experienced a significant change in a regime element and in eighteen of these instances, the regime has been ascribed a significant causal influence on this change. The changes identified in Germany predominantly indicate improvements achieved with respect to the completeness of information on policy options. Such changes occurred in the ozone regime, the regimes dealing with the environmental management of the Rhine, the Baltic Sea, or the reduction of transboundary pollution. These findings suggest that even countries with comprehensive research or administrative capacities can be influenced by new ideas or solutions that were developed in the context of a regime.

3. Institutional mechanisms and knowledge

It has been argued by cognitivists that institutions or social actors participating in the management of international programmes contribute to the communication of knowledge on cause-effect relationships or policy options to the broader transnational public. An institution-based explanation for the evolution of knowledge takes the existence of institutional mechanisms providing various functions for the evolution of consensual knowledge as a starting point for analysis.[16] Institutions are considered frameworks which allow the creation and expansion of epistemic communities or other networks of scientific, technical, and policy experts which then contribute to the strengthening of consensual knowledge. Institutions must be empowered by social actors who provide expertise and develop consensual knowledge. Four types of institutional functions that influence the evolution of knowledge on cause-effect relationships or policy options will be distinguished:

- *Scientific monitoring of the causes and effects* of an environmental problem is one of those functions frequently provided for in international environmental agreements. It leads to the collection of additional information that would be unavailable or less complete if states did not coordinate national monitoring or expand these efforts on an international level.
- *Research on the causes and effects of a transboundary problem* is another function which states intend to expand at international and national level by the establishment of international environmental regimes. International research programmes develop methodologies for the production and assessment of data, evaluate data provided by monitoring networks and other sources. They can also identify past and future trends from existing data, or focus on the implementation of qualitative studies on specific topics or issues that cannot be explored by the use of monitoring data.
- *Systems for the review of implementation* are important in the assessment of how far domestic measures chosen by member states will achieve sufficient levels of compliance. In this context, the review of implementation measures can help improve understanding of the feasibility of existing policies or inform about factors determining both the failure and success of national implementation.

---

[16] For studies dealing with the role of institutional mechanisms and scientific actors for the creation of consensual knowledge, see Andresen, S., Skodvin, T., and Underdal, A., *Science in international environmental regimes: between integrity and involvement*, Manchester (Manchester University Press) 1st edn 2000. There is a large number of case studies focussing on the role of knowledge as a factor that accounts for problem-solving effectiveness. Of particular interest are those detailed included in Young, O. R. (ed.), *The effectiveness of international environmental regimes: causal connections and behavioural mechanisms*, Cambridge Mass. (MIT Press) 1st edn 1999.

Table 1.4 *Institutional mechanisms in regime elements*

Regime	Scientific monitoring of the causes and effects of the problem* (Total/regime elements ending in 1998)	Research about the causes and effects of the problem (Total/regime elements ending in 1998)	Review of implementation (Total/regime elements ending in 1998)	Reviewing the adequacy of commitments (Total/regime elements ending in 1998)
Antarctic Regime	10/4	4/2	2/2	12/6
Baltic Sea Regime	10/6	10/6	10/6	10/6
Barents Sea Fisheries	2/2	2/2	2/2	0
Biodiversity Regime	2/2	2/2	2/2	0
CITES Regime	4/2	4/2	4/2	2/1
Climate Change Regime	6/4	6/4	6/4	6/4
Danube Regime	6/2	4/2	2/2	2/2
Desertification Regime	0	0	2/2	0
Great Lakes Regime	8/6	6/4	6/4	6/4
Hazardous Waste Regime	0	0	(1)**	2/0
IATTC Regime	6/4	6/4	4/4	2/2
ICCAT Regime	2/2	2/2	2/2	2/2
Whaling Regime	4/2	4/2	4/2	0
London Convention	10/4	10/4	2/2	0
LRTAP Regime	2/1	2/2	4/4	3/3
North Sea Regime	4/2	6/4	6/4	4/4
Oil Pollution Regime	0	0	4/2	0
Rhine Regime	8/8	8/8	2/2	6/6
Ramsar Regime	4/2	4/2	2/2	2/2
Black Sea Regime	4/4	4/4	2/2	2/2
South Pacific Fisheries	3/1	3/1	2/1	2/1
Stratospheric Ozone Regime	4/2	4/2	8/6	8/6
Tropical Timber Trade Regime	2/2	2/2	2/2	2/2

* Data before the oblique stroke relate to the total of elements coded for a regime. Data after relate to developments in elements of a regime which end in 1998. A total of 172 regime elements have been coded.
** Implementation review has been practised only in the context of the European Union.

- *Mechanisms which review the adequacy of commitments* assess whether existing international policies are effective in light of observed changes in the state of the environment, or of new technologies, or the policy options available for problem-solving. This role of institutions and the above-described functions can be seen in the reformulation of policies and the development of new international norms and rules.

Mechanisms for scientific monitoring and research were established in most regimes. In some regimes, regime components based on framework conventions also carry out these functions for other regime components. While there has been a tendency towards the establishment of these mechanisms on an international level, the Barents Sea fisheries regime is an example of Russia and Norway acting as the two sole regime members carrying out these functions on the national level. They also involved non-governmental organisations in various activities related to scientific research and monitoring. Both countries and non-governmental organisations exchanged and integrated their knowledge in joint meetings and working groups.[17] A similar situation occurred in the Great Lakes management regime. Major regime functions remained within the national authority of the USA and Canada, but a dense institutional framework and formalised channels of communication facilitated the exchange of data and scientific findings. A discursive setting has emerged in this regime within which scientific actors, policy-makers, local and regional communities, business or activist NGOs inform one another about important aspects of consensual knowledge. While the two regimes encompass only two members, the multilateral composition of membership caused states to establish these mechanisms primarily on the international level in most of the twenty-three regimes. This allows the integration of information and the creation of consensual knowledge. However, global and regional research- and monitoring networks would be ineffective if states did not continue or intensify their activities on a national or local level. Mechanisms for the review of implementation have been established in all regimes. In some components of the hazardous waste regime (e.g., Bamako and Waigani), these reviews were absent during the periods that were explored. Even though mechanisms for reviewing whether commitments were sufficient could be found in the majority of regimes, at least six regimes were lacking these mechanisms by the end of the twentieth century.

Which conclusions can be drawn in regard to the existence and operation of institutional mechanisms as a condition for the evolution of consensual knowledge? It is striking that strongly established understanding of the type of problem has emerged in regimes only if mechanisms for scientific monitoring and research have been established. On the other hand, existence of these

---

[17] See Stokke, O. S., Anderson, L. G., and Mirovitskaya, N., The Barents Sea fisheries, in Young (1999), op. cit., pp. 91–154; Honneland, G., Compliance in the fishery protection zone around Svalbard, *Ocean Development and Int'l Law* 29 (1998), pp. 339–360.

mechanisms has not been a guarantee of the emergence of strongly or very strongly established understandings. The structure of many problem issues obviously makes it far more difficult in single regimes to improve the level of consensual knowledge to a strong or very strong understanding of the type of problem. In addition, the institution itself can, to a great extent, only complement rather than fully replace the functions necessary for improving various components of consensual knowledge in environmental issue areas. Whilst such capacities are frequently lacking in developing countries, regimes can facilitate the establishment of information systems or of research and monitoring facilities that contribute to the improvement of consensual knowledge. The structure of the problem as an intervening variable is also a factor that can partly explain the emergence of predominantly medium completeness of information on policy options. The complexity of a problem can be a constraint to the development of policy options. At the end of the twentieth century there was still a demand in some regimes for the establishment of institutional mechanisms to review the sufficiency of commitments.

IV. Conclusion

Our measurements examine whether institutions have been designed properly and whether alternative solutions exist that make the operation of institutional mechanisms more effective. The expansion of institutional mechanisms used for improving the consensual knowledge in the issue area could be observed in almost any of the regimes explored. Whether or not regimes should be brought together under the umbrella of a single global environmental organisation or be more closely linked to special international organisations is a topic of ongoing debate. Proponents of the creation of a new Global Environmental Organisation whose powers would go beyond the present coordinating and catalytic role of the United Nations Environment Programme (UNEP) take other international governmental organisations as an example. They argue that a more centralised environmental organisation would lead to improvements in several respects: (i) it could integrate functions independently carried out by regimes into one organisational framework; (ii) it could improve capacity-building in developing countries or take on a coordinating role with respect to financial and technology transfer; (iii) it could further promote awareness about newly emerging environmental problems.[18]

There is certainly a need to integrate the functions among international regimes more effectively in the realms of monitoring, scientific research, the review of implementation or compliance, information management, and

---

[18] For a summary of this position see Biermann, F. and Simonis, U. E., Institutionelle Reform der Weltumweltpolitik? Zur politischen Debatte um die Gründung einer 'Weltumweltorganisation', *Zeitschrift für Internationale Beziehungen* 7 (2000), pp. 163–183.

administrative tasks. Functional integration does not inevitably require the creation of international government-like structures. It can also be achieved by institutional arrangements between various regimes or international organisations. It is doubtful whether a global institution like the World Trade Organization (WTO) can be used as a blueprint for the organisational restructuring of global environmental governance. The vast majority of transboundary environmental problems pertain to bilateral, regional, or multilateral contexts below the global level. A predominantly global framing of environmental problems would contradict the bilateral or regional character of many transboundary problems.[19] The reform of global environmental governance will have to respect the desire for decentralised institutions that can consider local and regional concerns. If global environmental governance will be restructured at some point it is open to conjecture whether all environmental regimes could be subject to the decision-making of international organisations. The suggestion of achieving 'closer integration of related or overlapping international environmental regimes' by the clustering of institutions stems from the insight that the existence of several hundreds of environmental regimes has caused a fragmentation of environmental governance systems.[20] Under these circumstances, the establishment of less complex units that carry out similar functions for a number of regimes on the international level could be a feasible solution that is realisable in a reasonably short period.

[19] For a critical discussion of the proposal demanding the establishment of a Global Environmental Organisation, see Gehring, T. and Oberthür, S., Was bringt die Weltumweltorganisation? Kooperationstheoretische Anmerkungen zur institutionellen Neuordnung der internationalen Umweltpolitik, *Zeitschrift für Internationale Beziehungen* 7 (2000), pp. 185–211.

[20] On the proposal of a clustering of environmental institutions, see Konrad von Moltke, Chapter 16.

PART VII

Improving the instruments of global governance

18

Regulatory competition and developing countries and the challenge for compliance push and pull measures

JOYEETA GUPTA

I. Introduction

Emissions trading[1] under the Marrakech Accords[2] and the Kyoto Protocol[3] to the United Nations Framework Convention on Climate Change (UNFCCC)[4] allow countries to trade emissions of greenhouse gases with each other. Although this scheme is presently limited to the developed countries, it is anticipated that as and when developing countries commit themselves to some kind of upper emission limit, they too can participate in this process. There is also considerable pressure on developing countries to take on some form of measurable commitment as of the second budget period, which is expected to begin in 2012. For economists this is logical and necessary, since emissions trading is an efficient solution to the problem of climate change.[5] Various formulae have been devised to facilitate allocations of initial emission entitlements or allowances that work in the interest of either the developed or the developing countries.[6]

This chapter has been supported by the research undertaken in the context of the Vrije Universiteit Project on the Law of Sustainable Development and the project Inter-governmental and Private Environmental Regimes and Compatibility with Good Governance, financed by the Netherlands Scientific Organisation. I thank the project members of the group on the Transnational Institutions on the Environment for their comments and in particular Peter Sand for his detailed comments.

[1] This instrument allows countries that have overused their emission allowance to buy emission units from other countries who have surplus emission allowances.
[2] Climate Change Secretariat, The Marrakech Accords and the Marrakech Declaration, Bonn, 2001.
[3] The Kyoto Protocol to the United Nations Framework Convention on Climate Change, 37 I.L.M (1997) 22.
[4] United Nations Framework Convention on Climate Change (UNFCCC), New York, 9 May 1992, in force 24 March 1994; 31 ILM (1992) 22.
[5] See e.g., the enormous literature on emissions trading.
[6] Phylipsen, G. J. M., Bode, J. W., Blok, K., Merkus, H., and Metz, B., A triptych sectoral approach to burden differentiation: GHG emissions in the European bubble, Energy Policy 26 (12) (1998), pp. 929–943; Meyer, A., Contraction and convergence: the global solution to climate change, Schumacher Briefings no. 5, Foxhole/Dartington/Totnes (Green Books for the Schumacher Society) 2000; Agarwal, A., Making the Kyoto Protocol work: ecological

The anticipated difficulties in reaching an amicable compromise were, however, seen as the reason that such a scheme would not work;[7] nevertheless, through a clever negotiating strategy, emissions trading is one of the instruments in the climate change regime.[8] But as someone who has grown up in a developing country, frequently visited developing countries, immersed herself in problems of developing countries, it is difficult for me to fathom that the international community does not realise that this instrument is doomed to failure since the majority of the countries of the world, including several of the East and Central European countries, just do not have the institutional wherewithal to cope with such a complex system with such high financial stakes. I also have doubts about the ability of the developed countries to develop an adequate system given the huge uncertainties in the science of emission inventories and sinks.[9]

Why did such an instrument emerge in the international arena? Because the USA included it in a draft Protocol text submitted to the Secretariat of the UNFCCC in 1996 that made absolutely clear that targets and timetables would only be acceptable in the context of flexible mechanisms including emission trading.[10] The USA had successful experience in domestic emissions trading.[11] It had no experience in international emissions trading. The European Union had no experience in domestic or international emissions trading; nor did the rest of the world. A year later during the negotiations in Kyoto, various elements were discussed and included. At the last minute, the USA was able to insert paragraph 16 bis on emissions trading (renamed Article 17) into the agreement.[12] Since then, the USA has withdrawn from the regime and now

and economic effectiveness and equity in the climate regime, New Delhi (CSE Statement) 2000; Banuri, T., Goran-Maler, K., Grubb, M., Jacobson, H. K., and Yamin, F., Equity and social considerations, in Bruce, J., Hoesung, L., and Haites, E. (eds.), *Climate change 1995: economic and social dimensions of climate change*, Contribution of Working Group III to the Second Assessment Report of the Intergovernmental Panel on Climate Change, Cambridge (Cambridge University Press) 1996, pp. 79–124; Baumert, K., Bhandari, R., and Kete, N., *What might a developing country climate commitment look like*, Climate Notes, Washington (World Resources Institute) 1999; Brazilian Proposal, Proposed elements of a protocol, FCCC/AGBM/1997/Misc.1/Add.3.

[7] See Shelling, T. C., The cost of combating global warming: facing the trade-offs, *Foreign Affairs* 76(6) (1997), pp. 8–14; Cooper, R. N., Toward a real global warming treaty, *Foreign Affairs* 77(2) (1998), pp. 66–79.

[8] See e.g., Yamin, F., The Kyoto Protocol: origins, assessment and future challenges, *Review of European Community and Int'l Environmental Law* 7(2) (1998), pp.113–127.

[9] There is a huge amount of uncertainty in the values of emissions by sources and absorbtions by sinks; see e.g. the IPCC reports. See also, Gupta, J., Olsthoorn, X., and Rotenberg, E., Scientific uncertainty and compliance with the Kyoto Protocol: clarifications and complications, *Environmental Science and Policy* 6(6) (2003), pp. 475–486.

[10] See also Gupta, J. and v.d. Grijp, N., Leadership in the climate change regime: the European Union in the looking glass, *Int'l J. Sustainable Development* 2(2) (1999), pp. 303–322, for a history of the negotiations between the European Union and the USA in relation to the Kyoto Protocol.

[11] There is a huge literature of SO_2 emissions trading, especially in the USA.

[12] See e.g., Yamin (1998), op. cit.

Europe and the rest of the world is left with an instrument that they have no experience to deal with. The EU is, however, bravely going ahead with developing a system for internal trading.[13] Subsequently at some later date, capacity-building exercises will probably be held in other countries to teach them how to participate effectively in this instrument.

This brief history indicates that very significant elements are introduced into international environmental treaties, but these are often not necessarily based on informed consent from the other parties, but are introduced by epistemic communities and, via the process of bargaining, somehow become mainstream ideas. I would not be surprised if countries, and especially developing countries at a later date, would have considerable difficulties in implementing the instrument effectively. This history has only been recounted here to provide the flavour of the kind of problem that this chapter intends to address. The above case is only one of a number of different types of problems that developing countries face when they negotiate and implement international environmental agreements.

This chapter focuses on the reasons why developing countries are often unable to comply with their commitments under international agreements. Compliance refers not only to rule consistent behaviour by states (outcomes) but also by the social actors within the countries leading to actual changes in the environment (impacts).[14] It first briefly examines the situation of developing countries in relation to international agreements (section II). It then goes on to expand on the elements of the theory on compliance pull and compliance push (section III). It borrows the concept of regulatory competition and applies it to the international context and analyses the implication of such regulatory competition for the legitimacy of the agreement and the sovereignty of nations (section IV). It then draws some conclusions (section V).

This chapter focuses on the specific problems faced by developing countries in the international negotiation process and in the implementation of international treaties. In doing so, it borrows empirical and legal evidence from the climate change regime.

II. Developing countries and compliance: pre and post-negotiation explanations

The fact that developing countries (and sometimes countries with economies in transition) tend to be in non-compliance with their international environmental agreements is not an unintuitive one. The reasoning, however, may be.

---

[13] See, e.g., the EU Green Paper on Emissions Trading within the European Union, COM(2000)87. The EU emissions trading scheme has become operational in 2005.
[14] Underdal, A., Hisschemöller, M., and von Moltke, K., The study of regime effectiveness: agenda setting paper for the concerted action workshop, paper for the Workshop on 16–18 October 1998, Noordwijk, Netherlands.

There is considerable empirical evidence that suggests that many of these countries are simply unable to meet the obligations they take on in the international arena. The post-negotiation explanation is simple and the one that is often discussed. International relations scholars often begin their analysis with 'output' (Treaty), 'outcome' (effect on domestic regulatory regimes), and 'impact' (effect on environment).[15] The literature points out that these countries lack the monitoring facilities, scientific capabilities, financial resources, manpower, public support, civic culture, political will, legal and administrative infrastructure, and an environmentally conscious civil society to implement these agreements.[16] This is referred to as involuntary non-compliance as opposed to voluntary non-compliance when countries consciously decide not to comply with an agreement.[17] The solution proposed is to develop institutions and capacity in these countries.[18] It is to promote the export of 'leap-frog' technologies to these countries so that they can make use of the available scientific and technical knowledge.[19] I do not want to labour this point further since it has been amply discussed in the literature.

But there are also prenegotiation explanations, which for some reason remain a relatively neglected element in the discussion of non-compliance. These include the fact that the international agenda is often developed by the industrialised countries and the problem is defined to suit their interests. As a result, the problem is seen as alien to domestic interests and concerns in developing countries. The theory of a *hollow mandate* explains why developing countries are likely to face several sustainability dilemmas[20] in the development of their

---

[15] Underdal, A., Hisschemöller, M., and von Moltke, K., op. cit.; Underdal, A. and Young, O. R., *Institutional dimensions of global change: a preliminary scoping report, Report for the International Human Dimensions Programme*, Bonn, 1996.

[16] Jacobson, H. K. and Weiss, E. B., Strengthening compliance with international environmental accords: preliminary observations from a collaborative project, *Global Governance* 1(2) (1995), pp. 119–148; Sand, P. H., Institution building to assist compliance with international environmental law, *Heidelberg J. of Int'l L.* 56(3) (1996), pp. 774–795. Grey, K. and Gupta, J., The United Nations climate change regime and Africa, in Gray, K. R. and Chaytor, B. (eds.), *Environmental law and policy in Africa*, Dordrecht (Kluwer Academic Publishers) 2002, pp. 60–81.

[17] Putnam, R., Diplomacy and domestic politics: the logic of two-level games, *International Organization* 42(2) (1988), pp. 427–460; Chayes, A. and Handler, A. C., On compliance, *International Organization* 47(2) (1993), pp. 175–205.

[18] See e.g., Sand, op. cit.

[19] See the Scientific Declaration of the Second World Climate Conference 1990; Intergovernmental Panel on Climate Change, *Special report on technology transfer*, Cambridge (Cambridge University Press) 2000; Hennikoff, J., Bridging the intellectual property debate: methods for facilitating technology transfer in environmental treaties, in Susskind, L. E., Moomaw, W. M., and Hill, T. L. (eds.), *Innovations in international environmental negotiation*, Cambridge, Mass. (Pon Books) 1997, pp. 48–59.

[20] The sustainability dilemmas include the dilemma on how to modernise without Westernising, how to survive without squandering resources, how to beg without mortgaging one's

national position and are unlikely to be in a position to have a well developed negotiating position in relation to environmental problems that have been primarily defined by the developed countries. The theory of the *defensive negotiating strategy* of developing countries explains why developing countries are unlikely to come up with a constructive regulatory option that serves their interests and is likely to work in the context of their countries (however different they may be from each other). The theory of *handicapped coalition-building power* explains why developing countries are unable to pool their knowledge together to come up with a common negotiating position in order to be able to negotiate effectively at international level. The theory of *handicapped negotiating power* explains why, despite the adoption of rules of procedure, the developing countries are unable to negotiate effectively within the context of the actual negotiations. The theory of the *structural imbalance in negotiating* explains why, even if the developing countries were in a position to push a constructive suggestion, it is likely to be unpackaged in such a way that it does not resemble the original proposal except in name. The competing *theories of problem solving* show that while for regime analysts, in the absence of a hegemonic leader, cooperation is only possible when issues are clearly delineated and identified, for true problem solvers, issues are possibly so closely interlinked that a process of dealing with single issues may not address the structural problems facing developing countries and hence may not put them in a position to be able to implement international agreements.[21]

Such prenegotiation explanations can also be used to argue why such treaties may be less legitimate in my perspective. One can argue that in general because the developing countries are facing a structural imbalance in knowledge and because they have a hollow mandate, a handicapped coalition-building power and a handicapped negotiation power, they are in not much of a position to influence the actual substantive content of a treaty. They are also often not in a position to withdraw from the negotiation process because of their realisation

---

resources, how to empower the private sector to solve public problems, how to demand equity internationally without providing it nationally, how to meet short-term economic interests without compromising on long-term interests, how to unite the G-77 without being reduced to support the absolute lowest common denominator. For details, see Gupta, J., Environment and development: towards a fair distribution of burdens and benefits, in Heins, J. J. F. and Thijs, G. D. (eds.), *Ontwikkelingsproblematiek: the winner takes it all? Verdelings Vraagstukken in de Wereld*, Themabundel Ontwikkelingsproblematiek no. 12, Amsterdam (Vrije Universiteit Amsterdam Press) 2002, pp. 35–50.

[21] See for details, Gupta, J., The Climate Convention: can a divided world unite?, in Briden, J. and Downing, T. E. (eds.), *Managing the Earth: the eleventh Linacre Lectures*, Oxford (Oxford University Press) 2002, pp. 129–156; Gupta, J., North-South aspects of the climate change issue: towards a negotiating theory and strategy for developing countries, *Int'l J. Sustainable Development* 3(2) (2000), pp. 115–135; Gupta, J., *The Climate Change Convention and developing countries: from conflict to consensus?*, Environment and Policy Series, Dordrecht (Kluwer Academic Publishers) 1997, pp. 256.

that being on the boat is better than being out of it. As a result, one can argue that the legitimacy of the process and outcome is at risk.[22]

The fact remains that we are witnessing an era of multiple environmental treaties and that developing countries are struggling to cope with these treaties. This is not only because such treaty negotiation is complex in itself, but also because it is no longer a one-off affair. The framework treaties call for continuous fine-tuning and what Jutta Brunnée (in Chapter 15) describes as a continuous interactional process that 'can help build the foundations for legitimate international environmental governance, and can provide important guidance to law-makers, even as they continue to operate within a formal, consent-based framework'.[23] This imposes an impossibly hard burden on the developing countries because it calls for 'staying power'.[24]

III. Compliance pull and compliance push mechanisms

Let us now turn to the features that make international law in general successful.[25] One can argue that the success of an international Treaty depends on the compliance pull[26] and compliance push elements that have been negotiated in the Treaty. Let me begin with a description of the latter idea first.

The 'compliance push' element refers to those Articles/ingredients of an international treaty that create an environment in which countries have a very strong incentive to comply with the agreement because it directly affects the national interests of a country. Compliance push mechanisms are often seen as the driving forces by rationalists and realists, by those who subscribe to the school of the logic of consequences. Traditionally, this focused primarily on the enforcement mechanisms. Increasingly, new mechanisms are supplementing such enforcement mechanisms. These include Articles on monitoring,

---

[22] Gupta, J., Legitimacy in the real world: a case study of the developing countries, non-governmental organisations and climate change, in Coicaud, J. and Heiskanen, V. (eds.) *The legitimacy of international organizations*, Tokyo (United Nations University Press) 1997, pp. 482–518.

[23] See Jutta Brunnée, Chapter 15.

[24] Gupta, J., *Climate change: regime development and treaty implementation in the context of unequal power relations*, Report O-00/02, Amsterdam (Institute for Environmental Studies) 2000.

[25] Koh, H. H., Why do nations obey international law? *Yale L. J.* 106 (1997), pp. 2599–2659; Sand, op. cit.; Simmons, B. A., Compliance with international agreements, *Annual Rev. Political Science* 1 (1998), pp. 75–93; Underdal, A., Explaining compliance and defection: three models, *European J. Int'l Relations* 4(1) (1998), pp. 5–30; Keohane, R. O., Haas, P. M., and Levy, M. A., The effectiveness of international environmental institutions, in Haas, P. M., Keohane, R. O., and Levy, M. A. (eds.), *Institutions for the Earth: sources of effective international environmental protection*, Cambridge, Mass. (MIT Press) 1993, pp. 3–26.

[26] For example, Franck talks of the inherent compliance pull of international rules; see Franck, T. M., *The power of legitimacy among nations*, Oxford (Oxford University Press) 1990.

reporting and review, and perhaps even articles on scientific cooperation that are included in several international treaties.[27] These Articles push countries to monitor the domestic implementation of international Treaties and to report on the activities taken domestically. Such reports are frequently subject to an independent review process. There are also mechanisms for dispute resolution. The mechanisms of reporting and monitoring push countries into an annually recurring cycle that can at best ensure that the implementation of the Treaty gets incrementally pushed, and at worst lead to a consultancy report that has no influence or impact domestically. A relatively new trend is that of transnational enforcement of environmental law defined as 'actions by private persons or non-governmental organisations (NGOs) in national courts or administrative bodies to secure compliance with environmental law, including both national and international, in cases involving more than one state, or a state and areas beyond the limits of national jurisdiction.'[28] However, while these trends exist to lesser or greater extent in different environmental Treaties, there is increasing recognition of the fact that developing countries are often in non-compliance but that 'punishing' such countries does not increase the likelihood of compliance.[29] Pushing them to comply, through obligations on reporting, is invariably dependent on the financial resources available for such compliance, and developing countries are becoming more and more reluctant to accept such responsibilities under different Treaties because of the stress it puts on their scarce national resources.

The 'compliance pull' element refers to those elements of an international Treaty that bind the countries to the Treaty. To some extent, these elements are seen as more important by those who subscribe to the logic of appropriateness.[30] The law of treaties emphasises that countries should negotiate in good faith, that there should be state consent, and it adopts the principle of *pacta sunt servanda*.[31] Franck argues that the mere existence of state consent is not adequate for ensuring that the Treaty will be implemented. He then suggests that there are four other criteria that need to be met in order to ensure the legitimacy of the agreement. These are: determinacy, symbolic validation,

---

[27] Birnie, P. and Boyle, A., *International law and the environment*, Oxford (Oxford University Press) 2002, p. 586.
[28] Report of the Committee on Transnational Enforcement of Environmental Law of the International Law Association, 2002.
[29] Chayes and Chayes Handler, op. cit.; Sand op. cit.; Keohane, R. O., Haas, P. M., and Levy, M. A., The effectiveness of international environmental institutions, in Haas, P. M., Keohane, R. O., and Levy, M. A. (eds.), *Institutions for the Earth: sources of effective international environmental protection*, Cambridge, Mass. (MIT Press), pp. 3–26.
[30] See e.g., the classic book: Henkin, L., *How nations behave: law and foreign policy*, New York (Council on Foreign Relations, Columbia University Press) 2nd edn 1979.
[31] The Convention on the Law of Treaties, Vienna, 23 May 1969, in force 27 January 1980; 8 ILM (1969) 679.

coherence, and adherence to a normative hierarchy.[32] In an earlier paper, I have argued that it is also of vital importance that there is real and substantive, and not just formal, agreement on the nature of the problem, that negotiators are well prepared for the negotiations, and that the negotiation process is fair in itself.[33] These factors also determine the legitimacy and broad-based support for the agreement. Table 18.1 presents a summary of compliance push and compliance pull elements in a modern environmental Treaty.

In this chapter, I would like to make the case that compliance pull elements are increasingly including Articles to promote implementation and non-compliance mechanisms, mechanisms that promote capacity-building and technology transfer, and mechanisms that promote the commitment of the developing countries by incorporating legitimacy. Thus, for example, the Marrakech Accords to the UNFCCC include detailed provisions on capacity-building and technology transfer.[34] However, the key point I want to make here is that the design of compliance pull and compliance push measures is such that it tends to take the post-negotiation problems of developing countries into account and tends to ignore the prenegotiation problems. Thus, the capacity-building provisions in the Marrakech Accords talk about helping countries set up inventories, prepare national reports and scenarios, etc.; less (if anything at all) is said about building the very institutions that can help the country in engaging constructively in the negotiations.

IV. Negotiation as regulatory competition

Let us then return to the problem of developing countries. If we are in agreement that developing countries have structural disabilities to engage effectively in international negotiations; and if we then agree that the negotiation outcome reflects the way countries have negotiated, then the only way to deal with the problem of non-compliance is to provide a one-way transfer of technology and capacity-building. But this is perhaps a far too simple explanation of the problem of international negotiations.

Let us turn to the theory of regulatory competition. This theory can be traced back to Charles Tietout who argued that different tax regulations in different regions of a country would lead to competition attracting residents and this would lead to increased welfare. The theory has considerably evolved since then and has been applied in many different contexts with several refinements regarding when social welfare would increase. This led to a debate as to when

---

[32] Franck, op. cit.; Franck, T. M., *Fairness in international law and institutions*, Oxford (Oxford University Press) 1995.
[33] See for details, Gupta (2001), op. cit.
[34] See Marrakech Accords to the UNFCCC, Decision of the Conference of the Parties taken in 2001, Decision 2/CP.7.

Table 18.1 Elements of compliance push and compliance pull

Item	Elements	Reason
Compliance push (logic of consequences)	Monitoring	Keeps control on impacts
	Reporting and reviewing	Fosters 'habits of compliance' (Chayes)
	Enforcement	Creates incentive for implementation
	Dispute resolution	Provides opportunities for addressing difference of opinion
	Scientific cooperation	Promotes convergence in relevant scientific knowledge
Compliance pull (logic of appropriateness)	Good faith	Fundamental assumption of international law supported by the idea of reciprocity
	State consent	Formal necessity
	Pacta sunt servanda	Fundamental assumption of international law
	Legal legitimacy	Characteristic of a rule to cause countries to adhere to it
	Paralegal legitimacy	Characteristic of the negotiating process that attracts countries to adhere to it
	Non-compliance mechanisms	Mechanism to help countries comply with the agreement when it is clear that they are unable to comply
	Technology transfer, financial assistance, capacity building	Mechanisms to help countries comply

regulatory competition between countries is useful for increasing welfare and when regulatory coordination is useful. Some argue that regulatory competition could lead to a 'race to the bottom', especially in the area of environmental protection. Others argue that the idea that such competition is a race to the bottom is overstated, and that there should perhaps be a balance between competition and cooperation and this should be referred to as the theory of co-opetition.[35]

There is another strand of thought emerging. This argues that low standards within various EU Member States can lead to social or environmental dumping; this problem can be addressed by regulatory harmonisation. While such regulatory harmonisation can lead to the adoption of the highest common denominator, because of the need for consensus and state consent, it can also lead to a situation in which countries with advanced domestic policies try to sell their policies to the European Union.[36] Some countries try to promote their own domestic regulatory system and solution to the international arena because of the intense domestic pressure to do so from diverse lobby groups.[37] The purpose of this competition is to minimise the cost of implementation and to minimise the competitive disadvantages for the domestic industry. In other words, if countries already have a carbon tax in place, then this is the instrument that they wish to sell to the supranational community, and if they do not have a domestic carbon tax, they will avoid accepting this instrument at supranational level.[38]

Let us extrapolate this experience to the international level. It is argued that in the international context, because of the need for consensus, the negotiated outcome tends to be the highest common denominator.[39] This would appear

---

[35] Esty, D. C. and Geradin, D., Regulatory co-opetition, in Esty, D. C. and Geradin, D. (eds.), *Regulatory competition and economic integration: comparative perspectives*, Oxford (Oxford University Press) 2001, pp. 30–47.

[36] See e.g., Héritier, A., The accommodation of diversity in European policy-making and its outcomes: regulatory policy as a patchwork, *J. European Public Policy* 3(2) (1996), pp. 149–176; Héritier, A., Knill, C., and Mingers, S., *Ringing the changes in Europe: regulatory competition and the redefinition of the state, Britain, France, Germany*, Berlin/New York (De Gruyter) 1996.

[37] Faure, M., Regulatory competition versus harmonisation in EU environmental law, in Esty, D. and Geradin, op. cit. pp. 263–286.

[38] In the case of the carbon tax, there are other reasons such as competition between the ideas of subsidiarity and competence; see Dahl, A., Competence and subsidiarity, in Gupta, J. and Grubb, M. (eds.), *Climate change and European leadership: a sustainable role for Europe*, Environment and Policy Series, Dordrecht (Kluwer Academic Publishers) 2000, pp. 203–220.

[39] Communicated by P. Sand as an improved version of what is argued in Sand, P., *Lessons learned in global environmental governance*, New York (World Resources Institute) 1990; building on Underdal, A.'s (1980) analysis of the politics of international fisheries management. See also Scasz, P. C., International norm-making, in Weiss, E. B. (ed.), *Environmental change and international law*, Tokyo (UN University) 1992, pp. 41–80, at 57, n. 21.

to be the logical conclusion of a rational discussion of consensus. At the same time, empirical evidence tends to point in slightly different directions. Highly specialised solutions are being devised by countries to deal with specific environmental problems. Those countries that are in a position to develop such solutions try and promote their solutions as the best epistemic solution to the problem. This leads to a highly technical discussion among those who understand the solution and then eventually one of these solutions is often adopted. The intense competition to sell such solutions to the international community is not just motivated by altruistic ideas about what is good for the global environment but is also rooted in domestic self-interest. This is because each country has its own system of dealing with problems. If it has to change its system, this can bring huge administrative costs to the country. This highly specialised form of competition is increasingly being recognised in the context of the European Union Member States.[40] This type of competition is also visible at the international level. This competition can be explained through public choice theory by arguing that the lobby groups within certain highly regulated countries want to protect their own interests by pushing for very high standards at European level. Or this can be explained by arguing that such competition in promoting standards maximises environmental protection at the European Union level.

Before going further, it might be useful to dwell on the appropriateness of using regulatory competition to refer to the situation described above. Some scientists argue that regulatory competition, cooperation and co-opetition presuppose respect for national sovereignty, and hence the use of this term in such a context is seen as inappropriate. Others would argue that regulatory competition should be used to refer only to the competition between different countries. On the other hand, one could also argue that at one end of the spectrum, regulatory competition refers to competing administrative regimes; at the other end of the spectrum, it refers to the intensified competition to ensure that the domestic administrative solution is the one that is used to harmonise the international standard. This can be depicted by the illustration in Figure 18.1.

The above figure shows that in the context of regulatory competition between different administrative systems, this can lead to a race to the top where each region tries to adopt the best policies that maximise welfare, but it can also lead under different circumstances to a situation of destructive competition and a race to the bottom when industry moves to the region with the lowest

---

[40] Börzel, T. A., Why there is no Southern problem: on environmental leaders and laggards in the EU, *J. European Public Policy*, 7(1) (2000), pp. 141–162; Börzel, T. and Gupta, J., A new North-South conflict? Regulatory competition in European and international environmental politics, Paper presented at the international Workshop on European Concerted Action on the Effective Implementation of Environmental Law, Barcelona, 9–11 November 2000.

Dimensions of Regulatory Competition

	Between states	Towards harmonisation		
High	Race to the top; maximises welfare	Power Politics; LCD of most powerful countries	Low	Compliance pull
Low	Race to the bottom/ destructive competition	Consensus politics; lowest common denominator	High	

(Environmental Protection on left axis; Compliance pull on right axis)

Figure 18.1 Regulatory competition

standards. At the other extreme, where countries compete to promote their own national policies at the international level, the competition can lead to the highest common denominator policy being adopted, which by virtue of the requirement for consensus is in fact a very low level of policy. This policy is likely to have a high compliance pull but will result in low environmental protection. But, under certain circumstances where Southern and other countries agree to complex solutions because they do not understand their implications or for other political or procedural reasons, it can lead to the adoption of a highly modern technique or solution which is likely to have a low compliance pull, but if successful, high environmental protection.

In this chapter I am focusing on the right hand side of Figure 18.1. While I am aware of the environmental risks of consensus that reflects the low level of the highest common denominator, I want to point to the challenges for compliance in the situation where regulatory competition leads to the adoption of a highly complex administrative solution.

Let me return to the argument in section II. Developing countries have difficulties in preparing for negotiations on complex scientific and political problems. I would argue that competition to promote regulatory solutions at the international level aggravates further the inability of the developing countries to come up with structural solutions and to negotiate them. Worse still, this leads to an inequitable distribution of costs between the countries that are successful in such a competition (in general one or more of the developed countries) and the rest (developing countries, countries with economies in transition, and possibly some of the other developed countries). This is because those who already have an administrative solution in place or experience with such a solution have lower implementation costs in comparison to those that have no familiarity with such a solution, either theoretical or practical. This is, in fact, responsible for creating new 'capacity' problems, in addition to old 'capacity' problems and it also undermines the legal and paralegal legitimacy of the agreement. Some political scientists and economists might be tempted to argue that investment in 'new' 'capacity-building and technology transfer' is then the side payment to get the developing countries on board,[41] while others may argue that since the problem developing countries face is one of capacity, the solution should be framed in terms of capacity and technology transfer. While not denying the importance of both as theoretical insights, I would be tempted to argue that the problem may not be so much 'new capacity' problems resulting from regulatory competition, but 'old capacity' problems. This is not to completely undermine the idea of 'leap-frogging', but to put forth some of my concerns with this idea.

The idea of regulatory competition could be healthy from the perspective of the market. Let the best system of regulation win. But I wonder if it is as simple as that. First, what we are seeing is that the regulatory ideas of the most powerful countries are the ones that get transferred to the international level, for example, emissions trading and the idea of joint implementation and the clean development mechanism. Secondly, there is no guarantee that these regulatory ideas are the best available to deal with the problem. Although the ultimate goal of several new environmental treaties is to achieve sustainable development, I am not convinced that the transfer of existing technologies does more than entrench developing countries into the very same technological trajectory that has led to the current environmental crises. Thirdly, the most powerful countries are also exporting competing regulatory ideas in the environmental field to the international treaty-making world, leading to contradictory outcomes. For example, HFC gases, which are essentially greenhouse gases, were promoted under the 1987 Montreal Protocol on Ozone Depleting Substances. Fourthly, the regulatory ideas being sold to the rest of the world may be most self-serving because they are the most cost-effective to the country exporting the idea and lead, hence, to an unfair imposition of costs on other countries. Fifthly, the most powerful countries are selling competing regulatory ideas in different regimes. For example, while on the one hand there is an enormous amount of emphasis being paid to political human rights, economic and social human rights are being neglected in international environmental Treaties. Some authors argue, for example, that the law of development is the neglected element of the newly developing law of sustainable development.[42] Sixthly, however appealing it may be to play the role of leader, the responsibility of transferring technologies and capacity-building will never be adequately fulfilled because of the unidirectional character and the continuous financial burden it imposes on the

---

[41] This is common for those who use coalition theory or rational actor models.
[42] Schrijver, N., On the eve of Rio plus ten: development – the neglected dimension in the international law of sustainable development, Dies Natalis, lecture at the Institute of Social Studies, The Hague, 11 October 2001; Fuentes, X., International law-making in the field of sustainable development: the unequal competition between development and the environment, *Int'l Environmental Agreements: Politics, Law and Economics* 2(2) (2001), pp. 109–133.

developed countries, and hence the solution is a dubious one at best. Seventhly, a key argument being put forth is that it is easier to implement new technologies in the green fields of the South, because this does not lead to the problem of stranded resources. Ironically, this leads to proposals to build renewable energy plants in developing countries, which the developed countries themselves find too expensive to put up domestically. The financial accounting for such projects is extremely unclear. On the contrary, success stories on technology diffusion show that precisely those technologies that have been successful in the West are the ones that become cheap enough for the South to purchase (e.g. telephones). Eighthly, the whole process of capacity-building and technology transfer seems to ignore the lessons learnt in development economics of the last fifty years regarding the appropriateness of leap-frog technologies and capacities.

Finally, I would like to develop further an idea put forth by Tariq Banuri.[43] He argues that the world is a Third World country, because all the features of the world exist in a Third World country. In other words, if we can find ways and means to help a Third World country come out of its Third World situation, we know how to address the problems of the global community. Let me translate this idea to the context of this chapter. The idea that the regulatory system or ideas that work in a highly developed country will work at the global level in an effort to help the rest of the world catch up with that highly developed country is a self-defeating idea. Such a system is extremely unlikely to work in other countries and in the globe as whole. The emissions trading system is a case in point. Instead, we have to look for solutions that are likely to work within the domestic context of developing countries and possibly upgrade these solutions to the global level if we really want to solve global environmental problems. To some extent, this idea is compatible with complex-adaptive system theory which argues that for strong and resilient management of a problem, it is vital that all the different parts of the network function independently to develop solutions and to adopt and implement them.[44]

V. Conclusion

This chapter has argued that the success or failure of an international environmental agreement depends on the inclusion of Articles and state practice that promote compliance pull and compliance push. Developing countries are in general unable to implement their commitments under the international environmental Treaties. This raises questions regarding the effective inclusion of ideas that promote both compliance pull and compliance push. The

---

[43] Banuri, T., The South and the governability of the planet: a question of justice, in Theys, J. (ed.), *The environment in the 21st century: the issues*, vol. I, Paris (Themis) 1996, pp. 405–414.

[44] See e.g., Homer-Dixon, T., *The ingenuity gap*, New York (Random House) 2000.

argument presented in this chapter is that in general there is a tendency among researchers to focus on the post-negotiation shortcomings of the developing countries in implementing international agreements. The realisation that these shortcomings are often rooted in the structural features of developing countries (lack of resources and institutions) has meant that the solution is framed in terms of, inter alia, promoting technology transfer and capacity-building. This chapter argues that the capacity problem being addressed by the environmental Treaties is the new capacity problem constructed by the regime as a result of the process of regulatory competition. In other words, through the process of regulatory competition, certain instruments and mechanisms that are well-developed or reasonably well-developed in the developed countries are pushed on to the international arena. Then it is argued that the developing countries do not have the relevant expertise. This implies that the developed countries have to create that capacity in the developing countries in order to implement the agreement.

My counter-argument is that the process of regulatory competition aggravates the existing problems of developing countries. It increases the burden on developing countries because the costs of implementation for them will be higher since the instruments proposed are often different from those instruments that the countries are familiar with. These increased costs are over and above other relevant costs. I argue that the highly technical and modern solutions being proposed in international treaties may actually be inappropriate solutions and not sustainable because of the one-way direction of the process. Furthermore, if we want to deal with environmental problems more structurally, we have to help developing countries deal with their own capacity problems and not the ones we have created. We have to provide capacity to help them compete in the process of regulatory competition by developing their own ideas of what is most likely to work in the context of their own countries.

19

Policy instrument innovation in the European Union: a realistic model for international environmental governance?

ANDREW JORDAN, RÜDIGER K. W. WURZEL, AND
ANTHONY R. ZITO

I. Environmental policy instruments: out with the old and in with the new?

The deployment of 'new' environmental policy instruments (NEPIs), namely market-based instruments (MBIs) such as eco-taxes and tradable permits, voluntary agreements (VAs), and informational devices such as eco-labels, has grown spectacularly in recent years. In 1987, the Organisation for Economic Cooperation and Development (OECD)[1] reported that most national environmental policies still relied upon a regulatory or 'command and control' mode of action, but since then the number of MBIs has grown 'substantially'.[2] Some estimates put the growth in MBIs in OECD countries at over 50 per cent between 1989 and 1995.[3] VAs, too, are becoming much more popular. In 1997, the European Environment Agency (EEA)[4] put the total in the European Union (EU) at around 300, with more and more being adopted each year.

The research underpinning this chapter was undertaken for a project entitled Innovation in Environmental Governance: A Comparative Analysis of New Environmental Policy Instruments which was generously funded by the Economic and Social Research Council (ESRC) under grant number L216252013. For more details, see www.uea.ac.uk/env/cserge/research/fut_governance/Home.htm An earlier version of this chapter was presented at the DFG Workshop on Transnational Institutions for the Environment (TIE), Justus-Liebig Universität Gießen, Germany, 20–21 June 2003. The authors are grateful to helpful comments by the participants and the editor, Professor Gerd Winter.

[1] OECD, *Managing the environment: the role of economic instruments*, Paris (OECD) 1994, p. 177.
[2] CEC, Database on environmental taxes in the EU Member States, consultancy prepared by Forum for the Future, July 2001, Brussels (CEC) 2000, p. 2.
[3] Ibid.
[4] European Environment Agency (EEA), *Environmental agreements: environmental effectiveness*, Copenhagen (EEA) 1997.

The putative shift from traditional ('command and control') regulation towards NEPIs is not, of course, confined to the EU Member States. Golub suggests that the eagerness to extend the environmental policy toolbox is producing a 'fundamental transition' around the globe.[5] In Japan, one estimate put the total number of VAs at around 30,000.[6] The US Environmental Protection Agency (USEPA) recently conducted an audit and discovered 'an enormous number' at the federal and state level, with 'literally thousands' at the substate level.[7] The sheer diversity of instruments now employed in the USA, the report continued, is also 'remarkable'.[8] There has even been a growing interest in and emerging experience with NEPIs in developing countries such as China.[9]

The reasons for the upsurge of NEPIs are complex and include cost-effectiveness considerations, competitive pressures from global markets, and the emergence of new concepts such as sustainable development which can no longer be implemented by relying merely on traditional regulations. We have assessed the underlying reasons for the increased uptake of NEPIs elsewhere.[10] This chapter instead aims to assess whether the recent NEPI innovation within the EU and its Member States could provide a model for other regions and states. In particular, it analyses whether the EU has facilitated or constrained the horizontal diffusion of 'new' policy tools. Our argument proceeds as follows. In section II we define NEPIs. Section III analyses the overall pattern of NEPI use and more traditional (or 'older') tools of environmental policy (i.e. regulation) in seven Member States and the EU. Section IV explains what role or roles the EU could conceivably play in the selection and possible diffusion of policy instruments, and section V relates these to the actual use of NEPIs both at the EU level and in Member States. Section VI assesses what lessons could be drawn from the EU's experience with adopting and implementing NEPIs to inform the development of environmental governance in other states and regions. We should, of course, be careful about drawing lessons from the EU's experience because the EU is not a typical regional organisation. It is also not a state, although it has some state-like characteristics. Furthermore, while the EU operates at a supranational level in Europe, it is considerably more complex than a conventional international regime. In fact, the EU enjoys some quasi-federal powers in the environmental sector. These limitations

---

[5] Golub, J. (ed.), *New instruments of environmental policy*, London (Routledge) 1998, p. xiii.

[6] Andrews, R. et al., *Voluntary agreements in environmental Policy*, Prague (University of Economics Press) 2001, p. 10.

[7] USEPA, *The United States experience with economic incentives for protecting the environment*, EPA 240-R-01-001, Washington DC (USEPA) 2001, pp. 23, 85.

[8] Ibid., p. ix.

[9] OECD, *Environmental taxes: recent developments in China and OECD countries*, Paris (OECD) 1999.

[10] Jordan, A. J., Wurzel, R. K.W. and Zito, A. R. (eds.), *New instruments of environmental governance*, Frank Cass (London) 2003.

notwithstanding, the EU's experience does still provide some important clues as to how 'new' policy tools might best be deployed in other regions and states. On closer examination, the EU's role in promoting the use of NEPIs is actually quite paradoxical. So, although there is widespread agreement that the EU has, at various times, helped to drive up national and international environmental standards,[11] and has actively explored NEPIs as a means of overcoming the poor implementation of regulation, its ability actually to adopt and/or promote NEPIs remains rather mixed.[12] We explore the reasons for this in more detail below. Finally, section VII draws some comparative conclusions.

In our analysis, we draw upon empirical examples from seven industrialised countries, namely Austria, Germany, Ireland, Finland, France, the Netherlands, and the United Kingdom, which have historically different levels of environmental performance and different experiences of NEPI use.[13] The Netherlands and (until recently) Germany are often portrayed as environmental 'leader' states, which forcefully advocate high environmental standards at home and in international settings.[14] However, while the Netherlands has a long history of experimenting with a wide range of different instruments, Germany has struggled to overcome the long tradition of being a 'high regulatory' state, although it has made wide use of VAs, most of which are, nonetheless, adopted 'in the shadow of the law'.[15] Austria and Finland also have strong environmental reputations, but whereas Finland pioneered the use of environmental taxes, adopting the world's first carbon dioxide tax in 1990, Austria has been a slower developer as regards MBIs. France, meanwhile, pioneered the use of certain types of VAs and MBIs as early as the 1970s, but these tools have only recently been extensively adopted across French environmental policy. The United Kingdom could be placed in a middle position as far as its environmental reputation is concerned, although it began to experiment enthusiastically with NEPIs in the 1990s. Finally, Ireland is often characterised as an environmental

---

[11] Jordan, A. J., *The Europeanisation of British environmental policy: a departmental perspective*, Basingstoke (Palgrave) 2002; Wurzel, R. K. W., *Environmental policy-making in Britain, Germany and the European Union: the Europeanisation of air and water pollution control*, Manchester (Manchester University Press) 2002; Zito, A. R., *Creating environmental policy in the European Union*, Basingstoke (Macmillan/Palgrave) 2000; see also Ludwig Krämer, Chapter 13.

[12] Jordan, A. J., Wurzel, R. K. W. and A. R. Zito, 'European governance and the transfer of 'new' environmental policy instruments', *Public Administration*, 81(3) (2003), pp. 555–574; Jordan, Wurzel, and Zito, *New instruments*, op. cit.

[13] The information on Finland, France, and Ireland is drawn from Jordan, Wurzel, and Zito, *New instruments*, op. cit.

[14] Liefferink, D. and Andersen, M., Strategies of the 'Green' Member States in EU Environmental Policy-Making, *J. European Public Policy*, 5(2) (1998), pp. 254–70.

[15] Héritier, A., Knill, C., and Mingers, S., *Ringing the changes in Europe: regulatory competition and the redefinition of the state, Britain, France and Germany*, Berlin (de Gruyter) 1996.

laggard state and even today, the extent of innovation with NEPIs has been very limited.

II. What are 'new' environmental policy instruments?

On a very general level, policy instruments are the 'myriad techniques at the disposal of governments to implement their policy objectives'.[16] There is no universally accepted definition of NEPIs, although the following four-fold distinction is widely accepted in the literature: (1) MBIs, (2) VAs, (3) informational devices, and (4) traditional regulation.[17]

1. Market-based instruments

A very broad definition of MBIs is that they are instruments that 'affect estimates of costs of alternative actions open to economic agents'.[18] The total number of MBIs used in OECD countries has grown steadily since the early 1970s, as has the range which now extends from subsidies through to emission charges and tradable permits.[19] The OECD distinguishes between four main types of MBI: taxes (including charges and levies); subsidies; tradable emission permits; and deposit refund schemes.[20] Charges and taxes are already widely used in Northern Europe, but tradable permit schemes are still relatively novel in most OECD countries outside the USA, where they first originated.

2. Voluntary agreements

The first VAs appeared in Japan in the 1960s and then later in France.[21] There is, however, no commonly agreed definition of what they are. The EEA defines VAs as 'covering only those commitments undertaken by firms and sector associations, which are the result of *negotiations* with public authorities and/or explicitly recognised by the authorities' (emphasis added),[22] but the EU Commission adopts a much more inclusive definition: 'agreements between industry and public authorities on the achievement of environmental objectives'.[23] The

---

[16] Howlett, M., Policy instruments, policy styles and policy implementation, *Policy Studies J.* 19(2) (1991), pp. 1–21, at 2.
[17] For more details see Jordan, Wurzel, and Zito, *New instruments*, op. cit.
[18] OECD (1994), op. cit. p. 17.
[19] OECD, *Evaluating economic instruments*, Paris (OECD) 1998.
[20] Ibid., pp. 7–9.
[21] Jordan, Wurzel, and Zito, *New instruments*, op. cit.   [22] EEA (1997), op. cit. p. 11.
[23] CEC, *Communication from the Commission on environmental agreements*, COM (96) 561 final, Brussels (CEC) 1996, p. 5.

OECD[24] also subscribes to this broader definition: 'voluntary commitments of the industry undertaken in order to pursue actions leading to the improvement of the environment'.

Börkey and Lévèque have helpfully provided a typology which differentiates between three different subtypes: unilateral commitments, public voluntary schemes, and negotiated agreements.[25] *Unilateral commitments* consist of environmental improvement programmes instigated by individual companies or by industry associations. Strictly speaking these are not really instruments of government, because they do not involve the state; they are instruments of governance because they offer industry a means to communicate its environmental commitment to the public. *Public voluntary schemes* (PVS) are established by public bodies, which define certain performance criteria and other conditions of membership. Individual companies are free to decide whether or not to join, although the scheme defines the criteria that have to be met. Most PVSs would qualify as an instrument of governance, although they still involve a great deal of government involvement in their design, adoption, and monitoring. Finally, *negotiated agreements* are more formal 'contracts' between industry and public authorities aimed at addressing particular environmental problems. They may be legally binding such as the Dutch 'covenants'. However, in some countries (such as Austria and Germany), VAs cannot be legally binding for constitutional reasons. Usually, their content is negotiated between industry and public bodies. Consequently, they are much closer to the government end of the government-governance spectrum than the other two subtypes. The OECD has put forward a similar typology which adds 'private agreements between polluters and pollutees' as a fourth category.[26]

3. Eco-labels

Eco-labels are relatively 'soft' policy instruments in comparison to regulation and MBIs (such as tradable permits and eco-taxes). They mainly rely on moral suasion by providing consumers with standardised information about the environmental impact of purchasing particular products and services.[27] The assumption is that this information will allow more informed comparisons to

---

[24] OECD, *Voluntary approaches for environmental policy*, Paris (OECD) 1999, p. 4.
[25] Börkey, P. and Lévèque, F., *Voluntary approaches for environmental protection in the EU*, Paris (OECD) 1998.
[26] OECD, *Voluntary approaches for environmental policy: effectiveness, efficiency and usage in policy mixes*, Paris (OECD) 2003.
[27] Jordan, A. J., Wurzel, R. K. W., Zito, A. R. and Brückner, L., Consumer responsibility-taking and national eco-labelling schemes in Europe, in Micheletti, M., Follesdal, A., and Stolle, D. (eds.), *Politics, products and markets: exploring political consumerism, past and present*, New Brunswick (Transaction Publishers) 2003, pp. 161–80.

Table 19.1 *The distribution of NEPIs by country, c. 2000*

	Eco-taxes	Tradable permits	Voluntary agreements	Eco-labels	Regulation
Austria	Medium	Low	Medium	Medium	Still dominant
Finland	High	Low	Medium	High	Still significant
France	Medium	Low	Low	Medium	Still dominant
Germany	Medium	Low	High	High	Still dominant
Ireland	Low	Low	Low	Low	Still dominant
Netherlands	High	Medium/high	High	Low	Still significant
United Kingdom	Medium	High	Low	Low	Still significant
EU	Low	Low/medium	Low	Low/medium	Still dominant

be made and, ultimately, encourage consumers to make more environmentally sustainable purchasing decisions in a similar manner as traditional regulatory standards. Businesses might then have a strong incentive to apply for an eco-label to avoid being competitively disadvantaged. However, eco-label schemes are less effective at changing producer behaviour in markets which are characterised by a low degree of environmental awareness, although they may help to raise public awareness.

III. Patterns of NEPI use

Table 19.1 provides a summary of the distribution of NEPIs across the eight countries and the EU. Rather than populate the cells with numbers,[28] we put forward a simple weighting to allow the reader to make comparisons between different instrument types.[29] Please note that the descriptors used offer a general assessment of NEPI use within each country in relation to the others in the study, rather than to some absolute baseline.

Two things are apparent. The first is that the diversity of instruments used has grown significantly since 1970. Thirty years ago, only a small number of countries had adopted what are now classified as NEPIs. Today, even the least innovative and environmentally ambitious countries (in our sample, Ireland) have a number of fully functioning NEPIs in place.

---

[28] This is actually not terribly meaningful for our purposes, as countries collect incomparable data based on competing definitions of the same instrument. Simple, quantitative measures may therefore obscure more than they reveal (e.g., with eco-labels, does one count the number of labels awarded or the total number of products/service groups within a particular scheme?), hence our more disaggregated, qualitative approach.

[29] For detailed data see Jordan, Wurzel, and Zito, *New instruments*, op. cit.

Secondly, although NEPIs are more popular and more widely used, they are much more popular in some countries (e.g. the Netherlands, Germany, and Finland) than others (e.g. Ireland). Significantly, even the most enthusiastic users of NEPIs have so far chosen to shun certain types of instruments. For instance, there are few VAs in Finland, the Netherlands was late in adopting a national eco-label scheme, and, prior to the EU-wide emissions trading system, tradable permits were not a feature of the German policy instrument mix. By contrast, some countries are enthusiastic about particular NEPIs (e.g. tradable permits in the United Kingdom) but fairly ambivalent about the rest. Moreover, as will be shown below, the same NEPI may be used in different ways across a range of countries.

Therefore, just as there were enduring differences in the way environmental regulation was applied in the past, there are differences in the way NEPIs are utilised today. The fact that different state actors show marked preferences for certain types of NEPIs has implications for the EU's involvement in shaping instrument choices, both nationally and at the EU level. Crucially, in order for the EU to adopt a new instrument, agreement must be reached amongst states as to whether it constitutes the most appropriate mechanism for dealing with a particular environmental problem. We shall show that securing this common agreement is difficult to achieve on the supranational level.

1. Market-based instruments

Japan adopted one of the first eco-taxes (on sulphur dioxide emissions) in 1974. The Nordic countries (such as Finland), the Netherlands, and France followed soon after with charges on water and air pollution. Germany adopted a wastewater levy in the mid-1970s, but this was not fully implemented until the early 1980s. The United Kingdom did not initiate national environmental taxes until the early to mid-1990s.[30] More recently, the United Kingdom has begun to pioneer the use of various highly innovative MBIs including waste taxes and (drawing upon US experience) tradable permits.[31] However, Ireland has barely started to adopt MBIs.

In general, though, the 'followers' are now beginning to catch up with the pioneers as MBIs are more widely applied across Europe.[32] However, the gap between the wealthier and the poorer European countries persists and, on some

---

[30] Jordan (2002), op. cit.; OECD, *Environmental taxes in OECD countries*, Paris (OECD) 1995.

[31] Wurzel, R. K. W., Varma, A., Jordan, A., and Zito A. R., Das britische Emissionshandelssystem: Design und erste Unternehmenserfahrungen, *Umweltwirtschaftsforum* 3 (2003), pp. 9–14.

[32] EEA, *Environmental taxes: recent developments in tools for integration and sustainable development*, Copenhagen (EEA) 2000.

criteria, may even be growing.[33] Thus, the pioneers have now moved on to more sophisticated ecological tax reforms (e.g. Germany), whereas the followers have still not made much progress with first generation MBIs such as simple effluent taxes and user charges.

The array of MBIs used has also evolved. In the 1970s, cost recovery charges dominated, but even at this relatively early stage in the evolution of modern environmental policy, environmentally beneficial subsidies were being used in countries as diverse as Austria, Germany, Finland, France, and the Netherlands.[34] Throughout the 1980s, they were joined by user charges and incentive taxes. Incentive taxes (such as lower tax rates for cars with catalytic converters and unleaded petrol) are particularly widely used in Austria, Finland, Germany, and the Netherlands.

In the 1990s, policy-makers began to experiment with 'second generation' approaches involving hypothecation (i.e. earmarking a certain portion of the revenue stream for particular (often environmentally beneficial) forms of spending).[35] In our sample of seven countries, Austria (landfill taxes), Finland (e.g. the oil waste levy), Germany (e.g. duty on mineral oils), and the United Kingdom (e.g. the landfill tax) formally 'earmark' the revenue from environmental taxes to environmental or other 'good' causes.

Environmental tax reform is the most advanced form of MBI currently deployed among the eight countries. Here again, there are clear leaders (the Netherlands, Finland, Germany, and the United Kingdom all adopted significant programmes in the late 1990s) and followers (Austria and especially Ireland). The Netherlands has moved towards a sophisticated mix of a wide range of policy instruments, while Germany has relied on a narrower mix. Importantly, there are still no eco-taxes at the EU level. Several states (initially the United Kingdom and more recently Spain) have consistently blocked the Commission's ability to innovate in this area. Consequently, the Commission is forced to rely heavily on regulation.

Finally, tradable permits were originally developed by the USA, but they are still relatively uncommon in Europe. On the insistence of the USA, tradable permits were included into the Kyoto climate change Protocol as a means of achieving climate change gas reduction. In our sample, only the United Kingdom[36] and the Netherlands have explored national tradable permit schemes prior to the EU Commission's proposal.[37] In the 1990s, the German government

---

[33] CEC (2000), op. cit.; Weale, A., Pridham, G., Cini, M., Konstadadkopulos, D. Porter, M., and Flynn, B., *Environmental governance in Europe: an even closer ecological union?*, Oxford (Oxford University Press) 2000.

[34] OECD, *Voluntary approaches*, op. cit. p. 5.

[35] CEC (2000), op. cit. p. 16.   [36] Wurzel, Varma, Jordan, and Zito, op. cit.

[37] CEC, Proposal for a Directive of the European Parliament and Council establishing a scheme for greenhouse gas emissions trading within the Community and amending Council Directive 96/61/EC, COM(2001) 581 final, 2001/0245, Brussels (CEC) 2001.

failed to persuade industry to take part in national pilot schemes.[38] Austria also edged towards the adoption of a national tradable permit pilot scheme when it became clear that it would have difficulties in fulfilling its Kyoto climate change commitments through VAs, eco-taxes, and traditional regulation.[39]

The uptake of tradable permitting recently gained a huge boost when the EU adopted a Commission proposal for an EU-wide emissions trading scheme, which became operational in 2005. By using this tool, the European Commission has been able to circumvent the legal restrictions on the adoption of eco-taxes at the EU level and gain a tighter grip on EU greenhouse gas emissions. The EU's scheme has since pushed innovation at the Member State level. Thus, several EU Member States (e.g. Germany) which were initially opposed to tradable permits, have now accepted them. National efforts to establish emissions trading permits in Austria were strongly driven by the EU Commission's proposal. France and Ireland remained circumspect about tradable permits for even longer but have since responded constructively to the proposed EU-wide scheme.

2. Voluntary agreements

The overall popularity of VAs has also grown significantly in all seven countries since the 1970s despite the fact that serious concerns have been raised about their effectiveness.[40] Most VAs are non-binding and voluntary, but some states are now experimenting with more formal and binding approaches. Overall, the most popular type of VA within the EU fifteen is the negotiated agreement.[41] Every EU state has adopted some form of VA, but the majority are to be found in the Netherlands and Germany, which together account for well over two-thirds of the VAs surveyed.[42] By 2002, the Netherlands (>100) and Germany (>130) alone had together more than 230 VAs in place.[43]

As with MBIs, the use of VAs varies significantly across Member States. In simple quantitative terms, the differences are quite stark. In 1996, the European Commission[44] reported the following distribution of VAs: Austria (25); Belgium (14), Denmark (16), Germany (80); Spain (6); Greece (0); Ireland (1);

---

[38] Wurzel, R. K. W., Jordan, A., Zito, A. R., and Brückner, L., From high regulatory state to social and ecological market economy? 'New' environmental policy instruments in Germany, in Jordan, A., Wurzel, R. K. W., and Zito, A. (eds.), *'New' instruments of environmental governance: national experiences and prospects*, London (Frank Cass) 2003, pp. 51–72.

[39] Wurzel, R. K. W., Brückner, L., Jordan, A., and Zito, A. R., Struggling to leave behind a highly regulatory past? 'New' environmental policy instruments in Austria, in Jordan, Wurzel, and Zito, op. cit. pp. 51–72.

[40] OECD (2003), op. cit.

[41] OECD, *Voluntary approaches*, op. cit.   [42] CEC (1996), op. cit.; EEA (1997), op. cit.

[43] Jordan, Wurzel, Zito (2003), op. cit.   [44] CEC (1996), op. cit.

Italy (8); Luxembourg (5); Netherlands (>100); Portugal (10); Sweden (13); the United Kingdom (c.10). The pattern of leaders and followers is therefore also apparent with respect to VAs: in this case Germany, France, and the Netherlands pioneered their use, with the rest following.

More interestingly, the intrinsic nature of the VAs also varies significantly across the seven countries. Thus, in the Netherlands, VAs supplement regulation rather than being an alternative to it; most of the recent Dutch VAs are legally binding contracts or 'covenants'.[45] In Germany, all VAs are non-binding, but they are often negotiated 'in the shadow of the law' and put forward by industry as a means of preempting regulation. Moreover, the Dutch covenants are negotiated within a fairly formalised negotiation process (between industrial and governmental actors) and stipulate clear monitoring requirements. German VAs, on the other hand, are arrived at in a much more informal or even ad hoc manner. They rarely put forward monitoring requirements, although there are a few notable exceptions (such the most recent climate change VA). Austria's VAs are all non-binding, while in France and Ireland about half the VAs are binding. VAs are not very common in the United Kingdom and those that do exist tend to be non-binding and very flexible.

The uptake of VAs at the EU level has remained low. By 2003, only twelve EU-wide environmental VAs have been adopted despite the EU Commission's continuing attempts to increase their uptake.[46] The low uptake on the EU level can be explained by transparency and legitimacy concerns about this NEPI which is adopted outside the formal decision-making procedures and thus fails to grant the European Parliament (or societal stakeholders) a say. Moreover, there are still unresolved questions regarding free-riders who try to gain a competitive advantage vis-à-vis rival firms by failing correctly to implement VAs.

3. Eco-labels

Germany adopted the world's first national eco-label scheme in 1978. Austria (1991), France (1992), and the Netherlands (1992) have all adopted national eco-label schemes. Finland has been actively participating in the Nordic Swan which is a multinational eco-label scheme that was adopted by the Nordic Council countries in 1989. Ireland and the United Kingdom have relied only on the EU eco-label. However, the EU eco-label scheme suffered from a cumbersome and non-transparent decision-making process and competition with Member State eco-label schemes. It has achieved only a low degree of producer acceptability and consumer recognition. By 2000, only forty-one EU eco-labels were

---

[45] Mol, A, Lauber, V., and Liefferink, D., *The voluntary approach to environmental policy*, Oxford (Oxford University Press) 2000.

[46] CEC, Communication from the Commission: Environmental agreements at Community level within the framework of the action plan on the simplification and improvement of the regulatory environment, COM(2002) 412 final, 17 July 2002, Brussels (CEC) 2002.

awarded (for fifteen EU Member States) compared to almost 4,000 national eco-labels under the German Blue Angel scheme. In 2000, a revision took place of the EU's eco-label scheme. It brought about some improvements in terms of stringency of the criteria and transparency of the decision-making process. However, the EU eco-label scheme's acceptance and its uptake have remained low.[47]

During the early 1990s, a rapid diffusion of eco-label schemes took place around the globe.[48] However, not all of them turned into successful eco-label schemes. The Austrian, French, and Dutch national eco-labels all suffer from a low take-up. And some countries never adopted a national eco-label scheme (Ireland and the United Kingdom). In 1994, a Global Eco-labelling Network (GEN) was set up.[49] Its aim is to promote and improve eco-labelling around the globe. By the end of 2001, twenty-six national and multinational eco-labelling organisations were members of GEN. However, GEN has remained a loose network amongst national and supranational eco-label schemes. It failed to influence significantly any of the successful (European) schemes.

The German Blue Angel acted as a catalyst but the followers did not simply copy it. Thus, the Austrian, Dutch, French, and the Nordic White Swan ecolabels put more emphasis on lifecycle analysis. Importantly, certain (national/regional) environmental *and* economic preferences are reflected in the various (national/regional) eco-label schemes. For example, Austria pioneered an eco-label for tourism, the Netherlands were first to extend the national eco-label scheme to the food sector and flours, and Finland regards forest certification as an important issue.

4. Regulation

Finally, amid all the discussion about the uptake and diffusion of NEPIs, it is easy to forget that regulation has not gone away even in leader states such as the Netherlands, Germany, and Finland. There has been no wholesale switch to NEPIs. In fact, NEPIs tend to be reserved for quite specific uses such as 'filling in the cracks' not covered by regulation or dealing with emerging issues such as climate change. There are a number of reasons for this. First, regulation often serves a supporting function for NEPIs, for example, regulations are often used to implement NEPIs, set the rules for their operation, and penalise defectors. Secondly, there is still strong domestic political support for continuing to use

---

[47] Jordan, Wurzel, Zito, Brückner, op. cit.
[48] Ibid.; Kern, K., Kissling-Näf, I., Landmann, U., and Mauch, C., Ecolabelling and forest certification as new environmental policy instruments: factors which impede and support diffusion, paper presented for the ECPR Workshop on the Politics of New Environmental Policy Instruments in Grenoble, 2001.
[49] Jordan, Wurzel, Zito, Brückner, op. cit.

regulation in countries (such as Austria, Finland, and Germany) that have relied heavily on it in the past.

Thirdly, regulation remains the main instrument of EU environmental policy, whereas as MBIs, VAs, and eco-labels have been used only very sparingly at the EU level. Apart from transparency and legitimacy issues, VAs are difficult to negotiate across borders especially when well established and large industry associations are absent (i.e. it is significant that the first EU VAs target the chemical and car industries and not farming or retailing). That said, in many countries the nature of regulation is changing into a more 'light handed' form. It is also being used less as a mainstay of policy and more as a 'support' for other, sometimes newer, tools. In the United Kingdom, the domestic integrated pollution control regime (i.e. regulation) shares many similarities with what continental states usually refer to as 'negotiated agreements underpinned by the law' (e.g. the Netherlands).

IV. The EU's role in instrument selection

Having sketched out the broad patterns of use in the different jurisdictions, we now turn to look at the EU's involvement. In general terms, the EU can fulfil a number of roles in relation to diffusion (i.e. horizontally between states) and transfer (i.e. vertically between the EU and the states). It can function as (1) a neutral arena for lesson drawing and diffusion; (2) a facilitating arena for horizontal policy instrument transfer; (3) a harmonisation arena for approximating policies and tools; (4) a competitive arena for regulatory competition between different tools; and (5) an independent, entrepreneurial actor for novel policy tools. By identifying and assessing the EU's different roles in facilitating and diffusing NEPIs, we should learn more about the possible spread of these 'new' tools of governance around the globe.

The neutral role (1) assumes that Member State policy instrument repertoires converge autonomously, without the EU's involvement. In scenarios 2, 3, and 4, the EU arena creates strong endogenous incentives for Member States to converge, while the fifth suggests a more 'top-down dynamic' where the EU plays a stronger entrepreneurial (or forcing) role in getting states to adopt NEPIs. Importantly, the different roles are not necessarily mutually exclusive.

1. The EU as a neutral arena for lesson drawing and diffusion

This scenario expects that EU Member States with similar policy problems and resources, as well as geographic proximity, will seek to emulate key aspects of another country's policy which are seen to be successful.[50] Dolowitz and Marsh

---

[50] Bennett, C., What is policy convergence and what causes it?, *British J. Political Science* 21 (1991), pp. 215–233.

use Rose's notion of 'lesson drawing' to distinguish voluntary policy transfer.[51] Here, frequent contact between Member State officials occurs, in part, due to the demands of the EU policy process. Equally, Member State officials may perceive the same policy threat which may lead them to consider emulation. In this scenario, policy instrument innovation within and between Member States may occur without a substantive contribution from the EU. For example, prior to the EU Commission's proposal for a Directive on emission trading, very few Member States had experience with tradable permits. Those that did (i.e. the Netherlands and the United Kingdom) drew lessons from existing schemes outside Europe (namely in the USA).[52] Similarly, as was mentioned above, the German eco-label scheme acted as a model for other countries without any real EU involvement.

In order to be sure that this scenario provides an accurate reflection of reality, we need to show that a NEPI was in use in one particular place/time and that other actors in different localities and at different points in time were aware of it, gathered information, and then adopted *and* implemented something very similar. There is an extensive literature on policy diffusion. Lesson drawing and horizontal diffusion can undoubtedly act as an important factor for the uptake of 'new' policies and/or tools. However, the fact that countries adopt a similar policy and/or policy tool, says little about how it is used in practice. We noted above the tendency for the same instrument to be defined and used in different ways across the EU.[53] To put it differently, the same type of NEPI may take on very different forms and functions in different national and/or supranational contexts. The above-mentioned example of VAs in the Netherlands and Germany are a good example of this.

2. The EU as a facilitating arena for horizontal policy instrument transfer

This scenario acknowledges that the complex web of actors and processes that surround EU policy-making create a breeding ground for policy networks (i.e. groups of scientists, experts, and officials) and epistemic communities. The EU creates the opportunity for Member States to showcase their approach to others and possibly to define the larger, regional agenda. The Dutch Environmental Policy Plan and the EU's Fifth and Sixth Environmental Action Programmes

---

[51] Dolowitz, D. and Marsh, D., Who learns from whom?, *Political Studies* XLN (1996), pp. 343–357.

[52] Zapfel, P. and Vainio, M., Pathways to European greenhouse gas emission trading: history and misconceptions, paper presented at the CATEP Workshop in Venice, 3–4 December 2001.

[53] See also Jordan, A. J., Wurzel, R. K. W., and Zito, A. R., European governance and the transfer of 'new' environmental policy instruments, *Public Administration*, 81(3) (2003), pp. 555–574.

(EAPs) all emphasised the need for a wider use of non-regulatory instruments and MBIs such as eco-taxes. However, the EU was unable to adopt an EU-wide eco-tax (i.e. the carbon dioxide/energy tax) due to the unanimity requirement (see above). A group of like-minded countries (including Austria, Finland, Germany, and the Netherlands) therefore met several times in the 1990s to discuss how national eco-taxes could be used without damaging the economic competitiveness. Horizontal (or inter Member State) policy instrument transfer may therefore be the result of the EU's inability to adopt a common NEPI (e.g. an eco-tax). It may also be indirectly 'forced' by the EU's decision to adopt ambitious policy goals. For example, because the Packaging Waste Directive legislation leaves unspecified the precise implementing policy instrument to be used, it has encouraged several Member States to adopt NEPIs such as VAs and (in the case of the United Kingdom) tradable permitting systems.

3. The EU as a harmonisation arena for approximating policies and policy tools

Bennett notes that convergence may be driven by the harmonisation of national policies within supranational organisations and regimes (e.g. the WTO).[54] This scenario includes EU measures taken to protect the Single European Market (SEM) which constitutes a vital goal for the EU.[55] Much of the EU's early environmental legislation (e.g. on car emission regulation) was justified by the need both to protect the environment *and* to avoid barriers of trade and distortions in competition. Importantly, legally binding legislation was, for a long time, considered to be the only effective (although not necessarily the most efficient) policy tool for dealing with pressing environmental problems while ensuring the free movement of goods, services, capital, and people within the SEM. Alternative policy tools (such as MBIs) were considered only after it was recognised that regulation would eventually produce diminishing marginal benefits at a time of increasing global economic competition. It could therefore be argued that, paradoxically, the SEM triggered the adoption of illiberal regulatory policy instruments, although it was informed by a (neo-)liberal market philosophy.[56]

4. The EU as an arena for regulatory competition between different policy tools

This fourth category recognises that the EU creates the conditions under which different Member States have a strong incentive to compete for economic advantage, or at least minimise regulatory adjustment costs. Because the EU integration process has led to a significant adjustment of national environmental policies and standards, Member States have a clear incentive to ensure that

---

[54] Bennett, op. cit.   [55] See also Ludwig Krämer, Chapter 13.   [56] Weale *et al.*, op. cit.

their national policies stay 'ahead of the EU game'.[57] If individual states have imposed regulations with significant costs on industry, the national government also may seek to ensure that other Member States are forced to impose similar legislation.[58] States that have more elaborate regulatory frameworks than the norm will be strongly interested in trying to shape the EU agenda according to their own regulatory patterns. Member States wish to avoid endangering the competitive position of their industries. Until recently, most Member States relied heavily on regulation as the main policy tool for tackling environmental problems on the national level. It is therefore unsurprising that Member States also pushed for common environmental regulation on the EU level, although some Member States (e.g. Austria, Finland, Germany, and the Netherlands) would have liked to see the adoption of EU-wide eco-taxes. Britain, which for long was opposed to EU-wide eco-taxes on sovereignty grounds, was, however, strongly motivated to develop a working national emissions trading system as a kind of model for the EU.[59]

5. The EU as an entrepreneur of novel policy tools

This last category recognises the substantial independent effect that EU actors can have on affecting Member State policies in such a way as to make them converge over time.[60] Most attention is often paid to the activities of the Commission as it seeks to expand the influence of the EU by looking for new policy initiatives. In terms of NEPIs, the Commission's past commitment to a carbon-dioxide/energy tax and its current desire to harmonise energy taxation, suggest a combination of motives, such as to expand the leadership position of the EU and to increase influence on key environmental and economic issues involving taxation.[61] As Jordan notes, the Commission has been highly successful in operating at the international level to develop policies that feed back into, and thereby strengthen, EU regulation as part of a complex multilevel game.[62] However, its legal competence to adopt NEPIs remains weak. Significantly, tradable permits are arguably the only type of NEPI which the Commission has successfully added to the EU's agenda against the wishes of most Member States.

---

[57] Héritier et al., op. cit.
[58] Ibid.   [59] Wurzel, Varma, Jordan, Zito, op. cit.
[60] Jordan, A. J., The Europeanisation of national government and policy: a departmental perspective, *British J. Political Science* 33(2) (2003), pp. 261–282; Jordan, A. J., Liefferink, D., and Fairbrass, J., The Europeanization of national environmental policy: a comparative analysis, in Barry, J., Baxter, B., and Dunphy, R. (eds.), *Europe, globalisation and sustainable development*, London (Routledge) 2004; see also Ludwig Krämer, Chapter 13.
[61] Zito, A. R., *Creating environmental policy in the European Union*, Basingstoke (Macmillan/Palgrave) 2000.
[62] Jordan, A. J., The construction of a multilevel environmental governance system, *Environment and Planning C: Government and Policy* 17 (1999), pp. 1–17.

V. The EU's role in shaping the pattern of NEPI use

Having explored the potential roles that the EU could play, we now take each instrument in turn, and try to establish precisely how it acted as well as search for underlying patterns and explanations.

1. Eco-taxes

The EU (and the OECD) have certainly stimulated the placement of eco-taxes on the national political agendas in several Member States. Thus, in many countries elements of the 'double dividend' argument (i.e. that eco-taxes can be beneficial for environmental *and* economic reasons) were factored into domestic thinking starting in the late 1980s, although the impact on national instrument choices was sometimes quite limited, e.g. the United Kingdom and France. Nevertheless, the overall development of eco-taxes within the EU suggests that most of their adoption was mainly due to domestic reasons (e.g. the need to raise additional revenue) and shaped decisively by the national context, notably as occurred in the Netherlands, France, and Germany (i.e. Roles 1 and 2). This may be partly due to the fact that the EU has failed (until very recently) even to harmonise the minimum level of national eco-taxes, let alone adopt an EU-wide carbon dioxide/energy tax. However, the EU Commission has played an important (albeit more 'negative') role in ensuring that national eco-tax adoption is in accordance with EU Treaty provisions such as the state aid rules (Role 3). For example, in 1999 the introduction of the German eco-tax reform had to be postponed by three months after the Commission raised serious concerns about generous tax exemptions for industrial high energy users.

2. Voluntary agreements

The EU Commission has made great efforts to create EU-wide VAs.[63] However, by 2003 there were only twelve EU-wide environmental VAs, although this type of NEPI has been widely used in Germany and the Netherlands (see above). The German and especially the Dutch VAs influenced the EU Commission's thinking but they did not trigger the widespread adoption of VAs on the EU level. In the Member States, consideration of this instrument tended to follow long established patterns of institutional and state–society relationships. Thus, the United Kingdom's limited number of VAs largely take the form of the traditional 'gentleman's agreement'. In Germany, VAs are often adopted 'in the shadow of the law' while in the Netherlands, legally binding covenants are seen as a useful supplement to traditional regulation.

---

[63] CEC (1996), op. cit.; CEC (2002), op. cit.

For VAs, therefore, Roles 1 and 2 appear to dominate. Serious concerns about the legitimacy (i.e. VAs are adopted outside the formal Treaty-based decision-making procedures). Thus far, treaty-based decision-making procedures), effectiveness (e.g. free-riders cannot be 'forced' to comply and may gain a competitive advantage), and efficiency concerns have prevented a more widespread adoption of VAs at the EU level. The EU has no harmonisation powers (Role 3) and its entrepreneurial role (Role 5) has been very limited largely due to a lack of Treaty competences. There has also been little competition between national VAs (Role 4), although Germany has recently demanded that voluntary industry commitments undertaken at the national level to reduce climate change gases be taken into account within the EU emissions trading scheme.

3. Eco-labels

The story of the eco-label schemes demonstrates a clear aspect of policy learning about the pioneering German system. Austria especially, but the Netherlands as well, looked to the German Blue Angel scheme (the Dutch also paying attention to the EU scheme) before setting up their national schemes, which however differed from the German scheme, focusing more on lifecycle analysis and on fitting the national domestic context (i.e. they took into account both national environmental and economic priorities, such as tourism in Austria's case and food production in the Dutch case). Indeed, the German experience provided almost a 'negative learning model' in the sense that the followers (Austria and the Netherlands) sought to improve on the functioning of the German system. Equally, the Dutch sought to avoid duplicating the European scheme while providing stricter criteria. Therefore, Roles 1 and 2 appear to have most shaped the adoption of this particular instrument. However, since the adoption of the EU eco-label, the EU has increasingly taken on Role 5 to push the practice (albeit slowly) into reluctant states such as Ireland and the United Kingdom. Importantly, apart from the Nordic Swan, none of the other eco-label schemes discussed in this chapter have secured anything like the wide acceptance amongst stakeholders as the German scheme.

4. Tradable permits

It is tradable permits where the clearest national convergence around an instrument has occurred. Lesson drawing (and to a very limited degree also policy instrument transfer) has occurred here, as many Member States scrutinised closely the US models (i.e. Roles 1 and 2). Nevertheless, the national pilot projects which the Netherlands and especially the United Kingdom have developed in the prelude to the EU scheme (i.e. Role 4) have all had strong national characteristics. For example, the United Kingdom's national emissions trading scheme is closely intertwined with the national climate change tax and the domestic climate change agreements which are VAs.[64] But the EU's successful efforts to develop a common emissions trading scheme to meet its climate change targets has decisively defined the future efforts in all of the seven Member States assessed in this chapter. At least in this respect, the Commission has managed to play the part of an external entrepreneur (i.e. Role 5).

VI. Lessons for other states and regions

Generally speaking, NEPIs have not (yet) been used widely on the international level which is still largely dominated by traditional regulatory instruments such as legally binding Treaties and Conventions. However, there are signs that certain types of NEPIs are increasingly considered as possible tools for environmental governance outside the EU and its Member States. What lessons could therefore be drawn from the EU's experience with NEPIs for other states and regions? Could the EU and its Member States act as a realistic model? We again explore these questions by taking each instrument in turn.

1. Market-based instruments

Emissions trading has now been endorsed by the Kyoto Protocol as a possible tool (for certain countries) for achieving climate change reduction targets. The EU's strenuous efforts to set up a functioning EU-wide emissions trading system by 2005 are to a large degree driven by the Kyoto Protocol (although other reasons also play a role, as was explained above). The EU is keen to gain practical experience with this NEPI by having in place a supranational emissions trading system before global trading is scheduled to start in 2008. A well functioning EU-wide emissions trading system would probably lead to a boost of emissions trading in other states and regions. Many EU Member States (and companies) are keen to get involved in global emissions trading. However, the experience from existing national emissions trading schemes (e.g. the United Kingdom) has raised fears that participants may simply trade not in emissions reductions but 'hot air' (i.e. reduction that would have occurred regardless of emissions trading). Consequently, allocations are bought and sold without an overall reduction in total greenhouse gas emissions, which does very little to avert the threat of climate change.[65] But there are indications that emissions trading, which has spread from the USA to Europe, is nonetheless gaining support in other states and regions.[66]

---

[64] Wurzel, Varma, Jordan, Zito, op. cit.
[65] Wurzel, Varma, Jordan, Zito, op. cit.   [66] Zapfel, Vainio, op. cit.

Eco-taxes constitute an important MBI which have been widely used in some (i.e. mainly Northern European) Member States in recent years.[67] However, the EU experience clearly shows that eco-taxes are very difficult to adopt above the national level (i.e. on the supranational or international level). Concerted actions by like-minded European pro-eco-tax countries had little impact on veto actors who blocked EU-wide eco-taxes on sovereignty grounds, although they have helped to spread knowledge about different national eco-tax schemes. International organisations such as the OECD and, although to a lesser degree, NGOs (such as Friends of the Earth and the European Environmental Bureau) and epistemic communities have diffused knowledge about the use of eco-taxes and kept this type of NEPI on the political agenda in many highly developed industrial countries. However, the EU's neutral and facilitating roles (Roles 1 and 2) failed to bring about any real innovation in the use of supranational eco-taxes. The Commission's attempts to act as an entrepreneur (Role 5) also ended in failure.

On one level, the EU should provide a good breeding ground for market-based instruments. After all, its Member States are at a similar level of economic development and share a common cultural and political heritage. They have also established a SEM. But securing political agreement between states on the need for supranational eco-taxes is still beyond the EU. Minimum tax harmonisation between certain groups of states and/or subregions therefore offers a more realistic model for other jurisdictions. Policy learning from other states is likely to be limited due to competitive pressures and ideological differences about eco-taxes.

2. Voluntary agreements

VAs are very popular in the Netherlands and Germany. However, by 2003, the EU had adopted only twelve common environmental VAs. Some transnational companies and trade associations have adopted voluntary environmental codes of conduct. However, these amount only to unilateral statements of intent. The participation in environmental management audit schemes (EMAS) has increased significantly in recent years. The EU's EMAS and the International Standard Organisation's 14001 standard both require companies to audit their environmental impact, establish internal monitoring systems, and where possible reduce negative environmental impacts while providing stakeholders with regular statements. In exchange, companies are granted an official confirmation (or logo). Although participation in both schemes is voluntary, firms are often driven to participate by pressure from their stakeholders, their competitors, or others firms in their supply chain. Policy-makers often encourage participation by easing the regulatory burden (e.g. fewer inspections). This should encourage greater self-responsibility, reduce central government involvement,

---

[67] Jordan, Wurzel, Zito, op. cit.; Weale *et al.*, op. cit.

and encourage better use of scarce resources. Critics, however, claim that the accreditation process is often opaque and overdominated by industry, while the environmental effectiveness of EMAS and ISO 14001 is at best unproven and at worst inferior to that of other instruments.

The EU's EMAS scheme, which was established in 1993, was relaunched in 2001 to make it more compatible with the ISO's scheme that is widely seen as the more lenient scheme.[68] The Commission had become increasingly concerned that European companies were shunning EMAS for the more globally recognised ISO standard. By 2002, the total number of EU registrations under the EMAS scheme was about 3,700, as opposed to nearly 20,000 certifications under ISO 14001. The main lesson to draw from the EU's experience with this instrument is that regionally more stringent NEPIs may be negatively affected (i.e. out-competed) by 'weaker' international standards.

3. Eco-labels

The aim of the GEN, which was set up in 1994, is to promote and improve eco-labelling around the globe. By the end of 2001, twenty-six national and multinational eco-labelling organisations were members of the GEN network. However, although member organisations have learned more about the various national and multinational schemes, there is little evidence that it has facilitated the dissemination of eco-label schemes around the globe. In fact, the global spread of national and multinational eco-label schemes, which are evaluated by independent third parties, has slowed down in recent years. Even the highly successful German Blue Angel scheme has suffered a decline in terms of the number of labelled products and services. These trends are partly the result of the huge proliferation of private self-declaratory eco-label schemes which put forward unverified and sometimes dubious environmental claims that have confused consumers.[69] The EU's experience with this instrument is also that regionally more ambitious schemes may run the risk of being out-competed by 'weaker' industry-led schemes. Moreover, the EU still has difficulties in gaining support for a supranational eco-label scheme from Member States which already had in place well recognised national schemes.

VII. Comparative conclusions

Clearly, the use of NEPIs is most certainly not 'limited' as some have claimed.[70] Far from it: the total number and diversity of NEPIs used in our seven countries has grown significantly, with environmental taxes, VAs, and eco-labels proving

---

[68] Golub, op. cit. p. 18.   [69] Jordan, Wurzel, Zito, Brückner, op. cit.
[70] Lafferty, W. and Meadowcroft, J., (eds.), Concluding perspectives, in Lafferty, W. and Meadowcroft, J. (eds.), *Implementing sustainable development*, Oxford (Oxford University Press) 2000, p. 452.

especially popular. In some countries, the adoption of NEPIs has been stunningly fast, to the extent that NEPIs are now the preferred instrument of new environmental policies in countries as diverse as the United Kingdom, Finland, and Germany. However, there are countries where the expansion of NEPI use is either proceeding much more slowly or barely at all (Ireland). And some other market-based NEPIs (e.g. tradable permits) have only recently been deployed, while some 'old' policy instruments (e.g. subsidies) are discredited.

The common perception that NEPIs are somehow sweeping uniformly across different national environmental protection systems does not, therefore, stand up to empirical testing. Some countries have adopted NEPIs much earlier than the rest. Rather than a broadly synchronous pattern of change, for each instrument it is possible to identify a set of leader states (the Netherlands, Germany, and Finland) and a set of followers (Ireland), with France and the United Kingdom adopting an intermediate position. Importantly, NEPIs are often put to different tasks and even appear to take on a different form in neighbouring countries.

Our analysis reveals that the pattern of NEPI use is, in fact, very highly differentiated both across and within individual countries. There are several aspects to this point. First, huge differences sometimes exist between the way in which instruments are used in different national (or regional) contexts. This strongly suggests that we should not easily assume that instruments from the same subtype (e.g. VAs) are functionally equivalent. On the face of it, there has been very little, if any, harmonisation in this particular aspect of EU environmental policy. One should therefore be sceptical about claims which suggest a widespread transfer of certain types of NEPIs has taken place.

Secondly, regulation often offers an important support function, giving authority to the agency designing and implementing a NEPI, establishing the rules governing its operation, penalising defectors, etc. But the state's involvement also extends way beyond the matter of regulating, to include the day-to-day administration of NEPIs (e.g. negotiating VAs, undertaking economic valuation studies, ensuring fair play, monitoring compliance, and penalising defectors). The total administrative load involved required to develop NEPIs can be surprisingly high. In the United Kingdom, the Environment Ministry devoted seventeen person years to negotiating just forty-two climate change VAs!

Thirdly, it is increasingly the case that policy instrument mixes rather than one single ('new' or 'old') tool of governance are used to tackle particular environmental problems (such as climate change). The future challenge at national, supranational, and global levels is how best to combine these policy instruments mixes in a manner that minimises the conflicts between instruments adopted at different levels of governance. Policy-makers should also remain open to the possibility that a NEPI may be used in different ways in different states and regions.

Fourthly, the EU's influence in shaping the prevailing pattern of NEPI use has been and remains very mixed. The EU has not adopted many VAs of its own, is struggling to develop a popular eco-label scheme, and has failed to generate consensus on the need for EU-wide eco-taxes. A strong entrepreneurial influence on the part of the EU can only really be detected with respect to tradable permits and, to a much lesser degree, eco-labels.

So, what lessons can be drawn from the EU's experience? Most NEPI activity seems to take place at the national level, even though most target and policy framing activity is now undertaken at the EU level. Many analysts concur that the EU has greatly influenced ('Europeanised') Member State environmental policies, but this influence does not appear to extend to the selection and implementation of policy tools, especially 'new' tools such as NEPIs. Why have so few NEPIs been adopted on the EU (and global) level despite widespread demands for more 'non-regulatory' instruments in recent years? One explanation is that even a supranational organisation such as the EU, which has 'quasi-federal' powers and relatively dense institutional rules, is highly constrained in its choice of policy instruments. Normally, policy instrument choices are presented predominantly as technical choices which are largely made on the basis of efficiency and effectiveness criteria.[71] However, although states allow the EU and/or international institutions to set certain environmental targets and deadlines, they are much more reluctant to cede control over instrument selection to higher authorities.

In some cases, the opposition to giving the EU a greater role is simply due to technical (i.e. efficiency and effectiveness) concerns. For example, VAs are difficult to engineer, monitor, and 'enforce' beyond the state level, especially in policy sectors which are characterised by a large number of relatively small firms. Concerns about free-riders are magnified at the supranational and, even more so, at the global level. However, there are also important economic and political impediments which militate against the uptake of certain NEPIs at the supranational and/or global level, as can best be seen in the EU's continuing failure to adopt a carbon dioxide/energy tax.

The other feature of the EU's use of NEPIs is that the overall pattern of use is, for the reasons identified above, highly variable. This is quite puzzling, as the EU is much more socially and economically homogeneous than other regions; it even has an explicit goal to harmonise its policies in relation to environmental protection. Clearly, those advocating the use of NEPIs at a global level will need to tolerate these national differences in use, or find some way to moderate them.

But does it actually matter if states adopt NEPIs in different forms at different times, and deploy them in often highly different ways? In one important sense, no. States adopt common policy objectives at the international level and in

---

[71] Majone, G., Choice among policy instruments for pollution control, *Policy Analysis* 2 (1976), pp. 677–715.

the EU, but, by and large, retain the right to determine the precise means of achieving them. In the EU, this 'right' is expressed in the formal definition of a Directive, the main instrument of EU environmental policy. That said, there are two circumstances in which we might consider the persistence of different national approaches and instruments to be a bad thing. First, if one country adopts a VA with its industry to reduce pollution, it could put it at a competitive disadvantage with similar industries in less heavily regulated neighbouring countries. The Commission has already pointed out that VAs should not interfere with the functioning of the SEM.[72] By their very nature, NEPIs which target products rather than processes are especially important to harmonise. However, the need to protect the operation of the SEM is a broad constraint within which states design and deploy NEPIs. It does not dictate the specific design features of a particular instrument.

Secondly, if different instruments have different environmental outcomes (i.e. some are more effective at tackling problems than others), then some stakeholders will legitimately ask whether the overall effort is fairly distributed. We have not explicitly addressed the question of environmental effectiveness in this chapter, but it is now being actively researched both by academics and international bodies.[73] The emerging consensus is that some instruments work better in some circumstances than others, but this is not the same thing as saying that every state should adopt the same instrument.

[72] CEC (1996), op. cit. p. 14.
[73] OECD (2003), op. cit.; EEA, *Environmental taxes: recent developments in tools for integration and sustainable development*, Copenhagen (EEA) 2000.

20

Financial instruments and cooperation in implementing international agreements for the global environment

CHARLOTTE STRECK

I. Introduction

Over the past thirty years, the effects of global environmental threats have become more and more significant. It also became obvious that the threat to the environment coincides with a development strategy which is based on the consumption of global goods to an extent that brings these resources to the edge of extinction, irreversible pollution, or destruction.[1] In order to avoid further deterioration of the global ecosystems, not only do consumption patterns in the North have to change, but the South needs to be assisted in pursuing a line of development that avoids the destructive pattern of industrialisation adopted in the developed parts of the northern and western hemispheres.

Developing countries are also more vulnerable to global change and are more frequently exposed to the negative impacts of environmental deterioration. They have weaker economies and institutions, limited access to capital and information and therefore less capacity to bear the shock, to respond, or to adapt to global change. Also, poverty reduction and intragenerational equity (as compared to intergenerational equity) are the overriding concerns of developing countries. Even if pollution may be lower in absolute terms in developing countries than in more highly developed ones, mitigation costs are high relative to the ability of developing countries to pay.[2]

The article represents the personal view of the author and should in no way be taken to represent the official view of any institution for which she works or with which she is associated.

[1] See for the debate on global public goods, Kaul, I., Grunberg, I., and Stern, I. (eds.), *Global public goods: international cooperation in the 21st century*, Oxford (Oxford University Press) 1999.

[2] See Bulato, L. and Sands, P., Financial resources and international funding mechanisms for the climate change convention, Center for International Environmental Law, Association of Small Island States (AOSIS) Background Paper No. 3, 1991, p. 2.

The South, by voicing its concerns about equity and the right of development at the UN Conference on Environment and Development (UNCED), held in 1992 in Rio de Janeiro,[3] helped the international community to recognise that the restraints posed by a narrow definition of interest must be loosened to allow for a broader understanding of interdependence and responsibility. Although the expectations of developing countries in Rio, to broaden the debate to press their claim not only for global environmental protection but also for poverty alleviation and promote a much wider form of sustainable development, failed,[4] the summit helped industrialised countries to understand that for developing countries the provision of funds is a condition for their participation in any effort to address global environmental concerns dear to the constituencies of Northern policy-makers.

In order to inveigle countries with lesser economic power into signing environmental conventions, the calls of developing countries for additional financial resources need to be addressed.[5] As industrialised nations from the North must take a major share of responsibility for creating the problem, they should facilitate developing countries' participation in international efforts addressing the problem without sacrificing their aspirations for welfare enhancement for their citizens. The recognition of this need has found its expression in a number of legal principles that govern international environmental action.[6] The polluter pays principle, as well as the innovative principle of *common but differentiated responsibilities* as included in Principle 7 of the Rio Declaration, laid the intellectual and ethical grounds for systems that include financial transfers from the North to the South, thereby helping the developing nations implement environmental policies and projects.[7] The principle of common but differentiated responsibilities is founded on the understanding that effective action based

---

[3] For a description of the confrontation of expectations of the South and the North at the occasion of the UNCED, see Shabecoff, P., *A name for peace: international environmentalism, sustainable development and democracy: a history of the international environmental movement*, Hanover, NH, (University Press of New England) 1996, p. 160.

[4] Jordan, A., Financing the UNCED agenda: the controversy over additionality, *Environment* 36(3) (1994), p. 26.

[5] For a detailed discussion of the concept of 'additionality' in the context of global environmental policy, see Jordan, op. cit. pp. 16–20 and 26–34.

[6] Such principles include the principle of sustainable utilisation of resources (Principle 2), sustainable production and consumption (Principle 8), the right of participation and access to information (Principle 10), the precautionary principle (approach) (Principle 15), or the obligation of prior and timely notification of relevant transboundary impacts (Principle19). The UN Conference on Environment and Development (UNCED) adopted the Rio Declaration on Environment and Development on 14 June 1992, 31 I.L.M. (1992) 874 ('Rio Declaration').

[7] Principle 7 of the Rio Declaration states that 'in view of the different contributions to global environmental degradation, States have common but differentiated responsibilities. Developed countries have acknowledged the responsibility that they bear in the international pursuit of sustainable development in view of the pressures their societies place on the global environment and of the technologies and financial resources they command'.

on environmental regimes has to take into account not only who is responsible for the problem but also the ability of a country to act and its exposure of negative consequences of (non) acting. Based on these principles, it is imperative that the global community makes a commitment to action and that such commitment is embedded in regimes and frameworks that allow their translation into concrete actions with assigned responsibilities. As a result of this new allocation of differentiated responsibilities, the last decade saw the emergence of mechanisms which govern the transfer of funds to the benefit of the global environment.

Today, financial mechanisms form an integral part of multilateral environmental agreements, such as the Montreal Protocol on Substances that Deplete the Ozone Layer,[8] the Convention on Biological Diversity,[9] the Framework Convention on Climate Change[10] and its Kyoto Protocol,[11] and the Stockholm Convention on Persistent Organic Pollutants.[12] This chapter focuses on the financial mechanisms implemented by states mobilising and providing financial means to achieving the objectives of multilateral environmental agreements and the compliance with obligations under such agreements. The chapter commences with a brief description of the funding mechanism established under the Montreal Protocol, the first funding mechanism to aid poorer countries to comply with their obligations under an international treaty. It will then give some background on the establishment and governance structure of the most important financial mechanism for the global environment: the Global Environment Facility (GEF). Thirdly, the chapter will focus on the provisions and innovative tools that involve broader sources of funds and provide for financial transfer in the emerging climate change regime, and compare these mechanisms with such mechanisms as provided for under the Montreal Protocol. The author will finally analyse the opportunities, advantages, and limits of these mechanisms and conclude with an outlook on how these innovative mechanisms could be integrated into the current system of environmental governance.

II. The Montreal Protocol and the Multilateral Fund

The Montreal Protocol, which governs the phase-out of production and consumption of ozone depleting substances, is of particular interest for the analysis

---

[8] 26 I.L.M. (1987) 1550, 16 September 1987 ('Montreal Protocol').
[9] Convention on Biological Diversity of 5 June 1992, 31 I.L.M. (1992) 818 ('Biodiversity Convention').
[10] United Nations Framework Convention on Climate Change, 9 May 1992, 31 I.L.M. (1992) 851 ('Climate Change Convention').
[11] The Kyoto Protocol to the Framework Convention on Climate Change, opened for Signature 16 March 1998, 37 ILM (1998) 22 (entered into force 16 February 2005).
[12] The Stockholm Convention was adopted in Stockholm, Sweden, 22 May 2001 and has not yet entered into force.

of financial mechanisms under multilateral environmental agreements. Many of the key features of the GEF, such as the incremental costs principle and the tripartite agreement between the World Bank,[13] the UN Environment Programme (UNEP), and the United Nations Development Programme (UNDP), were first mentioned during the design of the financial mechanism for the Montreal Protocol.

In 1985, the international community adopted the Vienna Convention for the Protection of the Ozone Layer[14] as the first international treaty expressing concerns about the depletion of the ozone layer. The Convention was followed only two years later by the Montreal Protocol which requires specific abatement measures and establishes phase-out schedules for chlorofluorocarbons (CFCs) and other ozone-depleting substances (ODS).[15] Whereas the negotiations of the Montreal Protocol reflect the recognition by developed countries that ethical considerations (involving the valuation of risk and intergenerational equity) were essential components of the economic analysis, developing countries and the claim for intragenerational equity played a minor role during the negotiations.[16] At the time the instruments were negotiated and adopted, the production and use of ODS by developing countries was negligible, although it was projected to grow substantially.[17] Article 5 of the Montreal Protocol grants developing country parties (Article 5 countries) with an annual consumption of ODS less than 0.3kg per capita, a grace period of ten years[18] before they have to engage in activities that reduce consumption and production of ODS.[19] Following the adoption of the Protocol, industrialised countries expected that the

---

[13] The World Bank is comprised of five associated institutions: the International Bank for Reconstruction and Development (IBRD), the International Development Association (IDA), the International Finance Corporation (IFC), the Multilateral Investment Guarantee Agency (MIGA), and the International Centre for the Settlement of Investment Disputes (ICSID). The 'World Bank' as used in this chapter refers to the IBRD and IDA.

[14] UNEP Doc. IG. 53/5; 26 I.L.M. (1987) 1529, 22 March 1985 ('Vienna Convention').

[15] Since the adoption of the Montreal Protocol, the Convention/Protocol has been mirrored by a number of other regimes. The Biosafety Protocol, for example, has been adopted under the Biodiversity Convention; the Kyoto Protocol under the Climate Change Convention.

[16] With regard to the recognition of the principle of intragenerational equity through the US Administration under President Reagan, see DeCanio, S., Economic analysis, environmental policy, and intergenerational justice in the Reagan administration: the case of the Montreal Protocol, *Int'l Env. Agreements* 3(4) (2003), pp. 299–321.

[17] It was estimated that India and China alone would account for one-third of the world's consumption of chlorofluorocarbons (CFCs) by 2008: Friends of the Earth, *Funding change: developing countries and the Montreal Protocol*, Washington DC (Friends of the Earth) 1990.

[18] This grace period has been renegotiated several times.

[19] Benedick, R. E., *Ozone diplomacy: new directions in safeguarding the planet*, Cambridge Mass. (Harvard University Press) 1991, p. 148 *et seq.* Industrialised nations, with less than 25 per cent of the world's population, which consume an estimated 88 per cent of CFCs; their per capita consumption was more than twenty times higher than that of the developing countries average.

transitional period in the use of CFCs and halons would trigger wide accession to the Treaty by developing countries.[20]

However, reality turned out to be different. The time lag did not provide sufficient incentive to join the Protocol and developing countries showed every sign of remaining outside the Treaty and the risk of potential large-scale non-accession to the Montreal Protocol became obvious. In 1989, only fourteen developing countries had ratified the Protocol, among them only three which accounted for a potentially increasing and high demand for CFCs and halons (Mexico, Nigeria, Venezuela).[21] In order to be willing to join the international effort and assume commitments under the Protocol, developing countries insisted on establishing a mechanism that would ensure industrialised countries made contributions to cover incremental costs of the phase-out and conversion of industries. Even though the Montreal Protocol had a provision for the transfer of technology, it was not binding or sufficiently specific. Instead, countries indicated their wish that the financial mechanism to be created under the auspices of the Protocol be based on four basic concepts:[22]

(1) a discrete multilateral trust fund to be established within UNEP to meet all incremental costs to developing countries of complying with the Protocol;
(2) legally enforceable obligations on industrialised countries to contribute to the fund, based on a distribution formula;
(3) supplemental contributions; and
(4) technology transfer to developing countries.

Whereas donor countries acknowledged the equity concerns, they preferred to channel funds through existing institutions. During the course of the negotiations, however, all parties developed a growing recognition that something new and different was required and gradually even donors began to use the term 'multilateral fund'.[23] There was also a widening agreement that the new structure should draw as much as possible on expertise in existing organisations, such as the World Bank and UNEP.[24] Finally, an agreement was reached and the Second Meeting of the Parties in London concluded in the establishment of the Multilateral Fund to Implement the Montreal Protocol (MLF) as the

---

[20] Another incentive for ratification was created through trade restrictions that allowed the parties to only trade in controlled substances with other member countries.
[21] Benedick, op.cit. p. 151: 'In contrast, virtually, every industrialised nation, large and small, had joined the protocol.'
[22] UNEP, Open-Ended Working Group of the Parties to the Montreal Protocol, First Session of the First Meeting, *Final Report*, UNEP/OzL.Pro.WG.I(1)/3, 25 August 1989, Nairobi, pp. 4, 6, 8, 9.
[23] Benedick, op.cit., p. 156.
[24] The USA initially stated that it would only support a mechanism located within the World Bank drawing on existing World Bank resources, and no additional contributions should be required from donor countries.

interim financial mechanism of the Montreal Protocol.[25] The MLF was established to provide financial and technical cooperation to Article 5 countries and to enable their compliance with the control measures of the Protocol, in addition to financing institutional strengthening and clearing-house functions. UNEP, UNDP, and the World Bank were identified as implementing agencies of the fund,[26] with an invitation to other agencies, in particular regional development banks, to cooperate and assist in carrying out the functions of the financial mechanism.[27] Contributions to the MLF were made voluntarily by all parties who do not act under Article 5 of the Protocol. Although developing countries had pushed unsuccessfully for legally enforceable obligations to contribute to the fund, the agreement on the MLF convinced major developing countries to join the Protocol. The fund was established as a mechanism with an initial size of US$160 million, which was later expanded to US$ 240 million when India and China joined the Protocol.

The MLF was the first fund established to help developing countries meet their obligations under an environmental treaty and therefore became the 'prototype' international funding agreement on the environment.[28] The MLF is an independent body managed by an Executive Committee which reports to the Meeting of the Parties. The Executive Committee consists of fourteen parties, equally split between developing and developed countries; the representation and voting structure within the MLF is aimed at an equitable distribution of powers.[29] The formal decision-making procedure of the Executive Committee involves a voting mechanism based on a double majority, comprising separate simple majorities among North and South.[30]

---

[25] The financial mechanism was established by Article 10 of the Montreal Protocol. The Fourth Meeting of the Parties to the Montreal Protocol (Copenhagen, 1992) confirmed the MLF as a permanent financial mechanism.

[26] The United Nations Industrial Development Organization (UNIDO) was added in October 2002 to the group of implementing agencies.

[27] Revisions to the Montreal Protocol agreed at the Fourth Meeting of the Parties to the Montreal Protocol on Substances that Deplete the Ozone Layer, Annex IV, Appendix IV, Terms of Reference of the Interim Multilateral Fund, B. Roles of the Implementing Agencies, para. 3, UNEP/OzL.Pro/2/3.

[28] Article 10 of the Montreal Protocol.

[29] Revisions to the Montreal Protocol agreed at the Fourth Meeting of the Parties to the Montreal Protocol on Substances to establish the financial mechanisms and the Terms of Reference of the Executive Committee: 'the Executive Committee shall consist of seven Parties from the group of Parties operating under paragraph 1 of Article 5 of the Protocol and seven Parties from the group of Parties not so operating. Each group shall select its Executive Committee members. The members of the Executive Committee shall be formally endorsed by the Meeting of the Parties'. UNEP/OzL.Pro/2/3, Annex IV, Appendix IV.

[30] The formal voting procedure of the Committee has yet to be tested, as to date all decisions of the Committee have been taken by consensus.

Management of the Fund through such a supervising committee has been particularly successful. Although the progress in decision-making by the Executive Committee was slow, it has gained experience over time and today functions as an efficient and independent body in administrating the MLF. The Committee has provided proof several times of its independence and it has shown the willingness to take unpopular decisions that safeguard the integrity of the Treaty. Just to cite two examples: the way the MLF was initially structured, developing countries did not need to forego funding during the period when their production was still increasing.[31] The time lag in Article 5 countries' obligations and the promise of funding created a certain mismatch in incentives to further expand the use and production of ODS while at the same time engaging in conversion projects which would receive funding from the MLF. As a response to this situation, the Committee decided that all plants built after 1995 would be ineligible for funding, whether for technology conversion or plant closure, and no Article 5 country would be allowed to build new plants after December of that year.[32]

Another example of the willingness of the Executive Committee to take decisions relates to the sector plans approved by the Executive Committee in recent years. In this context, funding for new commitments cannot be allocated to a country surpassing the initially calculated amount of funds necessary to finance the sector phase-out for a specific country. This provision effectively limits the opportunities for expansion in the ODS sector for developing countries, unless the countries are willing to finance the incremental costs of the phase-out with their own resources.

The MLF has functioned very efficiently and contributed to making the regime established by the Vienna Convention and the Montreal Protocol a story of success: since its inception, the fund has been replenished five times with contributions totaling US$1.61 billion. Almost all of the 140 developing country member parties have implemented phase-out programmes in their country with the assistance of the fund.[33] Projects under the MLF are prepared by the eligible countries together with the implementing agencies, which administer the funds given on a grant basis for ODS phase-out activities. UNEP implements

---

[31] See for an analysis of the problems related to the granting of a grace period to developing countries, Papasavva, S. and Moomaw, W. R., Adverse implications of the Montreal Protocol grace period for developing countries, *International Environmental Affairs* 9(4) (1997), p. 219.

[32] DeSombre, E. R., The experience of the Montreal Protocol: particularly remarkable, and remarkably particular, *UCLA J. Envt'l L. and Policy* 19 (2000/2001), pp. 49, 72.

[33] Even a successful operation is not free of disappointments though: at the Fifteenth Meeting of the Parties to the Montreal Protocol held in November 2003 in Nairobi, the USA asked for large exemptions of quantities of ozone-depleting substances from control measures (nominations for critical use of methyl bromide and conditions from granting critical use exemptions for methyl bromide).

supporting institutional strengthening programmes, maintains information networks and implements country programmes which describe the consumption of ODS, industry and policy structure in the country, and determines the country's action plan and national strategy for the phase-out of ODS. UNDP, UNIDO, and the World Bank provide funding for investment projects to phase out ODS and technical assistance.

The MLF operations implemented through the World Bank are governed by umbrella agreements concluded between the Bank and Article 5 countries. These innovative agreements provide an overarching legal arrangement in which the Bank and the countries agree to an indicative amount of funding to cover ODS phase-out activities even though specific subprojects have not yet been identified. This allows the Bank to sign only one grant agreement and channel subprojects under the umbrella agreement until the maximum amount of funds has been reached. The Bank has also used market-based instruments, such as an auctioning of grants in Chile in which private beneficiaries bid on confinancing grants for conversion of clean technologies. Another example of increasing the effectivness of MLF funding is the Chiller Replacement Programme in Thailand where MLF funds have been leveraged through concessional lending from revolving funds.

Today, the conversion of the biggest production plants has been concluded and project activities that help countries to fulfil their commitments under the Montreal Protocol are gradually moving from a project approach towards one that implements countries' sector plans. The World Bank, which has traditionally focused on the implementation of large conversion investment projects, currently implements the first series of projects that are based on the Executive Committee's approval of national sector plans to completely phase out the consumption of chlorofluorocarbons (see Figure 20.1). The experience gained by Article 5 countries in developing and implementing sector and national phase-out plans for ODS could have far-reaching impacts, in particular on the implementation of other global and regional environmental agreements, such as the Stockholm Convention on Persistent Organic Pollutants.

The ozone regime illustrates the need to distribute the burden and benefits of environmental protection in an equitable way. It demonstrates how a universally accepted regime can operate effectively in a spirit of trust and cooperation.[34]

---

[34] The compliance mechanism included in Annex III to the London Amendments to the Montreal Protocol further contributes to this spirit of cooperation as it relies primarily on self-reporting and assistance for countries that face justified difficulties in meeting their commitments. The procedure revolves around an autonomous body of the state parties, the Implementation Committee, made up of ten representatives of states elected by the Meeting of the Parties. For further detail, see German Advisory Council on Global Change, *New structures for global environmental policy*, London and Sterling, Va. (Earthscan) 2001, p. 94.

> Under this agreement the IBRD is providing a US$560,000 grant to the Bahamas to assist the Bahamas to phase out the use of ODS within its territory in accordance with the 'Terminal Management Phase-out Plan of The Bahamas'. The Project is divided into two parts. Part A involves providing grants to convert CFCs containing equipment to reduce the consumption of ODS. Grants will occur in the domestic refrigeration, commercial retail food refrigeration, transport refrigeration, commercial fisheries, and mobile air conditioning sectors. Part B involves providing technical assistance and supporting the Bahamas policy framework. This will be done through providing consultants' services, training, and office equipment, and carrying out training programmes and public awareness programmes about the CFCs and the phase-out of ODS.

Figure 20.1 Multilateral Fund for the Implementation of the Montreal Protocol, project example: The Bahamas, Terminal CFC Phase-out Management Plan

The financial mechanism acknowledges that developing countries have, on the one hand, to contribute to the international effort of tackling an environmental problem, but on the other hand, need appropriate assistance and funds to do so. The procedures governing the MLF are thus characterised by a balance struck between donor and recipient positions in the negotiations. Whereas the Meeting of the Parties is the ultimate body governing the financial mechanism, it is represented by an Executive Committee which closely monitors operations and supervises the activities implemented by a set of international organisations. It was also in the context of the Montreal Protocol that developing nations for the first time demanded 'new and additional' resources, a request which has been reiterated in many fora and with regard to all multilateral environmental agreements adopted since.[35] On the other hand, industrialised countries defined the costs that are incremental to the project and related to the global environmental benefit as a determining parameter to calculate the payments developing countries ought to receive to meet their compliance costs.

When the MLF was created, developed countries expressed concern that the newly established fund would create a precedent. In fact, the USA only agreed to the establishment of a multilateral fund, subject to the condition that this fund should base its assistance to developing country parties on the incremental costs approach, that it would be limited and unique in nature, and that it would not prejudice any other future arrangements the parties might develop

---

[35] In 1989, developed countries still assumed that it would be sufficient if they would reallocate some of their aid to environmental purposes without increasing its overall amount.

with respect to other environmental issues.[36] However, despite all attempts to limit the effect of the precedent set with the establishment of the MLF, the agreement to support projects and treaty compliance in developing countries through a financial mechanism established under an environmental convention set a model and precedent. All multilateral environmental agreements negotiated since then foresee financial transfers to assist developing countries to meet their treaty commitments.[37] It is in this context that the MLF helped to frame the principle of common but differentiated responsibilities. The world for the first time formally recognised that the richer countries, having caused more damage, had more responsibility when it came to addressing the existing damages and mitigating future deterioration. While the polluter pays principle allocates the duty to pay for damage caused, the principle of common but differentiated responsibilities takes a more comprehensive view and allocates responsibility taking into account economic conditions and fair burden-sharing in addressing environmental problems. The principle of common but differentiated responsibilities creates a global partnership to protect the environment; a partnership in which the partners bring different resources and problems to the table – where the successful achievement objective of the partnership depends on the cooperation among the various partners.

III. Global Environment Facility

In parallel to the negotiations that led to the creation of the MLF and upon the initiative of the French government, the World Bank conducted consultations for the establishment of a global environmental fund which would later become the GEF. The idea that triggered the GEF was to provide developing countries with funds which would constitute a 'small, but additional, financial incentive to tackle global environmental problems'.[38] While most countries of the Group of 77 (G77)[39] were generally supportive of such a fund, they stressed the fact

---

[36] See for further detail, Andersen, S. O. and Sarma, K. M., *Protecting the ozone layer: the United Nations history*, London (UNEP) 2003, p. 123; DeSombre, E. R. and Kauffman, J., The Montreal Protocol Multilateral Fund: partial success story, in Keohane, R. O. and Levy, M. A. (eds.), *Institutions for environmental aid: pitfalls and promise*, Boston, Mass. (MIT Press) 1996, pp. 89, 99.

[37] Whereas developing countries negotiated and continue to negotiate for individual and separate mechanisms that are modelled after the MLF, donor nations put forward and continue to support a consolidated global financial mechanism for all Conventions and instruments.

[38] Jordan, A., Paying the incremental costs of global environmental protection: the evolving role of the GEF, *Environment* 36(6) (1994), pp. 12, 13.

[39] The Group of 77 (G77) was established on 15 June 1964 by seventy-seven developing countries signatories of the Joint Declaration of the Seventy-Seven Countries issued at the end of the first session of the United Nations Conference on Trade and Development (UNCTAD) in Geneva. The G77 provides the umbrella for developing countries to negotiate in international fora (http://www.g77.org).

that the fund would have to be new and additional to funds already provided for regular development assistance. The negotiators agreed that the fund should be established as a pilot and should provide cofinancing to developing countries and those with economies in transition for projects with global environmental benefits. In creating the GEF, donor countries were keen to ensure that the new fund would only finance the 'incremental' costs of projects. Incremental costs were defined as the extra costs incurred in the process of redesigning an activity vis-à-vis a baseline plan – which is focused on achieving national benefits – in order to address global environmental concerns.[40] GEF funds should be used in the most efficient manner, over and above what developing countries aided by existing channels of development assistance were doing to protect the environment.[41] GEF finance would be made available for investment and technical assistance in four focal areas: global warming, biodiversity, international waters, and ozone depletion.[42] The responsibility for the implementation of such projects was meant to be shared between UNDP, UNEP, and the World Bank.[43]

In March 1991, the Board of Executive Directors of the World Bank approved the establishment of the GEF and the Global Environment Trust Fund (GETF).[44] Decisions by the Governing Council of the UNEP[45] and the Governing Council of the UNDP[46] supported the arrangement. Sixteen OECD countries and nine developing countries expressed their confidence in the newly created entity when they pledged some US$860 million to the GETF.[47] In order to avoid different levels of membership it was understood that all participants should contribute to the new facility. However, recipient countries were not obliged to be participants and contributors to the GEF in order to receive grants from the fund. This construction aimed to strengthen the partnership among the countries through eliminating the recipient versus the donor perspective. Developing countries as donor countries were expected to show a new

---

[40] Sjöberg, H., From idea to reality: the creation of the Global Environment Facility, GEF Working 10 Paper 1994, para. 1.02.
[41] Jordan, op. cit., pp. 12, 20.
[42] In October 2002 two additional focal areas were included in the GEF Instrument: land degradation and persistent organic pollutants.
[43] See Boisson de Chazournes, L., The Global Environment Facility galaxy: on linkages among institutions, in *Max Planck Yearbook of the United Nations III*, Leiden (Martinus Nijhoff Publishers) 1999, p. 243.
[44] Resolution 91–5 of the World Bank's Board of Executive Directors.
[45] Resolution 16/47 of the UNEP Council, 13 May 1991.
[46] Decision 92/16 of the UNDP Governing Council, 26 May 1991.
[47] Austria, Belgium, Brazil, Canada, China, Denmark, Egypt, Finland, France, Germany, India, Indonesia, Italy, Japan, Mexico, Morocco, the Netherlands, Norway, Pakistan, Spain, Sweden, Switzerland, Turkey, and the United Kingdom. In addition to their contributions to the core fund, Belgium, Japan and Switzerland had separate cofinancing arrangements.

commitment for the true aim of the GEF, creating benefits for the Earth as a whole.[48]

However, despite the effort to inspire a true sense of partnership into the fund, the fact that the GEF pilot was becoming practically a part of the World Bank provoked mistrust from non-governmental organisations (NGOs) and developing countries. The UNCED in 1992 in Rio de Janeiro proved to be a watershed in the history of the GEF. It entered the negotiations as a short-term, experimental pilot project and departed considerably strengthened, internationally endorsed and with a strong institutional mandate for the future.[49] Prior to UNCED, the donor countries had indicated clearly that they would only support a unified funding mechanism for all up-coming conventions. They wanted to avoid the proliferation of funds going along with the proliferation of environmental treaties. Instead, they envisioned the GEF as the financial mechanism for all future North–South financial transfers for environmental projects with global impact.[50] On the other hand, the developing countries, together with UNEP, called for one or several new 'green' funds. When developing countries reluctantly agreed to have the GEF as interim financial mechanism for the Biodiversity Convention and the Climate Change Convention, they made it clear that a permanent relationship between the Conventions and the GEF would be contingent on reforms that would ensure the GEF would promote further transparency, democracy, and universality of participation. Developing countries, UN agencies, and the majority of the NGOs were in favour of a mechanism with a governance structure more similar to the UN system.[51] They wanted the GEF to be based on universal membership and equal voting rights for each country. In addition to this, NGOs demanded more participation in GEF procedures and projects. On the other side, OECD countries and the World Bank preferred the governance structure of the Bretton Woods system and argued in favour of efficiency, cost effectiveness, effective management, and executive abilities. In order to integrate the GEF into the more UN-driven Conventions, and to make the GEF the financial mechanism for the Conventions, these differences had to be resolved and a compromise found. Negotiations on restructuring the GEF in 1994 therefore became one of the most interesting processes in international law and

---

[48] The developing countries were represented by seven nations only: India, China, Brazil, Morocco, Mexico, Zimbabwe, and Cote d' Ivoire.

[49] Jordan, A., Financing global environmental protection: the Global Environmental Facility, CSERGE GEC Working Paper, 92-137, 1994, p. 21.

[50] The developed countries stressed that environmental projects without any global relevance ought to be paid for by mainstreaming the regular development assistance. The GEF funds were restricted in the pilot as well as in the restructured GEF to projects with impacts on the global environment.

[51] See GEF, The GEF in the 21st century: a vision for strengthening the Global Environment Faciltiy, a Joint NGO Document, 1998 (Final Draft, 5 March 1998).

politics. The main points addressed in the restructuring negotiations were the following.

- *The legal establishment of the restructured GEF*: the G77, as much as the NGOs, preferred a body established independently of the World Bank either by a government endorsed 'treaty' approach, or by an interagency agreement. Eventually, the parties agreed to the establishment by a resolution of the three agencies, signed by the heads of the agencies, and approved by the governing bodies.
- *The governance structure of the new GEF*: while G77 pleaded for a universal Assembly, such as the General Assembly of the United Nations, OECD countries put forward the idea of a Council with similar rights and functions as the World Bank's Board of Executive Directors. The parties reached a compromise that included both elements. A Participants Assembly would be universal and representative, while the main decision-making body would be the GEF Council where representation would be based on constituencies and shares.
- *Distribution of the constituencies*: the OECD favoured a small and balanced Council, whereas the G77 requested the majority of Council members. The final agreement foresees a GEF Council comprised of thirty-two members, fourteen from OECD countries, sixteen from G77 and China, and two from countries of central and Eastern Europe and the former Soviet Union.
- *The decision-making procedure*: while the North supported the Bretton Woods model of contribution-weighted share and voting rights, the South was in favour of the democratic system of the United Nations (one country, one vote). As a compromise, the parties agreed that it would be generally understood that decisions would be based on consensus. Only if the Secretariat cannot reach consensus, will they resort to a formal vote. The voting system finally established has a double majority and integrates both systems.
- *Universal membership*: the developing countries made it a prerequisite for all further negotiations that the GEF would become open for all parties of the Conventions. Therefore, the mandatory membership contribution of the GEF pilot was unanimously abandoned.[52]

The restructured GEF has key operational principles based on the Conventions, the GEF Instrument,[53] and Council decisions. These principles have been translated into the Operational Strategy to which all projects have to conform. The Operational Strategy set out Operational Programmes, from Arid and

[52] Helen Sjöberg draws attention to how the policy had changed between 1991 and 1994. When the pilot was created the mandatory contributions were supported to promote a spirit of partnership. Three years later, the political viewpoint of universality was predominant.
[53] Eventually, two years after the Rio Conference, the Instrument for the Establishment of the Restructured Global Environment Facility was adopted in Geneva on 16 March 1994.

Semi-arid Zone Ecosystems to a Contaminant-Based Operational Programme. Both, the Operational Strategy and the operational programmes make clear the mission of the GEF and formulate its guidelines.[54] The GEF supports three broad types of projects in its focal areas. Apart from the Operational Programme, these are enabling activities, and short-term response measures.[55] GEF project types include small and medium size project activities, enabling activities, and full projects. Projects usually receive grants and concessional cofinancing of incremental project costs through GEF resources. In order to meet the eligibility criteria of the GEF, projects must reflect national or regional priorities, have the support of the country or countries involved, and improve the global environment. Enabling activities help countries to identify their needs and prepare for projects to help them meet their obligations under the Conventions. The GEF funds short-term response measures, but only if they are high priority and yield immediate benefits at low costs. GEF project examples include the Coastal and Biodiversity Management Programme in Guinea-Bissau, Sustainable Transport and Air Quality for Santiago Project in Santiago de Chile, and the Danube Strategic Partnership for Nutrient Reduction.[56]

In many ways, the GEF built on the example of the MLF. Both mechanisms aim at building bridges between developing country demands and industrialised country conditions. They do not just open another window of aid.[57] Instead, the fund as well as the facility are to meet the incremental costs encountered by developing countries when undertaking a project with additional global benefits; or, looked at from a different angle, development should not be penalised by expenses that could not be justified by domestic benefits.[58] In both cases, the voting mechanisms in the GEF Council and the Executive Board, respectively, are the result of a pragmatic compromise.[59] The reliance on existing agencies to implement policies and projects has also proven a successful model in both cases.

---

[54] GEF, Operational Strategy, 1996; as of December 2003 the GEF has fifteen operational programmes. See www.gefweb.org

[55] GEF, Operational Strategy, 1996, p. 7.

[56] The GEF pipeline of projects can be accessed through the GEF website, www.gefweb.org

[57] Neither does the Montreal Protocol which laid down many of the principles which govern the GEF. See Hurlbut, D., Beyond the Montreal Protocol: impact on nonparty states and lessons for future environmental protection regimes, *Colo. J. Int'l Envt'l L. and Policy* 4 (1993), pp. 344, 358.

[58] El-Ashry, M., Reflections on the GEF role in the protection of the ozone layer, in Andersen, S. O. and Sarma, K. M., *Protecting the ozone layer: the United Nations history*, London (UNEP) 2003, p. 251.

[59] Similar voting procedures have been proposed for the World Bank Board of Executive Directors, the CCD, and CBD. See also German Advisory Council on Global Change, *New structures for global environmental policy*, London and Sterling, Va. (Earthscan) 2001, p. 161.

However, the two mechanisms also show significant differences: whereas the funding to developing country parties under the MLF is limited to assisting these countries to meet their targets under the Montreal Protocol, the GEF has a broader mandate to support projects which contribute to the ultimate objectives of the Conventions and fit into the Operational Strategy of the GEF – as long as they fit into the incremental cost framework. While the MLF is an instrument established under the governing treaty (the Montreal Protocol), the GEF has been created to be assigned to serve the purposes of the UNFCCC, the CBD, later expanded to serve the Convention to Combat Desertification,[60] and the Stockholm Convention on Persistent Organic Pollutants.[61] Whereas the GEF operates under the 'guidance of the Conferences of the Parties' it is governed by its own rules and procedures and establishes an additional layer of structures and approvals. The relationship between the GEF and the Conferences of the Parties is critical to advancing the objectives of the Conventions in developing countries and to securing the support of those countries for the multilateral approach chosen by the Conventions. The Treaties also provide a framework under which the GEF and its implementing agencies can be held accountable. The relationship between the Conferences of the Parties and the GEF has therefore not always been easy, and it is a challenge for the GEF to respond to a 'proliferation of guidance and priorities' emanating from the Conferences of the Parties (COPs).[62]

Since 1991, the GEF has provided US$4.5 billion in grants and generated US$14.5 billion in cofinancing from other partners for projects in developing countries and countries with economies in transition (see Figure 20.2). This makes the GEF the biggest source of funding for projects with global environmental benefits in developing countries. Within this time, the GEF has undergone a constant evolutionary process. With the restructured GEF, leadership and responsibility shifted from the World Bank to the GEF Council. Developing and developed countries are actively involved in the Council; however, the balance of power within the Council is still weighted in favour of OECD countries. The major donors underline their demands for influence with policy recommendations linked to the replenishment procedure. Developing countries also have found it difficult in some instances to develop projects along the incremental cost principle which is not always easy to define and integrate in the national environmental priorities. It also leaves out aid for local priority problems. Nevertheless, increasing participation of developing countries in the GEF attests to a generally positive outlook of the GEF.

---

[60] International Convention to Combat Desertification in those Countries Experiencing Serious Drought and/or Desertification, particularly in Africa, 33 I.L.M. (1994) 1332.
[61] Stockholm Convention on Persistent Organic Pollutants ('POPs Convention'), 40 ILM (2001) 532.
[62] Joint Summary of the Chairs, GEF Council Meeting, 5–7 December 2001, para. 37.

> The GEF Efficient Street Lighting Programme is a climate change programme that will be administered by the IBRD. The project involves providing approximately US$730,000 to assist Argentina remove key barriers to energy conservation in the street lighting sector. These barriers include lack of information about viable energy saving opportunities in street lighting, access to commercial sources of financing, and increased transaction costs for initial installations. Properly developed and managed, efficient street lighting projects in Argentina offer energy savings of over 60 per cent, making them economically viable. The key to opening this market is demonstrating and replicating viable project finance and contract structures and security mechanisms.
>
> The project involves developing a project that will act as a model for structuring and financing future projects, developing a pipeline of new municipal street lighting projects, and increasing the capacity of private sector energy efficiency business to realise these projects. Saving energy used in street lighting will decrease energy demanded and correspondingly decrease the greenhouse gas emissions generated by energy production.

Figure 20.2 Global Environment Facility, project example: Argentina, Efficient Street Lighting Programme

Today the GEF is a remarkably open and flexible institution and has proven to be able to learn and adapt. However, lasting environmental improvement will not depend on the individual project but depends on a long-term policy change, prioritisation, trust, and continued funding long after the closing of the GEF project. The ultimate objective of the GEF is to mainstream global environmental concerns by expanding the horizons of decision-makers both in developing countries and the implementing agencies to include major global environmental issues as practical policy concerns encountered in their daily operations and considerations. Mainstreaming of environmental concerns is the most difficult challenge the GEF faces and has not yet been rewarded with convincing success. It is therefore a critical goal of the GEF intervention to strengthen the framework for sustainable environmental resources management in a country or a region. The effectiveness of the GEF must ultimately be demonstrated in results that convince governments and people in countries that are eligible for GEF funding that it is worthwhile to participate in international environmental agreements.[63] The GEF must communicate its objectives and increase its visibility to stakeholders and affected communities at the country level to ensure that GEF projects are country driven. Only if the host country has full ownership and understanding of the global benefits of

---

[63] GEF, *Focusing on the global environment: a decade of the GEF*, Second Overall Performance Study, 2002. http://www.gefweb.org/1Full_Report-FINAL-2-26-02.pdf, p. vv.

the project, will it help to mainstream the environment in the broader policy area.

IV. The UNFCCC and funding mechanisms under the Kyoto Protocol

The United Nations Framework Convention on Climate Change (UNFCCC) was opened for signature by the countries participating in the UNCED and came into force on 21 March 1994. Its ultimate objective is the 'stabilization of greenhouse gas concentrations at a level that would prevent dangerous anthropogenic interference with the climate system' (Article 2 of the UNFCCC). The Convention is also firmly based on the principle of common but differentiated responsibilities, which finds its expression in Article 4(2) where the industrialised countries and those with economies undergoing the transition to market economies (EITs) undertake to adopt policies and measures which will 'demonstrate that developed countries are taking the lead in modifying longer term trends in anthropogenic emissions consistent with the objective of the Convention'.

The Convention also includes a commitment to assist countries particularly vulnerable to the effects of climate change and to promote technology transfer. Article 4(7) goes even further when it makes developing country action conditional on the effective implementation of commitments under the UNFCCC and the transfer of resources and technologies.[64] This clause is a response to possible shortfalls of funding and related risks of developing countries to be exposed to commitments without secured funding in the case of the financial mechanism of the Montreal Protocol. Financial resources under the Convention are mobilised and administered by the GEF.

The Kyoto Protocol was adopted at the third session of the COP to the UNFCCC, held in Kyoto, Japan, on 11 December 1997. In contrast to the UNFCCC, it provides for specific Quantified Emission Limitation and Reduction Commitments (QELRCs) to be met by the countries listed in UNFCCC Annex I (industrialised countries and EITs, together 'Annex I countries') over the first commitment period, beginning in 2008 and ending in 2012. The Annex I countries agreed to reduce their greenhouse gas emissions by an average of 5.2 per cent below their 1990 levels. The Kyoto Protocol entered into force on 16 February 2005, ninety days after the Russian Federation ratified the treaty. With Russia's ratification, the Protocol achieved the double majority of being

---

[64] 'The extent to which developing country Parties will effectively implement their commitments under the Convention will depend on the effective implementation by developed country Parties of their commitment under the Convention relating to financial resources and transfer of technology.' The UN Convention on Biological Diversity contains a similar provision in Article 20(4), 31 I.L.M. (1992) 818.

ratified not only by fifty-five parties to the UNFCCC, but also by countries representing more than 55 per cent of the total 1990 carbon dioxide emissions of Annex I countries.

The Kyoto Protocol recognises that economic and social development and poverty reduction are the overriding priorities for non Annex I countries and that their emissions will, by necessity, grow as their material welfare improves. At the same time, many of the effects of global warming are likely to have very damaging effects on poorer countries. Rising sea levels, changes in rainfall, loss of subsistence crops, and increased disease are likely to hit poor people hardest. Therefore, the Climate Change Convention as well as the Kyoto Protocol foresee support of developing countries to assess the likely impacts of climate change, to mitigate its effects, and to build capacity to minimise the threat to their territory and people. To provide funding for mitigation and adaptation as well as capacity-building measures, industrialised countries will increase GEF replenishments and funding under bilateral and multilateral sources.

Additionally, three new funds will be set up: two under the UNFCCC and one under the Kyoto Protocol. The funds will promote adaptation, technology transfer, and mitigation activities in the energy, industry, and transport sectors. All three funds will be administered by the GEF. At the seventh COP held in 2001 in Marrakech, the European Community and its Member States, together with Canada, Iceland, New Zealand, Norway, and Switzerland, made political declaration on their preparedness collectively to contribute US$410 million annually by 2005,[65] with this level to be reviewed in 2008.

Recognising the importance of institutional flexibility and private sector involvement, the Kyoto Protocol also introduced three 'flexible mechanisms' which may be used to supplement domestic greenhouse gas mitigation action. Since greenhouse gases mix uniformly in the atmosphere, it is equivalent from an environmental standpoint to reduce emissions domestically or abroad. Achieving emission reductions outside of the national borders makes the costs of reaching national targets for industrialised countries cheaper and at the same time fosters the flow of investments and technology transfer to developing countries or countries with economies in transition. Through the flexible mechanisms, the Kyoto Protocol foresees the creation of markets for greenhouse gas emission reductions through project-based emission crediting or emission trading. Two of these instruments are available only to countries with qualified targets: Joint Implementation (JI) set forth in Article 6 and emission trading set forth in Article 17 of the Kyoto Protocol. In addition, the Kyoto mechanisms also include in Article 12 a Clean Development Mechanism (CDM), which

---

[65] See FCCC/CP/2001/13/add.1 Decision 7/CP.7 Recitals. The declaration does not contain any information on how this contribution will be distributed among the new funds, GEF replenishment, and bilateral measures.

aims to enhance cooperation among industrialised and developing countries to achieve sustainable development and reduce emissions.

JI and CDM projects are expected to generate emission reductions that, once certified by an operational entity, will become Certified Emission Reductions or CERs (for CDM projects), or Emission Reduction Units or ERUs (for JI projects), provided that the projects lead to real, measurable, and long-term benefits related to the mitigation of climate change and result in emission reductions that are additional to any that would occur in the absence of the project. Industrialised Annex I countries may then use CERs and ERUs to help comply with emission reductions obligations under Article 3 of the Kyoto Protocol.

By allowing for some form of outside purchase of emission credits, the Kyoto Protocol lays the ground for the so-called 'carbon market'. The carbon market is one of the few markets for environmental services currently in operation; and the only one with worldwide reach. Thus, it should not only generate large efficiency gains, but could also contribute substantially to sustainable development, since it can bring new public and private capital to economies in transition and developing countries, where abatement costs are, in general, lower than in industrialised countries. At the same time, financial mechanisms for technology transfer are critical to meeting the rapidly growing energy needs of developing countries, while also facilitating their participation in global efforts to reduce greenhouse gases.[66]

CDM and JI projects implement an activity which aims at the reduction of greenhouse emissions, which can be measured and, once it has been quantified and verified, be transferred between the participants in a carbon project. Such projects include renewable energy, energy efficiency, waste management, or afforestation projects. CDM and JI projects are governed by contracts which foresee a payment against the achievement of an activity that leads to the removal or mitigation of greenhouse gases. Forward purchase contracts, so-called Emission Reductions Purchase Agreements (ERPAs), are the most commonly used form of carbon contracts. These contracts do not regulate financial services, such as depth or equity financing, but govern exclusively the acquisition of defined emission reduction credits. Many CDM and JI contracts, including the one used by the World Bank Carbon Finance Business, are structured more like long-term supply or off-take agreements than financing agreements.

So far developed countries have done little to reduce their greenhouse gas emissions. The USA and Australia have expressed their intent not to ratify the Kyoto Protocol. Even those countries committed to the instrument and the process still have to show that they are able to change trends. Nonetheless,

---

[66] See Figueres, C. and Ivanova, M. H., Climate change: national interest or a global regime?, in Esty, D. C. and Ivanova, M. H. (eds.), *Global environmental governance: options and opportunities*, New Haven (Yale) 2002, pp. 1, 16.

the international carbon market sees a steady increase in the trade of emission rights generated by CDM and JI projects. The COP has fostered the market development through the authorisation of a 'prompt start' of the CDM, which makes it possible that CERs obtained during the period between 2000 and 2008 can be used to assist achieving compliance in the first commitment period.[67] In the year 2004 alone, 108 million of CO_2 equivalent tons of emission reductions (tCO_2e) have been contracted at prices ranging from US$3 to US$10 per tCO_2e; this represents an increase of 39 per cent compared to the previous year (78 million).[68] Since 1996, a total of 220 tCO_2e have been traded in the emerging market with a total value of between US$300–650 million. Although still sovereign buyers account for about three-quarters in investments in the CDM and JI, the participation of the private sector in the market is rapidly increasing.[69] Although prolonged insecurity on the entry into force of the Kyoto Protocol has long limited the growth of the market, the entry into force of the Kyoto Protocol, and the acceptance of CERs as a compliance tool under the EU Emissions Trading Scheme, have given the CDM and JI an additional push.

The CDM has been hailed by some analysts as an ingenious device to reconcile the goals of greenhouse gas abatement and sustainable development.[70] On the other hand, trading of emission rights is not bare of criticism. It has been claimed that it deviates funds and attention from domestic emission reduction and only resources for cheap mitigation options will be attracted (the so-called 'low-hanging fruit'), leaving developing countries to undertake the more expensive options themselves.[71] Additionally, there is some concern that the CDM will channel investment into projects of marginal social utility[72] or that the gains will not be shared fairly.[73] It also has been argued that not all

---

[67] Article 12.10 of the Kyoto Protocol.
[68] For more detail see Lecocq, F. and Capoor, K., *The World Bank, state and trends of the carbon market* (PCFplus Research, World Bank) 2005 (based on data and insights provided by Evolution Markets LLC, Natsource LLC, and PointCarbon), at www.carbonfinance.org
[69] It is also worth noting that data of private contractual arrangements with respect to carbon projects (especially JI and CDM) are not as easily accessible as data from sovereign purchases of CERs or ERUs.
[70] Goldemberg, J. (ed.), *Issues and opinions: the Clean Development Mechanism*, New York (UNDP) 1998; Haites, E. and Aslam, M. A., *The Kyoto mechanisms and global climate change*, Washington, DC (Pew Center on Global Climate Change) 2000.
[71] Agarwal, A. and Narain, S., *Addressing the challenge of climate change: equity, sustainability and economic effectiveness: how poor nations can help save the world*, New Delhi (Center for Science and Environment) 1999.
[72] Ibid.
[73] Parikh, J., IPCC response strategies unfair to the South, *Nature*, 10 December 1992, pp. 507–508; Parikh, J., North-South issues for climate change, *Economic and Political Weekly*, 5–12 November 1994, pp. 2940–2943; Parikh, J., North-South cooperation in

emission rights are transferable or exchangeable, but that there is a certain set of emissions associated with basic necessity consumption which should not be allowed to be traded.[74] However, experiences gained with the implementation of the CDM so far, conclude that the CDM does not touch the right to emit a certain amount of basic emissions. Since all CDM project activities require host country approval, the country has the chance to examine the benefits of the project for its sustainable development. The CDM also plays an important role in reducing the resource gap that projects that mitigate greenhouse gases face in developing countries.[75] Investors are often not willing to take the significant risks that are associated with investments in renewables, energy efficiency, and afforestation projects in developing countries. The mechanism allows developing countries to initiate and implement greenhouse gas mitigation projects and in return sell the CERs to Annex I countries or entities. These benefits help to outweigh many of the political concerns expressed with regard to the CDM.

Compared to the GEF or the MLF, which are more traditional financial mechanisms that ensure compliance and cooperation from developing countries, the Kyoto Protocol foresees the implementation of more innovative compliance mechanisms. However, the design of the mechanisms relies on the proven experience of existing mechanisms: with the Executive Board for the CDM, the UNFCCC COP created a structure similar to the Montreal Protocol's Executive Committee to oversee the implementation of the mechanism and the 'additionality' requirement under the JI and CDM, is a concept closely related to the incremental cost principle of the MLF and the GEF. The flexible mechanisms in general, and the CDM in particular, are among the most innovative aspects of the emerging climate change regime.

They address the problem of global warming on an international level and through mechanisms based on the principle of trading emission reduction offsets. The CDM provides the parties to the Kyoto Protocol with an instrument of mutual benefit for industrialised and developing parties while supporting project activities that create a win-win situation for project participants. The CDM also makes the Protocol more acceptable to G77 countries by channelling responsible investment their way while creating a tool for industrialised countries to off-set their domestic emissions.

The CDM provides a framework under which new collaborative network structures consisting of nation states and non-state actors can evolve. Such

climate change through joint implementation, *International Environmental Affairs* 7(1) (1995), pp. 22–43.

[74] Pan, J., Emission rights and their transferability, *International Environmental Agreements* 3 (2003), pp. 1–16.

[75] Beg, N. *et al.*, Linkages between climate change and sustainable development, *Climate Policy* 2 (2002), pp. 129–144.

> The Prototype Carbon Fund (PCF) is a World Bank-administered multidonor trust fund to purchase emission reductions from the CDM and JI project. In the case of the Jepirachi Wind Power Project, the PCF will purchase US$3.2 million dollars worth of emission reductions from the project. The project involves developing a wind farm that will be the first wind power plant linked to the Colombian grid, delivering around 68.3 GWh/year. By linking into the grid, the project will displace coal and natural gas generated power and will contribute to the abatement of CO_2, CH_4 and NO_2. The addition of wind energy will diversify energy sources and help stabilise seasonal fluctuations in Colombia's hydroelectric energy generating capacity. The wind farm will therefore contribute to lowering the thermal load during the dry season by providing sustainable electricity from a renewable resource. The PCF purchases an equivalent of 800,000 tons of CO_2 equivalent emission reductions over a time of a maximum of fifteen years.
>
> The transfer of new wind power technology will help Colombia nationally and the region locally. Nationally, it assists Colombia develop sustainably by giving Colombia access to a new source of renewable energy. It will assist the region locally by assisting the socio-economic development of the local Wayúu Indian community. The project goes beyond national requirements for local assistance, and will provide funding and electricity for a water desalinisation plant, the local school, health centre facilities, and refrigeration.

Figure 20.3 Prototype Carbon Fund, project example: Columbia, Jepirachi Wind Power Project

cross-sectoral networks[76] have been described as 'global public policy networks'[77] that go beyond traditional conceptions of special interest politics, giving non-state actors a variety of voluntary, semi-formal, and formal roles in the implementation process. The CDM aims to involve not just governments but a wide array of actors, including individuals, companies, and agencies whose

---

[76] Reinicke, W. and Deng, F., *Critical choices*, Ottawa (International Development Research Center) 2000; Reinicke, W., The other world wide web: global public policy networks, *Foreign Policy* (Winter 1999/2000), pp. 44–57; Reinicke, W., Policy cooperation in a post-interdependent world: a global order for sustainable growth, in Bakker, A. (ed.), *A global order for sustainable growth*, Amsterdam (Nederlands Instituut voor het Banken Effectenbedrijf) 1998; www.globalpublicpolicy.net; Thatcher, M., The development of policy network analyses: from the modes origins to overarching frameworks, *J. Theoretical Politics* (1998), p. 10; Messner, D., *The network society: economic development and international competitiveness as a problem of social governance*, London (Frank Cass) 1997.

[77] The author of this chapter also participated as a case study author in the Global Public Policy Network Project led by Wolfgang Reinicke and Francis Deng. The project took place in 1999 and 2000 and was sponsored by the UN Foundation. It aimed to provide strategic advice to Kofi Annan the Secretary General of the United Nations. The results of the GPPN Project are captured in Reinicke and Deng, op. cit.

behaviour does not change simply because governments have made international commitments. As a international mechanism relying on market forces, the CDM (i) builds a bridge between industrialised and developing countries, (ii) builds a platform for a coordinated approach for public and private entities to implement the Treaty, and (iii) integrates market-based mechanisms into the Treaty. The CDM provides an example of how economic instruments can leverage commitments under international treaties. It also shows how the principle of common but differentiated responsibilities can be taken beyond government commitments to increase flows of private investments in developing countries. The Kyoto Protocol hereby sets an important framework and creates a platform for the development and transfer of technology, as well as for leveraging financial resources. Binding phase-out targets under the Montreal Protocol effectively signalled to the market that research into alternatives would be profitable. In the case of the Kyoto Protocol, market mechanisms involve private sector companies in achieving emission reduction targets and help leveraging financial resources into developing countries.

V. Summary and outlook

More than ten years passed between the establishment of the Multilateral Fund under the Montreal Protocol, the establishment and formulation of the principles of the GEF, and the final negotiations on the implementation of the Kyoto Protocol. The MLF and the GEF were proposed and supported by different constituencies and represent in their governance structure other traditions. The flexible mechanisms under the Kyoto Protocol for the first time try to rely on market-based principles to provide for financial transfers to meet obligations under a treaty.

However, all three mechanisms discussed in this chapter describe how developing countries have to bear part of the burden to address global environmental problems with, however, the benefit of 'special considerations' which take into account the general weakness of developing countries to respond to environmental threats, the limited access to funds and technology, and their reduced responsibility for global environmental degradation. Developing countries are called upon to meet their part of the obligations, which consist in information-gathering as well as implementing their commitments under the treaties, to the extent they are equipped to do so with funding made available to fill the gap. It is therefore essential that agreements formulated in a treaty are broadly supported and self-enforcing in nature. This is vital as countries are free to decide whether to join a treaty, and international enforcement of non-compliance with a treaty is weak and not backed by any executive force. Negotiating a treaty that sustains near-universal participation and requires that each signatory to an agreement provide a substantial amount of environmental protection is the principal challenge to diplomacy.[78] Because many measures to protect global environmental resources depend on the cooperation of developing countries, these countries have gained over time negotiating power, and this manifests itself especially in their say on the use of funds.[79] This new negotiation power has led to the voting structure in the MLF and the GEF Council, which may serve as an example for other international processes.

However, financial resources mobilised through intergovernmental processes and international funds fall short. Parallel to efforts to obtain serious commitment by industrialised countries to assume responsibility for addressing international environmental concerns globally, innovative financial mechanisms must be developed and, where existing, strengthened. Such mechanisms help to enable steady funding for global environmental policy and at the same time create a degree of independence from the willingness of industrialised countries to provide funds.[80] For that purpose it is essential to promote the mobilisation of private resources for financing of activities with global environmental benefits. Such mechanisms include user charges, insurance solutions, or environmental lotteries. Market mechanisms are designed to use the forces of the market to achieve environmental benefits. Through the creation of a market new services commodities are defined, which give a price to externalities of production and consumption processes. The CDM demonstrates a step in the right direction. However, it is important to stress that the success of implementation partnerships and market mechanisms depend to a significant degree on the willingness of governments to set ambitious binding targets. The legal and political framework creates the nurturing context in which these mechanisms can live. Market mechanisms and partnerships on their own will never be a substitute for binding international commitments by governments, nor would such substitution be desirable. A robust legal framework can galvanise private initiatives and use the process of globalisation and its efficiencies to help channel funds into the developing world thereby promoting sustainable development.

[78] Barrett, S., Montreal versus Kyoto: international cooperation and the global environment, in Kaul, I., Grunberg, I., and Stern, M. A. (eds.), *Defining global public goods: international cooperation in the 21st century*, New York (UNDP) 1999, pp. 192, 193.
[79] Biermann, F., *Weltumweltpolitik zwischen Nord und Süd: Die neue Verhandlungsmacht der Entwicklungsländer*, Baden-Baden (Nomos) 1999.
[80] German Advisory Council on Global Change, *New structures for global environmental policy*, London and Sterling, Va. (Earthscan) 2001, p. 144.

PART VIII

Fundamental concepts of institutionalising common concern

21

Global environmental change and the nation state: sovereignty bounded?

PETER H. SAND

I. Introduction

In spite of early hopes for a 'fading away' of sovereignty in the face of global environmental challenges, recent codifications of international law have confirmed the creeping national enclosure of what were once considered common assets, e.g., exclusive economic zones under the Law of the Sea Convention 1982; and access to genetic resources, from the 1983 International Undertaking via the Biodiversity Convention 1992 to the Plant Gene Treaty 2001. Yet, because of their explicit limitation and qualification by 'common interest' obligations, these expanded sovereign rights of nation states must be considered *fiduciary* rather than proprietary. The emerging legal regime is one of international public trusteeship (sometimes referred to as guardianship or stewardship) over a widening range of environmental resources. This chapter traces the evolution of the public trust concept in modern environmental law and its ramifications for international law and governance, as reflected in proposals suggesting a new environmental mandate for the UN Trusteeship Council.

All revolutions have their iconoclastic phase. When international lawyers first embraced the global environmental revolution[1] – looking for icons to smash – they were eager to pick on the nation state as a target: not surprisingly, much of the early literature on international environmental law and governance started from a radical *critique* of territorial sovereignty, suspected to lurk at the roots of many transnational environmental problems; and from high hopes for an

---

Revised version of a paper presented at the 2001 Berlin Conference on the Human Dimensions of Global Environmental Change, first published in *Global Environmental Politics* 4(1) (2004), pp. 47–71 (with detailed bibliographical references not reproduced here). Helpful comments by Klaus Bosselmann, Steve Charnovitz, Hong Sik Cho, Rudolf Dolzer, Harrison C. Dunning, Wolfgang Durner, Jeremy Firestone, Peter M. Haas, Robert O. Keohane, Peider Könz, Elisabeth Mann Borgese, Sabine von Schorlemer, Maurice F. Strong, Paul C. Szasz, Ernst U. von Weizsäcker, Jonathan B. Wiener and Gerd Winter are gratefully acknowledged.

[1] Nicholson, M., *The environmental revolution: a guide for the masters of the new world*, London (Hodder & Stoughton) 1969.

'erosion' or 'perforation' of operational sovereignty, as the preferred solution to those problems.[2]

Reality turned out to be different, or so it seems. Not only did state sovereignty prove its resilience as an organising element for the post-Stockholm 1972 and post-Rio 1992 global ecologic order,[3] quite paradoxically, two of the most momentous recent developments in the worldwide codification of natural resources law resulted in a net expansion of national jurisdiction. First, the UN *Convention on the Law of the Sea* (UNCLOS 1982 Article 56) formally extended the sovereign rights of coastal states to the vast new area of 'exclusive economic zones' (EEZs),[4] estimated to contain 25 per cent of global primary production and 90 per cent of the world's fish catch.[5] Ten years later, the *Convention on Biological Diversity* (CBD 1992, Article 15(1)) extended sovereign rights to the even vaster range of plant and animal genetic resources,[6] thereby enclosing access to another major chunk of what had once been considered 'heritage of mankind'.[7] And most recently, the *International Treaty on Plant Genetic Resources for Food and Agriculture* (FAO Plant Gene Treaty 2001 Article 10(1)) bluntly put an end to that legal fiction:[8]

> In their relationship with other States, the Contracting Parties recognize the sovereign rights of States over their own plant genetic resources for food and agriculture, including that the authority to determine access to those resources rests with national governments and is subject to national legislation.

---

[2] e.g., see Falk, R. A., *This endangered planet: prospects and proposals for human survival*, New York (Vintage) 1971, p. 222; but see also Falk, R. A., Environmental protection in an era of globalization, *Yearbook of Int'l Environmental Law* 6 (1995), pp. 3–25, at 11: 'I now believe that this earlier analysis was badly mistaken in several key respects'.

[3] e.g., Perrez, F. X., *Cooperative sovereignty: from independence to interdependence in the structure of international environmental law*, The Hague (Kluwer Law International) 2000; and Sowers, J., Kohli, A., and Sorensen, G., States and sovereignty: Introduction, in Chasek, P. S. (ed.), *The global environment in the twenty-first century: prospects for international cooperation*, Tokyo (UN University Press) 2000, pp. 15–21.

[4] United Nations Convention on the Law of the Sea, adopted at Montego Bay on 10 December 1982, 21 I.L.M. (1982) 1261; see Attard, D. J., *The exclusive economic zone in international law*, Oxford (Clarendon) 1987; and Hafner, G., *Die seerechtliche Verteilung von Nutzungsrechten: Rechte der Binnenstaaten in der ausschließlichen Wirtschaftszone*, Vienna (Springer) 1987.

[5] Independent World Commission on the Oceans (IWCO), *The ocean: our future*, Cambridge (Cambridge University Press) 1998, p. 59.

[6] Convention on Biological Diversity, signed at the UN Conference on Environment and Development at Rio de Janeiro on 5 June 1992, 31 I.L.M. (1992) 818.

[7] International Undertaking on Plant Genetic Resources, adopted by Conference Resolution 8/83 of the Food and Agriculture Organization of the United Nations (FAO) at Rome on 23 November 1983, Article 1.

[8] International Treaty on Plant Genetic Resources for Food and Agriculture, adopted by FAO Conference Resolution 3/01 at Rome on 3 November 2001; see Raustiala, K. and Victor, D. G., The regime complex for plant genetic resources, *International Organization* 58 (2004), pp. 277–309.

So is the pendulum swinging back to the other extreme – to that 'formidable defensive concept'[9] of permanent sovereignty over natural resources, and its notorious 'obsession with territory'?[10] I don't really think so. True, the new treaty language seems to acknowledge that states can have their 'own' genetic resources, in the way in which the UNESCO *World Heritage Convention* recognised cultural and natural heritage sites as 'property, to whatever people they may belong'.[11] Yet the reference to ownership and property rights introduces an analogy to private property law here that is potentially misleading.[12] Just as the sovereign rights of coastal states in their maritime exclusive economic zones are qualified by specific obligations owed to other states and to the international community (UNCLOS Articles 61–70), the sovereign rights of 'countries of origin' over access to genetic resources *in situ* are matched by an obligation to facilitate access for other parties to the Biodiversity Convention (CBD Article 1(2)), by the catalogue of conservation duties spelled out in that Convention (Articles 5–14) and the 'multilateral system' established under the FAO Plant Gene Treaty (Article 10 (2)).

In both instances, such limitations on sovereignty have been justified by community interests designating certain areas or resources as a matter of 'common concern',[13] notwithstanding the fact that – unlike 'common heritage' in the global commons *outside* national jurisdiction, such as deep seabed or outer space areas – they may be situated squarely *within* the territorial boundaries of states. Given those built-in restrictions, however, the analogy to 'ownership' rights becomes so diluted as to evoke a different legal analogy altogether i.e., the role of the nation state becomes more akin to a kind of *public trusteeship* – an idea which has indeed been gaining ground in modern environmental law, and on which I will now focus.

The message is simple: the sovereign rights of nation states over certain environmental resources are not proprietary, but *fiduciary*. I will show this

---

[9] Allott, P., International law and international revolution: reconceiving the world, in Freestone, D. and Subedi, S. (eds.), *Contemporary issues in international law: a collection of the Josephine Onoh Memorial Lectures*, The Hague (Kluwer Law International) 2002, pp. 77–98, at 17.

[10] Scelle, G., Obsession du territoire, in Asbeck, van, F. M. *et al.* (eds.), *Symbolae Verzijl*, The Hague (Nijhoff) 1958, pp. 347–361.

[11] Convention for the Protection of the World Cultural and Natural Heritage, adopted by the UN Educational, Scientific and Cultural Organization (UNESCO) at Paris on 16 November 1972, 151 U.N.T.S. 1037 (fifth preambular paragraph). On the evolution of 'national' versus 'common' heritage concepts for cultural property, see e.g., von Schorlemer, S., *Internationaler Kulturgüterschutz: Ansätze zur Prävention im Frieden sowie im bewaffneten Konflikt*, Berlin (Duncker & Humblot) 1992, p. 564.

[12] Carty, A., *The decay of international law? A reappraisal of the limits of legal imagination in international affairs*, Manchester (Manchester University Press) 1986, p. 44.

[13] See e.g., Kornicker-Uhlmann, E. M., State community interests, ius cogens and protection of the global environment: developing criteria for peremptory norms, *Georgetown Int'l Environmental L. Rev.* 11(1998), pp. 101–135; and Durner, W., *Common goods: Statusprinzipien von Umweltgütern im Völkerrecht*, Baden-Baden (Nomos) 2001, pp. 234–275.

by reference to comparative environmental law, to so-called 'stewardship economics', and to public international law.

II. The public trust in comparative environmental law

The concept of public trusteeship for environmental resources has undergone a spectacular revival in the USA. A rather obscure, century-old US Supreme Court case (*Illinois Central Railroad* v. *People of the State of Illinois*),[14] rediscovered by a perceptive law professor,[15] became the starting point for a whole generation of innovative environmental law-making – from Michigan's Environmental Protection Act of 1970[16] to federal legislation such as the 'Superfund' Act of 1980 (CERCLA)[17] and the Oil Pollution Act of 1990,[18] and reflected in new constitutional provisions; for example, article 1(27) of the Pennsylvania Constitution (as amended on 18 May 1971) now reads:[19]

> Pennsylvania's natural resources are the common property of all the people, including generations yet to come. As trustee of these resources, the Commonwealth shall conserve and maintain them for the benefit of the people.

What, then, is the idea of public environmental trusteeship?[20] In very simplified language, it means that:

---

[14] US Supreme Court (5 December 1892), US Supreme Court Reports 146, pp. 387–476; see Kearney, J. D. and Merrill, T. W., The origins of the American public trust doctrine: what really happened in Illinois Central, *University of Chicago L. Rev.* 71 (2004), pp. 799–931.

[15] Sax, J. L., The public trust doctrine in natural resources law: effective judicial intervention, *Michigan L. Rev.* 68 (1970), pp. 471–556; see the Symposium on 'Takings, public trust, unhappy truths, and helpless giants': a review of Professor Joseph Sax's defense of the environment through academic scholarship, *Ecology L. Q.* 25 (1998), pp. 325–438.

[16] Michigan Environmental Protection Act, Public Act No. 127 of 27 July 1970; *Michigan L. Rev.* 70 (1972), p. 1004.

[17] Comprehensive Environmental Response, Compensation and Liability Act, US Public Law No. 96–510 of 11 December 1980; United States Code 42, 9601.

[18] Oil Pollution Act, US Public Law No. 101–380 of 18 August 1990, United States Code 33, 2701.

[19] Purdon's Pennsylvania Statutes Annotated, St. Paul, Minn. (West Publishing) 2000; see Kury, F. L., The environmental amendment to the Pennsylvania Constitution: twenty years later and largely untested, *Villanova Envt'l L. J.* 1 (1990), pp. 123–134; Kirsch, M. T., Upholding the public trust in state constitutions, *Duke L. J.* 46 (1997), pp. 1169–1210; and Dernbach, J. C., Taking the Pennsylvania Constitution seriously when it protects the environment, Part II: Environmental rights and public trust, *Dickinson L. Rev.* 104 (1999), pp. 97–164.

[20] e.g., see Johnson, R. W., Water pollution and the public trust, *Environmental Law* 19 (1989), pp. 485–513; Araiza, W. D., Democracy, distrust, and the public trust: process-based constitutional theory, the public trust doctrine, and the search for a substantive environmental value, *University of California Los Angeles L. Rev.* 45 (1997), pp. 385–452; and Lum, A. L., How goes the public trust doctrine: is the common law shaping environmental policy?, *Natural Resources and Environment* 18 (2003), pp. 73–75.

(a) certain natural resources, e.g., watercourses, wildlife, or wilderness areas, regardless of their allocation to public or private uses, are defined as part of an 'inalienable public trust';
(b) certain authorities, e.g., federal agencies, state governments, or indigenous tribal institutions, are designated as 'public trustees' for protection of those resources;
(c) every citizen, as 'beneficiary' of the trust, may invoke its terms to hold the trustees accountable and to obtain judicial protection against encroachments or deterioration.

The public trust doctrine is now well-established in US environmental law, albeit not uncontested – partly because of its manifest reliance on private property concepts, which some authors find ill-suited for what is typically public (administrative) law governing the management of natural resources. Even though its origins are claimed to go back to ancient Roman law, much of its methodology and terminology is essentially derived from the Anglo-American common law of charitable trusts, under which all beneficiaries are entitled to hold a trustee accountable.[21] Simultaneously, and initially modelled after Britain's *National Trust for Places of Historic Interest or Natural Beauty* (1894, confirmed by legislation since 1907),[22] the 'land trust movement' to preserve strategic natural areas for the public (conservancy by charitable title acquisition) has since spread throughout North America.[23] While courts in some common-law countries like Australia and Canada have been more reluctant to extend the environmental scope of public trusteeship,[24] it found enthusiastic reception in others: witness the Philippine Environmental Policy Decree of 1977 (Article 2), which proclaimed 'the responsibilities of each generation as trustee

---

[21] See Kötz, H., *Trust und Treuhand: eine rechtsvergleichende Darstellung des anglo-amerikanischen Trust und funktionsverwandter Institute des deutschen Rechts*, Göttingen (Vandenhoek & Ruprecht) 1963, p. 63; and Sheridan, L. A., Public and charitable trusts, in Wilson, W. A. (ed.), *Trusts and trust-like devices*, London (British Institute of International and Comparative Law) 1981, pp. 21–43, at 21.

[22] Waterson, M., *The National Trust: the first hundred years*, London (BBC Books and National Trust) 1994; Dwyer, J. and Hodge, I., *Countryside in trust: land management by conservation, recreation, and amenity organisations*, Chichester (Wiley) 1996; Garner, J. F. and Jones, B. L., *Countryside law*, Crayford (Shaw) 3rd edn 1997, p. 192.

[23] Davis, G. D., *Developing a land conservation strategy: a handbook for land trusts*, Elizabethtown, NY (Adirondack Land Trust) 1997; Abbott, G. Jr., *Saving special places: a centennial history of the Trustees of Reservations, pioneers of the Land Trust Movement*, Ipswich, Mass. (Trustees of Reservations) 1993; Fairfax, S. K. and Guenzler, D., *Conservation trusts*, Lawrence, Kans. (University Press of Kansas) 2001.

[24] Bates, G. M., *Environmental law in Australia*, Sydney (Butterworths) 4th edn 1995, p. 70; Maguire, J. C., Fashioning an equitable vision for public resource protection and development in Canada: the public trust doctrine revisited and reconceptualised, *J. Envt'l Law and Practice* 7 (1997), pp. 1–42; von Tigerstrom, B., The public trust doctrine in Canada, *J. Envt'l Law and Practice* 7 (1997), pp. 379–401; and Romy, I., *Mise en œuvre de la protection de l'environnement: des 'citizen suits' aux solutions suisses*, Fribourg (Éditions universitaires) 1997, p. 44.

and guardian of the environment for succeeding generations' (applied to the conservation of public forests in a widely quoted Supreme Court case, *Minors Oposa* v. *Factoran* 1993);[25] Eritrea's Environment Proclamation of 1996, which designated the state as 'custodian for the harmonised and integrated management and protection of the national environment and the sustainable use of natural resources' (Article 5);[26] South Africa's National Water Act of 1998, referring to the government as 'public trustee of the nation's water resources' (chs. 1 and 3); and India, where the Supreme Court in a landmark decision declared the public trust doctrine 'a part of the law of the land' (*Mehta* v. *Kemal Nath* 1996,[27] followed in two 1999 Supreme Court cases).[28]

Even more striking are similar developments in the environmental legislation of continental European countries, where the common law trust is generally considered *not* to be part of a national legal tradition.[29] In Sweden, for example, the Royal Academy of Sciences (and since 1964, the Nature Conservation Board) has been designated as public trustee for protected natural areas;[30] in Italy, the Court of Accounts (*Corte dei Conti*) (and since 1986, the Environment Ministry) acts as trustee for claims of damage to national heritage (*danno erariale*) in the field of natural resources that would otherwise remain without procedural representation.[31]

There are many historical precedents for the transnational diffusion of law, a cross-cultural process sometimes described as *mimesis*,[32] and not dissimilar to

---

[25] Supreme Court of the Philippines, Judgment of 30 July 1993, G. R. No. 101083, reprinted in 33 I.L.M. (1994) 168; see Allen, T., The Philippine children's case: recognizing legal standing for future generations, *Georgetown Int'l Envt'l L. Rev.* 6 (1994), pp. 713–741.

[26] UNEP/UNDP Joint Project on Environmental Law and Institutions in Africa, Compendium of Environmental Laws of African Countries 1 (Supplement), Nairobi (UN Environment Programme) 1997, 44.

[27] Supreme Court of India, Judgment of 13 December 1996, (1997) SSC 1, 388, reprinted in UNEP/UNDP Compendium of Judicial Decisions on Matters Related to Environment: National Decisions 1, Nairobi (UN Environment Programme) 1998, 259.

[28] See Deepak Singh, R., Response of Indian judiciary to environmental protection: some reflections, *Indian J. Int'l Law* 39 (1999), pp. 447–463, at 458; and Razzaque, J., Application of public trust doctrine in Indian environmental cases, *J. Envt'l Law* 13 (2001), pp. 221–234.

[29] e.g., the German Federal Supreme Court, in an often-quoted decision of 13 June 1984, considered the (private law) concept of the trust 'incompatible with the dogmatic foundations of German law': Klein, M. J., Testamentary Trust nach Common Law und funktionsverwandte deutsche Zivilrechtsinstitute: ein Rechtsvergleich, *Zeitschrift für Vergleichende Rechtswissenschaft* 101 (2002), pp. 175–199.

[30] Hillmo, T. and Lohm, U., Nature's ombudsmen: the evolution of environmental representation in Sweden, *Environment and History* 3 (1997), pp. 19–43.

[31] Francario, L., *Danni ambientali e tutela civile*, Napoli (Novene) 1990; and Bianchi, A., Harm to the environment in Italian practice: the interaction of international law and domestic law, in Wetterstein, P. (ed.), *Harm to the environment: the right to compensation and the assessment of damages*, Oxford (Clarendon Press) 1997, pp. 103–109.

[32] Toynbee, A. J., *A study of history: reconsiderations* 12, Oxford (Oxford University Press) 1961, p. 343.

the spread of innovative technologies – or of contagious diseases,[33] vindicating Mephisto's metaphor in *Faust I*:[34]

> All rights and laws are still transmitted
> like an eternal sickness of the race,
> from generation unto generation fitted
> and shifted round from place to place.

In the words of Roscoe Pound, 'the history of a system of law is largely a history of borrowing of legal materials from other legal systems, and of assimilation of materials from outside the law';[35] as already noted by Max Weber, that kind of reception across national boundaries typically occurs through social elites (*honoratiores*), such as judges and legislators.[36] Environmental law proved a particularly fertile ground for this 'horizontal' transfer of innovative concepts and institutions,[37] well illustrated by the public trust doctrine.

III. Stewardship economics and common goods

Recent economic literature, under the label of *stewardship economics*,[38] identifies 'fiduciary responsibilities' of society with regard to certain resources such as 'a fishery, a forest, the Internet, the air, the oceans, the ecological health of a stream, and so on';[39] i.e., a broad range of common

---

[33] Gould, P. R., *Spatial diffusion*, Washington, DC (Association of American Geographers) 1969, pp. 55–58.
[34] von Goethe, J. W., (1808) *Faust I* (English translation B. Taylor 1870) Oxford (Oxford University Press) 1932, p. 1: IV; as a lawyer, of course, Goethe knew what he was talking about.
[35] Watson, A., *Legal transplants: an approach to comparative law*, Edinburgh (Scottish Academic Press) 2nd edn 1993, p. 22.
[36] Rheinstein, M.,Types of receptions, in Leser, H. G. (ed.), *Max Rheinstein: Gesammelte Schriften* [Collected Works] 1, Tübingen (Mohr) 1979, pp. 261–268.
[37] Kern, K., Jörgens, H., and Jänicke, M., The diffusion of environmental policy innovations: a contribution to the globalisation of environmental policy, Discussion Paper FS II 01–302, Berlin (Wissenschaftszentrum) 2000; Wiener, J. B., Something borrowed for something blue: legal transplants and the evolution of global environmental law, *Ecology L. Q.* 27 (2001), pp. 1295–1371, at 1298.
[38] Young, M. and McCay, B. J., Building equity, stewardship, and resilience into market-based property right systems, in Hanna, S. and Munasinghe, M. (eds.), *Property rights in social and ecological context: concepts and case studies*, Washington, DC (World Bank) 1995, pp. 87–102, at 94; and Page, T., On the problem of achieving efficiency and equity, intergenerationally, *Land Economics* 73 (1997), pp. 580–596.
[39] Brown, P. G., *Ethics, economics and international relations: transparent sovereignty in the Commonwealth of life*, Edinburgh (Edinburgh University Press) 2000, p. 110; see also von Ciriacy-Wantrup, S. and Bishop, R. C., 'Common property' as a concept in natural resources policy, *Natural Resources J.* 15 (1975), pp. 713–727, at 725; and Scott, A., Trust law, sustainability, and responsible action, *Ecological Economics* 31 (1999), pp. 139–154, at 154.

goods,[40] 'environmental commons' in particular,[41] which (depending on criteria of public accessibility or excludability) are categorised either as global collective or 'public goods',[42] or as common property[43] or 'common pool resources' (CPRs).[44] There also is related interdisciplinary research with a focus on the economics of 'trust' as a general organising principle in social psychology,[45] which mirrors legal definitions of public trusteeship as 'preventing the destabilising disappointment of expectations held in common'.[46]

[40] Zacher, H. F., Erhaltung und Verteilung der natürlichen Gemeinschaftsgüter: eine elementare Aufgabe des Rechts, in Badura, P. and Scholz, R. (eds.), *Wege und Verfahren des Verfassungslebens: Festschrift für Peter Lerche zum 65. Geburtstag*, Munich (Beck) 1993, pp. 107–118; and Engel, C., Das Recht der Gemeinschaftsgüter, *Die Verwaltung* 30 (1997), pp. 429–479.

[41] Feld, L. P., Hart, A., Ostmann, A. and Pommerehne, W. W., Umweltgemeingüter?, *Zeitschrift für Wirtschafts- und Sozialwissenschaften* 117 (1997), pp. 107–144; and Ostmann, A., Grenzen ökonomischer Anreize für Umweltgemeingüter, *GAIA* 7 (1998), pp. 286–295.

[42] See Olson, M. Jr., *The logic of collective action: public goods and the theory of groups*, Cambridge, Mass. (Harvard University Press) rev. edn 1971; Murswiek, D., Die Nutzung öffentlicher Umweltgüter: Knappheit, Freiheit, Verteilungsgerechtigkeit, in Gröschner, R. and Morlock, M. (eds.), *Rechtsphilosophie und Rechtsdogmatik in Zeiten des Umbruchs*, Stuttgart (Steiner) 1997, pp. 207–222; Kaul, I., Grunberg, I., and Stern, M. A. (eds.), *Global public goods: international cooperation in the 21st century*, New York (Oxford University Press) 1999.

[43] International lawyers tend to use the term 'common property' in a different (spatial) sense, to designate *res communes* situated in the global commons outside national jurisdiction only, e.g., Wolfrum, R., *Die Internationalisierung staatsfreier Räume*, Berlin (Springer) 1984; and Boyle, A. E., Remedying harm to international common spaces and resources: compensation and other approaches, in Wetterstein, op. cit. pp. 83–100, at 83. But see the wider concept of '*domaine public international*' as used by Scelle, G., *Droit international public: Manuel élémentaire*, Paris (Domat-Montchrestien) 2nd edn 1944, p. 350; and the radically different use of the term – so as to exclude 'public' goods altogether – in natural resource economics (von Ciriacy-Wantrup and Bishop, op. cit. p. 715).

[44] Ostrom, E., *Governing the commons: the evolution of institutions for collective action*, Cambridge (Cambridge University Press) 1990; German translation by E. Schöller, *Die Verfassung der Allmende: jenseits von Staat und Macht*, Tübingen (Mohr Siebeck) 1999; Mitchell, R. B., International environmental common pool resources: more common than domestic but more difficult to manage, in Barkin, J. S. and Shambaugh, G. E. (eds.), *Anarchy and the environment: the international relations of common pool resources*, Albany (State University of New York Press) 1999, pp. 26–50; International Association for the Study of Common Property (IASCP) (ed.), *Constituting the commons: crafting sustainable commons in the new millennium*, papers of the Eighth Biennial Conference, Bloomington, Ind. (Indiana University) 2000; and IASCP (ed.), *The commons in an age of globalisation*, papers of the Ninth Biennial Conference, Victoria Falls (IASCP) 2001.

[45] Gambetta, D., *Trust: making and breaking cooperative relations*, New York (Blackwell) 1988; Ripperger, T., *Ökonomik des Vertrauens: Analyse eines Organisationsprinzips*, Tübingen (Mohr Siebeck) 1998; Engel, C., *Vertrauen: Ein Versuch*, Preprint 99/12, Bonn (Max-Planck-Projektgruppe Recht der Gemeinschaftsgüter) 1999; and Nooteboom, B., *Trust: forms, foundations, functions, failures and figures*, Cheltenham (Edward Elgar) 2002.

[46] Sax, J. L., Liberating the public trust doctrine from its historical shackles, *University of California-Davis L. Rev.* 14 (1980), pp. 185–194, at 187.

At the same time, the concept of stewardship has become the hallmark of two international pilot projects operated by environmental NGOs in cooperation with industry, for the use of economic instruments in natural resource management, in the form of 'eco-labels' for the global marketing of commodities claimed to be sustainably harvested: i.e., timber products certified by the *Forest Stewardship Council*,[47] and ocean fishery products certified by the *Marine Stewardship Council*.[48] The topic has thus ceased to be academic: transnational civil society groups, emerging as powerful actors in the environmental arena,[49] are beginning to develop and invoke their own tangible criteria for holding public trustees accountable.

IV. Environmental trusteeship in international law

How far, then, has the idea of public trusteeship for environmental resources progressed in the field of international law? To make things clear, I am *not* referring here to the 'trust funds' frequently used as mechanisms to finance international environmental regimes and projects, such as the *Global Environment Facility* (GEF) for which the World Bank serves as trustee[50] – even though their operational experience may also offer useful insights for global environmental governance[51] and for the further transnational harmonisation of legal rules.[52] What is at stake here, however, as object of the trust (or *corpus*, in the jargon of trust law), and as object of the rules, are *not* financial assets, but the environmental resources themselves.

---

[47] Kloven, K. M., Eco-labeling of sustainably harvested wood under the Forest Stewardship Council: seeing the forest for the trees, *Colorado J. Int'l Envt'l Law and Policy* 9 (1998), pp. 48–55; and Schmidt, E., The Forest Stewardship Council: using the market to promote responsible forestry, *Yearbook Int'l Co-operation on Environment and Development* 7 (1998), pp. 23–27.

[48] Freestone, D. and Makuch, Z., The new international environmental law of fisheries: the 1995 United Nations Straddling Stocks Agreement, *Yearbook Int'l Envt'l Law* 7 (1996), pp. 3–51, at 48.

[49] e.g., see Edwards, M. and Gaventa, J., *Global citizen action*, Boulder (Rienner) 2002; Oberthür, S. et al., *Participation of non-governmental organizations in international environmental governance: legal basis and practical experience*, Berlin (Ecologic) 2001.

[50] See Sand, P. H., Carrots without sticks? New financial mechanisms for global environmental agreements, *Max Planck Yearbook of United Nations Law* 3 (1999), pp. 363–388.

[51] Liu, J., Trust funds as mechanisms for sustainable development, in Bothe, M. and Sand, P. H. (eds.), *Environmental policy: from regulation to economic instruments*, The Hague (Martinus Nijhoff) 2002, pp. 269–295.

[52] e.g., compare Gold, J., Trust funds in international law: the contribution of the International Monetary Fund to a Code of Principles, *American J. Int'l Law* 72 (1978), pp. 856–866; and the Convention on the Law Applicable to Trusts and on Their Recognition, signed at The Hague on 1 July 1985, 23 I.L.M. (1984) 1389 (with an introduction in 25 I.L.M. (1986) 593).

The idea of treating at least part of these resources as 'inclusive' or 'internationally shared environment'[53] has, of course, a long tradition in international law, with regard to resources outside national jurisdiction, from *res communes omnium* to 'common heritage' doctrines;[54] and with regard to certain 'internal resources',[55] from doctrines of *bon voisinage* to 'shared natural resources'.[56] Proposals to make use of the public trust doctrine in an international environmental context date back to the 1893 *Bering Sea Fur Seal Arbitration*;[57] they resurfaced during preparations for the 1972 *Stockholm Declaration*[58] and the *World Heritage Convention*,[59] and have since been taken up by a number of international publicists, especially in the legal debate on intergenerational equity.[60]

Various forms of 'trusteeship', 'guardianship', 'custodianship', or 'stewardship' status have thus been suggested for the marine environment in coastal waters and exclusive economic zones; for certain continental shelf areas beyond the EEZ; for marine resources in specific regional seas such as the Mediterranean and the South Pacific; for living ocean resources in general; for Antarctica; for the global atmosphere; for all global commons; for rain forests in Latin America;

---

[53] McDougal, M. S. and Schneider, J., The protection of the environment and world public order: some recent developments, *Missouri L. J.* 45 (1974), pp. 1085–1124, at 1092; Handl, G., Territorial sovereignty and the problem of transnational sovereignty, *American J. Int'l Law* 69 (1975), pp. 50–76; and Schneider, J., *World public order of the environment: towards an international ecological law and organization*, Toronto (University of Toronto Press) 1979, p. 22.

[54] e.g., see Stocker, W., *Das Prinzip des Common Heritage of Mankind als Ausdruck des Staatengemeinschaftsinteresses im Völkerrecht*, Zürich (Schulthess) 1993; and Baslar, K., *The concept of the common heritage of mankind in international law*, The Hague (Nijhoff) 1998.

[55] Arsanjani, M. H., *International regulation of internal resources: a study of law and policy*, Charlottesville, Va. (University Press of Virginia) 1981.

[56] Adede, A. O., Utilization of shared natural resources: towards a code of conduct, *Environmental Policy and Law* 5 (1979), pp. 66–76; Barberis, J. A., *Los recursos naturales compartidos entre estados y el Derecho Internacional*, Madrid (Editorial Tecnos) 1979; and Reszat, P., *Gemeinsame Naturgüter im Völkerrecht: Eine Studie zur Knappheit natürlicher Ressourcen und den völkerrechtlichen Regeln zur Lösung von Nutzungskonflikten*, Munich (Beck) 2004.

[57] *Great Britain v. USA*, Arbitration Award (Paris, 15 August 1893) [1999] 1 International Environmental Law Reports 43.

[58] Sohn, L. B., The Stockholm Declaration on the Human Environment, *Harvard Int'l L. J.* 14 (1973), pp. 423–515, at 457; and Maggio, G. F., Inter/intra-generational equity: current applications under international law for promoting the sustainable development of natural resources, *Buffalo Environmental L. J.* 4 (1997), pp. 161–223, at 203.

[59] See n. 11 above; Gardner, R. N., *Blueprint for peace*, New York (McGraw Hill) 1966, p. 154; Train, R. E., A World Heritage Trust, in Gillette, E. R. (ed.), *Action for wilderness*, Washington, DC (Sierra Club) 1972, pp. 172–176; and Meyer, R. L., Travaux préparatoires for the UNESCO World Heritage Convention, *Earth L. J.* 2 (1976), pp. 45–81.

[60] Detailed bibliographical references in *Global Environmental Politics* 4(1) (2004), pp. 52–53 and 58–71.

for freshwater resources in the Middle East; for genetic resources or biological resources generally; or for all elements of the environment.[61]

In two cases dealing with marine resource conservation, the European Court of Justice declared all Member States 'trustees of the common interest';[62] and in a judgment interpreting the 1979 EU Bird Conservation Directive,[63] it considered wild birds 'a case where the *management of the common heritage is entrusted* to the member states in their respective territories'.[64] More recently, in his much-quoted separate opinion in the 1997 *Danube Dam* case, Judge Christopher G. Weeramantry of the International Court of Justice referred to a 'principle of trusteeship for earth resources'.[65]

In July 1997, UN Secretary-General Kofi Annan proposed, in his report on governance reform,[66] that the United Nations Trusteeship Council:

> be reconstituted as the forum through which Member States exercise their collective trusteeship for the integrity of the global environment and common areas such as the oceans, atmosphere and outer space. At the same time, it should serve to link the United Nations and civil society in addressing these areas of global concern, which require the active contribution of public, private and voluntary sectors.

The idea was not a new one. It had first been raised by Maurice Strong, legendary organiser of the Stockholm and Rio UN Conferences, in a 1988 speech to the World Federation of United Nations Associations in Halifax;[67] and by Maltese Foreign Minister Guido de Marco in his closing address as president of the forty-fifth UN General Assembly in 1991.[68] Initial reactions were rather sceptical, mainly because changing the mandate of the Trusteeship Council would require an amendment of the UN Charter,[69] and earlier attempts at

---

[61] See n. 60 above for source references.
[62] Case C-804/79, *European Commission* v. *United Kingdom* [1981] 1 ECR 1045 at para. 30; Case C-325/85, *Ireland* v. *European Commission* [1987] 3 ECR 5041, at para. 15.
[63] Council Directive 79/409/EEC of 2 April 1979 on the Conservation of Wild Birds [1979] OJ L103/1.
[64] Case C-339/87, *European Commission* v. *Netherlands* [1990] 1 ECR 851; [1993] 2 CMLR 360, at 885.
[65] International Court of Justice, Judgment in the *Case concerning the Gabcíkovo-Nagymaros Project (Hungary* v. *Slovakia)* [1997] ICJ Rep. 1; 37 I.L.M. (1998) 204 at 213; see also Weeramantry, C. G., *Nauru: environmental damage under international trusteeship*, Melbourne (Oxford University Press) 1992, p. 151.
[66] Report of the Secretary-General to the General Assembly, *Renewing the United Nations: a programme for reform*, UN Doc. A/51/950, 14 July 1997, para. 85.
[67] Reprinted in Strong, M. F., The United Nations in an interdependent world, *International Affairs* January 1989, pp. 11–21, at 20.
[68] See de Marco, G. and Bartolo, M., *Second generation United Nations: for peace in freedom in the 21st century*, London (Kegan Paul International) 1997.
[69] Szasz, P. C., Restructuring the international organizational framework, in Weiss, E. B. (ed.), *Environmental change and international law: new challenges and dimensions*, Tokyo (United Nations University Press) 1992, pp. 340–384, at 362.

extending that mandate to the Antarctic had failed.[70] But Strong has a reputation for never taking 'no' for an answer, and nobody was surprised therefore to see the idea resurface in the report of the *Commission on Global Governance*, of which he was a member,[71] and later in the UN reform proposals (for which he served as consultant), promptly endorsed by Malta's newly elected head of state.[72]

The 1997 UN report was followed by a note from the Secretary-General on the concept of trusteeship,[73] which regrettably entrusted the question to the proverbial UN committee: the *Task Force on Environment and Human Settlements*, chaired by the Executive Director of UNEP. The task force report to the General Assembly in October 1998 refrained from making any recommendations on the trusteeship issue.[74] Instead, the buck was passed to the *Open-ended Intergovernmental Group of Ministers on International Environmental Governance* launched by the UNEP Governing Council in February 2001, which predictably referred the matter to expert consultations, held in Cambridge in May 2001; the experts, in their wisdom, concluded that 'it would be very difficult to undertake measures that would affect the main organs established by the United Nations Charter, like the ECOSOC and the Trusteeship Council'.[75] As a result, the topic never even reached the agenda of the 2002 Johannesburg Summit on Sustainable Development.[76]

So is this just another one of those non-starters that periodically emerge in international institutions, only to die a slow 'death by committee'? I don't think so; and I believe it is worth taking a closer look at the idea of trusteeship, for a number of reasons.

---

[70] Wolfrum, op. cit. p. 49.

[71] Report of the Commission on Global Governance, *Our global neighbourhood*, Oxford (Oxford University Press) 1995, p. 251.

[72] de Marco, G., A renewed Trusteeship Council: guardian of future generations, First Arvid Pardo Memorial Lecture, in International Ocean Institute, *Proceedings of Pacem in Maribus XXVII*, Suva (10I) 1999; see also Mann Borgese, E., *The oceanic circle: governing the sea as a global resource*, Tokyo (UN University Press) 1998, pp. 164 and 195.

[73] Note by the Secretary-General on United Nations Reform Measures and Proposals, *A new concept of trusteeship*, UN Doc. A/52/849, 31 March 1998.

[74] Report of the Secretary-General to the General Assembly, *Environment and human settlements*, UN Doc. A/53/463, 6 October 1998; Agarwal, A., Narain, S., and Sharma, A., *Green politics: global environmental negotiations* 1, New Delhi (Centre for Science and Environment) 1999, p. 365; and Desai, B. H., Revitalizing international environmental institutions: the UN Task Force Report and beyond, *Indian J. Int'l Law* 40 (2001), pp. 455–504, at 486.

[75] Estrada Oyuela, R., *Expert consultations on international environmental governance (Cambridge, May 28–29, 2001): Chairman's summary*, Nairobi (UNEP IEG Working Document) 2001, p. 1.

[76] Sand, P. H., Environmental summitry and international law, *Yearbook of Int'l Envt'l Law* 13 (2002), pp. 3–15, at 35.

V. Prolegomena of a theory

In spite of the irritant amount of rhetoric surrounding it, the concept of public trusteeship is *not* a mere figure of speech or a utopian scenario, as some commentators and orators seem to assume. To begin with, the concept has respectable philosophical credentials: from the famous statement in John Locke's *Second Treatise on Civil Government* (1685), asserting that governments merely exercise a 'fiduciary trust' on behalf of their people,[77] to the suggestion by Roscoe Pound to limit the role of states in the management of common natural resources to 'a sort of guardianship for social purposes'.[78] That comes remarkably close indeed to Karl Marx:

> Selbst eine ganze Gesellschaft, eine Nation, ja alle gleichzeitigen Gesellschaften zusammengenommen sind nicht Eigentümer der Erde. Sie sind nur ihre Besitzer, ihre Nutznießer, und haben sie als *boni patres familias* den nachfolgenden Generationen verbessert zu hinterlassen.[79]

It seems to me that this fundamental *public* law dimension of trusteeship is often neglected in solely *private* law comparisons between Anglo-American trust law and other legal systems.[80] While it is true that the common law trust has historic parallels in European civil law (going back to the ancient Roman *fiducia* and *fideicommissum*), in the charitable *waqf* of Islamic law,[81] and in the

---

[77] Gough, J. W., Political trusteeship, in Gough, J. W. (ed.), *John Locke's political philosophy*, Oxford (Clarendon) 1973, pp. 154–192; Dunn, J., The concept of 'trust' in the politics of John Locke, in Rorty, R. (ed.), *Philosophy in history*, Cambridge (Cambridge University Press) 1984, pp. 279–301; and Brown, P. G., *Restoring the public trust: a fresh vision for progressive government in America*, Boston (Beacon Press) 1994.

[78] Pound, R., An introduction to the philosophy of law, New Haven, Conn. (Yale University Press) rev. edn of 1922 edn, 1954, p. 111.

[79] F. Engels (ed.), *Das Kapital* (1865) 1894 vol III, ch. 6, in *Karl Marx und Friedrich Engels Gesamtausgabe*, Berlin (Dietz) 1992, Pt 2, vol. IV, p. 718: 'Even society as a whole, a nation, or all contemporary societies taken together, are not owners of the Earth. They are merely its occupants, its usufructuaries; and as diligent guardians, must hand it down improved to subsequent generations' (author's translation; the reference to *bonus pater familias* (literally, 'good family father', i.e., caretaker, or guardian) of Roman law, in which Marx had been trained, defines a standard of care comparable to the due diligence of a common law trustee, as an 'ordinary prudent man dealing with the property of another'; Scott, op. cit. p. 145.)

[80] e.g., see Schwarz-Liebermann, H. A., *Vormundschaft und Treuhand des römischen und englischen Privatrechts in ihrer Anwendbarkeit auf völkerrechtlicher Ebene*, Tübingen (Mohr) 1951; Kötz, op. cit.; Waters, D. W. M., The institution of the trust in civil and common law, *Hague Academy of International Law Recueil des Cours* 252 (1995), pp. 113–454; Hansmann, H. and Mattei, U., The functions of trust law: a comparative legal and economic analaysis, *New York University L. Rev.* 73 (1998), pp. 434–479; Hayton, D. (ed.), *Modern international developments in trust law*, The Hague (Kluwer Law International) 1999; and Klein, op. cit.

[81] Fratcher, W. F., Trust, in *International Encyclopedia of Comparative Law* 6(11) (1973), pp. 84–141, at 108.

```
            Settlor
              •
             / \
            /   \
           /     \
  Trustee •───────• Beneficiary
```

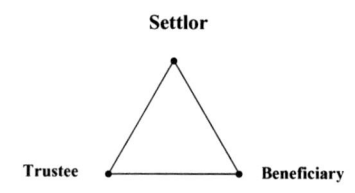

Figure 21.1 Trusteeship

moramati of African customary land law,[82] analogies from private property law do not suffice to explain public trusteeship. In particular, the instinctive inclination of German lawyers to consider the trust as equivalent to the private law *Treuhand*,[83] with its predominant focus on *bilateral* contractual relations between a settlor (*Treugeber*) and a trustee (*Treuhänder*),[84] has resulted in fatal misconceptions of public trusteeship in the environmental context – which instead is really *trilateral* (see Figure 21.1).

Another major source of misunderstanding is the frequent invocation of trusteeship metaphors without juridical content, a usage already encountered in the literature on common *cultural* heritage, often labelled 'comparable to

---

[82] Kenyatta, J., *Facing Mount Kenya: the traditional life of the Gikuyu*, Nairobi (Heinemann) reprint of 1938 edn, 1978, p. 32; and Ollennu, N. A., *Principles of customary land law in Ghana*, London (Sweet & Maxwell) 1962, p. 4.

[83] Not to be confused with the Treuhand-Anstalt, a unique administrative (fiscal) institution established after the fall of the Berlin Wall to privatise the former East German government's real estate holdings; see Seibel, W., Necessary illusions: the transformation of governance structures in the new Germany, *Tocqueville Review* 13 (1992), pp. 178–197; Fischer, W., Hax, H., and Schneider, H. K. (eds.), *Treuhandanstalt: the impossible challenge*, Berlin (Akademie-Verlag) 1996; and Seibel, W., *Verwaltete Illusionen: Die Treuhandanstalt und ihre Nachfolgeeinrichtungen 1990–1994*, Frankfurt and New York (Campus Publishers) 2005. Not surprisingly perhaps, the German Advisory Council on Global Change (Wissenschaftlicher Beirat Globale Umweltveränderungen, WBGU) mistook Kofi Annan's concept of UN environmental trusteeship (see n. 66 above) for a proposal to empower international '*Treuhandbehörden*' to levy fiscal charges on global common goods such as airspace, the high seas, geostationary orbits, and Antarctica; see WBGU (ed.), *Welt im Wandel: Neue Strukturen globaler Umweltpolitik*, Berlin (Springer) 2001, p. 183 (English translation, *World in transition: new structures for global environmental policy*, London (Earthscan) 2002); WBGU (ed.), *Charging the use of the global commons*, Berlin (Springer) 2002; reviewed by Sand, P. H., Vergemeinschaftung von Umweltgütern als Teil einer UN-Reform?, in Klein, E., Volger, H., and Weiss, N. (eds.), *Integrative Konzepte bei der Reform der Vereinten Nationen*, Potsdam (MenschenRechtsZentrum der Universität Potsdam) 2004, pp. 38–44.

[84] See Coing, H., *Die Treuhand kraft privaten Rechtsgeschäfts*, Munich (Beck) 1973; Grundmann, S., *Der Treuhandvertrag, insbesondere die werbende Treuhand*, Munich (Beck) 1997, p. 3; and Grundmann, S., Trust and Treuhand at the end of the 20th century: key problems and shift of interests, *American J. Comparative Law* 47 (1999), pp. 401–428.

GLOBAL ENVIRONMENTAL CHANGE AND THE NATION STATE 533

Community

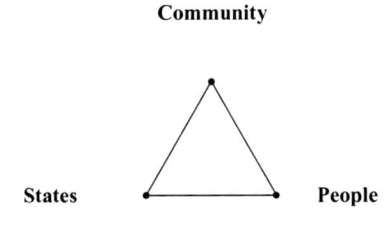

States ————— People

Figure 21.2 International environmental trusteeship

trusteeship in a *non-legal* sense'.[85] In environmental writings as well, whenever ethical terms like 'resource stewardship',[86] 'international/global stewardship',[87] 'man's stewardship or trustee responsibilities for Earth's natural resources and life systems'[88] or the role of states as '*Hüter* [guardians/keepers] *oder Treuhänder*' for the environment are invoked,[89] the focus tends to be on *bilateral* duties owed by the present generation of humankind – as trustee – to future generations or 'future humanity' as the beneficiaries.[90] These purely metaphoric formulations can hardly be taken as reflecting a trusteeship vision in the legal sense. Yet the *trilateral* legal structure of international public trusteeship over environmental resources[91] is easily expressed in Figure 21.2.

Admittedly, this oversimplified figure leaves a number of questions open for debate, starting with the definitions: of the community concerned as *settlor* (the global community? or the community of members of specific international regimes, e.g., contracting parties to a multilateral convention?); of the sovereign

---

[85] Stocker, op. cit. p. 123.
[86] Tarlock, A. D., Exclusive sovereignty versus sustainable development of a shared resource: the dilemma of Latin American rainforest management, *Texas Int'l L. J.* 32 (1997), pp. 37–66, at 66.
[87] Brown, J. L., Stewardship: An international perspective, *Environments J. Interdisciplinary Studies* 26(1) (1998), pp. 8–17; Lucas, P. H. C., Beresford, M., and Aitchison, J., Protected landscapes: global and local stewardship, *J. Interdisciplinary Studies* 26(1) (1998), pp. 18–26.
[88] Robinson, N. A., Editorial: stewardship, *Earth L. J.* 1 (1975), pp. 3–4, at 3.
[89] Calliess, C., Ansätze zur Subjektivierung von Gemeinwohlbelangen im Völkerrecht: das Beispiel des Umweltschutzes, *Zeitschrift für Umweltrecht* 11 (2000), pp. 246–257, at 247.
[90] e.g., see Busuttil, S., Agius, S., Inglott, P. S., and Macelli, T. (eds.), *Our responsibilities towards future generations: a programme of UNESCO and the International Environment Institute*, Malta (Foundation for International Studies) 1990; Gillespie, A., *International environmental law, policy and ethics*, Oxford (Clarendon Press) 1997, p. 107; Gaba, J. M., Environmental ethics and our moral relationship to future generations: future rights and present virtue, *Columbia J. Envt'l Law* 24 (1999), pp. 249–288; and von Bubnoff, D., *Der Schutz der künftigen Generationen im deutschen Umweltrecht: Leitbilder, Grundsätze und Instrumente eines dauerhaften Umweltschutzes*, Bielefeld (Erich Schmidt Verlag) 2001.
[91] Sand, P. H., Trusteeship for common pool resources? Zur Renaissance des Treuhandbegriffs im Umweltvölkerrecht, in von Schorlemer, S. (ed.), *Praxis-Handbuch UNO: Die Vereinten Nationen im Lichte globaler Herausforderungen*, Berlin (Springer) 2003, pp. 201–224.

entity concerned as public *trustee* (states only? or also intergovernmental institutions acting in areas outside national jurisdiction, e.g., the UN International Seabed Authority?); of the people concerned as *beneficiaries* (present *and* future civil society? individuals *and* groups?); and of the *corpus* of the trust (designated resources only? or the global commons? or the whole environment?).

There are essentially three options for the creation of an international environmental trust:

(a) by a specific trust 'deed' (*Widmung, affectation*)[92] designating a particular resource to be conserved for a beneficial purpose, e.g., the 'listing' of protected areas under the World Heritage Convention, through a process of formal nomination (by a host state) and conditioned acceptance (by a committee representing the member states), based on agreed criteria;[93]

(b) by a treaty designating an entire category of trust resources to be so conserved in all member states, e.g., the plant genetic resources included in Annex I of the FAO Plant Gene Treaty,[94] subject to ratification by the *in situ* states concerned; or

(c) arguably, by customary law or 'objective' extension of a conventional public trust regime to all states (*erga omnes*) regardless of their membership in the treaty, on the basis of objective natural criteria of the resource (*par nature*),[95] which would presumably in turn require some kind of declaratory or customary specification of the international community's 'common concern',[96] e.g., for the deep seabed (common heritage 'as a form of international trusteeship').[97]

Save for the last-mentioned hypothesis of an 'objective regime' – which remains controversial – the majority of international environmental trusts are likely to arise in one of the consensual forms described under options (a) and (b); hence, their legal effects will normally be limited to relations between parties to the multilateral regimes concerned. When defining the environmental resources of 'common concern' envisaged as objects of a global public trust – its *corpus*, as it were – the UN Trusteeship Council proposal seems to envisage the global commons in the first place;[98] however, as the examples of genetic bioresources and cultural/natural heritage illustrate, 'internal' resources situated *within* national jurisdiction could also be so designated if the community as settlor and the host

---

[92] Kiss, A. C., La notion de patrimoine commun de l'humanité, *Hague Academy of International Law Recueil des Cours* 175 (1982), pp. 109–256, at 229. Incidentally, the French term for 'trust funds' in UN terminology is '*fonds d'affectation*'; see UN Doc. ST/SGB/Financial Rules/1/Rev.3 (1985), paras. 106.3–106.4.

[93] See n. 11 above; Lyster, S., *International wildlife law: an analysis of international treaties concerned with the conservation of wildlife*, Cambridge (Grotius Publications) 1985, p. 211.

[94] See n. 8 above.   [95] Kiss, op. cit. p. 225.   [96] Durner, op. cit. p. 291.

[97] Boyle, op. cit. p. 84.

[98] Report of the UN Secretary-General, op. cit. p. 85; WBGU, op. cit.

state as trustee so agree. Hence, the trusteeship status of a resource is not at all incompatible with the legitimate exercise of sovereign rights by a host state, just as (and here the analogy from trust law seems perfectly appropriate) a common law trustee has legitimate property rights over the *corpus*, always provided those rights are exercised in accordance with the interests of the beneficiary and with the terms of the trust.

(That, incidentally, also applies to the exercise of sovereignty by administering authorities in trust territories under the post-war trusteeship system supervised by the Trusteeship Council,[99] and indeed in pre-Second World War 'mandate' territories – even though Woodrow Wilson's famous reference to the 'sacred trust of civilization' (*League of Nations Covenant* 1919, Article 22) turned out to be untranslatable into French and therefore all but lost its original Anglo-American legal meaning in the practice of the League of Nations.)[100]

Safeguarding the rights of beneficiaries is indeed a core function of environmental public trusteeship. While the balance between a trustee's current use and long-term conservation of the resource is the key *economic* issue (converging in the 'sustainable development' paradigm), public participation becomes the key *legal* issue: in order to 'enforce the terms of the trust against the trustee' (as it were in common law parlance), this may require *procedural* safeguards, including actionable rights to know, rights to be heard, and rights to challenge decisions, along the lines of the Aarhus Convention,[101] as well as *institutional* arrangements such as the empowerment of a 'Guardian' or 'Environmental

---

[99] Rouche, J., La souveraineté dans les territoires sous tutelle, *Revue Générale de Droit International Public* 58 (1954), pp. 399–437, at 419; Toussaint, C. E., *The trusteeship system of the United Nations*, London (Stevens & Sons) 1956. For a recent reassessment see Bain, W., The political theory of trusteeship and the twilight of international equality, *International Relations* 17 (2003), pp. 59–77; and on the 'representational' analogy with regard to trusteeship zone proposals for the law of the sea, Hafner, op. cit. pp. 91–95.

[100] The French text Covenant Article 22 had mistranslated 'sacred trust' as *'mission sacrée'* (the same in UN Charter Article 73), thereby shifting the legal metaphor from trusteeship to mandate, or agency. The similar German mistranslation from the Covenant used *heilige Aufgabe* (which became *Auftrag* in the UN Charter, hence *Auftragsverwaltung*). In the 1966 South West Africa case, the International Court of Justice initially treated the trusteeship concept as a 'moral ideal' only (*Ethiopia* v. *South Africa/Liberia* v. *South Africa*, 2nd phase judgment [1966] ICJ Rep. 6), but in the 1971 Namibia Advisory Opinion recognised it as creating rights and obligations between the trustee and the beneficiaries (*Legal Consequences for States of the Continued Presence of South Africa in Namibia/South-West Africa* [1971] ICJ Rep. 16).

[101] Convention on Access to Information, Public Participation in Decision-Making and Access to Justice in Environmental Matters, adopted by the United Nations Economic Commission for Europe (UN/ECE) at Aarhus, Denmark, on 25 June 1998; 38 I.L.M. (1999) 517. See Rose-Ackerman, S. and Halpaap, A. A., The Aarhus Convention and the politics of process: the political economy of procedural environmental rights, *Research in Law and Economics* 20 (2002), pp. 27–64.

High Commissioner' with rights of standing and legal representation on behalf of civil society.[102] In the case of public trusts operating in the context of conventional regimes, such as the World Heritage Convention, or the Biodiversity Convention and the FAO Plant Gene Treaty, existing treaty institutions may have to be adapted accordingly. In the case of free-standing 'objective' public trusts operating outside treaty regimes, the proposed environmental mandate for a reconstituted UN Trusteeship Council might serve a useful residual purpose, also in the hypothesis of jurisdictional disputes between overlapping trusts. The international community may even be said to have a responsibility towards the beneficiaries – i.e., transnational civil society – to ensure that they can enforce the terms of the trust against trustee states, through appropriate remedies and institutions, e.g., by the designation of representative civil bodies so as to overcome the 'democratic deficit' of global governance.[103]

VI. Conclusions

The broader question as to whether lessons learned from national environmental institutions can be extrapolated to the global environment seems to have intrigued not only international lawyers, but far more serious minds, including Nobel laureates in economics.[104] Public trusteeship for environmental resources typically raises a problem of 'scale': i.e., the transferability of empirical generalisations and causal inferences from one level to another in the dimensions of space and time.[105] What I have tried to show is that a transfer of the public trust concept from the national to the global level is conceivable,

---

[102] Sands, P. J., Protecting future generations: precedents and practicalities, in Agius, E. and Busuttil, S. (eds.), *Future generations and international law*, London (Earthscan) 1997, pp. 83–91, at 83; Orrego Vicuña, F. and Sohn, L., Responsibility and liability under international law for environmental damage, *Annuaire de l'Institut de Droit International* 1 (1997), pp. 288 and 341; and the IWCO Report, op. cit. p. 136.

[103] See generally Keohane, R. O., International institutions: can interdependence work?, *Foreign Policy* 110 (1998), pp. 82–96, at 91; Wirth, D. A., Globalizing the environment, in Cusimano, M. K. (ed.), *Beyond sovereignty: issues for a global agenda*, Boston (Bedford/St.Martin's) 2000, pp. 198–216, at 210; Edwards, M., NGOs and international economic policy-making: rights and responsibilities in the global arena, *World Economics* 2(3) (2001), pp. 127–137, at 136; Agarwal, A., Narain, S., Sharma, A., and Imchen, A., *Poles apart: global environmental negotiations 2*, New Delhi (Centre for Science and Environment) 2001, p. 38; and Scholte, J. A., Civil society and democracy in global governance, *Global Governance* 8 (2002), pp. 281–304.

[104] North, D. C., Dealing with a non-ergodic world: institutional economics, property rights, and the global environment, *Duke Environmental Law and Policy Forum* 10 (1999), pp. 1–12.

[105] Young, O. R., *The institutional dimensions of environmental change: fit, interplay, and scale*, Cambridge, Mass. (MIT Press) 2002, pp. 139–162.

feasible, and tolerable. It does *not* pose the 'threats to sovereignty' imagined by ultra-conservative US political scientists,[106] who have conjured up images of 'the black helicopters of the United Nations' invading Yellowstone National Park to carry out field inspections under the World Heritage Convention.[107] Ironically, that treaty, which now has 180 member states, goes back to an initiative by the USA, due mainly to the efforts of the first chairman of the US Council on Environmental Quality, Russell E. Train.[108] The essence of environmental public trusteeship, as embodied in the Convention, is the democratic *accountability* of states[109] for their management of trust resources in the interest of the beneficiaries – the world's 'peoples'.[110] As Robert Keohane puts it, 'in the long run, global governance will only be legitimate if there is a substantial measure of external accountability. Global governance can impose limits on powerful states and other powerful organizations, but it also helps the powerful, because they shape the terms of governance.'[111]

---

[106] Rabkin, J. A., *Why sovereignty matters*, AEI Studies on Global Environmental Policy, Washington, DC (American Enterprise Institute) 1998, p. 46.

[107] See n. 11 above. The occasion was a 1995 visit to the Park (at the invitation of the US government) by the UNESCO World Heritage Committee to hold hearings on potential threats to a 'listed' protected area from a mining development project in an adjacent area. The incident prompted – unsuccessful – legislative proposals for an American Land Sovereignty Protection Act (H. R. 3752, 104th Cong. 2nd Sess. 1996), providing for congressional approval of all public land designations under international agreements; see Gebert, D. L., Sovereignty under the World Heritage Convention: a questionable basis for limiting the federal land designation pursuant to international agreements, *Southern California Interdisciplinary L. J.* 7 (1998), pp. 427–444. There are subtle parallels in the European Union, where conservative German and British governments tried to stop the European Commission from undertaking field inspections of national protected areas, following a judgment of the European Court of Justice in which the Commission had challenged dyke construction projects in a German coastal zone 'listed' under the 1979 EU Bird Conservation Directive (see n. 63 above); Case C-57/89, *European Commission v. Germany* (Leybucht case) [1991] 1 ECR 383; see Baldock, D., The status of special protection areas for the protection of wild birds, *J. Envt'l Law* 4 (1992), pp. 139–144; and Krämer, L., *European environmental law casebook*, London (Sweet & Maxwell) 1993, p. 399.

[108] See n. 59 above.

[109] cf. Allott, P., *Eunomia: new order for a new world*, Oxford (Oxford University Press) 1990, p. 336 ('legal accountability for the exercise of social power'); Jonas, H., *Das Prinzip Verantwortung: Versuch einer Ethik für die technologische Zivilisation*, Frankfurt (Suhrkamp) 4th edn 1984, p. 174; English translation, *The imperative of responsibility: in search of an ethics for the technology age*, Chicago (University of Chicago Press) 1984, p. 90; Brown, op. cit. p. 142; and Fisher, E., The European Union in the age of accountability, *Oxford J. Legal Studies* 24 (2004), pp. 495–515.

[110] Rawls, J., *The law of peoples*, Cambridge, Mass. (Harvard University Press) 1999, p. 23.

[111] Keohane, R. O., *Global governance and democratic accountability*, Milliband Lecture, London (London School of Economics and Political Science) 2002, p. 29.

The public trust concept thus reinforces, rather than weakens, the 'sovereign legitimacy'[112] of environmental governance by nation states. There is little evidence, I am afraid, of the icon of territorial sovereignty 'fading away' into history.[113] All I can diagnose in this field is a palish new 'greening' of sovereignty[114] – and that is nothing to apologise for.

[112] Hochstetler, K., Clark, A. M., and Friedman, E. J., Sovereignty in the balance: claims and bargains at the UN Conferences on the Environment, Human Rights, and Women, *International Studies Q.* 44 (2000), pp. 591–614, at 611.

[113] Kiss, A. C., Commentary, in Weiss, op. cit. p. 13.

[114] cf. Litfin, K. T. (ed.), *The greening of sovereignty in world politics*, Cambridge, Mass. (MIT Press) 1998.

22

Whose environment? Concepts of commonality in international environmental law

MICHAEL BOTHE

I. The basic issue: distribution of jurisdiction – distribution of benefits

Environmental problems are natural phenomena. They are caused by human activities. But once so caused, they follow the laws of nature. Thus, they tend to ignore political boundaries drawn by man. But the regulatory powers to deal with these problems are distributed according to the principle of territorial jurisdiction. No state has jurisdictional powers outside its borders unless the state where such powers are exercised consents to it. That principle of the territorial distribution of regulatory powers is complemented by the principle of freedom in areas where there is no territorial jurisdiction.

The first problem triggered by this situation is that of effectiveness. How can a state deal effectively with a problem that has its origins elsewhere? Can it be expected that a state deals effectively with a problem the consequences of which are felt elsewhere? In economic terms, this is the problem of externalities. Activities of events taking place in one state have (positive or negative) effects on the territory of other states or in areas beyond national jurisdiction. These externalities pose the major problem in terms of both regulatory effectiveness and equitable allocation of burdens and benefits.

The territorial division of the land surface of the Earth has another, yet related consequence: the benefits derived from the resources situated in a particular territorial state belong to that state. This has been called the principle of sovereignty over national resources.[1] In areas beyond national jurisdiction, the rule of free appropriation on the basis 'first come, first served' prevails. Both rules of distribution[2] entail problems of distributional justice and environmental preservation. As to the principle of permanent sovereignty over national resources, the question of access to resources needed by other states, and the fair return for such access, is problematic. As to the resources in areas

---

[1] See in particular UN General Assembly Resolution 1803 (XVII) (1962).
[2] Wolfrum, R., Die Fischerei auf Hoher See, *Zeitschrift für ausländisches öffentliches Recht und Völkerrecht* 38 (1978), p. 659.

beyond national jurisdiction, the freedom of exploitation may boil down to the freedom of the fastest and strongest – which is not necessarily just in terms of distributional justice nor an optimal allocation of scarce resources.

The policy related to the use of natural resources and the preservation of the environment in a world which is divided into territorial states is loaded with conflict. Models for conflict resolution have to be sought. A basic idea behind this quest for appropriate solutions is that the environment of our planet Earth is a common asset which cannot properly be divided, which is shared by humankind at large. This is the fundamental concept of commonality which this chapter tries to explore in more detail by going through a number of typical conflict situations.

Private law analogies[3] are often suggested as a possible model. Territorial jurisdiction is compared to property. For the purposes of environmental protection, this chapter asks whether certain limitations on the use of private property, imposed to safeguard other private or public interest, can apply *mutatis mutandis* in the international sphere. A basic concept of private law is that the owner of a property is as a matter of principle free to use it as he or she likes, but not always so. Limitations are imposed upon the owner for reasons of the common weal. It may well be that the law prescribes that he or she has to share benefits with others. In this connection, the legal construction of a trust is often invoked.[4] This chapter suggests that these analogies are sometimes useful, but their value is limited.

II. Sovereignty over national resources and distributional justice: the problem of externalities

1. Traditional conflict in neighbourly relations

The first type of conflict which has to be solved at the international level is the situation where a pollution (emission) originating in one state causes damage in another state. The distributional question raised by that situation is: who bears that damage: the victim/victim state or the polluter/state of the polluter? It is now uncontroversial, as a matter of principle, that it is the polluter. The leading case is the *Trail Smelter* arbitral award.[5] It is based on a primary rule developed through a private law analogy: *sic utere tuo ut neminem laedas*. Formulated in terms of international law: each state is under an international legal duty to prevent acts or events on its territory which cause or are likely to cause damage on the territory of another state.[6] The corresponding

---

[3] The basic monograph on this concept still is Lauterpacht, H., *Private law sources and analogies of international law*, 1927, reprinted Hamden, Conn. (Archon) 1970.
[4] See Peter Sand, Chapter 21.   [5] RIAA 3 (1949), pp. 1903–1982.
[6] Sands, P., *Principles of international environmental law*, Cambridge (Cambridge University Press) 2nd edn 2003, p. 321 *et seq.*

secondary rule, derived from the principles of state responsibility, is that the state of origin owes compensation to be paid to the state suffering the damage. In terms of principles of environmental policy, this solution corresponds to the 'polluter pays' principle. In economic terms, it means that the external effects of the activity taking place on the territory of the state of origin are internalised. The result is, as a rule, an efficient allocation of a scarce resource (the receptive capacity of the environment). In terms of distributional justice, the result is considered to be 'just'. Be it noted that the scope of application of this rule is limited. It only applies to a situation where there is a point source of pollution and a 'point damage', i.e. damage to a defined individual property interest.

The second traditional type of conflict which has to be considered in neighbourly relations is that between upstream versus downstream riparians of a particular river. It presents, however, a much more complex set of externalities than the situation of transfrontier pollution just described. Although similar problems arise in the internal sphere of states, private law analogies are not really available as there are considerable differences in the water law systems of various states.[7] In earlier controversies, upstream and downstream states put forward incompatible claims: the absolute right of the upstream state to use a stream as it saw fit (absolute sovereignty, *Harmon* doctrine) and the absolute territorial integrity of the downstream state, meaning a duty of the upstream state not to alter the natural flow and quality of the waters of a river.[8] It is obvious that neither solution constitutes an efficient allocation of a scarce resource nor a just distribution. Thus, some accommodation on intermediate terms is necessary.[9] These conflicts have led to a broader approach, going beyond the upstream/downstream question, namely that of an international hydrographic system or drainage basin. The waters of the basin are considered as a 'shared resource'. The leading principle relating to conflicting claims of states belonging to the basin is that of 'equitable utilisation'. As formulated in the famous Helsinki Rules of the International Law Association[10] (Article IV) generally considered to reflect customary law: 'Each basin State is entitled, within its territory, to a reasonable and equitable share in the beneficial uses of the waters of an international drainage basin'. This principle is designed to ensure distributional justice. Its application also affects the question of transfrontier pollution. In this respect, the Rules contain a variation of the prohibition of transfrontier pollution developed above (Article X):

---

[7] Caponera, D., *Principles of water law and administration, national and international*, Rotterdam (Balkema) 1992.
[8] Barberis, J. A., International rivers, in Bernhardt, R. (ed.), EPIL II, p. 1364.
[9] Sands, op. cit. p. 461 *et seq.*
[10] Reproduced in Hohmann, H. (ed.), *Basic documents of international environmental law*, vol. I, London/Dordrecht/Boston (Graham and Trotman) 1992, p. 227.

> Consistent with the principle of equitable utilization of the waters of an international drainage basin, a State (a) must prevent any new form of water pollution ... which would cause substantial injury in the territory of a co-basin State, and (b) should take all reasonable measures to abate existing water pollution ... to such an extent that no substantial damage is caused in the territory of a co-basin State.

The Helsinki Rules also mention a number of 'relevant factors' to be considered in order to determine what is equitable in a particular case. But the principle of equitable utilisation can hardly be operationalised without the existence of procedural rules concerning that determination. That is the basic idea behind the creation of a number of international regimes for international water systems as shared natural resources.[11]

2. Dispersed physical externalities

It has already been pointed out above that the significance of the prohibition of transfrontier pollution is limited to cases of point sources leading to point damage. But the situation of non-point sources/non-point damage is more common and more difficult than that of clear-cut transfrontier pollution of the type just described. Most environmental problems are the aggregate result of environmental pollution and degradation from many sources, many of them remote from the places where the cumulative effects occur. This is true, in particular, for most cases of air pollution, for the environmental problems of climate change, for the degradation of soils, for the pollution of larger bodies of water. These problems cannot be solved by protective measures taken at the place where the damage occurs, they must be addressed by action taken at the various sources. This is indeed the way in which national environmental policies address these problems, in particular in the field of air pollution. The use of private law tort remedies has not proven helpful in these situations. In Germany, an attempt made by forest owners to sue collectively all power generation establishments for damages caused to those forests by SO_2 pollution have failed, for the reason indicated.[12]

The international dimension of this regulatory problem is obvious. The aggregate effects of small pollutions do not respect state boundaries. Although some states may contribute more than others to a particular problem of pollution, all states which do contribute to an environmental problem should take action against the respective sources situated within their territory. If only some did so and others not, this would be either ineffective or would create windfall

---

[11] Sands, op. cit. p. 447 *et seq.*; Beyerlin, U., *Umweltvölkerrecht*, München (Beck) 2000, p. 91 *et seq.*

[12] Entscheidungen des Bundesgerichtshofs in Zivilsachen (Federal Court Reports, Private Law) vol. 102, 363.

profits for the latter ones, which would be unjust in terms of distributional justice and inefficient in terms of environmental economics. This is the problem, for instance, raised by US non-participation with the Kyoto Protocol, but also by the non-participation of major polluters from newly industrialised countries, due account being taken of the fact that the question of distributional justice is different in the case of the latter. The example shows that the obvious solution to the problem is the creation of international regimes dealing with these problems by which the states undertake to take the necessary measures for dealing with a specific environmental problem.

But entering into such agreements is subject to the free will of sovereign states, at least as a matter of principle. This is the logical consequence of the principle of territorial sovereignty stated at the outset. Sovereignty considerations are still very important. For many, in particular so-called 'young' states, the symbolic value of their sovereignty is very high. But the insistence on the traditional concept of territorial sovereignty, 'permanent sovereignty over natural resources', also corresponds to a desire of private actors not to internalise external effects of their behaviour, and of their respective states to leave it that way. In this respect, the perceptions of political and economic interests may fatally converge.

The problem is aggravated by scientific uncertainties. If the externalities are not proven beyond doubt, the argument is always too easy that no action is required. The negotiating history of the climate change regime provides one of the examples for this major obstacle to international cooperation in solving environmental problems.[13]

Yet in the light of the existence of external effects, at least some of which cannot be denied, the question has to be asked, and is being asked, whether there are principles which limit territorial sovereignty and oblige states to internalise these external effects even in the absence of such agreements. Are there principles which reflect the fact that the environment, or rather certain elements of the environment, constitute a shared, a common asset of many or, as the case may be, of all states?

Two types of documents must be analysed in order to ascertain whether such principles exist or are about to develop: the first are the programmatic utterances produced by international bodies, the second are the Treaties themselves. The analysis of the latter may yield general principles underlying these Treaties.

The relevant documents reflect a tension between the desire to uphold the sovereignty interest but on the other hand to recognise some limitations imposed upon the freedom of states for the sake of environmental protection.

---

[13] Bothe, M., The United Nations Framework Convention on Climate Change: an unprecedented multilevel regulatory challenge, *Zeitschrift für ausländisches öffentliches Recht und Völkerrecht* 63 (2003), p. 239.

The first of these somewhat ambiguous formulations is contained in Principle 21 of the Stockholm Declaration of 1972:[14]

> States have, in accordance with the Charter of the United Nations and the principles of international law, the sovereign right to exploit their own natural resources pursuant to their own environmental policies, and the responsibility to ensure that activities within their jurisdiction and control do not cause damage to the environment of other States or of areas beyond the limits of national jurisdiction.

The essential question is whether 'damage' in this sense is only the 'point damage' envisaged in the prohibition of transfrontier pollution already explained, or whether the notion comprises in a more general way negative effects on the environment of other states. Though this is not clear, the term 'damage' suggests the former interpretation. To say the least, it is somewhat unclear to what extent the 'responsibility' enshrined in the second part of Principle 21 limits the 'sovereign right' recognised by the first part. Yet, the World Charter of Nature,[15] adopted ten years later by the UN General Assembly, uses the same language. So does Principle 2 of the Rio Declaration 1992.

It is in another aspect, namely that of a duty to cooperate, that the insistence on state sovereignty is somewhat mitigated if one compares the Stockholm and Rio Declarations. Article 24 of the Stockholm Declaration reads in part:

> Co-operation through multilateral or bilateral arrangements or other appropriate means is essential to effectively control, prevent, reduce and eliminate adverse environmental effects resulting from activities conducted in all spheres, in such a way that due account is taken of the sovereignty and interests of all States.

The duty to cooperate is somewhat stronger in the Rio Declaration (Principle 7):

> States shall co-operate in a spirit of global partnership to conserve, protect and restore the health and integrity of the Earth's ecosystem. In view of the different contributions to global environmental degradation, States have common but differentiated responsibilities.

In contradistinction to the 1972 text, the duty to cooperate is not subject to a sovereignty reservation. The provision speaks of the 'Earth's ecosystem', implying the oneness of that system, in contradistinction to the division of the Earth into territorial states. If the oneness is taken literally, the environment of the Earth becomes a shared resource, not one which is split into national bits and pieces. That provision is, of course, a compromise. The *quid pro quo* consists in the recognition by the developed countries that they have to shoulder a larger

---

[14] Hohmann, op. cit. p. 21.
[15] Resolution 37/7 of 28 October 1982; Hohmann, op. cit. p. 64.

burden for the sake of environmental preservation. This is indicated by the principle of 'common but differentiated responsibilities'.

The duty to cooperate constitutes a limitation on territorial sovereignty. But it is a limitation which is weaker than a procedural duty to consult other states or a substantive duty to take into account the needs to preserve the environment of other states. These duties exist only in respect of neighbouring states.

That being so, the question has to be asked whether an analysis of the relevant Treaties yields principles which go beyond that general duty to cooperate.

First, the legal regimes relating to environmental problems of the atmosphere will be analysed: the ECE Convention on Long-Range Transboundary Air Pollution (LRTAP), Geneva, 1979,[16] the Convention for the Protection of the Ozone Layer, Vienna, 1985,[17] with the Montreal Protocol, 1987,[18] and the United Nations Framework Convention on Climate Change (UNFCCC) 1992,[19] with the Kyoto Protocol of 1997.

The LRTAP Convention,[20] in its Preamble, emphasises the necessity of cooperation. But the object of the Convention goes beyond the traditional problem of transboundary pollution in the context of neighbourly relations. 'Long-range transboundary air pollution' is defined as 'air pollution . . . which has adverse effects [note: not 'causes damage'!] in the area under the jurisdiction of another State'. Thus, the Convention establishes a regime for the control of certain dispersed physical externalities. It is a Framework Convention which does no more than establish a procedural framework for dealing with the problem. Its many additional protocols prohibit or limit particular types of pollution,[21] i.e. regulate specific externalities. This entire treaty regime, thus, constitutes a concretisation of the general duty to cooperate.

The same holds true for the Vienna Convention for the Protection of the Ozone Layer 1985.[22] It also concerns a dispersed externality, namely the danger to human, animal, and plant health caused by the depletion of the ozone layer, a development already observed in the 1970s and forecast at the time.[23] It is attributed to the pollution by certain types of substances. Like the LRTAP Convention, it is a Framework Convention which sets up a procedural framework for dealing with a specific dispersed externality of certain human activities. Only two years later, it was implemented by the Montreal Protocol 1987[24] which provides for the phasing out of the production and use of specific ozone-depleting

---

[16] Hohmann, op. cit. p. 1650.   [17] Ibid., p. 1691.   [18] Ibid., p. 1704.
[19] 31 I.L.M. (1992) 849.   [20] Sands, op. cit. p. 324 *et seq.*
[21] Sulphur (1985, 1994), nitrogen oxides (1988), VOCs (1991), heavy metals (1998), acidification (1999).
[22] Sands, op cit. p. 342 *et seq.*
[23] Baker Röben, B., Protection of global atmospheric components, in Morrison, F. L. and Wolfrum, R. (eds.), *International, regional and national environmental law*, The Hague (Kluwer) 2000, p. 201, at 206.
[24] As amended 1990, 1992, 1995, 1997, 1999.

substances. The ozone layer protection regime thus constitutes another concretisation of the general duty to cooperate, but it contains two new distinctive features: the Montreal Protocol expressly recognises the precautionary principle as a basis for its provisions ('Determined to protect the ozone layer by taking precautionary measures to control equitably total global emissions of substances that deplete it'). In addition, both the Vienna Convention and the Montreal Protocol recognise the special situation of the developing countries, and the Protocol does so by imposing less stringent obligations on developing countries and by providing for financial assistance to be accorded to them in the implementation of their Treaty obligations. Thus, this regime is the first recognition of the precautionary principle and of that of common but differentiated responsibilities later expressly formulated in the Rio Declaration.

The next problem of particular externalities caused by the emission of certain substances which was taken up by the international community was that of climate modification.[25] The aggregate effect of the emission of certain gases leads to an increase of the global greenhouse effect which may produce a certain number of adverse consequences, in particular a sea level rise. The method of establishing a regime for solving this has been similar to that of the ozone protection regime, but in the case of climate change, the problems are much more complex and the interests at stake of a far greater importance. This means that the tension between the interests in combatting climate change and those of economic development is sharper, between developed and developing countries as well as between different developed countries, and that scientific uncertainty plays a greater role as a justification for not taking action. The UNFCCC 1992 establishes a general framework of cooperation and very soft obligations of states to limit the emission of greenhouse gases. It is expressly based on the principle of common but differentiated responsibilities, which means a greater burden for the developed countries; less stringent obligations for developing countries and a financial assistance given to them by the developed parties which is designed to cover the entire 'additional' cost of implementing the Convention. On the other hand, in the light of the persisting scientific uncertainties, the Convention is clearly based on the precautionary principle (Article 3(3)):

> The Parties should take precautionary measures to anticipate, prevent or minimize the causes of climate change and mitigate its adverse effects. Where there are serious threats of serious or irreversible damage, lack of full scientific certainty should not be used as a reason for postponing such measures.

In 1997, the UNFCCC was supplemented by the Kyoto Protocol. It gives a more precise content to the obligations of developed states by introducing 'quantified

---

[25] Sands, op. cit. p. 357 *et seq*; Bothe, op. cit.

emission limitation and reduction commitments' and at the same time by creating 'flexible mechanisms' (joint implementation, clean development mechanism, emissions trading) which address the question of the distribution of costs. They are designed to lead to a distribution of cost which is more efficient and/or more equitable. They allow to take into account the fact that these commitments may entail different unit costs for different countries, which is an element of economic efficiency, and that these costs may also have different effects for countries having a different degree of industrial development, which is a question of both equity and efficiency.

The international legal order, thus, has developed a systematic response to the problem of dispersed physical externalities in the field of air quality: once there is agreement on the problem, a regime is established that concretises the general duty to cooperate for solving the problem raised by these dispersed externalities. States are no longer free to disregard the external effects of specific activities taking place on their territories. In this sense, their territorial sovereignty is limited. But it is still respected as the pertinent regimes leave a considerable degree of choice to the states as to the manner in which they deal with the problem. As to the problem of distributional justice, each state has to take the required measures at its own cost. That corresponds to the polluter pays principle. That principle is, however, modified in favour of the developing countries. In relation to the LRTAP Convention, this problem does not arise, as this is a treaty among developed countries or countries in transition to a market economy. The two universal regimes, on the other hand, provide for two exceptions to a formally equal application of the principle: less stringent obligations for the developing countries and financial assistance granted to them in the implementation of their obligations. The Kyoto Protocol also addresses the question of distribution of the cost of implementation between the developed countries.

None of the three regimes discussed puts into question the principle of territorial sovereignty. The Preamble to the Vienna Convention restates Principle 21 of the Stockholm Declaration with its express recognition of state sovereignty, and the Preamble to the UNFCCC reaffirms 'the principle of sovereignty of States in international co-operation to address climate change'. What means 'commonality' in this context? There is no such thing as a UNECE air shed which could be designated as a common good. Is climate, is the integrity of the ozone layer, a common good? It can be so called as a *façon de parler*, but not as a notion entailing certain legal consequences. What is common is an environmental problem, the interest in solving this problem. There is an environmental interdependence. The legal answer to this phenomenon lies in a duty to cooperate to be concretised through international negotiations entailing, or resulting from, common responsibilities. The legal answer cannot be found in notions like common good, common resources, common heritage, or trust, notions which states are loath to accept because they put into question, in one way or the other, the comprehensive character of the territorial jurisdiction of states.

3. Preservation of species and spaces: what type of externality?

Turning to the question of the preservation of species and spaces, the question of externalities is to be posed in different ways. There are essentially two different ways in which the loss of a species in one state may affect other states. The question may be the exploitation of a species for economic purposes. The reduction of a population in one state may adversely affect the subsistence of the species in another state and thus cause economic loss in the latter. That is the case of a physical externality, already discussed.

But this economic concern is not the only one which has triggered measures of nature conservation both at the national and at the international level. There has always been an idealistic concern, an interest in the preservation of natural spaces and of species, which is often styled as 'amenity'.

In particular cases, it is not always possible to distinguish clearly the two types of externalities. In the light of the complexities of biosystems, the loss of particular species or habitats, of elements of particular ecosystems, may entail economic effects which are difficult to foresee. Thus, the preservation of species or spaces for idealistic reasons may also protect unknown economic interests.

How does international law deal with these hybrid externalities?

Nature protection is to a large extent a matter of regional regulation.[26] The rationale underlying the respective Conventions varies: nature conservation is, first, an important element of general regional cooperation. Thus, many of these Conventions have been concluded within the framework of existing regional organisations (Council of Europe, OAU (as it then was), ASEAN). This cooperation is part of regional solidarity. The external effects of national neglect of nature conservation are only marginally touched upon, for instance in the protection of migratory species.[27] The African Convention of 1968 goes farthest in the recognition of a responsibility towards mankind as a whole:

> Fully conscious that soil, water, flora and fauna resources constitute a capital of vital importance to mankind;

That may be interpreted to come close to the ideal of a trust. However, in view of the insistence on their sovereignty which characterises the political stance of developing countries, that interpretation would probably go too far.

---

[26] Examples: Berne Convention on the Protection of European Wildlife and Natural Habitats 1979; African Convention on the Protection of Nature and Natural Resources (Algiers, 1968); ASEAN Agreement on the Conservation of Nature and Natural Resources (Kuala Lumpur, 1985).
[27] Preamble to the Berne Convention.

A number of universal conventions also deal with specific aspects of nature conservation: the Convention on Wetlands (Ramsar, 1971), the Convention concerning the Protection of the World Cultural and Natural Heritage 1972, the Convention on International Trade in Endangered Species (CITES) 1973, the Convention on the Conservation of Migratory Species (Bonn, 1979). The most comprehensive and complex treaty is the Biodiversity Convention of 1992.

The Preamble to the Ramsar Convention addresses the underlying rationale in two different ways. It first recognises wetlands as a 'resource of great . . . value', without specifying who should benefit from it, but then pinpoints more precisely the externalities involved:

> Recognising that waterfowl in their seasonal migrations may transcend frontiers and so should be regarded as an international resource;

That phrase evokes the principles concerning shared resources already treated above.

The World Heritage Convention pursues a different, in a way more radical, approach. The central parts of the Preamble read as follows:

> Considering that deterioration or disappearance of any item of the cultural or natural heritage constitutes a harmful impoverishment of the heritage of all nations of the world,
>
> . . .
>
> Considering that parts of the cultural or natural heritage are of outstanding interest and therefore need to be preserved as part of the world heritage of mankind as a whole;
>
> Considering that, in view of the magnitude and gravity of the new dangers threatening them, it is incumbent on the international community as a whole to participate in the protection of the cultural and natural heritage of outstanding universal value, by the granting of collective assistance which, although not taking the place of action by the State concerned, will serve as an efficient complement thereto;

The word 'sovereignty' does not appear in this Preamble. It appears that national sovereignty is modified by a principle of common entitlement to the goods in question. This common entitlement gives the international community a *droit de regard* concerning national measures of preservation (but also entails its responsibility to grant assistance for that purpose). It may well be that this disrespect for national sovereignty is more apparent than real. Due to the relatively weak enforcement mechanism of the Convention, the practical impact of the Convention regime on the freedom of states to set their own priorities concerning conservation is very limited.

The text of CITES[28] does not adhere to this radical or progressive approach of the World Heritage Convention, but its impact on the freedom of national

---

[28] Sands, op. cit. p. 505 *et seq.*

decision-making in states where endangered species are situated is very real. The Preamble pays a lip service to state sovereignty:

> Recognising that peoples and States are and should be the best protectors of their own wild fauna and flora;

The measures which are at the centre of the regulatory approach of CITES, namely import restrictions for specimens exported in violation of the Convention, is styled as an 'addition' to these national measures of protection, but in reality, they constitute an imposition on the developing countries where the specimens originate by the developed (= importing) countries. That approach cannot be explained or justified unless one accepts the idea that the preservation of species constitutes a concern of all states. The concept is, thus, not very far from the world heritage principle promoted by the text of the 1972 Convention, but the sanctions provided under the regime are more effective.

The Migratory Species Convention 1979[29] resembles CITES in that it also contains a reference to state sovereignty which paraphrases the text of the relevant part of the Preamble to CITES. On the other hand, the Convention recognises a legally protected conservation interest of the international community:

> Recognising that wild animals in their innumerable forms are an irreplaceable part of the earth's natural system which must be conserved for the good of mankind;

On the other hand, the leverage which third states possess in relation to the 'range state' is far less effective than in the case of CITES.

The most complex addition to this series of treaties providing for the preservation of spaces or species is the Biodiversity Convention.[30] Earlier drafts had styled biodiversity as a 'common heritage of mankind', making biodiversity a common good comparable to the resources of the deep seabed. The essential difference between the seabed regime and biodiversity is, however, that the seabed is part of an area beyond national jurisdiction, while the elements of biodiversity are usually situated on national territory and are subject to the territorial sovereignty of states. Thus, to designate biodiversity as common heritage of mankind would have been unacceptable for most states. Thus, this concept was only adopted in a softer form, namely as 'common concern':

> Affirming that the conservation of biological diversity is a common concern of humankind;

But the drafters of the Convention take care to pay due respect to the principle of sovereignty. The following paragraph of the Preamble reads:

> Reaffirming that States have sovereign rights over their own biological resources,

---

[29] Ibid., p. 606 *et seq.*   [30] Ibid., p. 515 *et seq.*

Be it noted that the formulation does not use the definite article ('the sovereign right to exploit'). Thus, the Convention certainly restrains the scope of national freedom to deal with national biological resources as it pleases. On the other hand, the actual conservation obligations contained in the Convention are rather soft. Nevertheless, there is a *quid pro quo* which has induced the developing countries, which possess most of the world's biological resources, to accept that regime, namely an advantageous financial regime. First, as in the case of the Montreal Protocol and the UNFCCC, the developed countries have to reimburse the incremental cost which the developing countries have to pay for implementing the Convention. Secondly, access to their genetic resources is conditioned on a regime which grants them an equitable share of the benefits derived from an exported element of genetic resources.

What conclusion can be drawn from this analysis of Treaties related to the protection of species and spaces as to the notion of commonality on which they may be based? As to the elements of the environment covered by the respective Conventions, there exists a *droit de regard* of other states or of the organs of a treaty regime as to the way in which the state where these elements are situated treats them. The way in which this right is exercised is regulated by the particular Conventions in specific ways. The right may be stronger or weaker. The principle of state sovereignty is maintained. But the sovereignty is limited by these Conventions, yet not to an extent that the regime could be compared to a trust or a similar concept of private law. The approach adopted by the World Heritage Convention seems to get close to that concept – but only if one regards some ideological utterances of the Preamble and not the actual content of the obligations.

III. Areas beyond national jurisdiction : distributional justice challenged

It is in relation to areas beyond national jurisdiction, in particular the high seas, that the concept of commonality has traditionally played an important role. The principle of the freedom of the high seas (*mare liberum*) became established in the seventeeth century.[31] One of the essential contents of this principle is that it is not open to appropriation. Thus, the relevant private law analogy is not that of *res nullius*, but *res communis*. That invites a further analogy to a traditional concept of national law, the 'commons'. One speaks of 'global commons'.

1. *Compatibility of use*

Freedom of the high seas means a freedom of use, or more precisely of different uses, the freedoms of the high seas (in the plural!), the most important ones

---

[31] Graf Vitzthum, W., Raum und Umwelt im Völkerrecht, in Graf Vitzthum, W. (ed.), *Völkerrecht*, Berlin (de Gruyter) 3rd edn 2004, p. 401.

being navigation and fisheries. As all users enjoy as a matter of principle equal freedom, some accommodation must be found between conflicting uses. The exercise of these freedoms must be regulated by law. The regulatory problem is to limit these freedoms in a way which makes their exercise by various actors compatible. The principle that a particular use must be compatible with the general or common interest of other users is the most important principle of commonality in relation to the high seas. Article 87(2) of UNCLOS formulates the principle in this way:

> These freedoms shall be exercised by all States with due regard for the interests of other States in their exercise of the freedom of the high seas.

Specific conflicts may require specific rules. The law of warfare at sea, for instance, has developed particular rules for the conflict between the military use of the sea and commercial navigation, as the latter is not possible where fighting takes place. The issue of establishing special or exclusion zones is controversial in a number of details, but the principle that belligerents can establish zones where commercial shipping operates at its own risk is recognised.[32]

The question of the compatibility of uses becomes more acute where the exploitation of a renewable resource beyond its regenerative capacity is at stake. That is the case of high seas fisheries. In this situation, some kind of international administration or management is necessary, as catch limitations will not be observed without a corresponding restraint being exercised by the other relevant users. The principle that certain stocks may not be used beyond their capacity of regeneration is a part of the customary law relating to the use of the high seas as part of the concept of commonality. But it cannot be applied, so to say, automatically. Thus, it has been enshrined in a number of regional fisheries agreements[33] and also in some universal agreements concerning species which must be administered at the world level. An early example is the International Whaling Commission,[34] a recent one the 1995 Agreement Relating to the Conservation and Management of Straddling Fish Stocks and Highly Migratory Fish Stocks.[35]

In relation to the use of global commons, the concept of commonality is no longer reflected in a simple rule of freedom of use. Rather, it is implemented in particular regimes of resource management.

---

[32] Bothe, M., Friedenssicherung und Kriegsrecht, in Graf Vitzthum, op. cit. p. 646.
[33] For an overview, see Sands, op. cit. p. 584 *et seq.*
[34] Established by the International Convention for the Regulation of Whaling, 2 December 1946, Sands, P. and Gallizzi, P. (eds.), *Documents in international environmental law*, Cambridge (Cambridge University Press) 2nd edn 2004.
[35] Sands and Gallizzi, op. cit. p. 336.

2. Equal freedom for unequal actors?

The concept of commonality just described constitutes a concretisation and development of the principle that all states have an equal right to exercise the freedoms of the high seas and that the distributional results of this concept are generally acceptable. But this is not true in all respects.

The establishment of management regimes is not the only reaction to the regulatory challenges of the uses of the seas and the resulting question of the distribution of benefits. The other one is the reintroduction of a *mare clausum* concept for specific questions, i.e. the establishment of zones of exclusive jurisdiction over certain areas of the sea, be it only for limited purposes. That trend has been correctly called a 'terranisation' of the seas.[36] The examples are the development of the concept of the continental shelf and that of the exclusive economic zone. Both concepts provide for a redistribution of the benefits to be derived from the exploitation of the resources of those sea areas.

In the case of the continental shelf, it was the USA, once the technical possibilities and the economic importance of the exploitation of the resources of that area had become apparent, which claimed the exclusive jurisdiction over these resources.[37] That redistribution of benefits, in other words the removal of those benefits from the principle of commonality, very soon met with general agreement.

In relation to the exclusive economic zone,[38] the situation was somewhat more complex. The move to extend the jurisdiction of the coastal state beyond the traditional breadth of the territorial sea (three or at the utmost twelve nautical miles) was prompted by the fact that, on the one hand, the waters adjacent to the coast, but situated outside the territorial sea, had very rich living resources, but that the long distance fishing fleets of the developed countries exploited most of this wealth to the detriment of the technologically less advanced fleets of the neighbouring developing coastal states.

Thus, it was perceived that the traditional rule of the freedom of fisheries on the high seas yielded an unjust result as to the distribution of benefits, to the detriment of the developing countries. This prompted a number of developing coastal states to claim a territorial sea of 200nm. The outcome of the conflict was a compromise: an exclusive economic zone where the jurisdiction of the coastal state is not as comprehensive as it is in the territorial sea, but where the coastal state has a primary right to exploit these resources. This compromise was facilitated by the fact that certain developed countries possessing long coastlines had reassessed their interests and found that the new concept also favoured them, not only certain developing countries.

---

[36] Graf Vitzthum, op. cit. p. 398.   [37] So-called Truman Declaration.
[38] Gündling, L., Die exklusive Wirtschaftszone, *Zeitschrift für ausländisches öffentliches Recht und Völkerrecht* 38 (1978), p. 616.

On the other hand, this transfer of benefits to the coastal state goes hand in hand with certain responsibilities. In particular in relation to the living resources of the EEZ, the coastal state: 'shall ensure . . . that the maintenance of the living resources . . . is not endangered by over-exploitation'.[39]

In relation to those resources which present particular problems of externalities (migratory species), there are specific duties of cooperation.[40]

The other and very different example of a redistribution of benefits as compared to the traditional notion of the freedoms of the high seas is the establishment of a specific exploration and exploitation regime for the resources of the deep seabed. In this case, too, there was an attempt to compensate North-South disparities. The resources of the deep seabed, lying at the bottom of waters more than 10,000m deep, can only be exploited by technologically advanced countries which have the economic resources to make the necessary investment. The freedom of exploiting these resources would thus serve the benefit of these countries only, unless a redistribution of the benefits could be achieved. The latter is the purpose of the concept of common heritage of mankind. Those resources being declared the common heritage of mankind, there exploitation is a privilege granted by the international community which receives, in return, a part of the benefits for the purpose of redistribution to the developing countries. Although, technically speaking, this regime is now in force, it is not operational because no enterprise is, for the time being, interested in exploiting these resources. The reasons are economic: this type of mining is so expensive that the market price of these commodities could not match the production cost. Thus, the concept of common heritage of humankind is an idea of considerable historic interest – which so far has not been put into practice.

IV. Distributional justice between generations or intergenerational equity

Not only interlocal, but also intertemporal externalities present a regulatory challenge for international environmental policy and law. It is obvious that measures now taken in relation to the environment have effects in the future, near or distant. Since the first adoption of documents concerning environmental policy, this need to take intertemporal externalities into account is formulated as a concern for future generations. A few quotations from the abundant wealth of documents, both political and legal, must suffice. Principle 1 of the Stockholm Declaration 1972: 'Man . . . bears a solemn responsibility to protect and improve the environment for present and future generations'; Principle 3 of the Rio Declaration 1992: 'The right to development must be fulfilled so

---

[39] Article 61 UNCLOS.   [40] Articles 64, 66, 67 UNCLOS.

as to equitably meet developmental and environmental needs of present and future generations'.

The latter provision expressly refers to 'equity'. Indeed, the need to take intertemporal externalities into account is often formulated as a requirement of intergenerational equity.[41]

This basic approach is uncontroversial. Implementing it in practice is, however, a different matter. It involves, first, the question whether and to what extent intergenerational equity is a legal principle, and secondly, how the principle can be operationalised. It is particularly in this context that the private law analogy of a trust comes to one's mind. If the resources of the Earth are only held in trust for the benefit of future generations, that appears to be a solid basis for a legal obligation to treat the object of the trust with due care.

So far, the analogy is plausible. But it is not able to give an answer to a number of further relevant questions: who is the trustee? All states? Every human being? Who could be entitled to represent the beneficiary of the trust who, by definition, does not yet exist? And what is the yardstick of permissible use of the environment by the present generation?

As to the representation of the beneficiary, one could argue on the basis of a public trust doctrine, it is everybody.[42] But that conclusion would be highly problematic, for two reasons: first, it would mean that the public trust doctrine is a general principle of law recognised throughout the nations of the world – but this is far from being the case. Secondly, it is highly questionable, to say the least, to allow any self-appointed claimant before whatever jurisdiction to enforce the trust. It is an analogy which invites the powerful to act unilaterally in order to enforce what he considers most beneficial for the world at large, including future generations. If procedures are devised to make sure that intergenerational equity is duly taken into account in decisions concerning the use and exploitation of resources, some screening of those able to serve as the attorney of future generations would be necessary. In other words, a regulated procedure is necessary. I will revert to this question.

As to the question of the yardstick, two other (yet related) principles have been introduced into the legal and political discourse which are now widely recognised: the first one is the principle of sustainable development. This relationship between intergenerational equity and sustainable development is clearly expressed in the report of the Brundtland Commission: 'development that meets the needs of the present without compromising the ability of future

---

[41] Epiney, A. and Scheyli, M., *Strukturprinzipien des Umweltvölkerrechts*, Bern (Stämpfli) 1998, p. 45 *et seq.*

[42] In terms of procedural law, this raises the question of standing. On the question of standing and intergenerational equity, see ILA, Committee on Sustainable Development, Fifth and Final Report, in *Report of the Seventieth Conference*, New Delhi (ILA) 2002, p. 380, at 393.

generations to meet their own needs'.[43] This sentence, which is generally cited with approval, makes it clear that sustainable development is a means to ensure intergenerational equity.[44]

The principle of sustainable development is enshrined in so many laws and treaties that one can hardly doubt its character as being a rule of general international law. Yet, its ability to serve as a yardstick in deciding concrete cases is very limited. Its content is relatively clear only where it refers to the use of one particular resource. In particular, in relation to the living resources of the seas, this principle is formulated in various Treaties as 'maximum sustainable yield'.

If one leaves this area of resource management to address more general issues of environment and development, the concept loses its concrete content and becomes a general notion which needs further normative steps in order to be effectively applied. It is nothing more and nothing less that a principle of good governance.

A major regulatory tool to concretise and implement the principle of sustainable development is the precautionary principle. It requires that measures for the preservation of the environment must not only be taken when there is already a clear danger that damage to certain elements of the environment or in particular to human health will otherwise occur (protection principle), but also when this is not (yet?) the case because the danger is remote or the damage uncertain. There are essentially two justifications for this requirement. The first one is the element of uncertainty. In this perspective, the precautionary principle is a means, so to say, to be on the safe side. The second one is the idea of leaving space for future uses of the same resource. It is in this perspective that the precautionary principle becomes a tool for ensuring sustainable development.

The precautionary principle is enshrined in a great number of international instruments.[45] Various formulations stress the two aspects of the principle in different ways.

Principle 15 of the Rio Declaration reads:

> In order to protect the environment, the precautionary approach shall be widely applied by States according to their capacities. Where there are threats of serious or irreversible damage, lack of full scientific certainty shall not be used as reason for postponing cost-effective measures to prevent environmental degradation.

That formulation stresses the uncertainty element. But as it is in particular the danger of 'irreversible' damage which triggers the application of the precautionary approach, there is also the element of sustainability and intergenerational

---

[43] World Commission on Environment and Development, *Our common future*, Oxford (Oxford University Press) 1987, p. 43.
[44] Epiney and Scheyli, op. cit. p. 55. [45] Sands, op. cit. p. 266 *et seq.*

equity: where a damage which occurs is irreversible, future generations are definitely deprived of the resource concerned.

It is also to be noted that the word 'approach' is used instead of principle. The diplomats assembled in Rio were apparently reluctant to call it a principle, a term which would have given a higher legal dignity to this rule. In addition, the approach is only to be applied by states 'according to their capabilities'. It shows that the precautionary principle cannot mean that everything possible has to be done, but that choices are to be made which balance environmental concerns against other relevant interests, in particular economic ones.

The element of uncertainty is reflected in a different way in the Convention for the protection of the marine environment of the north-east Atlantic:

> Article 2(2)
> The Contracting Parties shall apply:
> (a) the precautionary principle, by virtue of which preventive measures are to be taken when there are reasonable grounds for concern that substances or energy introduced, directly or indirectly, into the marine environment may bring about hazards to human health, harm living resources and marine ecosystems, damage amenities or interfere with other legitimate uses of the sea, even when there is no conclusive evidence of causal relationship between the inputs and the effects;

In contradistinction to the formulation of the Rio Declaration, which stresses the 'serious or irreversible damage' as the decisive criterion, it is the degree of probability of harm ('reasonable grounds for concern') which in this provision triggers the need to take action. This, too, shows that the application of the precautionary principle is subject to different emphasis of its various elements, i.e. it is a rule which is in constant need of concretisation.

The formulation of the Rio Declaration may still leave some doubt as to whether the precautionary principle has become a part of customary international environmental law. But since then, it has been included in many treaties,[46] and it has been recognised, although perhaps not in very certain terms, by international judicial or quasi-judicial bodies, namely the International Tribunal on the Law of the Sea in the *Southern Bluefin Tuna* case[47] and the Appellate Body of the WTO dispute settlement system.[48] It is thus safe to conclude that it is nowadays a rule of customary international law.

We can thus conclude that there are now at least two legal principles which ensure some degree of intergenerational equity. The need for a construction based on a private law analogy of trust seems to be questionable.

---

[46] See n. 45 above.
[47] 38 I.L.M. (1999) 1624. ITLOS did not expressly apply the precautionary principle, but did so for all practical purposes, cf. para. 90 of the judgment.
[48] In particular in the *Shrimps–Turtle* case, 38 I.L.M. (1999) 118, see Sands, op. cit. p. 965 *et seq.*

V. Conclusions

International environmental law has developed a number of leading principles in order to deal with the problem of externalities, both interlocal and intertemporal. These principles are specific ones for particular conflict situations and types of externalities and reflect the idea of commonality in different ways. In practical terms, these principles are more meaningful than certain private law analogies, as for instance the construction of a trust. Just to recapitulate the most important ones: *sic utere tuo*, equitable utilisation, duty to cooperate, common concern, common but differentiated responsibilities, common heritage, common heritage of mankind, sustainable development, precautionary principle.

The place of private law analogies in international law largely depends on the availability of judicial pronouncements. It is through judicial law development, through case law, that private law analogies have found their way into positive international law. As the culture of judicial and quasi-judicial dispute settlement develops in international relations (and it does develop), the chances of the success of similar constructions increase.

23

Globalising environmental liability: the interplay of national and international law

A. E. BOYLE

I. Introduction

Liability for loss or damage is an elementary feature of a legal system; it remains an important part of most systems of environmental law even when supplemented or in part superseded by regulatory regimes, risk avoidance procedures, and criminal penalties. In international law, liability for transboundary damage, based on analogies going back to Roman law, is one of the oldest concepts available in interstate disputes. An international arbitral award, delivered in 1938 and 1941, is the seminal judicial contribution to the international law on the subject.[1] Since then, however, there has been only limited judicial elaboration at an international level, and the precise character of this elementary concept remains unsettled.[2] On the most widely held view, the responsibility of states for transboundary damage depends principally on objective fault, i.e. a failure to act with due care or diligence, or a breach of treaty, or the commission of a prohibited act. If states can be held more generally responsible without showing fault, the examples remain at best exceptional and questionable.[3] The principle of state responsibility for transboundary damage is not in doubt, however. It has been incorporated in treaties,[4]

This chapter is reprinted with permission from *Journal of Environmental Law* 17 (2005), pp. 3–26. I am indebted to the International Law Commission, and especially to Special Rapporteur P. S. Rao, for enabling me to attend their debates in 2002 and 2003 and for many useful discussions. Funding for these visits was provided by the Leverhulme Trust. I am also grateful to Jutta Brunnée and Caroline Foster for comments on an earlier draft of this article and to Pierre Harcourt for sharing insights gained at the ILC while researching his LLM dissertation. They bear no responsibility for any of the views or misconceptions that follow.

[1] *Trail Smelter Arbitration* (1939) 33 AJIL 182 and (1941) 35 AJIL 684.
[2] See in particular *Corfu Channel Case* [1949] ICJ Rep. 1. [3] See section II.
[4] e.g. UN Convention on the Law of the Sea 1982, Article 235; UN Watercourses Convention 1997, Article 5.

recognised in the law of state responsibility,[5] and invoked by the UN Security Council.[6]

In the 1960s and 1970s, a number of civil liability and compensation Conventions were negotiated in order to address two of the most hazardous and significant transboundary risks: oil pollution at sea and nuclear accidents.[7] They represent an alternative approach to liability for transboundary damage. Instead of relying on the responsibility of states in international law, these Conventions address the civil liability of ship-owners or the operators of nuclear installations. Although further such sectoral agreements have since been concluded,[8] there remains no global treaty on civil liability for transboundary pollution or damage, and few of these additional agreements are in force or widely ratified. To that extent, the general availability of civil law remedies for transboundary damage cannot be assumed.

With the deficiencies of the existing law in mind, the UN Conference on the Human Environment in 1972 called on states 'to develop further the international law regarding liability and compensation for the victims of pollution and other environmental damage caused by activities within the jurisdiction or control of such states'.[9] Six years later, the International Law Commission (ILC) embarked unsuspectingly on an odyssey now entering its twenty-eighth year and entitled 'Liability for Injurious Consequences of Acts Not Prohibited by International Law'. In this improbable guise, the ILC has slowly and uncertainly

---

[5] ILC, 2001 Articles on the Responsibility of States for Internationally Wrongful Acts, reproduced with commentaries in Crawford, J. (ed.), *The International Law Commission's Articles on State Responsibility*, Cambridge (Cambridge University Press) 2002.

[6] UNSC Resolution 687 (1991) holds Iraq responsible for damage to other states, including environmental damage, arising from its illegal invasion of Kuwait. The UN Compensation Commission was created to administer claims for compensation.

[7] Paris Convention on Third Party Liability in the Field of Nuclear Energy 1960 (in force 1968); Brussels Convention on the Liability of the Operators of Nuclear Ships 1962 (not in force); 1963 Brussels Agreement Supplementary to the Convention on Third Party Liability etc. 1960 (in force 1974); Vienna Convention on Civil Liability for Nuclear Damage 1963 (in force 1977, to be replaced by 1997 Protocol, not in force); International Convention on Civil Liability for Oil Pollution Damage 1969 (in force 1975, replaced by 1992 Convention, in force 1996); Brussels Convention related to Civil Liability in the field of Maritime Carriage of Nuclear Material 1971 (in force 1975); Convention on the Establishment of an International Fund for Compensation for Oil Pollution Damage 1971 (in force 1978, replaced by 1992 Convention, in force 1996); Convention on Civil Liability for Oil Pollution Damage resulting from Exploration for and Exploitation of Seabed Mineral Resources 1977 (not in force).

[8] See n. 44 below. The 2003 UNECE Protocol on Civil Liability and Compensation (the 'Kiev Protocol') is the closest analogue to the ILC's own Principles, but it is European in scope and confined to transboundary damage caused by industrial accidents on transboundary rivers and lakes. While there are significant differences between the two regimes, it is clear from the ILC commentary that this agreement has provided useful guidance for the Commission on certain issues.

[9] 1972 Stockholm Declaration on the Human Environment, Principle 22.

grappled with the task identified by the Stockholm Conference and reiterated in 1992 by the Rio Conference on Environment and Development.[10]

In an attempt to move beyond the limitations of the existing law on state responsibility, the ILC's 1996 draft Articles would have made states strictly liable for significant transboundary harm caused by an activity covered by the Articles.[11] The obligation to compensate other states would not have covered unforeseeable risks, but would have included harm which the source state could not prevent by exercising due diligence.[12] In this situation, the harm would in effect be unavoidable and there would be no fault on the part of the state. At the same time, the ILC's 1996 proposals for no fault liability did not place the source state in the same position as if it were at fault in failing to regulate the harmful activity. The scope of reparation would have been more limited under this version of no fault liability: there would be no obligation to compensate in full for the loss or afford *restitutio in integrum*, but only to compensate 'in accordance with the principle that the victim of harm should not be left to bear the entire loss'.[13] The level of compensation would thus be determined by negotiation, having regard to various factors.[14] In effect, what was required as part of a balance of interests between the parties was equitable compensation rather than full compensation.

These were relatively novel proposals, however, and they did not rest on any clear foundation in general international law. A decision was taken in 1997 to suspend further consideration of liability for damage and concentrate instead on other related but less controversial issues. The draft Articles on the Prevention of Transboundary Harm adopted in 2001 thus codify only the legal framework for regulation and management of activities which pose a risk of transboundary harm.[15] There is little in them of relevance to liability, except for a non-discrimination principle which governs transboundary access to 'judicial or other procedures' for preventive remedies and redress, and a

---

[10] 1992 Rio Declaration on Environment and Development, Principle 13.
[11] 1996 ILC draft Article 5. For the full text of the 1996 draft see Report of the Working Group on International Liability etc., Report of the ILC UNGAOR A/51/10 (1996), Annex 1, p. 235. For a brief resumé see Boyle, A. E. and Freestone, D. (eds.), *International law and sustainable development*, Oxford (Oxford University Press) 1999 pp. 73–85; La Fayette, L. de, The ILC and international liability: a commentary, *RECIEL* 6 (1997), pp. 321–333.
[12] Under 1996 draft Article 1 this obligation would apply both to activities where there was a risk of harm and those which merely caused harm. Cf. *Corfu Channel Case* [1949] ICJ Rep. 1, in which it was held that Albania both knew of the risk and could have prevented the harm. Similarly, the *Trail Smelter* case appears to be an example of liability for harm which was foreseeable and preventable, although it is true that the arbitral award also makes provision for future liability which is not dependent on failure to take preventive measures.
[13] 1996 draft Article 21, on which see Report of the Working Group on International Liability etc., in ILC Report (1996), op. cit. Annex 1, p. 320.
[14] See n. 67 below.   [15] See ILC Report, UN GAOR A/56/10 (2001), paras 366–436.

savings clause for obligations under other Treaties or customary international law. The possibility of adopting additional provisions on liability for damage was thus left open.

Certain governments and some members of the ILC believed, and continue to believe, that the liability of states for transboundary damage has been adequately dealt with in the wider context of the ILC's Articles on State Responsibility, and that no development of the existing law is necessary.[16] We will return to this question below. Nevertheless, in 2001, largely at the behest of developing states, the General Assembly requested the ILC to resume work on liability, 'bearing in mind the interrelationship between prevention and liability, and taking into account the developments in international law and comments by Governments'.[17] This suggests a recognition by at least some governments that existing law on liability for transboundary damage remains insufficient and that some additional measures are necessary. Faced with such an express request from the UN General Assembly, however unwelcome, the ILC had little choice but to agree to reinstate the topic on its agenda in 2002.

The most fundamental question confronted by the ILC was whether to continue to focus on extending the strict liability of states in international law along the lines envisaged in 1996. However meritorious that idea may be in theory, few governments, in whatever context, have shown any enthusiasm for accepting that no fault liability for damage caused by activities within their jurisdiction should fall on states themselves. Marking an important change of direction since 1996, the ILC has not returned to this model of loss allocation. In the current Special Rapporteur's words:

> The hesitation to peg State liability to strict liability is also understandable. It is mainly due to an assessment that in international practice, as between States, that form of liability is not accepted for activities that are considered as lawful to pursue in their domestic jurisdiction in accordance with their sovereign rights.[18]

Thus, for essentially pragmatic rather than principled reasons, the ILC has opted instead to concentrate on alternative approaches, focused on 'loss allocation among different actors involved in the operations of the hazardous activities'.[19] These actors are much more likely to be corporations and other private parties than states. Rather than making states directly responsible in international law to compensate for damage, the ILC's intention is that states should make provision for other actors to compensate transboundary damage through national law. States would still remain responsible for their own fault in international law. Essentially, however, the ILC's work would now have to build much more

[16] 2003 ILC Report, para. 178. See also the 2002 ILC Report.
[17] UNGA Res. 56/82 (2001).
[18] ILC, Special Rapporteur's Second Report on Injurious Consequences etc., 2003, para. 22.
[19] ILC Report (2003), op. cit. para. 168.

directly on the private law civil liability models already adopted for oil, nuclear, and other environmental risks.

The ILC proceeded quickly and in 2004 a set of draft Principles was adopted and sent to states for consultation.[20] If they prove acceptable, the ILC's principles may thus establish for the first time a genuinely global regime of civil liability for transboundary damage. Although not confined to environmental claims, these are likely to constitute the most significant category covered by the draft Principles.

II. Who should be liable for transboundary harm: states or private parties?

Why should the ILC address the question of civil liability for transboundary damage and why is its concluded work on state responsibility and the management of transboundary risk not sufficient for the purpose? There are at least two answers. First, as we saw in the introduction, it is far from clear that states are fully responsible in international law for damage to neighbouring states. While undoubtedly responsible for transboundary damage caused in breach of obligation,[21] damage caused without such a breach is not covered by the ILC State Responsibility Articles.[22] For example, transboundary pollution damage resulting from the activities of industry or business will not in normal circumstances be attributable to the source state in international law.[23] State responsibility will usually be based on breach of an obligation of due diligence in the regulation and control of such potentially harmful activities. This will not cover damage resulting from events that are either unforeseeable or unavoidable using reasonable diligence.[24] In these circumstances, the state itself is not at fault and the loss will not be recoverable in international law.[25] The ILC

---

[20] See ILC Report, GAOR A/59/10 (2004), paras 158–176. For preparatory work see ILC Report, GAOR A/57/10 (2002), paras 430–457; Special Rapporteur Rao's First Report A/CN.4/531 (2003); 2003 ILC Report, GAOR A/58/10, paras 154–231; Special Rapporteur Rao's Second Report A/CN.4/540 (2004).

[21] *Trail Smelter Arbitration* (1939) 33 AJIL 182 and (1941) 35 AJIL 684; *Corfu Channel Case* [1949] ICJ Rep. 1; UN Convention on the Law of the Sea 1982, Articles 192–199 and 235; 1992 Rio Declaration, Principle 2. It is important to appreciate that none of these authorities prohibits transboundary harm. States are only required to take measures to prevent, reduce, and control harm. That does not preclude the possibility that certain harmful activities may be prohibited, such as atmospheric nuclear tests or ocean dumping of waste.

[22] 2001 ILC Articles on State Responsibility, Article 2.

[23] 2001 ILC Articles on State Responsibility, Articles 4–11, and commentary in Crawford, op. cit.

[24] See e.g., *Corfu Channel Case* [1949] ICJ Rep. 1; UN Convention on the Law of the Sea 1982, Article 139.

[25] ILC Report (2004), op. cit., commentary to Principle 1, para. 8.

work thus proceeds from the entirely reasonable assumption that transboundary damage may still happen, however diligent the state has been in regulating and controlling the harmful activity, and that some alternative form of redress is desirable.

Even though it may not be at fault in such cases, the arguments for shifting the burden of unavoidable loss back to the source state are strong, particularly where the source is an ultra-hazardous activity such as a nuclear power plant. In the absence of reciprocal acceptance of risk, or some common benefit, making the victim state suffer in the event of unforeseeable or unavoidable harm is not an attractive policy.[26] The underlying assumption here is that it is inequitable to leave the burden to lie where it falls merely because the source state has acted with all due diligence. The injured state can neither control the activities which cause such harm nor does it necessarily benefit from them, however socially or economically desirable they may be to the source state.

The problem of inequity in the present law can readily be observed in the relationship between states using nuclear power and those non-nuclear states which cannot avoid the risks posed by nuclear accidents such as Chernobyl: the latter have no veto over their neighbours' use of nuclear power and no guarantee of indemnity for accidental harm. Accidents may happen even in the best regulated and managed installations: their occurrence does not necessarily indicate any failure of due diligence or breach of duty by the state. Nor is due diligence always an easy standard to administer unless clearly accepted international standards defining the content of this duty can be identified.[27] A heavy burden of proof will be placed on the state which has to establish a failure of due diligence. In the case of complex processes, such as nuclear reactors, this will be especially difficult unless liberal inferences of fact are allowed, or the burden of proof is placed on the source state.[28]

These examples illustrate why the Commission spent so long attempting to develop a principle of strict liability applicable to states. The only clear precedent for no fault liability of this kind is the Space Objects Liability Convention 1972 under which a launching state is absolutely liable for any damage resulting from the crash of a spacecraft launched from its territory.[29] Some support might

---

[26] See Quentin-Baxter, R., in *YbILC*, 2(1) (1981), pp. 113–118; Barboza, J., in *YbILC* 2(1) (1986), p. 160; Handl, G., Après Tchernobyl: quelques réflexions sur le programme législatif multilateral a l'ordre du jour, *RGDIP* 92 (1988), p. 50.
[27] As for example in the Convention on Nuclear Safety 1994.
[28] Cf. *Corfu Channel Case* [1949] ICJ Rep. 1, at 18 where the court did allow certain inferences from the fact of Albania's exclusive territorial control; McCaffrey, S., in *YbILC* 2(2) (1988), p. 30, para. 167, suggests that due diligence is 'essentially a defence' and thus 'the burden of proving it should lie with the state of origin'.
[29] See Cosmos 954 Claim 18 I.L.M. (1979) 902. For a much more doubtful but possible example see the *Trail Smelter Arbitration*, n. 12 above.

also be derived from general principles of law based on analogy with strict liability legislation, but the application of such a principle to pollution or other forms of transboundary damage is far from universally supported in national or international law.[30] The arguments for continuing to develop international law in the direction of making states strictly liable for harm caused by hazardous activities remain strong; the problem with this approach, as we saw earlier, is simply its political unacceptability.

Secondly, even where a state is potentially responsible in international law, to whatever extent, it is far from clear that states should be the only or even the principal source of recourse for those injured by transboundary damage. Claiming compensation from a government for pollution caused by industry undermines the polluter pays principle.[31] Favouring interstate claims in such cases allows governments to subsidise their industries by accepting responsibility for transboundary costs. Allowing direct recourse against the enterprise causing the damage would do more to facilitate implementation of a 'polluter pays' approach to the allocation of transboundary costs than making states a guarantor for industry.[32]

Moreover, only governments can bring international claims against another state. Even if they are willing to proceed, which they may not be, finding a forum with jurisdiction will depend on the consent of the other state. This may not be easy to obtain. In practice very few cases claiming liability for transboundary damage have been handled in this way. Thus it will usually be simpler, quicker, and economically more efficient to make those who cause pollution or other forms of damage pay, rather than states. From this perspective, state responsibility and the liability of states are and should be no more than residual sources of redress. Having eschewed state liability as a solution, the ILC's principles necessarily assume that any scheme of redress for transboundary damage should principally address the civil liability of private parties. To that extent it recognises the reality that many, if not most, transboundary environmental problems are mainly caused by and affect private parties, rather than states as such.

---

[30] Commission of the European Communities, *Green Paper on Remedying Environmental Damage*, COM (93) 47 (1993), para. 2.2.1; Lefeber, R. *Transboundary environmental interference and the origin of state liability*, The Hague (Kluwer) 1996, pp. 182–183, 276–279.

[31] See 1992 Rio Declaration on Environment and Development, Principle 16. The polluter pays principle is also part of OECD and EC environmental policy.

[32] See *Vellore Citizens Welfare Forum* v. *Union of India* (1996) 5 SCC 647, where the Indian Supreme Court relied on the principle to justify imposition of absolute liability on the polluter both for injury to private parties and for environmental reinstatement costs which the government would otherwise have borne.

III. Transboundary civil liability: the options

Liability, and liability treaties, are not a panacea for pollution or environmental damage or other forms of transboundary harm, and sceptics rightly question whether they have had much impact on industry or contribute to improving standards.[33] This is not the place to pursue such a socio-legal enquiry, and in any event the principal purpose of liability is to secure redress for victims, not necessarily to influence the behaviour of defendants. Accepting for the moment that the ILC's task is to outline the provision states should make for transboundary civil liability and compensation, the question which then arises is how this should be done. It was apparent to the ILC that it had several options, not necessarily exclusive of each other:

- an access to justice approach, i.e. ensure that states make effective recourse against the relevant private party available through national law for victims of transboundary harm;
- a conflict of laws approach, i.e. facilitating transboundary civil litigation through forum shopping and other procedural reforms;
- a harmonisation approach, i.e. ensure that national laws set internationally acceptable standards of liability, jurisdiction, availability of remedies, etc;
- a compensation approach, i.e. ensure that compensation is available to cover situations where liability is limited or inadequate, or to spread the burden equitably between the party liable for the harm or pollution, the industry, and (possibly) the state.

As we shall see in the next section, there are elements of most of these approaches in the ILC's draft Principles, which draw heavily on existing law and precedents in this field. To understand how far the ILC has been creative, or has built on generally accepted principles, it is necessary to outline briefly the present position.

1. A minimalist approach: access to justice

Already codified in Article 15 of the ILC's 2001 Articles on Transboundary Harm and in Article 32 of the UN Watercourses Convention 1997, a right of non-discriminatory access to remedies in national law gives victims of transboundary pollution or damage direct recourse to local remedies in the state where the source of the harm is located. Given the ILC's consistent endorsement of the non-discrimination principle, we can for present purposes assume that it already reflects existing international law.

---

[33] See Brunnée, J., Of sense and sensibility: reflections on international liability regimes as tools for environmental protection, *ICLQ* 53 (2004), p. 351; Bergkamp, L., *Liability and the environment: private and public law aspects of civil liability for environmental harm in an international context*, The Hague (Kluwer) 2001.

Is non-discriminatory access to justice enough to meet the needs of an international civil liability regime? Not if there is no liability in national law or if existing liability is inadequate. Non-discrimination leaves the host state free to define both the scope and content of the liability, determine applicable law, and afford remedies, provided they are equally available to foreign and domestic claimants. This is the most minimalist solution, and in some cases it will be no solution at all if the state chooses to make no provision for liability, or denies any remedy, or confers immunity on defendants.

However, Principle 10 of the Rio Declaration does require states to go further by providing '*Effective* access to judicial proceedings, including redress and remedy'. For the same reason, the ILA 1996 Watercourses Articles require states to provide a basic minimum standard of redress:

> States, individually or jointly, shall ensure the availability of *prompt, adequate and effective* administrative and judicial remedies for persons in another State who suffer or may suffer damage.[34]

Underlying both of these formulations is the understanding that non-discriminatory access to national remedies may not of itself be enough to satisfy an international standard of access to justice.[35] Moreover, the failure of a state to provide adequate redress to its own citizens for pollution or other forms of damage may in sufficiently serious cases also violate the rights to life, health, private life, property, and freedom to dispose of natural resources under international human rights agreements.[36] These rights provide an additional basis

---

[34] 1996 Helsinki Articles on International Watercourses, Article 2(1), in ILA, *Report of the 62nd Conference*, London (ILA) 1997. See also UNCLOS 1982, Article 235(2), which similarly requires states to ensure that recourse is available within their legal system for 'prompt and adequate compensation or other relief in respect of damage caused by pollution of the marine environment'.

[35] The Arhus Convention on Access to Information etc. in Environmental Matters 1998, Article 9, guarantees access to justice, including 'adequate and effective remedies', and Article 6 of the European Convention on Human Rights also guarantees access to justice. In *Al-Adsani* v. *United Kindom* (2001) 34 EHRR 273; *Fogarty* v. *United Kindom* (2001) 34 EHRR 302, and *McElhinney* v. *Ireland* (2001) 34 EHRR 322, the ECtHR held that this Article does not itself guarantee any particular content in substantive law; Article 6(1) could not be used to create a substantive civil right that had no legal basis in the state concerned. The ECtHR also indicated that the state could not 'remove from the jurisdiction of the courts a whole range of civil claims or confer immunities from civil liability on large groups or categories of persons'. It is an open question how far these cases can support an argument for substantive liability for damage, although they are more likely to do so if used in combination with the cases cited in n. 36 below.

[36] ECtHR: *Lopez Ostra* v. *Spain* (1994) 20 EHRR 277; *Guerra* v. *Italy* (1998) 26 EHRR 357; *LCB* v. *United Kingdom* (1999) 27 EHRR 212; *Hatton* v. *United Kingdom*, 2003; African Commission on Human and Peoples' Rights: *Social and Economic Rights Action Centre* v. *Nigeria*, Comm. No.115/96 (2002) (The 'Ogoni' case); IACHR: *Yanomani Indians* v. *Brazil*, Decision 7615, *Inter-American YB on Hum. Rts* (1985), p. 264.

for a minimum standard of liability or compensation. In such cases, transboundary claimants would then be entitled on a non-discriminatory basis to the same standard of treatment as those within the jurisdiction of the forum state. Perhaps the most important aspect of the draft liability Principles adopted by the ILC is that for the first time the Commission has accepted the arguments for setting a minimum standard of timely and effective redress. We return to this point below.

Nevertheless, even if a legal system is adequate on all these grounds, access to it is only helpful to the victim who is willing and able to sue in the place where the defendant is domiciled or in which it operates. Where this is not the case, the possibility of forum shopping and of litigating transboundary cases in the plaintiff's own state are important alternatives to access to justice in the source state.

2. Transboundary civil litigation: forum shopping

Private international law generally affords victims of transboundary harm a choice of forum in which to sue. What choices are available in any particular legal system will depend on the jurisdictional rules of that legal system. Not all legal systems will exercise jurisdiction over damage abroad, even if it is caused by activities within their jurisdiction.[37] However, the most widely accepted general principle is that proceedings may be brought (a) in the courts of the place where damage occurs (i.e. the transboundary victim's own state), or (b) in the place where harmful activity is located, or (c) in the place where the defendant is domiciled.[38] Such a broad jurisdictional choice creates obvious problems of uncertainty for industry about where it will be sued and under which legal systems it will be liable, and of expense or complexity for the plaintiff in establishing where it is possible or best to sue. But it also has several significant advantages. First, as we have seen, it enables injured transboundary

---

[37] See e.g., *British South Africa Company* v. *Compania de Moçambique* [1893] AC 602; *Hesperides Hotels Ltd* v. *Muftizade* [1979] AC 508; *Albert* v. *Frazer Companies Ltd* [1937] 1 DLR 39; *Dagi* v. *Broken Hill Proprietary Co. Ltd* (1997) 1 Victoria Rep. 428. UK courts now have jurisdiction over torts affecting immovable property outside the United Kingdom under s. 30 of the Civil Jurisdiction and Judgments Act 1982. See generally Bernasconi, C., Civil liability resulting from transfrontier damage: a case for the Hague Conference?, *Hague YIL* (1999), pp. 102–106.

[38] See respectively Case 21/76, *Handelskwekerij G. J. Bier* v. *Mines de Potasse d'Alsace* [1976] ECR 11-1735; *Re Union Carbide Corp.* 634 F. Supp. 842 (1986); *In re Oil Spill by Amoco Cadiz* 954 F. 2d 1279 (1992). All three jurisdictional bases are recognised by the Brussels Convention on Jurisdiction and the Enforcement of Judgments 1968, Articles 2 and 5 (replaced by Council Regulation EC/44/2001 of 22 December 2000 on jurisdiction and the recognition and enforcement of judgments in civil and commercial matters [2001] OJ L12, 16 January 2001 (in force 1 March 2002), and by the 2003 Kiev Protocol on Civil Liability and Compensation, Article 13.

victims to sue at home. Secondly, it also enables multinational corporations to be sued wherever there is the greatest likelihood of success, including in their home jurisdiction. One obstacle to such suits is the discretionary refusal of jurisdiction on grounds of *forum non conveniens*. This poses a problem in the USA when a foreign plaintiff sues a US domiciled defendant for injury abroad.[39] In other common law jurisdictions *forum non conveniens* is not applied when to do so would amount to a denial of justice.[40] The principle of *forum non conveniens* is unknown in civil law systems; it may also be inconsistent with contemporary human rights standards for access to justice.[41]

In contrast to these jurisdictional questions, no general principle exists for choice of law rules in transboundary torts. These rules are determined by the law of the forum. *Lex loci delicti, lex fori, lex domicili*, most favourable law, all are employed by different states. National practice has not so far been harmonised by the Hague Conference on Private International Law.[42]

An important question for the ILC was whether it wanted to address any of these matters relating to transboundary litigation. Private international law has not traditionally been part of the Commission's mandate. The Hague Conference has both a mandate and the necessary expertise to undertake the task.[43] But is the task worth undertaking? Harmonising choice of law rules for transboundary torts is not a method for allocating loss and will do little to promote justice for the victims. It is unlikely to answer the General Assembly's call for progress on liability. Forum shopping is already a reasonably well-established phenomenon; where there are presently obstacles, as in the USA, it is far from certain that whatever the ILC proposes would lead to material change in national law.

The main reason why forum shopping is important is that it reminds us that victims of transboundary torts are not necessarily obliged to sue in a foreign court. Given that the location of the damage will normally provide the necessary jurisdictional basis, the plaintiff will usually have the choice of suing at home if the legal system of the other state is inadequate or unfavourable. So long as they are non-discriminatory, it is open to the courts or the legislature of the plaintiff's own state to determine what liability standards it wishes to apply

---

[39] See *Re Union Carbide Corp.* 634 F. Supp. 842 (1986); *Aguinda v. Texaco Inc.*, 142 F. Supp. 2d 534 (2001).
[40] Cf. *Lubbe v. Cape plc* [2000] 1 WLR 1545.
[41] Ibid., per Lord Hope. See generally UN Covenant on Civil and Political Rights 1966, Article 14.
[42] See Report of the Committee on Transnational Enforcement of Environmental Law, *ILA Report of the 70th Conference*, Berlin (ILA) 2004.
[43] For a preliminary study see Bernasconi, C., Civil liability resulting from transfrontier damage: a case for the Hague Conference? *Hague YbIL* (1999), p. 35. The Hague Conference decided not to proceed with the subject.

in transboundary tort claims and what choice of law rules to adopt. It is not necessary for international law or the ILC to regulate such choices.

Nevertheless, in any scheme of transboundary civil liability there must be a forum in which to sue. The one contribution the ILC could make here is to ensure that the source state should enable its courts to exercise jurisdiction over activities taking place within its territory or control. We return to this question below.

3. Civil liability and compensation schemes

International harmonisation of civil liability for accidental damage is an important part of many schemes for regulating the transboundary risks of hazardous activities. It can contribute to simplifying the burden facing injured plaintiffs, while at the same time clarifying the responsibilities of defendants; it can also be a means of avoiding conflict of laws problems by ensuring that common liability standards apply in all the participating jurisdictions. There are benefits in the reduction of unpredictability, complexity, and cost of litigation. Insofar as harmonisation may also bring about a more equitable balance between the interests of plaintiffs and defendants, it helps to create shared expectations on a regional or global basis which may make the risks posed by hazardous activities more socially acceptable to those likely to be affected.

The main features of most of the civil liability treaties are that they establish a common scheme of strict liability in national law, usually channelled to the owner or operator of the vessel or installation (but in certain circumstances with a right of recourse against other parties), limited in amount, and supported by compulsory insurance and compensation funds, which will provide an assurance of additional compensation.[44] Although compensation limits have not always been realistic, civil liability Conventions of this kind afford litigants significant benefits. The plaintiff will usually know who to sue. There is no need to prove negligence, but it must still be shown that the damage was caused by the relevant accident. Problems of choice of law are minimised or eliminated; the

---

[44] In addition to those listed in n. 7 above, see also 1992 Convention on Civil Liability for Oil Pollution Damage 1992 ('CLC') (in force 1996); Convention on the Establishment of an International Fund for Compensation for Oil Pollution Damage 1992 ('Fund Convention') (in force 1996); Convention on Civil Liability for Activities Dangerous to the Environment 1993 ('Lugano Convention'); Convention on Liability and Compensation for the Carriage of Hazardous and Noxious Substances by Sea 1996 ('HNS Convention'); 1997 Protocol on Civil Liability for Nuclear Damage and Convention on Supplementary Compensation; 1999 Protocol on Liability and Compensation for Damage resulting from Transboundary Movements of Hazardous Waste; Convention on Civil Liability for Bunker Oil Pollution Damage 2001; 2003 Protocol on Civil Liability and Compensation for Damage caused by the Transboundary Effects of Industrial Accidents on Transboundary Waters ('Kiev Protocol'). Save where noted, none of these agreements are known to be in force at the time of writing.

applicable law will mainly be that laid down in the relevant Convention. There are clear rules on which court has jurisdiction over any proceedings. Judgments are enforceable internationally.

With the exception of the Council of Europe's Lugano Convention, which is considered below, none of the schemes follows the polluter pays principle in its simplest form. Although there are differences in the way each scheme allocates losses, in the case of pollution from ships' cargoes or nuclear installations the burden of major losses is borne initially by the owner of the vessel or operator of the installation up to the specified limit, then respectively by the industry or states concerned, and beyond that limit it falls on the innocent victim, or must be recovered in interstate claims. Three features require further explanation: the preference for no fault liability, the 'channelling' of liability, and the allocation of loss through compensation schemes.

(a) No fault liability

The choice of strict, or in exceptional cases absolute, liability is an invariable feature of all of the international liability Conventions. There are several reasons for this choice:

- it relieves courts of the difficult task of setting appropriate standards of reasonable care and plaintiffs of the burden of proving breach of those standards in relatively complex and technical industrial processes or installations;
- it would be unjust and inappropriate to make plaintiffs shoulder a heavy burden of proof where the risks of an activity are acceptable only because of its social utility; this argument is particularly strong in cases where the injured victims are in countries which derive no benefit from the activity which causes the damage;
- the risk of very serious or widespread damage, despite its low probability, places most of the activities covered by these Conventions in the ultrahazardous category.

Fault in most cases remains relevant only exceptionally, notably where third parties are implicated, or where owners or operators are themselves acting intentionally or recklessly in causing the damage.[45] In the case of nuclear accidents, fault is relevant only insofar as it allows the operator a right of recourse against any party intentionally causing the damage.[46] In some cases, however, there is broader provision for additional fault liability, including negligence. Under the 1999 Protocol on Liability for Transboundary Waste any person whose failure to comply with laws implementing the Basel Convention on Transboundary Movements of Hazardous Waste 1989 or whose wrongful, intentional, reckless,

---

[45] See e.g., CLC 1992, Articles 3 and 5(2); Lugano Convention 1993, Article 8(b).
[46] Paris Convention on Third Party Liability 1960, Article 6(f); 1997 Protocol on Civil Liability for Nuclear Damage, Article 4(2).

or negligent acts or omissions result in waste causing damage will be liable. While making operators strictly liable for transboundary damage caused by industrial accidents, the 2003 Kiev Protocol also retains additional fault-based liability as provided for by national law.

All the liability Conventions allow the operator or owner certain defences, including armed conflict and natural disasters. Beyond that there is some diversity in practice. The Lugano Convention, for example, allows the widest range of defences, the nuclear liability Conventions the narrowest. For this reason it is sometimes suggested that nuclear liability is absolute rather than simply strict. These are differences of detail and degree, however, not of fundamental principle.

(b) Channelling of liability

The channelling of no fault liability to the owner/operator is a feature of most of the liability Conventions, but unlike strict liability, it is by no means a universally accepted principle. Channelling to the owner/operator also means different things:

- In the case of ships carrying oil or hazardous and noxious substances (where the owner is liable) no action may be brought against the charterers, the crew, a pilot, or salvor, or the servants or agents of any of these.[47] Other potential defendants remain open to suit outside the terms of the Conventions. However, the Bunker Fuel Convention 2001 takes a different approach to pollution from ships and makes the owner, charterer, manager, and operator jointly and severally liable, thus spreading rather than channelling the liability.
- In the case of nuclear installations, nuclear powered ships, and ships carrying radioactive material, only the operator may be sued.[48] All other potential defendants are excluded, including the designers, builders, suppliers, contractors, employees, and so on. However, the nuclear liability Conventions do recognise that there may be several operators, including carriers of nuclear materials and handlers of nuclear waste. In the event of an accident involving multiple operators, liability is also joint and several.
- In the case of damage resulting from the transboundary movement and disposal of waste, no single operator is liable at all stages.[49] Instead, generators, exporters, importers, and disposers are all potentially liable at different stages of the waste's journey to its eventual destination. In general, during export

---

[47] CLC 1992, Article 3(4); HNS Convention 1996, Article 7(5).

[48] Paris Convention on Third Party Liability 1960; Brussels Convention on Nuclear Ships 1962; 1963 Brussels Supplementary Agreement; Vienna Convention on Civil Liability 1963; Convention on Oil Pollution Damage 1992; Brussels Convention on Maritime Carriage of Nuclear Material 1971.

[49] 1999 Protocol on Liability and Compensation for Transboundary Movements of Hazardous Waste.

and transit the person who notifies the states concerned of a proposed transboundary movement of waste will be liable (this will be either the generator or the exporter of the waste); then the ultimate disposer of the waste assumes liability once possession is transferred. Additional rules determine who is liable where there is no notification, or where waste is returned to the state of origin. Where several parties are liable, which is clearly possible, liability is joint and several.

Channelling of liability has the advantages of simplifying the plaintiff's identification of a defendant and establishing a clear line of responsibility. The choice of the owner or operator as the focus of liability is based on the assumption that these parties respectively will be in the best position to exercise effective control of a ship or nuclear installation and to insure it. On the other hand, as the examples of the Bunker Fuel Convention and the Protocol on Liability for Transboundary Waste show, channelling of liability to a single owner or operator is not always a realistic option, and the choice of 'owner/operator liability' without more would represent in some cases too simplistic a solution without a broader definition of these terms. However, where, as in these two examples, there may be several 'owners' or 'operators', joint and several liability will enable the plaintiff to pursue the most solvent and if necessary spread the burden of compensation more widely than is possible under the CLC or Nuclear Liability Conventions. The broader the definition of 'operator', the larger the potential pool of solvent defendants; however, the larger the pool of defendants the harder it may be to know which to sue.

(c) Allocation of loss

Limitation of liability at relatively low levels in most of the conventional schemes recognises that owners of ships or operators of nuclear installations cannot realistically be held liable for the full cost of serious accidents. This is why such schemes also make provision for the payment of additional and usually much greater sums out of compensation funds. The essential point in these two examples is that the cost of accidents does not fall exclusively on the owner/operator, but is shared respectively by the owner/operator and the industry or states concerned. In the case of bunker fuel and hazardous waste the liability, though limited in amount, is spread across several parties, unlike other schemes. In the latter case supplementary compensation is available only to developing state parties or economies in transition. This limitation is not a feature of other compensation schemes. Another difference is that the fund is financed by voluntary contributions from the parties to the Convention. There is no requirement for industry to contribute. Not all liability Conventions make provision for limited liability or additional compensation funding: the Lugano Convention 1993 and the 2003 Kiev Protocol are notable exceptions.

(d) Common principles or diverse solutions?

Three important points about allocation of loss stand out when examining existing civil liability and compensation schemes. First, strict liability is the universally accepted standard, albeit with minor variations in the permitted defences. The ILC scheme does not depart from this basic element. Secondly, as already noted, liability is not consistently attributed to a single 'operator'. There is no common view on the question who should be made liable, or on channelling to a single defendant. Significantly, while the ILC scheme chooses to focus liability on operators, it also allows for alternatives. Thirdly, while most liability schemes spread the burden of loss through additional compensation schemes, each scheme has its own unique funding arrangements. There is no common pattern. In some cases, states carry the ultimate burden of residual compensation funding, as well as a residual liability in the event of operator insolvency; in others, the costs are borne wholly by industry. This makes them difficult models from which to derive any general scheme of loss allocation that might secure universal agreement beyond the proposition that some such provision should be made. More than that, it may also suggest that different contexts require different solutions. So far only one attempt has been made to delineate a general scheme of liability for hazardous activities: the Council of Europe's Lugano Convention 1993.

(e) Lugano Convention on Civil Liability for Damage resulting from Activities Dangerous to the Environment 1993

This Convention is the only existing scheme for comprehensive harmonisation of environmental liability in Europe, or elsewhere. It is not limited to transboundary harm but, like the nuclear liability Conventions, it imposes a common scheme of strict liability for damage caused by dangerous activities or dangerous substances on the operator or operators of the activity in question. It is the only conventional scheme in which liability is not limited in amount and to that extent reflects the polluter pays principle more closely than other Treaties under which the loss is spread. There is no provision for additional compensation funds. The intention is that the unlimited liability of the operator will be assured by compulsory insurance or other financial security. 'Damage' is widely defined and covers reasonable measures of prevention or reinstatement of environmental harm, as well as injury to persons and property.[50] For this purpose the 'environment' is also broadly defined and includes natural resources, cultural heritage property, and 'characteristic aspects of the landscape'. Jurisdiction is based on the forum shopping provisions of the Brussels Convention on Civil Jurisdiction and Judgments 1968.

---

[50] See La Fayette, L. de, in Bowman, M. and Boyle, A. E. (eds.), *Environmental damage in international and comparative law*, Oxford (Oxford University Press) 2002, ch. 9.

This scheme otherwise shares most of the main features of the more specialised liability regimes. Its main weakness, however, is that eleven years after adoption it has still attracted no ratifications, and appears likely to have no impact in Europe unless the EC decides to participate. Lack of participation is a problem with most of the liability schemes; at best it casts some doubt on their acceptability or relevance.[51] The prospect of possibly extensive changes to national tort law is one reason for this hesitation; the selective application of strict liability in some areas but not others may be another, insofar as it changes fundamental concepts of national law. The Lugano Convention provided an obvious model for the ILC to draw upon, but the main risk had it tried to follow this approach was that it would prove overprescriptive and result in an outcome unwelcome to many states. If such a solution is unappealing even in Europe what chance of success would it have elsewhere?

IV. The Commission's 2004 Draft Liability Principles

Certain political realities thus limit the ILC's room for creativity. Making states liable for all transboundary damage, or going beyond the existing limits of state responsibility as already codified, do not appear likely to become acceptable to many governments for the reasons already outlined above. Drafting a complex harmonisation Convention along the lines of the Lugano Convention 1993 seems unlikely to attract greater support at a global level than it has attracted in Europe. Reforming the relevant rules of private international law and tackling the concept of *forum non conveniens* to facilitate transboundary litigation would take the ILC into new areas where it lacks expertise and would compete head on with other bodies. Non-discriminatory access to justice has already been reiterated as a basic right, but would have to be supplemented by some conception of minimum redress to be fully effective. If that were possible, it could enhance the utility of forum shopping and have beneficial effects on national liability laws in general.

The draft liability Principles adopted by the ILC in 2004 are far from radical, and in that respect they fully reflect the Commission's traditional conservatism and caution. Three preliminary points are important. First, the scheme is without prejudice to other existing or future liability regimes, or to the existing responsibility of states in international law.[52] In that sense it is residual, and states are free to and are indeed encouraged to negotiate other arrangements.[53] Secondly, as presently drafted, it has no obligatory components. Unusually for the ILC, the final text is pure soft law, employing the term 'should' rather than 'shall' throughout. The commentary explains that:

---

[51] Churchill, R., Civil liability litigation for environmental damage by means of treaties: progress, problems and prospects, *YbIEL* 12 (2001), p. 3.
[52] See General Commentary, paras 6 and 7, and section V.   [53] See Principle 7.

the Commission concluded that recommended draft principles would have the advantage of not requiring a potentially unachievable harmonisation of national laws and legal systems. It is also of the view that the goal of widespread acceptance of the substantive provisions is more likely to be met if they are cast as recommended draft principles.[54]

In this respect the final text differs from the Special Rapporteur's initial drafting, although the ILC's report does indicate a willingness to think again in the light of comments. As we shall see below, such a rethink may be very desirable. Thirdly, the principles apply only to physical damage caused by 'activities which involve a risk of causing significant transboundary harm'.[55] This is the same test used in the ILC's 2001 Articles on Prevention of Transboundary Harm. The most important consequence of this definition is that, like the House of Lords decision on strict liability in the *Cambridge Water* case, there will be no liability where damage could not have been foreseen.[56] To that extent, some damage will still go uncompensated and the innocent victims must continue to bear such losses.

1. The core principle: prompt, adequate, and effective compensation?

Principle 3 sets out the objective of the draft Principles:

> The present draft principles aim at ensuring prompt and adequate compensation to natural or legal persons, including states, that are victims of transboundary damage, including damage to the environment.

In its commentary, the ILC offers a slightly expanded formulation, referring to 'compensation that is predictable, equitable, expeditious and cost effective'. Principle 4 reiterates the same general point by calling for states to take 'necessary measures' to ensure the availability of prompt and adequate compensation for transboundary victims.[57] Here we can see immediately that the ILC envisages more than simply opening up national procedures to non-discriminatory access. At the heart of its scheme is an international standard for compensation – a standard of promptness and adequacy which affects not only the compensation itself but the procedures and remedies through which it is to be obtained. Thus Principle 6(1) refers to the provision of 'appropriate procedures',[58] and

---

[54] ILC Report (2004), op. cit., General Commentary, para. 14.   [55] Principle 1.
[56] *Cambridge Water Co. v. Eastern Counties Leather plc* [1994] 1 All ER 53. See ILC Report (2004), op. cit., commentary to Principle 1, para. 10.
[57] 'Each state should take necessary measures to ensure that prompt and adequate compensation is available for victims of transboundary damage caused by hazardous activities located within its territory or otherwise under its jurisdiction or control.'
[58] 'States should provide appropriate procedures to ensure that compensation is provided in furtherance of draft principle 4 to victims of transboundary damage from hazardous activities.'

Principle 6(3) specifies that domestic law should provide 'effective remedies', and mechanisms that are 'no less prompt, adequate and effective' than those available to nationals.[59] While the rest of the scheme is essentially flexible and open to implementation in a wide variety of ways, the intention is that whatever measures are taken should promote and be compatible with the fundamental objective set out in Principle 3. This element of the ILC scheme could represent potentially its most significant contribution to the progressive development of the subject. As we saw earlier, it is not new, and builds on existing law, but it is the first occasion on which such a core principle has been articulated in such general terms.

The appearance of creativity is deceptive, however. An important question not directly addressed by the ILC is whether this core principle should be offered in soft law terms, as at present, or formulated instead as the one obligatory element of an otherwise optional scheme. The commentary to Principle 3 raises the issue obliquely by referring to the polluter pays principle as a possible basis for prompt and adequate compensation. Here, the ILC is understandably cautious. Pointing to the difficulty posed by the principle's inherent generality and diversity in application, it notes that a recent arbitral decision has held that it is not part of general international law, despite references in several Treaties. It is doubtful whether the ILC really believes the polluter pays principle is a legally binding norm that requires states to make compensation available; at the same time it is evidently willing to take account of the underlying policy endorsed in Principle 16 of the 1992 Rio Declaration.[60]

But if the ILC is clearly right in its treatment of the polluter pays principle, is it right to adopt a soft law formulation of its own core principle? Could it have concluded either that there is, or should be, a right to prompt adequate and effective compensation for transboundary damage in international law, or an obligation to make procedures for obtaining such compensation available? The ILC itself refers to the *Trail Smelter Arbitration* as authority: 'the basic principle established in that case entailed a duty of a state to ensure payment of prompt and adequate compensation for any transboundary damage'.[61] Moreover, as we saw earlier, Principle 10 of the Rio Declaration, Article 235(2) of UNCLOS 1982, Article 2(1) of the 1996 ILA Helsinki Articles on International Watercourses,

---

[59] 'To the extent necessary for the purpose of providing compensation in furtherance of draft principle 4, each State should ensure that its domestic administrative and judicial mechanisms possess the necessary competence and provide effective remedies to such victims. These mechanisms should not be less prompt, adequate and effective than those available to its nationals and should include appropriate access to information necessary to pursue such mechanisms.'

[60] See commentary to Principle 3, paras 7–13.

[61] ILC Report (2004), op. cit. commentary to Principle 4, para. 11. See also commentary to Principle 6, para. 7.

and human rights precedents,[62] all suggest that there are international standards of compensation for victims of transboundary damage, though they do not go very far in defining them. An alternative foundation would draw from precedents on the taking of property in international law, making the obvious analogy between a taking of property and damage by pollution.[63]

There is arguably enough material here on which to build something more than a soft law compensation principle. The ILC does not normally differentiate between the codification of existing international law and the progressive development of new law. In reality, its endorsement has not infrequently proved sufficient to endow what might otherwise have been regarded as *lex ferenda* with enough added authority to elevate it into law.[64] As Professor Crawford has observed:

> What the ILC can do is to consolidate developments in a particular area of law, making them part of the *droit acquis* . . . it is progressive when seen against a background of slow development of the international community and its institutional need for a coherent body of law.[65]

On this occasion, the ILC has been too cautious. While the Special Rapporteur may initially have been overprescriptive in his proposals for a draft civil liability treaty, the ILC risks wasting its energy on a draft which is not prescriptive enough. It is one thing to leave a wide discretion to states in giving effect to the core objective of the draft; soft law recommendations on the elements of a liability regime are appropriate for that purpose. It is quite another to leave the entire draft lacking in any basic obligation to make anything available to claimants. This represents only the illusion of progress over the present situation: indeed, it may be retrograde insofar as existing law arguably goes further.

The ILC's 2003 report had used a different test, requiring states to ensure 'equitable and expeditious compensation and relief to victims of transboundary harm'.[66] The ILC did not indicate what factors would determine whether compensation is 'equitable'. It is not obvious that the equitable factors listed in

---

[62] See n. 36 above.
[63] See e.g., *Sporrong and Lönnroth v. Sweden* (1983) 5 EHRR 617, where planning blight was held to constitute a taking of property without compensation, contrary to Article 1 of Protocol 1 to the European Convention on Human Rights. The 'prompt, adequate and effective' standard is not universally accepted, however. See Amerasinghe, C. F., Issues of compensation for the taking of alien property in the light of recent cases and practice, *ICLQ* 41 (1992), p. 22. The author notes the very different formulations employed in state practice, UN resolutions, regional human rights Treaties and international arbitral awards and concludes that full compensation is not appropriate in all cases.
[64] See e.g., *Gabcikovo-Nagymaros Case* [1997] ICJ Rep. 7.
[65] Crawford, J., former member of the ILC, letter to the author, 7 October 1997.
[66] ILC Report (2003), op. cit. para. 174(c)(12).

Article 10 of the 2001 Articles on Prevention of Transboundary Harm[67] would be equally relevant when transposed from a regime aimed at interstate relations to one intended to make polluters or others who cause harm liable for the losses incurred by otherwise innocent victims. The fundamental question at issue here is how far such victims should be fully compensated for their losses; equitable compensation, however calculated, is unlikely to be as generous or as predictable as prompt, adequate, and effective compensation.[68] From that point of view the ILC is right to abandon the attempt to invoke equity for inappropriate purposes. Nevertheless, even an obligation to make provision for equitable compensation may be preferable to a purely soft law recommendation to pay prompt, adequate, and effective compensation.

As they presently stand, it must be doubtful whether the ILC's 2004 draft Principles give effect to the wishes of the General Assembly or the Rio Conference, because they do nothing to clarify, codify, or develop the international law underpinning the Commission's proposed model of a liability regime. This is a house built on water, without foundations, or any visible means of support. The single most obvious way in which states could transform the present draft Principles into a workable exercise in progressive development would be to make Principles 4(1), 6(1), and 6(3) obligatory,[69] leaving the remainder of

---

[67] In establishing an equitable regime for the management of transboundary risks, Article 10 requires all relevant factors to be taken into account, including:

(a) the degree of risk of significant transboundary harm and of the availability of means of preventing such harm, or minimising the risk thereof or repairing the harm;
(b) the importance of the activity, taking into account its overall advantages of a social, economic and technical character for the state of origin in relation to the potential harm for the state likely to be affected;
(c) the risk of significant harm to the environment and the availability of means of preventing such harm, or minimising the risk thereof or restoring the environment;
(d) the *degree* to which the state of origin and, as appropriate, the state likely to be affected *are* prepared to contribute to the costs of prevention;
(e) the *economic* viability of the activity in relation to the costs of prevention and to the possibility of carrying out the activity elsewhere or by other means or replacing it with an alternative activity;
(f) the *standards* of prevention which the state likely to be affected applies to the same or comparable activities and the standards applied in comparable regional or international practice.

[68] The Space Objects Liability Convention 1972, Article 12, provides that compensation shall be determined in accordance with 'international law and the principles of justice and *equity*', but must be sufficient to restore the injured party 'to the condition which would have existed if the damage had not occurred'. In a claim made following the crash of Cosmos 954, Canada did not seek its full costs of $14 million, but claimed $6 million and settled for $3 million.

[69] See nn. 57–59 above.

the articles optional.[70] In that way, if states do not negotiate or ratify liability treaties, or implement the draft in some other way, there will still be some underlying legal obligation on which other states can rely in the event of transboundary harm that goes uncompensated. What is needed is to recognise that states are responsible, not for transboundary harm, but *for failing to make adequate provision to compensate* those who suffer loss from transboundary harm. Only if the draft formulates this core element as a legal obligation will it have the desired effect, or indeed any effect.

2. The ILC's model of a civil liability regime

In its 2003 Report, the ILC started from the assumption that there is a duty to compensate which states would be free to discharge in various ways:

> the review did not suggest that the duty to compensate would best be discharged by negotiating a particular form of liability convention. The duty could equally well be discharged by forum shopping and allowing the plaintiff to sue in the most favourable jurisdiction, or by negotiating an ad hoc settlement.[71]

While the ILC has now abandoned any hint of a duty to compensate, its suggested elements for a liability regime remain, as we have seen, both residual and optional. Any other approach would have required the ILC to design a draft Treaty that, for reasons already explored, would almost certainly share the same fate as all the other unratified liability Treaties. Nevertheless, the essential elements of the ILC scheme are very similar to the general principles found in existing civil liability Treaties. While this cannot be viewed as an exercise in codifying customary international law, it does show how the ILC can make use of general principles of law as 'an indication of policy and principle'.[72]

(a) Liability

Principle 4(2) of the ILC's 2004 draft provides that liability 'should not require proof of fault'. The commentary accepts the argument that the hazardous activities carry inherent risks and that it would be unjust and inappropriate to require proof of fault when accidents do happen. It notes the adoption of strict liability in Treaties and in national law, and on this point refers to its own draft as 'a measure of progressive development of international law'.[73] Principle 4(2) also provides that any conditions, limitations, or exceptions to such liability should be consistent with the core objective of prompt and adequate compensation.

---

[70] Even in treaties, the intermingling of hard and soft law terminology is not unknown: see UNCLOS 1982, Article 123.
[71] ILC Report (2003), op. cit. para. 174 (a).
[72] Lord McNair, *South West Africa Case* [1950] ICJ Rep. 148.
[73] Commentary to Principle 4, paras 15–17.

The option of limiting liability, also found in many of the existing civil liability Conventions, must be seen in this light; it will presumably be acceptable to the extent that other additional sources of compensation are made available, as envisaged in Principles 4(4) and (5). Moreover, where the operator has relied successfully on available defences, the ILC nevertheless envisages that compensation will be forthcoming either *ex gratia* from the state or from additional compensation funds.[74]

(b) Operator liability

Principle 4 envisages that the 'operator' of the harmful activity will be made primarily liable, but it also allows 'where appropriate' for liability to be imposed on some other person or entity. While the commentary views operator liability as an application of the polluter pays principle, the recognition that others may more appropriately be held liable shows how little guidance can be derived from that concept. The commentary refers to the need for 'flexibility' in this respect.[75] 'Operator' is defined as meaning 'any person in command or control of the activity at the time the incident causing transboundary damage occurs'.[76] The ILC recognises that Treaty definitions vary with the nature of the activity,[77] but the intention is to encapsulate all these possibilities within one portmanteau concept of 'effective control of the risk at the time of the accident or the most effective ability to provide compensation'.[78] This latter understanding is broad enough to cover even the lender liability found in US law. In practice, the ILC's draft seems to assume that there may be more than one operator and, by implication, that liability may be joint and several.

(c) Compensation funding

The ILC's Principles assume that even after holding an operator primarily liable, there may still be a need for states to take additional measures to ensure the availability of adequate compensation. First, it recommends that operator liability should be backed by insurance or other financial security to ensure redress even if the operator is insolvent.[79] Secondly, additional compensation funding should also be provided, as in many of the existing Conventions. It is not prescriptive about who should provide the funds – industry, if appropriate – or if the measures available are insufficient then it should fall to states to ensure additional resources are allocated.[80]

---

[74] Commentary to Principle 4, para. 29. [75] Commentary to Principle 6, para. 13.
[76] Principle 2(e). [77] Commentary to Principle 2, para. 27.
[78] Commentary to Principle 4, para. 12.
[79] Principle 4(3) and commentary, paras 30–34.
[80] Principles 4(4) and (5), and commentary, paras 35–36.

(d) Damage

The ILC's definition of damage successfully replicates the treatment of environmental damage in the more modern liability treaties, and is consistent with the practice of the UN Compensation Commission (UNCC) and developments in national law.[81] Thus, draft Principle 2(a) expressly includes damage to cultural property, the costs of reasonable measures of reinstatement of the environment, and reasonable response measures. 'Environment' is also defined broadly, including natural resources, and in terms that would cover ecosystems, biological diversity, and aesthetic values.[82] While acknowledging that there is no universal definition of the term, the ILC rightly observes that its own definition 'helps put in perspective the scope of remedial action required'. In one respect, the ILC's draft is potentially more progressive, however, because Principle 2(a)(iii) envisages liability for environmental damage *per se*, unrelated to the cost of response or restoration measures.[83] While some national laws already allow recovery of compensation for pure environmental damage, no previous liability agreement has gone this far.[84] There are well-known problems of valuation and standing which such claims give rise to. The ILC says nothing on the question of valuation, and it does not define who is a 'victim' for the purpose of suing, but its commentary notes that the term can include groups of persons, local authorities, NGOs, public trustees, and states.[85]

(e) Forum

Principle 6 envisages that 'appropriate procedures' will be provided, and goes on to refer both to domestic administrative and judicial mechanisms and international claims settlement procedures. The latter must be both 'expeditious and involve minimal expense', and the commentary refers *inter alia* to the UNCC as an example.[86] Clearly, there is a wide variety of possibilities here, and litigation before national courts is only one such option.

If litigation is envisaged, then some provision for jurisdiction will be essential to give effect to Principle 6 in those states which presently deny jurisdiction

---

[81] See Commentary to Principle 2, at paras 1–21. For a fuller analysis of recent trends see Bowman, M. and Boyle, A. E. (eds.), *Environmental damage in international and comparative law*, Oxford (Oxford University Press) 2002.

[82] Principle 2(b), and commentary, paras 14–17.

[83] See Commentary to Principle 2, para. 12. See also Special Rapporteur's Second Report, op. cit. para. 31.

[84] Compare 2004 Protocol to Amend the Paris Convention on Third Party Liability in the Field of Nuclear Energy, Article 1B; Convention on Civil Liability for Oil Pollution Damage 1992, Article 1(6). See La Fayette, L. de, in Bowman and Boyle, op. cit. ch. 9.

[85] Commentary to Principle 3, paras 3–6. The focus on 'victims' reflects Principle 13 of the 1992 Rio Declaration on Environment and Development.

[86] See n. 98 below.

in the case of damage abroad.[87] The draft does not spell out any specific rule, although the commentary mentions the forum shopping rules found in the Lugano Convention and in EU law. Principle 6(3) recommends only that states ensure their courts possess the necessary competence. Principle 8, which indicates that states 'should' adopt any legislative, regulatory, and administrative measures necessary to implement the Principles would also seem to suggest as much, although the commentary does not touch on the issue. To that extent, but no more, the ILC has addressed some of the private international law matters which arise in transboundary civil litigation. It carefully notes that Principle 6 does not alleviate the choice of law problems referred to above, but calls on states to promote further harmonisation.[88]

V. Unresolved matters: the relationship with the law of state responsibility

Whatever conception of loss allocation finally emerges from the ILC's work, if it entails access to remedies in national law the potential impact on interstate claims will become important. The ILC's 2004 Report notes that: 'The draft principles are therefore without prejudice to the rules relating to state responsibility and any claim that may lie under those rules'.[89] It seems clear that the ILC envisages civil liability and state responsibility as potentially complementary regimes. Nevertheless, members of the ILC have been notably divided on this question.[90]

In general, international law, interstate claims involving responsibility for injury to aliens, or violation of human rights norms, are normally conditional on the prior exhaustion of local remedies, which usually entails resort to the relevant national legal system as a preferred means of redress. Only if justice is effectively denied, or if no redress is available, will an international claim then be admissible.[91] It has been suggested in the ILC's work on diplomatic protection that the local remedies rule is inapplicable in cases of transboundary harm because there is no voluntary link or territorial connection between the victim and the respondent state.[92] The underlying idea is that the injured party must have voluntarily assumed the risk of being subject to the jurisdiction of a foreign state. The ILC's 2004 Report takes the following view:

---

[87] See n. 37 above.   [88] Commentary to Principle 6, para. 8.
[89] General Commentary, para. 7.   [90] See ILC Report (2002), op. cit. paras. 220–228.
[91] *ELSI* Case [1989] ICJ Rep. 15, paras 50–63; ILC, 2001 Articles on State Responsibility, Article 44(b).
[92] ILC Report (2002), op. cit. paras. 204–208, 220–228; ILC Report (2004), op. cit., Commentary to Article 10(c), draft Articles on Diplomatic Protection.

even where effective local remedies exist, it would be unreasonable and unfair to require an injured person to exhaust local remedies where his property has suffered environmental harm caused by pollution, radioactive fallout or a fallen space object emanating from a State in which his property is not situated.[93]

Draft Article 16(c) on Diplomatic Protection thus excludes the local remedies rule where there is no 'relevant connection' between the injured party and the state responsible. On this view, governments would remain free to make an interstate claim on behalf of anyone affected by transboundary damage without first exhausting local remedies. If local remedies need not be exhausted in such cases, then interstate claims become a primary remedy (in cases where the responsibility in international law of another state could be established). Use of local remedies will simply be an optional addition or alternative. Is this desirable?

Particularly in cases where the damage is widespread, and the victims are poor, it may be that governmental action at interstate level is the only realistic option. The UNCC's procedures for bringing compensation claims against Iraq are the most recent example of governments espousing claims in international law on behalf of a mass of individual victims.[94] Whether such claimants should be left to their local remedies would in this case be a matter for their own government to decide.

The contrary view, that local remedies should be exhausted when adequate and available, would leave interstate claims as a residual option to be exercised only when local remedies have been unsuccessfully exhausted or do not exist.[95] The preference of states for non-discriminatory access to national remedies, civil liability, and compensation schemes is already well established. Is it not desirable to encourage or recognise this trend by applying the local remedies rule to interstate claims for transboundary harm, even if the victims are 'involuntary'? In cases where the claimants are too numerous or poor to bring their own claims to court, governments could assume the right to do so on their behalf and consolidate them in a mass claims process, as has already happened in the *Bhopal* case.[96] Moreover, where the scale of damage and the number

---

[93] ILC Report (2004), op. cit., Commentary to Article 16(c), draft Articles on Diplomatic Protection, para. 7.
[94] See Kazazi, M., Environmental damage in the practice of the UN Compensation Commission, in Bowman and Boyle, op. cit. p. 111.
[95] In *Trail Smelter* there were no local remedies to exhaust: Canadian courts had no jurisdiction over damage abroad. In the Chernobyl disaster there were also no local remedies because there was no liability under Soviet law. But in the Sandoz pollution disaster on the Rhine, local remedies did exist and were used.
[96] The Bhopal Gas Leak Disaster (Processing of Claims) Act 1985 gave the Government of India the exclusive right to represent Indian plaintiffs in Indian courts and elsewhere in connection with the disaster.

and impecuniousity of potential claimants makes it unreasonable to proceed through national courts, the local remedies rule would, on the terms codified by the ILC, be inapplicable anyway.[97]

Given this very substantial qualification, which would cover all the hard cases identified in the ILC's debates, it is not obvious why the absence of a relevant connection with the respondent state should also exclude the local remedies rule even where the injured victims would suffer no hardship in pursuing local remedies. The ILC accepts that the authority in support of the voluntary link requirement is limited and contradictory, and its conclusion is tentative. Ultimately, this is a question of deciding which view is preferable.

VI. Conclusions

No one could reasonably suggest that the ILC has been at the forefront of the development of international environmental law. There is nothing in the present draft that challenges that record. But it is not the ILC's job to engage in radical law-making, and to expect otherwise is to miss the point. Codification and progressive development of the law on a basis acceptable to states in general is inevitably a rather more modest task. Nevertheless, the work of the ILC has been important and often influential in identifying, updating, and reshaping contemporary international law.

The present draft Principles represent a novel departure for the ILC in several ways. First, to a more significant degree than many other ILC projects, it has involved working mostly with general principles of law drawn mainly from liability treaties and national law. Secondly, while the Principles offer a model to which states may wish to conform, they are intended as no more than guidance – an indication of how a liability regime might ideally look. This accounts for their ostensibly soft law character, itself an unusual outcome for the ILC.

The draft Principles successfully reflect the modern development of civil liability treaties, without in any way compromising or altering those which presently exist. This is a notable achievement, but it may also be a double-edged attribute. On the one hand, it is prudent to build on what states themselves have already negotiated. On the other, the reluctance of states to ratify those same Treaties may indicate a less than wholehearted commitment to the idea of shifting the focus away from state responsibility for transboundary harm in favour of civil liability and individual access to justice. Only time will tell

---

[97] ILC Report (2004), op. cit., draft Articles on Diplomatic Protection, draft Article 16: 'Local remedies do not need to be exhausted where: (a) the local remedies provide no reasonable possibility of effective redress; (b) there is undue delay in the remedial process which is attributable to the State alleged to be responsible; (c) there is no relevant connection between the injured person and the State alleged to be responsible or the circumstances of the case otherwise make the exhaustion of local remedies unreasonable; (d) the State alleged to be responsible has waived the requirement that local remedies be exhausted.'

whether the ILC has made the right choice. Given the reluctance of states to extend their own liability on a no fault basis, it is difficult to see what other choice the ILC could have made in 2002.

The most obvious weakness of the present draft is the failure to require states as a matter of legal obligation to make provision for adequate redress in the event of transboundary damage. As we saw earlier, access to justice based on prompt and adequate compensation represents the foundation of the whole draft; it was originally envisaged as an obligatory element, and so it should have remained. Failure to address this deficiency will not only undermine the draft, it will also undermine existing developments in international law, already reflected in the Rio Declaration and regional and global treaties. Moreover, it is inconsistent with the ILC's otherwise sensible and successful codification of the law on the management of transboundary risk in 2001. The Commission rightly recognises that states must remain free to undertake beneficial activities even if they do pose a risk for other states, but its 2001 Articles on the Prevention of Transboundary Harm subject that freedom to certain conditions, including environmental impact assessment, notification, consultation, and cooperation. All these provisions the ILC itself regards as legally obligatory. The one condition missing from the 2001 Articles is that states make provision for liability or compensation in the event of foreseeable transboundary damage. If the present draft Principles on liability are adopted as drafted, states will remain free to engage in harmful activities without any obligation to provide effective remedies or redress for transboundary damage unless they are themselves at fault. That is exactly the defect which the ILC was invited to rectify when it began work on the topic in 1978.

Surprising as it may seem, the ILC, perhaps nearing the end of its twenty-seven-year odyssey, may yet find itself contributing as much to environmental rights as to liability. This would surely be right. Without casting doubt on the utility of interstate claims for transboundary damage (though they are most remarkable by their paucity), the more practical approach is to guarantee the innocent victims access to justice and adequate redress against those who cause transboundary harm, without making this entirely dependent on the willingness of governments to act for them, or to pay the costs of transboundary damage generated by others. Where such recourse is not provided, then states themselves should remain responsible for compensating the damage. That seems, to this author, the right balance between private law redress and interstate claims.

24

The legal nature of environmental principles in international, EU, and exemplary national law

GERD WINTER

Much has been said about the semantic content of various environmental as well as other principles, but there is less clarity about their legal nature. This chapter will propose a general concept of principles which can be applied to all levels of the law, national, regional, as well as international. The concept views principles as a transmission belt between societal common sense and the law. If seen in this light, principles can help to accelerate the making of environmental law, so much needed at a time of asynchronie between the speed of global environmental change and the slowness of institutional response. I will begin with a short overview of the rhetoric of environmental 'principles', and develop a definition of 'principle' suggesting that there are different definitions for different legal contexts in which 'principles' appear.

I. Overview of environmental propositions called principles

In international law, three environmental propositions are widely cited as principles, namely the sovereign right of states over their natural resources, the procedural duty between states to cooperate in mitigating environmental risks and emergencies, and the substantive duty to prevent, reduce, and control imminent and serious environmental harm.[1] These principles are recognised as rules of international customary law. They can also be regarded as 'principles of international law'. The third – prevention of serious harm – may even qualify as a 'principle of peremptory law' (*ius cogens*).

Precaution, meaning the duty to take measures even in situations of uncertain but possibly serious risks, has been much discussed as a candidate for a fourth rule of international customary law. However, although many scholars call precaution a principle,[2] neither the International Court of Justice (ICJ)[3]

---

[1] Birnie, P., and Boyle, A., *International law and the environment*, Oxford (Oxford University Press) 2nd edn 2002.
[2] Cf. Birnie and Boyle, op. cit. p. 120.
[3] *Case concerning the Gabcikovo-Nagymaros Dam*, judgment of 25 September 1997, ICJ, at paras 111–114.

nor the International Tribunal for the Law of the Sea[4] nor other international dispute settlement bodies like the WTO Appellate Body[5] have yet been bold enough to take the step to afford the principle the status of international custom. Nor is it regarded a 'general principle of law recognised by civilised nations' in the sense of Article 38 ICJ Statute (as long as by 'law' it is understood national law) because not many domestic environmental law systems have as yet ventured into precautionary legislation. Nevertheless, precaution does appear as a principle in several international Treaties,[6] but as such it is binding only *inter partes*.

More environmental 'principles' have been established by Treaties, such as, notably, the polluter pays principle, the principle of transparency and participation, the principle of joint but separate responsibility, and the principle of sustainability.[7] Equitable access to natural resources and the duty of the state of effective management are significant complementary principles propagated by those authors who write from the background of societies where inequality is tremendous and the administration widely ineffective.[8] But none of these has been attributed the status of customary law.

In the EU, environmental propositions have been codified in Article 174 EC Treaty. Some of them – precaution, prevention, rectification at source, and polluter pays – are called principles, others – preserving, protecting, and improving the quality of the environment at a 'high level' – are called objectives. A most interesting European contribution to the international debate is the integration principle, meaning that environmental requirements must be integrated into the definition and implementation of all other Community policies and activities (Article 6 EC Treaty). It is noteworthy that sustainability is not directly named as a principle of environmental policy but is seen as both a task of the EU (Article 2 EC Treaty) and a qualification of the 'principle' of integration (Article 6 EC Treaty).[9]

---

[4] ITLOS comes close, though, to formulating such a principle in its order of provisional measures of 28 August 1999 in the *Bluefin Tuna* case, saying at para. 77: 'Considering that, in the view of the Tribunal, the parties should in the circumstances act with prudence and caution to ensure that effective conservation measures are taken to prevent serious harm to the stock of southern bluefin tuna'.

[5] *EC-Measures concerning Meat and Meat Products*, Appellate Body Report, January 1998, WT/DS26/AB/R and WT/DS48/AB/R, paras 120–125 and n. 93.

[6] For an overview see de Sadeleer, N., *Environmental principles*, Oxford (Oxford University Press) 2002, p. 94.

[7] Cf. Birnie and Boyle, op. cit. p. 79 *et seq*.; de Sadeleer, op. cit. p. 23 *et seq*.; Sands, P., *Principles of international environmental law*, Cambridge (Cambridge University Press) 2nd edn 2003; Epiney, A. and Scheyli, M., *Umweltvölkerrecht*, Bern (Stämpfli) 2000.

[8] See Leme Machado, P. A., *Direito ambiental brasileiro*, Sao Paulo (Malheiros Editores) 11th edn 2003, pp. 47, 87 *et seq.*

[9] The draft Constitution retains the principles and objectives as listed above. Only slight changes have been made. The integration principle appears twice, namely as a basic right

Many more environmental 'principles' can be found in EC secondary law, such as the principle of integrated pollution prevention and control, the principle of free access to environmental information, the principle of environmental impact assessment, etc. Such 'principles' characterise the core idea or background theory of the individual provisions in the pertinent legal act.

On the national level, Germany and Brazil may be cited as two opposing cases. Germany is parsimonious and Brazil rich in constitutional principles of environmental protection. In the German Constitution, disregarding the rules on competences there is only one article referring to the environment. In Article 20a it is provided that the state must protect the natural conditions of life. In addition, jurisprudence of the Federal Constitutional Court has developed an objective duty of the state to protect human health and a subjective right of the individual to ask for such protection. There is, however, no subjective right to a livable environment. German law does also rarely lay down principles by ordinary legislation. The principles are mostly doctrinal constructions abstracted out of more precise norms of specific laws. For instance, precaution is part of a complex norm of the German Federal Immission Prevention Act which carefully circumscribes how far precaution can go. The same is true with regard to laws concretising the principles of rectification at source, polluter pays, and sustainable use of natural resources.

By contrast, Article 225 of the Brazilian Constitution establishes a much greater number of propositions which are called principles by legal doctrine, including everyone's right to an ecologically balanced environment, prevention and precaution, the duty of public authorities to defend the environment and to preserve it for future generations, the duty to prepare environmental impact assessments, the duty of the polluter to repair environmental damage, and precautionary management of risks.[10]

The overview of international, regional (EU), and national law shows that the term principle is used with many different meanings. Sometimes, a principle is binding law. As such it can be situated on the level of ordinary or of higher ranked law. It may, in international law, figure as a 'general principle of law' or as a 'principle of international law' or even as a fundamental principle having the status of *ius cogens*. Sometimes principles are understood as ideals or policies which deserve to become law but have no legal value. In yet other contexts, 'principle' is meant to indicate the core idea of a number of single provisions. Considering this diversity we will now attempt to develop a more systematic view of the legal nature of principles.

(Article II-37) and as a principle (Article III-4). Sustainability has been included in the objectives of the relations of the EU with the wider world. The new, somewhat pretentious, formula is that the EU shall 'contribute to the sustainable development of the earth' (Part I Title I Article 3 (4)).

[10] Although precaution is not explicitely mentioned, jurisprudence has read it into Article 225. See Leme Machado, op. cit. p. 67.

II. The legal nature of environmental principles

In search of definitions for a term it is advisable to consider the hermeneutic context in which the term will be used. That context can be one of:

(1) feeding new ideas into the evolution of law;
(2) structuring and shaping legal rules;
(3) measuring ordinary norms against more fundamental norms;
(4) reviewing the application of principles.

As we shall see, in each of these contexts the definition of what is meant by 'principle' varies.

1. Feeding new ideas into the legal process: principles of policy and of law

Legal and political discourses often refer to 'principles' when new ideas are recommended for law reform. In that context, principles of policy must be distinguished from principles of law. Even if a principle is contained in a law it is not necessarily a principle of law. The legislator must have intended to give the principle such effect. The policy character of a proposition contained in a legal text can be deduced either from its express wording (e.g. if a postulate is called a task, a value, an objective, or something else) or from the vagueness of the language expressing it. For instance, sustainable development is called a task of the EU in Article 2 EC Treaty, and if understood in the broadest sense of bridging ecological, social, and economic concerns it lacks determinable content. For these two reasons it is not a legal principle. It has been proposed that it should therefore be called a policy or an ideal.[11]

Besides legislation, principles of legal value can also emerge from legal custom, i.e. the common sense of the legal profession and broader societal beliefs based on the experience derived from social practice. This is the very source of principles in the common law systems, but it is also well known in the civil law systems as a corollary to statutory law.[12] Many judgments which have created new principles have based their arguments on experience and common sense rather than on the text of laws. Usually, practice and common sense will first be framed and propagated as principles of policy before a court takes the step to accept it as a principle of law.[13]

---

[11] See for a distinction of ideals and policies, Verschuuren, J., *Principles of environmental law*, Baden-Baden (Nomos) 2003, p. 19.

[12] For an in-depth analysis of the relationship between principles and codified law, see Esser, J., *Grundsatz und Norm*, Tuebingen (Mohr) 1964, p. 141. See also his observation (at 223) that there has emerged a convergence of Continental axiomatic and Anglo-American topical thought.

[13] Esser, op. cit. p. 137.

Sometimes, principles of law will emerge as a result of political will and decision rather than of lengthy professional disputes. This is the case when they appear in constitutions and codifications, or in landmark decisions of courts. For instance, precaution was introduced into German law in 1974 as a result of a clear political priority of a new (the social and free democrats) coalition. An example for a landmark judgment is the introduction of strict liability by an English court in 1868.[14]

It has been suggested that the content of legal principles can only be individual rights, not public interests.[15] However, there is ample evidence that legal practice has also established legal principles of respect for the public interest. For instance, the public interest in occupational and consumer health protection has for long been accepted as a counter-principle to economic freedoms. Public interests in environmental protection are more recent examples.

As exemplified earlier, principles rhetoric is particularly common in international law. Clarity about definitions can be reached if legal principles are more precisely distinguished from policy principles on the one side and legal rules on the other. Legal principles are at the bottom of the triad of sources of international law: customary law, treaty law, and – most openly – the principles of the legal orders of civilised nations.[16] 'Principles of international law' have been added by legal practice as a further notion, the precise status of which has remained somewhat elusive.

As shown above, more 'principles' than those recognised as international law are brought into play in more open debates of law development. However, discussing 'principles' of sustainability, precaution, etc., legal scholars do not always make clear if they expound principles of policy or of law.[17] For instance, in its 1995 Report, the UN Expert Group on Identification of Principles of International Law proposed nineteen 'principles and concepts' leaving open which ones were 'firmly established in international law' and which ones were 'only in process of gaining relevance in international law'.[18] More clarity can

---

[14] *Rylands v. Fletcher* (1868) LR 3 HL 330. Cf. Bell, St., *Ball and Bell on environmental law*, London (Blackstone) 4th edn. 1997, p. 193.

[15] According to R. Dworkin, principles are to be distinguished from 'policies' that serve not individual but collective goals: 'Arguments of principle are arguments intended to establish an individual right; arguments of policy are arguments intended to establish a collective goal. Principles are propositions that describe rights; policies are propositions that describe goals'. (Dworkin, R., *Taking rights seriously*, Cambridge (Harvard University Press) 1977, p. 90).

[16] It will later be argued that these 'principles' are in fact rules of international law.

[17] See, as an example, the notion of '*Strukturprinzipien*' as proposed by Epiney and Scheyli, op. cit. p. 75 *et seq*. Likewise, Philippe Sands in his comprehensive book on international environmental law covers both policy and legal principles.

[18] Cited in Beyerlin, U., 'Prinzipien' im Umweltvölkerrecht – ein pathologisches Phänomen?, in Cremer, H.-J., Giegerich, Th., Richter, D., and Zimmermann, A. (eds.), *Tradition und Weltoffenheit des Rechts, Festschrift für Helmut Steinberger*, Berlin (Springer) 2002, p. 31.

be derived from a suggestion made by Wilfried Lang that 'three different categories of principles of a decreasing legally binding/compulsory nature' should be distinguished, i.e. 'principles of existing international environmental law', 'principles of emerging international environmental law', and 'potential principles of international environmental law'.[19] Whilst the first are legal principles and the latter two policy principles, the distinction between an 'emerging' and a 'potential' legal value enriches the understanding of the role of policy principles. This transformation of principles of policy into principles of law proves the 'constructivist' power of the international legal discourse.[20]

In consequence, we may envisage a sequence of emerging law comprising principles of policy, principles of law, and finally rules of law. Principles of policy emerge out of societal and political experiences and interpretations. The legal profession and the political entrepreneurs draw on them when introducing legal principles by means of case law, statutory law, constitutions, and international treaties, be it that they postulate the principle as such, be it that they establish more concrete rules which are based on such principle.

2. Structuring and shaping the law: principles and rules

(Legal) principles and rules have often been opposed as different compositions of the law. Principles are basic ideas 'behind' a diversity of rules. They stand in the *background of rules* and influence their interpretation and application. They enhance the normative power of rules, advise how to interpret them, help to fill regulatory gaps, guide discretionary powers, and inform about necessary exceptions to a rule.[21] For instance, according to the German Federal Law on Soil Protection the authorities have discretion to deal with past land contamination. They have the choice of making one or more out of the following persons responsible: the original polluter, his or her legal successor, the owner of the land, and the holder of physical control of the land. The polluter pays principle, which is regarded as a principle although not explicitly stated by the law, has been used to fetter this discretion to the effect that the original polluter, if still available, should primarily be addressed.

> Like this author, Beyerlin advocates a clear distinction between propositions of policy and law, but defining principles as an ideal ('*ideales Sollen*') he denies the existence of legal principles (see op. cit. p. 51 *et seq.*). I believe this neglects the constructivist potential of legal principles.

[19] Lang, W., UN-Principles and international environmental law, *Max Planck Yearbook of United Nations* 3 (1999), p. 157, at 171.

[20] Koskenniemi, M., General principles: reflexions on constructivist thinking in international law, in Koskenniemi, M. (ed.), *Sources of international law*, Aldershot (Ashgate) 2000, p. 359, at 397.

[21] For more functions of principles, e.g. in relation to extra-legal negotiation and self-regulation, see Verschuuren, op. cit. p. 38 *et seq.*

A major characteristic of principles much propagated by the German philosopher Robert Alexy is that *principles are open for balancing against other principles whilst rules have to be applied in any case.* Whilst principles are committed to one objective or value and must be compromised if conflicting with opposing principles, rules are conclusive.[22] Rules may, however, provide that exceptions are possible. Often such exceptions will be door openers for concerns which represent a counter-principle to the principle which primarily stands behind the rule.[23] For instance, according to the German Federal Immission Prevention Act (*Bundesimmissionsschutzgesetz*) the competent authority is entitled to order a firm to take improvement measures if after the issuance of the primary authorisation scientific progress has revealed new environmental risks or produced better abatement technology. The order is, however, not allowed if the economic burden involved is unproportional. Here, the rule reflecting the principle of environmental protection is relativised by an exception representing the principle of economic freedom.

Rules can even be formulated in a way which allows the balancing of opposing principles *within* the scope of the rule. For instance, fundamental rights such as the right to economic freedom are constructed to include first the prima facie protection of certain activities (such as economic undertakings) and secondly the possibility of interference with the protected realm if reasons of public interest (such as environmental concerns) so require.[24]

Sometimes principles can be uncompromising. This is the case if they are of extremely high value, and if the core of the principle is at stake. For instance, according to the German Constitution the essential requirements of human dignity are absolute. They may not be relativised by other principles. In these cases, the principle is in fact a rule.

If a rule provides for the balancing of opposed principles there is no general norm establishing absolute cardinal or even ordinal ranks between conflicting principles. The law may nevertheless characterise a principle to be of particular importance. If so, the principle has, in the concrete case, a prima facie

---

[22] Alexy, R., *Theorie der Grundrechte*, Frankfurt (Suhrkamp) 2nd edn 1994, p. 71; Borowski, M., *Grundrechte als Prinzipien*, Baden-Baden (Nomos) 1998, p. 67.

[23] Alexy, op. cit. p. 88.

[24] This is very controversial in the German debate on the doctrinal construction of basic rights. Many authors understand a basic right as a conglomerate of principles. They regard basic freedoms as principles which can be balanced against public concerns and conflicting basic rights. They speak of rules only with regard to those specific propositions which case law develops for certain categories of cases. Cf. Ruehl, U., *Tatsachen – Interpretationen – Wertungen*, Baden-Baden (Nomos) 1998, p. 384. I believe that this conception neglects the specific terms of balancing which constitutions often provide. There is no reason why rules should not be conceived to be open for balancing if they circumscribe the kind of conflicting interests to be considered and give direction on how to do the balancing. There is also room to distinguish between more general and open rules, on the one side, and more concrete and closed rules, on the other.

priority over conflicting principles.[25] In consequence, the burden of proof is shifted to the defender of the counter-principle.[26] For instance, German land use planning law prescribes that the authorities must consider and adequately balance all interests affected by a zoning plan. Those interests include interests of housing, of trade and industry, of transportation, of environmental and nature protection, etc. The law says that some of the interests are to be respected 'as far as possible'. For instance, land used for agriculture, forestry, or housing will be converted for other uses only if this is unavoidable.[27] This means that to develop such land for, e.g. industrial or transportation purposes would be a prima facie violation of the principle. The burden of proving that in this case industrial use is a priority will be shifted to the development interests.

An example of a quite sophisticated rule of balancing opposing principles is contained in Article 6(4) of the Habitat Directive 92/43/EEC. As a starting point, the protected demands of the rare species and habitats are given priority over interests in their use. However, compelling public interests in the project can overcome this protection. Such interests must again give way if the affected species or habitats are listed as a priority. The priority is again reversed if the public interest in the project is particularly indispensable (such as the interests of public health and safety).

Absent legal prioritisation, all principles are equal in an abstract sense. The relative weight of principles will then change with the given individual circumstances and can therefore only be determined in the concrete case. One rule recognised in such circumstances is that the more one principle will be impaired by a solution, the weightier must the prevailing principle be.[28]

At the level of international law, the distinction between legal principles and rules can also play a clarifying role. Sands cites the umpire in an arbitration case as proposing the following distinction:[29]

> A 'rule'..., is essentially practical and, moreover, binding... [T]here are rules of art as there are rules of government while 'principle' expresses a general truth, which guides our action, serves as a theoretical basis for the various acts of our life, and the application of which to reality produces a given consequence.

Although the legal character of both rules and principles could have been made clearer in this statement, it does present an example for the role of principles as background theories or basic ideas of individual rules. Other than in national law, the evolution of international principles is often not such that there are first individual rules in the 'foreground' from which principles are then abstracted. More often the principle precedes the rule[30] – but rules must be construed on

---

[25] Alexy, op. cit. p. 88 *et seq.* [26] Alexy, op. cit. p. 146.
[27] Article 1a(2) sentence 2 Construction Code. [28] Alexy, op. cit. p. 146.
[29] Sands, op. cit. p. 233. [30] Koskenniemi, op. cit. p. 371.

its basis, because as explained above principles are too general and open for balancing with counter-principles to be directly applicable in a concrete case. Even if there are not yet detailed rules for a case the recourse to principles does not mean that the principle is directly applied. The court will then normally – if only implicitly – deduce a new rule from the broader principle.

Often the term 'principle' is used for an international norm but in fact what is discussed is a rule in the sense here proposed. This is true for the general principles of international law, some of which have the character of rules, and in particular those which even have the status of peremptory norms.[31] For the sake of clarity they should better be called 'general rules of international law'. Even the 'general principles of law' in the sense of Article 38(1) lit. (c) ICJ Statute, if consulted as a source of international law, will often more precisely be rules (such as e.g., the rule of compensation for damage, the rule of returning unjust enrichment, the rule of good faith).[32] The environmental propositions cited earlier as recognised international custom, i.e. the duties to prevent serious harm and to cooperate, are also not principles but rules. By contrast, precaution in its common understanding cannot be understood as a rule. It can, however, be regarded as a principle (a principle of law, to be sure) if by principle we mean a proposition which is open for balancing against conflicting principles. Based on such principle we may even devise precaution as a rule if opposing principles such as economic freedom are built into the formula. With this qualification, a rule of precaution might be framed as follows:[33]

> States cannot rely on scientific uncertainty to justify inaction when there is enough evidence to establish the possibility of a risk of serious harm, even if there is as yet no proof of harm. In determining whether and how far to apply precautionary measures, states may take account of their capabilities, their economic and social priorities, the cost-effectiveness of preventive measures, and the nature and degree of the environmental risk.

If relativised in this way, precaution may be more easily acceptable as a principle and even as a rule of international law.

3. Measuring law against higher law: ordinary and fundamental principles

Principles and their corresponding rules can be situated on the same level of a hierarchy of norms. This is the normal situation where principles play their proper role by serving as a source for interpreting rules, filling gaps in the rules, guiding the use of discretion, etc. For instance, as mentioned before, the

---

[31] See e.g., Brownlie, I., *Public international law*, Oxford (Clarendon Press) 5th edn 1998, p. 19.
[32] Esser, op. cit. p. 140.
[33] The phrasing is based on Birnie and Boyle, op. cit. p. 120.

precautionary principle stands behind its more precise and complex emanation laid down in the German Federal Immission Prevention Act.

Principles and rules can also be situated on different hierarchical levels of the law. There are internal hierarchies of the levels of national, regional, and even international law between ordinary law and higher ranked law controlling the ordinary law, i.e. constitutional law prevailing over national ordinary law, EC primary law commanding EC secondary law, and international peremptory law commanding international 'ordinary' law. This internal 'constitutional' hierarchy *within* each level is to be distinguished from the external hierarchy *between* levels which we might call the federal hierarchy: EC law has supremacy over national law, and depending on certain conditions international law can also have supremacy over national or regional law. The higher level can be one of constitutional law or one of EC or international law. I have mentioned examples of such higher ranked principles earlier, for instance, the protection of the natural conditions of life contained in article 20a of the German Constitution, the achievement of a high level of environmental protection in Article 174 EC Treaty, and the prevention of serious harm as a principle of international customary law.

If a principle has been laid down on a higher 'constitutional' or 'federal' level the crucial question is whether these principles have the power to render rules ranked on a lower level in the hierarchy inapplicable if the latter contradict the principle. I suggest that the answer is: not directly. The constitutional, supranational, or international principle must first have been transformed into a rule. Only rules can be attributed the effect of invalidating lower rank principles and rules.[34]

This implies, first of all, that we must be more careful with calling propositions rules or principles. The higher the level in the norm pyramid, the more willing we are to call a proposition a principle, although upon closer look it may be framed as a rule which already contains the balancing of different opposing principles.

For instance, article 20a of the German Constitution contains a qualification saying that the principle of environmental protection is binding only 'in the framework of the constitutional order'. This is generally understood to mean that environmental protection must be balanced against other principles such as property and economic freedom.[35] For this inclusion of countervailing

---

[34] Contrastingly, R. Alexy proposes to apply principles directly if only in a more open way which allows for the balancing of principles with colliding other principles. I do not follow Alexy because his theory would hinder the emergence of principles out of common sense and common practice. The discourse about new principles would be loaded with the 'threat' that all of what is accepted would already be applicable law. The dynamic potential of principles is, I believe, based on their somewhat elusive status behind the scenes.

[35] Jarass, H. D., *Grundgesetz für die Bundesrepublik Deutschland*, München (Beck) 5th edn 2000, Article 20a note 9.

principles into a balancing relationship, article 20a of the German Constitution must be regarded as a rule, an open one, for sure, but not a principle. Basic rights, too, can be understood to establish rules on balancing opposing principles. For instance, the basic right to health may be relativised by other principles of public interest. The fact that one principle (the protection of human health) was made a basic right has the effect that the protected freedom has a prima facie priority over the principles protecting public interests. The latter bear the burden of proving their *secunda facie* preponderance.

Likewise, the principles contained in Article 174 EC Treaty can only become operative if transformed into rules. This means that they must be formulated in a more complex way than by merely restating the principle. Opposing principles must be integrated into the rule, such as the principles of proportionality and the principles representing economic freedoms. Only via a complex and more precise rule can a principle render a national law inapplicable. This can be shown if we consider ECJ jurisprudence on fundamental rights under Article 6 EU Treaty.

It is true that European courts have only rarely had the opportunity of expressing themselves on rules combining basic rights with environmental protection principles. In comparison to the frequent opposition of basic rights and environmental protection in German domestic law, it is astonishing how seldom fundamental rights in the EU have been invoked as a bulwark against Community environmental measures (though this can sometimes be explained by the restrictive standing requirements of Article 230(4) EC Treaty).

Standley, however, can be seen as a case which does oppose fundamental rights and Community environmental principles. Standley, a farmer, brought an action against British laws which were founded upon a Community Directive. That Directive prescribed that the Member States must designate bodies of water with high levels of nitrate and limit intensive animal husbandry in the corresponding zones. Standley argued (unsuccessfully) that this was an interference with his property right. In response, the ECJ stated that the exercise of basic property rights could be subjected to limitations in so far as:

> those restrictions in fact correspond to objectives of general interest pursued by the Community and do not constitute a disproportionate and intolerable interference, impairing the very substance of the rights guaranteed.[36]

The protection of public health can be such an objective. The Directive serves these ends, as the ECJ briefly indicated, in a way that follows the principle of proportionality.[37] Thus, the principle of protection of public health was integrated into the basic right to private property. This right was construed as a

---

[36] Case C-293/93, *Standley* [1999] ECR I-2603, ECJ, at para. 54.   [37] Ibid., paras 54, 56.

complex rule on balancing property and human health interests. In the *Standley* case, this rule was not considered to be violated by the incriminated Directive.

In international law, the term 'general principles of international law' is often used to denominate certain fundamental propositions.[38] There are two deeper reasons which justify the fundamental character of such general principles: one is sovereignty, the other morality. Sovereignty is the core structure of the international system since the Westfalian peace. It is the basis of fundamental principles like the equality of states, non-intervention into internal affairs, and the prohibition of aggression. Morality is the basis of fundamental human rights such as the prohibition of slavery, torture, and crimes against humanity. Some legal scholars argue that the 'general principles of international law' have legal force only if they are at the same time international custom. The ICJ has, however, hardly cared about this. It has repeatedly referred to those principles as if they stand on their own, allowing it to be concluded that they are an additional source of international law. Indeed, one might argue that it is the very fundamentality of these principles which give them legal value.

For some (but not all) of the general principles of international law, their fundamental character is reason enough to attribute to them the status of a peremptory norm.[39] As *ius cogens*, they have the potential to render an ordinary international norm (in particular an international contract) inapplicable.[40] This proves that even in international law, the difference between two levels of the law – ordinary and 'constitutional' – has emerged.

4. Principles and the separation of powers: empowering and commanding principles

It is normally the task of the judiciary to elaborate, in the framework of existing legislation and case law, the principles and rules appropriate to solve the social problem brought to its attention. If, however, the problem was first tackled by the other branches of government and the courts are asked to check the legality or constitutionality of these decisions, the courts usually practise some measure of judicial self-restraint. By this they pay tribute to the fact that also other powers are legitimated to interpret and shape the law. Speaking in terms

---

[38] See, on the history and potential of this source of international law, Cassese, A., *International law*, Oxford (Oxford University Press) 2001, p. 155.

[39] Whether this implies a functionalist, naturalist, or consensualist conception of international law would require more in-depth analysis. For an overview of the '*Geltungsgründe*' of international law, see Ipsen, K., *Völkerrecht*, München (Beck) 5th edn 2004, p. 7.

[40] See Article 53 of the Vienna Convention on the Law of Treaties. Defining a 'peremptory norm of general international law' as 'a norm accepted and recognised by the international community of States as a whole', the article accepts a 'constructivist' element which transcends *consuetudo* as postulated by the definition of customary law.

of principles one could also say that the courts bring a counter-principle into play, i.e. judicial self-restraint in political matters.

Judicial self-restraint has different effects depending on whether the legislature or executive branch has already taken a decision or whether they have remained inactive. This is especially significant with principles that either empower or command government to take action. Judicial practice shows that if a governmental body has actually made use of a principle empowering it, the courts will tend to accept even a rather broad reading of the principle. For instance, they will be prepared to uphold a quite far-reaching understanding of precaution which the legislature may claim for promulgating a legal act, and confine themselves to checking if counter-principles were adequately considered.[41] If the governmental body has, however, remained passive although the principle may oblige it to take action, the courts will adopt a more minimalist reading as binding in order not to impose their own understanding of the principle. In addition, as the inactive governmental body has not expressed itself on potentially opposing principles, the courts will normally defer to their attitude and apply only a loose arbitrariness test, recognising that this is largely a political matter reserved to the democratically legitimated bodies.

We shall prove this hypothesis by comparing judgments of the European courts in relation to law providing powers and law commanding action.

(a) Context of providing powers

In the 'BSE' ('mad cow disease') case, the EU had taken legal measures directed against the export of British beef to other Member States. The ECJ was asked by Britain to check if the competence basis, namely that for agricultural policy, had duely been applied. Referring to the environmental policy principles and the principle of integration of these principles into other policies, the ECJ supported the Commission's rather broad concept of precaution:

> Where there is uncertainty as to the existence or extent of risks to human health, the institutions may take protective measures without having to wait until the reality and seriousness of those risks become fully apparent.[42]

It might appear as if the ECJ applied the precautionary principle directly.[43] In fact, however, it used the principle in order to form a rule on competences, which

---

[41] For examples see Scott, J. and Vos, E., The ambivalence of the precautionary principle, in Joerges, Chr., and Dehousse, R. (ed.), *Good governance in Europe's integrated market*, New York (Oxford University Press) 2002, p. 260.

[42] Case C-180/96, *United Kingdom v. Commission* [1998] ECR I-2265, ECJ, para. 99; the phrase was again invoked in Joint Cases T-74/00, T-76/00, *Artegodan v. Commission*, [2000] ECR II-327, CFI, para. 184.

[43] Confusingly, the court in *United Kingdom v. Commission*, n. 42 above, at para. 100 refers to the prevention rather than precautionary principle, but both principles are in fact combined: precaution for characterising the risk situation, and prevention for characterising the measure to be taken.

it is true is not openly expounded. This implicit rule says that an EC competence to take precautionary measures has priority over subsidiarity considerations,[44] for the simple reason that a Member State will be unwilling to act if it is economically affected by the precautionary measure (as Britain was in the 'BSE' case).

The ECJ's ruling in 'BSE' was affirmed by the Court of First Instance (CFI) in cases concerning the use of basic rights. In *Bergaderm*, a company which claimed compensation from the Commission for damage caused by an investigation into the risk of using the chemical 'psoralen' in its sun products, the CFI approved the Commission's action.[45] In *Pfizer*, the CFI took a somewhat more active role in qualifying the precautionary principle:[46]

> Rather, it follows from the Community Courts' interpretation of the precautionary principle that a preventive measure may be taken only if the risk, although the reality and extent thereof have not been 'fully' demonstrated by conclusive scientific evidence, appears nevertheless to be adequately backed up by the scientific data available at the time when the measure was taken.

Along the same lines, the ECJ expressed itself in the *Monsanto* case concerning a safeguard clause established on the ground of Article 95(10) EC Treaty.[47] The court, once more assuming a broad understanding of precaution, said that the safeguard clause introduced by legislation on novel food could be used for precautionary measures but that such measures had to be based on a risk assessment:

> Nevertheless, those measures can be adopted only if the Member State has first carried out a risk assessment which is as complete as possible given the particular circumstances of the individual case, from which it is apparent that, in the light of the precautionary principle, the implementation of such measures is necessary in order to ensure that novel foods do not present danger for the consumer, in accordance with the first indent of Article 3(1) of Regulation No. 258/97.[48]

(b) Context of commanding action

A commanding function can be attributed to the principles when they make specifications for the exercise by Community organs of a rule on competences, thereby encouraging rather than limiting action. The obligation that the

---

[44] Cf. Kraemer, L., *EC environmental law*, London (Sweet & Maxwell) 5th edn 2003, p. 15.
[45] Case T-199/96, *Laboratoires Pharmaceutiques Bergaderm SA and Goupil* v. *Commission* [1998] ECR II-2805, CFI, para. 66.
[46] Case T-13/99, *Pfizer* v. *Commission* [2002] ECR, CFI, para. 144.
[47] Case C-263/01, *Monsanto*, judgment of 9 September 2003, ECJ.
[48] At para. 107 of the judgment.

commanding function imposes is even more marked when, in a situation of otherwise complete passivity or even political resistance, it constitutes a rule compelling the EU's organs to act.

The ECJ gives the EU organs wide discretion in such cases. In *Safety High Tech*, following its usual jurisprudence, it stated that:

> in view of the need to strike a balance between certain of the objectives and principles mentioned in Article 130r and of the complexity of the implementation of those criteria, review by the Court must necessarily be limited to the question whether the Council, by adopting the Regulation, committed a manifest error of appraisal regarding the conditions for the application of Article 130r of the Treaty.[49]

The judicial self-restraint exposed in this rule is explained by the necessity to strike a balance between opposing principles and the complexity of the implementation of those principles. In more general terms, we can conclude that if the rule is very open, i.e. if it is only providing for a fair balancing of principles without giving specific guidance, the courts allow for wide legislatory discretion, thereby avoiding replacing the legislator's appreciation by their own.

Nevertheless, some more guidance than the mere arbitrariness test may be derived from a closer look at the meaning, aim, and conditions of the principles. A core and a penumbra of the principles may be distinguished, the core fettering the discretionary margin of the legislator. The core could be defined somewhat in the way of *a maiore ad minus*: where measures combatting uncertain risks may be regarded as an extension of the principle of environmental protection, measures to defend against imminent and serious dangers should be taken as a legal obligation. If in this way the core of principles is identified it can also be taken to already constitute the relevant rule. For if the core is affected there will hardly remain space for bringing opposing principles into the shaping of the rule.

Genuine cases in which a Community measure absolutely, and not only in relation to others, remains below an attainable level of protection have not yet found explicit treatment by the European courts. However, the ECJ in the case of *Safety High Tech* does imply the possibility that an environmental protection measure can fail to attain the high level of environmental protection required by Article 174 EC Treaty. In the case, the court found this standard was in fact met, as a comparison with the laxer measures of a pertinent international

---

[49] Case C-284/95, *Safety High Tech* [1998] ECR I-4301, ECJ, para. 37. The German Federal Constitutional Court has expressed itself in a similar way. See, for instance, the case where the neighbour of an airport complained that the authorities had not taken appropriate protection measures. The court ruled that there was no 'evident' violation of the constitutional duty of the state to protect the individual (BVerfGE 56, 54 *et seq.*, at 80).

agreement (the Montreal Protocol) showed. Because the ECJ treated this issue only implicitly, the question cannot, however, be considered as decided.

The ECJ has expressed itself on commanding functions mostly in the somewhat ironical cases where it was the addressee of a Community measure who complained that the Community measure did not go far enough. The plaintiffs in such cases, whose environmentally injurious acts were enjoined by Community law, argued that the EU failed also (or instead) to punish the other 'sinners'. The argument can be designated as a version of the NIMBY ('not in my backyard') principle. The more normal case – where a Community organ, a Member State, or a third party who would benefit from the Community measure but deems it insufficient, files the complaint – has not yet been decided by the courts.

Safety High Tech is particularly relevant as an example of the NIMBY situation. A Regulation for the protection of the stratospheric ozone layer prohibited the use of partially halogenated CFCs. The producer, Safety High Tech, argued that CFCs could not be singled out and forbidden without also forbidding halones, for halones (without controversy) have a higher potential than CFCs for destruction of the ozone layer and, in addition (unlike CFCs), also have a greenhouse effect. Because of the failure to consider the greenhouse potential of halones, the general command of the protection of the environment was violated; further, because of the failure to consider halones' higher potential to destroy the ozone layer, the specific command of a 'high level of protection' was also violated. The ECJ replied, on the basis of ex Article 130r (now Article 174) EC Treaty, that:

> it does not follow from those provisions that Article 130r(1) of the Treaty requires the Community legislature, whenever it adopts measures to preserve, protect and improve the environment in order to deal with a specific environmental problem, to adopt at the same time measures relating to the environment as a whole.[50]

Although this answer is basically reasonable, the court could have gone somewhat further by making use of a German legal construct, namely the *Konzeptgebot* (planned approach). The *Konzeptgebot*, which was introduced by the Federal Administrative Court (*Bundesverwaltungsgericht*) may be invoked in situations in which a complex set of problems must urgently be solved but are difficult to handle because of limited instrumental and administration capacity. Due to this complexity the issues do not have to be solved in one stroke. Rather, the public authorities may go step-by-step, singling out individual actors, if this is based on a broader plan providing for systematic further action in the future.

In *Safety High Tech*, the application of the *Konzeptgebot* would have meant to ask for an overall plan for the phasing out of both CFCs and halones. It seems

---

[50] *Safety High-Tech*, n. 49 above, at para. 44.

that in fact there was such a plan, in fulfilment of the obligations of the Montreal Protocol. It was defensible to first tackle CFCs, where ready substitutes exist, and then to address the thornier question of halones (which have since indeed been banned).

In international law, all subjects of this law (i.e. the states) being equal, the courts cannot defer to a discretionary margin of some and take a hard look at the attitude of others. They must conclusively express themselves on the status and content of the legal principles. For instance, the WTO Appellate Body in the *Hormones* case[51] had to decide whether precaution is a principle of (customary or GATT) law. It could not argue that because the EU was democratically legitimated to produce its own understanding of precaution, a discretionary margin of appreciation had to be recognised, for the opponents – the USA and other states – enjoy equal rights. The Appellate Body could nevertheless have, once and for all, adopted the proposal submitted above, i.e. a more modest version of a precautionary rule which internalises countervailing principles into a balancing relationship.

III. Conclusion

There is a multitude of meanings of 'principle', and many a discussion is hampered because different meanings are used, unexplicated, at the same time. Therefore, whenever the term 'principle' is introduced, the speaker should make the meaning explicit. A proposition can be a principle of policy or of law. Principles of law are to be distinguished from rules of law; they are basic ideas informing rules, and whilst rules are conclusive, principles are open for balancing with opposing principles. Principles of law can be ordinary principles or fundamental principles, the latter often having a constitutional or secondary level status.

This terminology can be applied to all levels of the law, national, regional, and international.

Distinguishing between different kinds of principles can also enhance the understanding of the evolution of law. Principles of policy and of law serve as a transmission belt between common experience and common sense, on the one side, and rules, on the other.

Principles and rules as defined in this chapter may also help to accelerate the creation of international law so desperately needed in the globalised world. Principles may more readily be accepted as having legal value if their openness for balancing with countervailing principles is taken into account. Rules may more readily be accepted if formulated to construct bridges between conflicting principles. For instance, the precautionary principle can in that way be

---

[51] See n. 5 above.

formulated as a principle of law and even as a rule of international customary law.

Distinguishing between ordinary and fundamental principles may help to clarify and foster the evolution of secondary or constitutional law as a fundament of, and control for, primary law.

Looking at principles in the framework of both the systems of separation of powers and of equality of states makes it understandable why courts sometimes support a very broad interpretation of a principle and sometimes narrow it down to a minimalist core.

INDEX

Aarhus Convention
   environmental information, 209–210, 246–248, 424
   globalising, 354
   implementation, 223
   public participation, 341, 354
   and transition economies, 362–363, 373, 380
Abkhazia, 379
access to justice, 566–568, 575, 582–583
acid rain, 82, 438
advocacy, meaning, 114
advocacy networks, 112
Afghanistan, 379
Agenda, 5–9, 80, 135, 208, 217, 310, 321
albedo, meaning, 4
Alderson, K, 140
Alexy, Robert, 593
Amazon, 114
Amoco Cadiz, 218
Amu-Daria River, 379
Annan, Kofi, 529
Antarctic regime
   consensual knowledge, 436, 439, 442
   Conventions, 433
   regime elements, 436
   Secretariat, 414
   trusteeship, 528
   understanding, 27, 39
   and USA, 27, 289–290
Antarctica, 61–62, 68
Anthropocene Age, 1
anti-globalisation movement, 112
Aral Sea, 361, 364, 379, 380
Aral Sea syndrome, 7
Arato, Andrew, 126–129, 133, 134, 136, 143–144

Arctic Council, 290
Arctic Ocean, 59, 60–61
Arctic regime, and USA, 289–290
Argentina, GEF project, 508, 508
Armenia, 378
Arrhenius, Svante, 68, 73
Arts, Bas, 96
Asbestos case, 262–263, 264–265
ASEAN, 357
Asian Tigers syndrome, 7, 13
Atlantic, 557
atmosphere
   acid rain, 82, 438
   and climate system, 50–51
   cluster of agreements, 419
   Conventions, 547
   LRTAP Convention, 430, 545
Australia, 347, 511, 523
Austria
   assistance to transition economies, 365
   eco-labels, 479, 480, 486
   eco-taxes, 477, 483, 484
   environmental regulation, 472
   environmental subsidies, 477
   labelling of tropical timber, 256
   landfill taxes, 477
   tradable permits, 478
   voluntary agreements, 474, 478, 479
Azerbaijan, 378

Bahamas, 501, 501–502
Bahía Declaration on Chemical Safety, 312–313
Baltic Sea, 364, 439–442
Banuri, Tariq, 468
Barents Sea, 434, 450

Basel Convention
  approach, 344
  scope, 318
  strict liability, 571
  and USA, 275–276, 345
Bauer, E., 71
Baynes, Kenneth, 143
Beck, Ulrich, 92–93
Beef Hormones dispute, 301–302, 603
Belgium, 478
Belize, 255
Bergaderm case, 600
Bering Sea Fur Seal Arbitration, 528
Bering Strait, 63
Bernstein, Steven, 134, 135
best practical means principle, 208, 219
Bhopal disaster, 15, 167–171, 174, 218, 305, 584
biodiversity
  Conventions, 343–344
  emergence of issue, 427
  and USA, 291–292
Biodiversity Convention
  access to genetic resources, 31, 521
  and GEF, 504
  and NGOs, 96
  scope, 418
  and sovereignty, 519, 520, 550–551
  trusteeship, 536
  and USA, 28, 291–292, 345
Black Sea, 436
Börkey, P, 474
Brazil, 89, 589
Bremerhaven, 47
bribery, 203
Bribery Convention, 17, 214
Broecker, Wally, 73
Brownlie, I, 187
Brundtland Report, 135, 555
Brussels Convention, 212–213, 574
BSE case, 599–600
Bulgaria, 359, 360, 367–368, 375
Bull, Hedley, 140
Bunker Fuel Convention, 572, 573
bureaucratic networks. *See* transnational bureaucratic networks
Busch, P-O, 243
Bush, George Sr, 275, 286, 291
Bush, George W, 276, 291, 295, 300
Buzan, Barry, 142
Byrd, Senator, 293

Cambodia, 255
Canada, 235, 285, 301–302, 424, 443–444, 447, 450, 510, 523
Cape disaster, 218
carbon dioxide
  carbon pumps, 46
  and climate change, 68–70, 73
  greenhouse gas, 73
  increase, 42
  percentage in atmosphere, 4–5
  records, 46
carbon market, 511
carbon taxes. *See* eco-taxes
Cartagena Protocol on Biosafety, and USA, 28, 292
Caspian Sea, 364, 379, 381
Caucasus, 378–380, 381
Cenozoic Age, 40
Central Asia, 378–380
CFCs, 306, 437, 496, 497, 501, 501–502, 602–603
Charnovitz, Steve, 255, 257
Chayes, Abram and Antonia Handler, 391–392, 393–394
Chechnya, 379
chemical safety
  activities, 312–320
  actors, 307–312
  agenda setting, 312–313, 323
  Bahia Declaration, 312–313, 323
  Basel Convention. *See* Basel Convention
  Bhopal disaster, 15, 167–171, 174, 218, 305, 584
  catastrophes, 305–307
  CFCs, 306, 437, 496, 497, 501, 501–502, 602–603
  cluster of agreements, 420
  efficacy of networks, 326
  empirical research in German MNEs, 154–157
  evaluation, 326–329
  GHS hazard classification and labelling, 18, 316–317, 322, 327

INDEX

chemical safety (*cont.*)
good laboratory practice (GLP), 313–314, 322
IGOs, 321–325
industrial importance, 305
information gathering, 313–317
Inter-Organization Programme for the Sound Management of Chemicals (IOMC), 309, 310–311, 321
inter-organisational agreements, 309–311
International Conference on Chemical Safety, 310
International Council of Chemical Associations, 312, 315
International Forum on Chemical Safety, 309, 310, 321
international organisations, 308–309
International Programme on Chemical Safety (IPCS), 309, 315–316, 321
IPCS activities, 315–316
labelling, 316–317
legal protection of networks, 328–329
legitimacy of networks, 326–328
London Guidelines, 318–319, 322
NGOs, 323
OECD SIDS programme, 314–315, 326
OECD Test Guidelines, 18, 314, 322
ozone layer Conventions, 319
PIC procedures, 318–319
POP Convention, 319, 321, 322, 344, 420
POPs, 306
private actors, 311–312
risk management, 318–320
Rotterdam Convention, 318, 322, 344, 420
rule-making, 320–324
self-regulation of German MNEs, 14–15, 157–174
ship anti-fouling paints, 320
soft law, 322–326
toxic ignorance, 306
transnational bureaucratic networks, 17–18, 307–320

Chemical Weapons Convention, and USA, 280–281
Cheney, Dick, 295
Chernobyl, 564
Chile, 500
China, 13, 19, 347, 471, 498
CITES
approach, 343
listing species, 425
scope, 418
state sovereignty, 549–550
and USA, 27, 288
civil liability
access to justice, 566–568, 575, 582–583
allocation of losses, 573
alternative solutions to MNE problem, 224
channelling of liability, 572–573
compensation schemes, 210, 566, 570–575
conflict of law, 211–212, 220, 566, 568–570
corporate responsibility, 182–186
criminal liability of MNEs, 214
damage definition, 582
direct responsibility of MNEs in international law, 191–198
diversity of solutions, 574
domestic laws, 186–191
extra-territorial jurisdiction, 211–212, 214–215, 220–221
extra-territorial jurisdiction over MNEs, 212, 213–215
forum shopping, 568–570, 574
future framework of transboundary MNE liability, 218–224
harmonisation approach, 566
ILC draft articles, 190, 208–209, 219, 561–565, 566, 575–583, 585–586
ILC model, 580–583
international civil liability scheme, 205–218
international forum, 215
international principles, 145–146, 185, 207, 208, 219–220
limits, 573, 581
local remedies rule, 583–585

civil liability (*cont.*)
  Lugano Convention, 572, 573, 574–575
  meaning of responsibility, 181–182
  MNE structures of evasion, 202, 215–218, 222–223
  multinational enterprises (MNEs), 17, 179, 200–203
  operator liability, 581
  and polluter pays principle, 571
  precautionary measures, 213–214
  remedies against MNEs, 221
  state funding, 581
  and state liability, 583–585
  strict liability, 571–572, 580–581, 591
  transboundary damage, 566–575
civil society. *See* global civil society
Claussen, Eileen, 138
Claussen, M, 71, 73
Clean Development Mechanism, 30, 510–515
climate change treaties
  consensual knowledge, 442
  cornerstones, 245
  emission targets, 245
  and GEF, 504
  Intergovernmental Panel on Climate Change, 422
  Kyoto Protocol. *See* Kyoto Protocol
  Marrakech Accords, 455, 462
  and policy convergence, 245–246
  UNFCCC. *See* UN Framework Convention on Climate Change
  and USA, 292–296, 324, 445, 456–457
climate changes
  adapting or abating, 2–3
  and carbon dioxide, 68–70
  causes, 4–5, 67–75
  Cenozoic Age, 40
  climate history, 66–75
  consequences, 75
  and El Niño, 40
  energy balance of the Earth, 44, 66
  expected warming, 42, 75
  greenhouse effect, 44–46
  historical observations, 37–38
  Holocene Age, 1, 40, 68, 73
  ice ages, 42, 68, 75
  inherent variability, 37–39
  Last Glacial Maximum, 40
  last millennium, 40
  Little Ice Age, 38, 40, 75
  Middle Ages, 73
  multiple causation, 546–547
  new Ice Age, 68
  outlook, 65
  paleo-climatic methods, 38, 71
  planetary motions, 67–68
  Pleistocene Age, 40
  precipitations, 42
  reconstructed temperature averages, 37–38
  scientific uncertainties, 543
  signs of past changes, 66
  sun luminosity, 70–71
  temperature records, 37, 42–56
  UNFCCC. *See* UN Framework Convention on Climate Change
  variables, calculation, 67
climate system
  atmosphere, 50–51
  components, 4, 49–65
  cryosphere, 55–65
  interactions, 49
  mechanisms, 47–49
  oceans, 51–55
Clinton, Bill, 275, 279, 287, 292
clusters of agreements
  actors, 428
  capacity building, 417
  cluster groups, 417–422
  communications, 416
  Conferences of the Parties, 412–413
  conservation cluster, 418–419
  development assistance, 415
  dispute resolution, 424–426
  domestic distribution of responsibilities, 426–428
  electronic clustering, 416
  environmental assessments, 423
  extractive resources cluster, 421–422, 423, 469
  finances, 414–416
  global atmosphere cluster, 419
  hazardous substances cluster, 420
  implementation reviews, 416–417, 424

clusters of agreements (*cont.*)
  joint institutions, 422–426
  marine environment cluster, 420–421
  monitoring, 423
  national coordination, 426–428
  need for, 409–412
  public participation, 423–424
  regime budgets, 415
  scientific assessments, 422–423
  Secretariats, 414
  subsidiary bodies, 413
  subsidies, 415–416
  transparency, 423–424
codes of conduct, transnational corporations, 204–205, 216
Cohen, Jean, 126–129, 133, 134, 136, 143–144
Columbia, 514, 514
Commission on Global Governance, 135
common but differentiated responsibilities
  international law principle, 588
  Kyoto Protocol, 546–547
  meaning, 494–495
  Montreal Protocol, 546
  Multilateral Fund, 502
  Rio Declaration, 29, 33, 145–146, 494–495, 544–545
  scope, 515
  UNFCCC, 509, 546
common resources
  dispersed pollution sources, 542–548
  global commons, 551–554
  high seas, 551–554
  intergenerational responsibilities, 554–557
  international rivers, 541–542
  neighbourly principles, 540–542
  principles, 554
  sic utere tuo ut neminem laedas, 540–541
  species and spaces, 548–551
  state responsibility, 540–542
  and state sovereignty, 542–548
  stewardship economics, 525–527
  trusteeship, 522–525, 555
communications, international environmental regimes, 416

Communism, 127
communitarians, 123, 125–126
competition, regulatory competition, 462–468, 469, 483–484
compliance. *See* treaty compliance
conflict of law, transboundary damage, 211–212, 220, 566, 568–570
conservation agreements, 418–419
conservationism, 93
constructivists, 10, 118–119, 132
consumers
  environmental effects, 102, 103
  and global governance, 102–104
  greening, 10
  sufficiency revolution, 104
  and sustainable development, 103–104
contaminated land syndrome, 7
continental shelf, 553
Conventions. *See* treaties
cooperation. *See* international cooperation
Council of Europe, 110, 209, 210
Crawford, J, 181, 578
criminal liability, MNEs, 194, 214, 221–222
critical theory, 126–129
Croatia, 375
cryosphere
  albedo, 4
  components, 55–58
  generally, 55–65
  ice sheets, 62–63, 68
  ice shelves, 61–62
  land, 63–65
  sea ice, 58–61
  snow, 58
culture
  core ideas, 82
  cultural pluralisation, 84
  cultural theory, 92–93
  and institution building, 81–82, 83
  myths of nature, 92
Czech Republic, 366, 369
Czechoslovakia, 359, 360

Daimler Chrysler, 138
Dansgaard-Oescherger events, 71–72
Danube Dam case, 529

democracy
  concept, 129
  cosmopolitan democracy, 130
  deliberative, 131–133
  and global civil society, 121–122, 130–133, 139–140, 141–142
  and transnational bureaucratic networks, 326–328
Denmark, 242, 243, 478
deposit-refund schemes, 473
detraditionalisation, 10, 84
developed countries
  environmental awareness, 90
  and global civil society, 142–143
  hegemonic development model, 91–92
  liberalism, 126
  lifestyle, 9
  motor vehicle stock, 102
developing countries
  See also common but differentiated responsibilities
  capacity building, 462, 467, 468, 469
  defensive negotiating strategies, 459
  environmental awareness, 89
  environmental protection by MNEs, 150–154
  Global Environment Fund, 502–509
  handicapped coalition building power, 459
  hollow mandates, 458
  and Kyoto Protocol, 510
  and Montreal Protocol, 496, 546
  negotiations as regulatory competition, 462–468, 469
  non-compliance with Conventions, 30–31, 457–460
  and polluter pays principle, 547
  pre-negotiation problems, 458–460
  priorities, 347
  special consideration, 515–516
  tradable permits, 455–456, 468
  Vienna Convention, 546
  vulnerabilities, 493–495
development
  assistance, 415
  hegemonic Western model, 91–92
development banks, and USA, 299
diffusion. *See* policy diffusion

dignity principle, 593
diplomatic protection, local remedies rule, 583–585
discourse coalitions, 82
discourse theory, 11, 82
dispute resolution
  clustered agreements, 424–426
  ECJ environmental disputes, 349–350
  European Union, 339–340, 353–354
  investment agreements, 426, 452
Dolowitz, D, 481
dolphins, 260, 297, 437
domestic regulation, 22, 186–191
Downs, George, 392–394
Dryzek, David, 130, 131, 132
dust bowl syndrome, 5
Dworkin, Ronald, 270

Earth
  rotation, 50, 67–68
  system analysis, 1, 4–9, 33
Earth Negotiation Bulletin, 115
eco-dumping, 286, 464
eco-labels
  Austria, 479, 480, 486
  Denmark, 242
  EU influence, 486
  EU model, 489
  EU patterns of use, 479
  European Union, 242
  Finland, 479, 480
  France, 479, 480
  Germany, 243, 479, 480, 482, 486, 489
  Global Eco-labelling Network, 480, 489
  Ireland, 480, 486
  Netherlands, 242, 476, 479, 480, 486
  new environmental policy instrument, 470, 474–475
  Nordic Swan, 479, 480
  policy diffusion, 242
  spread of schemes, 23, 231, 242, 251, 272
  tropical timber, 256
  United Kingdom, 242, 480, 486
eco-taxes
  Austria, 477, 483, 484

INDEX

eco-taxes (*cont.*)
  Denmark, 243
  diffusion of energy/carbon taxes, 237, 239, 242, 243, 252
  EU influence, 485
  EU model, 487–488
  European Union, 483
  Finland, 476, 477, 483, 484
  France, 476, 477, 485
  Germany, 476, 477, 483, 484, 485
  Ireland, 477
  Japan, 476
  landfill taxes, 477
  Netherlands, 243, 476, 477, 483, 484, 485
  new environmental policy instruments, 23, 470, 473
  United Kingdom, 476, 477, 485
  wastewater levies, 476
economic freedom, 593
ECOSOC, 18
El Niño, 40
emission reduction purchase agreements, 511
emission targets, 245
emissions trading. *See* tradable permits
endangered species. *See* CITES
energy/carbon taxes. *See* eco-taxes
English School, 140
environmental awareness
  concerns, 88–90
  conservationism, 93
  cultural theory, 92–93
  environmentalism, 93
  and global governance, 87–94
  Health of the Planet survey, 89–90
  master frames, 93
  patchwork of behaviours, 90–92
  social construction of risks, 92–94
environmental Conventions. *See* international environmental regimes; treaties
environmental impact assessments, 208, 209, 220, 341–342, 367–368, 371–372
environmental interaction, stages, 1–2

environmental liability. *See* civil liability; state responsibility
environmental management and auditing systems (EMAS), 488–489
environmental management systems, 208
environmental policies
  coercive policy transfer, 228
  convergence mechanisms, 228–230, 244–248
  diffusion. *See* policy diffusion
  harmonisation, 228, 242, 252, 283
  innovation, 229, 230–231
  new policies. *See* new environmental policy instruments
environmental principles
  See also specific principles
  balancing, 593–594
  Brazil, 589
  concept, 32–33, 587
  Conventions, 145–146, 185, 207, 208
  customary law, 587
  ECJ jurisprudence, 599–603
  emergence, 590–592
  European Union, 588–589
  Germany, 589
  hierarchy, 595–598
  jus cogens,, 587, 598
  legal nature, 590–603
  ordinary and fundamental principles, 595–598
  overview, 587–589
  and separation of powers, 598–603
  versus rules, 592–595
environmentalism, 93
epistemic communities, 113
Equitorial Guinea, 255
erga omnes obligations, 534
Eritrea, 524
Estonia, green party, 360
European Court of Human Rights, 210, 372
European Court of Justice
  access by environmental NGOs, 341
  environmental dispute resolution, 349–350

European Court of Justice (*cont.*)
  environmental jurisprudence, 599–603
  interstate use, 340
  role, 335
  trusteeship of common resources, 529
European Union
  accession of transition economies, 20, 364–365, 373–375
  acquis communautaire, 244
  Agenda, 375
  Asbestos case, 262–263, 264–265
  Beef Hormones disputes, 301–302, 603
  Bird Directive, 529
  competition, 465
  convergence mechanisms, 244
  decision-making, 337, 351–352
  dispute resolution, 339–340, 353–354
  ECJ. *See* European Court of Justice
  energy/carbon taxes, 243
  energy-efficient labels, 242
  environmental concerns, 88
  environmental dumping, 464
  environmental impact assessments, 341–342
  environmental information, 374
  environmental law, 209
  environmental management and auditing systems (EMAS), 488–489
  environmental policy development, 335–336, 350–351
  environmental policy diffusion, 241–242
  environmental principles, 588–589
  environmental regulation model, 348–355
  European Commission, 334, 348–349
  European Council, 334–335
  European Environment Agency, 338, 348
  European Parliament, 334
  financing climate change conventions, 510
  future accessions, 375
  GMO dispute with USA, 302
  Habitats Directive, 594
  harmonisation of environmental standards, 19, 271, 337, 483
  implementation of environmental law, 337–339, 352–353
  institutions, 334–335, 348–350
  integrated product policy, 268
  integration of environmental policies, 341–342, 355
  legal hierarchy, 596, 597–598
  NEPI model, 486, 487, 489, 491–492
  new environmental policy instruments (NEPIs), 23, 470, 475, 481, 485–487
  packaging waste, 483
  paradigm of regional integration, 24
  PHARE programme, 364, 367
  policy instrument selection, 484
  public participation, 340–341, 354–355
  regulatory competition, 483–484
  renewable energy, 242, 243–244
  single market, 483
  Smokestack Syndrome, 13
  Structural Funds, 340
  sustainable development, 333, 590
  TACIS, 365
  tradable permits, 456–457, 482, 486
  transboundary environmental liability, 210
  transparency, 341, 354–355
  trusteeship of common resources, 529
  Tuna Regulation, 255
  WTO environmental disputes, 28, 262–263, 301–302
exclusive economic zones, 31, 421, 519, 520, 521, 553, 554
extra-territorial jurisdiction
  multinational enterprises (MNEs), 211–212, 213–215, 220–221
  process and production measures, 258, 267, 269

Fabricius, Johann, 70
Falk, Richard, 141
favela syndrome, 7
fiducia, 531

financial instruments
  Clean Development Mechanism, 30, 510–515
  GEF. *See* Global Environment Facility
  international regimes, 29–30, 495
  Jeripachi Wind Power Project, 514, 514
  Kyoto Protocol, 509–515
  market mechanisms, 516
  Montreal Protocol, 495–502
  Multilateral Fund, 29, 495–502
  UNFCCC, 509–510
Finland
  eco-labels, 479, 480
  eco-taxes, 476, 477, 483, 484
  environmental regulation, 472
  environmental subsidies, 477
  new environmental policy instruments, 476
  oil waste levy, 477
  voluntary agreements, 476
Finnemore, Martha, 132
fisheries, 552
Fisheries Jurisdiction case, 269
flora and fauna, 548–551
Food and Agriculture Organisation (FAO), 31, 308, 310, 322, 534, 536
Ford Motors, 138
foreign direct investment, 150–154
Forest Stewardship Council, 527
forests, 246, 528, 542
forum non conveniens, 213, 300, 569, 575
forum shopping, 568–570, 574
Foucault, Michel, 82, 177
Foundation for International Environmental Law and Development (FIELD), 114
France
  eco-labels, 479, 480
  eco-taxes, 476, 477, 485
  energy-efficient labelling, 242
  environmental subsidies, 477
  tradable permits, 478
  voluntary agreements, 472–473, 479
Franck, Thomas, 393, 395–396
French, Hilary, 360
Friedmann, W., 187

Friis-Christensen, E, 70
Fuller, Lon, 394–395
fundamentalist backlashes, 84–85
Funtowitz, S., 100

G-7, 237
G-77, 502, 505
Galilei, Galileo, 37
game theory, 392
gasoline, US import restrictions, 296
GATT. *See* WTO/GATT
generational responsibilities, 554–557
genetic resources
  access to, 31, 519
  state sovereignty, 520, 521
  trusteeship, 529
genetically modified organisms, 302
Georgia, 378
Germany
  Advisory Council on Global Change (WBGU), 5–9
  assistance to transition economies, 365
  chemical industry self-regulation, 14–15
  consensual knowledge, 443
  constitutional right to safe environment, 361
  East Germany, 359
  eco-labels, 479, 480, 482, 486, 489
  eco-taxes, 243, 476, 477, 483, 484, 485
  environmental concerns, 89
  environmental impact, 20
  environmental pace-setter, 472
  environmental principles, 589
  environmental subsidies, 477
  forest damage, 542
  hierarchy of principles, 596–597
  human dignity principle, 593
  knowledge of policy options, 447
  Konzeptgebot, 602–603
  new environmental policy instruments, 476
  planning law, 594
  precautionary principle, 591, 596
  proportionality, 593
  and soft law, 327
  soil protection, 592

Germany (*cont.*)
  tradable permits, 476, 477, 478
  Treuhand, 532
  voluntary agreements, 474, 478, 479, 485, 488
  waste recycling, 13
Giddens, Anthony, 163, 170
glaciers, 42, 66–67
global civil society
  and absence of state, 11, 130–133
  activities, 113–122
  advocacy, 114
  advocacy networks, 112
  agenda setting, 113–114
  and classic liberals, 123–125
  colonisation, 134–139
  and communitarians, 123, 125–126
  concept, 10–11, 106–108
  and critical theory, 126–129
  current political discourse, 123–126
  and democracy, 121–122, 130–133, 139–140, 141–142
  elements, 10, 94–98, 106, 109–113, 134
  emancipatory potential, 123
  emergence, 10–11
  Eurocentric concept, 142–143
  for profit entities, 134–139
  international norm creation, 114–116
  international norm implementation, 116–117
  international relations discourses, 139
  IR constructivists, 118–119, 132
  IR discourses, 117–122
  lobbying, 114
  NGOs. *See* NGOs
  observer status, 115
  political theory, 122–129
  purism, 134–139
  social movement theory, 119–120
  social movements, 11, 86, 111–112
  solidarity, 139
  strategies, 115–116
  transnational corporations, 112–113
global commons
  compatibility of use, 551
  equal freedom for unequal actors, 553–554
  and jurisdiction, 551–554
  and USA, 297–298
Global Compact, 180, 192, 194, 197
Global Environment Facility (GEF)
  Argentina project, 508, 508
  cluster of agreements, 415–416
  decision-making, 505
  governance structure, 505
  operation, 29–30, 502–509
  scope, 507, 510
  trusteeship, 527
  universal membership, 505
global environmental governance
  concept, 11–13, 80
  cooperation. *See* international cooperation
  definition of global governance, 135
  and democracy, 130–133
  economic and social standards, 345–346
  emerging key actors, 10–11, 94–104
  and environmental awareness, 87–94
  existing situation, 342–348
  fair regulation, 105
  overarching constitution, 15
  and process and production measures (PPM), 267–274
  and science, 98–102
  self-regulation. *See* self-regulation
  social macro-trends, 83–87
  societal conditions for institution-building, 9–10, 83
  societal preconditions, 80
  standards. *See* international standards
  and transnational civil society, 94–98
global federal union, vision, 2
global mind, 9–11
global subject, 9
globalisation
  effect, 10
  McDonaldisation, 85
  phenomenon, 85–86
  transnational protest movements, 86
Goethe, J. W. von, 525
Golub, J., 471
good faith, negotiations, 461
Goose Bay, Labrador, 47
Gore, Albert, 287

governance. *See* global environmental governance
Gramsci, Antonio, 127, 134, 135
Great Lakes, 443–444, 447, 450
Greece, 479
Green Planners Network, 239
green revolution syndrome, 7
greenhouse effect, 44–46
greenhouse gases, 73, 467
Greenland, 38, 56, 62, 71
Grenadines, 256–265
Grotius, Hugo, 140, 141
grounded theory, 119
Gulf Stream, 47, 53, 55

Haas, Peter, 101, 113
Habermas, Jürgen, 127–128, 143–145
habitats, 594
Hague Conference, 569
Hajer, Maarten, 82
halons, 497
Hart, H L A, 270
Havel, Vaclav, 359
hazardous waste
    Basel Convention, 275–276, 318, 344, 571
    civil liability, 571, 573
    Liability Protocol, 276
    review of Convention implementation, 450
    Russian Arctic, 290
    toxic waste, 154, 290
    transport, 207, 210
hegemony, USA, 27–28, 303–304
Heinrich events, 72
Held, David, 130
Helsinki Convention, 364, 439
Helsinki Rules, 541–542, 567, 577
heritage sites, 521
    See also World Heritage Convention
high seas
    compatibility of use, 551
    equal freedom for unequal actors, 553–554
    fisheries, 552
    jurisdiction, 551–554
    seabed, 534, 550, 554
    UNCLOS. *See* UNCLOS
Holocene Age, 1, 40, 68, 73
Honduras, 256–265

Howse, Robert, 255
human rights
    and Alien Tort Claims Act, 300–301
    Central Asia, 378
    international regulation of MNEs, 203
    MNE norms, 16, 180, 192, 193, 196–198, 217
    transition economies, 372
    Universal Declaration of Human Rights, 278
    and USA, 278
Hungary, 359, 367, 368
Hurrell, A, 140
Hyde, C. C., 189

IBM, 187
ice ages, 42, 68, 75
ice sheets, 62–63, 68
ice shelves, 61–62
Iceland, 38, 510
IMF, 201, 413
implementation of Conventions
    clustered agreements, 416–417, 424
    environmental Conventions, 346
    EU law, 337–339, 352–353
    review systems, 448
    Trade Policy Review Mechanism, 424
India, 347, 498, 524
individualisation, 10, 84
Indonesia, 347
information, right to
    Aarhus Convention. *See* Aarhus Convention
    European Union, 374
    principle of international environmental law, 209–210, 220
    Rio Declaration, 246
    spread of environmental information provisions, 250
injunctions, 213–214, 221
institutions
    analysis, requirements, 2–4
    common principles, 32
    contradictory role, 2
    culture, 81–82, 83
    definition, 12
    discourse theory, 82
    emerging key actors, 94–104

institutions (*cont.*)
  focuses
    framework for self-regulation, 12
    institutionalised policy transfer, 233
    institutionalist theory, 10
    interests, 81, 83
    and knowledge evolution, 448–451
    polyarchy, 2
    power, 81, 83
    relations with society and nature, 3–4
    social laws, 13
    societal preconditions, 9–10, 83
Inter-American Tropical Tuna Convention, 437
Inter-Organization Programme for the Sound Management of Chemicals (IOMC), 309, 310–311, 321
Intergovernmental Panel on Climate Change (IPCC), 101–102
International Chamber of Commerce, 182
International Commission for the Conservation of Atlantic Tuna, 256–265
international community, 140, 141
International Conference on Chemical Safety (ICCS), 310
international cooperation
  and environmental policy convergence, 244
  LRTAP Convention, 545
  Montreal Protocol, 545–546
  and process and production measures, 268–271
  Rio Declaration, 544–545
  and state sovereignty, 545
  Stockholm Declaration, 544
  UNFCCC, 546
  Vienna Convention, 545
  World Heritage Convention, 549
International Court of Justice
  Connally reservation, 279
  Fisheries Jurisdiction case, 269
  general principles of law, 595, 598
  LaGrand case, 279
  Nicaragua case, 279
  and precautionary principle, 587
  role, 424
  and USA, 278–279
international crimes, 207
International Criminal Court, 207, 215, 219, 223, 279–280, 294
international criminal tribunals, 280
international environmental regimes
  clustering. *See* clusters of agreements
  complexity, 409
  compliance. *See* treaty compliance
  consensual knowledge, 431
  definition, 12
  effectiveness, 25–31
  financial instruments. *See* financial instruments
  generally, 342–348
  and hegemonic states, 27–28, 303–304
  implementation of Conventions, 346
  lack of coordination, 25–26
  patchwork of MNE control, 203–205
  persuasive authority, 185
  and policy convergence, 245–247
  policy options, understanding, 26–27, 444–447
  principles. *See* environmental principles
  public trusteeship, 527–530
  reform, 409
  scientific monitoring, 448
  Secretariats, 411, 414
  state responsibility, 186–191
  survey, 342, 344–345
  treaties. *See* treaties
  and USA, 283–301, 344, 356
International Forum on Chemical Safety, 309, 310
International Institute for Sustainable Development, 114
International Labour Organization (ILO), 192, 204, 308, 309, 310, 345
international law
  application of principles to private entities, 196
  binding effect, 396–401
  and corporate responsibility, 16–17, 182–186
  criminal responsibility, 194

international law (*cont.*)
  general principles, 595, 598
  and global civil society, 117–122
  interactional international law, 394–396, 401
  IRD. *See* International Regimes Database (IRD)
  neighbourly principles, 540–542
  and self-regulation, 185
  sources, 591
  UN principles, 591
International Law Association, Helsinki Rules, 541–542, 567, 577
International Law Commission
  civil liability model, 580–583
  conflict of laws, 569–570
  corporate responsibility, 181
  diplomatic protection, 583–585
  draft articles on transboundary liability, 187–188, 190, 208–209, 561–565, 566, 575–583, 585–586
  meaning of responsibility, 181
  MNE human rights responsibilities, 180, 196–198
  role, 585
  state responsibility, 32, 181, 560–563
  strict liability principle, 574
International Maritime Organization (IMO), 420–421
International Regimes Database (IRD)
  design and coding, 431–436
  nature, 431
  regime elements, 433
international relations theory
  English School, 140
  and global civil society, 117–122, 139
International Seabed Authority, 534
international society, 141–142
international standards
  economic and social, 345–346
  ISO 1400 Series, 14, 272, 488–489
  and process and production measures, 271–272
International Tribunal for the Law of the Sea (ITLOS), 420, 588
International Tropical Timber Organisation, 256

investment
  dispute resolution mechanisms, 426, 452
  international regulation of MNEs, 203
Iran Hostages case, 279
Iraq, UN compensation scheme, 584
IRD. *See* International Regimes Database (IRD)
Ireland
  eco-labels, 480, 486
  eco-taxes, 477
  new environmental policy instruments, 476
  sluggish environmental regulation, 472, 475
  tradable permits, 478
  voluntary agreements, 479
Islamic fundamentalism, 85
Islamic law, 531
Italy, 242, 524

Japan
  assistance to transition economies, 365
  eco-taxes, 476
  new environmental policy instruments, 471
  Smokestack Syndrome, 13
  US alignment, 347
  voluntary agreements, 473
  whale oil, 13
  whaling, 298
Johannesburg Summit (WSSD)
  and MNE liability, 202
  MNE responsibilities, 193
  Plan of Implementation, 208, 295
  priorities, 347
  results, 409
  strategies of developed countries, 135
  and USA, 295, 298, 345
Jordan, A. J., 484
jurisdiction
  areas beyond national jurisdictions, 551–554
  Brussels Convention, 212–213
  extra-territorial. *See* extra-territorial jurisdiction

jurisdiction (*cont.*)
  Fisheries Jurisdiction case, 269
  forum non conveniens, 213, 300, 569, 575
  International Court of Justice, 279
  territorial jurisdiction, 539–540
  transboundary damage, 540–542
  UNCLOS, 270
jus cogens, 587, 598

Kaldor, Mary, 133, 142
Katanga Syndrome, 5
Kazakhstan, 378, 379
Keane, John, 134, 139
Keck, Margaret, 112, 114, 120
Keeling, Charles, 45
Kelsen, H., 186
Kent, J., 102
Keohane, Robert, 131, 537
Kern, Kristine, 231
Kiev Protocol 2003, 573
knowledge
  impact of regimes on, 436–451
  and institutional mechanisms, 448–451
  and international regimes, 431
  International Regimes Database, 431–436
  nature of problems, 437–444
  policy options, 26–27, 444–447
knowledge society, 10, 86–87, 98
Koester, Veit, 342
Kubatzki, C., 73
Kuroshio, 55
Kyoto Protocol
  approach, 343
  business involvement, 137, 138
  Clean Development Mechanism, 30, 510–515
  common but differentiated responsibilities, 546–547
  compliance, 28–29, 402–405, 406
  compliance procedures, 398–401
  and developing countries, 510
  financial mechanisms, 30
  funding mechanisms, 509–515
  NGO strategies, 115
  and policy options, 445
  tradable permits, 455, 456–457, 477, 487
  and USA, 28, 293–296, 324, 445, 456–457, 511, 543
Kyrgyzstan, 378

labelling. *See* eco-labels
labour standards, 345
land, 63–65
landfill taxes, 477
Lang, Wilfried, 592
Lassen, Knud, 70–71
Latvia, 360, 373
Laurentide ice sheet, 73
law of the sea
  cluster of agreements, 420–421
  equal freedom for unequal actors, 553–554
  fisheries, 552
  flag state jurisdiction, 421
  jurisdiction over common territories, 551–554
  marine pollution, 207, 420–421
  seabed, 534, 550, 554
  tribunal, 420, 588
  UNCLOS. *See* UNCLOS
League of Nations, 277, 278, 324, 535
Lévèque, F., 474
lex mercatoria,, 184
Liability Protocol, 276
liberalism
  classic liberals and global civil society, 123–125
  egalitarian liberals, 126
  liberal environmentalism, 134–136
Lithuania, Green Party, 360
Little Ice Age, 38, 40
lobbying, 114
local remedies rule, 583–585
Locke, John, 124, 531
Long, Bill, 236
LRTAP Convention, 430, 545
Lugano Convention, 572, 573, 574–575
Luhmann, Niklas, 175
Luxembourg, 479

Major Accident Syndrome, 7
Malanczuk, P., 187
Malaysia, 347

Maldives, 348
mandamus actions, 213–214
Marco, Guido de, 529
marine pollution, 207, 210, 291, 320, 420–421, 572
Marine Stewardship Council, 95, 527
MARPOL, 291
Marrakech Accords, 455, 462
Marsh, D., 481
Marx, Karl, 129, 531
Mass Tourism Syndrome, 7
material flow analysis, 103
Mauna Loa curve, 45
McDonaldisation, 85
MEAs. *See* treaties
Mediterranean Sea, 528
MERCOSUR, 357
Mexico, 89, 347, 497
Middle Ages, climate, 73
Migratory Species Convention, 550
Milankovitch Theory, 48, 67, 68
Millennium Ecosystem Assessment, 413, 423
Minamata disease, 305–306
Moldan, Bedrich, 360
Moldova, 361
Monsanto case, 600
Montreal Protocol
  cooperation, 545–546
  compliance, 404
  HFC gases, 467
  Multilateral Fund, 29, 495–502
  precautionary principle, 546
  and USA, 27
morality, 598
moramati, 532
multilevel governance
  overarching principles, 31–33
  patterns of interaction, 13
  polyarchy of institutions, 2
  requirement, 12
  thesis, 2
multilateral environmental agreements. *See* treaties
Multilateral Fund, 29, 495–502
multinational enterprises (MNEs)
  alternative solutions for transboundary damage, 224
  application of international law principle to, 196
  codes of conduct, 204–205, 216
  conflict of law, 211–212, 220
  corporate responsibility, 182–186
  corporate veil, 218
  criminal liability, 194, 214, 221–222
  de facto control, 216, 223
  direct responsibility in international law, 191–198
  domestic regulation, 186–191
  empirical research problems, 154–157
  environmental disasters, 218, 220
  environmental liability, 17, 179, 200–203
  environmental protection, 149–154
  extra-territorial jurisdiction, 211–212, 213–215, 220–221
  fragmentation, 176
  future framework of transboundary liability, 218–224
  and global civil society, 137–139
  and Global Compact, 180, 192, 197
  human rights norms, 16, 180, 192, 196–198, 217
  internal audits, 163–167
  international civil liability scheme, 16–17, 205–218
  international forum of environmental disputes, 215
  international law patchwork, 203–205
  international legal personality, 187, 194
  non-legal instruments, 203, 204–205
  OECD guidelines, 17, 191–192, 193, 194, 208, 211, 214–215
  part of global civil society, 112–113
  parties to treaties, 195
  principles of international liability, 145–146, 185, 207, 208, 219–220
  remedies for transboundary environmental liability, 221
  self-regulation, 14–16, 157–174, 183
  status, 137–139
  structures and evasion of liability, 202, 215–218, 222–223
Myers, N., 102

NAFTA, 281, 285–287, 357, 426
national regulation. *See* state regulation
natural resources
  equitable access, 588
  public trusteeship, 522–525
  shared resources. *See* common resources
  sovereignty over, 539–551
neo-liberalism
neo-realism, 81
Netherlands
  assistance to transition economies, 365
  eco-labels, 242, 476, 479, 480, 486
  eco-taxes, 243, 476, 477, 483, 484, 485
  environmental pace-setter, 253, 472
  environmental policy development, 245
  Environmental Policy Plan, 482
  environmental subsidies, 477
  new environmental policy instruments, 476
  tradable permits, 477, 482
  voluntary agreements, 478, 479, 485, 488
new environmental policy instruments (NEPIs)
  eco-labels. *See* eco-labels
  eco-taxes. *See* eco-taxes
  EU and patterns of use, 485–487
  EU influence, 484, 491
  EU model, 486, 487, 489, 491–492
  European Union, 23, 470
  growth, 470–473, 489–490
  market-based instruments, 473, 476, 487–488
  nature, 470, 473–475
  negotiated agreements, 474
  patterns of use in Europe, 475, 481, 485–487, 490
  public voluntary schemes, 474
  and regulation, 481, 490
  subsidies, 473, 477
  tradable permits. *See* tradable permits
  unilateral commitments, 474
  voluntary agreements. *See* voluntary agreements
New York Convention. *See* UN Framework Convention on Climate Change
New Zealand, 347, 510
NGOs
  See also global civil society
  and Aarhus Convention, 363
  activities, 111, 113–122
  business NGOs, 137–139
  and chemical safety, 323
  compliance proceedings, 461–462
  and democracy, 130–133
  ECJ access, 341
  epistemic communities, 113
  explosion of activity, 106, 109–113
  funding, 111
  institutionalist theory, 10
  international norm creation, 114–116
  international norm implementation, 116–117
  legitimacy, 11, 97–98
  nature, 109–111
  observer status, 115
  role in treaty-making, 96, 116, 133
  strategies, 115–116
  transition economies, 370, 381–383
  and transnational bureaucratic networks, 327–328
  transnational civil society, 7–10, 94–98
Nicaragua case, 279
Nigeria, 497
Nikitin case, 369, 372
Nixon, Richard, 287
non-state actors
  See also global civil society
  activities, 113–122
  consumers, 102–104
  and democracy, 130–133
  emerging actors, 94–104, 106, 109–113, 134
  and European Union, 340–341
  for profit entities, 134–139
  legitimacy, 97–98
  science, 98–102
  transnational. *See* global civil society

North Atlantic, 55
North Atlantic Current, 53
Norway, 42, 52, 245, 298, 365, 450
Nowotny, H, 100
nuclear liability, 210, 572
Nuremberg trial, 279
Nye, J. S., 131
NIMBY, 602

Oberthür, S., 114, 116, 133
observer status, 115
oceans
  carbon pumps, 46
  and climate system, 4, 51–55
  counter-currents, 55
  currents, 5, 55
  gas storage, 54–55
  global hydrological cycle, 53–54
  heat storage, 53
  heat transport, 53
  water source, 53–54
OECD
  Bribery Convention, 17, 214
  and chemical safety, 309, 310, 314–315
  country reviews, 417
  and energy/carbon taxes, 237
  environmental performance review programme, 237, 352–353
  Green Planners Network, 239
  guidelines for MNEs, 17, 191–192, 193, 194, 204, 208, 211, 214–215
  new environmental policy instruments, 470
  policy diffusion, 22, 236
  SIDS programme, 314–315, 326
  Test Guidelines, 18, 314, 322
  voluntary agreements, 474
oil pollution, 207, 208, 210
Olleson, S, 181
OPEC, 295
Organisation of African Unity, 548
OSCE, 363
Oslo Convention, 410
Ottawa Convention on Landmines, 223
Overexploitation Syndrome, 5
ozone layer
  and CFCs, 306, 437–438, 496, 497, 501, 501–502, 602–603

Conventions, 288–289, 319, 343
Montreal Protocol 1987 *See* Montreal Protocol
Vienna Convention. *See* Vienna Convention 1985

Pacific Islands, 436
pacta sunt servanda, 461
Panama, Isthmus of, 64
Paris Convention, 410
Paulus, Andreas, 142
Permanent Court of International Arbitration, 215
Peru, 300
pesticides, 308
Pew Centre on Global Climate Change, 138
Pfizer case, 600
PHARE programme, 364, 367
Philippines, 64, 89, 523
Plant Gene Treaty, 519, 520, 521, 534, 536
Pleistocene Age, 40
Poland, 359, 369
policy diffusion
  benchmarking activities, 237–238
  direct policy transfer, 233
  driving factors, 231–252
  energy/carbon taxes, 237, 239, 242, 243, 252
  energy efficient labels, 23, 231, 242, 251, 272
  horizontal diffusion, 241–242
  institutional instruments, types, 239–241
  institutionalised policy transfer, 233, 235–244
  and international trade, 251–252
  and international treaties, 245–247
  meaning, 229
  model production, 238
  multilateral environmental discourses, 236–237
  and other convergence mechanisms, 228–230, 244–248, 252, 283
  and policy characteristics, 248
  and power, 252–253
  renewable energy, 242, 243–244

policy diffusion (*cont.*)
  and soft law, 246–248
  and state proximity, 233–235
policy instruments
  EU role in selection, 484
  financial. *See* financial instruments
  new. *See* new environmental policy instruments (NEPIs)
polluter pays principle
  and compensation schemes, 571
  and developing countries, 547
  German soil protection regime, 592
  Lugano Convention, 574
  principle of international environmental law, 208, 220, 502, 588
  Rio Conference, 494
  transboundary damage liability, 565
POP Convention, 319, 321, 322, 344, 420
POPs, 306
Portugal, 479
post-Communist states. *See* transition economies
Pound, Roscoe, 525, 531
poverty, 89, 379
power
  geography of power, 201
  and institution-building, 10, 81, 83
  legitimacy, 81
  and policy diffusion, 252–253
  purchasing power, 21–22
precautionary measures, 213–214
precautionary principle
  ECJ jurisprudence, 599, 600
  Germany, 591, 596
  Global Compact, 197
  Montreal Protocol, 546
  nature, 33
  North-East Atlantic Convention, 557
  principle of international environmental law, 208, 219, 556–557, 587–588, 595
  Rio Declaration, 556–557
  UNFCCC, 546
principles
  balancing, 593–594
  emergence, 590–592

environmental law. *See* environmental principles
  general principles of law, 595, 598
  hierarchy, 595–598
  jus cogens, 587, 598
  ordinary and fundamental principles, 595–598
  and separation of powers, 598–603
  sources of international law, 591
  versus rules, 592–595
Prior Informed Consent Convention. *See* Rotterdam Convention
process and production measures (ppms)
  and Article XX GATT exemptions, 265–267
  comparative advantages, 257–258
  examples, 255–256
  extra-territoriality, 258, 267, 269
  global environmental governance, 267–274
  international cooperation, 268–271
  international standardisation, 271–272
  legality, 254–255
  product-related and non-product-related, 256–257
  pros and cons, 257–258
  purchasing power of importers, 21–22
  tuna cases, 254, 259–260, 265–266, 297–298
  unilateralism, 258, 267, 268–269, 272–274
  US Shrimp/Turtle case, 255, 256, 260, 266, 268, 297–298
  and WTO/GATT, 255, 256, 259–267, 272–273
Prototype Carbon Fund, 514, 514

race to the bottom, 19, 464
rain forests, 528
Ramsar Convention, 359, 418, 549
Rao, Pemmaraju Sreenivasa, 188
Ravetz, J., 100
Reagan, Ronald, 276, 279, 345
Regan, Donald, 255
regional environmental governance, EU model, 23–25, 356–357

renewable energy, 242, 243–244
res communis, 551
research, objectives, 2–3
responsibility
    corporate responsibility, 181, 182–186
    criminal responsibility, 194
    direct responsibility of MNEs in international law, 191–198
    domestic regulation of MNEs, 186–191
    meaning, 15, 181–182
    MNE responsibility scheme, 205–218
    MNEs and environmental harm, 17, 179, 200–203
    states. *See* state responsibility
Rio Conference
    and developing countries, 494
    effects, 22, 409
    and Global Environment Facility (GEF), 504
    and global governance
    NGO participation, 115
    policy diffusion, 239
    sustainable development, 135
Rio Declaration
    See also common but differentiated responsibilities
    access to justice, 567
    compensation rights, 577
    environmental information, 246
    and ILC articles on transboundary liability, 579–580
    intergenerational responsibilities, 554
    international cooperation, 544–545
    precautionary principle, 556–557
    Principle 16, 577
    state responsibility for transboundary damage, 561
    state sovereignty, 544
    unilateral environmental actions (Article 21), 267
    use of principles, 208
risk management, chemicals, 318–320
Risse, Thomas, 113, 136
rivers, transboundary rivers, 541–542
Roman law, 523, 531, 559

Romania, 360, 375
Ronne-Filchner ice shelf, 61
Roosevelt, Eleanor, 278
Roosevelt, F. D., 277
Roosevelt, Theodore, 276
Ross ice shelf, 61
Rotterdam Convention, 318, 322, 344, 420
rules, versus principles, 592–595
Rural Exodus Syndrome, 5
Russia
    absence of environment ministry, 427
    Aral Sea, 361, 364
    and Barents Sea, 450
    Caspian Sea, 364
    constitutional right to safe environment, 360
    environmental protection, 368–369, 376–380
    environmental socialism, 347
    Nikitin case, 369, 372
    radioactive waste disposal, 377
    resource exploitation ethos, 20
    river diversion, 60–61
    Sava River Framework Agreement, 364
    toxic waste in Russian Arctic, 290
    UNEP role, 363
Rwanda, 280

Sachs, Wolfgang, 91–92
Safety High Tech case, 601–603
Sahara, 73
Sahel syndrome, 5, 13
Saint-Vincent, 256–265
Sands, Philippe, 594
Scalet, S., 124
Schmidtz, D., 124
Schweizerhalle disaster, 305
science
    assessment of clustered agreements, 422–423
    criteria, 100
    and global environmental governance, 98–102
    monitoring, 448, 450
    uncertainties, 99, 543
Scottish Enlightenment, 124

sea. *See* law of the sea
sea ice, 58–61
seabed, 534, 550, 554
seals, 289
security, and environment, 363–364
self-regulation
  by states, 18–21
  effectiveness, 158
  institutional framework, 12
  interlegality, 174–178
  internal audits, 163–167
  internal differentiation, 158
  and international law, 185
  methodology, 167–171, 174
  multinational enterprises (MNEs), 157–174, 183
  normative anchoring, 158
  private self-regulation as transnational law, 157–174
  problem proximity, 158
  societal self-regulation, 13–17, 25
  specialised organs, 158–159
  state of research, 162–167
  transition economies, 20–21
  transnational fields of practice, 178
  transnational self-regulatory systems, 159–162
separation of powers, 598–603
Seveso disaster, 218, 305
ship pollution, 210, 291, 320, 342, 572
Shrimp/Turtle case, 255, 256, 260, 266, 268
sic utere tuo ut neminem laedas, 540–541
Sikkink, Kathryn, 112, 114, 120
Slovak Republic, 360, 369
Slovenia, environmental laws, 360
Smokestack Syndrome, 7, 13
snow, 42, 58
social conditions
  cultural pluralisation, 84
  detraditionalisation, 84
  environmental awareness, 87–94
  fundamentalist backlashes, 84–85
  globalisation, 85–86
  individualisation, 84
  institution-building, 9–10, 83
  knowledge society, 86–87
  macro-trends for global governance, 83–87
social movements
  new social movements, 119–120
  part of global civil society, 111–112
  radicalisation of global civil society discourse, 136
  social movement theory, 119–120, 129
  transnational protest movements, 86
socialism, 81
soft law, 12, 16, 246–248, 322–326, 389–390, 396–397
solidarity, 139
South Africa, trusteeship of natural resources, 524
South Korea, 13, 347
South Pacific, 528
Southern African Development Community (SADC), 357
Southern Bluefin Tuna case, 557
Southern Ocean, 59
sovereignty. *See* state sovereignty
Soviet countries. *See* transition economies
Space Objects Liability Convention, 564
Spain, 244, 478
species preservation
  biodiversity. *See* biodiversity; Biodiversity Convention
  CITES, 549–550
  Migratory Species Convention, 550
  RAMSAR, 359, 549
  and state sovereignty, 548–551
SPS Agreement, 301
Stalin, Joseph, 277
Standley case, 597–598
state responsibility
  and civil liability, 583–585
  ILC draft articles, 32, 181, 560–563
  international environmental law, 186–191
  Stockholm Declaration, 182
  transboundary damage, 541, 559–563
  transboundary rivers, 541–542
state sovereignty
  Biodiversity Convention, 550–551

changing meaning, 121
CITES, 549–550
and common resources, 542–548
and cooperation obligations, 545
and global commons, 551–554
Migratory Species Convention, 550
over natural resources, 539–551
and preservation of species and spaces, 548–551
principle of international law, 598
public trusteeship, 521, 522, 537
Stockholm Declaration, 544
survival
and treaties, 324
UNFCCC, 547
Vienna Convention, 547
states
See also non-state actors
and global civil society, 11, 130–133
governance without state, 131
mutual influence, 21–23
purchasing power, 21–22
regulation, 18–21, 22, 186–191
responsibility. *See* state responsibility
state-centric view of international society, 140, 141
state of origin principle, 19
Westphalian state, 141
stewardship economics, 525–527
Stockholm Conference, 22
Stockholm Declaration
common resources, 544
intergenerational responsibilities, 554
international cooperation, 544
principles, 287
state responsibility for transboundary damage, 182, 560
state sovereignty, 544
trusteeship, 528
use of principles, 208
storylines, 82
straddling fish stocks, 552
Strong, Maurice, 529
subsidies, 415–416, 477
subsistence economies, 1
sufficiency revolution, 104
sun, and climate change, 70–71
sustainable development

and consumers, 103–104
EU principle, 333, 590
international law principle, 93, 555–556, 588
MNE policies, 217
Rio Conference, 80, 135
Sweden, 479, 524
Switzerland, 365, 510
syndrome analysis
development syndromes, 7
sink syndromes, 7
utilisation syndromes, 5–7
WBGU proposals, 5–9
Syr-Daria River, 379

TACIS, 365
Tajikistan, 378, 379
TBT Agreement, 256
technical barriers to trade, 256
temperature averages
expected warming, 42
nineteenth/twentieth century, 37
outlook, 65
reconstruction, 37–38
variations, 42–56
Teubner, G, 184, 193
Thailand, 500
Thejll, Peter, 71
Third World. *See* developing countries
Tietout, Charles, 462
timber, tropical, 256
Tisza River Basin, 364
Tokyo trials, 279
Tönnies, Ferdinand, 142
Toope, Stephen, 394
Torricelli, Evangelista, 37
tradable permits
Austria, 478
climate change Conventions, 455–457
critique, 511–513
developing countries, 455–456, 468
EU influence, 486
EU model, 487
European Union, 482
France, 478
Germany, 476, 477, 478
Ireland, 478

626   INDEX

tradable permits (cont.)
  Kyoto Protocol, 455, 456–457, 477, 487
  Netherlands, 477, 482
  new environmental policy instruments, 23, 470
  new market-based instruments, 23, 470, 473
  patterns of use, 477–478
  United Kingdom, 476, 477, 482, 484, 486
  USA, 456–457, 473, 477
trade
  See also WTO/GATT
  ppms. See process and production measures
  purchasing power of states, 21–22
  unilateral trade measures, 22, 258, 267, 268–269, 272–274
traditions, detraditionalisation, 84
Trail Smelter case, 285, 540, 559, 577
Train, Russell, 537
transboundary damage
  See also common resources
  civil liability, 566–575
  definition of damage, 582
  effective compensation principle, 576–580
  ILC civil liability model, 580–583
  ILC draft articles, 561–565, 566, 575–583, 585–586
  liability issues, 559–563
  neighbourly principles, 540–542
  state or private liability, 563–565, 583–585
  Trail Smelter case, 285, 540, 559, 577
transition economies
  assistance from non-EU countries, 365
  Caucasus, 378–380, 381
  Central Asia, 378–380
  convergence, 359–363, 383
  divergence, 361–375, 383
  ecological euphoria period, 360–361, 366
  environment and security, 363–364
  environmental challenges, 380–383
  environmental impact assessments, 368, 371–372

environmental jurisprudence, 372–373
environmental law development, 20–21, 366–375
environmental movements, 382
environmental socialism, 347
EU membership, 364–365, 373–375
NGOs, 370, 381–383
PHARE programme, 364, 367
post-EU accession, 375–376
TACIS, 365
transnational bureaucratic networks
  chemical industry, 307–320
  efficacy, 326
  evaluation, 326–329
  generally, 17–18
  IGOs, 321–325
  legal protection, 328–329
  legitimacy, 326–328
  NGOs, 327–328
  soft law, 322–326
  structures and rule-making, 320–324
  transparency, 328
transparency
  clustered agreements, 423–424
  European Union, 341, 354–355
  principle of international environmental law, 208, 209–210, 220, 588
  transnational bureaucratic networks, 328
treaties
  clustering. See clusters of agreements
  compliance. See treaty compliance
  Conferences of the Parties, 412–413
  environment. See international environmental regimes
  Framework Protocol model, 116, 133, 397
  future treaty on international corporate liability, 218–224
  implementation. See implementation of Conventions
  legitimacy, 461–462
  MNEs as parties, 195
  negotiating principles, 461
  negotiations as regulatory competition, 462–468

and policy convergence, 245–247
procedures, 17, 397–398
public participation treaty, 26
regulating MNEs, 16–17
soft law, 389–390, 396–397
subjectivity, 17
subsidiary bodies, 413
substance, 16–17
treaty compliance, 28–29
  binding effect of international law, 396–401
  challenge, 383
  compliance continuum, 402–407
  compliance pull mechanisms
  compliance push mechanisms, 460–461
  constructivist approach, 391, 394–396, 407–408
  developing countries, 30–31, 457–460
  enforcement model, 392–394, 408
  interactional approach, 394–396, 401, 407–408
  Kyoto Protocol, 398–401, 402–405, 406
  managerial approach, 391–392, 393–394, 408
  negotiations as regulatory competition, 462–468
  NGO legal actions, 461–462
  non-compliance procedures, 387–389
  persuasion and facilitation, 406–407
  power of legitimacy, 395–396
  soft law, 389–390, 396–397
  theoretical perspectives, 391–396
  voluntary and non-voluntary non-compliance, 458
Treuhand, 532
trusteeship
  common environmental resources, 555
  international environmental law, 527–530
  public trusteeship of environmental resources, 522–525
  public trusteeship theory, 31–32, 531–536

sovereignty as public trusteeship, 521, 522
stewardship economics, 525–527
tuna
  Inter-American Tropical Tuna Convention, 437
  regulation, 256
  Southern Bluefin Tuna case, 557
  WTO/GATT cases, 254, 259–260, 265–266, 297–298
Turkmenistan, 378, 379

Ukraine, 360, 369
UN Framework Convention on Climate Change
  common but differentiated responsibilities, 509, 546
  funding mechanism, 509–510
  international cooperation, 546
  and NGOs, 96
  precautionary principle, 546
  scientific uncertainty, 99
  scope, 419
  state sovereignty, 547
  and USA, 292–293
UNCLOS
  compatible use of high seas, 552
  compensation rights, 577
  competing jurisdictions, 270
  exclusive economic zones, 31, 519, 520, 521
  principles, 208
  and USA, 28, 290
UNDP, 192, 496, 498, 500, 503
UNECE
  Aarhus Convention. *See* Aarhus Convention
  and chemical industry, 308
  Convention on Transboundary Effects of Industrial Accidents, 209, 217–218
  membership, 424
UNEP
  and chemical safety, 308, 309, 310
  Global Compact, 192
  and Global Environment Facility (GEF), 503
  and hazardous substances, 420
  Multilateral Fund, 496, 498, 499

UNEP (*cont.*)
  reform of international
    environmental law, 409
  regional environmental governance,
    356, 420, 421
  regional seas programme, 420, 421
  role, 26, 356
  and transition economies, 363
  and USA, 27, 287
UNESCO, 521, 528
UNFCCC. *See* UN Framework
    Convention on Climate Change
UNIDO, 308, 310, 500
unilateralism
  process and production measures,
    22, 258, 267, 268–269, 272–274
  USA, 28, 276, 296–301
Unilever, 95, 187
Union Carbide, 163, 170
United Kingdom
  assistance to transition economies,
    365
  eco-labels, 242, 480, 486
  eco-taxes, 476, 477, 485
  environmental regulation, 481
  landfill tax, 477
  new environmental policy
    instruments, 472
  Shrimp/Turtle case, 255, 256
  strict liability, 591
  tradable permits, 476, 477, 482, 484,
    486
  trusteeship of natural resources, 523
  voluntary agreements, 479, 485
United Nations
  Global Compact, 180, 192, 194, 197
  human rights subcommission, 180,
    192, 193, 217
  Industrial Development
    Organisation, 192
  instruments of MNE control, 204
  International Seabed Authority, 534
  NGO participation, 110
  principles of international law, 591
  public private partnerships, 194
  state responsibility for
    transboundary damage, 560
  Trusteeship Council, 529, 534, 535,
    536

UNEP. *See* UNEP
  and USA, 277
Universal Declaration of Human
    Rights 1948, 278
Urban Sprawl Syndrome, 7
USA
  and Aarhus Convention, 424
  absence of environment portfolio,
    427
  Alien Tort Claims Act, 28, 189–190,
    300–301
  and Antarctic regime, 27, 289–290
  assistance to transition economies,
    365
  and Basel Convention, 275–276
  Beef Hormones dispute with EU,
    301–302, 603
  biodiversity Conventions, 291–292
  Bipartisan Trade Promotion
    Authority Act 2002, 287
  Californian automobile standards,
    27, 284
  and Chemical Weapons Convention,
    280–281
  and CITES, 27
  climate change Conventions,
    292–296, 324, 445, 456–457
  consensual knowledge, 443
  constitutional constraints, 282–283
  consumer society
  continental shelf, 553
  and development banks, 299
  environmental hindrance, 24
  environmental law, 284
  environmental treaty-making
    practice, 285–290
  EU environmental disputes, 301–302
  Fishermen's Protective Act 1967,
    298–299
  Fishery Conservation and
    Management Act 1976, 299
  gasoline import restrictions, 296
  and global commons, 297–298
  GMO dispute with EU, 302
  Great Lakes management, 443–444,
    447, 450
  hegemony, 27–28, 303–304
  and International Court of Justice,
    278–279

and International Criminal Court, 279–280, 294
and international environmental law, 283–301, 344, 356
and international human rights, 278
and international law, 275
Iran Hostages case, 279
isolationism, 27, 276, 290–296
and Johannesburg Summit, 135
and knowledge of policy options, 447
and Kyoto Protocol, 28, 293–296, 324, 445, 456–457, 511, 543
lender liability, 581
and MARPOL, 291
missionary ethos, 20, 27
and Multilateral Fund, 501
multilateralism, 27, 276–277
NAFTA, 281, 285–287
National Research Council, 423
new environmental policy instruments, 471
non-submission to international environmental treaties, 290–296, 350
ozone layer Conventions, 288–289
polar treaties, 289–290
policy diffusion, 235
political heritage constraints, 282
Shrimp/Turtle case, 255, 256, 260, 266, 268, 297–298
Smokestack Syndrome, 13
tradable permits, 456–457, 473, 477
Trail Smelter arbitration, 285, 540
trusteeship of environmental resources, 522–523
tuna cases, 254, 259–260, 265–266, 297–298
and UNCLOS, 28, 290
and UNEP, 287
unilateralism, 28, 276, 296–301
and United Nations, 277
Uruguay Round Agreements Act 1994, 281–282
whales, protection of, 298–299
and World Heritage Convention, 537
and WTO, 281–282, 296–298

Uzbekistan, 378, 379

Vainio, M, 487
Vavrousek, Josef, 359, 360
Venezuela, CFCs and halons, 497
Versailles Treaty, 277
Vienna Convention 1985, 496, 545, 546, 547
Viking settlements, 38
volcanoes, 64
voluntary agreements
  Austria, 474, 477, 478, 479
  Belgium, 478
  Denmark, 478
  EU influence, 485–486
  EU model, 488–489
  Finland, 476
  France, 472–473, 479
  Germany, 474, 478, 479, 485, 488
  Greece, 479
  growth, 470
  Ireland, 479
  Japan, 473
  Luxembourg, 479
  nature, 473–474
  Netherlands, 478, 479, 485, 488
  patterns of use, 478–479
  Portugal, 479
  problems, 491
  Spain, 478
  Sweden, 479
  targets, 481
  United Kingdom, 479, 485
Vorontsov, Nikolai, 360
Vostok, Antarctica, 46, 67, 69

Walzer, Michael, 146
Wapner, Paul, 135
waqf, 531
Washington, George, 276
waste
  1999 Protocol, 571
  dumping at sea, 207, 342
  EU Packaging Waste Directive, 483
  hazardous. *See* hazardous waste
  London Convention, 442
  transport liability, 572, 573
Waste Dumping Syndrome, 7
Watercourses Convention, 566

Weber, Max, 81, 159, 160, 525
Weddell Sea, 55, 61
Weil, Proper, 185, 390
Wernstedt, K, 377
wetlands, 359, 549
whaling
  change in consensual knowledge, 443
  International Whaling Commission, 552
  and USA, 298–299
  Whaling Convention, 298
Wilson, Woodrow, 277, 535
wind power, 514, 514
World Bank
  annual meeting, 413
  Carbon Finance Business, 511
  and Global Environment Facility (GEF), 29, 502, 503, 504–505, 507, 527
  Jeripachi Wind Power Project, 514, 514
  Multilateral Fund, 496, 498, 500–501
World Charter of Nature, 544
World Commission on Dams, 95
World Health Organisation (WHO), 308, 309, 310
World Heritage Convention, 528, 534, 536, 537, 549, 551
world society, 79, 80
World Watch Insitute, 114
WSSD. *See* Johannesburg Summit (WSSD)

WTO/GATT
  Article XX exemptions, 265–267, 286, 297–298
  country reviews, 417
  EC Asbestos case, 262–263, 264–265
  EC Beef Hormones dispute, 301–302, 603
  EC GMO dispute, 302
  environmental considerations, 21–22
  environmental impact, 25
  EU environmental disputes, 28
  governance model, 452
  non-discrimination principle, 21–22
  precautionary principle, 557, 588
  process and production measures, 255, 256, 259–267, 272–273
  Seattle and Cancún demonstrations, 347, 357
  SPS Agreement, 301
  TBT Agreement, 256
  Trade Policy Review Mechanism, 424
  tuna cases, 254, 259–260, 265–266, 297–298
  and USA, 28, 281–282, 296–298
  US Shrimp/Turtle case, 255, 256, 260, 266, 268, 297–298

Yeltsin, Boris, 359
Yugoslavia, 280

Zapfel, P, 487
Zürn, Michael, 130

CPSIA information can be obtained at www.ICGtesting.com
Printed in the USA
LVOW130800271212

313411LV00001B/60/P

9 780521 173438